The 11th Missouri
Volunteer Infantry
in the Civil War

ALSO BY DENNIS W. BELCHER

*The 10th Kentucky Volunteer Infantry in the Civil War:
A History and Roster* (McFarland, 2009)

The 11th Missouri Volunteer Infantry in the Civil War

A History and Roster

Dennis W. Belcher

McFarland & Company, Inc., Publishers
Jefferson, North Carolina, and London

LIBRARY OF CONGRESS CATALOGUING-IN-PUBLICATION DATA

Belcher, Dennis W., 1950–
The 11th Missouri Volunteer Infantry in the Civil War :
a history and roster / Dennis W. Belcher.
p. cm.
Includes bibliographical references and index.

ISBN 978-0-7864-4882-1
softcover : 50# alkaline paper ∞

1. United States. Army. Missouri Infantry Regiment, 11th (1861–1866)
2. Missouri — History — Civil War, 1861–1865 — Regimental histories.
3. United States — History — Civil War, 1861–1865 — Regimental histories.
4. Soldiers — Missouri — Registers.   5. Soldiers — Missouri — Correspondence.
6. United States — History — Civil War, 1861–1865 — Registers.   7. United
States — History — Civil War, 1861–1865 — Campaigns.   I. Title.
E517.511th.B45   2011   973.7'478 — dc23   2011033635

BRITISH LIBRARY CATALOGUING DATA ARE AVAILABLE

© 2011 Dennis W. Belcher. All rights reserved

*No part of this book may be reproduced or transmitted in any form
or by any means, electronic or mechanical, including photocopying
or recording, or by any information storage and retrieval system,
without permission in writing from the publisher.*

On the cover: *Siege of Vicksburg*, color print,
1888 (Library of Congress).

Manufactured in the United States of America

*McFarland & Company, Inc., Publishers
Box 611, Jefferson, North Carolina 28640
www.mcfarlandpub.com*

For Larry and Cecil

Table of Contents

Acknowledgments ix
Preface 1

1. Organizing the 11th Missouri Infantry and Battle of Fredericktown ... 5
2. Point Pleasant and Siege of Corinth 35
3. Battle of Iuka 61
4. Battle of Corinth 81
5. Siege of Vicksburg 104
6. End of the 11th Missouri and Reorganization 140
7. Abbeville, Pursuit of Price, and Battle of Nashville 170
8. Battle of Spanish Fort and Occupation in Alabama 204
9. Postwar Biographical Information 230

Appendix A: 11th Missouri Volunteer Infantry Roster 243
Appendix B: 11th Missouri Veteran Volunteer Infantry Roster 271
Appendix C: Wartime Letters of Men of the 11th Missouri Infantry 299
Notes 321
Bibliography 329
Index 333

Acknowledgments

I want to thank the numerous people who have made this project possible. I offer my grateful appreciation to those who have read and assisted in making this a presentable work. I also express my appreciation to the local historians in Illinois who provided invaluable assistance with the biographical information on the men of the 11th Missouri Infantry, including John King, Lawrence County; Jan Doan, Richland County; David Foote, Crawford County; and Curt Mann, Sangamon County.

I am very grateful for Jonathan Webb Deiss' diligent efforts at the Library of Congress to find letters, regimental records and other sources of information regarding the 11th Missouri Infantry. I thank Steve Mitchell of the Missouri Archives for his willingness to assist in this project and for allowing me access to primary sources on the 11th Missouri Infantry.

The historians at the National Parks Service have proven to be invaluable in the completion of this book, including Tom Parson at the Shiloh National Battlefield, Terrence Winschel at the Vicksburg National Battlefield, and Connie Langum and Jeff Patrick at the Wilson's Creek National Battlefield. Their assistance was very valuable, including allowing me to utilize photographs, providing reference assistance with the *National Tribune*, assistance in map production and also for reading a draft of the book. The National Parks Service is truly "America's Best Idea." I am particularly grateful to Connie Langum for her ability to locate and willingness to share many of the photographic images used in this book. Because the 11th Missouri was heavily involved in northern Mississippi, Tom Parson offered excellent advice and assistance in sections of the book on Iuka, Corinth, Tupelo and Oxford. Finally, Terrence Winschel was an excellent advisor to the Vicksburg Campaign and graciously furnished resources regarding the attack on Stockade Redan on May 22, 1863. These historians were so very helpful as I moved through the book. They willingly provided their expertise and I am forever grateful to them for this.

In addition, Robert Schulz, Civil War historian and Missouri author, graciously reviewed much of this book and his comments were instructive and helpful. I also want to thank author and Civil War historian Jim McGhee for assistance with the section of this book regarding the Battle of Fredericktown. I am grateful to Jim Kay, Nashville Battlefield Preservation Society, for his assistance with the section on the Battle of Nashville. Jim furnished information on the battle, provided photographs and reviewed the section on Nashville. All of these people reviewed and made excellent comments and suggestions on the material that is included.

I also want to acknowledge and express my gratitude to George Skoch who worked tirelessly on constructing the maps for this book. George's expertise in map production is amazing and he does an outstanding job, despite my assistance.

See, a people is coming from the land of the north,
A great nation is stirring from the farthest parts of the earth.
They grasp the bow and the javelin,
They are cruel and have no mercy,
Their sound is like the roaring sea.

—Jeremiah 6:22–23 (NRSV)

Preface

The 11th Regiment Missouri Volunteer Infantry had many nicknames in the Civil War, and if nicknames were a measure of the fighting ability of a regiment, then the 11th Missouri was one of the best. The regiment was first part of the "Eagle Brigade," a nickname it carried throughout the war. Then it shared a nickname as part of "Mower's Jack Ass Cavalry" for its speed and endurance in marching. Finally, it was part of Major General Andrew J. Smith's Guerrillas. The regiment was never nicknamed the "Fightin' Eleventh," although that is a name it perhaps deserves. The men of the 11th Missouri Infantry were "men of iron" and they rank among the elite of the Union soldiers of the Civil War, but little has been formally recorded about this regiment. Although it has been identified as one of the 300 top regiments of the Civil War, its history was neglected by both Missouri and Illinois.

Most of the men of this regiment (nine of the ten companies) were from Illinois but they fought under a Missouri flag. The regiment was actually two: first, the 11th Regiment Missouri Volunteer Infantry, which served for three years from August 1861 through August 1864; then it was re-formed as the 11th Missouri Veteran Volunteer Infantry, and this regiment served from August 1864 through January 1866. The 11th Missouri Infantry was one of Fox's Fighting 300 regiments of the Civil War, but this Union regiment was not what it seemed. Even though it was the 11th Missouri Infantry, its beginnings were as the First Missouri Rifles, and in fact, many in the regiment referred to themselves in this manner for several months after being mustered. Then the initial commanding colonel was not destined to lead the regiment; and in less than 60 days from being mustered, the command was taken from the colonel and he was replaced with a regular army commander.

The history of the 11th Missouri Infantry is one of the utmost bravery and loyalty to the Constitution of the United States. The regiment was just the type needed in the Civil War; the men were hard-as-nails and would follow their commanders "into hell if they ordered." Their story included numerous engagements: Fredericktown, Island No. 10, Siege of Corinth, Iuka, Corinth, Jackson, Vicksburg, Mechanicsville, Red River, Tupelo, Abbeville, Hurricane Creek, pursuit of Price, Nashville, and the battle of Spanish Fort. In these engagements the soldiers of this regiment fought with their hearts, souls, and blood, and many of them made the ultimate sacrifice. Although officially 285 men of the regiment died, many more never recovered from the service and died soon after returning home. The soldiers spent four and a half years in the West, and were fortunate to serve under outstanding leadership.

The story of the 11th Missouri has been preserved in many accounts of the official records of the Civil War, but also many letters exist to give personal accounts of the soldiers who served in it. Captain William Stewart, Company K, chronicled the regiment's activities in 1861 and 1862. The regimental chaplain, Samuel Baldridge, described actions in a series of letters in 1862. Sergeant Charles Treadway wrote a series of letters covering the time period 1862–1865. Also, Captain George Adams wrote some excellent letters describing Vicksburg and the Battle of Spanish Fort. Several sets of letters were also collected from the pension records of soldiers from the regiment, including Eugene Page, William Notestine, Alzono Thomas, John Treadway, John Collins, William Haskins, James Mulhall, Abraham Norris, William Chapman, Luther Vance, and Anderson Campbell. Duncan McCall published a memoir of the regiment that described firsthand the events during the first three years of the war. Finally, the accounts of the war and events of the 11th Missouri were preserved by the most prodigious letter writer of all, Doctor Thomas Hawley, whose letters cover the entire period of the war. These firsthand accounts were very important in defining the character of the 11th Missouri Infantry.

A few points need to be made about this book. Civil War records can be very complete but at the same time contain many errors. Many of the firsthand accounts need to be tempered with established historical facts. This is particularly true in descriptions of the events of battles where there is often a tendency to exaggerate the successes of the conflict. Determining a roster of men for the 11th Missouri Infantry and the 11th Missouri Veteran Infantry was a huge challenge. There are, at least, three primary sources for the roster. A descriptive work for the regiment can be found at the Missouri Archives, a second set of descriptive rolls is located at the National Archives, and finally, the carded information of the soldiers of the regiment can be found at the Missouri State Archives. Fortunately, these three sources have a consistent record of the soldiers, but there are differences among them. This makes a definitive list of soldiers in the regiment very difficult. In addition, some soldiers are shown as various different individuals because of differences in spelling—such as Columbus Wroe, Columbus Rowe, and Columbus Rove (a single individual). As a result, there are surely some errors in the regimental rosters located in Appendix A and Appendix B.

In regard to desertions, it should be noted that in the Civil War desertions were commonplace. It should also be noted that this was a time of poor communication and often the soldiers were illiterate. There were remarkably few desertions in the 11th Missouri Infantry and there were many desertions in the 11th Missouri Veteran Infantry. While reviewing the Compiled Service Records of the regiment, there were several accounts of records of desertions which were expunged from soldiers' records after the war was over. In many cases soldiers were sick or wounded, returned home to convalesce and were unable to return to the regiment. For whatever reason, the situation was not communicated to the regiment and the whereabouts of the soldier was unknown. A report stating a soldier was a deserter does not always tell the whole story. The appendices of this book report the regimental descriptive rolls for the regiment and if a desertion was expunged, this would have occurred after the war and may not be shown in the regimental rosters. I suggest that Compiled Service Records be reviewed before it is concluded that desertions were factual.

The 11th Missouri was considered a western regiment and did not fight in the grand battles of the East. But, the regiment proved itself worthy in many of the great battles in the West. Many readers will not be familiar with the commanders of the corps, divisions and brigades in which the regiment served but it is important to remember the names of Joseph Plummer, Joseph Mower, John McArthur and Andrew J. Smith. Much is made of the blunders of officers in the Civil War, but this set of officers was almost unprecedented in the quality of their leadership. These men never failed the regiment.

Finally, the story of the regiment needed to be told. It was called on many times to turn the tide of a battle and always responded without hesitation. Its soldiers fought against two angry Confederate regiments at Iuka, they repelled the Confederates at Battery Robinett at Corinth, they assaulted the impossible Stockade Redan at Vicksburg as rows of them were cut down and they broke Hood's line at Nashville, again charging through a barrage of musket and artillery fire.

Chapter 1

Organizing the 11th Missouri Infantry and Battle of Fredericktown

"The dead and the wounded were strewn in every direction, and often, commingled in one common mass, would be found the dead horses and their vanquished riders."
— Sergeant William Cleland, Company F, 11th Missouri

Missouri in 1861

The election of Abraham Lincoln in the border states was by no means a reassurance that the citizens of these states were having their political needs met. In Missouri, Lincoln carried only St. Louis and Gasconade counties in the election of 1860. In the 1860 presidential election, Missouri narrowly sided with Stephen Douglas, while John Bell, a Constitutional Unionist, ran second, and Lincoln ran a weak fourth with only 17,028 votes. Because Lincoln lost so decidedly in Missouri, this served as a point of contention that Missourians were not represented politically and a secession movement found fertile ground. Missouri was a divided state and had had clashes, including involvement in Kansas for several years regarding the slavery issues in that state. Claiborne Fox Jackson, Missouri's fourteenth governor, held the top political post in 1861 having been elected from the Democratic Party in 1860. Missouri leaned toward compromise as the clouds gathered and the Civil War loomed; but, as the lines became clearly drawn on the issues driving the country toward war, Jackson's position was revealed. He placed the "current crisis squarely at the feet of Northern abolitionists who threatened millions of dollars of Southern slave property."[1] He also felt the Southern states were being pushed into a position of inequality with the North, which was anything but constitutional and the Union was already abandoned.

Jackson and his lieutenant governor, Thomas Reynolds, began to take actions within the state in anticipation of Missouri's secession, but St. Louis would be instrumental in determining the direction the state would go. Not only was it the most populated area of the state, but it also housed the United States military arsenal with a very large number of muskets, powder, and other military supplies. Politically, St. Louis' mayor, Oliver Filley, and Congressman Frank Blair were "Free-Soilers" and Blair was a personal friend of newly elected President

Abraham Lincoln. Governor Jackson knew that if St. Louis was to be drawn to support secession, actions would have be taken to accomplish this task.

Missouri, a growing and changing state, was not a large plantation state; and despite areas like "Little Dixie," located in central Missouri and populated with residents from Kentucky, Virginia, and North Carolina, in 1861 Northern and foreign-born residents outnumbered the Southern born residents. In addition, economically, Missouri was dissimilar to states like Mississippi, Alabama, Georgia, and South Carolina. The debate regarding the national situation intensified when Ft. Sumter was shelled and Missouri, while leaning toward preservation of the Union and compromise, was being pushed to decide where its allegiance would lie. After Ft. Sumter, Abraham Lincoln called for 75,000 three-month volunteers and Missouri was asked to furnish 4,000 of these men; but Governor Jackson flatly refused to provide them.

Paramilitary organizations had been assembled prior to the Ft. Sumter incident, particularly in the St. Louis area where pro–Southern Minute Men and pro-Northern Home Guards were being trained in response to the deteriorating state and national situation. Governor Jackson's refusal to furnish the 4,000 recruits requested by Lincoln offered an opportunity for the pro-Union Home Guards to be mustered into service. The commander of the Union military forces in St. Louis was Captain Nathaniel Lyon, a hard-line, pro–Union military officer whose experience in Kansas during the time when Missourians attempted to force Kansas to become a slave-holding state hardened his resolve against the South.

As Lyon mustered the Home Guards into service, the importance of protecting and controlling the St. Louis arsenal was clear. Lyon sent the military supplies that were not essential for the operation of the arsenal to Illinois and then moved to better protect the supplies that remained, should the arsenal be attacked. Lyon was also given authority to enlist 10,000 men to protect St. Louis and other parts of Missouri. The best laid plans of Governor Jackson seemed to be slipping away, but he began a plan to muster the state militia to better protect the rest of the state and counter Lyon's increased number of pro–Union troops being recruited. Jackson also sent a request to the officials within the Confederate States of America seeking military aid and was rewarded with artillery and other supplies being secretly shipped to the state. In addition, Jackson was "confident that Missouri would furnish 100,000 to the Southern cause."[2]

While the St. Louis arsenal served as Lyon's base, General Daniel Frost established Camp Jackson at Lindell's Grove, an open area just northwest of the city limits of St. Louis, which contained about 700 men who were part of the Missouri Volunteer State Militia. The military supplies that Governor Jackson had requested from the Confederate government arrived at Camp Jackson, but the crates remained unopened. Captain Lyon felt that Camp Jackson posed an immediate threat, and he became aware that the arms which had arrived were confiscated from the United States Army arsenal in Baton Rouge. Lyon used the possession of these arms as a way to rid himself of Camp Jackson. On May 10, 1861, the Union forces, about 7,000 strong, surrounded the Southern camp of 700 men which, when faced with such disproportionate odds, surrendered. The captured men were marched toward the United States arsenal, and during the march tragedy occurred. The most common explanation of the events which resulted in bloodshed was that as the men were marched, a crowd formed along the path made up of citizens from both sides; and, as luck would have it, "having been treated rather unceremoniously, the drunk whipped out a pistol and fired toward the troops, who stopped in place and loosed a volley over the heads of the crowd."[3] Another explanation for the cause of the bloodshed was that a boy about fifteen years old threw a clod of dirt and hit a mounted officer. Then a volley was fired. Nevertheless, the inexperienced recruits had fired and the result was a riot in which 28 people were killed and many others wounded.

This event in St. Louis ended any hope of compromise throughout the state, as citizens of Missouri chose their sides. The inflexibility of Governor Jackson and the equally aggressive and inflexible Nathaniel Lyon polarized an already difficult situation. On May 9 through May 11, 1861, Governor Jackson pushed through bills in the state legislature funding and authorizing the enrollment of all able-bodied men to protect the state. These newly enlisted men became part of the Missouri State Guard which was commanded by ex-governor Sterling Price. In the meantime, the pro-Union forces in St. Louis were given authority to capture all illegal arms and contraband.

As the state continued to divide, the Harney-Price Agreement was reached as the State Guard and the Union soldiers were being mustered into service. It was agreed that the State Guard would maintain order within the state and the Union troops would be given authority to maintain order in the St. Louis area. This temporary solution initially calmed the situation, but the extremists on both sides were not happy with the compromise. Governor Jackson used this time to strengthen his efforts to guide Missouri toward the Confederacy and General Nathaniel Lyon continued to push for greater enlistments for the Union side. Finally a meeting was held on June 11, 1861, between Nathaniel Lyon, Sterling Price and Governor Jackson; and after four hours it became apparent that no agreement could be reached. Lyon was quoted as stating that rather than give up any part of Missouri to non–Union control, "I would see you, and you, and you, and every man, woman, and child in the state dead and buried."[4]

At this point, any hope of peace within Missouri was lost. By the next morning, General Sterling Price communicated to the Missouri State Guard there would be open hostility with the Union army. The Missouri executive government in Jefferson City left the capital on June 13, and on June 15 General Lyon arrived there with 2,000 troops. The pro-Southern troops of Governor Jackson and Price moved to the southwestern part of Missouri in July, and Union troops from Kansas, Iowa, and Illinois joined Captain Nathaniel Lyon's Union troops in St. Louis.

In early July 1861, Major General John C. Frémont was placed in command of the Union forces in Missouri and began to seek out the Confederate forces under the command of General and ex-governor Sterling Price who commanded the Missouri State Guard. "Governor Jackson issued a call for a special session of the legislature to meet at Nesho, Mo., on October 21, 1861. Only a few members met. They passed an act of secession declaring Missouri's withdrawal from the Union. The United States government never regarded Missouri as out of the Union, but the Confederacy accepted this secession act as legal."[5] The official secession of the state of Missouri was signed by governor in-exile, Jackson, on November 2, 1861, and later approved by the Confederate congress.

Within the wake of the elected civil government of Missouri being on the run from the advancing Union troops, the state convention was recalled to determine Missouri's future. During the convention, it was decided to overturn the militia or State Guard initiative approved under Governor Jackson's administration. The delegates of the convention also elected Hamilton R. Gamble and Willard Hall as governor and lieutenant governor, respectively. While these actions were possibly illegal, since only the General Assembly held the power to impeach elected officials, the critical situation of 1861 necessitated these measures. The convention also decided that general elections would be held in November to fill those elected governmental offices that were vacant. Newly elected governor Gamble was a native Virginian who migrated to Missouri. He held a law degree from Yale University and had risen to serve as a justice of the Missouri Supreme Court. Gamble demonstrated his leadership and influence as he guided Missouri through these difficult times.

Major General John C. Frémont assumed command of the newly organized Western

Department with headquarters at St. Louis. Soon after the Battle of Wilson's Creek, on August 30, 1861, he proclaimed martial law, arrested active secessionists, suspended the publication of newspapers charged with disloyalty, and issued a proclamation assuming the government of the state and announcing that he would free the slaves of those in arms against the Union. When pressured to soften his position, Frémont refused to withdraw his proclamation, and on September 2, the president declared Frémont's actions as unauthorized and premature. The declaration of martial law was made without consultation of the newly forming state government and Governor Hamilton Gamble and others strongly opposed this action. The second serious error that Frémont made was arresting Congressman Frank Blair who had sent a message to Washington about what he thought was Frémont's unsatisfactory performance. Frémont was relieved of his command on November 2, 1861, after many complaints had been made regarding his administration, but in March 1862, he was placed in command of the Mountain Department of Virginia, Tennessee and Kentucky. However, not everyone was happy with Frémont's removal. Captain William Stewart of Company K, 11th Missouri Infantry, wrote to his parents in a letter dated September 23, 1861, that Frémont's removal was a "heavy blow upon us in Mo. for his policy was the best that could have been adopted for the state, and the most effectual that could have been used to drive rebellion out of Missouri."[6]

Frémont's controversial proclamation was published in the *Missouri Democrat* newspaper:

Headquarters of the Western Department
St. Louis, August 30, 1861.

Circumstances, in my judgment, of sufficient urgency, render it necessary that the commanding general of this Department should assume the administrative powers of the State. Its disorganized condition, the helplessness of the civil authority, the total insecurity of life, and the devastation of property by bands of murderers and marauders, who infest nearly every county of the State, and avail themselves of the public misfortunes and the vicinity of a hostile force to gratify private and neighborhood vengeance, and who find an enemy wherever they find plunder, finally demand the severest measures to repress the daily increasing crimes and outrages which are driving off the inhabitants and ruining the State.

In this condition, the public safety and the success of our arms require unity of purpose, without let or hindrance, to the prompt administration of affairs.

In order, therefore, to suppress disorder, to maintain as far as now practicable the public peace, and to give security and protection to the persons and property of loyal citizens, I do hereby extend and declare established Martial Law throughout the State of Missouri.

The lines of the Army of Occupation in this State are for the present declared to extend from Leavenworth by way of the posts of Jefferson City, Rolla, and Ironton, to Cape Girardeau, on the Mississippi River.

All persons who shall be taken with arms in their hands within these lines shall be tried by Court-Martial, and if found guilty will be shot.

The property, real and personal, of all persons, in the State of Missouri, who shall take up arms against the United States, or who shall be directly proven to have taken an active part with their enemies in the field, is declared to be confiscated to the public use, and their Slaves, if any they have, are hereby declared Free men.

All persons who shall be proven to have destroyed, after the publication of this order, railroad tracks, bridges, or telegraphs, shall suffer the extreme penalty of the law.

All persons engaged in Treasonable correspondence, in giving or procuring aid to the Enemies of the United States, in fomenting tumults, in disturbing the public tranquility by creating and circulating false reports or incendiary documents, are in their own interests warned that they are exposing themselves to sudden and severe punishment.

All persons who have been led away from their allegiance, are required to return to their homes forthwith; any such absence, without sufficient cause, will be held to be presumptive evidence against them.

General Nathaniel Lyon at the Battle of Wilson's Creek (Library of Congress).

The object of this declaration is to place in the hands of the Military authorities the power to give instantaneous effect to existing laws, and to supply such deficiencies as the conditions of War demand. But this is not intended to suspend the ordinary Tribunals of the Country, where the Law will be administered by Civil officers in the usual manner, and with their customary authority, while the same can be exercised.

The commanding general will labor vigilantly for the public Welfare, and in his efforts for their safety hopes to obtain not only the acquiescence, but the active support of the Loyal People of the Country.

    J. C. FRÉMONT
    Major-General Commanding.[7]

So, as North-South factionalization was strengthening in Missouri, the Battle of Wilson's Creek was fought near Springfield, Missouri on August 10, 1861, and demonstrated to the Missourians that the new war would be vicious and hard fought. The battle resulted in approximately 2,500 casualties, including the death of Nathaniel Lyon, and was considered a Confederate victory. The Union army withdrew to Rolla but the Confederates were in no condition to pursue them.

The 11th Missouri Infantry

It was during this time of division and unrest the 11th Missouri Infantry was called to arms and organized. The 11th Missouri Infantry was mustered into service as a regiment shortly before the Battle of Wilson's Creek on August 6, and the real threat of a fighting war with Confederates in Missouri was soon a reality. After being mustered into service at Jefferson

Barracks in St. Louis, Missouri, the 11th Missouri was immediately under command of Captain David Bayles who took command of the regiment as its colonel; and on August 6, 1861, Bayles moved the regiment to Cape Girardeau, Missouri. The regiment arrived there on the August 7 and went into camp.

The 11th Missouri Infantry considered itself the "Missouri Rifles," which notation was found on company records through 1861, before fully assuming the identity as the 11th Missouri Infantry. While the First Missouri Rifle Battalion was being formed in the summer of 1861, it was temporarily assigned as part of the First Missouri Infantry regiment and was stationed at Phelps County, Missouri. The Missouri Rifles moved from Rolla to St. Louis to be mustered as the 11th Regiment Missouri Volunteer Infantry, and because there were not enough men to form a regiment, additional men were needed to completely fill the ranks. The new recruits joined with the First Missouri Rifles in St. Louis. In addition to David Bayles, Captain Rufus Saxton was instrumental in organizing the 11th Missouri Infantry; however, confusion about the leadership and identity of the regiment carried through September 1861.

Saxton, who was important in the formation of the First Missouri Rifles and helped organize

Rufus Saxton, an important figure in organizing the 11th Missouri, who transferred before ever commanding the regiment (Library of Congress).

the 11th Missouri Infantry, had a strong military background. Rufus Saxton was a native of Greenfield, Massachusetts, being born October 19, 1824. Saxton attended Deerfield Academy in Massachusetts and worked on the family farm until, at age of 20, he received appointment to West Point from which he graduated in 1849, leaving as a 2nd Lieutenant. In 1853-1854 he explored and surveyed the Rocky Mountains for the Northern Pacific Railroad. He was commanding an artillery unit at the St. Louis Arsenal when the Civil War began in April

1861. He also assisted Nathaniel Lyon in his actions at Camp Jackson and was named his Chief Quartermaster. In 1862, he was promoted Brigadier General and assumed command of Harpers Ferry.[8]

The 11th Missouri Infantry was a contradiction, because although this regiment was a Missouri regiment, in fact, nine of the ten companies contained almost all of the recruits originating from Illinois. Only Company K could be called a Missouri company. The summary of the original command for the regiment is shown below:

REGIMENTAL STAFF	AUGUST 1861	PLACE OF ORIGIN OF THE COMPANY
Colonel	David Bayles	
Lt. Colonel		
Major		
Adjutant	Charles Brookings	
Quarter Master	George Henry	
Surgeon	Thomas Smith	
Asst. Surgeon	Eli Bowyer	
Chaplain	Joseph Brooks	
Company A		
Captain	William Panabaker	Lawrence County, Illinois
1st Lieutenant	Menomen O'Donnell	
2nd Lieutenant	Charles Orr	
Company B		
Captain	Andrew Weber	Sangamon County, Illinois
1st Lieutenant	Jesse Lloyd	
2nd Lieutenant	James W. Wilson	
Company C		
Captain	Moses Warner	Springfield/Loami, Illinois
1st Lieutenant	William Perce	
2nd Lieutenant	Modesta Green	
Company D		
Captain	Clark Hendee	Clay and Pike County, Illinois
1st Lieutenant	Clark Bentley	
2nd Lieutenant	George Henry	
Company E		
Captain	Benjamin Livingston	Olney, Fairview, and Stringtown, Illinois
1st Lieutenant	Abner Bail	
2nd Lieutenant	Jacob Blew	
Company F		
Captain	Amos Singleton	Xenia and Flora, Illinois
1st Lieutenant	William Colclasure	
2nd Lieutenant	Benjamin McConnell	
Company G		
Captain	William Mieure	Lawrence County, Illinois
1st Lieutenant	Charles Carter	
2nd Lieutenant	Benjamin Laird	
Company H		
Captain	Thomas Dollahan	Crawford County and Sumner, Illinois
1st Lieutenant	William Boatright	
2nd Lieutenant	Harley Kingsbury	

	AUGUST 1861	PLACE OF ORIGIN OF THE COMPANY
Company I		
Captain	William Barnum	Bethel, Concord, and Meredosia, Illinois
1st Lieutenant	James Hummer	
2nd Lieutenant	Charles Osgood	
Company K		
Captain	William Stewart	Franklin, Phelps, and St. Louis counties, Missouri
1st Lieutenant	Wilson Duggans	
2nd Lieutenant	Charles Foster	

The months of August through October were defining times for the 11th Missouri and the regiment was very busy. Initially, Colonel David Bayles assumed command of the regiment; but by the end of September he was superseded by newly promoted Joseph Plummer. David Bayles was a native of Ohio and had military experience, having fought in the Mexican War. Prior to the beginning of the war he worked as a "collector, water license" in St. Louis. Bayles recruited men for the First Missouri Rifles with his friend Captain Saxton; and according to correspondence from Bayles to Francis Blair in March 1862, he explained it was intended that Saxton would command the First Missouri Rifles and Bayles would serve as his subordinate, presumably lieutenant colonel. However, Saxton was promoted as colonel and was transferred out of Missouri, which resulted in Bayles assuming command of the regiment; and David Bayles was mustered into the regiment as colonel in command of the 11th Missouri on August 6, 1861.

After being mustered as a regiment on August 6 in St. Louis, the 11th Missouri immediately boarded a riverboat and headed south arriving at Cape Girardeau, Missouri, on August 7. The men found that being an infantry regiment was not going to be the daily praise and glory they imagined, because the men were assigned the unloading of the boat. The 27-year-old Sangamon County, Illinois, farmer, Private Duncan McCall, Company B, recorded, "It was hard work, as we had to roll the barrels and hogsheads up a very high hill. But being strong and healthy, we soon put every thing on shore. We carried our traps into the second story of an old mill, which was deserted."[9] Captain William Stewart, Company K, wrote to his parents, "When we arrived the weather was excessively hot and continued so until 2 o'clock to-day when rain came up and to-night at 9 o'clock it still continues, but we have everything pleasant in our tents…. We now have 3000 men here and can withstand an attack of 10,000 men at least…. Our Colonel, Col. Saxton is one of the most popular military men in the west, and we will follow him wherever he shall lead us."[10]

Preparation for defenses in the oncoming war had recently begun at Cape Girardeau, considered the front in the conflict with the South. At this time the defenses consisted of an unfinished small fort with no guns mounted. The new Union defenders were informed an attack was likely. Early in the occupation of Cape Girardeau, the Confederates harassed the Union forces resulting in the wounding of Captain Clark Hendee, Company D, and two other soldiers of the 11th Missouri. Volleys had been exchanged in the evening, but little could be seen in the dark. Captain William Stewart recorded this raid in a letter to his family on August 10. "After waiting a while with my command on the left wing, the 2nd post of honor in the regiment, the rebel scouts came up in the dark (about 2 o'clock) and fired into my wing dropping two men in the company next to me. At this that Company fell into confusion and began firing right into my Company. I ordered my men to fall back out of range of the fire, which they did, escaping most marvelously, with a few hats shot to pieces and some heads burnt."[11] Obviously, the newly forming regiment had much to learn and their training would be important in how they would face their true enemy.

1. Organizing the 11th Missouri Infantry and Battle of Fredericktown 13

This event was also described in a letter by Private John Treadway, Company E. John Treadway was a 29-year-old hoop maker from Fairview, Illinois, and was the company musician. Treadway began his letter by relating that the regiment was camped at Cape Girardeau and estimated 4000 Southern troops threatened their camp. He also indicated the pro–Southern population and troops were exceeding hard on the pro–Northern local population, forcing them to leave the area. Treadway indicated his company resided in a large mill which had been owned by a man with Southern sympathies who had departed from Cape Girardeau. The rest of the regiment lived in two other mills, which also were used as shelter for the arriving Union troops. Treadway recorded the account of the skirmish, "Since I commenced this I have bin in quite a battle. There was one reported killed and 2 wounded. I have seen the wounded men. One of them is shot through the shoulder close to the top of the lungs. It is thought he will get well. Some of our men was in a close place that is those that was on picet guard. John Crawford and Milt Akey was out. Then one of the guard fires. They have to all fire and then run to the main body of the army. Some of the guards saw some of the enemy and fired at them. All of the guard fired and the enemy then fired on them. Milt Akey fired his gun and started to run and there was a man shot at him not more than ten feet of Milt rushed on him ... and knocked him down and fought him untell they saw others running up then he run. It was a very bold act and shows that he will fight. But when he come to find he was one of our own men, he is hurt very bad but not dangerous but the worst danger there was out [we] did not know that was a guard out there and as soon as they shot they thought that they was all enemys and they commenced firing at them. Capt. Hendy [Hendee] was struck with two balls. One only through his blanket and one tuched his arm and then he give orders to fire and then nearly all the regiment shot. John was running towards us and he found the balls flying so fast around him that they was cutting all the weeds down and then he got behind a wood pile but the main body of the enemy did not show themselves. They found that we was ready for them and they backed out.... We was taken out about eleven oclock up one hill and kept there untell morning."[12]

John Treadway, who was a musician, recorded he could not find his drum and grabbed the first thing he could find which was a musket. Private Treadway realized he was part of the infantry, regardless whether he was a musician or infantryman. The next morning blood was found on the ground and one horse was dead. The account of the skirmish clearly showed confusion on both sides. The unfortunate John Treadway died of consumption shortly after writing this letter in December 1861.

In addition to the conflict with their Southern foes, early camp life at Cape Girardeau was unpleasant, and as the Union army struggled to supply the forming regiments, many basics were missing. In a letter written by the 11th Missouri's doctor, Thomas Hawley, he indicated the initial problems resulted from lack of sanitation and proper supply. The uniforms had not arrived for the men even after three weeks in the new army. In addition, the first note was made that the command structure for the regiment was not complete despite the regimental elections. "Yesterday we had 120 patients, ⅔ of the diseases.... For many no blankets, coats and half naked. They have promises of uniforms tomorrow at the farthest. Dr. Smith, Rev. Brooks & Col Bayles are neither here nor have been for 2 weeks."[13]

On August 28, 1861, the regiment began its first military expedition to Perryville, Missouri, "and was gone seven days, capturing quite a number of rebels, breaking several rebel recruiting stations, and marching about seventy-five miles."[14] When the 11th Missouri advanced on Perryville, a German ball was in progress. The regiment advanced on the town from four directions and the town was taken by surprise. The citizens soon went home and the regiment enjoyed themselves. Private Duncan McCall, Company B, recorded, "Whiskey flowed quite freely, and the officers and men had a good time generally…. There was plenty here, and the people invited the soldiers to dine with them."[15] Private Luther Vance, Company I, wrote about the action at Perryville, "We went to a little town called Peryville — We took 200 secesionest and made them take the oath. All but one. We kep him and fetched him to the Cape to have his trial. He belong in a secesionest company. We stade there about 5 days then went to Camp Jackson about 40 miles from Perryville. They told us that we would have a fight thare back."[16] Upon returning to Cape Girardeau, the regiment spent the next days in drill and constructing the defenses of the city.

After returning to Cape Girardeau, the soldiers of the 11th Missouri Infantry were given their uniforms, and tragically, the regiment recorded that Private William Ford, Company B, drowned while washing himself before he put on his new blue uniform. William Ford was an 18-year-old farmer from Sangamon County, Illinois, and drowned on September 4, 1861. His drowning followed the drowning of Samuel Brown who died on August 24, 1861, in the Mississippi River. The drowning of Samuel Brown was the first recorded death for the regiment. Brown was an English-born farmer from Lawrence County, Illinois. Also in August, Private Jeremiah Miller's finger was accidentally shot off and Private Miller was later discharged from service in 1862 for disability.[17]

After returning from Perryville, three companies of the 11th Missouri Infantry were sent on a scouting expedition near Cape Girardeau. The soldiers had marched for twelve hours when, at 9:00 P.M., they found themselves surrounded by a large group of cavalry armed with squirrel rifles and shotguns. The skirmish was detailed by Captain Moses Warner, Company C, who told that in "the darkness some confusion at first arose, the mounted men of the two detachments becoming mixed up without recognizing each other."[18] This incident was described in the *Camp Fremont Register*, a newspaper published under the direction of the 11th Missouri Infantry while they were posted at Cape Girardeau. Warner further described the clash when his soldiers encountered the Southerners and his detachment was surrounded and "attacked in the rear, but coming to an 'about face,' opened upon them a brisk fire, killing eight, and capturing three, together with a few horses and other property."[19] The enemy consisted of about 200 mounted rebels and the clash was unplanned by both groups as they collided with one another unexpectedly. It was at this skirmish that the first member of the 11th Missouri Infantry died in action as a result of the conflict with the Confederates. Private Maurice Denizet was killed in action in the skirmish with the enemy in Dallas, Missouri, in Bollinger County. Private Denizet had just enlisted in the regiment on September 16 and eight days later he proved to be the regiment's first loss to enemy fire. Private Denizet was born in 1841 in France and had immigrated to Perryville, Missouri, with his family. He was 20 years old and had been working as a farm laborer before his enlistment. Private Denizet's death was described in one of Captain William Stewart's letters he sent to his parents. Captain Stewart wrote on September 26, 1861, that the 11th Missouri had "a small fight with some rebel cavalry, in which one of our men was killed by being shot through the head."[20] Stewart reported ten rebels were killed in the incident.

Dr. Thomas Hawley from Lawrence County, Illinois, became the 11th Missouri Infantry's regimental surgeon later in the war. He was a prolific letter writer and his letters have been preserved which recorded many details about the regiment. Hawley was initially mustered in as hospital steward. His letters continued throughout the war. Dr. Hawley was born on February 20, 1837, in Dayton, Ohio, and graduated from the St. Louis Medical College in 1861. He was the son of the Rev. Nelson Hawley. Dr. Hawley commented about the early command of the 11th Missouri Infantry in letter he wrote on September 8, 1861, from Cape Girardeau, Missouri. "We have had an election in the regiment lately for field officers.

The 11th Missouri was stationed at Cape Girardeau, Missouri (*Frank Leslie's Illustrated History of the Civil War*).

Col D. Bayles was unanimously chosen as such. Capt. Pennabaker, Lt. Col., Capt. Livingston as Major. Dr. Smith's office was confirmed with Dr. Bowyer and mine. Most of men now have their uniforms & look well. Not many of the officers have theirs for they have to go to St. Louis and as yet have not had the time. Col. Bayles is now commander of this post. As Col. Marsh is gone and is now on his way to Cairo. Our troops have charge of the breast works and artillery. From this and a few other reasons, we conclude if possible that we may remain here for a few weeks longer."[21]

In a surprising turn of events, the command of the 11th Missouri Infantry was transferred to Colonel Joseph Plummer who had participated in the Battle of Wilson's Creek and had gained recognition from his superiors. David Bayles, disappointed, was mustered out, honorably, from the army on September 30, 1861, after appealing unsuccessfully with General Frémont.[22] Newly appointed Colonel Joseph Plummer was an excellent soldier. He was born on November 15, 1861, in Barre, Massachusetts, and he was a schoolteacher after completing his education. In 1837, he obtained an appointment to the United Stated Military Academy at West Point, New York. He graduated and was commissioned as a 2nd lieutenant in 1841 and joined the United States Army. Plummer did not participate in the Mexican-American War due to illness. He served on the Texas frontier from 1848 to 1861. In 1852, he was promoted to the rank of captain in the U.S. Infantry. He married Frances Hagner and the couple had one son, Satterlee Plummer.[23]

Joseph Plummer was commissioned as the colonel of the 11th Missouri Infantry on September 24, 1861, and assumed command of the regiment at its first station at Cape Girardeau, Missouri. By the time Colonel Plummer joined the 11th Missouri Infantry, he was carrying a remembrance from the Battle of Wilson's Creek, a wound that would later play a significant part as a cause for his death.

Needless to say, Colonel David Bayles was not happy about Plummer commanding the regiment he had worked hard to organize; but General John C. Frémont deemed it necessary that the 11th Missouri Infantry be commanded by a trained and experienced officer. David Bayles later wrote that Frémont admitted to him that Joseph Plummer was given command of the 11th Missouri because he thought Bayles was only a lieutenant colonel. Frémont couldn't correct this mistake immediately because he was actively pursuing the enemy. Frémont was relieved of his command and no action was taken to correct the "wrong" done to Bayles. Despite Bayles' desire to command the 11th Missouri Infantry, he was not greatly missed by the regiment. Duncan McCall recalled that Bayles was a captain who had enlisted for 3 months service only. McCall also described Bayles, "He was very severe on us. We had to drill eight hours a day, and there was a great deal of fatigue duty to do."[24] Even after being superseded by Plummer, David Bayles tried to gain control of the 11th Missouri, gaining an order in May 1862 to travel and assume command of the regiment, but there is no evidence that he ever commanded the regiment after September 1861. On January 23, 1863, Special Order 37 revoked David Bayle's reinstatement as the 11th Missouri's colonel stating, "Special Order # 108, Series 1862, reinstated Colonel D. Bayles 11th Missouri Volunteers in his command is hereby revoked, he being unfit for duty on account of disability."[25] Bayles suffered from dropsy and general debility. Even the Report of the Adjutant General in 1863 failed to show him as colonel of the regiment, but did acknowledge his role in organizing the 11th Missouri. David Bayles' health failed him in 1862 and he died in St. Louis in 1863, never commanding the 11th Missouri Infantry again.

This effectively ended the confusion about the command of the 11th Missouri and the regiment was commanded by an excellent colonel and professional soldier which was the first step in making the 11th Missouri an efficient fighting regiment.

On September 29, Dr. Hawley wrote again to his family regarding the command of the 11th Missouri and the fact that Colonel Joseph Plummer was in command of the regiment. Hawley's approval of Plummer was evident in his letter: "We are under command of another Col or he soon will take command. I was introduced to him today and like his appearance much better than the present commander and least for good sound

Colonel Joseph Plummer, Massachusetts native, who served at the Battle of Wilson's Creek, assumed command the 11th Missouri Infantry (National Archives).

judgment. Col Plummer was a former captain in the regular service and commanded with distinguished bravery at Wilson Creek."[26] In another letter on October 2, Dr. Hawley was even more emphatic about the replacement of David Bayles by Colonel Plummer as commander of the regiment. "All are well pleased with the change of commanders. Col. Plummer is a thorough military man of the regular army and our former Col had not the knowledge, experience or judgment that the present one has."[27]

In October, in order to control the discipline of the soldiers and minimize the influence that external forces had on the regiment, Colonel Plummer issued General Order 20, which stated, "All persons keeping saloons or house of public resort where alcoholic liquors are kept, are prohibited from selling the same to soldiers of this command."[28] The need to control the alcohol consumption was evident due to several incidents that occurred with the regiment including the altercation between Private William McCready, Company A, and Private John McGinley, also from Company A. A fight broke out between the two in which alcohol was involved, which resulted in McCready "biting a piece off his ear." McCready faced a court-martial due to his actions.

When Colonel Bayles was replaced with Colonel Joseph Plummer, the command structure of the regiment was changed. The new officers of the regiment are listed in the table below:

REGIMENTAL STAFF	SEPTEMBER 1861		
Colonel	Joseph Plummer		
Lt. Colonel	William Panabaker		
Major	Benjamin Livingston		
Adjutant	Charles Brookings		
Quarter Master	George Henry		
Surgeon	Thomas Smith		
Asst. Surgeon	Eli Bowyer		
Chaplain	Joseph Brooks		
Company A		*Company F*	
Captain	Cyrenus Elliott	Captain	Amos Singleton
1st Lieutenant	Menomen O'Donnell	1st Lieutenant	William Colclasure
2nd Lieutenant	Charles Orr	2nd Lieutenant	Edward Gannon
Company B		*Company G*	
Captain	Andrew Weber	Captain	William Mieure
1st Lieutenant	Jesse Lloyd	1st Lieutenant	Charles Carter
2nd Lieutenant	James W Wilson	2nd Lieutenant	Benjamin Laird
Company C		*Company H*	
Captain	Moses Warner	Captain	Thomas Dollahan
1st Lieutenant	William Perce	1st Lieutenant	Willlliam Boatright
2nd Lieutenant	Modesta Green	2nd Lieutenant	Harley Kingsbury
Company D		*Company I*	
Captain	Clark Hendee	Captain	William Barnum
1st Lieutenant	Clark Bentley	1st Lieutenant	James Hummer
2nd Lieutenant	J. W. Cowperthwaite	2nd Lieutenant	Charles Osgood
Company E		*Company K*	
Captain	Charles Hollister	Captain	William Stewart
1st Lieutenant	Abner Bail	1st Lieutenant	Wilson Duggans
2nd Lieutenant	Jacob Blew	2nd Lieutenant	Charles Foster

By October 1861, the officers of the 11th Missouri Infantry were in place, but this group of men constantly changed throughout the war. Already, Colonel Rufus Saxton and David Bayles were no longer with the regiment.

The Officers and Men of the 11th Missouri Infantry

The officers and men of the 11th Missouri were a varied group of people. Specific information on the officers of the regiment was found in the 11th Missouri Descriptive Roll, U.S. Census records, biographies, and through pension records.

Company A. Captain William Panabaker, the first captain of the company, was elected as lieutenant colonel in September and handled the day-to-day command of the regiment while Colonel Plummer served as brigade commander. By October, the new captain of Company A was Dr. Cyrenus Elliott. Cyrenus Elliott, 43 years old, was a native of Ohio and was a physician, as was William Panabaker before him. Elliott was living in Poseyville, Indiana, prior to the war.

Company A's 1st lieutenant was Menomen O'Donnell, a native Irishman, who lived in Bridgeport, Illinois, prior to the war. Lieutenant O'Donnell was a married farmer prior to his enlistment. The 2nd lieutenant was Charles M. Orr, a single farmer who also lived in Bridgeport, Illinois. Lieutenant Orr had served three months with the Eighth Illinois Infantry prior to joining the 11th Missouri Infantry.

The enlisted men of Company A were almost exclusively from Lawrence County, Illinois. Sixty-one men listed Bridgeport as their residence, thirty listed Sumner and one soldier had resided in Lawrenceville. Only one person was from Hadley, Illinois, two were from Venice, Illinois, and finally, one soldier listed Poseyville, Indiana, as his place of residence. The recruits for Company A were mostly farmers, and 90 of the 97 enlistees indicated this to be their occupation. In addition, there were two millers, one blacksmith, one carpenter, one peddler, one cooper, one schoolteacher and one physician in Company A.

Company B. Captain Andrew Weber was a 21-year-old unmarried farmer from Springfield, Illinois. He was instrumental in organizing Company B for the 11th Missouri Infantry; and because the county quotas were full for the Illinois regiments, he committed his men to fight for Missouri. The 1st lieutenant of Company B was Jesse Lloyd, a married merchant also from Springfield, Illinois. Lieutenant Lloyd was 24 years old at the time of his enlistment. James W. Wilson was elected 2nd lieutenant for Company B. Lieutenant Wilson was born on December 28, 1835, the son of Clinton Wilson, and he was an unmarried farmer, living in Springfield, Illinois, at the time of his enlistment.

The enlisted men of Company B were primarily from Sangamon County, Illinois, where the Illinois state capital was located. Ninety-one of the enlistees indicated that Sangamon County was their residence, one soldier had resided in Chippewa, Illinois, and one soldier listed Cape Girardeau, Missouri, as his residence. This company consisted primarily of farmers with 83 soldiers listing farming as their occupation. In addition, there were two carpenters, one mechanic, one

Captain Andrew Weber, Company B, a farmer from Springfield, Illinois (courtesy Civil War Museum at Wilson's Creek National Battlefield).

hotel runner, one printer, one baker, one soldier, one tailor, one painter and one blacksmith in the company.

Company C. Moses Warner was elected captain of Company C in September 1861. Moses Warner was a 30-year-old railroad conductor living in Springfield, Illinois. Captain Warner had also served as a deputy city marshal in Springfield prior to the war. First Lieutenant William Perce was a constable and broom maker prior to his enlistment. He was 43 years old, a native of Ohio, and lived in Springfield, Illinois. Modesta Green was the company's 2nd lieutenant and was born in New Jersey before moving to Springfield. He was a married carpenter before his enlistment.

The enlisted men of Company C were predominantly from Sangamon County, Illinois, representing the towns of Springfield, Dawson, Loami, Waverly, Pleasant Plains, Verdin, and Mechanicsburg. Eighty-one of the soldiers of this company listed a Sangamon County location as their residence. In addition, one soldier was from Pike County, Illinois, one from Logan County, Illinois, one from Cape Girardeau, Missouri, and two from Perryville, Missouri.

Lieutenant James Wilson, Company B, a farmer from Springfield, Illinois (USAMHI).

Many of the soldiers from this company were farmers, but many other occupations were represented. Thirty-six enlistees indicated that farming was their occupation. The company also contained 8 carpenters, 2 blacksmiths, 2 butchers, 4 bricklayers/stone masons, 2 physicians, 2 merchant/manufacturers, 1 schoolteacher, 2 clerks, 1 tobacconist, 20 laborers, 1 gunsmith, 2 millers, 1 joiner, and 1 teamster.

Company D. Thirty-six-year-old, Vermont-native, Captain Clark Hendee was a physician prior to his enlistment. He was instrumental in forming Company D from Clay County, Illinois, and he personally paid to transport the men of Company D to St. Louis for enlistment. Clark Bentley was elected 1st lieutenant. Lieutenant Bentley was a 33-year-old painter living in Louisiana, Missouri, and he was born in New York. First Lieutenant Bentley resigned in early September without specifying a reason for his resignation. Second Lieutenant George Henry was an attorney prior to his enlistment. Lieutenant Henry was a native of Ohio and lived in Clay County, Illinois. Lieutenant Henry was soon promoted as regimental quartermaster. Next, John W. Cowperthwait was commissioned 2nd lieutenant to replace George Henry and after Lieutenant Henry's promotion and Clark Bentley's resignation, Cowperthwait was appointed 1st lieutenant for Company D. Lieutenant Cowperthwait was a native Missourian and he was a 26-year-old engineer living in St. Louis prior to entering service with the 11th Missouri Infantry. When John Cowperthwait was promoted to the rank of 1st lieutenant, Missouri native, minister and farmer, Mark Sappington, was promoted to the rank of 2nd lieutenant. Mark Sappington was living in Clay County, Illinois, prior to his enlistment.

The enlisted men in Company D were primarily from Clay County, Illinois, but also represented many other locations. Fifty-eight men listed Clay County, Illinois, as their residence. Also from Illinois, eleven men were from Pike County, one from Madison County and one from Wayne County. There were several Missouri men in this company. Four men were from Louisiana, seven from Franklin County, two from Crawford County, two from St. Louis, one from Phelps County, one from Boone County, three from Gasconade County and one from Point Pleasant, Missouri.

The peace-time occupations of the men enlisting in Company D were farmers (68), minister (1), schoolteacher (1), carpenters (13), stonecutter (1), blacksmith (4), laborers (7), cooper (1), tailor (1) raft pilot (1), saddler (1) and cabinet maker (1).

Company E. The first captain of Company E was Benjamin Livingston. He was 30 years old and a lawyer living in Olney, Illinois, prior to the war; but he was soon elected as major for the 11th Missouri regiment in October 1861. Charles Hollister succeeded Benjamin Livingston as captain. Charles Hollister was also from Olney, Illinois. First Lieutenant Abner Bail was also from Olney, Illinois. Abner Bail was a married saddler prior to his enlistment, and he was an experienced soldier having fought in the Seventh U.S. regiment of infantry in the Mexican War. Finally, 2nd Lieutenant Jacob Blew of Claremont, Illinois, completed the officers of Company E. Lieutenant Blew, married, was a farmer prior to his enlistment.

The enlisted men of Company E represented various locations with the greatest concentration of enlistees coming from Richland County, Illinois. Fifty-four men enlisted from the Richland County towns of Olney, Noble, Claremont, Stringtown and Calhoun. Seventeen men enlisted from Fairview, Illinois, one from Jasper County, Illinois, one from Paris, Illinois, one from Sumner, Illinois, two from St. Louis, Missouri, one from Carondelet, Missouri, five from Hadley, Missouri, one from Clay City, Illinois, and one from Cape Girardeau, Missouri.

As with the other companies, most of the prewar occupations for the men enlisting in Company E was farmer. The company had 58 farmers, one brick layer, two laborers, two hoop makers, four carpenters, one wagon maker, two saddlers, one salesman, one minister, one physician, two railroaders, two shoemakers, one clerk, one wood cutter, one plasterer, one painter, two coopers, two blacksmiths and one machinist.

Company F. Amos Singleton was elected as the captain of Company F in September 1861. Captain Singleton was a 27-year-old carpenter and native of Ohio. He was married and living in Xenia, Illinois, at his enlistment. William Colclasure was 1st lieutenant of Company F. Colclasure was 36 years old and a farmer living in Xenia, Illinois, also. He was mustered into service as a private and he was a native of Tennessee. Second Lieutenant Benjamin McConnell served only a short period of time and resigned by the end of August 1861. Lieutenant McConnell was also a resident of Xenia, Illinois. By October 1861, Edward Gannon was promoted to the rank of 2nd lieutenant. Gannon was a 25-year-old moulder from Cape Girardeau and he was a native of Pennsylvania.

The recruits for Company F were primarily from Clay County, Illinois, and sixty-eight of the recruits listed Xenia as their residence and another sixteen listed Flora as their residence.

Only four men listed Salem, Illinois, as their prewar residence. The recruits were primarily farmers with sixty-five soldiers listing farming as their occupations. The other recruits had various occupations — ropemaker (1), blacksmith (7), shoemaker (4), carpenter (3), machinist (1), cooper (3), laborer (3), and carriage maker (1).

Company G. The officers of Company G, William Mieure, Charles Carter and Benjamin Laird, were all residents of Lawrence County, Illinois. Captain William Mieure was a 40-year-old merchant prior to the war. First Lieutenant Charles Carter, a 21-year-old native of Ohio, was another of many physicians who served in the 11th Missouri Infantry. Forty-one-year-old attorney, Benjamin Laird, was the 2nd lieutenant for Company G. Lieutenant Laird was married and a native of Pennsylvania.

Company G was a Lawrence County, Illinois, based company with seventy-nine of the enlistees indicating that either Lawrenceville or Lawrence County was their home. Of the remaining recruits — one soldier was from Scott County, Missouri, one from Sparta, Illinois, two were from St. Louis, Missouri, and one each from Dallas and Perryville, Missouri. The majority of the recruits were farmers. Sixty-five of the recruits indicated that this was their prewar occupation. In addition, the following occupations were also listed by the new recruits — teacher (1), shoemaker (1), moulder (3), engineer (1), blacksmith (2), painter (1), carpenter (6), merchant (1), mason (1), clerk (2), plasterer (1), musician (1), and wagon maker (1).

Company H. Captain Thomas Dollahan was elected to command Company H. William Boatright was elected 1st lieutenant. Second Lieutenant Harley Kingsbury was also elected in September 1861. Captain Thomas Theodore Dollahan was a 33-year-old native of Ohio and blacksmith residing in Lawrence County, Illinois, prior to his enlistment. First Lieutenant William Boatright was born near Robinson, Illinois, in 1835 and was a farmer from Crawford County, Illinois, prior to the war.

Company H consisted predominantly of men from Sumner, Illinois, but this regiment also included a number of soldiers from Crawford County, Illinois. Of the records that listed place of residence, sixty-five enlistees indicated that Sumner was their home. Seven men from St. Louis enlisted in this regiment as did one man from Cape Girardeau, Missouri. Sixty-eight of the enlistees indicated farming was their occupation. The remainder of company included men with various occupations: one bookkeeper, one clerk, two carpenters, one harness maker, one saddler, three schoolteachers, two blacksmiths, one shoemaker, one miner and one laborer.

Company I. Thirty-two-year-old William Barnum was elected captain of Company I when the regiment was organized. William Barnum was a married merchant living in Springfield, Illinois, prior to the war. Barnum was born in New Jersey and had immigrated to Illinois. William Barnum worked in the wholesale grocery business in the 1850s. He also studied law and was admitted to the Illinois bar in 1859. He organized a company of sharpshooters which became Company I. The marksmanship of the company proved to be a valuable skill as the company faced the war ahead. Barnum's 1st lieutenant was James Hummer, a 38-year-old, married minister from Bethel, Illinois. Charles Osgood was the company's 2nd lieutenant. Osgood was 23 years old and a physician and farmer, who lived in Bethel, Illinois, prior to his enlistment.

The recruits from Company I indicated various locations for their residences but Bethel, Illinois, was the home of the largest number of men of this company with forty-five men indicating this was their home. In addition, all the men indicated an Illinois location as their home including: Cass County (1), Versailles (4), Barry (9), Exeter (2), Coopertown (4),

Virginia (1), Meredosia (11), Concord (10), Morgan County (3), Beardstown (3), Brown County (1), Arenzville (1), Whitehall (1) and Glasco (2). Eighty-three of the recruits indicated that farming was their occupation. In addition, there were two carpenters, two ministers, one wagon maker, one cooper, one shoemaker, one teacher, two blacksmiths and one cook who enlisted in Company I.

Company K. William Stewart ably led Company K through the first three years of the war and provided excellent insight into the actions of the regiment through a series of letters that have been preserved. Captain William Stewart was an attorney residing in St. Louis, Missouri, at the beginning of the war. Stewart held a masters of arts degree awarded by Indiana Asbury College and was native of Indiana, born in 1831. He established his law practice in St. Louis in 1858 and continued in that capacity until he enlisted in the First Missouri Rifle Battalion in April 1861. After three months, he assumed the command of the only "Missouri Company" in the 11th Missouri Infantry.

Wilson Duggans was elected as 1st lieutenant of Company K. Lieutenant Duggans was born in 1832 and was a merchant and resident of Springfield, Illinois. Duggans was a native Ohioan and had moved to Springfield in 1855. Second Lieutenant Charles Foster, also an attorney from St. Louis, rounded out the command of Company K. He was 20 years old at the time of his enlistment.

The recruits for Company K contained the highest percentage of Missourians in the regiment. The largest number of recruits resided in Franklin County, Missouri, and thirty-four enlistees came from this location. In addition, other soldiers came from various Missouri communities including Cape Girardeau (1), Gasconade County (1), St. Louis (9), Rolla (5), Pike County (2), Perryville (1), Point Pleasant (1) and New Madrid (2). Company K was also composed of men from Illinois communities, including Flora (2), Sangamon County (4), Sumner (12), Bridgeport (4), Springfield (1), Lawrence County (2), Pike County (1), and DuQuoin (1). There were sixty-nine men who indicated farming was their occupation. In addition, there was one miller, one merchant, three blacksmiths, one pilot, three laborers, one teamster, one nail cutter, one miner, one joiner, three peddlers, one gunsmith, one machinist, and one physician.

Chaplain. The 11th Missouri Infantry's chaplain was Joseph Brooks, a native of Ohio, who was born on November 1, 1821. Brooks attended Indiana Asbury University and became a minister of the Methodist

Captain William Stewart, Company K, an attorney from St. Louis, chronicled the events of the 11th Missouri in the early part of the war through a series of letters (courtesy Civil War Museum at Wilson's Creek National Battlefield).

Episcopal Church after his ordination in 1840. He moved to St. Louis in 1856 and established himself as a strict abolitionist. He also edited the *Central Christian Advocate* while in St. Louis. Joseph Brooks quickly became a chaplain in the war, first with the First Missouri Artillery and then with the 11th Missouri Infantry. He was forty years old when he became a member of the 11th Missouri.[29]

Above: The religious needs of the 11th Missouri were placed under the care of the Rev. Joseph Brooks, the first chaplain of the 11th Missouri Infantry (Butler Center for Arkansas Studies).

Surgeon. Dr. Thomas Smith was elected as the first regimental surgeon of the 11th Missouri Infantry. Dr. Smith was the oldest person in the history of the regiment. Thomas Smith was born on July 17, 1808, in Lancaster, Pennsylvania. At the age of 20 he married Martha McKay and began teaching school. When he was 28, his wife died and he moved to western Pennsylvania and began studying medicine under the tutelage of Dr. John Hassen. By 1843, he had remarried and moved to Cincinnati, Ohio. In 1848, he graduated from medical school with honors and began to practice medicine in Cincinnati. By 1854, he had moved to Keokuk, Iowa, and later, to St. Louis in hopes of improving the health of his second wife. In 1861, he joined the 11th Missouri

Left: Dr. Thomas Hawley, Hospital Steward and prodigious letter writer (Francis Warrington Dawson Collection, Duke University Rare Book, Manuscript and Special Collections Library).

Infantry.[30] Dr. Smith led an excellent group of physicians, including Dr. Eli Bowyer, Assistant Surgeon, and Dr. Thomas Hawley, Hospital Steward.

Battle of Fredericktown

In September and October, the 11th Missouri was heavily involved in patrolling, guard duty and building the fortifications of Cape Girardeau in anticipation of an attack. The days were filled with drills and physical work in building the fortifications around the city. The typical day for the men of the regiment was completely filled with duties and training.

Reveille	5:30 A.M.	Dinner	12:30 P.M.
Sick Call	6:30 A.M.	Fatigue	1 P.M.
Breakfast	7 A.M.	Recall from Fatigue	5 P.M.
Fatigue	8 A.M.	Retreat	Sunset
Guard Mounting	9 A.M.	Tattoo	9 P.M.
Recall from Fatigue	12 P.M.	Taps	9:30 P.M.[31]
First Sergts Call	12:30 P.M.		

The regimental bugler, Private Robert Burcher, Company F, was a 24-year-old blacksmith from Flora, Illinois, and was greeted with distain at 5:30 A.M. but his notes were welcome at 9:30 P.M.

While the 11th Missouri Infantry was beginning the initial phases of the war, the Confederate forces were intent on swinging Missouri to their side of the conflict; and after the success at Wilson's Creek, Brigadier General Meriwether "Jeff" Thompson wanted to be the instrument to make Missouri part of the Confederacy. General Albert Sidney Johnston and Major General Leonidas Polk at Confederate headquarters in Columbus, Kentucky, sent a message to Jeff Thompson on September 29, 1861, directing him to move his command near Farmington, Missouri, and to cut the Ironton Railroad line. "Ever eager to strike a blow, the irrepressible Thompson quickly prepared his troops for the expedition in compliance with Johnston's directive."[32] In addition to threatening St. Louis, the goal was to draw Union attention to Thompson to relieve pressure on the command of Sterling Price in southwest Missouri and also to embarrass and weaken the Union control of the southeastern part of the state. The 11th Missouri's first real challenge of the war was with General Jeff Thompson's Missouri State Guards.

Brigadier General M. "Jeff" Thompson was born on January 22, 1826, in Harpers Ferry, Virginia. Jeff was a nickname he acquired in his youth by his friendship to a local African American, Jeff Carlyle. Thompson was educated in Charles Town, Virginia, and his initial military training came as he commanded the school's militia company. He was the son of an army paymaster. He applied for admission to West Point and the Virginia Military Institute but was denied. He moved west in the 1840 and made St. Joseph, Missouri, his home, and he became mayor of the city. He was active in various businesses and he became colonel and inspector of the Fourth Military District of the Missouri militia. Although Thompson was not initially a secessionist, John Brown's raid on Harpers Ferry and his belief that northern business interests did not represent the needs of the south, caused him to become a southern supporter.[33] Immediately after hearing about the news of Fort Sumter, Thompson overtly sided with the new Confederacy.

Thompson initially assumed the rank of lieutenant colonel in a battalion of infantry from Ripley County, Missouri, and soon was promoted to brigadier general of the First Division of the First Military District in Missouri. By August 1, he was calling for recruits from southeastern Missouri and soon began his assault on the Union forces in the southeastern part of the state. On October 1, 1861, General M. Jeff Thompson began a raid to destroy railroads and bridges near Pilot Knob, Ironton, and Fredericktown, Missouri. Thompson led a total command of 3,000 men in the fall of 1861. Thompson wrote on October 11, 1861, "Dear General: I march from this point in the morning. I will burn the bridge over Big River, near the tunnel on Wednesday night, with 500 dragoons. My infantry will be in Fredericktown on the same night. If I succeed in destroying the bridge and the tunnel, I will march back towards Ironton, with all forces I can collect from your district, hope you will join us as soon as possible, that we may take Ironton and then march on St. Louis or General Price."[34] Thompson commanded troops of the Missouri State Guard at this point in the war. Even through the Missouri State Guard were sympathetic to the Confederate cause, these were not officially Confederate troops.

General M. Jeff Thompson, Missouri State Guard commander at the Battle of Fredericktown (courtesy Civil War Museum at Wilson's Creek National Battlefield).

On October 15, General Thompson reported that he had captured the Big River Bridge near Blackwell Station and "killed a number of the enemy and took 45 prisoners, captured 66 muskets, and quantity of overcoats, etc."[35] Those captured were from the 33rd Illinois Infantry which suffered 1 killed and 11 wounded. In addition, 45 men were captured, but were paroled and released. Thompson's forces suffered two killed and six wounded.

Also on October 15, 1861, Union Colonel William Carlin was informed that Potosi, Missouri, had been threatened by Confederate troops numbering about 400 on the day before and he had dispatched 300 men of the 38th Illinois Infantry commanded by Major D. H. Gilbert and four companies of the First Indiana Cavalry commanded by Colonel Conrad Baker to meet this threat. Carlin soon became aware that instead of 400 Confederates pushing into southern Missouri, the attacking force was 3,000 strong and was commanded by General Jeff Thompson.[36]

Colonel Carlin immediately informed Brigadier General Ulysses Grant that Jeff Thompson's Missouri State Guard was massed in Farmington, Missouri, and on the October 18 Grant was aware that Carlin's troops had been driven back towards Pilot Knob and he was facing a enemy which might exceed 5,000 men. The military operations in southeast Missouri were under the command of General Grant who was located in Cairo, Illinois. Colonel William Carlin, commander of the 38th Illinois and commander of the Union forces in Ironton, knew that he was a likely target for the marauding Confederates. Colonel Carlin sent a request for assistance to his commander, General Grant, and Grant responded with a message to Colonel Joseph Plummer. Plummer was in

Colonel William Carlin, "a somewhat austere, high strung man, ... an excellent soldier, and feverishly anxious to do his duty" (Library of Congress).

command of the Union forces at Cape Girardeau, and Grant directed him to proceed to block any further advances by General Thompson by marching to Colonel Carlin's assistance. In addition to Plummer's men, two Union regiments stationed in Jackson, Missouri, were ordered to move as quickly as possible to coordinate with Colonel Carlin's troops in Ironton. On October 17, two more infantry regiments and a battery of artillery were dispatched from St. Louis along with a cavalry regiment. Grant understood the need for haste, and in his message to Plummer he emphasized that the expedition should be "moved with all dispatch." On October 18, Grant sent a second message to Plummer directing him to march upon Fredericktown and "drive out all armed bodies now threatening Iron Mountain Railroad and destroy them if possible."[37]

The First Indiana Cavalry attacked the Missouri State Guard force under command of Colonel Aden Lowe on October 17. Lieutenant E. M. Joel, 29th Missouri Infantry, reported that the First Indiana Cavalry attacked the Confederates and then fell back into an ambush that was coordinated with Colonel John Alexander's 21st Illinois Infantry and that the Southern troops "suffered severely and fell back with heavy loss."[38] On October 19, Lieutenant Joel reported the enemy was expected to attack at four different locations. Colonel Carlin's intent was to engage Thompson, but faced with four points of attack and believing he was outnumbered, decided to remain in a defensive posture.

Prior to confronting Thompson's troops, the issue of who commanded the Union troops into battle had to be decided. With two Union columns uniting to battle the enemy and both columns command by colonels, there was disagreement of who would command the Union forces prior to the Battle of Fredericktown. Colonel William Carlin commanded the largest number of men but he held the same rank as Plummer who commanded the second wing of the Union force pursuing Thompson. Colonel Plummer felt he had command of the expedition based on General Grant's orders, but Colonel Carlin claimed command based on the date of his commission being earlier than that of Plummer's. Colonel Plummer had combat experience during the Battle of Wilson's Creek while Colonel Carlin had yet to lead men in battle in the Civil War. Colonel Leonard Ross of the 17th Illinois Infantry under Plummer's command settled the matter because his commission superseded both Plummer and Carlin. Colonel Ross was part of Plummer's force advancing from Cape Girardeau. Also, being a colonel, he threatened to claim the right of command for Plummer, because of his commission date. Carlin grudgingly allowed command of the expedition to go to Plummer. Despite the resolution of command, friction continued throughout the battle, and Colonel Carlin wrote in his after-action report, "But as he [Plummer] had not manifested that sense of justice and delicacy towards me and my command that was demanded by truth, I have felt compelled to make this report."[39]

Colonel William Carlin, a native of Illinois, was related to the sixth governor of Illinois, and he was part of the West Point Class of 1850. After his graduation he was part of the Sixth U.S. Infantry and he had ten years experience with Indian warfare, including fighting the Sioux and Cheyenne. He was also involved in action against the Mormons in 1858. Carlin had the opportunity to be under the command of Albert Sidney Johnston. He was serving as a captain in the U.S. Infantry prior to the war and he assumed the command of the 38th Illinois Volunteer Infantry in August 1861.

General Jeff Thompson reported that he arrived at 10:00 A.M. in Fredericktown on October 17 with an estimated 1,200 Union troops marching toward him. He prophetically stated "My men are prepared to fight."[40]

On October 20, Thompson reported he intercepted a dispatch from Colonel Plummer revealing his intent to stop Thompson's retreat. Thompson's knowledge of the Union plan allowed him to remove his supply train 12 miles to the rear of Fredericktown to prevent Plummer from capturing his supplies. Then Thompson marched back toward Fredericktown on October 21, starting his march at 1:00 A.M., where he planned to occupy the town before the arrival of Plummer and Carlin's forces. But when he arrived, he found Fredericktown occupied with "double our numbers."[41] Realizing the disparity in numbers precluded a direct assault on Plummer's Union troops, Thompson moved his Missouri State Guard about a mile south of Fredericktown and an ambush was prepared using a combination of infantry, artillery, and cavalry. Thompson "planned to strike a quick blow from ambush and then retreat."[42] The Union pursuers were anticipated to run headlong into the trap and be caught in a vicious and deadly crossfire by Thompson's men.

Plummer's 1,500 troops began their march from Cape Girardeau on October 18. Plummer's original plan was to march toward Farmington, but he changed his destination once finding Thompson near Fredericktown. He had planned to cut the Confederate route of retreat, should they decide to move south, but having his dispatch intercepted gave Thompson advance knowledge of the Union plan to attack on the 21st, thwarting Plummer's plan to capture the supply train. Thompson's advanced knowledge of Plummer's plan gave him the advantage to anticipate the events as they unfolded. Carlin's 3,000 men from Pilot Knob had also moved to Fredericktown and Plummer's men arrived at noon. So Thompson's forces lay in wait for the two Union columns just south of Fredericktown with his artillery concealed to surprise the unsuspecting prey. But the Union force received assistance from local citizens and was able to avoid Thompson's surprise attack.

As the two forces converged on Fredericktown, the numbers favored the Union force. Thompson's command of approximately 1,200 men faced the combined forces of Plummer (1,500 men) and Carlin (3,000 men).[43] As the 11th Missouri moved toward this small town in southeastern Missouri, the march was a pleasant one, as Duncan McCall recalled, "When we started the rain was falling sufficient to make it pleasant marching during the whole trip."[44] Although the march was not difficult for the soldiers, the trip was not without hazards. A soldier of the 20th Illinois was "accidentally shot by leaning his head upon the muzzle of his gun."[45] By October 18, the 11th Missouri had marched to Cane Creek and reached Dallas, Missouri, on October 19 only to find the village almost absent of male residents who were overwhelming aligned with the Confederacy. General Thompson planned to attack Plummer's column as they marched before the two columns united but Plummer took a different route thus avoiding the trap. Private Duncan McCall of the 11th Missouri wrote that Thompson's trap was revealed through the help of a local citizen: "We were marching as if it were to our destruction, when an old negro warned us of the danger. He informed Plummer where the rebels were posted."[46]

The Union forces, which converged on Fredericktown, were under the overall command of Colonel Plummer and the 11th Missouri was commanded by Lieutenant Colonel William E. Panabaker. The other regiments that participated in the Battle of Fredericktown included were:

UNION

Colonel J. B. Plummer	Colonel William Carlin
17th Illinois Infantry Regiment	21st Illinois Infantry Regiment
20th Illinois Infantry Regiment	33rd Illinois Infantry Regiment
11th Missouri Infantry Regiment	38th Illinois Infantry Regiment
Stewart's Cavalry Company	8th Wisconsin Infantry Regiment
Langen's Cavalry Company	6 Companies, 1st Indiana Cavalry
1 Section, Taylor's Battery	Hawkin's Company Missouri Cavalry
Battery, Missouri Light Artillery	
2 Purcell's Howitzers	

MISSOURI STATE GUARD
Brigadier General M. Jeff Thompson

3rd Infantry Regiment — Colonel Aden Lowe (k)
Lieutenant Colonel Isaac Hedgpeth
Jennings Battalion
Rapley's Battalion
2nd Regiment — Colonel Farmer
4th Regiment — Colonel Waugh
2nd Dragoons
3rd Cavalry Regiment

At noon on October 21, 1861, with the Missouri State Guard trap being set, Thompson's skirmishers were sent forward, as planned, and withdrew into the jaws of the trap as planned. Captain Warren Stewart and the men of Stewart's Cavalry moved forward to follow the "bait," but the Union cavalrymen were wise enough to reconnoiter the field to their front. They found the trap that had been set and quickly returned to Fredericktown to report the positions of the Southern units in their front. As the 11th Missouri prepared for its first battle of the war, "Thompson deployed his undersized regiments and battalions in echelon ... thereby providing each unit supporting fire when it withdrew according to the overall plan."[47]

While the 11th Missouri was commanded by Colonel Joseph Plummer, the direct command for the regiment during this battle was that of Lieutenant Colonel William Panabaker. William Panabaker was one of the most interesting and versatile commanders in the war. Panabaker, a physician by occupation, was born in Virginia in 1822 and had served in the army during the Mexican War. "Dr. Panabaker was a soldier, a physician, a farmer and a very efficient itinerant Methodist minister. After his return to Lawrence County, [Illinois] he was very much interested in the Olive Branch Church. He had gone West with, or soon after the forty-niners, during the California gold rush. By this time he was a practicing physician and while in the vicinity of Yuba City and Maryville, California he treated several men from Lawrence County, Illinois who were trying to share in the riches of the California gold rush. Dr. Panabaker returned to Lawrence County around 1856 and bought land adjoining his friend James Eaton, whom he had treated in the gold fields."[48]

When the Civil War broke out, Illinois had so many volunteers in response to Lincoln's call that many chose to enlist in Missouri regiments. Dr. Panabaker was requested to organize and drill these troops. Some of these volunteers, suspecting that the doctor was not too sympathetic to the Northern cause, went to Missouri to enlist in other regiments. Meanwhile Dr. Panabaker organized another company which he took to Missouri, and in conjunction with another veteran of the Mexican War, trained his company. This colorful individual was leading the 11th Missouri Infantry into the regiment's first full battle of the war, just two months after they enlisted.

As the Union columns approached Fredericktown, the 11th Missouri was split, by company, into two groups. One group was ordered to protect the supply train, and the other marched forward with the other infantry regiments. Five companies of the 11th Missouri—Company A, Lieutenant Menomen O'Donnell; Company C, Captain Moses Warner; Company D, Captain Clark Hendee; Company F, Captain Amos Singleton; and Company K, Captain William Stewart—marched in the rear of the 17th Illinois as that regiment deployed to meet Colonel Aden Lowe's infantry which was hidden in a cornfield. Company B, Captain Andrew Weber; Company G, Lieutenant Charles Carter; Company H, Captain Thomas Dollahan; and Company I, Lieutenant James Hummer, were detached to guard the baggage train. At 10:00 A.M., Company D was also ordered to guard duty around the Union supply train.

The Union attack began 1:00 P.M. as the Union column approached the trap set by Thompson. Carlin reinforced Plummer's force with Colonel John Alexander's 21st Illinois, Colonel Charles Hovey's 33rd Illinois, 38th Illinois, six companies of Colonel Baker's First Indiana Cavalry, and Hescock's section of artillery.[49]

Colonel Leonard Ross' 17th Illinois Volunteer Infantry was leading the Union column. Ross deployed into line of battle just to the south of Fredericktown and one section of Taylor's battery immediately opened fire and the enemy responded with four artillery pieces that were concealed on the facing slope about 600 yards away. As Ross' 17th Illinois moved forward, the 11th Missouri formed on the right and the 20th Illinois Infantry formed on the left. As the Union infantry moved forward, they found Aden Lowe's Southern infantry concealed in a cornfield directly in their front when a furious volley was sent toward the Union infantry. The Eighth Wisconsin, much to their chagrin, was held in reserve. Two additional sections of artillery (Captain Manter's and Lieutenant Hescock's) soon joined the duel that was underway across the cornfield.

The 11th Missouri's Sergeant William Cleland recorded, "Then commenced the battle in right good earnest. The rain of bullets, shot and shell, at first was truly terrific.... We, however, returned their fire with equal determination."[50] The Federal line that faced Lowe consisted of 4 companies of the 11th Missouri Infantry, the 17th Illinois Infantry and the 20th Illinois infantry. As volleys were exchanged with Lowe's Missouri State Guard infantry, it was evident that Lowe was in the unenviable situation of commanding the regiment that held the forward position in Thompson's trap. As the Union infantry advanced, Lowe had to find a way to disengage from the two and a half regiments of blue coats that faced his troops.

Duncan McCall recorded that Thompson "had planted two batteries, so that, when we got close enough they could rake our ranks. Plummer ordered up a battery and opened on them. Blank cartridges were fired from our side, and they replied with shot and shell, doing no damage, as they shot over us. The 17th Illinois and part of the 11th Missouri were ordered forward, and advanced and poured in a heavy volley of musketry."[51]

The Union regiments quickly fell into line to meet their foe. Lieutenant Colonel Panabaker was ordered to support White's battery and advanced with it to the "extreme front" and remained with it through to the end of the battle. Panabaker moved the 11th Missouri in line of battle as Union troops advanced. The four companies of the 11th Missouri lined to the left of an artillery piece that had been pushed forward to meet the Confederate threat to their front. Colonel Leonard Ross' 17th Illinois Infantry advanced forward and moved to face the opposing infantry under command of Colonel Aden Lowe hidden in a cornfield directly in front of forming Union line. As a result the 17th Illinois was involved in some of the hottest exchanges with the Southerners.

As Ross and Panabaker moved directly opposite Lowe's Third Infantry regiment, "small arms fire erupted in the cornfield as Federal skirmishers approached the fence line where Lowe's units lay concealed."[52] The four companies, A, C, F and K, of the 11th Missouri moved forward with the 17th Illinois "until the enemy were driven from their position and completely routed."[53] So heavy was the musket fire, the smallest cover proved to be invaluable. Local citizen R. C. Arnett related a story from Colonel Ross who stated a large apple tree saved his life during the battle, as he got to the cornfield and stood beside the apple tree, the Confederates opened fire and "the bark was literally torn off the tree and I did not get a scratch."[54] Colonel C. C. Marsh's 20th Illinois also advanced forward and flanked Lowe's Confederates and being flanked the Confederates could not withdraw without heavy losses. The 11th Missouri, 20th Illinois and the 17th Illinois again moved forward. As the battle began to turn serious, Colonel Aden Lowe was shot in the head and died instantly, and Lowe's command fell to Lieutenant Colonel Isaac Hedgpeth. Lowe's Home Guard troops fell back with heavy loss.

As the Missouri State Guard began to retreat, Colonel C. C. Marsh, 20th Illinois Infantry, described the situation, "The Infantry of Colonel Lowe commenced to retreating from the cornfield and the shelter of the fences. They thus exposed themselves to the raking fire from my left wing which was pouring in with terrible effect."[55]

Captain William Stewart, Company K of the 11th Missouri Infantry, recorded the battle as he led his troops, "My company was given the second position of importance in the whole battle line because (as the Col' told me) they were the best drilled. And though we were exposed to a continual fire from the cannon and muskets of the enemy, not a single one of my men was killed or wounded, though several guns and garments were struck and the grounds ploughed up around us. Our boys stood in line and poured in a continual volley of Minnie balls, making a stream of fire all along the line, without cessation, and slaying the rebels horribly.... There was battery of our cannon placed right behind and above our men, we being on the slope and the cannon on the hill, with the rebels in the hollow and other slope and hill. When (5000) five thousand on each side got in earnest in the firing of muskets and

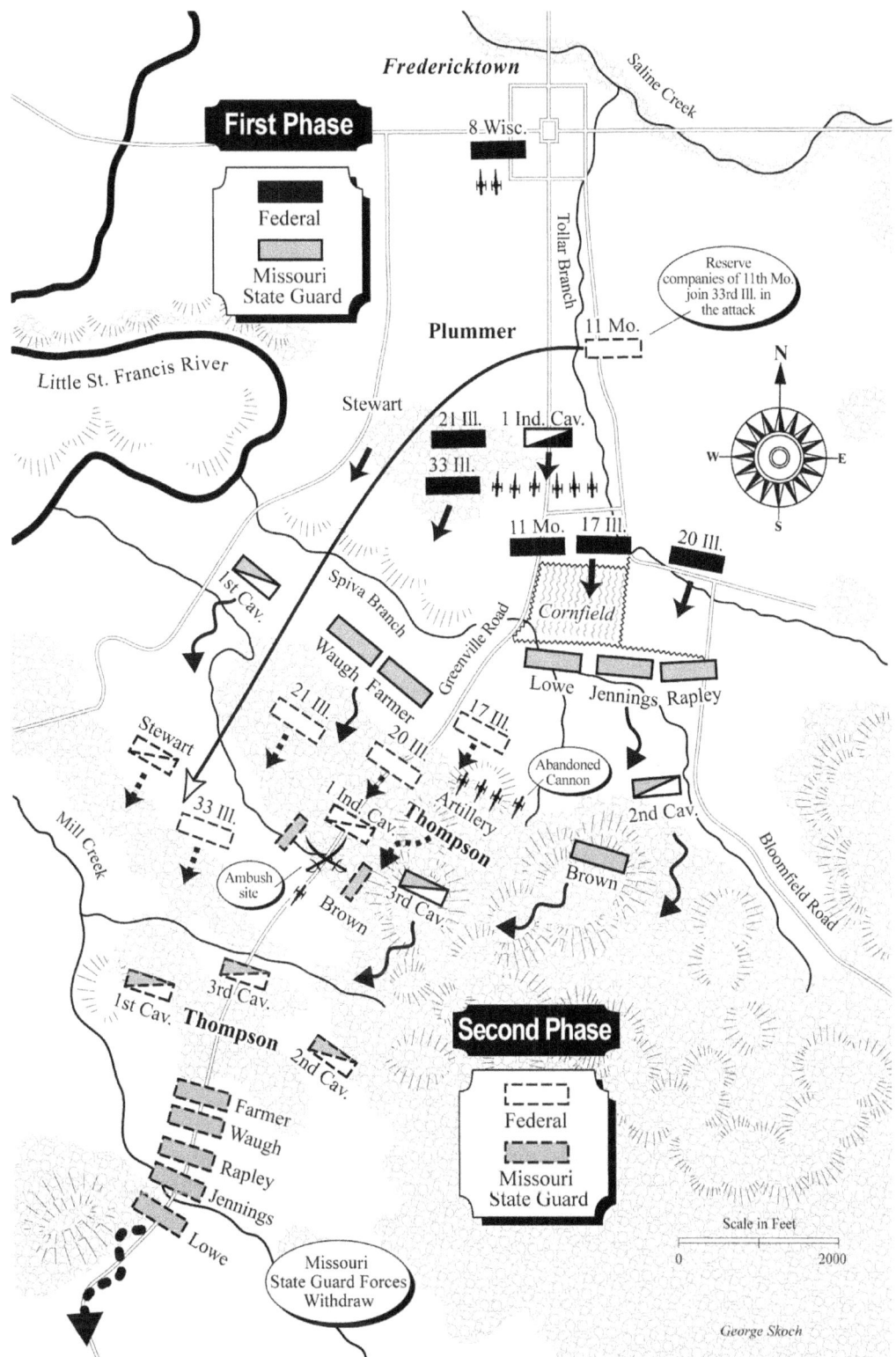

The Battle of Fredericktown, October 21, 1861. Four companies of the 11th Missouri Infantry attacked with the 17th Illinois Infantry. During the second phase of the battle, the remaining companies attacked with the 33rd Illinois Infantry.

cannon the scent and the sound were magnificent."⁵⁶ Captain Stewart's first battle caused him to overestimate the number of combatants.

As Colonel Aden Lowe's infantry shifted their front to meet the threat of Colonel Ross' 17th Illinois, they were subjected to a vigorous fire from the muskets of the 11th Missouri. The battle intensified with the infantry volleys and the Union artillery continued to exchange fire with Thompson's artillery. As Lowe's infantry was losing their battle to hold their line, they finally began their retreat, and as they gave way the Union troops flooded toward them. Sergeant William Cleland, 11th Missouri, explained that Union infantry "drove them from their ambuscade with great destruction of life. After an hour's hard fighting they began to retreat. We followed them through field and bush."⁵⁷

As the battle progressed, Thompson knew that his plans were not working, and Lowe's inability to disengage was where the plan began to fall apart. General Thompson's description of the part of the battle where the 11th Missouri was involved: "We returned their fire with one 12-pounder and one of our sixes. This we kept up for thirty minutes, when their line, having advanced within musket range of Lowe's regiments..., a galling fire was opened upon it, which was only returned when Lowe's men could get dead aim. The object of which Lowe was placed having been accomplished, he should have fallen back." The numbers of the Union forces began to tell, "I ordered a retreat by the right wing.... I continued my retreat to this place which is 26 miles from Fredericktown."⁵⁸

Colonel Aden Lowe's infantry was intended to engage the Union forces and fall back pulling the bluecoats into an ambush. However, Lowe did not withdraw, whether unable to disengage from such a large force or failed to do so. Regardless, he was killed as he faced the Union infantry directly in his front. After Lowe's death, Thompson reported that the Union artillery then found the range of his own artillery. Thompson ordered a retreat of his right wing, which resulted in significant casualties. At the battle progressed, it became evident that the Union army's baggage train was not under threat from the enemy and the remaining companies of the 11th Missouri were moved into the battle. They were ordered forward with the artillery and then moved to the right of the 33rd Illinois as this regiment advanced. These companies advanced under enemy fire until the left wing of the enemy was driven from the field.

Colonel Joseph Plummer recorded, "We met the rebels and repulsed them, after a fight which lasted about two and a half hours, resulting in a loss to the rebels of about six hundred in killed, wounded and prisoners. The enemy could not stand it, and fled, leaving us the masters of the field. The First Indiana cavalry made a charge, and Major Gavitt was killed. We lost about twenty-five men, in killed and wounded. The 17th and 20th Illinois charged and took a battery. Col. Lowe was killed on the rebel side, and Thompson's army all dispersed."⁵⁹

The First Indiana Cavalry was ordered to pursue the retreating soldiers of the Missouri State Guard and unfortunately, found that the State Guards still had plenty of fight left. The First Indiana charged ahead after the retreating Southerners and captured a piece of artillery but was riddled by enemy fire killing Captain Highman and Major Gavitt. But the Union forces proved too much for Thompson's troops, and their retreat now became general and they were pursued by Colonel Plummer's forces until dark. By the next morning Colonel Plummer reported that he had pursued the enemy 10 miles along the Greenville Road. Thompson retreated 26 miles to Greenville by October 22 and declared the battle a defeat.⁶⁰

Colonel Plummer reported 158 dead from Thompson's force and an additional 38 wounded, 80 captured. The Union loss reported by Plummer was 6 killed and 60 wounded.

After the battle, the Union soldiers turned their vengeance on the town of Fredericktown, believing the local citizens were working with the enemy. Plummer reported that six or seven buildings were burned before the officers could the stop the destruction of the town. Thompson's remarks about his reception in Fredericktown and the surrounding area of Missouri tend to shed some light on the Union reaction toward the town and citizens after the battle. "I found, however, the hearts of the people were all right, and from New Madrid to Big River Bridge, we have been welcomed in the most flattering and encouraging manner."[61] In addition, a description has been preserved by a citizen of Fredericktown, R. C. Arnett, who was only twelve years old at the time of the battle, "When the Confederates left town on Sunday afternoon, my mother, with my sister and myself, started home after bidding good-bye to her son, brothers, nephews, and relatives" [part of Thompson's force]. October 21 "was a nice, cool, frosty, crisp morning.... General Thompson, after talking a while, trying to answer all the girls' questions in relation to where this, and that one was, turned to my mother and asked if she knew of any white man he could trust to go into town and find out, if Col. Ross had gotten in yet from the Cape."[62] It was the 12-year-old Arnett who volunteered to go to Fredericktown as a spy for General Thompson.

The 11th Missouri's Lieutenant Colonel William Panabaker reported the vigorous fighting of the men directly under his command, "although exposed to the hottest fire of the enemy, the officers and men fought like veterans, displaying a coolness and bravery worthy of the cause for which they were fighting."[63] The 11th Missouri Infantry entered the battle with 460 men present and one man was killed and four were wounded. Sergeant Richard Smith, Company F, a 44-year-old, married shoemaker from Xenia, Illinois, was the one fatality of the 11th Missouri Infantry. Sergeant Smith was born in England and had immigrated to Illinois. Among the wounded were Charles Clark, Company A, "badly wounded with a ball in the thigh,"[64] and one man in Company C, Private Daniel Gantz, was also "severely wounded."[65] Charles Clark was a 23-year-old farmer from Sumner, Illinois, and Daniel Gantz was a 21-year-old farmer from Mechanicsburg, Illinois. Both soldiers were treated and returned to service with the 11th Missouri. In addition to these casualties, two soldiers were wounded slightly, Caleb Powell and John Powell, both in Company F. Caleb Powell had a "slight wound" and John Powell was wounded "slightly by a spent ball." Caleb and John Powell were 19 and 22 years old, respectively, and both were farmers from Xenia, Illinois.

Sergeant William Cleland reported the condition of the battlefield: "You can have no conception of the awful sight presented by the field after the battle. The dead and the wounded were strewn in every direction, and often, commingled in one common mass, would be found the dead horses and their vanquished riders. Some were crying for water to quench their parched thirst; others for aid to be disentangled from the bodies of their once respected companions."[66]

The description provided by Major John Schofield, who commanded the batteries in the action during the of Battle of Fredericktown was printed in the *New York Times* on Sunday, October 27, 1861, and explained the fate of Jeff Thompson's soldiers who were captured. "Fifty prisoners taken in the battle of Fredericktown have been put to work on the trenches in Cape Girardeau."[67] Schofield's accounts claim this victory was the most complete of any yet achieved by the Union army during the war so far.

A personal summary of the experience of the Battle of Fredericktown, Missouri, was summarized by Captain William Stewart, Company K, in a letter to his family. "When we left there we had discovered that 7 of our men were killed and about 50 wounded, while we had buried 232 of the rebels. About 500 of their men were wounded.... I never enjoyed anything so much in my life. Though this continual firing lasted for near two hours, our boys seemed very disappointed when it ceased. Our firing did so much execution that the rebels could not stand it but fled with us after them. Our Regiment was put in pursuit with Major Schofield's Battery but after running them four or five miles that night could not catch them.

Next day we went 25 miles further but finding Jeff Thompson['s] Army all scattered we had nothing more to pursue and next day we returned to Fredericktown, and then by forced marches returned to the Cape here. I cannot begin to give you a description of the battle-field after the battle was over. Just think of 300 dead men, 300 wounded, a lot of horses killed and wounded, the wounded men crying out with the most hideous groans and moans and the dead men, some mangled to pieces, some with their heads shot off, some with their bowels torn out, and you will have some idea of the ravages of war.... My men fought bravely and well and obeyed my orders strictly. I never felt cooler in my life. Our beautiful flag was right by the side of my men and they sustained it nobly. The Battle was fought on Monday, the 21 of Oct. and last night the 25th we returned to our quarters having marched 30 miles yesterday. This forced march was because we expected Gen. Hardee to make an attack upon Cape Girardeau who is very close to us with 10,000 men. We are all hoping strongly that he will come on and try us."[68]

Sergeant George W. Gould, Company A, a farmer from Sumner, Illinois, fought in the Battle of Fredericktown, Missouri (courtesy Edwin Gould Jr.).

The victory at Fredericktown was very important for the men of the 11th Missouri Infantry because this was the first face-to-face battle with the enemy. The regiment performed well and stood across from Lowe's concealed and well-prepared enemy. Certainly the odds favored the Federal forces but the battle was regiment against regiment. The soldiers of the 11th Missouri gave as good as they received. This was the regiment's first test and they passed; but there were more and bigger tests yet to come.

On October 27, 1861, General Grant sent a message of congratulations stating that the troops "have done nobly" and prophetically stated that it "goes to prove that much more may be expected when the country and our great cause calls upon them."[69] On November 23, 1861, Grant sent another message regarding Colonel Plummer. "I would further most heartily recommend that Colonel Plummer be returned to this command with his rank confirmed by competent authority. This I conceive due him for gallantry displayed in the battle of Wilson's Creek ... and for the entire credit which is due him for bringing on and fighting the battle of Fredericktown, where our arms were covered with an important victory."[70]

CHAPTER 2

Point Pleasant and Siege of Corinth

"This was a very pretty little exploit for the numbers engaged, and did great credit to Colonel Mower and his troops."
— General David Stanley

After the Battle of Fredericktown, the 11th Missouri Infantry returned to Cape Girardeau and remained there until November 5 when they proceeded on an expedition with the 17th Illinois and 10th Iowa infantries in the area of the Whitewater River located about 20 miles from Cape Girardeau, but the march proved to be uneventful for the regiment. The march was intended to meet and do battle with another group of Confederates reputed to be greater than 15,000 strong, but they were not found when the Union forces arrived. The regiment returned to camp on November 10, and after this expedition, they went into quarters at Cape Girardeau for the remainder of the winter. While stationed at Cape Girardeau, the Union forces continued to build the city's defenses into a formidable stronghold against any potential Southern attacks. As for the day-to-day life for the men, William Stewart reported the winter quarters were quite comfortable and it was pleasant to spend the entire winter there. For enlisted men, Charles Treadway summarized his experiences at Cape Girardeau in the winter of 1861–1862, "We have lots of fun out here and thare is lots of purty girls out here but nothing compared to the Illinois girls."[1] Dr. Thomas Hawley also enjoyed Cape Girardeau and stated, "Yet, I say that I love this city of Marble and think it would be a very pleasant home."[2] But, Dr. Hawley and the rest of the medical staff of the 11th Missouri had a difficult time with disease. On November 30, 1861, Dr. Hawley lamented the problem with measles and typhoid fever and he stated, "We have lost nearly twenty since first coming here."[3] In the cold, dark nights of winter the men's thoughts turned to the purpose of being in uniform. On January 4, 1862, Dr. Hawley wrote to his family and said, "Oh, how I wish for peace to end this terrible war. We cannot count the unnumbered tears and groans of a mighty nation mourning for lost brave and dear hearts."[4] The 11th Missouri would have four long years ahead of them.

The first four months of the war were filled disease, as the regiment struggled to control the illnesses among the soldiers, and a total of 30 men died before the end of 1861. Two men were killed in action, 26 died of diseases (fever, typhoid fever, consumption, and measles), and two accidentally drowned. Among those who died was the unusual situation of Corporal William Laughlin, Company A, who died of "cold inducing paralysis" that was contracted resulting in death within a few hours. William Laughlin, 29, was a farmer from Bridgeport, Illinois.

On November 5, 1861, the 11th Missouri Infantry lost their first officer in the field when Captain William Mieure, Company G, died of typhoid fever in Cape Girardeau. Captain Mieure was a 41-year-old merchant from Lawrenceville, Illinois, and was instrumental in raising his company. A letter from regimental surgeon, Thomas Smith, described Captain Mieure as being "in a very feeble state of health having been sick for several weeks with a case of malarious fever."[5] Private John Collins, Company G, wrote of Captain Mieure's and Corporal George McKelvey's deaths which were long and arduous: "I guess you will be very much surprised to hear of the death of George McKelvey who died last evening and also Captain Mieure today. I regret the loss of both of them. I suppose Capt. Mieure's remains will start home today or tomorrow. George will be buried in the graveyard. They was both sick about forty days with the fever."[6] The command of Company G passed to 1st Lieutenant Charles Carter, a 21-year-old physician, also from Lawrenceville, Illinois. Lieutenant Carter was promoted to rank of captain after William Mieure's death.[7] Captain Mieure's death was a bitter event to his cousin Thomas Mieure, who continued to serve the company as a sergeant and was promoted to the rank of lieutenant later in the war.

Company D also had changes in the command structure beginning in November 1861 when 1st Lieutenant Clark Bentley resigned. Sergeant Mark Sappington was promoted to the rank of 2nd lieutenant. The 31-year-old Sappington was a minister and a resident of Clay County, Illinois, prior to his enlistment. Second Lieutenant J. W. Cowperthwait was promoted to the rank of 1st lieutenant to replace Bentley.

In addition to the men who died in the regiment, the 11th Missouri Infantry began to lose men for various reasons, including disability, desertion, and transfers. Men who were discharged were ones who were physically disabled through some medical malady.

11th Missouri Infantry Regimental Losses Through 1861

	AUG/SEPTEMBER	**OCTOBER**	**NOVEMBER**	**DECEMBER**
Discharged	Bucklers, Herman (C)	Powers, William (G)	Miller, John (B)	Askren, Samuel (A)
		Powers, William (G)	Courtney, Liberty Sgt. (I)	Armstrong, John (B)
	Salisbury, Orlando (H)	Thompson, Alonzo (H)	McMahan, Hugh (B)	McGuire, James (C)
	Davis, Edwin (A)	Berry, Thomas (I)		
	Manning, John (C)	Davis, William (I)		Cochran, John (G)
	Weiser, Benjamin (H)	Manning, William (K)		Hopkins, Horatio N. Sgt. (G)
				Decker, James (F)
				Bay, William (K)
Died	Tade, Alexander Sgt. (E)	Pettyjohn, Richard (D)	Turley, Theodore (B)	Laughlin, William Corp. (A)
	Brown, Samuel (G)	Meyers, James K (E)	Meyers, Joseph (C)	Grandstaff, Isaac Wagoner (B)
	Ferguson, Anderson (H)	Garmon, Robert (I)	Smith, John (C)	Hicks, William (H)
	Keirn, John (H)	Russell, James (I)	Conley, James Corp (D)	Headley, James Sgt. (B)
	Kimball, Joseph A (I)	Smith, Richard Sgt. (F)	Gallaspie/Gillespie, Willis (E)	
	Orr, Elijah B. (I)		Treadway, John Musician (E)	
	Johns, Sweptson (K)		McKelvey, George Corp. (G)	

	AUG/SEPTEMBER	OCTOBER	NOVEMBER	DECEMBER
	Denezet, Morris (C)		Mieure, William Capt. (G)	
	Ford, William (B)		Elliott, Edgar (I)	
			Hummer, George Corp. (I)	
			Duncan, John (K)	
			Flinn, Patrick (G)	
Deserted	Johns, Ellis C. (H)	Pollack, John (H)		
	Turner, Charles N. (H)			
	Miller, David C. (I)			
	Thomas, Elijah (I)			
Killed In Action	Denezet, Morris (C)	Smith, Richard Sgt. (F)		
Resigned	McConnel, Benjamin 2nd Lt. (F)			
	Bentley, Clark 1st Lt. (D)			

Court-Martial of Lieutenant Benjamin Laird

In December 1861, Lieutenant Benjamin Laird faced a court-martial for "disrespectful language against Charles M. Carter, Capt. of Company D 11th Regt Missouri Volunteers to wit, calling the said Charles M. Carter Capt. of Company D 11th Reg. Mo. Vols. a rascal and a thief," and the same charge was made for calling Major Benjamin Livingston a rascal and thief. Laird also allegedly called Major Livingston a "damned ignoramus, a damned rascal and a damned thief." The fourth charge Laird faced was he became intoxicated and troublesome at the headquarters of the regiment. The fifth charge specified he called Colonel Joseph Plummer a "drunken sod and that he did not know what he was doing half his time." Finally, Lieutenant Laird was charged with calling Lieutenant John Cowperthwait "a damned son of a bitch." These events occurred in December 1861, a month that Lieutenant Laird would have liked to forget. Many of the officers of the regiment became involved in this court-martial and were called to give testimony in the trial.[8]

This was a particularly unpleasant court marital which involved several of the officers of the regiment in the proceedings with various allegations being made in regard to all parties. Laird was a 40-year-old attorney when he enlisted in the 11th Missouri, and personal animosity existed with several of the officers due to events that occurred prior to the war. The major factor prompting the actions and subsequent charges was the failure of 2nd Lieutenant Laird to gain a promotion. It should be remembered that Captain William Mieure died in November 1861 and his position was filled by 1st Lieutenant Charles Carter. Laird was the 2nd lieutenant in Company G. However, Edward Gannon was promoted to the rank of 1st lieutenant over Benjamin Laird. This was almost certainly a blow to Laird's ego that resulted in the explosive events which followed. It was known within the regiment that Major Livingston and Captain Carter opposed Laird's promotion, and Carter even threatened to resign if Laird was promoted.

The bad feelings carried over from before the war coupled with the lost promotion resulted in tempers flaring and words being exchanged. The result of the court was that Benjamin Laird was found not guilty on all charges, but by end of 1862 he had resigned from the regiment.

1862 — Point Pleasant, New Madrid, and Island No. 10

In March 1862, the regimental commander of the 11th Missouri Infantry, Colonel Joseph Plummer, was promoted to the rank of Brigadier General effective October 22, 1861. With Plummer's promotion command of the 11th Missouri fell to William Panabaker who retained the rank of lieutenant colonel until a regimental colonel was appointed. General Plummer's promotion allowed him to assume command of the Fifth Division of John Pope's Army of the Mississippi.

Morale within the 11th Missouri Infantry was high during the winter of 1861–1862. Captain William Stewart wrote in a letter on January 12, 1862, about the reputation of the regiment and also about his respect for Colonel Plummer. "Our regiment (the Eleventh United States Volunteer of Missouri) has quite a name for courage and fighting ability — and they will no doubt be assigned important work to do. And whatever that may be you may rest assured that it will try to do it, while life shall last. Col. Plummer is our Colonel and a braver or better officer does not live."[9]

The Mississippi River was of great strategic value to both sides throughout the Civil War. Obviously, it was a route of commerce, but it also was an important artery for troops to move from one location to another. From a defensive standpoint, it was important that the enemy did not show up unexpectedly at an important geographic location or at a key city, such as Memphis, New Orleans, and St. Louis. Cape Girardeau was initially the southernmost city in firm control by Federal troops in eastern Missouri, and by the end of 1861, the Union troops were planning a way to expand their control of the river. On November 7, 1861, Brigadier General Ulysses Grant fought the Confederate troops of Brigadier General Gideon Pillow in the Battle of Belmont, Missouri. At this battle, Grant overran the Confederate camp and destroyed it before he was forced to retreat. The next step in expanding control of the western banks of the Mississippi River was New Madrid, Missouri, which was 175 miles south of St. Louis. New Madrid is located in a great bend, the Madrid Bend, of the Mississippi River and was selected as a strategic location by the Confederates because, by land, a road led directly from this location to St. Louis. Just upriver from New Madrid lay Island No. 10, located in the middle of the Mississippi River, which when fortified was an imposing obstacle to any Northern vessel trying to move south down the river. However, leadership of the Confederate army felt Columbus, Kentucky, was a better site from which to defend the river; and New Madrid became the second line of defense, should Columbus fall or become ineffective in protecting the river. While the 11th Missouri Infantry spent the winter in quarters enhancing the fortifications at Cape Girardeau, two Arkansas infantry regiments worked diligently on the defenses at New Madrid and the Island. Three main batteries were added to the island and five more batteries were added in a redoubt on the Tennessee side of the river.

The capture of Forts Henry and Donelson by Union forces in February 1862 on the Tennessee and Cumberland Rivers put the Confederate defenses at Columbus in a non-defensible position. This elevated the value of New Madrid and Island No. 10's strategic importance in preventing the Union forces from splitting the South by controlling the Mississippi River. Confederate Brigadier General John McCown arrived to assume command at New Madrid in late February and began to fortify the Confederate position. When the Confederate defenses had been enhanced, the armament in the Madrid Bend was impressive. There were 24 artillery pieces mounted on the shore and another 19 cannons on the island. In addition, nine cannons were placed on floating batteries. Another 12 heavy guns were placed in New Madrid, creating a formidable defensive line. McCown's Chief of Artillery, Brigadier General James Trudeau, arrived on March 1 to assume command of the artillery. The ground forces at New Madrid were also strengthened with additional infantry regiments and artillery companies. Brigadier General Alexander P. Stewart was placed in command of New Madrid and he immediately ordered a new fort be constructed on the eastern edge of town. Island No. 10 and five shore batteries on the Tennessee side of the river were reinforced with additional infantry regiments, cavalry, and a regiment of artillery.

In February 1862, Brigadier General John Pope assumed control of the Union forces which opposed the Confederates at New Madrid, Missouri, and Island No. 10. John Pope was a 39-year-old son of a judge from Illinois with political connections that directly linked him to the president. His experience was somewhat limited, but he had served in the Mexican War as part of Zachary Taylor's staff. The Union Army of the Mississippi under command of Brigadier General John Pope began their movement on New Madrid in late February, arriving in Commerce, Missouri, on February 25, 1862. Pope decided to unite his army at Commerce, Missouri, and began his march toward New Madrid through some of the most adverse wet and muddy conditions. The advance scouts reached the outskirts of New Madrid on March 2. On March 3, the remainder of the Union force arrived having slogged through the Missouri mud. Recognizing the threat to the city, the exiled Missouri legislature, which had relocated to New Madrid, left the city and moved further south under protection of the 11th Missouri's old foe, Brigadier General M. Jeff Thompson.

The 11th Missouri Infantry and their brigade were ordered to board the steamer *Empress* on February 26 and were transported to Commerce to be united with the rest of Pope's Army of the Mississippi. Approximately 570 men, excluding regimental staff, left Cape Girardeau to join Pope's army.[10] The advancing Union army was harassed by General Jeff Thompson's troops as they moved further south. The march was difficult, as described by Duncan McCall, "Rain fell that day, and made it hard marching for us."[11] Typical army food awaited the soldiers who breakfasted on coffee and hard crackers.

On the eve of the 11th Missouri's departure from Cape Girardeau, Captain William Stewart again wrote to his parents, "Today we received our orders and tomorrow will start for Dixie. We are already now except striking the tents which will take us about five minutes. Of course I cannot tell exactly our route, although our first work will be to clean out New Madrid and then proceed southward."[12]

Pope's Army marched to New Madrid and Island No. 10 (Florida Center for Instructional Technology).

Once arriving at New Madrid, the 11th Missouri Infantry was part of the army that was shelled by the Confederate defenders. As the Union army advanced on New Madrid, the 11th Missouri and its brigade were positioned on the right side of Plummer's Fifth Division. As the army advanced, the Confederate defenders retreated to their defenses and their artillery fired away at the advancing blue-coated soldiers with an "unremitting fire of solid shot and shell from the gunboats and their works, 24-pounder shot, shells from 32-pound and 64-pounders, besides missles from guns of smaller caliber."[13] Captain William Stewart recorded, "Our boys could dodge balls and shells while they fell and bursted all around us. Our regiment sat down and ate a lunch right among their shells."[14] After evaluating the Southern defenses on March 7, 1862, General Pope ordered a probe against the defenders but the units were repulsed by the heavy guns. The attack was led by Brigadier General David Stanley's, Colonel W.H. Worthington's, and Brigadier General David Palmer's divisions of Pope's army. After this attack, General Pope developed a plan which would lay siege to the city.

Meanwhile, the 11th Missouri Infantry was put into action as part of General Plummer's Fifth Division, supplemented with the a squadron from each of the Second and Third Michigan Cavalry, four pieces of Powell's Battery M of the First Missouri Light Artillery and an engineer company. This force was ordered to march five miles south of New Madrid to Point Pleasant and prevent Confederate reinforcements, naval or ground, from advancing on the city from the south. Again, the marching was difficult for the regiment. Private Duncan McCall recorded, "We marched nearly all night, and at last came to a halt, and we were ordered to lay down without any fire and make ourselves as comfortable as possible."[15] Many of the men of the regiment had no blankets or cover, which had been left at Sikeston before the march to Point Pleasant. The men had marched through mud and water that was over the tops of their shoes as they slogged through a cold March night. Captain Stewart, in a letter written to his parents, described the night of March 6, "We started about 1 o'clock, and that snowy cold and muddy night, camped in a cornfield without fires. I slept on a pile of cornstalks with my 1st Lieutenant Wilson A. Duggans, with one blanket over us. In the morning our blanket was covered with snow."[16] Once Plummer's division reached Point Pleasant, they occupied the town, and havoc was unleashed upon the town with looting and destruction being widespread. Plummer set up the divisional headquarters about a mile from the river. The Confederate gunboats attempted to force Plummer's Division, about 3,000 strong including artillery, to retreat from their position on the shore, but they were unsuccessful. Later that day, Plummer's men entrenched themselves on the bank of the river. Their first two targets, the Confederate transports, *Mary Keane*, and the *Kentucky*, were surprised by artillery fire and volleys from the infantry of the Union force occupying Point Pleasant. The *CSS Pontchartrain*, a Confederate gunboat captained by John Dunnington, moved down river to deal with the Union forces that occupied the western edge of the Mississippi River. "Seeing a white flag on shore, Dunnington cautiously steered his vessel to within forty yards. A devastating volley of musketry opened, killing one aboard and wounding two others."[17] That evening the 11th Missouri and the rest of Plummer's division dug in and had the advantage of the levee as a natural defense. Although the Confederate navy tried for three nights to dislodge Plummer's men, they were unable to do so and they were forced into a "stationary position opposite Point Pleasant."[18]

But soon the Confederates had had enough of Plummer's men being unopposed at Point Pleasant, and by noon on March 9, two guns from Pointe Coupee Artillery Battery had been placed directly opposite on the Tennessee side of the river. It was Plummer's time to experience an artillery barrage, but the shelling had little impact on Union position. According to Cloyd Bryner, author of the history of the 47th Illinois Infantry, "A Confederate battery of heavy

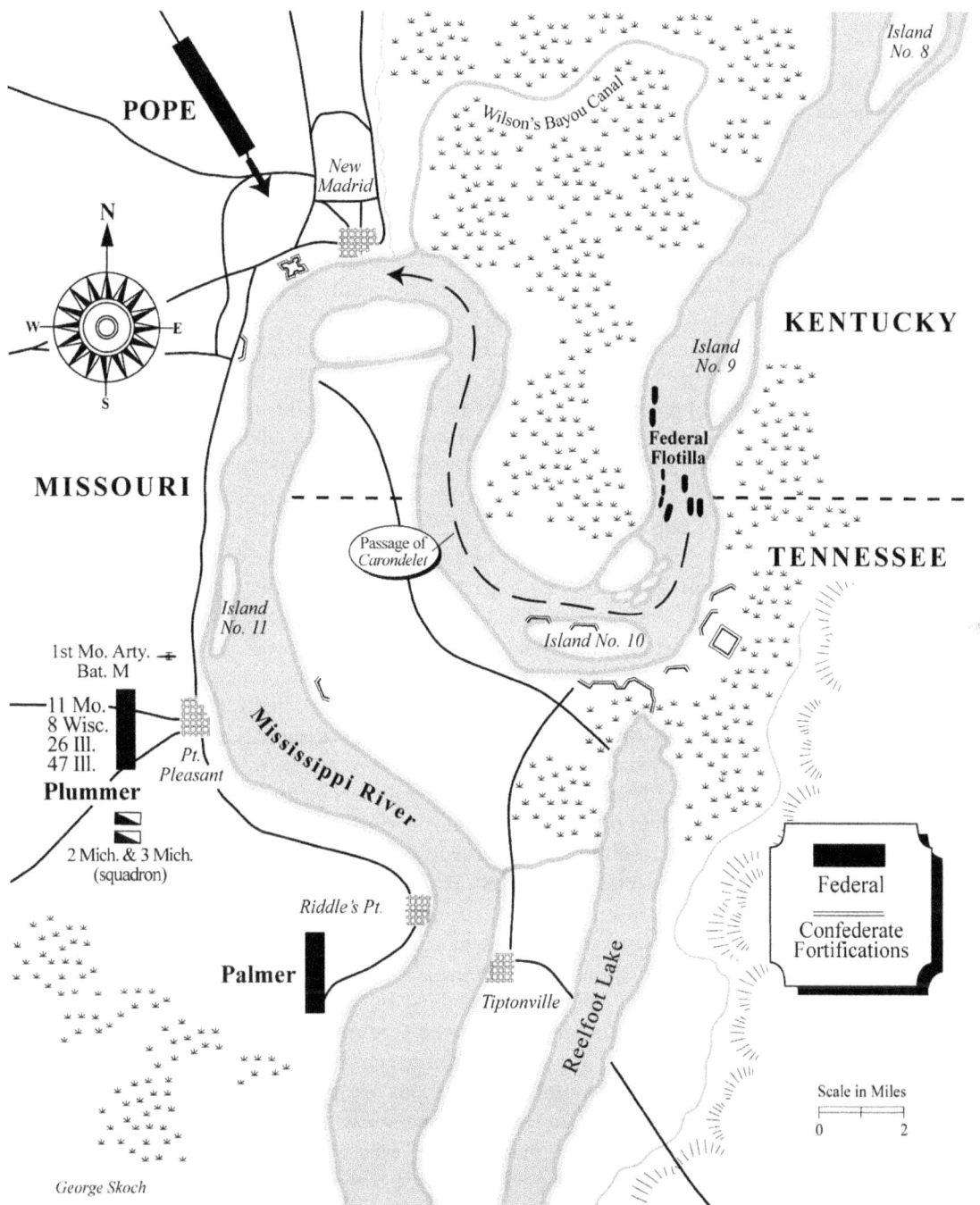

The Siege of Island No. 10, February 28, 1862–April 8, 1862. The 11th Missouri Infantry occupied Point Pleasant, Missouri, as part of Plummer's division during the siege.

guns was planted on the opposite shore and opened fire on the 13th — the only result being the spoiling of a pot of good mush which was hit by a solid shot and scattered far and wide."[19]

Despite Plummer's success, Confederate naval vessels were able to slip by his position during the night. One unanswered question in the Island No. 10 siege is why the Confederates never tried to force General Plummer's command to retreat using ground forces. The commander of the Confederate forces at New Madrid, General John McCown, was an experienced soldier and he knew he had a fight on his hands. McCown, a native of Tennessee and a West Point graduate of the class of 1840, observed the ranks of blue-coated soldiers and the armada of Union gunboats. He needed reinforcements if he was going to hold Island No. 10 and New Madrid. McCown strenuously requested that reinforcements should be sent to relieve the siege, but Confederate General Pierre Beauregard thought he could defeat the Union army in Tennessee and then move to relieve the pressure at the Island. McCown was on his own until he could be relieved by Beauregard. Pope and the Union Army of the Mississippi were determined to take New Madrid and the Island. In the words of Duncan McCall, "We had come to stay for awhile, and we were determined on it."[20]

Captain Stewart's letter on March 29 described the conflict from the eyes of members of the 11th Missouri, "They have tried often to land and take our batteries, but our boys killed so many of their pilots and men with our excellent rifles, that the boats had to back out every time. They have shot near a thousand shells and round shot at us, and as yet have killed but one man and one horse. The town is completely riddled with their balls, but our boys have learned to dodge them."[21] The shells fired on the 11th Missouri Infantry had little affect because the shells tended to just flop into the mud when they struck.

In a daring scheme, the 11th Missouri's 1st Lieutenant Menomen O'Donnell, Company A, gained permission to raid the artillery battery across the river. Lieutenant William Snow, Company K, who was a farmer in Franklin County, Missouri, in peace time, described the attempt to silence the newly fortified Confederate artillery. "Lieut. O'Donnell said that if they would let him have 12 picked men he would go over and spike their guns. He did and I was one of the 12. We crossed the river at midnight on a dark night and drifted down to opposite the guns, when the rebel sentinel sang out, 'Who goes there?' Lieut. O'Donnell told them he was a friend and wanted to see the General in command. At least 1,000 men raised up from behind the guns."[22] Needless to say, the attempt to spike the guns was not successful as the raiders drifted away into the night. Also, during the occupation of Point Pleasant, one member of the 11th Missouri, Henry Koch, Company C, was injured when he was shot in the left foot when a musket accidentally discharged. He lost all of his toes as a result of his injury. Henry Koch was a 37-year-old butcher from Springfield, Illinois.

As the siege of New Madrid continued, Union reinforcements totaling 6,000 men were moved into the conflict. The Union army brought their heavy artillery forward, three 24-pounders and an 8-inch howitzer, and exchanged fire with the heavy guns of the forts. Captain Joseph A. Mower, First U.S. Infantry, commanded the siege guns outside New Madrid. Captain Mower was soon to become a very important person to the 11th Missouri Infantry. On March 13, over 100 men were killed or wounded in a vicious artillery duel at New Madrid. As a result, General McCown met with Confederate General Alexander P. Stewart and they concluded that New Madrid could not be defended and evacuated the town during the night. When the Union troops gained control of New Madrid, they immediately began utilizing the captured guns as a way of completely preventing any hope of naval support to those left on Island No. 10 up river. But the Island still had to be taken.

Shortly after the end of the siege of New Madrid, the Fifth Division, which included the 11th Missouri, was reinforced with the arrival of the Eighth Wisconsin Infantry and the Seventh Illinois Cavalry. By this time, Plummer had reinforced his artillery: "Two-man rifle pits lined the riverbank for a half mile. The battery [at Point Pleasant] consisted of two 10-pounder Parrot rifles and two 13-pounder English rifles."[23]

When the Eighth Wisconsin Infantry joined Plummer's Division and Colonel John Loomis' Second Brigade, they brought along with them "Old Abe" and soon the brigade was nicknamed the Eagle Brigade. Old Abe was a bald eagle. It is unclear whether Old Abe was

Bombardment of Island No. 10 (Florida Center for Instructional Technology).

male or female, but the mascot was part of the regiment and soon designated the entire brigade as the Eagle Brigade. The eagle was captured by a Chippewa Indian in Price County, Wisconsin, and traded to Mrs. Margaret McCann; but the eagle became too large for the McCann family. Next Old Abe was sold to Lieutenant James McGuire of the Eighth Wisconsin, and the regiment and Old Abe joined the brigade permanently. Old Abe rode on a standard "consisting of a pole and copy of the shield from the Great Seal of the United States."[24] The Eighth Wisconsin and Old Abe remained brigaded with the 11th Missouri through victory and defeat to the end of the war.

The Union navy began the initial assault on Island No. 10 on March 15 and intensified their efforts on March 16, including utilizing 10 mortars. Late in the afternoon, the 27th Illinois Infantry landed on the Missouri shore opposite the Island with the Second Illinois Artillery, Battery I; and by 6:00 P.M., the land-based artillery began shelling the Island. On March 17, the Union attacked with the *USS Benton, USS Cincinnati, USS St. Louis, USS Mound City,* and *USS Carondelet.* On March 18, shelling from the Union gunboats continued along with the mortar barrages, but the Island was not taken and the siege continued through the end of March.

Because of the formidable defenses on Island No. 10, Pope had to consider another way around this obstacle, so he decided a canal could be dug through the peninsula east of New Madrid. Over a two week period the canal was dug which entered the Mississippi River west of the Island and east of New Madrid. On April 2, after weeks of constructing a canal bypass of Island No. 10, four transports and five barges emerged from St. John's Bayou moving much needed reinforcement south of the Island. Although the canal was not deep or large enough for gunboats, transports and supply vessels were able to avoid the island and move safely to New Madrid. On April 4, the ironclad *USS Carondelet* made a night run past the Island and on April 6 the gunboat *USS Pittsburg* also ran past. Two Union warships were safely at New Madrid making sure that no Confederate naval reinforcements would threaten the Union siege. On the morning of April 7, the Union warships began shelling and destroying Confederate batteries. Union infantry was transported to Watson's Landing, on the Tennessee side of the river just south of Island No. 10, and troops also landed at Tiptonville and moved inland. When New Madrid was evacuated, General John McCown was replaced with Brigadier General William Mackall. The Confederate forces under command of Mackall, trapped on a peninsula of land with no exit, moved south to Tiptonville to try to escape the noose that was being tightened. The Union forces had landed at Tiptonville and blocked his last hope to escape, so on April 8, Mackall surrendered. Also, troops on the Island, finding their shore support gone, formally surrendered on April 8. Part of General Plummer's command made up the force of Union troops transported to land at Tiptonville but remained at the landing. There is no evidence that the 11th Missouri moved to Tiptonville.

The siege of Island No. 10 was by no means an equal contest. By March 31, 1862, the Union Army fielded greater than 25,000 combatants and the Confederates had approximately 7,400 men in the Island No. 10 conflict. Reports of the number of men captured at Madrid Bend varied, with General Pope reporting greater than 7,000, but more likely 4,000 men captured. No one from the 11th Missouri was killed and only one was wounded in this action. It should also be noted that by the time the Island surrendered, the affect of exposure and weather began to seriously affect the men of the 11th Missouri with companies reporting double-digit counts of soldiers who were listed as sick. The regiment needed warm weather and better living conditions.

Below is listed the 11th Missouri Infantry soldiers who died or were discharged during the first three months of 1862. None had died in battle but disease claimed eighteen lives. Among those who died in the first three months of 1862 was Sergeant Thomas Manning. On February 13, 1862, the company records for Company K recorded Sergeant Thomas Manning was killed while serving as Sergeant of the Picket when he was shot accidentally by Private George Nicholson. Manning, 22 years old, was an unmarried miller from Franklin County, Missouri.

11th Missouri Infantry Regimental Losses
January 1862 Through March 31, 1862[25]

	JANUARY	FEBRUARY	MARCH
Discharged	Bensley, Jesse Musician (E)		Friend, Samuel P. (D)
	Babcock, William (F)		Tibbs, William (E)
Died	Clifton, David (A)	McEntire, John (C)	Besley, James (A-K)
	Young, Benjamin (A)	Wilson, William O. B. (E)	Nigh, Nathaniel (A)
		Manning, Thomas Sgt. (K)	Huffmaster, Daniel (C)
	Jordan, Thomas (F)	McGaughley, Edward (D)	Bland, William (E)
	Byrnes, William (I)		Clancy, Edward (E)
			Surtherland, William (F)
			Mullhall, James (G)
			Caughlen, Bernard (K)
			Price, Edward (K)
			Thompson, Willis (I)
Desertion		Fitzgerald, James J. (E)	

Bombardment of Island No. 10 (Florida Center for Instructional Technology).

Captain William Stewart recorded the feelings of the men of the 11th Missouri after the fall of Island No. 10. "We are all in high glee and fine spirits. I never before realized the grandeur and sublimity of the power of a free government when once called into exercise. I can now understand more than ever before, the glorious meaning of that patriotic passion called 'love of country.'"[26]

Meanwhile in southwestern Tennessee on April 6–7, the Battle of Shiloh was fought resulting in the Confederate Army's withdrawal toward Corinth, Mississippi. During the Battle of Shiloh, General Albert Sidney Johnston was killed, and command of Johnston's Army of Mississippi fell to Pierre Beauregard. The strategy for Pope's army after the victory at Island No. 10 was to advance southward and open up the Mississippi River, but Fort Pillow was another Confederate stronghold where a siege would be necessary. Fort Pillow was 40–50 miles north of Memphis and was fortified with extensive defenses and batteries of cannon that controlled the river. Rather than stagnate Pope's Army of the Mississippi in another two month siege, the Union army moved eastward to capitalize on the situation in west-central Tennessee. The Confederate defeat at Shiloh resulted in a strong Union force in a position to begin advancing into Mississippi. Pope's Army was called to add to the Union strategic initiative that resulted with the victory at Shiloh. The Confederates were clearly on the defensive and the Union plan was to drive the recently defeated Confederate army deeper into Mississippi.

After Island No. 10 surrendered, the 11th Missouri with the rest of their division remained in New Madrid until April 13; and then boarded the steamboat, *Hannibal City*, and moved ever south down the Mississippi River to Mosquito Point, Arkansas, which was near Fort Pillow. The name of this place was indicative of what the men had to experience: "a continual singing in our ears by these torments."[27] Captain William Stewart described Mosquito Point as "the mosquitoes innumerable, large, and powerful."[28] The regiment remained in camp for two days. On April 17 the regiment was moved again by the steamboat, *Hannibal City*, which journeyed up the Tennessee River to Hamburg, Tennessee, arriving on April 22, 1862.

As a footnote to what should have been an uneventful passage from Mosquito Point to Hamburg, the unfortunate Private Jeremiah Carroll, Company K, accidentally fell overboard while on the Hannibal City near Paducah, Kentucky, and drowned.[29] The cause of his accident is not known, but Irish-born Jeremiah Carroll was 33 years old, a married farmer from Sumner, Illinois.

Corinth was an important railway junction in northern Mississippi and three Union armies were converging on this location in an attempt to destroy Beauregard's army. The Union armies advancing on Corinth were the Army of the Ohio, commanded by Major General Don Carlos Buell, the Army of Western Tennessee commanded by Major General George Thomas, and the Army of the Mississippi commanded by Major General John Pope. It was Pope's army which included the 11th Missouri Infantry, and these three armies combined more than 120,000 men.

Corinth was the junction of the Memphis & Charleston Railroad (east-west) and the Mobile & Ohio Railroad (north-south); and these railroads were critical to the movement of supplies in the mid-south. These railroads were the longest railroads in the Confederacy. The Memphis & Charleston was the direct line between the Mississippi River and the Atlantic seaboard. Corinth was located in Tishomingo County in the northeastern part of Mississippi, and in 1861 the population of Corinth was approximately 1,200 people.

Regimental Changes

Colonel Joseph Plummer was promoted to rank of brigadier general and given divisional command at the Battle at New Madrid. Lieutenant Colonel William Panabaker had been commanding the 11th Missouri since Plummer assumed brigade command in Cape Girardeau; but once Plummer was given divisional command, there was need to fill the position of colonel for the regiment. The 11th Missouri Infantry received praise and attention and was becoming known as a regiment that helped their colonel receive the next promotion, a star on the shoulder. This tradition would continue. Joseph Plummer, a graduate of 1841 class of West Point, had been a major in the Eighth U.S. Infantry prior to becoming colonel of the 11th Missouri. As general of the division, he recommended Vermont native, Joseph Mower, also a regular army officer, to be his successor. Mower attended Norwich University for two years beginning in 1843. He enlisted in the United States Army Engineers in 1847 and fought in the Mexican War until 1848. He was appointed to the rank of 2nd lieutenant in the First United States Infantry in 1855 and served in the army in Texas until the beginning of the Civil War. Mower held the rank of captain at the beginning of the war and commanded artillery batteries in the siege of New Madrid, Missouri, until his promotion to the rank of major in the 11th Missouri Infantry in May 1862. Mower would refine his reputation as a fighter and was a rough-and-tumble type of commander who would fight whenever he could. The new commanding officer of the 11th Missouri would lead these men into the jaws of death and never back down; and his regiment gladly followed him. Confusion about David Bayles' status regarding the command of the 11th Missouri continued in May 1862, and therefore, Mower was not promoted to the rank of colonel initially. However, it soon became evident that Bayles' failing health prevented him from rejoining the regiment and Mower quickly gained command of the regiment.

In addition to Joseph Mower assuming command of the regiment, several other command changes occurred during the first four months of 1862. Surgeon Thomas Smith resigned and was replaced with Dr. Melancthon Fish. The role of regimental surgeon was not an easy one, especially early in the war when sanitary conditions often led to diseases spreading throughout the regiment. The stress of caring for the sick men also greatly affected the medical staff. This was the case resulting in the resignation of Dr. Thomas Smith, who resigned on April 4, 1862, and in his letter of resignation he stated the extreme "labors of the past two months having so impaired my health, as to render it necessary that I should have some relaxation from active duty for a time."[30] Chaplain Joseph Brooks resigned and was replaced by Samuel

Baldridge. The Rev. Joseph Brooks left the 11th Missouri Infantry to join the 33rd Missouri Infantry which was commanded by his brother. The Rev. Brooks left a rather cryptic resignation letter stating, "A condition of things having arisen within this command which will hinder the profitable exercise of the function of my office,"[31] and this led to his resignation.

On April 1, 1862, Captain Andrew Weber, Company B, was promoted to major, replacing Benjamin Livingston who had resigned in November 1861. Major Livingston found himself being "unfit for duty more than one half of the time" and felt compelled to leave the service of the army on April 3, 1862. Captain Weber was replaced by Jesse Lloyd. The newly promoted Captain Jesse Lloyd was a merchant living in Springfield, Illinois, prior to his enlistment. This allowed 2nd Lieutenant James Wilson the opportunity to be promoted to 1st lieutenant of Company B and Major Andrew Weber's bother, George Weber, was promoted to the rank of 2nd lieutenant. George Weber was a married farmer living in Sangamon County, Illinois, prior to the war. In March 1862, 1st Lieutenant William Perce resigned as 1st lieutenant in Company C, resulting in Modesta Green's promotion to that rank and James Lott was promoted to 2nd lieutenant of the company. Lieutenant Perce resigned on April 3, 1862, and stated his resignation "is because my health has been sick for the several months past that I have been unable to serve much of the time."[32] James Lott was a native Pennsylvanian and was a married carpenter living in Springfield, Illinois, prior to the war. No doubt his experience in Springfield Light Artillery and his connections to the Republican party prepared Lott for his promotion.[33] In Company F, 2nd Lieutenant Edward Gannon accepted the position of 1st lieutenant in Company G. Gannon was an unmarried moulder from Cape Girardeau. In March, William Cleland was promoted to the rank of 2nd lieutenant in Company F. The Massachusetts born Cleland had enlisted in the First Missouri Rifles early in 1861, and he was a bookkeeper in St. Louis prior to the war. Finally, in April 1862 in Company I, 1st Lieutenant James Hummer resigned and was replaced by 2nd Lieutenant Charles Osgood. Osgood, a native of Ohio, was a physician living in Bethel, Illinois, prior to the war. Lieutenant Hummer cited his reason for resignation as the actions of the war exacerbated an injury he had incurred 16 years prior when he was thrown from a horse. John Hathorn was promoted to the rank of 2nd lieutenant filling Osgood's old post. Hathorn, also an Ohio native, was a miller living in Bethel, Illinois, prior to the war.

It is important to note that not all changes occurred without strife, and a good example of one such event was the appointment of Dr. Melancthon Fish as regimental surgeon. After Dr. Smith's resignation, all of the officers of the 11th Missouri signed a document on April 14, 1862, requesting Dr. Eli Bowyer be appointed surgeon indicating, "Whereas Asst Surgeon Eli Bowyer has laboured arduously with the Eleventh Regiment Mo Vols since the organization of the Regiment, as asst Surgeon, not only having performed his duties in that capacity but having during the greater portion of the time performed the duties of Regimental Surgeon, giving entire satisfaction to all, he has become endeared to us by exhibitions of his skills as a physician and surgeon

First Lieutenant James A Lott, company C, was a native Pennsylvanian and a married carpenter living in Springfield, Illinois, prior to the war (author's collection).

and by his deportment as a gentleman. And whereas a vacancy having occurred by the resignation of Dr. Thos Smith Regt Surgeon. Dr. Eli Bowyer having been recommended (a copy of said recommendation and endorsement is here with enclosed) but Dr. Eli Bowyer not having been appointed in accordance with the desire of regiment but one Dr Melanchthon Fish an entire stranger having been appointed."[34] All of the regimental officers signed the document, but the decision was not changed. By all indication, Dr. Melancthon Fish was an exemplary doctor, and even though he was not initially chosen by the officers, he was selected by the governor of Missouri to fill this position and did an excellent job as surgeon. Dr. Fish had worked at the hospital at the Jefferson Barracks in St. Louis and had received great praise for his efforts at that facility.

Dr. Fish was born in Delaware County, New York, in 1828. He was 5 feet 7 inches tall with hazel eyes and dark brown hair. He worked as a schoolteacher and lived in various locations, including Texas, and tutored at the Wesleyan Seminary in Michigan from 1847–1848. He also served for six years in China as vice-consul. By all indications, he was a talented, highly energetic and excellent physician.

Advance on Corinth, Mississippi

Organization of the Army of the Mississippi, Maj. Gen. John Pope Commanding, April 30, 1862.[35]

SECOND DIVISION
BRIG. GEN. DAVID S. STANLEY

SECOND BRIGADE
BRIG. GEN. J.B. PLUMMER

26th Illinois, Col. J. M. Loomis
47th Illinois, Col. J. Bryner
11th Missouri, Lieut. Col. W. E. Panabaker
8th Wisconsin, Col. R. C. Murphy
2d Iowa Battery, Capt. N. T. Spoor

After arriving at Hamburg, Tennessee, the army spent the next week in organizing transportation and improving the roads so that soldiers and supplies could be moved. But, by April 27 the army was on the move traveling 5 miles toward Corinth, and on April 29 the enemy was found "in force"[36] when the cavalry reconnoitered two miles further toward Corinth. By May 1, General David Stanley's Second Division entered Mississippi and soon made contact with Union troops on his flanks. The Army of the Mississippi was reorganized after the Battle of Island No. 10 and General Joseph Plummer was appointed to brigade command reporting to the divisional commander David Stanley. Stanley would command the 11th Missouri's division throughout 1862 through significant and bloody battles. Stanley was an Ohio native and he graduated from West Point in 1852. The 33-year-old Stanley had fought in Wilson's Creek campaign, and he was also present during the siege of New Madrid and Island No. 10.

On May 3, General John Pope reported the reconnaissance of Farmington, Mississippi, found the enemy in strength of about 4,500 men, supported by artillery in the town. Stanley's Division camped on Seven Mile Creek on the Farmington Road on May 4 and suffered through cold rains for several days. Moving the army was a difficult task, and even Confederate Brigadier General Patton Anderson reported, "The roads are in wretched condition."[37] Duncan McCall described his march toward Corinth, "Owing to the bad roads, a succession of mud holes and hills, and height of the streams which had overflowed their banks, by which several mules were drowned, our advance was most difficult and laborious."[38] The Confederates did not make the advance easy, "We had a fight almost every day."[39] The three Union armies pressed toward the Confederates who were entrenched at Corinth. Buell's Army of the Ohio held the center, the Army of the Tennessee held the Union right and John Pope's Army of the Mississippi advanced along a ridge road and was positioned on the Union left.

Colonel Mower, realizing that his regiment had been in the field for several months and involved in hard campaigning, noticed a problem and set about making sure that his regiment was safe and healthy. On May 5, 1862, Mower issued an order to the regiment, "It having been reported to the Colonel Commanding the Regiment that the men in his command are infested with vermin, he orders that a thorough inspection to made by the officers commanding the different companies, and men found with them on their persons or clothes be reported at Sick Call, to the Regimental Surgeon."[40] Mower realized that he needed a healthy regiment if they were to be able to fight.

On May 8, the army was again on the march and it passed through Farmington, Mississippi, about 4 east miles of Corinth, and the Confederate pickets were driven before the advance. A brigade was sent to probe the defenses and drove the Confederates into the main entrenchments of Corinth. The Union brigade pushed forward until it came under the range of the cannons in the enemy's main line of defense. Beauregard's Confederates were not idle as the Union army slowly advanced on Corinth. Being outnumbered, Beauregard utilized the terrain to his advantage and had to wait for Pope to make a mistake. On May 8, Pope ordered Brigadier General David Stanley's Second Division and Brigadier General Eleazer Paine's First Division to within range of the Confederate cannons at Corinth, but he lost contact with Major General Don Carlos Buell's Army of the Ohio on his flank. Realizing that he was exposed and vulnerable to a Confederate attack by being so far in front of his support, Pope withdrew to the relative position of Buell's line. As he withdrew, he decided to leave Colonel John Loomis' brigade in the town of Farmington.

Colonel Loomis was commanding Stanley's Second Brigade, which was officially commanded by General Joseph Plummer who was sick and absent. The exposure to the elements that occurred during the March and April expedition to Point Pleasant had taken its toll on General Plummer. Therefore, the command of the Second Brigade fell to Colonel J. M. Loomis of the 26th Illinois Infantry.

Loomis' occupation of Farmington posed a threat to Beauregard because the Union troops were within two miles of the Memphis & Charleston Railroad and also within four miles from the Mobile & Ohio Railroad. The Mobile & Ohio Railroad was particularly important to the defenses of Corinth. The threat to Beauregard's supply line and Loomis' isolated position provided the impetus for a Confederate attack. Major General Earl Van Dorn's Army of the West was ordered northward to strike Pope's army. On the evening of May 8, Van Dorn positioned his three divisions to strike Pope with Brigadier General James H. Trapier's division forming on the left, Brigadier Daniel Ruggles' division holding the center and Major General Sterling Price forming to the right. Van Dorn shifted his forces further east on the morning of May 9 and then attacked.

On the morning of May 9, the Confederates attacked the rear of Stanley's Division, hoping to envelope at least a brigade; and the brigade receiving the blow was Second Brigade commanded by Colonel J. M. Loomis, which consisted of the 26th Illinois, 47th Illinois, Eighth Wisconsin and the 11th Missouri infantries. The Confederates attacked early in the morning, and Colonel Loomis reported, "Skirmish firing commenced in front of Farmington and continued at intervals until about 9 o'clock, when Major Jefferson [8th Wisconsin Infantry], commanding advance guard, reported that without reinforcements he could not hold the ground.... General John Palmer's reinforcements arrived and went to the front"⁴¹ to relieve the Eighth Wisconsin. Loomis recorded, "I had made preparations to withdraw the brigade, considering myself relieved, when General Stanley, having arrived, ordered one regiment across the swamp on our left to occupy the high, clear ground, to hold it, and prevent the planting of batteries there. I ordered Colonel Mower, Eleventh Missouri Volunteers, to that point, and they performed the duty well, held the position, and thus prevented the possibility of a flank movement against our left."⁴² Duncan McCall of the 11th Missouri described the opening of the engagement, "Early the next morning our ears were saluted with the heavy boom of cannon ... for the rebels were pouring the shot and shell."⁴³ Confederate Divisional Commander Brigadier General Daniel Ruggles of Braxton Bragg's Corps reported that finding the enemy ahead of him, he deployed the batteries of Hodgson's Louisiana, Ducatel's Orleans Guards and Hoxton's Tennessee artillery to begin shelling the Union forces and awaited the attack of Major General Earl Van Dorn's troops scheduled to join the fight on his right. Finally, Robertson's battery also joined in the artillery barrage.⁴⁴

On the previous day, General Pope prophetically reported from Farmington, Mississippi, "Judging from the very feeble resistance offered to our advance on any of the roads leading to Corinth and the ease with which close reconnaissance was made, I am inclined to think either the enemy is evacuating or that he desires to draw us in on this road."⁴⁵ Pope soon was aware the enemy was not evacuating.

In Loomis' report of the action at Farmington, he stated that a Confederate battery, located about a mile away on the brigade's left, began shelling the most forward units of the brigade. Soon thereafter, another Confederate battery opened

Colonel J. M. Loomis, commanded the 2nd Brigade in the engagement at Farmington, Mississippi (Library of Congress).

up on the brigade's right. Hescock's Union First Missouri Light Artillery, Battery G, located the Confederate batteries and began to return fire. "The skirmishers and battle line of General Palmer's brigade covered our front from right to left, and considerable fighting occurred."[46] Under fire from the enemy's artillery, Loomis ordered the 47th Illinois, Eighth Wisconsin, and 26th Illinois infantries to lay down behind a ridge because with General's Palmers troops advancing, these regiments could not fire without hitting their own troops. Spoor's Second Iowa Light Artillery battery was ordered to a position to counter fire the enemy's batteries. The battle began to intensify and Loomis stated, "We suffered considerably from the fire of the enemy."[47] After relieving the advanced Union troops, General Palmer's brigade began to withdraw, resulting in 47th Illinois and Eighth Wisconsin infantries becoming the front line. These regiments were ordered to open fire on the advancing enemy "which order they promptly and with effect obeyed."[48]

The 26th Illinois was directed to change their front to face the oncoming Confederates and open fire. As the withdrawing Union forces flowed through the Second Brigade's lines, the

Colonel Joseph Mower, new commander of the 11th Missouri. "No officer was better fitted for hard campaigning" (Library of Congress).

26th Illinois unleashed a volley into the Confederates. "The fire of these three regiments checked the advance of the enemy and compelled a portion of their line to retire under cover."[49] Confusion occurred within the Union forces when the 26th Illinois, which had moved to face the enemy, was surprised by a cavalry charge coming from their rear. Loomis was incredulous that he had had no indication that this was happening. This was the charge of the Second Iowa Cavalry, which was thrown forward by the order of Brigadier General Halbert Paine to stop the advance of the rebels. The cavalry charged from the rear of Loomis' infantry without any warning and spooked the troops. The Second Iowa Cavalry recorded 51 casualties for May 9 as a result their charge on the attacking Confederates, which represented the largest number of casualties of any unit for the battle at Farmington. Loomis gave the order for his infantry to cease fire while the cavalry charged. The 26th Illinois Infantry quickly reformed after their surprise from the rear and along with the Eighth Wisconsin again began firing at the gray-clad foes. Confusion continued as Loomis began searching for Spoor's battery, which was supposed to fire at the Confederate artillery, but he could not find them. Loomis had to be lamenting the role of brigade commander as he watched his own regiment begin to withdraw to the right of the original line, much to his chagrin. He asked the 26th Illinois' Lieutenant Colonel Tinkham why he was moving. "He answered, 'By order of General Paine' and that he was further ordered by him to retire by right of companies to the rear into the swamp, which movement was executed."[50] Meanwhile, the remaining two regiments, the 47th Illinois and Eighth Wisconsin, were still in line firing forward.

As the battle intensified, General Pope reported, "The enemy has advanced in such heavy force that the infantry command on opposite sides of creek could not retain their position."⁵¹ To Loomis' relief, General John Palmer arrived and directed him to form a new line at the edge of a swamp and under cover. Loomis was able to withdraw the 47th Illinois and Eighth Wisconsin and he united three regiments when he ordered the 26th Illinois to reform with the other two regiments.

But the Second Brigade had four regiments. The 11th Missouri Infantry was obediently holding their ground under the command of Colonel Joseph Mower in his first command of the regiment in a fighting situation. He was ordered to hold this ground, and hold it he would, even though his brigade was withdrawing. Luckily for the 11th Missouri, Captain Temple Clark, assistant adjutant general, gave the order for the regiment to withdraw. William Stewart recorded, "Our regiment had the most dangerous position and was the last regiment off the field.... The whole country in front was black with the advancing foe."⁵² The main body of the Union force was withdrawing and the 11th Missouri was stoutly holding their ground and itching to get into the fight. Captain Clark's order came just in time because the regiment was dangerously close to being surrounded. Duncan McCall recorded, "Our regiment, the 11th Missouri, was formed in line of battle, within a short distance of a rebel

General John Pope, commander of the Army of the Mississippi at Farmington. "He desires to draw us in on this road" (Library of Congress).

battery, which was shelling our men with pretty good effect; they never fired a shot at us. Their object was to flank us and take all prisoners.... He [Mower] was riding up and down the lines, surveying with an eagle eye the operations of the enemy, when he perceived their intentions was to flank us, and he ordered us to about face and retreat. We double-quicked about two miles."⁵³ A third defensive battle line was being formed under the order of General Palmer, but General Stanley wanted the brigade to form in front of its own camp. The isolated 11th Missouri was assigned to "protect the bridge on the main approach and some stores,"⁵⁴ having made its way back to the main body. Finally the Union lines were stabilized and the Confederate attack halted. Loomis recorded, "Of the conduct of your officers and men I cannot speak in terms of too high praise."⁵⁵

Colonel Loomis' brigade recorded 64 killed and wounded in the engagement at Farmington. The bridge across the creek was burned by the enemy. The Confederate loss was reported as 8 killed, 2 missing and 89 wounded, while the Federal forces lost more heavily, the casualties being 16 killed, 148 wounded and 14 captured or missing.[56]

General Pope's final message of May 9, stated "All is quiet. Our pickets occupy the bridge across Seven Mile Creek, which is half a mile in the swamp and near the farther side. My impression is that the enemy has retired, but he may possibly be massing forces on our left, as the cars have been very busy last night and to-day as far as Glendale. I shall have early notice if it is so."[57] But the Battle at Farmington was over, and, at least for Colonel Loomis, it was a day of confusion and conflicting orders. General Stanley, in his official report, stated, "As Brigadier-General Palmer has made a full report and commanded, it not deemed necessary to repeat any of the incidents of the fight."[58] General Pope's attention was drawn to the manner in which the engagement of Farmington was conducted, and he sent a clear order showing his disapproval in the actions of some in the recent engagement in General Order 46 on May 14, 1862. "The Major General Cmndg was much mortified in the skirmish of the 9th inst. To learn of a number of this command who skulked to the rear to be out of danger. They are a disgrace to the army and their country."[59] In a Regimental General Order, the new colonel for the 11th Missouri Infantry demonstrated an almost instinctive ability to lead by immediately supporting his regiment's efforts on May 9, "The Col Comdg takes pleasure in announcing the above order No. 46 does not apply to this regiment in any instance."[60] The leadership ability of Mower was immediately felt by the 11th Missouri, as Mower reassured his men that they had performed well. The 11th Missouri had nearly been cutoff and captured, but the regiment was able to find its way back to the Union lines and there were no casualties reported for the day. It was fortunate for the Union Army that the full plan of the Confederate attack did not take place. Colonel Loomis found himself in a precarious situation in Confederate attack facing Ruggles' Division with two additional divisions prepared to strike. "Van Dorn, alerted that Buell had moved a division forward to reinforce Pope, did not attempt to force his way across the stream, but led his troops back to their camps."[61] After the clash with Confederates at Farmington on May 9, better coordination of the three Union armies was needed. Pope's advance position made it possible for an attack to be made on his troops.

On May 17, the three Union armies again began to advance toward Corinth, with Pope advancing through Farmington on the army's left, Buell in the center, and General George Thomas commanding the third army on the right. As the Union forces advanced, the Confederates were pushed to within two miles of their defensive fortifications outside Corinth. Skirmishes were a daily event for the advancing armies. On May 18, General Henry Halleck reported that Major General William T. Sherman's division had lost 8 men killed and 31 wounded in skirmishes with Confederate defenders. The advance not only faced Confederate skirmishers, but the advance was hampered by the inhospitable terrain. Halleck reported that the terrain was so marshy and woody that advancing was treacherous. Again, General Beauregard determined it was time to strike the Union advanced units. On May 22, Beauregard tried to push the blue-coated soldiers back but was unsuccessful. Beauregard planned an all-out assault on Union armies and concentrated his entire force with the intent to punish the Federal troops before they could entrench before Corinth. The attack did not come to fruition because one key of Beauregard's plan was missing. General Earl Van Dorn was unable to get his Army of the West into position. Being outnumbered more than 2:1 (120,000 to 53,000), the situation was becoming critical for the Southern defenders.

Ever encouraging his commanders toward victory, President Lincoln sent a message on May 24, "I believe you and the brave officers and men with you can and will get the victory at Corinth."[62] Also on May 24, the 11th Missouri got back into action. Five companies of the 11th

Missouri were ordered to drive in Confederates pickets and with Companies H and F acting as skirmishers, the companies charged the Confederate defenders, only to find them gone. As the companies pushed ahead, they emerged from some dense timber where they were seen by Confederate defenders who sent a volley of musket fire into the 11th Missouri and also began to shell them. The 11th Missouri returned fire and the Confederates continued their withdrawal. Three of the 11th Missouri infantrymen were wounded in the exchange. The details of the skirmish were recorded by General David Stanley, "I being officer of the day, and the enemy's firing upon our pickets having become exceedingly annoying and insolent, it was deemed advisable by General Pope to drive them from their positions. I selected for this purpose five companies of the Eleventh Missouri, Colonel Mower commanding, and five companies of the Thirty-ninth Ohio, Major Noyes commanding, with Dees' Third Michigan Battery. Getting in front of our pickets, we soon found the position of the enemy, and after throwing some rounds of shell with great accuracy into their reserves, Colonel Mower charged the wood occupied by the enemy with five companies of the Eleventh Missouri, driving the enemy before him. The enemy had three regiments of infantry and a battalion of cavalry, and after being driven from their first position they tried to make a stand in the open field. Coming out of the woods with the members of my staff, I found myself within a few hundred yards of their front, but, I suppose thinking us their officers, they made no attempt to molest us. I rode back and apprised Colonel Mower, who, concealing his force, advanced on the enemy until within musket range, and gave them a volley that started them scampering in all directions for the cover of the woods. I then brought down two of Dees' Parrott guns and threw a dozen shells into Corinth. The two men of the Eleventh Missouri were badly wounded. We could not learn the loss of the enemy. We took one prisoner; one of their wounded also, who soon died, and we know of several of their dead left in the woods. The battalion of the Thirty-ninth Ohio was kept as a support for Dees' battery. Considering the disparity of numbers this was a very pretty little exploit for the numbers engaged, and did great credit to Colonel Mower and his troops."[63]

On May 28, Halleck reported that Pope's Army on the Union left flank had received the greatest resistance that day and had lost 25 killed or wounded, while their enemy had left 30 dead on the field after a skirmish. The 11th Missouri moved forward with Pope's artillery and dug their own rifle pits, but the immediate task was to protect the cannons. Although the Confederates tried to force the men protecting the cannons to withdraw, they were unsuccessful. General David Stanley reported on May 28 that his "division moved forward 1¼ miles, and halted near the White House on Bridge Creek, presenting a diagonal double line to Corinth, the right flank nearest the enemy's main work and the front facing a large earthwork battery erected by the enemy south of the Memphis and Charleston Railroad. This battery was silent for several hours until about noon."[64] Stanley ordered his artillery batteries to begin firing on the Confederate position, which resulted in an artillery duel between the respective batteries. While this took place, the Union soldiers were able to continue their entrenching activities until about 3:00 P.M. At that time, three Confederate columns attacked Stanley's division while Stanley was still under artillery fire, but Stanley reported that his division repulsed the enemy. Stanley's division reported that over 50 Confederate soldiers were buried after the attack. After Stanley handled this attack, the Confederates did not bother his division for two days, and Stanley was able to move very close to the Confederate defenses at Corinth. By May 29, he had entrenched his division securely in place.

The 11th Missouri spent May 29 in their rifle pits. The Union armies again pressed forward and by late May had pushed within a 1,000 yards of the Confederate fortifications and began to establish positions for large siege cannon (20 pound Parrotts) to be used against the defenders. By May 29, Pope's artillery began shelling the Confederates. Orders were sent that a general assault on Corinth was to begin on May 30, and according to Duncan McCall, "Everything being ready, the ball was to open on the morrow."[65] The men had prepared and were ready to charge the Confederate defenses; however, having already lost the ability to protect the railroads, Beauregard ordered a withdrawal from Corinth on the evening of May 29. The Confederates retreated south toward Baldwyn and finally about 50 miles south to Tupelo. Union forces moved into the abandoned defenses on May 30 and John Pope's Army of the Mississippi pressed forward to pursue the retreating Confederates. Union General Henry Halleck reported, "For miles out of the town the roads are filled with arms, haversacks, etc., thrown away by his flying troops."[66] Halleck reported that he had captured as many as 2,000 prisoners.

During the push on the fortifications of Corinth, at least eight men from 11th Missouri Infantry were killed or severely injured. The regimental service records recorded the following were killed or wounded during the advance:

Marion Turner	Company A	Died of wounds
John Lyons	Company C	Died of wounds
Levi Messer	Company E	Gunshot wound
George Grate	Company E	Died of wounds
Thomas Haws	Company F	Gunshot wound
Ezekiel Waldrop	Company H	Gunshot wound later discharged
Thomas Wilkinson	Company H	Died of gunshot wound
Edmond Bower	Company I	Died of gunshot wound

Fox's records for regimental losses recorded that the 11th Missouri Infantry totaled three men killed and another 22 wounded in the Siege of Corinth in May 1862.[67]

The evacuation of Corinth, May 1862 (Library of Congress).

Despite the weariness that was present in the Union army, morale was good. The Confederate foe had taken flight. The 11th Missouri's Private Anderson Campbell, Company K, a native of Tennessee and farmer from Sumner, Illinois, described his view of the events in letter to his family. "We are in Missippi under marching orders now. I gess you have heard that Corinth is evacuated and the rebels is gone and we are going to start after them in the morning. We have been on gard for 48 hours.... I think the secesh is about plaid out and it is getting dark and I must quit writing soon."[68]

Sergeant James Scott, Company B, from the 10th Kentucky Infantry, also involved in the advance on Corinth, wrote a letter to his parents on June 18, 1862, and described the situation near Corinth, Mississippi. He described the poor marching conditions, including swamps, and the men attacked by scorpions and the ever ubiquitous mosquitoes. Sergeant Scott also lamented the conditions of the citizens in Corinth. Although the Union forces had sufficient food, "it is pretty ruff and the citizens round here is bound to starve unless the government furnishes them something to eat."[69] Sergeant Scott's impression was that the Confederate Army had foraged all the food from the local citizens and that the local men were forced into the army. Sergeant Scott stated, "I think they have all gone home."[70]

The climate of Mississippi was oppressive for wool-clad soldiers of blue as they moved into the hot summer months. The heat, humidity, and mosquitoes took their toll on the men of the 11th Missouri and resulted in the resignation of 2nd Lieutenant Harley Kingsbury, Company H, whose health gave out on him near Corinth. Lieutenant Kingsbury stated in his resignation, "I find that the heat of this climate has increased my disability until I am nearly completely prostrated. Duty to myself, my family and my country demands my resignation."[71] Harley Kingsbury was replaced by newly promoted 2nd Lieutenant Edwin Applegate. Applegate, a native Ohioan, was a 21-year-old carpenter from Sumner, Illinois. In the case of Lieutenant Harley Kingsbury, the war was not over for him. He returned home and recovered his health, then enlisted in the 64th Illinois Infantry. Kingsbury returned to the field and died in Atlanta campaign with his new regiment.

Captain Thomas Dollahan, Company H, resigned in June 1862, due chronic diarrhea and infection of his lungs. 1st Lieutenant William Boatright was promoted to the rank of captain in June. Lewis Gray was promoted to the rank of 2nd lieutenant.

Captain George Henry, Company D, an attorney from Clay County, Illinois (author's collection).

First Lieutenant Wilson Duggans, Company K, also resigned due to the exertions placed on him in this harsh environment, stating, "I have been sick half the time, ... but the fatigue and exposure that I have undergone since my arrival at Hamburg, Tennessee April 22/62 have prostrated me."[72] On June 13, 1862, Captain William Stewart wrote, "My 1st Lieut. W. A. Duggans of Springfield, Illinois has resigned on acct of sickness. Lt. Foster formerly 2nd Lieut. is now 1st Lieut. and Sergt. Kendall 2nd Lieut."[73] When Wilson Duggans resigned, he was replaced with 2nd Lieutenant Charles Foster and Cyrus Kendall was promoted to the rank of 2nd lieutenant. Cyrus Kendall was an attorney from Clay County, Illinois. Kendall was 24 years old, married and a native of Pennsylvania.

The captain of Company D, Clark Hendee, resigned in July 1862. He was replaced with the regimental quartermaster, George Henry. George Henry was a native Ohioan, and an attorney from Clay County, Illinois, prior to his enlistment. Able Pickrell was appointed to the post of regimental quartermaster. Pickrell was a 29-year-old farmer from Sangamon County, Illinois, prior to his enlistment.

First Lieutenant William Colclasure, Company F, a veteran of the Mexican War, also resigned in June 1862, citing ill health as reason. Colclasure was replaced with the current 2nd lieutenant of Company F, William Cleland. The new 2nd lieutenant for Company F was John Finlay. Finlay was a schoolteacher prior to enlisting in the 11th Missouri Infantry from Xenia, Illinois.

By June 4, Pope had pushed 30 miles south of Corinth and reported as many as 10,000 prisoners; and by June 9, Pope was 50 miles south and reported Beauregard was at Saltillo and estimates of prisoners were at 20,000–30,000 men. General Beauregard stated the estimates by Union commanders could not be further from the truth. The 11th Missouri remained in Boonville, Mississippi, for several days and then returned to Clear Creek near Corinth, Mississippi. One of the 11th Missouri Infantry had the misfortune of being severely injured when a tree fell on his tent. Captain William Stewart described, "In the rear of my tent was a tall dead tree without limbs. Two officers and I were in the tent, when the tree began cracking, some person called to us to look out. We all started. I, one way, and the other two another way, but I happened to run right under the tree as it struck the tent. The tent poles struck me on the shoulders and sent me whirling about a rod, and this saved my life for the heavy tree smashed through the tent and fell right where I was struck with the tent poles and ... was crushed as flat as a pancake."[74] The soldier that was injured in this incident was Private Charles Gillen, Company G. Private Gillen was discharged as a result of this accident in November 1862.

Even celebrations proved to be dangerous in the Civil War. Private William Haskins, Company G, of the 11th Missouri recorded the celebration on July 4, 1862, "It is very sickly here at this time. It is so hot that the soldiers can't live hardly. So no more on that. Well something about the fourth of July, we did not have much of a time here. They were celebrating by firing cannons. There was a poor fellow that got his hand shot off and blowed about a rod and powder burned him until he was perfectly black."[75]

In August 1862, tragic news reached the men of the 11th Missouri Infantry when General Joseph Plummer died. It will be recalled that Plummer was wounded in the Battle of Wilson's Creek in August 1861, and he suffered ill health since that time, despite the fact that his performance was so excellent he had been promoted to the rank of general during the past twelve months. In May, while 11th Missouri marched toward Corinth, Plummer was sick and later consulted a Baltimore physician to try to combat his debility. However, on August 9, almost twelve months to the day of his wounding at Wilsons Creek, Plummer died. He died from "congestion of the brain secondary to his wounds, hepatic derangement and the fatigues and exposures to active campaigning."[76] Plummer's loss was severe news for the men of the 11th Missouri and the Union army.

The regiment remained at Clear Creek until August 18 enjoying the rest and time needed to recuperate after being on the march since late February. It was time for the regiment to regain its strength and military bearing. The days were filled with guard duty, drill and dress parades. The brigade was under the command of Colonel Robert Murphy of the Eighth Wisconsin who "drilled us in the battalion drill in the morning, brigade drill in the afternoon."[77] Also in August, the 11th Missouri lost the services of their much respected Lieutenant Colonel William Panabaker who was injured while riding his horse through one of the swamps near Corinth. Being unable to recover from the injury and therefore accompany the regiment, Panabaker resigned his commission. He was replaced with Major Andrew J. Weber who was previously the captain in Company B. The regimental drills lasted while the regiment remained at Clear Creek.

On August 23, Captain Stewart reported, "We had preaching this morning by our Chaplain. He is a young man but quite earnest and forcible. He is popular so far. He has been with us about a month, is a Presbyterian from Illinois named Baldridge."[78] Samuel Coulter Baldridge had taken the spiritual reins of a very difficult regiment, the 11th Missouri Infantry. Baldridge was born on August 6, 1829, in Vermillion County, Indiana, and had graduated from Hanover College in 1849. He then attended the New Albany Presbyterian Theological Seminary until 1852. The Presbyterian Church licensed him to preach in 1853, and he was ordained on October 15, 1854. Baldridge was the minister of the Friendsville, Illinois, Presbyterian Church prior to his enlistment.

Also in August, Sergeant Silas Renick, Company F, was detached from the 11th Missouri and sent to Palymyra, Missouri, to attempt to gain new recruits for the regiment. What should have been safe and easy duty for Sergeant Renick turned into a fight for his life when he was attacked by guerrillas outside of Palmyra. While defending himself from the ruffians he was shot with a shotgun in the left elbow and side to such an extent that he was discharged in December 1862. The 28-year-old Sergeant Renick was a farmer from Xenia, Illinois, in his civilian life.

One of the most selfless actions by a captain in the regiment occurred in July 1862 when Captain and Dr. Clark Hendee resigned his commission, feeling that he had lost the confidence of his command. His resignation letter stated:

> Sir
> I hereby tender my resignation of my commission to take effect immediately and unconditionally. Having seen evidence of a state of feeling among the enlisted men in my command satisfies me that their efficiency might be materially enhanced by a change of commanders is the reason that has induced me to resign.[79]

Obviously Captain Hendee wanted the best for his men and something triggered the belief that someone else might be better suited to command his company. This was an interesting turn of events due to Hendee's obvious importance in organizing the company and even paying to transport the men to St. Louis with his own money.

Extracts from the Civil War diary of Sergeant David McKnight, Company D, did not mention Captain Hendee's resignation. His diary recorded the regiment spent most of the time in camp at Camp Gaylord, Mississippi, and the regiment marched to Tuscumbia, Alabama, on August 18 and remained in camp from August 23 to the end of the month.[80] The summer of 1862 was coming to a close but September and October would bring new challenges for the regiment.

11th Missouri Infantry Regimental Losses April 1862 Through August 31, 1862

	APRIL	MAY	JUNE	JULY/AUGUST
Discharged	Green, George (K)	Haas, Elias (B)	Askren, William (A)	Fish, Thomas (A)
		Samson, William (B)	Dunnaway, Charles (B)	Shaw, Oliver (A)
		Kirkham, Kirkland, William (E)	Pohlman, John (B)	Utter, Thomas (A)
		Redick, James (G)	Fleece, James (C)	Williams, John (D)
		Henderson, Francis (I)	Bartley, Thomas (A)	Wright, James Sgt. (E)
		Johnson, George (I)		McDonnell Columbus Corp. (F)
		Miras, John (I)		
		Reed, Moses (H)		Hoover, Jonathan (G)
				Kyger, George (G)
				Pickering, Francis (H)
				Scyoc, John (H)
				Waldrop, Ezekial (H)
				Hamilton, Noah Sgt. (I)
				Bosley, Phillip (I)
				Snowden, Willis (I)
				Sweat, Nephi (I)
				Thomas, Jeremiah (I)
				Cable, Alfred (K)
				Schriner, Herman (K)
				Williams, John (K)
				Woodland, James (K)
Died	Guenterman, Robert (D)	Turner, Marion/Marvin (A)	Chapman, Thomas L. (A)	Newell, Thomas (A)
	Carroll, Jeremiah (K)	Jordan, John M. (C)	Yates, Benjamin (A)	Beckman/Buckman, Charles H. (C)
		Gibson, Henry A. (D)	Lyons, John (C)	Jump, George (D)
		Grate, George (E)	Smith, Lewis (D)	Blackledge, Martin (F)
		Howland, John (E)	Smith, William (D)	Cummins, William Corp (F)
		Ayers, William, Drummer (F)	Pickering, James (H)	Power, Robert (F)
		Powell, Thomas (F)		Davis, William (G)
		Bathe, John (G)	Bower, Edmond (I)	Shields, Samuel Corp. (G)
		Branstuller, John (G)	Chapman, James H. (I)	Haskins, William (G)
		Raines/Renix, George (G)	Rook, William (I)	Beathard, Thomas (I)
		Ethel, James Corp. (I)		Hood, William Reg. Musician
		Bay, Martin (K)		
		Johnson, Eli (K)		
		Pursley, David (K)		
		Wade, Albert M. Sgt. (K)		

	APRIL	MAY	JUNE	JULY/AUGUST
Deserted	Murry, John (B)			
	Holt, John (E)			
	Thompson, John (G)			
Transferred Out				
Resigned	Brooks, Joseph Chaplain, F&S	Hummer, James 1st Lt. (I)	Dollahan, Thomas Captain (H)	Hendee, Clark Captain (C)
	Livingston, Benjamin Major — F&S		Colclasure, William Lt. (F)	
	Smith, Thomas Surgeon, F&S		Duggans, Wilson Lt. (K)	
	Perce, William 1st Lt. (B)			

Chapter 3

Battle of Iuka

"The heavy pall of sulphurous smoke that hung like a breath from Hell."
— The Rev. Samuel Baldridge

After the Siege of Corinth and the pursuit of Beauregard's army, it was a rejuvenated 11th Missouri Infantry that marched toward Iuka, Mississippi, in September 1862. The first part of the summer found the heat oppressive and marching was almost intolerable, but conditions improved as the months passed. In September, the 11th Missouri Infantry was led for the first time into battle by "Fightin' Joseph Mower" who was also referred to as "The Wolf" because of his predilection for riding up and down the battle line and also for his inherent ability for battle. Mower was the type of a regimental and brigade commander chosen to lead soldiers into the heat of battle, and he would be called upon to do this repeatedly. The regiment had been mustered into service slightly over a year before and had yet to really be tested in battle with an enemy that would stand and fight. The test was about to be faced, ironically, with an enemy commanded by a fellow Missourian, Major General Sterling Price. Price was a native Virginian, was active in the Missouri legislature, and had even served in the U.S. House of Representatives. He was elected governor of Missouri and served from 1853–1857. His military experience extended to his service in the Mexican War when he commanded the Second Regiment, Missouri Mounted Volunteer Cavalry. Sterling Price began the war striving for neutrality for Missouri and commanded the Missouri State Guards, as an attempt to keep the state from sliding into war; but the state had chosen to align with the Union cause. Price committed his talents for the Confederacy, and by the summer and fall of 1861, he had fought at Wilson's Creek and captured 3,500 Union soldiers in Lexington, Missouri, which added to his growing reputation within the Confederate army.

John Meyers, 11th Missouri Infantry (USAMHI).

On March 7–8, 1862, Sterling Price led Confederate troops in the Battle of Pea Ridge in Arkansas. By April 1862, Price had been rewarded for his service in the Confederacy by being commissioned as a major general. The 11th Missouri Infantry would face this fellow Missourian in the upcoming Battle of Iuka.

During the summer of 1862, General Pierre Beauregard's health had declined after he was forced to withdraw from Corinth, and he left the army without authorization and traveled to Mobile to convalesce. With Beauregard's exit, General Braxton Bragg assumed control of the Confederate Army in the west. Henry Halleck's three Union Armies had pushed Beauregard out of Corinth in June. Since June, the Union army gained control of Memphis and the three armies separated to carry the war to different areas of the South. By the first week in June, Don Carlos Buell's Army of the Ohio had pressed toward Chattanooga, Sherman's forces were sent to repair and guard the railroad west toward Memphis and General John McClernand was sent to Bolivar, Tennessee. Pope's army was given the job of improving the old Confederate defenses in Corinth to meet the Union objectives of keeping the railroads functioning as a source of supplies and as a way of rapidly moving troops. Controlling the railroads gave the Union forces an opportunity to move east, west or south rapidly.

Due to his success at Island No. 10, New Madrid, and Corinth, General John Pope was summoned to Washington in mid–June; and he would ultimately assume command of the Army of Virginia and have the dubious honor of facing General Robert E. Lee in the Second Battle of Bull Run. On June 26, the command of the Army of the Mississippi was ably filled by Major General William Rosecrans. Ohioan William Starke Rosecrans was born in 1819 and graduated 5th in his class at West Point in 1842. Rosecrans was an engineer in the army until his resignation in 1854. Prior to the war Rosecrans ran a kerosene factory in Cincinnati, and he received a commission as a colonel serving as General George McClellan's aide early in the Civil War. He was promoted to the rank of brigadier general and distinguished himself in action at Rich Mountain, Virginia. Serving under McClelland was revealing to Rosecrans when McClelland failed to acknowledge much of the success at Rich Mountain was due to Rosecrans' efforts. As a result, Rosecrans requested a transfer to the western theater of the Civil War rather than serving under McClelland in the east.

Also, during the summer of 1862, Henry Halleck was given the command as General in Chief in Washington and General Ulysses Grant was the made the commander of the District of West Tennessee commanding the previously mentioned Union forces, but he did not command Buell's Army of the Ohio. Grant's command included the Army of the Mississippi with its 25,000 men and the Army of the Tennessee with over 38,000 men.

For the Army of the Mississippi stationed at Corinth, Rosecrans and Grant decided to enhance the defenses at Corinth including the fortification of the six earthen lunettes or forts. "Each had high parapets, ten-foot-wide ditches in front, and embrasures for cannons."[1] The batteries were named Lathrop, Tanrath, Phillips, Madison, Williams and Robinett. The six batteries were placed within one-half mile of the railroad junction and these fortifications proved to be very important for the 11th Missouri, particularly, in October 1862. Finally, a seventh fort, Powell, was completed the evening of October 3. Also, in June 1862, Major General Henry Halleck ordered the construction of six artillery redoubts (Batteries A through F) and these redoubts were designed to continue the original Confederate earthworks all the way around the city.

Things did not stay static for long as a stalemate had existed between Bragg's Army and Grant's since June; but in late July, Bragg decided to take the offensive. He intended to move the bulk of his army toward Chattanooga in eastern Tennessee to stabilize the situation where pro–Union sentiment was high. Bragg decided to take the war out of Mississippi and strike Buell's Army of the Ohio, and he planned to leave Mississippi in the hands of General John Forney who commanded the Army of the Gulf, General Earl Van Dorn to protect Vicksburg with 16,000 men and finally Sterling Price with his Army of the West who commanded the District of Tennessee. As Bragg moved to face Buell, he ultimately decided to strike northward into Kentucky and confronted Buell at Perryville, Kentucky, in October 1862.

For Price, who was responsible for the Confederate activities in northern Mississippi and western Tennessee, several problems concerned him. Some of his Missouri troops wanted to return to their home state and not fight in Mississippi, but Price knew he had to deal with the task at hand. He convinced his troops that their need was in Mississippi and they would later return to Missouri. The Missouri troops had not had a pleasant experience since they had left their home state, but these troops were welcome in Mississippi. Price's major problem was that he was given the responsibility for northern Mississippi and western Tennessee, but had too few soldiers for this vast territory. Also, Bragg was "exhorting him to hold the line of the Mobile and Ohio Railroad and keep Grant and Rosecrans from reinforcing Buell."[2] Given this task, he was left to his own devices without specific orders. Price wrote that the success of General Bragg's movements into Tennessee and Kentucky "depends on the promptness and boldness of our movements and the ability which we shall manifest to avail ourselves of our present advantages."[3]

Private John McDonel, Company H, 11th Missouri Infantry, a native Mississippian who was living in Cape Girardeau at the beginning of the war (Abraham Lincoln Presidential Library & Museum).

By September, Grant placed two divisions of the Army of the Mississippi at Jacinto, Danville, Rienzi and Corinth under the command of Major General William Rosecrans. This was Grant's left wing. Major General Edward Ord occupied the center of Grant's forces and Major General William Sherman, at Memphis, occupied Grant's right.

Price felt compelled to take action on Rosecrans' Union forces at Corinth to prevent the Army of the Mississippi from uniting with Buell. He was also being told that the movement of Bragg drew the Union forces in Tennessee and northern Mississippi eastward and that Price would have an excellent opportunity to attack Rosecrans. Price, ever diligent, tried to develop a plan to move northward, but he felt that he needed additional troops. He requested that Earl Van Dorn's troops join in his advance and suggested that the best strategy would be the concentration of their forces to overwhelm the remaining Union defenders in northern Mississippi, but Van Dorn denied any assistance. Van Dorn felt his forces were needed to deal with the Union threat near Vicksburg where the Union army had begun digging a canal opposite the city. Van Dorn was also concerned about the Union actions in Louisiana where the Federal forces had increased their activity and threatened Port Hudson.

Price was again urged to "press the enemy closely in West Tennessee,"[4] but he was given no clear direction of how he was expected to proceed without assistance from other Confederate forces. He felt that an attack on Rosecrans' Army of the Mississippi was rash; however, he did order General Frank Armstrong's cavalry to conduct a reconnaissance into Union-held western Tennessee to determine the strength and location of Federal troops. Without permission, Armstrong changed his orders to conduct a raid. Even though he was able to capture over 200 prisoners, he was defeated at Britton's Lane, Tennessee. Meanwhile in early September, Bragg was moving toward Kentucky and he was continuing to challenge the Army of the Ohio. As predicted, Union forces from the west were beginning to be shifted to Buell, leaving Rosecrans with only two divisions (commanded by Brigadier General David Stanley and Brigadier General Charles Hamilton) to defend the Corinth area of Mississippi. There were also three additional divisions from the Army of the Tennessee near Corinth. The Union vulnerability was becoming evident as the troops left this area and Frank Armstrong's cavalry penetrated into Tennessee.

Finally on September 1, a message from Braxton Bragg forced Price to take action when Bragg informed Price that he was successful in drawing Buell toward Nashville and Price was formally ordered to prevent the unification of Rosecrans and Buell. Although Price hoped that Van Dorn would send troops to his assistance, when this yielded no positive outcome, he decided he could wait no longer. Bragg and Major General Kirby Smith were striking into Kentucky and they needed Price to strike Rosecrans as part of the "grand offensive."[5] Bragg erroneously believed Rosecrans was about to cross into Tennessee to reinforce Buell. In reality, Rosecrans had no plans of moving from the Corinth area of Mississippi.

Price's force of 12,000 men was divided into two divisions. The first division was commanded by Brigadier General Henry Little and consisted of 4 brigades of infantry:

Confederate Forces at Iuka[6]

MAJOR GENERAL STERLING PRICE — ARMY OF THE WEST
1ST DIVISION — BRIGADIER GENERAL HENRY LITTLE

1st Brigade — Colonel Elijah Gates
16th Arkansas, 2nd Missouri, 3rd Missouri, 1st Missouri Dismounted Cavalry, Wade's Missouri Battery

2nd Brigade — Brigadier General Louis Hébert
14th Arkansas, 17th Arkansas, 3rd Louisiana, 40th Mississippi, 1st Texas Legion, 3rd Texas Dismounted Cavalry, Dawson's St. Louis Battery, Clark's Missouri Battery

3rd Brigade — Brigadier General Martin Green
7th Mississippi Battalion, 43rd Mississippi, 4th Missouri, 6th Missouri, 3rd Missouri Dismounted Cavalry, Guibor's Missouri Battery, Landis' Missouri Battery

4th Brigade — Colonel John Martin
37th Alabama, 36th Mississippi, 37th Mississippi, 38th Mississippi

Cavalry — Brigadier General Frank Armstrong
Adam's Mississippi Regiment, 2nd Arkansas, 2nd Missouri, 1st Mississippi Partisan Rangers, 4th Mississippi Cavalry

Price's second division, which trailed behind Little's, was commanded by Brigadier General Dabney Maury. Although Maury played an important role in the upcoming battle by preventing Major General Edward Ord's three divisions from entering Iuka from the north, Maury would not be actively involved in the battle at Iuka. By September 5, Little's division had advanced to Saltillo, Mississippi, about 5 miles north of Tupelo, and Maury moved into Baldwyn, Mississippi, which had just been vacated by Little. So the advance upon Iuka had begun. The commander of Price's First Division was Henry Little, a native of Maryland. Little was the son of a member of the U.S. House of Representatives, Peter Little, and at the age of 45, Little had Price's full confidence. Little was an experienced soldier having served in U.S. Infantry after he graduated from West Point in 1839.

As Bragg had predicted, the Union Army in northern Mississippi was slowly losing men to support Buell in Tennessee; and the final two divisions of Rosecrans' force stationed at Corinth assisted Halbert Paine's and John Mitchell's divisions in their crossing of the Tennessee River near Tuscumbia, Alabama. Despite the loss of combat troops from northern Mississippi and western Tennessee, it was critical to hold onto the gains that were won earlier in the year. Corinth was won in the action in May 1862 and was a vital junction of two major railroads. Rosecrans believed that in addition to Corinth, a strategic location that needed to be defended was Eastport, Mississippi, which was the best river port on this section of the Tennessee River. Eastport was just a few miles north of Iuka, and to protect Eastport, Iuka needed to be held.

The Rev. Samuel Baldridge, chaplain of the 11th Missouri, wrote to his brother-in-law on August 27 while the regiment was stationed at Tuscumbia. The Rev. Baldridge was obviously struggling with the moral life of the men of the regiment. "I find some cases of piety, many cases of seriousness, but more of utter recklessness.... We are very pleasantly located, on a height E. of Tuscumbia."[7] Baldridge reported the oppressiveness of the heat from 10:00 A.M. until 5:00 P.M., and he was quickly learning that the 11th Missouri was a rough and rowdy regiment.

On September 8, Price received communication from Bragg that he interpreted to be an order to follow Rosecrans toward Nashville, where Bragg perceived him to be moving. Already on the move, Price intended to do just that, and if he found any Union forces in Iuka, he would defeat them and move steadily northward. By September 11, Price's Army of the West was advancing closer to Iuka, but his movements did not go unnoticed by Union scouts and cavalry that remained in northeastern Mississippi. So Grant became aware an engagement with Price was likely, but he was unsure if Price intended to attack Corinth or Iuka. Rosecrans began to concentrate his forces at Jacinto, Mississippi, and he ordered Colonel Robert Murphy's Second Brigade of Stanley's Division to remain at Iuka with orders to protect the railroad and Union stores there. Murphy's brigade included the 26th Illinois, 47th Iowa, 11th Missouri, Eighth Wisconsin, Second Battery of the Iowa Light Artillery, and the Third Battery of the Michigan Light Artillery.

In a letter, Captain William Stewart, Company K, 11th Missouri, wrote to his family, he described the activities of some of the Union troops during this time at Iuka. "The 6th we came out of Iuka 7 miles into a nest of Guerrillas and have been skirmishing with them ever since. We have pitched our camp with orders to cleanout the country around here which you may be sure we will do. Gen. Price with a large Army is not far off, but we are watching him."[8]

Clearly, Rosecrans and Price were closing in on one another, but confusion was evident on both sides and neither Rosecrans nor Price knew exactly where the other force was.

In northeastern Mississippi, Iuka was a small town with a population of about 300 people, and for the most part, its importance was the fact that it was Union supply depot. Colonel Robert Murphy commanded the Second Brigade of the General David Stanley's Second Division of Rosecrans' Army of the Mississippi and was the colonel of the Eighth Wisconsin Infantry. In war, Robert Murphy was not lucky, and luck is important. At 8:00 A.M. on September 13, the Second Brigade's pickets were attacked outside of Iuka by Price's advance troops, General Frank Armstrong's cavalry. There were attacks and counterattacks throughout the morning. Murphy determined from prisoners, Price's main force of infantry was following behind Armstrong's cavalry. To give Murphy his credit, he tried to contact Rosecrans for orders, but the telegraph was down and all the couriers that he dispatched failed to return. Murphy was alone in Iuka, and he did not know for how long or the extent of the force he was facing. As part of Murphy's Brigade, the 11th Missouri held their ground throughout the day of September 13, and at 2:00 A.M. on September 14, Murphy sent a wagon train westward toward Corinth, with the infantry following at daybreak.

Receiving dispatches from Armstrong about Murphy's brigade defending Iuka, Price planned an infantry attack on the morning of September 14, but he was surprised to find his prey gone. Price force-marched his men as he approached Iuka, desiring to overwhelm Murphy's brigade and nearly exhausting his men in the process. Murphy had marched from Iuka; however, Murphy had orders to destroy the Union supplies which he failed to do and Price's men enjoyed their bounty. Although Price had captured Iuka, he was still struggling with developing a plan to complete the orders preventing Rosecrans from becoming united with Buell; and so his only conclusion was to move westward to find Rosecrans' main force and attack him.

Price's intent was to follow what he thought was Rosecrans' withdrawal to Nashville, but Rosecrans was still in Corinth; and, likewise, Rosecrans was confused about Price's purpose for attacking Iuka. Regardless, Colonel Robert Murphy's time as brigade commander was over. The ire of both Grant and Rosecrans focused on Murphy, and they were greatly disappointed in his decision to abandon Iuka. Murphy was immediately relieved of command and brought up on charges. With Murphy's exit, Rosecrans gave command of the Second Brigade to Joseph Mower, colonel of the 11th Missouri Infantry. Mower was making a meteoric rise in command. In April, Mower was a captain in the U.S. Infantry, now five months later he had advanced from regimental commander to brigade command. Mower was a "scrappy, hard-drinking Vermonter, he had entered the army during the Mexican War as a private.... Already Mower made an enviable record for himself as one of the most reliable regimental commanders in Rosecrans army, when sober."[9] When Mower was given command of the brigade, command of the 11th Missouri Infantry was passed to Major Andrew J. Weber. While the Second Brigade had gained an excellent brigade commander, it was obvious that the events leading to the brigade leaving Iuka was an embarrassment to everyone. Neither Duncan McCall nor William Stewart reported on this event in any of their correspondence.

Confederate Major General Sterling Price (courtesy Civil War Museum at Wilson's Creek National Battlefield).

With Price in Iuka, Grant and Rosecrans felt they needed to attack Price before he could unite with Van Dorn's command. Grant, Ord, and Rosecrans maneuvered to cut off and destroy Price's isolated divisions. By September 16, Mower advanced toward Iuka traveling by rail from Corinth to Burnsville, about halfway between the two towns. He then detrained and began a march eastward to gather information about Price for Rosecrans and Grant. His march was hard and swift and earned his brigade the nickname of "Joe Mower's Jack Ass Cavalry."[10] By 4:00 P.M. Mower discovered the Confederate pickets from Frank Armstrong's cavalry about six miles west of Iuka. Companies E and F of the 11th Missouri were deployed forward to find the enemy. Private William Gilliard, Company F, described the reconnaissance of Iuka. "We moved out in the open with our entire force. Cos. F and G [E], under command of Capt. W. W. Cleland moved rapidly across the field. When we got nearly across the enemy's skirmishers opened fire on us, but we went forward with a rush until we reached the top of a hill, where we could see Iuka."[11] Armstrong raised the alarm within Price's camp and the Confederates fell into a defensive line. Mower ended the day about a mile from Price's defenses near Iuka and sent word back to Rosecrans and Grant that 12,000 Confederate soldiers occupied Iuka.

After determining the size of the Confederate force he faced and anticipating Van Dorn would move to combine his forces with Price, Grant decided to attack Price before this could happen. Grant decided to send 15,000 men — 6,000 with General Edward Ord and 9,000 with Rosecrans — to battle Price's 12,000 Confederates. If Van Dorn and Price combined, Grant felt he would be outnumbered 2 to 1.

Rosecrans was ordered to lead his remaining two divisions, under the command of Brigadier General Charles Hamilton and Brigadier General David Stanley, as a unified force in a flanking movement against Price by sending them toward Iuka along the Fulton Road while Ord advanced from the northwest. General Hamilton planned to send troops to the east of Iuka and Price would be boxed in on three sides with the Tennessee River blocking his north. This was accepted as the best plan and the Union troops began their march on Iuka beginning on September 17. Often coordinated attacks in the Civil War went awry because communication was difficult and proper timing was so difficult to accomplish. The plan was good, the implementation was the challenge. This was to be the case at Iuka in September 1862.

As the 11th Missouri reconnoitered the area around Iuka, a group of foragers looking for watermelons were captured. Although soldiers from the regiment set out immediately to rescue the soldiers, they were unsuccessful. The men from the regiment who were captured included:

William Hutenhow	Company B
Michael English	Company B
Charles Simmons	Company E
William Couch	Company E
William Hardy	Company E
Luther Zimmerman	Company H

The Union Forces at Iuka

ARMY OF THE MISSISSIPPI.— MAJOR GENERAL WILLIAM S. ROSECRANS. SECOND DIVISION, BRIG. GEN. DAVID S. STANLEY.

First Brigade, Col. John W. Fuller
27th Ohio, 39th Ohio, 43rd Ohio, 63rd Ohio, Battery M 1st Missouri Artillery, 8th Wisconsin Battery, 2nd U.S. Artillery

Second Brigade, Col. Joseph A. Mower
26th Illinois, 47th Illinois, **11th Missouri**, 8th Wisconsin, 2nd Iowa Battery.

THIRD DIVISION, BRIG. GEN. C. S. HAMILTON.

First Brigade, Col. John E. Sanborn
48th Indiana, 5th Iowa, 16th Iowa, 4th Minnesota, 26th Missouri, 11th Ohio Battery

Second Brigade, Brig.-Gen. Jeremiah C. Sullivan
10th Iowa, 17th Iowa, 10th Missouri, 24th Missouri, 80th Ohio, 12th Wisconsin Battery

CAVALRY DIVISION, COL. JOHN K. MIZNER

2nd Iowa, 7th Kansas: 3rd Michigan. Unattached. Jenks' Co., Illinois Cavalry.

Price knew the Union infantry was near and expected a fight at any time. On the morning of September 19, General Earl Van Dorn finally sent a communication stating that Price should move from Iuka to combine his forces with Van Dorn and that Corinth would be his target. After months of being on his own, Price was relieved to be given any kind of direction at all. Before Price could implement this order, he had to deal with Grant's army which was converging on his troops.

On September 18, General David Stanley's Second Division was to have marched and to be approaching Iuka, but his guide led him in the wrong direction and he was already behind schedule. Stanley started toward Barnett's Crossroad at 4:30 A.M. on September 19 while trying to make up time. The plan called for the attack to begin at dawn but that was no longer practical.

So that morning, Hamilton and Stanley's divisions were marching swiftly toward Price. Ord understood his orders from Grant, but he was delayed several times because Rosecrans' divisions were late. Because of the delays, Grant eventually ordered Ord to commence his attack when he heard Rosecrans initiate the battle. Communication was very difficult during the Civil War. Grant anticipated an attack by Ord in the early afternoon when the firing began, therefore, relieving pressure on Hamilton and Stanley. Due to further problems in coordinating the attacks, the stage was set for a difficult afternoon for Ord's comrades in Rosecrans' two divisions.

An interesting event occurred on September 19; Grant received a telegram stating that General Robert E. Lee had been defeated at the Battle of Antietam. Grant had the telegram carried across the lines and urged Price to lay down his arms and surrender. As might be expected, Price refused to do so. Price stated that he doubted the report, but that the news "would only move him and his soldiers to greater exertions in behalf of their country."[12]

General David Stanley, 2nd Division commander at the Battle of Iuka (Library of Congress).

The exchange of fire between Rosecrans and Price occurred at noon when the Second Iowa Cavalry commanded by Colonel Edward Hatch pushed some of Falkner's First Mississippi Rangers back from Peyton's Mill. The Battle of Iuka had begun. Hamilton's First Brigade commanded by Colonel John Sanborn had advanced to Cartersville, boxing Price on three sides. At noon, Rosecrans discovered an error; he thought Hamilton and Mower's brigades would be within supporting distance while traveling down the Jacinto and Fulton Roads, but they were five miles apart. Rosecrans feared that Price would defeat each division in detail, and he quickly made efforts to remedy this situation when he ordered the divisions to proceed up Jacinto Road together. However, the action left the Fulton Road unprotected should Price attempt to retreat. Also Rosecrans still thought Ord would engage Price shortly, allowing his divisions to take advantage of their position. So, a great plan was not proceeding smoothly.

The conflict at Iuka began to develop in earnest at 1:30 P.M. when the Third Michigan Cavalry screening Sanborn's brigade ran into Frank Armstrong's Confederate Cavalry, First Mississippi Partisan Rangers, along the Jacinto Road about four miles west of Iuka. The cavalry fell into line and was positioned to move the defenders out of the way near the Moore house. As the Confederate cavalry gave way, General Hamilton ordered the Moore house to be set afire. Duncan McCall recorded the 11th Missouri marched past the house, which was burned and two cavalry troopers had been killed there.

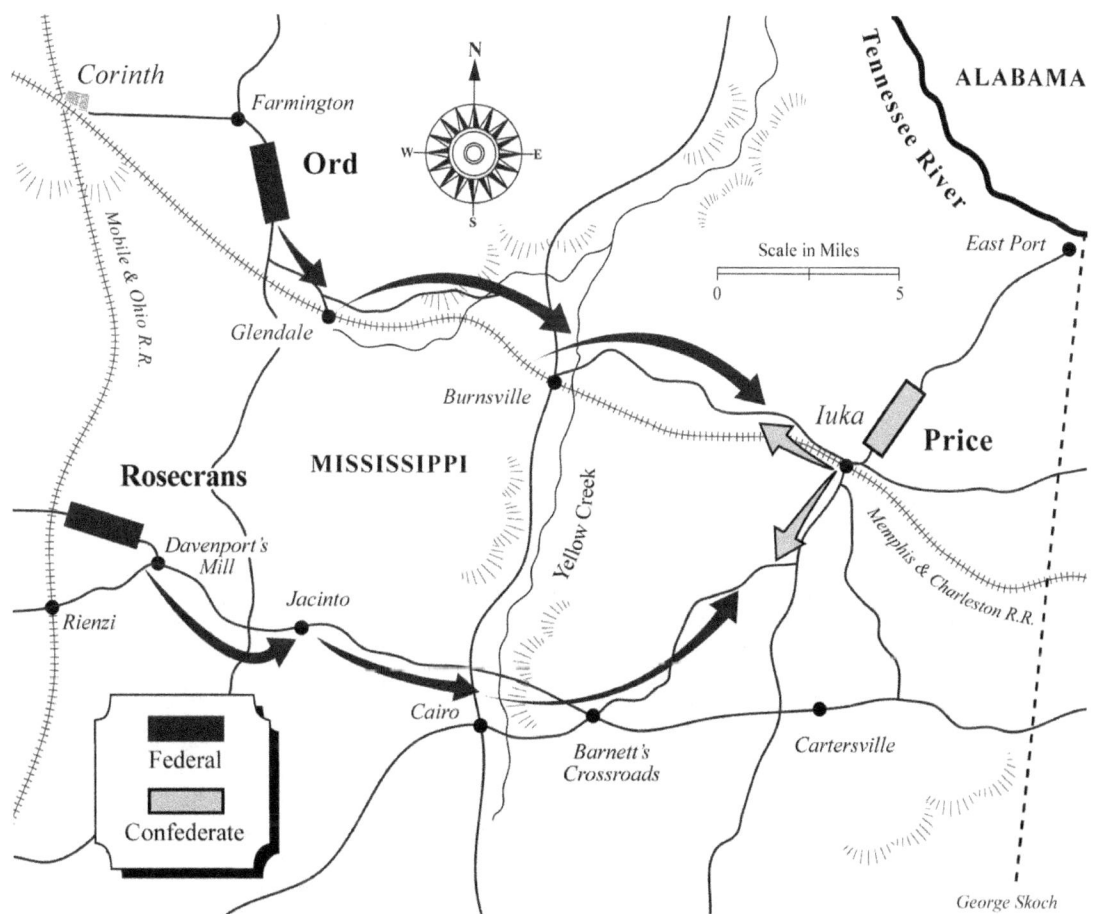

The Union approach to Iuka, September 1862.

By 3:00 P.M., Sanborn had pushed another mile closer to Iuka and traveled northward along the Jacinto Road until he reached the Ricks Farm, which was about two miles west of Iuka. The Union infantry marched to a meeting house at the fork in the road, and being unsure of where Price's main force was located, probed forward with skirmishers. At 4:00 P.M., the 26th Missouri Infantry found Price's infantry about three-quarters of a mile west of Iuka. The 26th Missouri Infantry discovered Brigadier General Louis Hébert's Second Brigade, which was supported by artillery. Hébert's infantry was forming a battle line on a high knoll, and the 26th Missouri, located on a low ridge, faced them across a ravine. Faris' Confederate Missouri artillery quickly began shelling Sanborn's men and quickly came under fire in return from the Missourians as the Union artillery was unlimbered. As Hébert's men fell into line, the Third Texas Cavalry (Dismounted) formed a skirmish line and moved toward the bottom of the ravine.

More Federal and Southern regiments began falling into line. Sanborn unlimbered the 11th Battery of the Ohio Light Artillery, which began to duel across the ravine. The Fifth Iowa Infantry fell in line to the right followed by the 48th Indiana Infantry on the left of the Union line. Soon, the Fourth Minnesota Infantry completed the front line of defense for Sanborn by positioning itself to the left of the 48th Indiana. The 26th Missouri moved into the Union line to the right and rear of the Fifth Iowa, and the 16th Iowa was positioned behind the 48th Indiana. Likewise, Hébert deployed his regiments, including the First Texas Legion on his right, 14/17 Combined Arkansas Infantry in the center and the Third Louisiana on the left. The 40th Mississippi was positioned in the rear of these regiments. The Texans were not happy.

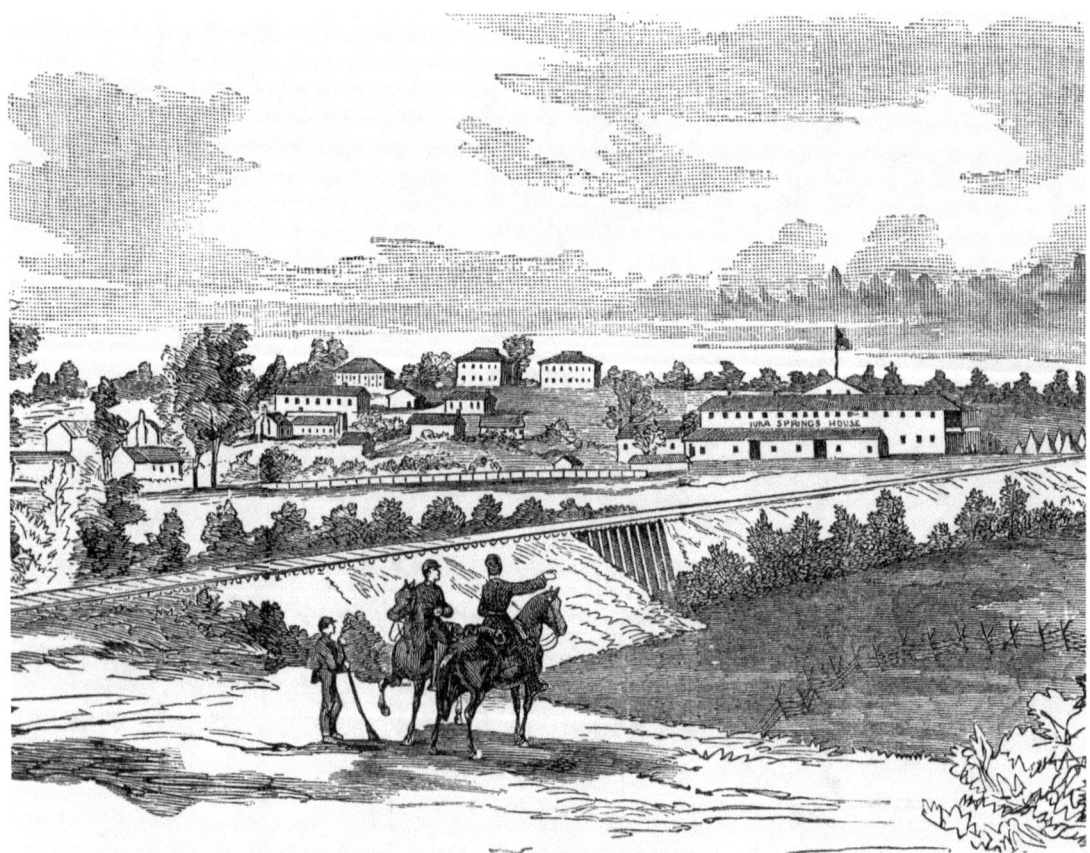

Iuka, Mississippi, site of the battle on September 19, 1862 (Florida Center for Instructional Technology).

"Still bitter over their transfer to the infantry, the Texans entered their first major dismounted combat poorly prepared for the experience. The men were still armed with their old double barrel shotguns."[13] Due to the poor condition of their mounts, the cavalry was relegated to dismounted duty.

By 5:00 P.M. additional regiments were concentrating on the ridges. Sullivan's Union brigade, including the 80th Ohio, 17th Ohio, 10th Iowa, and 10th Missouri infantries, filled in throughout the Union line. The 12th Wisconsin Artillery completed the Union line by anchoring the extreme left.

Hébert pressed forward and fire erupted from both sides, but Hébert did not have enough men to defeat Hamilton's division. Hébert's dilemma was soon solved when his divisional commander, Brigadier General Henry Little, arrived with Colonel John Martin's Third Brigade, which resulted in the 37th and 38th Mississippi infantries being placed to the right of the First Texas Legion and the 37th Alabama and 36th Mississippi infantries moved to the left of Hébert's line. At 5:15 P.M., Little began his attack. According to historian Peter Cozzens, "Hébert's brigade, numbering 1,774 officers and men, and Martins' brigade, some 1,600 strong, moved forward to do battle with 2,200 Federals of Sanborn, and, in close proximity, a similar number under Sullivan."[14]

One of the initial objectives of Little's assault on the Union line was to eliminate the 11th Ohio Artillery, which had been placed in a forward position to fire on Little's men. As the Confederates advanced, the First Texas Legion and the Third Texas Cavalry (Dismounted) emerged from the ravine and delivered a "point blank" volley into the green 48th Indiana Infantry, which gave way falling back over the ridge to their rear. This left the 11th Ohio Artillery unprotected on its left.[15]

When the 48th Indiana broke, Colonel Sanborn ordered the soldiers to stand and fight and pulled his pistol and killed two men who refused. The 16th Iowa held the position in the rear of the 48th Indiana and was ordered to prepare to receive the Texans as they chased the 48th Indiana rearward. For some reason, the 16th Iowa did not allow the 48th Indiana to pass through their lines before they released a volley "killing more Indianans than had died from Rebel bullets."[16] Colonel Sanborn ordered the 16th Iowa to charge the Texans, which they did, sending the southerners back over the ridge. The situation was only slightly better on the Confederate side. As the Texans tried to regroup after falling back, they came under fire from their own men. At 6:00 P.M., the 16th Iowa advanced on the hill to exchange volleys with the Texans, but when the 16th Iowa's Colonel Alexander Chambers was shot from his saddle, the regiment became unnerved and broke for the rear.

While the Texans were handling the Indianans and Iowans, on the right of the 11th Ohio Artillery, the Fifth Iowa was battling the Third Louisiana. These regiments exchanged volleys for 15 minutes and the Fifth Iowa's bayonet charge drove the Louisiana regiment back into the ravine. The Third Louisiana regrouped and pushed forward again, only to be driven back with a second bayonet charge. To complicate matters for the Fifth Iowa, they began to receive enfilading fire from the Texans on their left.

Sanborn needed to stabilize his line and shore up the position lost by the 16th Iowa and 48th Indiana. The 26th Missouri regiment was ordered to split into groups of companies to fill the gaps, but as the regiment was moving into place, volleys from the Confederates riddled the regiment and soon they were retreating with 60 percent of the men killed or wounded. When the 26th Missouri withdrew, the Third Louisiana completed their thrust up the ridge with the Fifth Iowa giving way. The 40th Mississippi also advanced forward on the left of the Third Louisiana and the 37th Alabama and 36th Mississippi moved forward. As the Union infantry was giving way, the loss to the 11th Ohio Artillery was terrible. The gunners "stood by the cannon to the last," but soon the 11th Ohio Artillery fell to the Confederate onslaught. "Of the 54 cannoneers, 46 were hit."[17]

Of Sanborn's five regiments, only the Fourth Minnesota remained unbloodied and intact. Sullivan's regiments were yet to be engaged, but they were scattered throughout the Union line. Martin's Confederate brigade advanced, and it seemed the Southern regiments could not be stopped, but they paused. The light was fading, but more importantly, General Henry Little had just been killed on the field; and this caused the Confederate attack to stall. The pause was critical for the Union army as Sanborn tried to rally his troops. Soon Confederate divisional command was passed from the dead Little to Louis Hébert, and the battle resumed its ferocity.

General Sullivan, watching the Union regiments of Sanborn's brigade fold, knew he had to take the situation in hand or else all would be lost. He ordered the 80th Ohio and the 17th Iowa forward to stem the surge of butternut soldiers streaming over the ridge. Through a series of almost unbelievable events, Colonel John Rankin of the 17th Iowa fell from his horse, unconscious, and command passed to Captain John Young; companies became separated; and when another captain in the regiment was also shot, the regiment panicked and ran to the rear. It was the 80th Ohio which held the Texans long enough for Sullivan to rally and piece together a defensive line made up parts of the Fourth Minnesota, 48th Indiana and 16th Iowa, and they again pushed the Texans back only to be pushed back themselves.

Rosecrans' earlier fear his divisions would be defeated in detail seemed close to becoming a reality. Finally, David Stanley's division was emerging on the scene. Stanley rode forward to meet with Sanborn and assess the situation. Sanborn's response to General Stanley, when asked where he needed help, was to send reinforcements as soon as possible or the day would be lost. Joseph Mower's Jack Ass Cavalry was leading the way and at the head of the column was the 11th Missouri Infantry hustling forward to the sound of battle. The regimental strength of the 11th Missouri, according to the company morning reports, was nearly 500 men.[18] With Colonel Joseph Mower in command of the brigade, Major Andrew Weber commanded the 11th Missouri. Major Andrew Weber reported the regiments in front of the 11th Missouri did not move forward, but his regiment moved forward at double-quick time and cheered as they went. The 11th Missouri Infantry wanted to get into the fight, and it looked like they were going to get the chance. As the 11th Missouri moved forward, they moved to the extreme right of the Union line in an effort to reach the field as soon as possible. Joseph Mower accompanied the regiment to the front. The 47th Illinois, 26th Illinois, and the Eighth Wisconsin arrived on the scene later.

As the 11th Missouri prepared to move forward and to the right of the Fifth Iowa, they marched in four columns, loaded their muskets and marched forward at double-quick time. As the regiment advanced, they shifted their formation from column to battle line as they crossed a field on the extreme right of the Union line. They passed though a wooded area, and as soon as they emerged from the woods, they came "face to face with an enemy line of battle, thirty yards away."[19] The 11th Missouri fired the first volley and there was no return fire. Major Andrew Weber recorded all became clear when a soldier ran forward from the regiment to their front, "For God's sake, stop firing into your own men, you are firing into the Thirty-seventh Mississippi."[20] With that the Missourians cheered and sent a second volley into the 37th Alabama and the 36th Mississippi infantries. The quote referring to the 37th Mississippi was in error, because the 11th Missouri was facing two startled and angry Confederate regiments,

Opposite: **The Battle of Iuka, September 19, 1862. The 11th Missouri Infantry engaged the 36th Mississippi and 37th Alabama on the right flank of the Union line.**

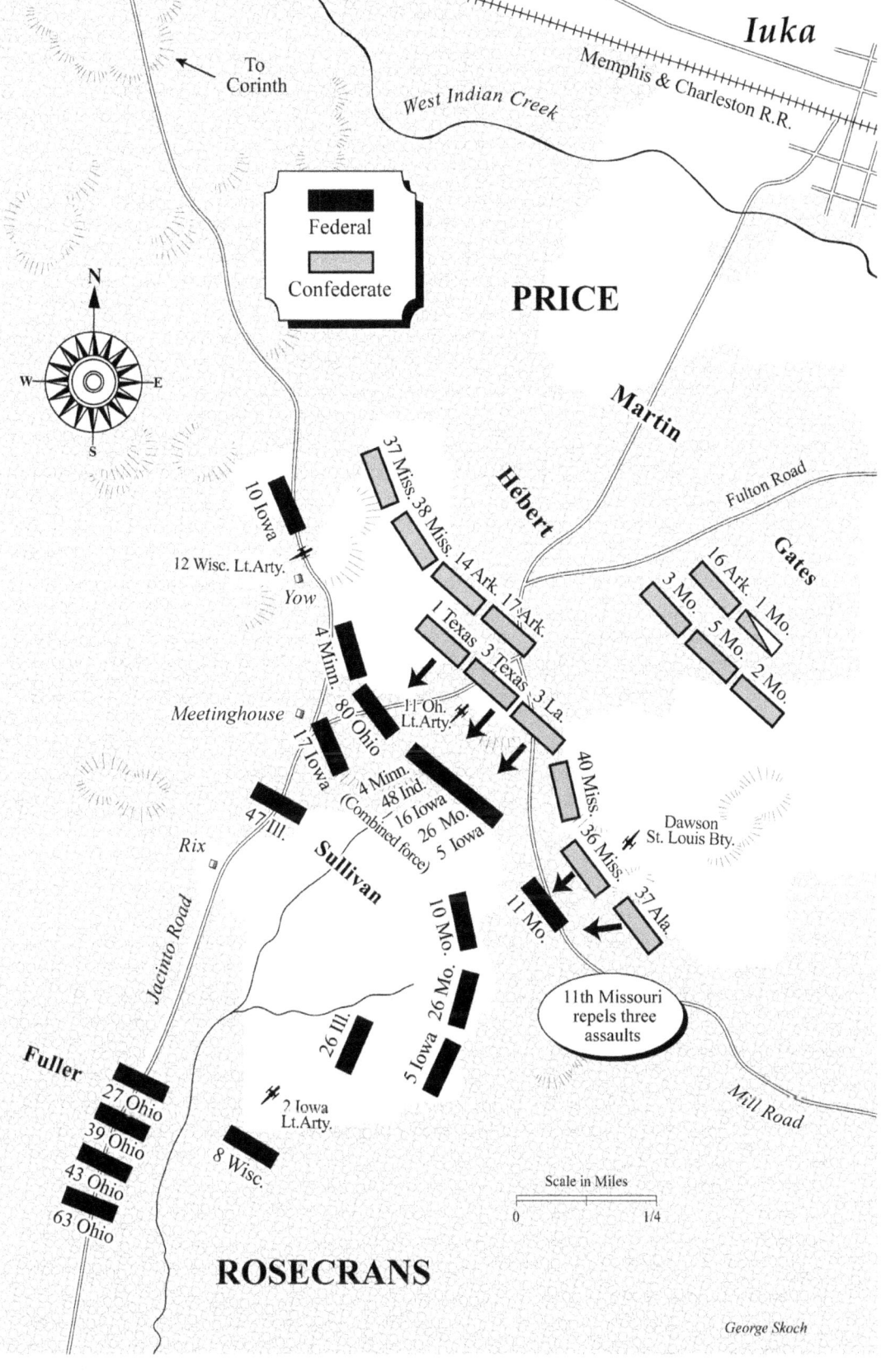

the 37th Alabama infantry and the 36th Mississippi Infantry, not the 37th Mississippi. If the pause, which stalled the Confederate attack when Little was killed, had not occurred, it would have been likely that the 11th Missouri would have been surprised instead of the 37th Alabama and 36th Mississippi; but that was not the case. The hardnosed 11th Missouri made their presence known and were determined to hold their ground.

The two battle lines set about firing volleys into one another. Major Weber of the 11th Missouri reported that the smoke was so thick that "an object could not be seen five paces distant."[21] The 37th Alabama and 36th Mississippi regiments ran forward in a bayonet charge with hopes of pushing the 11th Missouri back, but this regiment did not give. The 11th Missouri, fighting for its life, "repelled three charges in brutal, close quarter fighting."[22] Major Weber reported that the enemy was received on the point of the bayonet and shot off. In many cases the officers placed their pistols directly in the faces of the Confederate attackers and fired. "The rebels approached so close that they used their revolvers; but as the smoke had darkened where we were, they fortunately did no damage, except scorch some of the boys' faces with powder. When we discovered the rebels in such close proximity to us we were ordered to fire, which order we obeyed with alacrity, and volley after volley was poured into their advancing columns. They threw column after column against our lines to break them and cut their way out, but unable to succeed."[23] The Rev. Samuel Baldridge described the battle, "But no words can describe the scene. O the awful roar of musketry, sharp and wicked, murderous. overwhelming — now & then the hollow horrible crash of a cannon loaded with canister & the heavy pall of sulphurous smoke that hung like a breath from Hell."[24] The 11th Missouri and their Confederate foes fought for nearly an hour before the Alabamians and Mississippians stopped their attacks and withdrew. The 11th Missouri, with no ammunition remaining, slowly pulled back. The day was over. The official report of the 11th Missouri showed that 7 men were killed, 64 wounded and 3 were missing.

Of the battle, Captain William Stewart wrote, "For 2 hours or three during the battle, my life couldn't have been insured for more than twenty five cents at the highest. There has been no Regiment in the whole war that fought more desperately for over two hours than the 11th Mo. did in that battle."[25] Stewart reported the 11th Missouri had the advantage of being on lower ground and the Confederate musket fire went over the regiment. The Confederate regiments recorded 13 dead and 64 wounded during the battle. The after-battle reports from the 36th Mississippi and the 37th Alabama are not recorded, but officers of the 37th Alabama suffered greatly in the battle with the 11th Missouri. These two regiments entered the battle with 626 men. In the 37th Alabama, both Colonel James F. Dowdell and Lieutenant Colonel Alexander A. Greene were among the wounded with Greene the more seriously of the two. Next, the 37th Alabama's Major William F. Slaton was shot from his horse so intense was the battle on both sides of the line.

Meanwhile the rest of the battle was winding down as darkness halted the bloodshed. General Rosecrans said of the 11th Missouri's battle, "As the first came bearing down upon the 11th Missouri, and when within 20 paces, an officer of the rebel ranks sprang forward and shouted, 'Don't fire upon your friends, the Thirty-seventh Mississippi.' He was answered by a volley which drove them back in confusion. The Second Brigade followed, and in the dusk of evening and the smoke of battle reached the very front of the 11th Missouri. The roar of musketry was terrific, but Mower met the shock and stood firm. The rebels recoiled and the firing ceased throughout the line. The troops rested on their arms."[26] Rosecrans summarized the regiments battle results, "The 11th Missouri, which, under the gallant Mower, met and discomfited two rebel brigades, and having exhausted every cartridge, held its ground until darkness and the withdrawal of the rebels enabled him to replenish."[27]

General Stanley's said of the 11th Missouri actions, "The only regiment that became heavily engaged was the 11th Missouri. This regiment stood its ground under a storm of musketry, which they repaid with double interest."[28] Finally Colonel Mower's recorded his pride in the action of the 11th Missouri: "The 11th behaved with the greatest gallantry and determination, both officers and men standing to their posts in the midst of a most deadly fire. Where all did their duty so well I can hardly mention any particular persons, without appearing to be guilty of partiality. Major Weber encouraged the men by his presence and coolness under the fire of the enemy."[29]

After the battle, the 10th Missouri moved up to relieve the position held by the 11th Missouri. The 11th Missouri replenished their ammunition and lay down to rest from their struggle with Martin's regiments. They had no blankets and huddled together to keep off the cold, but all had a restless night expecting to renew the battle in the morning.

Of those killed in the battle was Captain Amos Singleton of Company F, "one of the best officers."[30] Captain Singleton was a 28-year-old native from Ohio, and he was a married carpenter prior to enlisting. His loss was sorely felt by the regiment. Also Lieutenant William Cleland, acting regimental adjutant, was wounded in a fall when his horse was killed under him. Lieutenant Charles Osgood, Company I, was severely wounded in his chest when he was struck by a minié ball near his right shoulder, shattering his clavicle. Captain Moses Warner, Company C, Lieutenant John Cowperthwait, Company D, and Lieutenant Charles Foster, Company K, were also slightly wounded by balls fired by the soldiers of the 37th Alabama and 36th Mississippi.

Among the wounded at Iuka was Lieutenant John Cowperthwait, Company D. He was an engineer from St. Louis prior to his enlistment (courtesy Civil War Museum at Wilson's Creek National Battlefield).

Private Eugene Page wrote to his mother and described the actions of the 11th Missouri

Infantry, "Well I must tell you a little about my last soldier'n. I have been in the bigest fight that has eve been in the west. But as it was God's will I come out sound while many of my friends fell down around. The fight commensed a little before sundown. Our regiment was marched up a little after dark and one too or three regiments running. These officers could not rally them atoll. Our regiments stood and fought 2 too brigades one our and ten minutes. They charged on us too times but we cept them back. We crossed bainets several times our ammunition ran out and we was ordered to fall back. Our loss killed and wounded was 80. The rebles was over three hundred. They said they had fought many a regiment but they never come across one but what they could back before."[31] Eugene Page later succumbed to smallpox and died at Memphis, Tennessee, on February 16, 1863. He was 23 years old, stood 6' 1" tall and, ironically, had been born in Marshall, Virginia.

The 11th Missouri had developed quite a reputation as a fighting regiment. They were Mower's regiment and the only regiment of the brigade to fight in the Battle of Iuka. The 11th Missouri wanted to fight, and even though the cost was high, the regiment reveled in the recognition that they received. According to William Stewart, "Our Regiment is known and bragged on throughout the whole Army."[32] Of the regiments that fought on September 19, the 11th Missouri proved its ability to stand and fight. The regiment was bloodied with 74 casualties but the men knew that they could face death and stand their ground. The regiment had evolved this day and the presence of Joe Mower helped them become who they were, one of the best.

For the 11th Missouri, seven men were killed in action[33]:

John B Robinson	Corp	B	Killed
Fred W Schauburg	Pvt.	B	Killed
Emmanuel Lidey	Sgt.	G	Killed
Isaac BedfordAct.	Sgt.-Major	H	Killed
William Chapman	Pvt.	I	Killed
John Easton	Pvt.	I	Killed
Marshall Osborne	Sgt.	K	Killed

In addition to these, the following men subsequently died from their wounds[34]:

Daniel Dutton	Corp.	A	Mortally
George Moore	Pvt.	A	Body
McKelly, Crawford	Pvt.	D	Leg
John Cunningham	Sgt.	F	KIA
Amos Singleton	Capt.	F	Chest
Bedford Clark	Pvt.	G	Thigh
Luther Vance	Pvt.	I	Head
Albert Baymer	Pvt.	I	Body

Also, three men were listed as missing after the battle[35]:

James Hantsey	Pvt.	C	Missing
Daniel Cuppy	Pvt.	C	Missing
Thomas Capps	Pvt.	C	Missing

The remaining list of men made up the casualty list for the 11th Missouri, which was recorded by Dr. Thomas Hawley.

"Adjutants Report of Killed & Wounded in the 11th Mo Inf V in Engagement Near Iuka Sept 19, 1862 (Total 74 Killed & Wounded – Killed and Mortally Wounded 12 – Missing 3 Leaving Wounded 59)." [36]

Company A
Samuel Bourn	Pvt.	Shoulder	Severely
Alex Brooks	Pvt.	Side	Severely
John Lappin	Pvt.	Arm	Slightly
William McGuire	Pvt.	Thigh	Slightly
Edward Raridan	Pvt.	Leg	Slightly

Company B
Antonio Bush	Pvt.	Hip	Dangerously
Thomas Pugh	Pvt.	Side	Slightly
Andrew Reed	Pvt.	Left Arm	Badly
Charles Ross	Pvt.	Face	Slightly
Sylvester Turner	Pvt.	Neck	Severely

Company C
Moses Warner	Capt.	Leg	Slightly
William Roney	Corp.	Hip	Severely
John Byrd	Pvt.	Head	Slightly
John Hami/Hime	Pvt.	Ankle	Severely
Martin Hogue	Pvt.	Foot	Slightly
Samuel Neal	Pvt.	—	Slightly
John Rose	Pvt.	Foot	Severely
Montgomery Sweet	Pvt.	Shoulder	Severely

Company D
John Cowperthwait	1st Lt.	Shoulder	Slightly
Melkert Burton	Pvt.	Arm	Severely
James Davis	Pvt.	Leg	Slightly
John Gross	Pvt.	Arm	Slightly
Dios Hagle	Pvt.	Leg	Severely
Jasper Shockley	Pvt.	Head	Slightly

Company E
John D Bail	Sgt.	Arm	Severely
John Perry	Pvt.	Leg	Severely

Company F
William Cleland	1st Lt.	—	Horse Killed Under Him
John Lawson	Sgt.	Head	Severely
Elias Draper	Corp.	Hip	Severely
Garret Sutherland	Corp.	Thigh	Severely
William Doyle	Pvt.	Shoulder	Severely
David Harman	Pvt.	Arm	Severely
Jesse McLean	Pvt.	Thigh	Severely
James Robertson	Pvt.	Side	Dangerously

Company G
George Quick	Corp.	Head	Severely
Patrick Norton	Corp.	Neck	Slightly
General Adams	Pvt.	Breast	Severely

John Able	Pvt.	Both legs	Severely
Jacob Cochran	Pvt.	Leg	Slight
Edwin Kueff	Pvt.	Shoulder	Slight
George Lehr	Pvt.	Leg	Slight
Franklin Lewis	Pvt.	Thigh	Severely
Jonathan Mumpower	Pvt.	Leg	Slight
Lewis Swagler	Pvt.	Thigh	Severely
Thomas Wallace	Pvt.	Ankle	Slight
Company H			
Joseph/Josiah Adams	Pvt.	Head	Slight
Samuel Daniels	Pvt.	Breast	Slight
Henry Kaley	Pvt.	Arm	Slight
Timothy Kerney	Pvt.	Leg	Slight
Jonathan Moran	Pvt.	Thigh	Severely
John Mills	Pvt.	Neck	Severely
Company I			
Charles Osgood	1st Lt.	Chest	Severely
Cyrus Spicer	Sgt.	Face	Severely
William Capper	Corp	Breast	Mortally
John Seager	Pvt.	Abdomen	Mortally
Cyrus Baul/Bail	Pvt.	Hand	Slightly
Company K			
Charles Foster	1st Lt.	Leg	Slight

One incident of the battle was reported by Private Anderson Campbell, Company K, in letter to his family. "I supposed that you heard [Marshall] Osborne was killed at Iuka Springs. He never shot of his gun. We just marched up in line to the edge of woods and he was shot before we fired a shot."[37] The losses were significant and maybe more meaningful when expressed in the letters sent to the families of the men who were killed. In October, Newton Preston, Company I, sent such a letter to the sister of William Chapman who was killed at Iuka, "He died a true soldier. I deeply sympathize with you in your loss. You wanted to know if he was buried decently. He was buried as decently as he could under the circumstances. He was buried with his blanket around him but his grave is sufficiently deep to keep him from being exposed."[38]

Charles Treadway, Company A, wrote of the action of the regiment on September 30, 1862, about the recent battle, "It was one of the serious sights I ever saw. Thare was a good many kill and wounded some with broken arms and some with broken legs, some shot through the head, some wounded one way, and some an other. George [Moore] was shot through the breast and badly wounded. It is sad news to relate to ones friends. But if one is killed in the service of this country, they die in a good and just cause. There has been many a good man that has fallen on the battle field in the struggle of their country and their last words 'stand by them stares and stripes that shine so bright that I have died for. For I have stood by them my last time.'"[39]

The wounded were moved away from the battlefield and suffered through the night. The wounded from both sides were taken to respective field hospitals, "where every major building had been converted into a hospital. Federal surgeons performed amputations by candlelight, operating without anesthetics."[40] The Union hospital was established at the Rick's house about a half mile to the rear of the battle line where the surgeons made their best attempts to save lives. Corporal William Copper, Company I, was wounded at Iuka, and even the smallest kindness proved to be significant "as he lay wounded on his gum blanket waiting his turn for the Surgeon's attention. As he lay in the twilight a man on a horse came up, and dismounting, perceived him. He came to him and, kneeling down, asked where he was wounded. Comrade Copper told him, and the man said: 'Where is your blanket; you are very cold?' Upon being told that the blanket was in his knapsack, piled up with the other knapsacks of the company, the man said again: 'You are very cold; I have a blanket on my saddle which you shall have if I never get another.'"[41] Corporal Copper never learned the identity of man on the horse, but kept the blanket for the rest of his life.

After the battle, Sterling Price met with his divisional commanders, Dabney Maury and Louis Hébert, and decided to move south to Baldwyn the next morning. They needed to meet up with Van Dorn, but Maury and Price had expected an attack from Ord. They were puzzled about Ord who had failed to attack at all during the day.

During the evening, Stanley's division moved into the front of the Union line while Hamilton's men were moved into a reserve role, and Grant gave Stanley orders to attack in the morning. Stanley, who felt he was outnumbered, said, "I feel I shall be killed tomorrow, but your orders will be obeyed."[42] Price wanted to stay and fight but he was persuaded by his subordinates to retire from the field. By the next morning Price had withdrawn from Iuka down the unguarded Fulton Road, and as Stanley's men moved forward, they found the carnage from the previous day's battle, as they marched past bodies, dead horses and destruction.

Among the wounded was 1st Lieutenant William W. Cleland, Company F, whose horse was shot from beneath him (courtesy Civil War Museum at Wilson's Creek National Battlefield).

Rosecrans questioned Ord about his failure to attack, and Ord pulled a copy of the orders he received from Grant directing him to postpone the attack until he heard the sound of battle. Ord recorded his responses to Grant about his actions on the afternoon of October 4: "At the same time you directed me to move my whole force forward to within 4 miles of Iuka, and there await sounds of an engagement between Rosecrans and the enemy before engaging the latter."[43] The order was also supposed to have been given to Rosecrans, which he never received. Certainly Ord's failure to act at Iuka was questionable despite his order, but Ord also claimed he was in an acoustical shadow that prevented him from hearing the battle. Grant had expected Ord to start his attack when he heard battle commence. Regardless, there was a great deal of anger within the Army of the Mississippi towards Ord and Grant. Captain William Stewart, Company K, stated, "If Grant had come up the whole rebel Army would have been captured or killed. But Gen. Grant was dead drunk and couldn't bring up his Army."[44] This claim was without foundation, but the comment showed the anger of the soldiers of Stanley's and Hamilton's divisions facing Price alone on September 19. Ord advanced on the morning of September 20 to Iuka and also found that Price had marched south.

Many in the Confederate army felt that they had won the day, but some of the officers were concerned that Price intended them not to resume the conflict the next day. Price ordered his army to move southward by way of the Fulton Road, which was unoccupied due to Rosecrans decision to move forward with Hamilton's and Stanley's divisions along the Jacinto Road in their attack the afternoon before. Price was forced to leave his seriously wounded in Iuka and some of his supplies, but he was packed and gone by daylight. He had accomplished a tricky maneuver by extricating his men from Rosecrans and Ord, and he did this by beginning his march at 3:00 A.M. By 2:00 P.M. Price was more than eight miles from Iuka.

Private George Lehr, Company G, suffered a leg wound at Iuka — postwar photograph (USAMHI).

The exact losses of either side for the Battle of Iuka may never be known, but the medical director for the Army of the Mississippi placed the Confederate casualties at 520 killed, 1,300 wounded and 181 captured. Price reported his casualties at 535 — killed, 85; wounded, 410; captured or missing, 40. Rosecrans estimated Confederate losses at 385 killed, 692 wounded and 361 captured. Rosecrans reported the Union losses as 141 killed, 613 wounded, and 36 captured.

Some authorities claim a Union victory at Iuka because Price was forced to retreat southward, but clearly Price's Confederates manhandled the Union infantry in battle. Price was able to escape to combine his forces with Van Dorn, but Grant was able to force Price out of Iuka. If it was a Union victory, it was one that did not receive many accolades.

Chapter 4

Battle of Corinth

"When the 11th was ordered to charge. They rose, fired a volley into their ranks and charged with bayonets."
— Private Duncan McCall

Within two weeks of the Battle of Iuka, the 11th Missouri Infantry was again challenged in the Battle of Corinth which was fought on October 3–4, 1862. The 11th Missouri Infantry, a bloodied but proven regiment, basked in their success, being the only regiment from their brigade to be engaged in the Battle of Iuka and being personally commanded by the popular brigade commander Colonel Joseph Mower and regimental commander Major Andrew Weber. Charles Treadway, Company A, predicted an upcoming battle in a letter he wrote on September 30, 1862, "We are expecting a fight at this place all the time."[1]

Sterling Price's army slipped from the trap that William Rosecrans and Ulysses Grant had set for him on September 19 after introducing the Union troops in Rosecrans' army to a new level of ferocity in battle. The Confederates withdrew from Iuka to Baldwyn, Mississippi, with the intent of meeting General Earl Van Dorn's main force.

General Earl Van Dorn was a colorful and inconsistent military commander, born in Mississippi in 1820. He attended West Point, graduating in 1842 and finishing 52nd in a class of 56. Van Dorn served in both the Mexican War and also in the conflict with the Seminoles in Florida. He was promoted to the rank of captain in the Second U.S. Cavalry in 1855 where he served with Albert Sidney Johnston, Robert E. Lee, William Hardee and John Bell Hood. Van Dorn offered his military skills to his home state and to the Confederacy at the beginning of the Civil War. He began his service with the state of Mississippi and was commissioned a colonel in the new Confederate army in 1861. In 1862, Van Dorn was promoted to the rank of major general and was given command of the Trans-Mississippi District of the Confederate Army. His forces were defeated at the Battle of Pea Ridge, but in October 1862, Van Dorn was determined to deal with the Union forces located near Corinth, Mississippi.

Van Dorn's stated plan was to drive Grant's forces out of Mississippi and West Tennessee all the way to the Ohio River. Then he intended to reinforce Bragg in Kentucky, but the first step in completing this was to destroy the Union garrison at Corinth. Even if he couldn't drive them to the Ohio River, he could distract them to such an extent they would not unite with Buell's Army of the Ohio. Van Dorn planned to unite his forces with those of General Sterling Price at Ripley, Mississippi, and then, believing the Federal remnants near Corinth to be vulnerable from a concentrated attack, he intended to strike Corinth before Union reinforcements

The Battle of Corinth (Library of Congress).

could concentrate their scattered forces. This situation was exactly what Ulysses Grant feared and which had precipitated the Union attack on Price at Iuka. Van Dorn felt that "swiftness and surprise were critical."[2] The combined Confederate force marched northward and entered Tennessee. Then the cavalry began to destroy the railroads leading to Corinth, thus preventing the rapid reinforcement of the Union troops there. Because the Union forces were scattered at various locations, including Memphis, Bolivar, Jackson and other minor outposts, Van Dorn's thrust into Tennessee was a feint. His objective was to strike Corinth before the Federals could react. Both actions were designed to surprise and isolate Corinth. Corinth was a fortified city that Beauregard abandoned in May, and the fortifications had been enhanced by the Union since that time; but the overall design of the fortifications were intimately known to Van Dorn, who felt he could exploit their weaknesses. General Rosecrans continued the work of improving the fortifications immediately after the Battle of Iuka, utilizing what troops he had on hand to complete the task. He utilized "colored engineer troops organized into squads of twenty-five each, headed by a man detailed from the line or the

Confederate Major General Earl Van Dorn (courtesy Civil War Museum at Wilson's Creek National Battlefield).

quartermaster's department, and commanded by Captain William B. Gaw, a competent engineer."[3]

Van Dorn was adamant that for success he needed to attack Corinth immediately, and he planned to strike Rosecrans with three divisions. Van Dorn wrote, "The troops were in fine spirits, and the whole Army of West Tennessee seemed eager to emulate the armies of the Potomac and of Kentucky. No army ever marched to battle with prouder steps, more hopeful countenance, or with more courage than marched the Army of West Tennessee out of Ripley on the morning of September 29, on its way to Corinth."[4] With the Confederate offensives of Bragg in Kentucky and Lee in Virginia, it was important Van Dorn and Price play their part in the Confederate grand offensive occurring across the country. Van Dorn's command included Price's Army of West Tennessee, General Louis Hébert's First Division, General Dabney Maury Division, and General Mansfield Lowell's Division of the District of Mississippi. General Frank Armstrong's cavalry was attached to Price. Mansfield Lowell's division was the first to begin their march on September 29, and Price's two divisions began their march on September 30. So, within two weeks of the Battle of Iuka, the Confederates were marching again. This time the Confederate force was larger by one division — Price with 14,363 men and Lowell with 7,000, for a total greater than 21,000 men.

The Confederate Forces — September 29–October 4, 1862[5]

Army of West Tennessee — Major General Earl Van Dorn

PRICE'S CORPS OR ARMY OF THE WEST — MAJOR GENERAL STERLING PRICE

UNATTACHED

1st Mississippi Partisan Rangers
2nd Mississippi Cavalry

FIRST DIVISION — BRIG. GENERAL LOUIS HÉBERT, BRIG. GENERAL MARTIN E. GREEN

First Brigade Col. Elijah Gates

16th Arkansas Infantry, 2nd Missouri Infantry, 3rd Missouri Infantry, 5th Missouri Infantry, 1st Missouri Cavalry (dismounted), Missouri Battery

Second Brigade Col. W. Bruce Colbert

14th Arkansas, 17th Arkansas, 2nd Louisiana, 40th Mississippi, 1st Texas Legion, 3rd Texas Cavalry (Dismounted), Clark's (Mo.) Battery, St. Louis (MO) Battery

Third Brigade Brig. Gen. Martin E. Green, Col. W. H. Moore

7th Mississippi Infantry Battalion, 43rd Mississippi Infantry, 4th Missouri Infantry, 6th Missouri Infantry, 3rd Missouri Cavalry (Dismounted), Missouri Battery (Guibor), Missouri Battery (Landis)

Fourth Brigade Col. John D. Martin, Col. Robert McLain

37th Alabama Infantry, 36th Mississippi, 37th Mississippi, 38th Mississippi (battery attached to this brigade not identified).

MAURY'S DIVISION — BRIG. GEN. DABNEY H. MAURY

Moore's Brigade Brig. Gen. John C. Moore

42d Alabama Infantry, 15th Arkansas Infantry, 23rd Arkansas Infantry, 35th Mississippi Infantry, 2nd Texas Infantry, Missouri Battery (Bledsoe)

Cabell's Brigade Brig. Gen. William L. Cabell

18th Arkansas Infantry, 19th Arkansas Infantry, 20th Arkansas Infantry, 21st Arkansas Infantry, Arkansas Infantry Battalion (Jones'), Arkansas Infantry Battalion (Rapley's), Arkansas (Appeal) Battery

Phifer's Brigade Brig. Gen. C. W. Phifer
3rd Arkansas Cavalry, 6th Texas Cavalry, 9th Texas Cavalry, Stirman's Sharp-shooters, Arkansas Battery (McNally's)

Cavalry Brig. Gen. Frank C. Armstrong
2nd Arkansas Cavalry, Adam's Mississippi Cavalry, 2nd Missouri Cavalry

Reserve Artillery
Tenn. Battery (Hoxton's), Lieut. Thomas F. Tobin, Alabama Battery

DISTRICT OF THE MISSISSIPPI
FIRST DIVISION — MAJ. GEN. MANSFIELD LOVELL

First Brigade Brig. Gen. Albert Rust
4th Alabama Infantry Battalion, 31st Alabama Infantry, 35th Alabama Infantry, 9th Arkansas Infantry, 3rd Kentucky Infantry, 7th Kentucky Infantry, Mississippi (Hudson) Battery

Second Brigade (composition not fully reported) Brig. Gen. J. B. Villepigue
33rd Mississippi Infantry, 39th Mississippi Infantry

Third Brigade Brig. Gen. John S. Bowen
6th Mississippi Infantry, 15th Mississippi Infantry, 22nd Mississippi Infantry, Mississippi Infantry Battalion, 1st Missouri — Lieut.-Col. A. C. Riley, Louisiana (Watson) Battery

Cavalry Brigade Col. W. H. Jackson
1st Mississippi Cavalry, 7th Tennessee Cavalry

Despite Van Dorn's confidence, not all of his brigade or divisional commanders were confident about attacking the heavily fortified Corinth. Facing Van Dorn in this fortified city were two Union divisions totaling 10,000 men — General Thomas Davies' Second Division and General Thomas McKean's Sixth Division. Van Dorn faced two lines of earthworks. The defensive line included the original Confederate defenses of the "Beauregard Line" and the inner "Rosecrans Line" made up of forts. Breastworks and abattises served as the primary defenses, but the anchors in the defenses were heavily constructed forts containing artillery batteries in lunettes named Robinett, Williams, Madison, Powell, Phillips, Tanrath, and Lothrop. Rosecrans had two remaining divisions — Stanley's, which had seen little action at Iuka (except for the 11th Missouri Infantry), and Hamilton's (of which Sanborn's brigade had been chewed up at Iuka) — positioned around Corinth in defensive screens attempting to keep Van Dorn at bay.

Van Dorn's plan was to march north into Tennessee and turn east and attack Corinth from the northwest. This meant that Van Dorn would face both lines of Union defenses, but he hoped that speed and concentration of force would allow him to win the day. By the end of September, Rosecrans was relatively sure that Van Dorn planned to attack, but his exact location was unknown. In addition to Corinth, Van Dorn's possible targets were Jackson, 50 miles north, and Bolivar, Tennessee, 35 miles northwest. Rosecrans drove his men to strengthen the defenses even more; and by October 1, he ordered Hamilton's division to move closer to Corinth. Stanley's division was ordered northward and just west of Corinth near the Hatchie River near Kossuth. On October 1, the 11th Missouri Infantry and their brigade were awakened and marched all day reaching Kossuth at midnight. The regimental strength of the 11th Missouri in early October 1862 was slightly less than 450 men. The presence of the enemy had been detected near Chewalla, Tennessee, and Rosecrans was trying to place his men where they could be moved to support wherever the blow would fall. Facing Van Dorn were four Union divisions, but the risk was ever present that Van Dorn could strike single divisions and defeat the Union in detail.

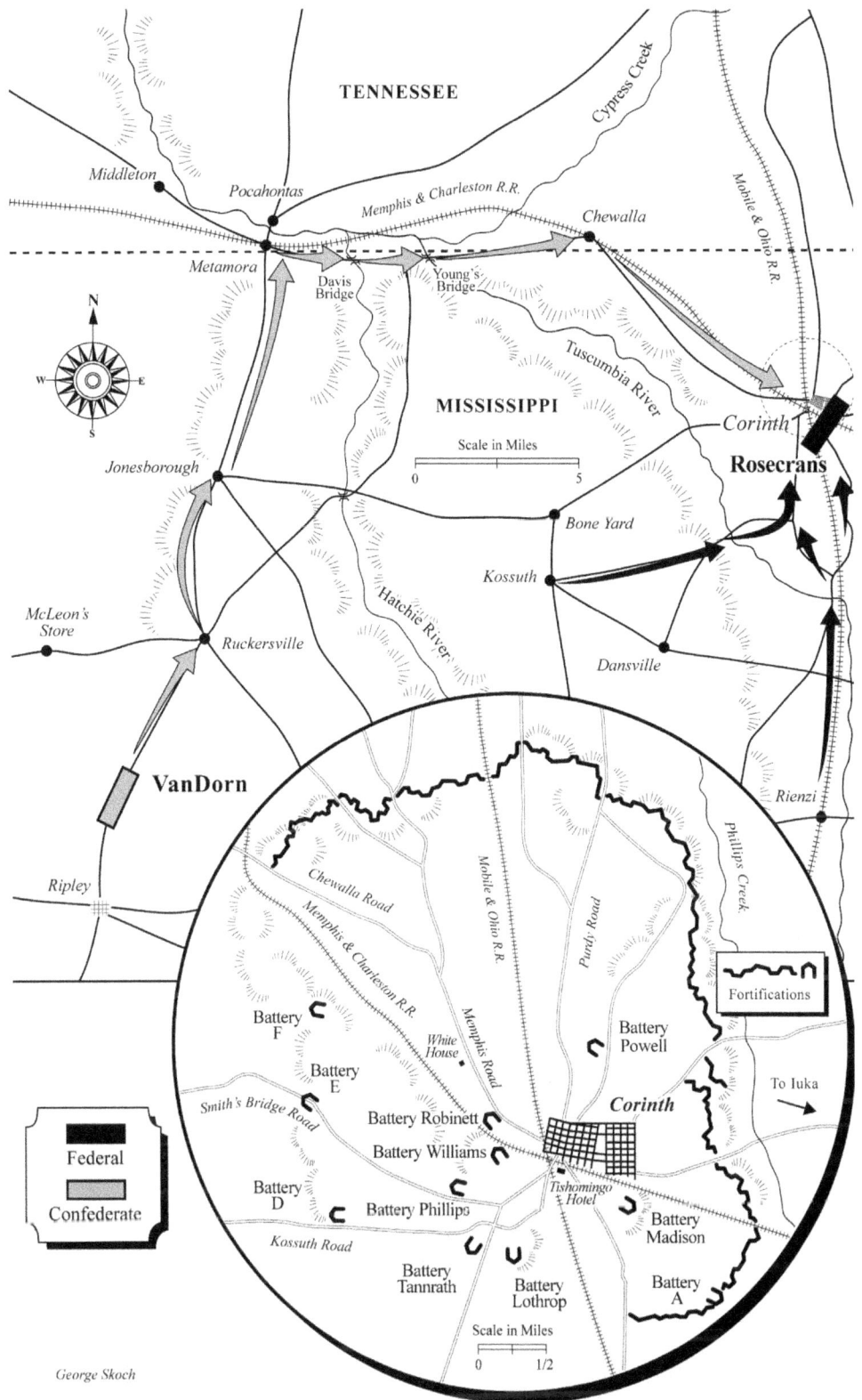

The Union and Confederate movements at Corinth. The Union and Confederate armies converged on the heavily fortified town of Corinth.

The Union Forces[6]

ARMY OF WEST TENNESSEE — MAJOR GENERAL WILLIAM S. ROSECRANS
SECOND DIVISION — BRIG. GEN. DAVID S. STANLEY

First Brigade Col. John W. Fuller
27th Ohio Infantry, 39th Ohio Infantry, 43rd Ohio Infantry, 63rd Ohio Infantry, Jenks' Co., Illinois Cavalry, 3rd Michigan Battery, 8th Wisconsin Battery Section F, 2nd U.S. Artillery

Second Brigade Col. Joseph A. Mower
26th Illinois Infantry, 47th Illinois Infantry, 5th Minnesota Infantry, **11th Missouri Infantry**, 8th Wisconsin Infantry, 2nd Iowa Battery

THIRD DIVISION — BRIG. GEN. CHARLES S. HAMILTON

Escort C, 5th Missouri Cavalry

First Brigade Brig. Gen. Napoleon B. Buford
48th Indiana Infantry, 59th Indiana Infantry, 5th Iowa Infantry , 4th Minnesota Infantry, 26th Missouri Infantry , Section M 1st Missouri Artillery , 11th Ohio Battery

Second Brigade Brig. Gen. Jeremiah C. Sullivan, Col. Samuel A. Holmes
56th Illinois Infantry , 10th Iowa Infantry, 17th Iowa Infantry, 10th Missouri Infantry, 24th Missouri Infantry, 80th Ohio Infantry, 6th Wisconsin Battery, 12th Wisconsin Battery

CAVAALRY DIVISION — COL. JOHN K. MIZNER

(Division organized into two brigades with Col. Edward Hatch commanding the First and Col. Albert L. Lee the Second.)
11th Illinois Cavalry, 2nd Iowa Cavalry, 7th Kansas Cavalry, 3rd Michigan Cavalry, 5th Ohio Cavalry

UNATTACHED

64th Illinois (Yates' Sharpshooters) — Capt. John Morrill, 1st U.S. (6 co's, siege artillery) — Capt. G. A. Williams

ARMY OF WEST TENNESSEE
SECOND DIVISION — BRIG. GEN. THOMAS A. DAVIES

First Brigade Brig. Gen. Pleasant A. Hackleman, Col. Thomas W. Sweeny
52nd Illinois Infantry, 2nd Iowa Infantry, 7th Iowa Infantry
Union Brigade (composed of detachments of 58th Illinois, and 8th, 12th , and 14th Iowa) Lieut. Col. John P. Coulter

Second Brigade Brig. Gen. Richard J. Oglesby, Col. August Mersy
9th Illinois Infantry, 12th Illinois Infantry, 22nd Ohio Infantry, 81st Ohio Infantry

Third Brigade Col. Silas D. Baldwin (w), Col. John V. Du Bois
7th Illinois Infantry, 50th Illinois Infantry, 57th Illinois Infantry

Artillery Maj. George H. Stone
Section D, 1st Missouri Artillery, Section H, 1st Missouri Artillery, Section I, 1st Missouri Artillery , K, 1st Missouri Artillery

Unattached
14th Missouri (Western Sharp-shooters) — Col. Patrick E. Burke

SIXTH DIVISION — BRIG. GEN. THOMAS J. MCKEAN

First Brigade Col. Benjamin Allen, Brig. Gen. John McArthur
21st Missouri, 16th Wisconsin, 17th Wisconsin

Second Brigade Col. John M. Oliver

Indpt. Co., Illinois Cavalry, 15th Michigan Infantry, 18th Missouri Infantry (4 co's), 14th Wisconsin Infantry, 18th Wisconsin Infantry

Third Brigade Col. Marcellus M. Crocker

11th Iowa Infantry, 13th Iowa Infantry, 15th Iowa Infantry, 16th Iowa

Artillery Capt. Andrew Hickenlooper

Section F, 2nd Illinois Artillery, 1st Minnesota Artillery, 3rd Ohio Artillery, 5th Ohio Artillery, 10th Ohio Artillery

Defenses of Corinth

1st U.S. Infantry (6 companies), "B" 2nd Illinois Light Artillery

The terrain around Corinth consisted of low rolling hills with oak trees and often swampy bottoms near the streams that flowed through the region. Corinth was located on low and flat terrain. The strategic importance of Corinth was as a crossroads of the Mobile & Ohio Railroad and also the Memphis & Charleston Railroad. In addition, Corinth was only 90 miles east of Memphis, and to control Corinth was to control supplies and transportation for the region.

On October 2, the Union cavalry detected Van Dorn's advancing infantry near the junction of Chewalla and Kossuth Roads. Later on October 2, the Confederates pushed the Union advance pickets from Colonel John Oliver's Second Brigade, McKean's Division, to within four miles north and west of Corinth. General Rosecrans, becoming more concerned about the proximity of Van Dorn, was still unsure whether the attack would be in Tennessee or at Corinth; but of one thing he was sure, it was imperative to concentrate his scattered command together. McKean's Sixth Division (5,300 men) was located northwest of Corinth and was the closest to Van Dorn. General Thomas Davies' division (3,200 men) was already located south of Corinth. General Hamilton's division (3,700 men) was camped two miles south of Corinth, and Stanley's Division (3,500 men), which included the 11th Missouri Infantry, was about 10 miles west of Corinth near Kossuth, Mississippi. After midnight on October 2, General Rosecrans sent the message for his troops to begin their move to concentrate at Corinth; but, unfortunately, General Van Dorn was already poised to attack the next morning.

In Cloyd Bryner's history of the 47th Illinois Infantry, he recorded, "At one o'clock in the morning, the brigade was aroused; two days rations hastily prepared — easily enough when you have only to choose between pickled pork raw and pickled pork fried with your 'hard tack.' The 'hard tack' (army bread) was not unlike water wafers and when fresh, good; when mouldy, intolerable; when only wormy, if hungry enough, you are not fastidious."[7]

General Hamilton's division began marching at daybreak, General Davies' was moving at 7:00 A.M., and General David Stanley, being the greatest distance away from Corinth, began marching at 3:00 A.M. On the Confederate side of the battle, Van Dorn had his men marching toward Corinth at 4:00 A.M. He had to cover ten miles before he could sweep over Corinth before reinforcements could arrive.

All were converging on Corinth.

The Battle Begins

The first clash of these two forces occurred northwest of Corinth at Alexander's Crossroads about three miles from Corinth, when Lovell's advance units ran into Colonel John Oliver's Second Brigade of McKean's Division. Oliver's job, although greatly outnumbered, was to hold the enemy until the Union forces could prepare a proper defense. Lovell's attack began at 7:00 A.M. Oliver fell back across Cane Creek and attempted to destroy the bridge, thus slowing Lovell. Lovell pressed Oliver backward until he came to the old Confederate earthworks, which he established as his next defensive position. At 8:00 A.M., General John McArthur of McKean's division, seeing Oliver's situation unfold, ordered his First Brigade forward to support him.

McArthur's closest support was Colonel Marcellus Crocker's Iowa Brigade (11th, 13th, 15th and 16th Iowa Infantry regiments) still about a mile away. As the conflict started to develop near Oliver, Rosecrans rushed General Thomas Davies' Second Division to join Oliver and McArthur. Other Federal divisions were moving toward the battle. "General Charles Hamilton had his division a mile and half northeast of Corinth, watching the Monterey and Purdy Roads. The head of Stanley's column was still at least two hours away and Davies' division was only then entering town."[8]

Van Dorn's Confederates began the battle near Cane Creek, while Rosecrans frantically tried to pull his scattered troops together. Van Dorn opened the battle in a splendid and terrible fashion as he marched toward Oliver in line of battle with all of his army. By 9:00 A.M., the battle began in earnest, as the First Missouri Light Artillery and a remnant of the First Minnesota Light Artillery began shelling the advancing Confederates. General McArthur marched the 21st Missouri Infantry and the 16th Wisconsin Infantry to aid Oliver in his defense. Oliver and McArthur were hastily arranging their regiments into a defensive line when they observed General Thomas Davies' division marching to their right with about 3,000 men.

At 10:00 A.M. the Confederate Infantry slammed into McArthur's defenders and they were "irresistible."[9] The attack on McArthur and Oliver came from three sides, and although the Union defenders tried to hold their ground, they were propelled backward from the sheer force of the Confederate assault. By 1:00 P.M., the entire Union line was retreating toward Corinth. While the main body of the Confederate line paused to reorganize, General John Moore's brigade of the 15th Arkansas Infantry, 23rd Arkansas, Second Texas, 35th Mississippi and the 42nd Alabama decided to press forward and took advantage of a gap in the Union line between McArthur and Davies.

After Moore's success in penetrating the Union line, McArthur organized what regiments could be rallied after being pushed backwards and counterattacked. Moore's brigade was halted and repelled, but by 3:00 P.M., McArthur was again retreating towards Corinth as the full force of Van Dorn's attack proceeded.

Rosecrans was steadily being pushed back, and he called on Stanley's Division to assist in stopping the Confederate attack. Rosecrans had confidence Mower's brigade would fight and called on him to slow the Confederate attack. Rosecrans sent a message to Stanley stating, "The general commanding directs you to send a brigade across on to the Chewalla road, through the woods by shortest cut; re-enforce Davies from your left, close in, in conformity with that movement. You had better send Mower."[10] Mower had marched hard from Kossuth and his men were tired and suffered from lack of water. In Mower's battle report, he stated that he had reached the Corinth earthworks around noon and was resting. All of Mower's regiments were present except for the Fifth Minnesota, which had been detached to guard the Smith Bridge Road over the Tuscumbia River. Although the men of Mower's brigade were tired, the men of Davies' division were exhausted from fighting their relentless Confederate adversary.

Finally, at 4:30 P.M., General Joseph Mower's brigade emerged onto the battlefield coming to the assistance of General Thomas Davies' Division about one-half mile north of Corinth. General Stanley reported, "These troops moved off promptly and with loud cheers, although sadly distressed for the want of water. This force consisted of the Twenty-sixth and Forty-seventh Illinois, the Eleventh Missouri, the Eighth Wisconsin, and Spoor's battery."[11] Much to the chagrin of Mower, the first volley from General Martin Green's Confederate First Division sent his lead regiment, the 26th Illinois Infantry, scampering away.

Mower's remaining three regiments, however, entered into the battle with gusto. The 11th Missouri Infantry replaced the 52nd Illinois regiment. The Eighth Wisconsin Infantry moved forward to replace the position previously held by Seventh Iowa Infantry and the Second Iowa Infantry. The 47th Illinois Infantry filed to the left of the Eighth Wisconsin covering the front vacated by three infantry regiments withdrawing to the rear. The new regiments were immediately under fire. Mower's brigade had been marching throughout the day, and he had to be questioning what he had been thrown into.

Prior to entering the battle, Duncan McCall indicated that after all the heavy marching, the regiment was parched and was suffering greatly for lack of water. He recorded that as the regiment was preparing to enter the battle, there was a momentarily halt and stillness. "'What was it that made us so still?' All at once everything seemed quiet. It was a calm before an approaching storm."[12]

As the Union regiments withdrew from the fighting where they had been engaged since 3:30 P.M., the 11th Missouri, Eighth Wisconsin, and 47th Illinois held their ground but were three regiments being flanked by Van Dorn's advancing infantry. Missourian fought Missourian in this battle as the Confederate Third Missouri Infantry began an "enfilading fire on the Federal Eleventh Missouri."[13] The 11th Missouri adjusted their line to meet this threat, as the 47th Illinois moved to meet the threat of General C. W. Phifer's brigade of Dabney Maury's Division, consisting of the Third Arkansas Cavalry, the Sixth Texas Cavalry, Ninth Texas Cavalry and Stirman's Sharpshooters. The 47th Illinois made a gallant bayonet charge, temporarily pushing Phifer's Confederates backward, before the reinforcing Confederate troops forced

Battle of Corinth (Library of Congress).

them to give way. The 47th Illinois recorded over 100 casualties and the regiment lost their colonel in this courageous charge. The Eighth Wisconsin held the center of the brigade.

Major Andrew Weber described the 11th Missouri's actions on the afternoon of October 3: "We found ourselves in front of an open field, in which there was but few of the enemy, but their solid columns could be distinctly seen advancing on our right and left flanks, where were stationed the Twenty-sixth and Forty-seventh Illinois and Eighth Wisconsin respectively. The whole fire of my right wing was to the right oblique and that of my left oblique. Just as our ammunition was expended Colonel Mower was informed from Colonel (or General) Sweeny that the forces on both our flanks had retired and unless we fell back at once we would be outflanked. We did so in good order and took position with the rest of the brigade between the two central forts, commanded by Captain Williams, of the First U.S. Infantry."[14]

The 11th Missouri and the Eighth Wisconsin were facing six infantry regiments bearing down on them from Green's Brigade. The 11th Missouri faced the Third Missouri Infantry, detached from Gates brigade, which was moving into the flank of the 11th Missouri and pouring an enfilading fire into their ranks. To the right of the Third Missouri was the 43rd Mississippi, the Sixth Missouri, the Seventh Mississippi Battalion and both the Third Missouri Cavalry and Fourth Missouri Infantry. More detail of the battle was recounted by Duncan McCall who stated that one soldier in Company B was shot through the head and was killed. He also stated that most of the firing was at long range but fighting was personal and that "the firing was quite brisk for a time."[15]

As the situation deteriorated around the 47th Illinois and Eighth Wisconsin, Mower left the 11th Missouri to handle the Confederates the regiment faced to the best of its ability. After fighting for 30 minutes with the enemy on three sides, the regiment fell back toward Corinth. Next, the Eighth Wisconsin gave way and retired to Corinth. But certainly Mower's three regiments, which after marching throughout the day were thrown into battle facing Phifer's and Green's brigades, could not be expected to stem the Confederate assault. As the day ended, Rosecrans had been roughly shoved backwards into Corinth, but he finally had his troops in one place and he did have the advantage of the defenses of Corinth as he looked for a renewed fighting the next morning.

It has been reported that one cause for the collapse of the Eighth Wisconsin Infantry was the dispensing of whiskey by the quartermaster to the regiment before entering the engagement. Even the Eighth Wisconsin's mascot "Old Abe," a bald eagle, was nearly lost when a Confederate bullet cut the rope that bound him to his perch.[16]

The evening of October 3 was a busy one for the medical staff of the Union army, as it had been a bloody day, but surgeons were prepared as much as possible to handle the medical duties. "Night fell; the roar of artillery and sharp crack of musketry replaced by the cries of the wounded."[17] A commissary depot had recently been constructed to also serve as a hospital, but it proved not to be large enough to handle all the wounded. So hospitals were established at the Tishomingo Hotel and the Corinth House to handle the overflow.

Van Dorn recorded at the end of the first day's battle, "I had been in hopes that one day's operation would end the contest and decide who should be the victors on this bloody field. But a ten miles' march over a parched country on dusty roads without water, getting into line of battle in forest and undergrowth, and the more than equal activity and determined courage displayed by the enemy, commanded by one of the ablest generals in the United States army, who threw all possible obstacles in our way.... One hour more of daylight and victory would have soothed our grief for the loss of the gallant dead who sleep on that lost but not dishonored

Opposite: **The Confederate brigades force Mower's retreat, October 3, 1862.**

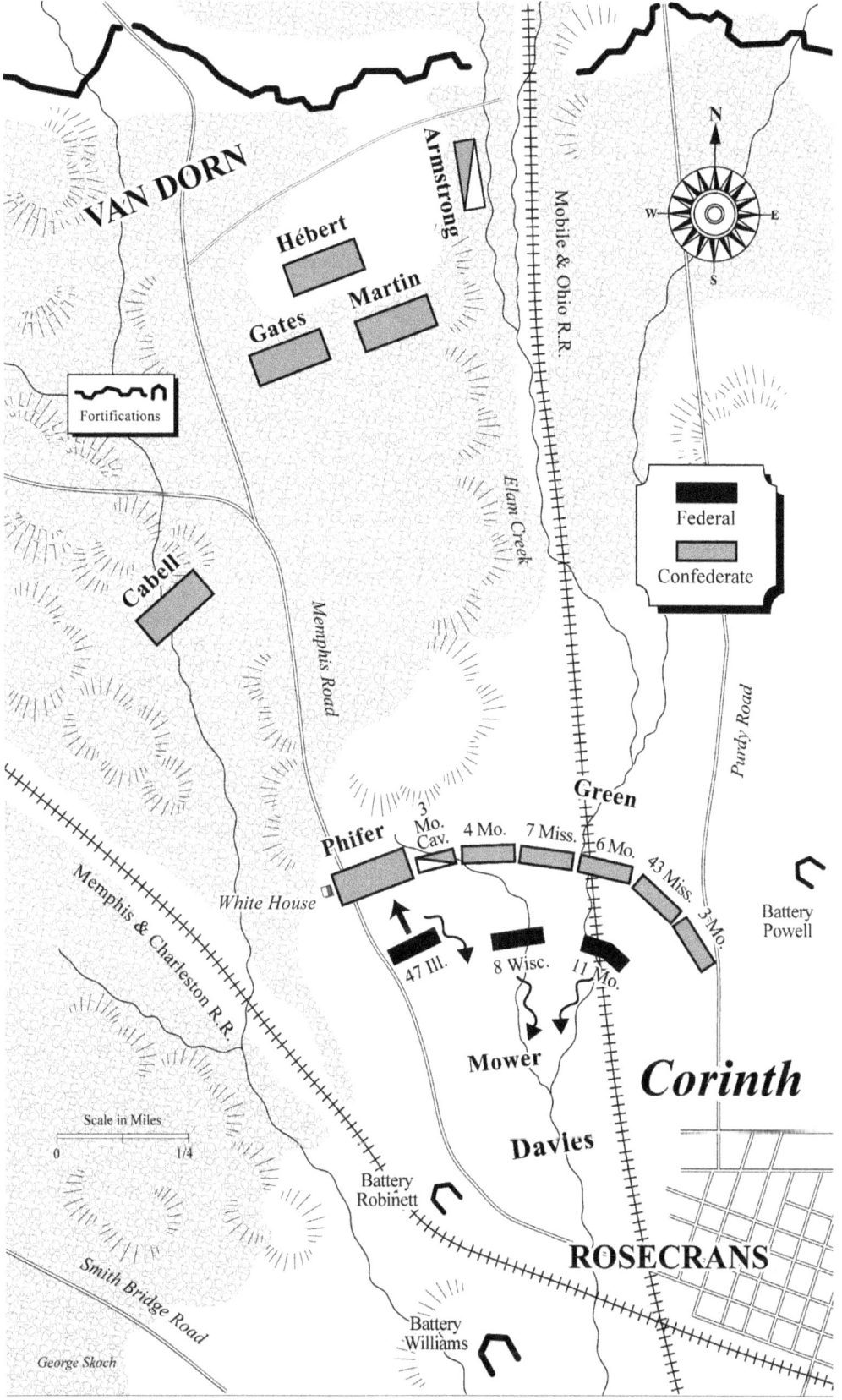

field."[18] Although Van Dorn had most of the day of October 3 his way, Rosecrans scrambled to pull his defense together and was determined to stop his foe. October 4 would begin with the Union firmly positioned behind the defenses of the city.

At 11:30 P.M. on October 3, General Rosecrans sent an optimistic message to General Grant referring to the actions of the day, as he described his defensive line and his attitude about the inevitable battle on the 4th. "Our left — McKean and Stanley — occupies Price's new line; right Hamilton and Davies — rests north of the town on the rebel works, stretched across to join Stanley in the bottom near Halleck's old headquarters. They appear to be still in the angle of the roads. If they fight us to-morrow I think we shall whip them."[19]

Battle of Corinth — October 4

On the morning of October 4, Van Dorn had high hopes of finishing the job he had started the day before. The attacking Confederate army was positioned with Price in an angle to the north of Corinth between the Memphis & Charleston Railroad and the Mobile & Ohio Railroad. Lovell was to the west of the Corinth with his left flank on the Memphis & Charleston Railroad. On the left of the Union line was the entrenched battery — Phillips; and Battery Robinett was at the center of the Union defenses. Davies' division held the center of the Union line supported by Battery Powell, and Hamilton held the right of the Union line. Battery Phillips served as the western most entrenched battery of the Union line. Batteries Tanrath and Lothrop were directed away from the attackers and were not significant in the upcoming battle. During the night Van Dorn had not been idle, establishing his own artillery within 600 yards of Battery Robinett. The 11th Missouri Infantry had been detached from Mower's brigade and was positioned behind Battery Robinett during the night to support Colonel Fuller's Ohio brigade (27th Ohio, 39th Ohio, 63rd Ohio, 43rd Ohio).

On October 4, the Confederate artillery began firing on Corinth at 4 A.M. and the Union artillery returned fire at dawn. The artillery duel lasted about a half and hour, and by 9:00 A.M., the artillery action was diminished as lines of gray-coated soldiers emerged from the woods intent on pushing Rosecrans' army out of Corinth. The initial Confederate attack consisted of four brigades advancing *en echelon* from Van Dorn's left to right, first striking Davies. Next Van Dorn attacked Stanley's division and then Hamilton's division. General Price's divisions (Maury and Green) drove forward, and the Union line yielded as they were pushed to the north side of the square in Corinth. As Brigadier General Dabney Maury's and Brigadier General Martin E. Green's soldiers drove forward, the men of Brigadier General Thomas Davies' division were thrown back across the Memphis & Charleston Railroad tracks. Having penetrated the Union line, Maury and Green failed to break it. The Union reserves converged on the Confederate attackers from all sides. Unable to stand the counterattack, the Confederates were repulsed and thrown back. "Caught in a counter-attack converging on the crossover from the south, east, and west, the Confederates who remained in town were soon driven back in disorder."[20] The Union line proved too much and the battle along the Union right flank was over.

For the 11th Missouri Infantry, the regiment had to wait for their appointment with Price's Confederates. Major Andrew Weber recorded, "The morning of the 4th found us in the same position, facing the west. About 4.30 A.M. we were awakened by a shell from a 12-pounder howitzer, which the enemy had during the night succeeded in placing within 400 or 500 yards of us."[21] The 11th Missouri Infantry suffered through the artillery barrage along with everyone else. "Nearly all the shells passed over us and went crashing through the town,"

Duncan McCall recalled. The Union artillery "soon silenced the rebel guns, killing most of their horses."[22] Prior to the Confederate attack, Confederate sharpshooters began picking off targets within the Union line; and in return, Union artillery and soldiers attempted to reduce their effectiveness, and "many a rebel paid the penalty of climbing a tree, being picked off by our sharpshooters."[23]

The 11th Missouri's Captain George Henry, Company D, recorded the artillery battle of the morning. "Heavy cannonading under which the men were obliged to maintain their position was endured with undaunted courage."[24] As the battle raged on the right, Mansfield Lovell's division attacked the Union left about 20 minutes after Hébert/Green's division attacked the right. At 10:30 A.M., Dabney Maury's division, without Cabell's Brigade, began their attack on the Union line near Battery Robinett, where the 11th Missouri was located. The Union artillery blasted away at the advancing lines of Confederate soldiers shelling them with "grape and canister until within 50 yards" of Battery Robinett.[25] The Confederate line had to advance 250 yards under the fire of the three 20-pound parrot rifles in Battery Robinett, while also being exposed to the fire of Battery Williams which contained five 30-pound Parrott rifles. Colonel John Fuller's Ohio Brigade defended the right and left of Battery Robinett with four regiments: 43rd Ohio to the left of Battery Robinett and the 63rd Ohio, 27th Ohio and 39th Ohio, from left to right of the battery. "Presupposing that the Sixty-third would collapse, Fuller placed the Eleventh Missouri twenty-five yards behind them. General Stanley shared Fuller's concern, and he placed himself and his staff behind the Sixty-third."[26] Maury's soldiers "advanced in solid column from the north. When I saw them coming I changed my front and laid down, with bayonets fixed, about 40 paces in rear of the Sixty-third Ohio,"[27] Major Andrew Weber reported.

Captain Oscar Jackson of the 63rd Ohio Infantry watched as Confederates marched toward them and reported, "Not a sound was a heard but they looked as if they intended to walk over us. I afterwards stood a bayonet charge when the enemy came at us on the double-quick with a yell and it was not as trying on the nerves as that steady, solemn advance."[28]

Colonel John Fuller stated that at 11:00 A.M. he observed Maury's division emerge from the woods to their front in four columns. General Phifer's Texas and Arkansas brigade was the first troops onto the battlefield. General Moore's Brigade consisting of the 42nd Alabama, 15th Arkansas, 23rd Arkansas, 35th Mississippi and Second Texas infantries formed to the right. The Ohio regiments (63rd, 39th and 27th) waited until the columns reached to within 100 yards of their lines and opened with a volley. Then the Confederates charged their primary target, the 63rd Ohio. "In a few minutes the fusillade became general along the whole line of the Army of the West, and Cabell's brigade was ordered in to support of Gates' brigade, the next on Phifer's left. The brigades of Generals Moore, Phifer, and Cabell were gallantly led by their commanders to the assault of the enemy's works in the heart of Corinth."[29]

The 42nd Alabama attacked the 43rd Ohio and the Sixth and Ninth Texas Cavalry (Dismounted) attacked the 27th and 39th Ohio. The 35th Mississippi and Second Texas concentrated their attack on the 63rd Ohio and Battery Robinett. The battle raged with heavy losses on both sides, but none so fierce as the battle near the 63rd Ohio and Battery Robinett. The 63rd Ohio's first volley struck the first line of attackers but the Confederates to their front relentlessly attacked the Union defenders. The 63rd Ohio held on until they were nearly wiped out, losing nearly half their men. Colonel John Sprague, commander of the 63rd Ohio, recorded, "Every officer and man of my command seemed to put forth superhuman exertions to hold our position, but no troops could long stand against such unequal odds pouring a fire upon front and flank. Out of 13 line officers 9 were killed or wounded and 45 per cent of my whole force had shared the same fate, to say nothing of the number necessarily detailed to carry off the wounded."[30]

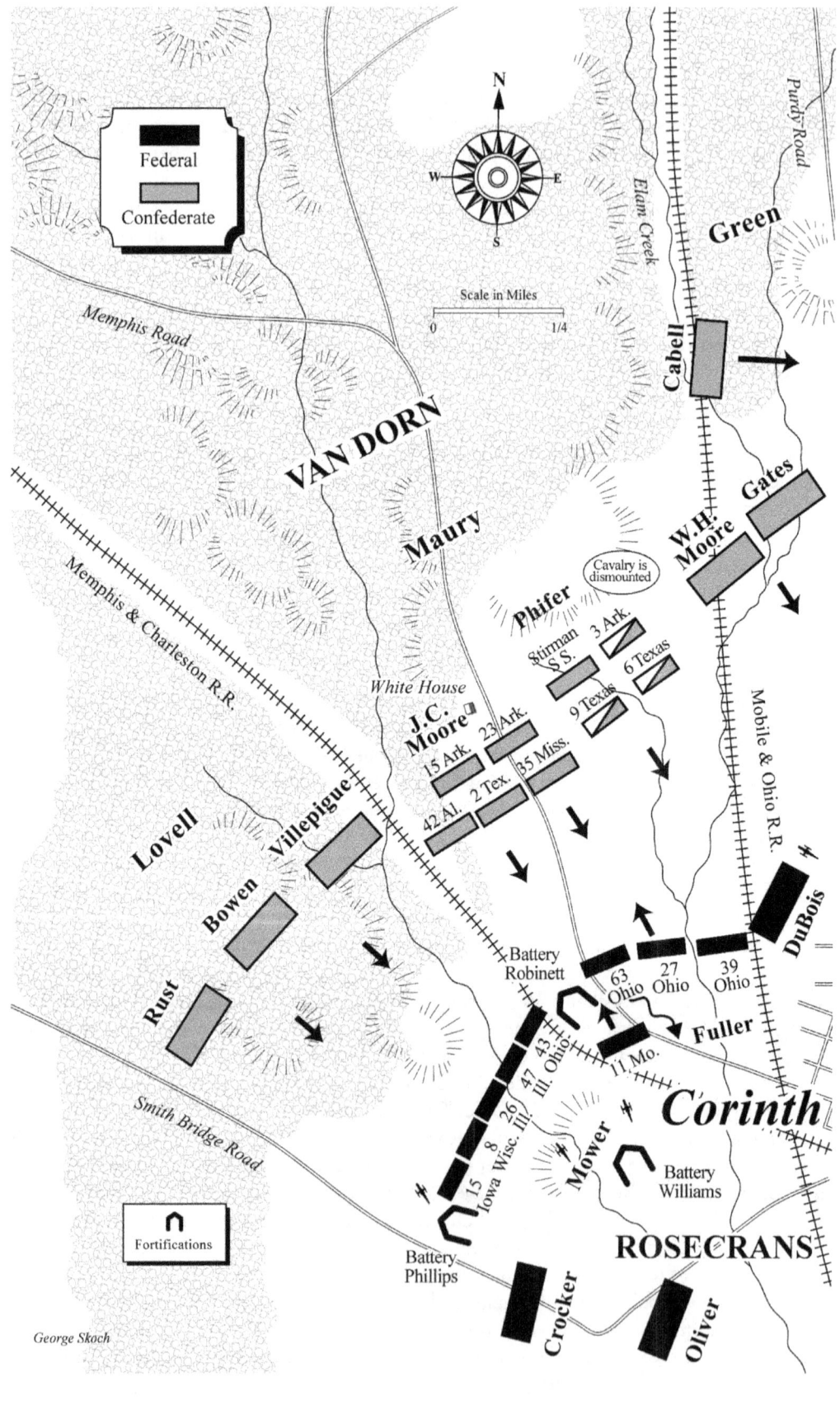

The 11th Missouri's Duncan McCall described the Confederate attack. "The rebels came on in solid column, and as they emerged from the woods their colors were thrown to the breeze and proudly waved over the sons of the South. They steadily advanced ... our men waiting in line of battle to receive them. There was nothing to them, and volley after volley of musketry was poured into their advancing columns. As one man fell another took his place; and still they came on, firing as they came."[31]

The Confederate infantry made two charges into the ranks of the defenders, but were repulsed. The Confederate attack was an impressive sight as rows of soldiers advanced with the intent on silencing the battery and breaking the Union line. The artillerymen at Battery Robinett fought with the same intensity as the rest of Union line, and the advancing Confederate lines fell under the barrage of the shell and canister from the Union artillery. The third attack was spearheaded by Colonel William P. Rogers' Second Texas, which pushed forward. The 63rd Ohio had been victim of Confederate sharpshooters and received the brunt of the previous attacks. The third Confederate assault on the Union line near Battery Robinett caused the 63rd Ohio to give way; and Colonel John Fuller, on the scene, "yelled to the commander of the 11th Missouri to be ready to charge the moment the Sixty-third faltered."[32] As the left hand companies of the 63rd Ohio fell back, the "Missourians opened their files to let the Ohioans by, then fired. They reloaded and fired again. The enemy kept coming. When the rebels were thirty yards away, the Missourians raised a yell and charged."[33]

Colonel John Sprague's 63rd Ohio took the brunt of Dabney Maury's attack (Library of Congress).

Major Weber had watched in awe at the losses of the 63rd Ohio: "Quite a number of the officers and men of this regiment were killed or wounded."[34] The 63rd lost more than 60 percent of its officers, reported over 130 casualties for the battle, and was repelled backward. "At this moment the Eleventh Missouri sprang to their feet and received a volley, which, for the instant, staggered them. The next they pressed forward with heroic gallantry, and the Twenty-seventh Ohio, whose left had fallen back slightly joining in the movement, and uniting their flanks, the two regiments rushed in splendid style upon the enemy, instantly routing him and driving him in utter confusion from the field, which was thickly strewn with his dead and wounded."[35]

Several accounts of the 11th Missouri's charge at Battery Robinett have been preserved. Major Weber said of their attack, "When they [63rd Ohio] fell back ... we arose with a yell and charged them. Though the enemy had thus far been successful, when met at the bayonet

Opposite: Repulsing the Confederate attack at Battery Robinett. As the 63rd Ohio gave way, the 11th Missouri and 27th Ohio counterattack stopped the Confederate advance.

point he turned and fled ignominiously. We retook the fort and then fired our first shot, and having every advantage of the confusion of the enemy, piled the ground with his killed and wounded. In front of our line fell Colonel Rogers, Second Texas, commanding brigade."[36] Colonel Rogers was reported to be the fifth color bearer of the Texans, so determined was he to achieve his objective. Even the Union soldiers who participated in the defense near Battery Robinett had praise for the dedication, skill and sacrifice of those soldiers who attacked over and over again.

Duncan McCall recalled the attackers "firing as they came, led on by the brave Col. Rogers of the 2nd Texas cavalry. The 63rd Ohio, also the 27th, were doing their best to keep them back, but still they came on, and planted their colors on the fort, when the 11th was ordered to charge. They rose, fired a volley into their ranks and charged with bayonets, when the rebels broke and fled in all directions, not being able to stand cold steel. Col. Rogers was ordered to surrender as prisoner of war, but he would not, but kept shooting his revolver and giving command to his men, when one of the regulars shot him in the side with a revolver, and one of company B shot him through the breast. Several other officers were killed and lay close to him. A horse was laying dead and a man by his side; another laid a little in the rear; he had been struck by a shell in the head, and lay with his hand grasping some hair and brains; his head was nothing but a shell, the brains being scattered all over the ground. But few ever reached the woods that made the charge, and their loss must have been terrible."[37] For the 11th Missouri, the Color Guard suffered severely during the charge on Battery Robinett when the color sergeant, James Fyffe was wounded and another "seven guards were also killed or wounded."[38]

Lieutenant William S. Snow, Company K, recorded that Colonel Rogers fell "leading his men in an attempt to plant the rebel flag in the fort, and he and his horse lay together, his left leg under the horse."[39] According to Ephraim M. Eckley, Company E, "the 11th Mo. Went into that breach, many of the Ohio boys fell in with that regiment and met the enemy in the final struggle, in which he was driven from the field. 'God bless you, 11th Mo.!' Was Col Fuller's greeting, in a broken voice, as that regiment went into action."[40] Captain George Henry, Company D, reported, "Then, with fixed bayonets, at double-quick, we met the rebel column.... At the moment we commenced our charge, Gen. Rogers — he was then Brevet Brigadier-General — with at least two of his staff were charging upon our lines. At that instant he and Lieut. Foster of his staff, fell."[41] Captain Henry recalled, "None of the enemy got inside the embrasure. We then expected the enemy to reform and make another charge. I was ordered to take a position in the ditch in front of the guns of the battery, to do which we had to remove out of the ditch 47 dead and wounded rebels."[42] It is important to note that at the assault on Battery Robinett, the Confederates had not entered the defenses nor planted any flags inside, as some accounts report. Captain George Henry's account is the more accurate of the accounts regarding Battery Robinett.

"We fired several volleys and went in with the bayonet, and did our full share in turning the rebs back," recalled Lieutenant James McNeal, Company H.[43] "When the Johnnies were falling back, yet in close musket range, some strange officer came to our regiment and ordered us to cease firing. As some of the boys paid no attention to his orders, he threatened to strike them with his sword. They turned, and the point of the bayonet convinced him that he was in the wrong crowd. Who was he? Some of our boys thought it was Col. Fuller, others that it was some rebel."[44]

Duncan McCall recorded, "You can judge for yourself how bloody now was the conflict here and along the whole line. Twenty-five dead lay in the ditch, whose bodies we had to remove, in order to occupy it, so that if the rebels returned we would be prepared for them, and as we had gathered up the rebels' guns we were well supplied. Two of the boys had fifteen guns, and most of them had two."[45]

"Most gloriously did they obey this command and the enemy sent as chaff before the wind," according to the records of Company D.[46] The records of 11th Missouri, Company K, recorded, "A battle so glorious to our arms and so disastrous to our enemies — making that remarkable charge at 'Battery Robinett' which closed the battle."[47]

Colonel John Fuller's praise for the 11th Missouri, which valiantly supported his brigade, could not have been higher. "Major Weber, commanding the Eleventh Missouri, though not attached to this brigade, fought under my command during the action, and displayed so much of the true soldier and handled his regiment with so much skill that I should do injustice to my own feelings did I fail to speak of him in this connection. He is doubtless one of the best officers in this division, and deserves great praise for his conduct during the battle.[48]

Van Dorn's attack had been repulsed all along the Union line and his troops began to withdraw.

After the battle was over, General Rosecrans rode through the Union defenses and "was cheered most heartily."[49] In the evening, when Gen. Rosecrans rode into the ranks of the 11th Missouri Infantry and announced the defeat and "retreat of the Johnnies, he praised the 11th Mo. for their fighting qualities, as displayed at the battle of Iuka and gave the 11th Mo. credit for the repulse of the Johnnies at Battery Robinett."[50]

The 11th Missouri's Captain William Stewart's father died in Missouri at this time, so his generally eloquent descriptions of events are missing. However, he wrote in a letter, "You have no doubt seen the details of the battles [Iuka and Corinth] in the newspapers. I have no time now to write details. Our Regiment (the 11th Mo) did nobly and won a great name. In our bayonet charge in recapturing the Fort at Corinth we lost 63 men. This charge was one of the most brilliant affairs of the war."[51] In a letter on October 17, William Stewart stated that the new motto for the 11th Missouri entering the battles of Iuka and Corinth was "victory or death, and our brave boys stuck to the motto most determinedly."[52]

The 11th Missouri lost one officer and six enlisted men killed in action, one officer and 61 enlisted men wounded and five missing. Captain Charles Hollister, Company E, was killed while leading his company in the charge. Also killed were James Fair, Company K, Francis French, Company A, John Guthrie, Company A, James Smith, Company B, Joel Smith, Company B, and Abraham Williams, Company D.

Summary of Casualties of the 11th Missouri Infantry at Corinth October 3–4,

Regimental Staff			
Joseph Mower	Col	Neck	
Company A			
Elisha Day	Pvt	Head	Slightly
Francis French	Sgt.	KIA	
John Gutherie	Pvt	KIA	
Edward Heath	Pvt	Side	Slightly
John McAplin	Pvt	Side	Severely — Died
Riel Plummer	Pvt	Head	Died
Wesley Sievert	Pvt	Ankle	Slight
Company B			
James Callaway	Pvt	Arm, shoulder, side	Severe

Name	Rank	Wound	Severity
John Driscol	Pvt	Wounded and missing	
Marion Hall	Pvt	Hand, side	
Thomas Hall	Pvt	Arm	Slight
Joseph Hanna	Pvt	Head	Severe
Charles Ross	Pvt	Lung	Severely
James C Smith	Pvt	KIA	
Joel Smith	Pvt	KIA	
Company C			
John Buchanan	Pvt	Shoulder	Severe
Jacob Caine/Cine	Pvt	Wounded in camp	
Benjamin Lightfoot	Corp.	Shoulder, thigh	Severely
Henry McHaley	Pvt	Breast	Severely
Patrick Mehan	Pvt	Knee	Died in October
Samuel Neal	Pvt	Hand	
William Simmons	Corp.	Arm, Back	Slight
Company D			
Charles Apperson	Pvt	Foot	Slight
William Eaton	Corp.	Breast	Severe
Lancaster Fields	Corp.	Wounded	Severe — Died
Samuel P. Friend	Pvt	Side	
Calder Gibson	Pvt	Breast	Severely
Riley Jump	Pvt	Leg	Slight
Crawford McNally	Pvt	Leg	Died
David McKnight	Sgt.	Neck, Shoulder	Severely
William McKnight	Pvt	Head, Leg	Slightly
John Pridemore	Pvt	Side, Chest	Slightly, Severe
Henry Smith	Pvt	Shoulder	Severe
Williams, Abraham	Pvt	KIA	
Company E			
Dennis Brown	Pvt	Left Leg	Severe
Andrew Egan	Corp.	Face	
William Eckey	Corp.	Hand	Slight
Ephraim Eckley	Pvt	Breast	Slight
Alvin Eckley	Corp.	Thigh	Severe
Zachariah Herrington	Pvt	Thigh	Severely
Charles Hollister	Capt.	KIA	
George Hood	Pvt	Head	Slight
Alvin Eckley	Corp.	Leg	Severe
John R. Rolen	Pvt	Side	Severely
Company F			
Eugene Robinson	Pvt	Chest	Died
William F. Rollen	Pvt	Arm	Slightly
Company G			
Granville Bernier	Pvt	Hand	Slight
James Cummings	Pvt	Hand	Slightly
James Fyffe	Corp.	Arm	Severely
George Lehr	Pvt	Leg	

Samuel Ream	Pvt	Both legs	Severely — Died
Joseph Rivers	Pvt	Neck	Severely
Company H			
Franklin Anderson	Pvt	Wounded	
David P. Henry	Corp.	Leg, amputated	Severely
John Laird	Pvt	Shoulder	Severely
Company I			
Harrison Davis	Corp.	Breast	Slightly
David Johnson	Corp.	Leg	Died
Company K			
John Bay	Pvt	Hand	Slight
James Fair	Pvt	KIA	
John Foster	Corp.	Breast	Severe
Cyrus Kendall	Lt.	Leg, shoulder	Slight
Patrick McCue	Pvt	Wrist	

Another member of the regiment and brigade was wounded during this battle, Colonel Joseph Mower. While the 11th Missouri Infantry was detached from the rest of Mower's brigade, their beloved colonel, Joseph Mower, was having personal problems of his own. At 8 A.M. on October 4, he received orders from General Stanley to take a group of skirmishers to determine the position of the Confederate forces that faced Stanley's division. There are two accounts of this reconnaissance. One reports that General Stanley asked for five volunteers from every company in the division to reconnoiter the enemy positions. Stanley took half the volunteers and Colonel Mower took the second half. The second story reported that Mower, always personally involved with the action, took two companies from each regiment along the Memphis Railroad because he wanted to dislodge the enemy's sharpshooters, which "were at that time causing considerable annoyance."[53] Both accounts state that Mower was successful in driving the sharpshooters about three-quarters of a mile when the skirmishing party ran into the main lines of the Confederates. Mower reported, "My men received several volleys from them, some shots reaching us from the rear of our left."[54] Mower assumed the fire was from friendly troops and rode away to stop the firing, when he found himself surrounded by butternut-clad soldiers. While trying to escape, he was wounded with a gunshot wound to the neck and was captured. The initial reports made to General Stanley and General Rosecrans indicated that Mower had been shot and killed. Wounded, he was taken to the Confederate camp, but the battle was turning into a defeat for his captors. During some confusion which occurred in camp, he was able to escape as the Confederate retreat began. When Colonel Mower went into battle, he had removed his designation of rank and only wore a common blouse, and because of this he was not closely guarded. He received cheers as he rode into the Union camp on a Confederate horse he had stolen. The rumor of Mower's brigade being intoxicated on the prior day rankled Mower, so when he approached Rosecrans, he said, "Yes, General, but if they had reported me for being 'shot in the neck' today instead of yesterday, it would have been correct."[55] Rosecrans reported that Mower had been unjustly accused of allowing his brigade to be intoxicated on the previous day.

Known as a hard drinking, hard fighting commander, Mower's assertion of innocence in regard to the consumption of alcohol was somewhat challenged by Peter Cozzens in his book, *The Darkest Days of the War: The Battles of Iuka and Corinth*, when he states that Colonel Mower "had kept warm with a bottle during the night and ... was too drunk to distinguish"[56] the Confederate troops he encountered from the friendly Union troops on the day of his capture.

Confederate dead at Battery Robinett (Library of Congress).

In defeat, General Sterling Price described the gallantry and glory of the battle which had been so bravely fought. "They have won to their sisters and daughters the distinguished honor, set before them by a general of their love and admiration upon the event of an impending battle upon the same field, of the proud exclamation, 'My brother, father, was at the great battle of Corinth.'"[57]

On October 13, 1862, the 11th Missouri Infantry's Private Anderson Campbell wrote to his family regarding the Battle of Corinth. "I was not killed or wounded. John McAlpin was wounded. Hiram Umfleet is wounded.... We are at Corinth Mississippi now. We have a battle at Corinth.... They were skirmishing about a half a day and the rebels then made a charge on one of our forts and tuck it and then we charged and tuck it back in about twenty minutes. The rebels charged again and missed us and then we fight about 1 hour and the rebels ran. I have nothing of importance to write."[58] The differences in the description of the battle from Price and Campbell cannot be overlooked.

The loss to the 11th Missouri was heavy and the final toll wasn't measured until later, as men died and the wounded who lived often times never returned to the regiment. The full extent of the extensive injuries, even for those who lived, may be expressed in the case of Benjamin Lightfoot, Company C, who was shot three times — one shot entered his lung and was unable to be removed, another ball entered his right shoulder and the third ball entered his hip. There was also evidence that a ball passed along his cheek and struck his ear as it passed by. The ball remained in his lung and lameness resulted from the hip wound. Corporal Lightfoot spent a year convalescing and received his discharge in August 1864.

In addition to the seven men who were killed in action at Corinth, another nine subsequently died as a result of their wounds. Another thirteen men were permanently injured and subsequently discharged as a result of the Battle of Corinth. The men who subsequently died of their wounds were:

Lancaster Fields	Company D
David Johnson	Company I
John McAlpin	Company A
Patrick Mahan	Company C
Crawford McNally	Company D
Riel Plummer	Company A
Samuel Ream	Company G
Eugene Robinson	Company F
William Sievert	Company A

William Sievert died on October 13 of wounds he received accidentally at Kossuth on October 1, two days before the battle.

At the end of the battle on October 4, the Union army had lost 355 men killed, 1,841 men wounded and 324 missing in action. Another 570 men were killed or wounded at the action at Davis Bridge by Major General Stephen Hurlbut's attempt to block Van Dorn's Confederate army retreat across the Hatchie River. The Southern losses were estimated at 505 men killed, 2,150 wounded and 2,183 missing during the battle; and an additional 400–500 men killed or wounded at Davis Bridge.[59] The victory by Rosecrans at Corinth, while not destroying Van Dorn's army, did open the door for the actions that would take place in 1863. General Grant, sensing that the Confederate forces in Mississippi were weakened, seized the strategic initiative and targeted the fortress at Vicksburg as his goal in the new year.

The losses to the 11th Missouri in September and October 1862 were significant. The once large and formidable regiment was being whittled down due to the battle losses, medical losses and sickness. In October, Major Andrew Weber sent an appeal to the governor of Missouri.

Hd Quarters 11th Mo Vol Inft[60]
Corinth Mississippi
October 30th 1862
Governor
   I would most respectfully beg leave to state the condition of the Regiment which has been under my command for the past six weeks. We were mustered into service on the 3rd of August 1861, by Capt. Tracy, and since that time have been doing active service. First under Gen Plummer, the Colonel, and since under Col. Jos A Mower of the 1st U.S. Inft. 'Tis not my intention to tell what we have done, I would refer you to General Rosecrans or any officer of the Army of the Mississippi. We report but five hundred and 20 enlisted men present. Present and absent we have six hundred and ninety-three, 693. For over four months we have had officers trying to recruit, laboring under peculiar disadvantages. They have succeeded in enlisting but two, 2, men. Though a Missouri regiment the men are mostly from Illinois, we cannot recruit among the personal friends of the regt and the consequence is — we cannot hope by our own simple efforts to fill up the standard.

I would most earnestly ask — can you send us some men! If upon you find we have not proven ourselves deserving. If we have not always well done our duty, then heed not our entreaty. If we have, then listen to our call for help. We have tried long and hard to help ourselves, but in vain, and as a last resort fall back to you — Our Commander in Chief,

Respectfully submitted by
    Your most
    Obt Servt
    A. J. Weber
    Major Comdg Regt

To — His Excellency H R Gamble Governor of Missouri

Private Newton Preston, Company I, also lamented the losses the 11th Missouri had suffered in the battles at Iuka and Corinth. He stated the regiment was so reduced in numbers that there were rumors that he regiment was going to be transferred to a heavy artillery unit. He stated, "We have only got 180 effective men in the regt."[61] Preston went on to hope for peace, "Our glorious country will have to be saved and the sooner the better. I am willing to do my part towards saving it. I am in hopes that this bloody war will soon come to a close and we can live in peace hereafter. What a good time we could all have this winter if the war [was] to close now but it seems very likely that we will be in service for some time yet."[62]

Sergeant Horace E. Brown, Company C, fought in the Battle of Corinth (courtesy Nancy Glaiberman).

11th Missouri Infantry Regimental Losses September–December 1862

	SEPTEMBER	OCTOBER	NOVEMBER/DECEMBER
Discharged		Seamon/Seeemon, William (C)	Bonner, Charles W. Musician (A)
	Hailey, John (B)	Anderson, Andrew (E)	
	Hood, William F. (B)	Blew, John (E)	Bishop, Elisha S. (A)
	Anderson, Franklin (H)	Blackledge, Gideon (F)	Bourn, Samuel (A)
	McClanahan, James M. Sgt. (K)	Black, Joseph (G)	Buchanan, John (A)

	SEPTEMBER	OCTOBER	NOVEMBER/DECEMBER
	Wade, William H. (K)	Sandiford, Samuel J. (G)	
	Cunningham, John Sgt. (F)	McColpin, George R. (H)	Smithers, Henry (B)
		McKinney, James (D)	Hime/Hine, John Wagoner (C)
		Umfleet, Hiram (A)	Barger, James N. (C)
		Wilson, Shelby (D)	Cook/Koch, Henry (C)
			Hami, William/John (C)
			Rose, John H. (C)
			Sweet, Montgomery (C)
			Erwin, John (D)
			Brown, Dennis (E)
			Pear, John (E)
			Gilligan, James (F)
			Pease, John T. (E)
			Harman, David (F)
			Gillen, Charles (G)
			Swagler, Lewis (G)
			Conrad, John (H)
			Copper, William H. (I)
			Filey, William H. (I)
			Mason, William T. (I)
			Seager, John C. (I)
			Shreves, Thomas J (I).
			Thorburn, Robert Sgt. (K)
			McGinley, John (K)
			Sullins, Nathan Corp (K)
Died	Robinson, John (B)	Baymer, Albert (I)	Flinn, Patrick (G)
	Schaburg, Frederick (B)	Bedford, Isaac Sgt. (I)	Burns, William (I)
	Chapman, William (I)	McAlpin, John (A)	Heither, Nathaniel (A)
	Lidey, Emmanuel Corp. (G)	Mehan, Patrick (C)	
	Vance, Luther (I)	Williams, Abraham (D)	
	Wilkinson, Thomas (A)	Clark, Bedford (G)	
	Moore, George H. (A)	Fair, James W. Corp. (F)	
	Easton, John G. (I)	French, Francis M. Sgt. (A)	
	Singleton, Amos Captain	Gutherie, John W. (A)	
		Hollister, Charles Captain (E)	
	Clark, Bedford (G)	Robinson. Eugene (F)	
	Osborne, Marshall (K)	Smith, Joel F. (B)	
		Dutton/Dulton Daniel C. (A)	
		Fields, Lancaster Corp (D)	
		Smith, James C. (B)	
		Reams, Samuel (G)	
		Haltermont, Andrew (F-K)	
		Johnson, David Corp (I)	
		Sievert, William (A)	
		Smith, Emmanuel (K)	
Deserted			Lambert, Hezekiah (G)
Resigned		Orr, Charles 2nd Lt. (A)	Panabaker, William E. (Lt. Colonel)
		Laird, Benjamin Lt. (G)	
Missing		Black, Andrew (C)	

Chapter 5

Siege of Vicksburg

"The narrow sunken road became increasingly encumbered with war's grisly harvest."
— Edwin Bearss

On October 5, 1862, the 11th Missouri Infantry and other regiments from Rosecrans' army began their pursuit of Van Dorn's retreating Confederate army after the Battle of Corinth. When the 11th Missouri encountered streams, they often found them guarded by Confederate rear guards and were forced to find alternate routes. The trail of the Confederate army was a series of discarded supplies, including guns, tents, cooking utensils, flour, and other army materials. Duncan McCall reported that many stragglers were found, captured and paroled and every house "contained either dead or sick soldiers."[1] Finally the pursuit ended near Ripley, Mississippi, and the regiment was ordered to establish pickets. The supplies caught up with the regiment, and McCall recalled, "We had sweet potatoes and fresh meat a plenty."[2] The regiment, through a series of starts and stops, began its return march to Corinth. The 11th Missouri Infantry returned to Corinth on October 12, and because of Colonel Mower's gunshot wound to his neck, the brigade was placed under the temporary command of Colonel John M. Loomis of the 26th Illinois. Duncan McCall recorded, "Every soldier was ordered to report with spade and shovel for fatigue duty and we had to work from day to day until we considered Corinth impregnable."[3]

Once the regiment returned to Corinth, the army was reorganized and the 11th Missouri Infantry became part of the Department of the Tennessee. The 11th Missouri was still commanded by the battle-tested Major Andrew Weber.

Organization of troops in the Department of the Tennessee, Maj. Gen. U.S. Grant, Commanding, November 10, 1862.

STANLEY'S DIVISION — BRIG. GEN. DAVID S. STANLEY
Second Brigade — Col. John M. Loomis

26th Illinois, Maj. Robert A. Gillmore
47th Illinois, Capt. George A. Williams
5th Minnesota, Col. Lucius F. Hubbard
11th Missouri, Maj. Andrew J. Weber
8th Wisconsin, Lieut. Col. George W. Robbins
2nd Iowa Baty., Lieut. Daniel P. Walling

With increasing confidence that the Confederate forces in Mississippi were weakened, Grant implemented a strategy to strike toward Vicksburg. In the fall of 1862, the 11th Missouri Infantry became part of General Grant's overland march toward Vicksburg. Throughout the war, it seemed that the regiment would have a connection to the Mississippi River — first by being garrisoned at Cape Girardeau, then participating in the siege of New Madrid and the taking of Island No. 10, and now focusing on Vicksburg. The Mississippi River was still important to the Confederacy, but now the great river became the backbone of the Union supply and communication system. The river became an important feature for the opposing armies because in 1862 the river was about a half mile wide in places and the speed of the current made navigation very difficult. In addition, operating near the river was difficult because of the swampy approaches. Perhaps one of the most poetic and prophetic descriptions of the Vicksburg campaign was offered by the 11th Missouri Infantry's Dr. Thomas Hawley, referring to Vicksburg's control of the Mississippi River: "When the broad bosom of the father of waters is no longer tarnished" by the Rebels and "it must, shall and will be forever free ... although its dark waters may be changed to red by the flow of human blood."[4] After Memphis fell into Union hands, the Federal navy began probing southward toward Vicksburg; and after New Orleans fell under the control of David Farragut's warships, the area around Vicksburg was the sole remaining Confederate stronghold on the Mississippi River. Farragut's naval vessels advanced upriver to Vicksburg in the summer of 1862, and stayed in the area for two months before moving south again. However, the sight of the Union warships at Vicksburg alerted the Confederates to the looming Union threat and they enhanced fortifications around the city as a result.

Confederate Lieutenant General John Pemberton commanded the Department of Mississippi and East Louisiana beginning in October 1862. He also commanded the Confederate garrison at Vicksburg and other Confederate forts along the Mississippi River. In addition, he commanded the Confederate field forces that were facing Grant's army then advancing toward Vicksburg. Pemberton was a formidable opponent. Pemberton, born in Philadelphia in 1814, graduated as part of the class of 1837 at West Point. He had military experience in both the Seminole and Mexican wars prior to the Civil War. Grant knew he would have to face Pemberton if he was successful in bringing his army to the gates of Vicksburg. Grant began his Central Mississippi Campaign in November 1862 with the intent of ultimately capturing Pemberton's citadel at Vicksburg. He planned to move south along two routes. The first route was taken by Major General William T. Sherman who moved downstream from Memphis to the Yazoo River just north of Vicksburg. Grant's other wing moved south along the railroads through north central Mississippi. According to Grant's plan, both forces converged on Vicksburg.

In early November the 11th Missouri Infantry marched with supply trains to Grand Junction, Tennessee. From there the men moved south with the army to Cold Water, Mississippi, then to Oxford, skirmishing daily. Where the Confederates prepared formidable defenses, the Union army was able to flank the positions and remove the immediate threats to its advance. The 11th Missouri's Captain William Stewart described the Mississippi territory the regiment was travelling through: "We are now in a rich portion of Dixie. Immense cotton and cornfields cover the entire country. The corn feeds our animals, the Negroes [men] make our roads, and the women pick cotton, which goes North. A planter is not respectable unless he owns 2000 acres of land and from one to three hundred Negroes. Ladies are scarce, particularly the handsome kind."[5]

Also in November, Brigadier General David Stanley was promoted and transferred to the Army of the Cumberland, commanded by General William Rosecrans. Initially, Stanley assumed command of the cavalry for the Army of the Cumberland. Brigadier General Leonard

Ross from Illinois assumed Stanley's old divisional command. Ross had previously served with the 11th Missouri in the Battle of Fredericktown. While Mower was recuperating from the wound he received at Corinth, the brigade command temporarily passed to John Loomis of the 26th Illinois. The 11th Missouri Infantry's chaplain wrote, "Our Col. Mower has been recommended for promotion to Brig. General. He was wounded & taken prisoner on the 4th & when the enemy were routed they were in such a hurry that they forgot to take their prisoners along. The Col in a frenzied panic got on a horse & headed for Corinth & no person took time to question & so he came in."[6]

On December 17, General Earl Van Dorn launched a raid against Grant that halted the advancing Union line. Earl Van Dorn's reputation had fallen after the Battle of Corinth when Van Dorn's leadership had come under scrutiny, and he even faced a court of inquiry. On December 17, Van Dorn led his force from Grenada, Mississippi, with the intent of capturing and destroying the Union supply depot in Holly Springs. A large Christmas celebration was held in Holly Springs on the evening of December 19, and Van Dorn struck the city early on the morning of December 20. Despite the cold weather, Van Dorn's men overwhelmed the pickets and found most the Union defenders asleep. While skirmishing took place during the capture, virtually the entire garrison of 2,000 men was captured. It was reported that the ladies of Holly Springs stood in their yards cheering as Van Dorn's cavalry accomplished their task. The Confederates took advantage of the Union supplies and destroyed the rest. Van Dorn also freed a number of Confederate prisoners. The result of this raid only superficially relates to the history of the 11th Missouri Infantry, because the garrison commander of Holly Springs was none other than Colonel Robert Murphy of the Eighth Wisconsin Infantry. It should be recalled Colonel Murphy was also in charge of the Union supply depot in Iuka, Mississippi, in September 1862, which General Sterling Price overwhelmed and captured prior to the Battle of Iuka. Colonel Murphy had been found not guilty in a court-martial for his actions at Iuka when he faced the charges of misbehaving in the face of the enemy and shamefully abandoning a post which he had been commanded to defend. He had been reassigned to duty under the command of General Stanley.

The controversy of who was at fault for the loss of Holly Springs continued. But whether Grant should have had stronger defenses, did cavalry commander Colonel T. Lyle Dickey, Fourth Illinois Cavalry, know of the impending attack, or was Colonel Murphy again at fault, is unimportant; because Colonel Murphy received the blame. Colonel Murphy wrote, "My fate is most mortifying. I have wished a hundred times to-day that I had been killed. I have done all in my power — in truth, my force was inadequate. I have foreseen this and have so advised. No works here, and no force to put in them if they were here, and yet I know General Grant is not to blame; he has done all for the best, and so did I. I have obeyed orders, and have been unfortunate in so doing. The misfortune of war is mine."[7] The unfortunate Colonel Murphy was be summarily dismissed from the service of the Union army on January 10, 1863.

Van Dorn's raid on Holly Springs succeeded in halting Grant's central Mississippi march, resulting in the recall of the 11th Missouri to Corinth, Mississippi. The 11th Missouri Infantry had two men captured in Van Dorn's raid on Holly Springs. The regimental quartermaster, Lieutenant Abel Pickrell, and Private William Bascue were both captured in the raid on Holly Springs. Both men were located at the supply depot as part of their quartermaster duties, but they had the bad luck of being at the wrong place at the wrong time. In addition, Dr. Thomas Hawley was captured and paroled at Holly Springs. Another of the soldiers, Peter Workman, Company C, of the 11th Missouri Infantry was wounded in an unfortunate event on December 16, 1862, near Oxford. Private Workman was returning from picket duty and while cooking his supper was "accidentally shot in the right arm and side, the ball passing through him, and lodging in the opposite side. The man [responsible] was a desperado, named John Clair, who having become enraged at some other of his comrades, fired the ball accidentally, struck."[8] The unfortunate Peter Workman was discharged and later died as a result of this wound on November 18, 1864.

Confederate General Earl Van Dorn's raid on Holly Springs stopped Grant's plan to attack Vicksburg by a land route through Mississippi. Sherman's advance was also halted when his troops were repulsed at the Battle of Chickasaw Bayou on December 29, 1862. As Grant reformulated his plan to capture Vicksburg, these setbacks convinced him that he needed a river-based attack. So, by January 30, 1863, he established his headquarters at Milliken's Bend, Louisiana, a mere 10 miles west of Vicksburg, and decided to use the Mississippi River as the route for concentrating his troops and supplies prior to his attack on Vicksburg.

On January 1, 1863, the bloodied and now recovered commander of the 11th Missouri, General Joseph Mower, returned to duty. The regiment began a march toward Corinth, which led through La Grange, and then to Grand Junction where the regiment spent ten days on guard duty. The regiment again passed through Oxford, Mississippi, and marched onward to Corinth through terrible road conditions and cold, rainy weather. By January 20, the 11th Missouri moved to Germantown, Tennessee, (fifteen miles from Memphis). They remained there through January and most of February 1863, where much of their time was spent protecting railroads from attacks of guerrillas and Confederate cavalry. Foraging continued to be a daily task, but the area around Germantown was picked clean of food and wood. Dr. Thomas Hawley reported that the weather "had been nothing but rain and drizzle and drizzle and rain for the past 3 weeks, instead of the cold spell as we used to have up north.... I think this element mud will do as much toward ending the war as the rebels."[9]

The supplies for the 11th Missouri were scare in the winter of 1862–1863 due to the irregularity of the railroad being open for transportation, so the men were authorized to forage for supplies. The local population was squeezed by the Union army and often by their loyalty for local troops. While foraging, the 11th Missouri located stolen Union supplies. The frustration by the regiment was expressed by Duncan McCall, "It was stolen at the time of the raid, as the citizens participated in it. They said they had just received it from Memphis, but our men were not to be deceived by such stories, and would take most all of it from them. Some of them had protection papers, which did not save them, as the soldiers had got tired of listening to such professions of unionism and loyalty as these men made, there being little friendship for the Yankees existing amongst them at this time."[10] Also, in January 1863, Private William Moses Baker, Company B, was shot and killed by a local citizen while foraging. Also four soldiers of the 11th Missouri were captured on February 17 and managed to escape. "Some men belonging to the Eleventh Missouri went out in an ambulance yesterday and were taken prisoners. Four of them were taken by two rebels, though they had a revolver among them. They came in to day."[11]

After being in service for 18 months, Dr. Thomas Hawley wrote in a letter to his family, "Oh how I wish for peace to end this terrible war. We count the unnumbered tears and groans of a mighty nation mourning for lost brave and dear hearts. But we must have an honorable peace."[12]

Regimental Changes

The formal religious efforts for the 11th Missouri were abandoned in January, 1863, when the regiment's second chaplain, Samuel Baldrige, resigned his post on January 5. The Rev.

Baldridge wrote in his letter of resignation, "Convinced by a long & earnest trial of my inability to work the moral & spiritual welfare of your gallant command in a manner to satisfy my own conscience or the just demands of the government."[13] The Rev. Baldridge also cited a severe domestic calamity as the final cause for his resignation.

Other changes within the officers' rank of the regiment included the resignation of Charles M. Orr, Company A. Orr was replaced with William Pickrell who now held the rank of 2nd lieutenant. William Pickrell was a clerk who lived in Mechanicsburg, Illinois, prior to the war.

The Battles of Iuka and Corinth resulted in the death of two captains, Charles Hollister, Company E, and Amos Singleton, Company F. In Company E, 1st Lieutenant Abner Bail was promoted to the rank of captain, and 2nd Lieutenant Jacob Blew was promoted to the rank of 1st lieutenant. The newly appointed 2nd lieutenant was Elmore Ridgely. The 31-year-old Ridgely was a married carpenter living in Olney, Illinois, prior to the war.

In Company F, 1st Lieutenant William Cleland was promoted to the rank of captain, 2nd Lieutenant John Finlay was promoted to the rank of 1st lieutenant. Dr. Elias Weir was promoted to the rank of 2nd lieutenant for the company. Dr. Weir was another of the several physicians that had joined the 11th Missouri; 45 years old, he was a Tennessee native and was one of the older officers in the regiment. Lieutenant Weir was married and Xenia, Illinois, was his home prior to the war.

The regiment also lost the services of Lieutenant Benjamin Laird, Company G, through unfortunate circumstances. Lieutenant Laird's daughter died in the autumn of 1862, and his wife "lost her reason becoming deranged in consequence of the burning death of my little daughter. I have still four children helpless and unprotected."[14] Life continued back home as well as in the war, and it is often forgotten how one influences one's actions in the other. In this case, the tragedy that occurred at Benjamin Laird's home resulted in his exit from the regiment. Lieutenant Laird was replaced with newly promoted 2nd Lieutenant David Bailey. Bailey was 21 years old and was a farmer from St. Louis, Missouri, prior to the war.

Regimental Assistant Surgeon Eli Bowyer was recommended for the post of regimental major prior to Samuel Baldridge's resignation. The Rev. Samuel Baldridge wrote, "Dr. Bowyer is recommended for promotion as major & I fear that when his commission comes it will break up our pleasant intimacy. The Major's place in the encampment is to the right of the Col.'s marker & the Chaplain's, on the left. So we would be separated."[15] Bowyer's promotion to the rank of major occurred in December 1862. Major Andrew J. Weber was promoted to the rank of lieutenant colonel in November 1862.

Furloughs in Memphis

Sometimes battle-hardened soldiers have a difficult adjustment to non-military situations. This appeared to be the case with the men of the 11th Missouri, who had been constantly on duty for eighteen months, when they finally were granted furloughs in Memphis in the winter months of 1862–1863.

The soldiers of the 11th Missouri ran into some trouble in Memphis early in 1863 as some of the regiment were settling their accounts at Curley's Rooming House. There was a verbal exchange between one of the soldiers of the 47th Illinois Infantry and someone in a second story window of the rooming house. When the soldier pulled his revolver to shoot the man, Owen "Dug" Prentice of the 11th Missouri snatched the revolver quickly out of the soldier's hand and hid it under his coat and walked away. The soldier from the 47th Illinois Infantry did not know who took the revolver, but a woman from the rooming house pointed out Prentice, who then faced her and said, "I'll stop her noise."[16] He pulled the revolver and shot at the window where she was yelling. This silenced the altercation. The rough and rowdy 11th Missouri Infantry had too much time on its hands.

A second incident occurred while the regiment was in Memphis which was recorded by Corporal Joseph Jones, Company C. The regimental adjutant, Lieutenant Charles Brookings, marched a squad of men from the 11th Missouri into a theater. The group walked to the front of the theater that was filled with other people and told those occupants, "Those seats are reserved for the Eleventh Mo." After a verbal altercation, the seats were given to the men of the 11th Missouri. Next, Jones reported, "The curtain did not rise to suit the boys, who shot on the stage, and several times the company was encored by shots at the stage. The audience was about half made up of ladies and other citizens of Memphis, who made their exits as fast as possible."[17] This exploit virtually ruined the theater for the rest of the winter.

Thankfully for the residents of Memphis, the 11th Missouri moved to Helena, Arkansas, then to Young's Point, Louisiana, and finally to Duckport, Louisiana, from February 13 to February 20. The regiment's reputation as a fighting unit certainly helped keep morale high, but the winter was long and boring for many of the men. As the regiment

Private Owen Prentice, Company C, involved in the altercation at Curley's Rooming House in Memphis (courtesy Civil War Museum at Wilson's Creek National Battlefield).

moved toward Helena, Arkansas, again it made a nuisance of itself as it landed in new locations, as described by Duncan McCall: "Several of the boys left the boat, got a little the worse for liquor, and becoming quite noisy. General Benjamin Prentiss [commander at Helena] ordered his men to arrest them, but they were unable to do so, owing to the resistance made. Revolvers were drawn, missiles thrown, and the guard driven from the ground, but they soon returned with reinforcements."[18] Joseph Jones, Company C, recorded the problem occurred when "our boys making themselves too free with things they came in contact with." Lieutenant Colonel Andrew Weber became aware of the problem and sent Captain Modesta Green to take his company and retrieve the errant soldiers of the regiment. Green himself became involved in a "scrap" and the result "became a 'free for all.'"[19] Colonel Mower had to come ashore and escort his brigade back aboard the boats. The guard lined up in front of the boats as a show of authority and to ensure the men stayed on the boats. The regiment then pummeled the guards and General Prentiss with coal. The regiment was transported a couple of miles down river where it established camp on Chuckaluck Island and where the men could do no further harm.

Maybe the payment for the brigade's rowdiness was its stay on Chuckaluck Island, which was described as follows: "Crowded in narrow quarters between the Mississippi River and a black bayou were tents, wagons, cannons, mules and men; the campaign against Vicksburg thus far a failure; small-pox and measles raging; toads, lizards and snakes infesting the soldiers' quarters; everybody suffering from malaria."[20]

Excavating the canal opposite Vicksburg (Library of Congress).

Arriving at Duckport, Louisiana, a town which no longer existed, the 11th Missouri took possession. The town had been destroyed by the Union army before the regiment arrived, but the regiment remained in place from February 20 until May. Vicksburg was a very impressive defensive obstacle with artillery that could sink any vessel moving past the city's guns. In June 1862, work had commenced on excavating a canal that might allow vessels to move south without passing the fortress' guns. A canal was constructed to a depth of 13 feet deep and 18 feet wide, but by the end of July, work on the canal ceased. In January 1863, construction on the canal began again, as Grant prepared his assault on Vicksburg. As construction continued, a rising Mississippi River flooded the excavated canal. Because of the flooded canal, further excavation required dredging equipment, which was fired upon by Confederate artillery. The brigade spent much of its time at Duckport digging the canal but abandoned the project in late April when the Mississippi River level lowered and made the canal useless. While at Duckport, Private Charles Treadway of Company A wrote he thought the war was nearly over, "I think the rebell is lasting longer than I contracted for. The opinions of the soldiers in general is that the dog is near dead in the South and that they come back to the union before long."[21] Private Alonzo Thomas wrote in a letter of his canal digging experiences and stated this was a "rather funny way to take Vicksburgh."[22]

Additional Changes in Regimental Officers

By May 1, a few additional changes occurred within the officers' ranks of the regiment. Dr. Thomas Hawley was finally assigned to the regiment as assistant surgeon. Dr. Hawley was a voice of the regiment and had struggled to be appointed as regimental surgeon or assistant surgeon. This was accomplished in the spring of 1863, and Dr. Hawley remained with the regiment throughout the remainder of the war.

Captain Moses Warner, Company C, resigned in the spring of 1863, and he was replaced with the company's 1st lieutenant, Modesta Green, and 2nd Lieutenant James Lott was promoted to the rank of 1st lieutenant. Captain Warner had lost the sight in his right eye at this point in the war and the condition was so serious that continued service in the 11th Missouri risked the loss of sight in his left eye. Harrison Withrow was promoted to the rank of 2nd lieutenant. Withrow was a 22-year-old farmer from Loami, Illinois, prior to the war. In Company I, Captain William Barnum, was promoted to the rank of lieutenant colonel on the regimental staff and 1st Lieutenant Charles Osgood was named the new captain for Company I. It is unknown why Barnum was promoted over the existing regimental major, Eli Bowyer, but Barnum's promotion elevated his rank from captain in Company I to lieutenant colonel when A. J. Weber received his much-deserved promotion to full colonel.

Grant's Vicksburg Campaign Begins

Grant determined that his assault on Vicksburg would be a land-based attack, which needed an eastern land-based approach. Grant needed to get his army from the western side of the

Running the batteries (Florida Center for Instructional Technology).

Mississippi River to the east in preparation for the ultimate infantry assault on Vicksburg. Admiral David Dixon Porter's eight gunboats and three transports "ran the batteries" at Vicksburg, and the boats provided the protection and means of getting Grant's army across the river. Henry O'Neil, Company F, 7th Missouri Infantry and later Company A of the 11th Missouri Veteran Infantry, recorded when running the batteries trying to reach Perkins Landing south of Vicksburg, "When the rebel gunners would pull the lanyards to fire their pieces the flashes would light up their faces with a red glow. McGuire noticing this he turned to the Colonel, who was intently watching their manuvers [sic], and said: 'See the bloody spalpeens blush whin they be firing on the Sthars and Sthripes."[23] Once the army crossed the river, it was opposed by Confederate Major General John Bowen's four brigades, but the Union troops were successful in crossing the Mississippi River. In April Grant had reorganized his forces which approached Vicksburg into three corps under the command of Major General John McClernand, Major General William T. Sherman, and Major General James McPherson. These three corps were ordered by Grant to advance northeast and continue with a plan designed to sever Vicksburg's supplies and communications by destroying the railroad linking the fortress with Jackson, Mississippi. With the reorganization of the army, the 11th Missouri Infantry had been assigned to Sherman's XV Corps.

FIFTEENTH ARMY CORPS — MAJ. GEN. WILLIAM T. SHERMAN[24]
THIRD DIVISION — BRIG. GEN. JAMES M. TUTTLE

Second Brigade — Brig. Gen. Joseph A. Mower
47th Illinois, Lieut. Col. Samuel R. Baker
5th Minnesota, Col. Lucius F. Hubbard
11th Missouri: Col. Andrew J. Weber
Lieut. Col. William L. Barnum
8th Wisconsin, Col. George W. Robbins

When the Union Army was reorganized in April 1863, the 11th Missouri Infantry continued to serve under the brigade command of General Joseph Mower and it became part of Brigadier General James Tuttle's division. Tuttle was described as follows: "In size General Tuttle is above the medium, with broad, square shoulders, and weighing one hundred and ninety pounds. He has a sanguine, bilious temperament; light, florid complexion; and gray eyes. His mental and physical organism seem to be in perfect sympathy; for he is slow of speech, and slow in action. He has none of the dash of Sheridan; — he is more like General Grant — slow and sure. Ordinarily he does not draw conclusions rapidly; but, if the circumstances be such as to give him no time for deliberation, he seems equal to emergencies, for his judgments are nearly always correct. He is naturally modest, unassuming and unostentatious. He has large hope, but little self-esteem, and lacks confidence in his own ability. But he is stubborn, and his deliberate opinions are not easily shaken."[25] Tuttle was born in Ohio in 1823 and moved to Iowa in 1846 where he had been sheriff, recorder, and treasurer for the county. In 1861, he organized a company for the Second Iowa Infantry and later was promoted to divisional command in Sherman's XV Corps.

Battle of Jackson, Mississippi

The 11th Missouri's Company K records show the regiment began its movement toward Mississippi on May 2 arriving at Hard Times Landing, a distance of 61 miles from the origination of the march from Duckport, Louisiana. The regiment crossed into Mississippi on May

6. Once Grant's army moved into Mississippi, it suffered a supply problem with food and ammunition being scarce. The 11th Missouri advanced on Mississippi Springs on May 12 and then moved toward Jackson, Mississippi, arriving on May 14.

Sergeant George Adams, Company I, recorded that as the 11th Missouri marched, the weather was warm and the roads were dusty. He described the countryside and the destruction caused by an advancing army: "Some fine houses. No one at home. One house supposed to have 30 thousand dollars worth of furniture in it. It were burned."[26]

On May 12, McClernand's corps was attacked by Brigadier General John Gregg's Confederate brigade at Raymond, Mississippi, which alerted Grant to the danger that other Confederate forces might attack his right flank. Therefore, Grant turned toward Jackson, Mississippi, which he concluded needed to be neutralized before he could attack Vicksburg. Jackson was the capital of one of the most staunchly supportive states of the Southern cause in the Civil War. Jackson was a reservoir of supplies and a railroad hub for Mississippi; and if Pemberton was to survive with the Mississippi River under Union control, Jackson was a critical source of supplies and reinforcements for the Confederate army in the state.

General James Tuttle commanded the 3rd Division of Sherman's XV Corps during the Vicksburg Campaign (Library of Congress).

The Union attack on Jackson included McPherson's Corps approaching from the northwest and Sherman approaching from the southwest. Torrential rain turned the dusty roads into mud and the marching was difficult. "So hard was the rain that McPherson had delayed attacking lest water fill the cartridge boxes of his men as they reached for their paper wrapped ammunition."[27]

The regimental strength of the 11th Missouri Infantry was recorded on the morning reports each company completed; however, when on the march, the company morning reports were suspended. The regimental strength on May 10, 1863, was 361 men reporting for duty, or about 38 percent of the maximum regimental strength. As the regiment advanced on Jackson, Mississippi, it encountered the first Confederate defenders on May 13 when the regiment began exchanging fire with pickets.

General James Tuttle wrote regarding the events of May 13, "After a brisk firing for a few minutes between them and my advance guard, I ordered the leading brigade, General Mower commanding, to deploy on the right of the road, and the next, General Matthies commanding, on the left, holding the other, General Buckland's, in reserve. In this position we advanced about one-fourth of a mile, and, finding no enemy in force, bivouacked for the night, my advance guard occupying Mississippi Springs."[28]

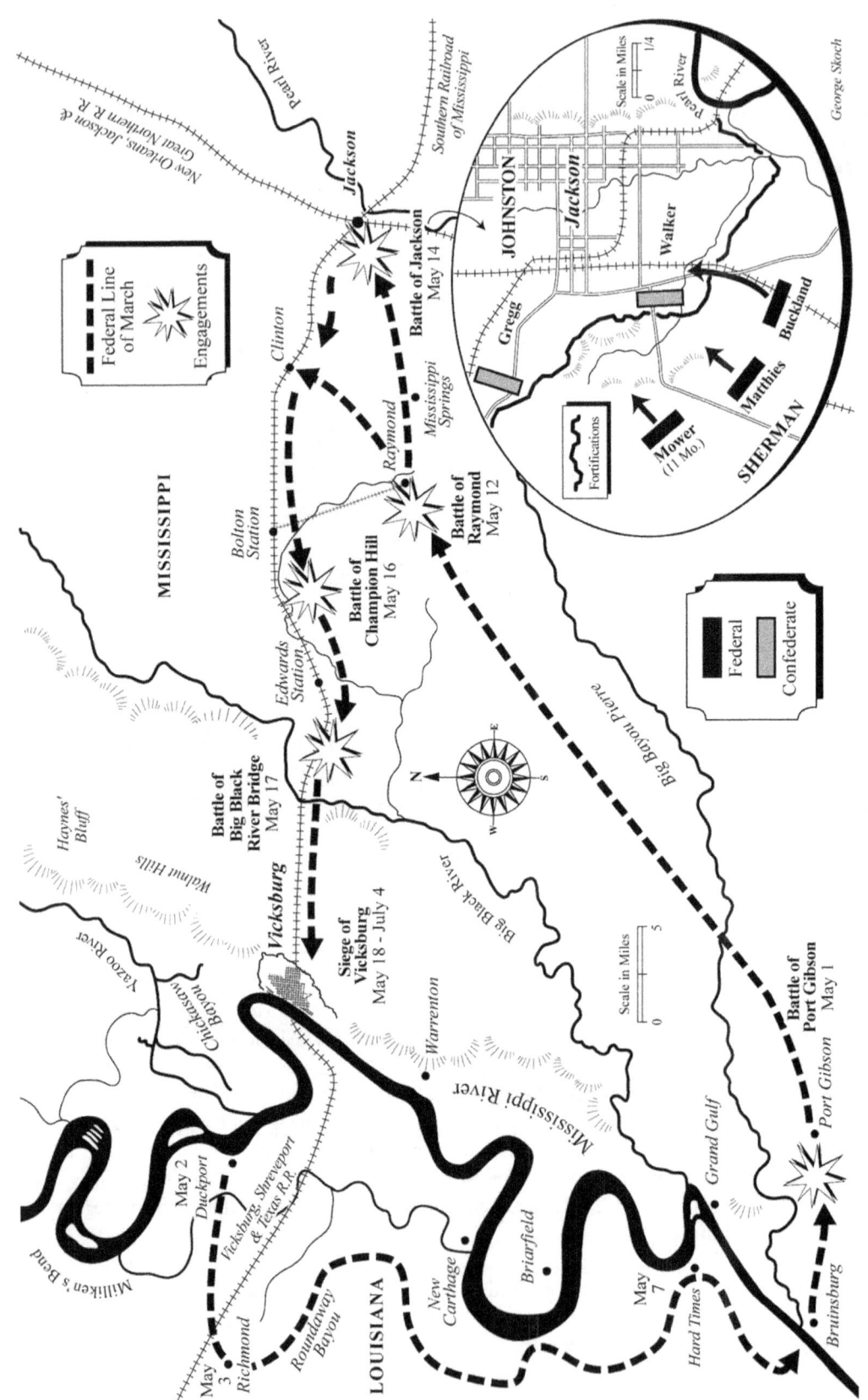

Grant's campaign on Vicksburg, May 1863.

As the Battle of Jackson began on May 14, the 11th Missouri started its advance at daybreak and marched about a mile before encountering the advance guard of Confederate defenders. The clash occurred about 2.5 miles from Jackson. While pushing toward Jackson, Mower's brigade advanced on the right side of the road and was shelled by a Confederate battery. The Second Iowa Artillery opened fire in return and silenced the Confederate artillery within a half an hour. Tuttle reported, "We drove the enemy before us until the artillery from the works around Jackson opened a brisk fire upon us."[29] The 11th Missouri Company C records recorded, "We drove the enemy from the town & took possession of the place."[30]

The advance on Jackson was described by Colonel Lucius Hubbard of one of the 11th Missouri's sister regiments, Fifth Minnesota Infantry: "We then advanced and charged through the timber at double-quick, the enemy rapidly retiring within his intrenchments near the precinct of the town. Here he made another stand, and obstinately disputed our farther progress. The fight continued for more than an hour, but was confined principally to artillery, the infantry occupying a position of shelter. At about 5 P.M. the order 'forward' was given. All supposing we were about to assault the enemy's works in our front, with bayonets fixed and with exultant shouts the line moved forward at a run. It was soon discovered, however, that the enemy had evacuated, and that the charge would be a bloodless one. The enemy had made a precipitate exit from the town, leaving all his artillery to fall an easy capture into our hands."[31]

The Fifth Minnesota was the leading regiment as the brigade advanced toward Jackson, but when the brigade was within two miles of Jackson, the 11th Missouri was placed as the advance regiment. Companies B and F of the 11th Missouri and part of the 47th Illinois Infantry were deployed as skirmishers. The Second Iowa Artillery was unlimbered and fired on Confederate batteries that were firing on the advancing Union troops. Tuttle ordered his brigade forward, and as they advanced across an open field, they received a volley of musket fire from the Confederate skirmishers. No harm was done to the advancing Union infantry, and soon the Confederate skirmishers fell back before the advancing troops. The regiment advanced and stopped before the defensive works and the 95th Ohio Infantry flanked the defenses and found "but few men inside their works."[32]

Confederate General Joe Johnston arrived in Jackson on May 13 and after finding only 6,000 defenders and the Union army bearing down on Jackson, he sent a message to Secretary of War, James A. Seddon, stating, "I am too late."[33] Tuttle also reported that his division captured 10 artillery pieces and captured about 150 of the gunners as the town was taken. Tuttle's division lost 5 killed and 21 wounded. The losses of the Mower's brigade and the 11th Missouri were:

Second Brigade Losses — Battle of Jackson

	Killed	Wounded	Missing
47th Illinois	1	3	0
5th Minnesota	0	0	0
11th Missouri	0	6	3
8th Wisconsin	0	0	0
Total Second Brigade	1	9	3

Sherman ordered the arsenal buildings, the government foundry, a gun-carriage facility, a carpentry shop and paint shops to be destroyed. Sherman also reported, "The penitentiary was burned, I think, by some convicts who had been set free by the Confederate authorities; also a very valuable cotton factory.... Other buildings were destroyed in Jackson by some mischievous soldiers (who could not be detected) which was not justified by the rules of war, including the Catholic church and Confederate Hotel — the former resulting from accidental circumstances and the latter from malice."[34]

Sergeant Joe Browning, Company H, of the 11th Missouri Infantry, described the Confederate exit of Jackson, "When they had to abandon the place they burned enough old-fashioned sugar to have lasted the army during the war, it seemed to me, and left their clothing, supplies, knapsacks, etc., thinking they couldn't use them."[35] Browning liked the Confederate knapsacks so much better than the one he was issued, he used a captured knapsack for the remainder of the war. Browning also was part of the force that liberated prisoners from the Jackson penitentiary and some of these men enlisted in the Union army so grateful were they for their release.

After capturing Jackson, the brigade was assigned as provost-guard, and General Mower was given command of the post. His task was to maintain order among the Union troops and the camp followers. Sherman wrote, "Yet many acts of pillage occurred that I regret, arising from the effect of some bad rum found concealed in the stores of the town."[36] The other brigades of Tuttle's division set about the tasks Sherman had identified for them.

The 11th Missouri Infantry marched to the Hinds County Courthouse, and because it was raining, located a warehouse which it used for the post. Duncan McCall stated as "soon as the soldiers gained possession of the place they commenced the work of plunder. The stores were broken open, everything of value was taken, and most every soldier in the brigade was dressed in citizens' clothes. Whiskey was plenty, and a good many of the boys got drunk. Guards were placed over the town, but they were of no avail, and the soldiers distributed shoes to the citizens, and almost everything that could be got was given to them, as these things were owned by the speculators, and were sold to the people of the town at the highest price."[37]

William Sherman commanded the XV Corps during the Vicksburg Campaign (National Archives).

Ambrose Armitage of the Eighth Wisconsin wrote in his dairy, "Jayhawking, thieving, plundering and drinking have been going on at a fearful rate all day in spite of the guard. Most of the men are drunk to night. Stores have been broken open.... Several buildings have burned."[38]

The 11th Missouri Infantry remained in Jackson for two nights and one day, and marched out of town to the sound of "Dixie." Many of the buildings had been burned or looted and the citizens of Jackson were glad to see them leave. Some soldiers remained in the city to maintain order, but as soon as the Union infantry departed, Confederate cavalry rode into the city and captured anyone who could not get away. The colonel of the 47th Illinois Infantry, which was brigaded with the 11th Missouri Infantry, returned to Jackson where he was confronted by Confederate cavalry and was ordered to surrender, but was killed when he refused to do so.

Although the official records reported three men of the 11th Missouri were captured in the advance on Jackson, Mississippi, in May, 1863, Compiled Service Records showed there were eleven men captured and taken prisoner, including seven men who were captured by the Confederate cavalry after the regiment left Jackson on the march toward Vicksburg. These men were:

Soldier	Company	Date	Place of capture
Fred McNeal	Company H	May 11	Edwards Depot
David Salisbury	Company H	May 11	Edwards Depot
John Dowdrick	Company B	May 12	Raymond
John/James Gallagher	Company B	May 12	Raymond
Hiram Easley	Company F	May 16	Jackson
Samuel Jones	Company E	May 16	Jackson
John Karns	Company C	May 16	Jackson
Joseph Kelly	Company C	May 16	Jackson
James Michaels	Company C	May 16	Jackson
Reuben Mills	Company K	May 16	Jackson
Fleming Talday	Company B	May 16	Jackson

Grant Moves on Vicksburg

Grant's strategy for preventing Confederate attacks on his flanks was temporarily successful when he captured Jackson. He next turned his attention to his primary objective—Vicksburg. General John Pemberton was under the command of General Joe Johnston who had arrived on May 13, just prior to the battle on May 14 as Jackson was being neutralized by Sherman and McPherson. Johnston ordered Pemberton's troops to be moved eastward from Edwards to meet and unite his forces with Johnston's. As Pemberton attempted to fulfill these orders, he was surprised by Grant's army near Champion Hill. The Battle of Champion Hill was fought on May 16, and the result was the Union army pushed Pemberton back to the Big Black River. In addition, one of the Confederate divisions failed to reach the bridges leading back to the rest of the Pemberton's forces. This division was lost to Pemberton, but was united with Johnston's forces instead.

On May 17, all three of Grant's corps advanced on the Big Black River, crossing at various locations. A Confederate rearguard was defeated as Grant pressed onward. After suffering from the unstoppable advance by Grant, the Confederate army retreated to the defenses of the "Gibraltar of the West"—Vicksburg. By May 18, the three Union corps were positioned around Vicksburg with McClernand's corps on the left, McPherson in the center and Sherman on the right. Sherman's corps occupied Haynes' Bluff, which overlooked the Yazoo River. As long as Union forces controlled this area, it provided a conduit for supplies and reinforcements from the Mississippi River. Thus Grant was fully supplied and Pemberton was cutoff.

General Joseph Mower was a highly respected and appreciated commander, and the men of the 11th Missouri made every effort to show their appreciation to him. Despite the rigorous marching in Mississippi, the regiment found time to do so. On Monday, May 18, the 11th Missouri Infantry presented its beloved Colonel Mower with a "splendid chestnut horse."[39] The horse was purchased by the privates of the regiment because Mower had lost so many mounts during the battles. He was reported to be at a loss for words, this being such a surprise, and he made a few remarks to the men of the 11th Missouri.

Grant's march from the Mississippi River through Jackson and then on to Vicksburg was an outstanding success. Historian Michael Ballard summarized the Vicksburg Campaign,

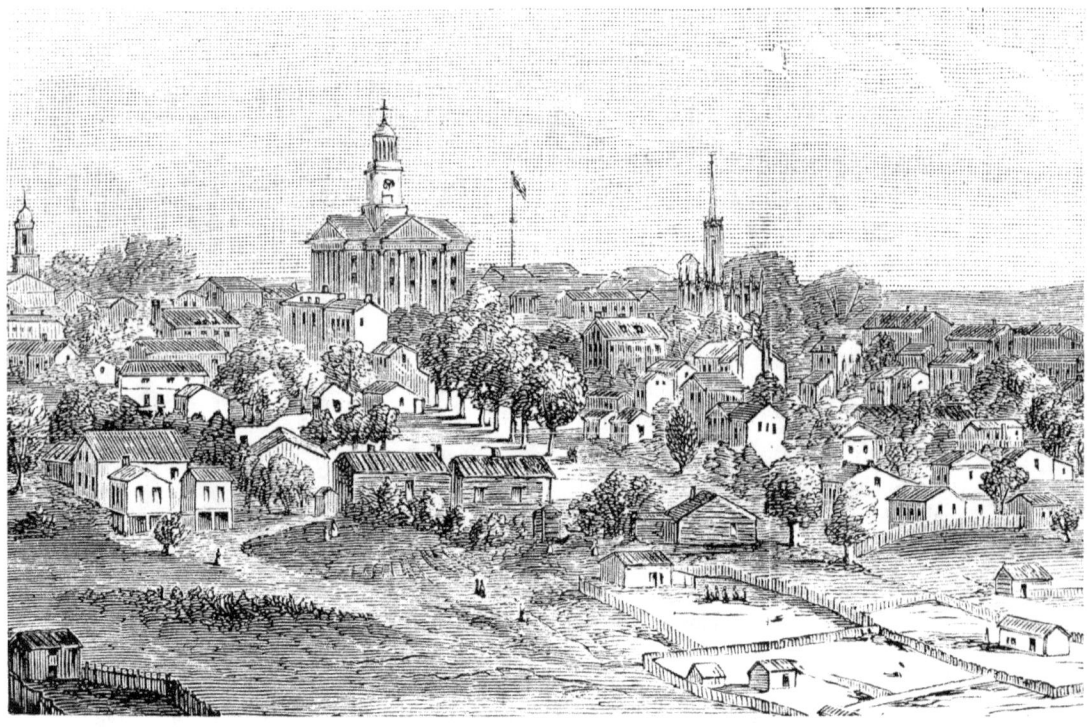

Vicksburg during the Civil War (Florida Center for Instructional Technology).

"Thus far, all that could go wrong for Pemberton had gone wrong."[40] Since the beginning of May, Grant had marched to the east and captured the capital, fought five battles and was confidently marching to his military objective. As the campaign unfolded for Grant, he had been highly successful, so far. It is not surprising that he felt the Confederate defenders at Vicksburg had lost the will to fight. Grant felt that with the series of defeats the Confederate army had just suffered, another strong push could easily break Pemberton's defenses and Vicksburg could be claimed. There was also the need on Grant's part to quickly take the city before he was attacked by Joe Johnston's men out in the countryside. Grant decided he would strike the Southern line on May 19 in a hastily planned assault to capitalize on the momentum of the Union army's successes. Sherman decided his assault would be carried out by General Frank Blair's Second Division, which would attack Stockade Redan, a fortified area on the northeastern part of the Confederate defenses. At 9:00 A.M. on May 19, the Union artillery began pounding the Confederate defenses. At 2:00 P.M., General Blair sent three brigades to attack the Confederate line near Stockade Redan. As the artillery from both sides bombarded each other, the infantry assault began with most of the attackers stopping part of the way up the hill to the Confederate works. Only Captain Edward Washington's First Battalion, 13th U.S. Infantry, part of Colonel Giles Smith's brigade, made it to the ditch in front of Stockade Redan. A few men from other regiments also joined them there. "Not until nightfall were they able to withdraw to Union lines. Sergeant Nelson succeeded in bringing back the regimental colors. He had four bullet holes in his clothes. There were eighteen holes in the flag and two pieces of canister and one musket ball in the staff. Private Patrick Moher dragged the national colors to safety, with the flagstaff in three pieces and fifty-six holes in the flag. The assault of 19 May

Opposite: **The Siege of Vicksburg, May 1863.**

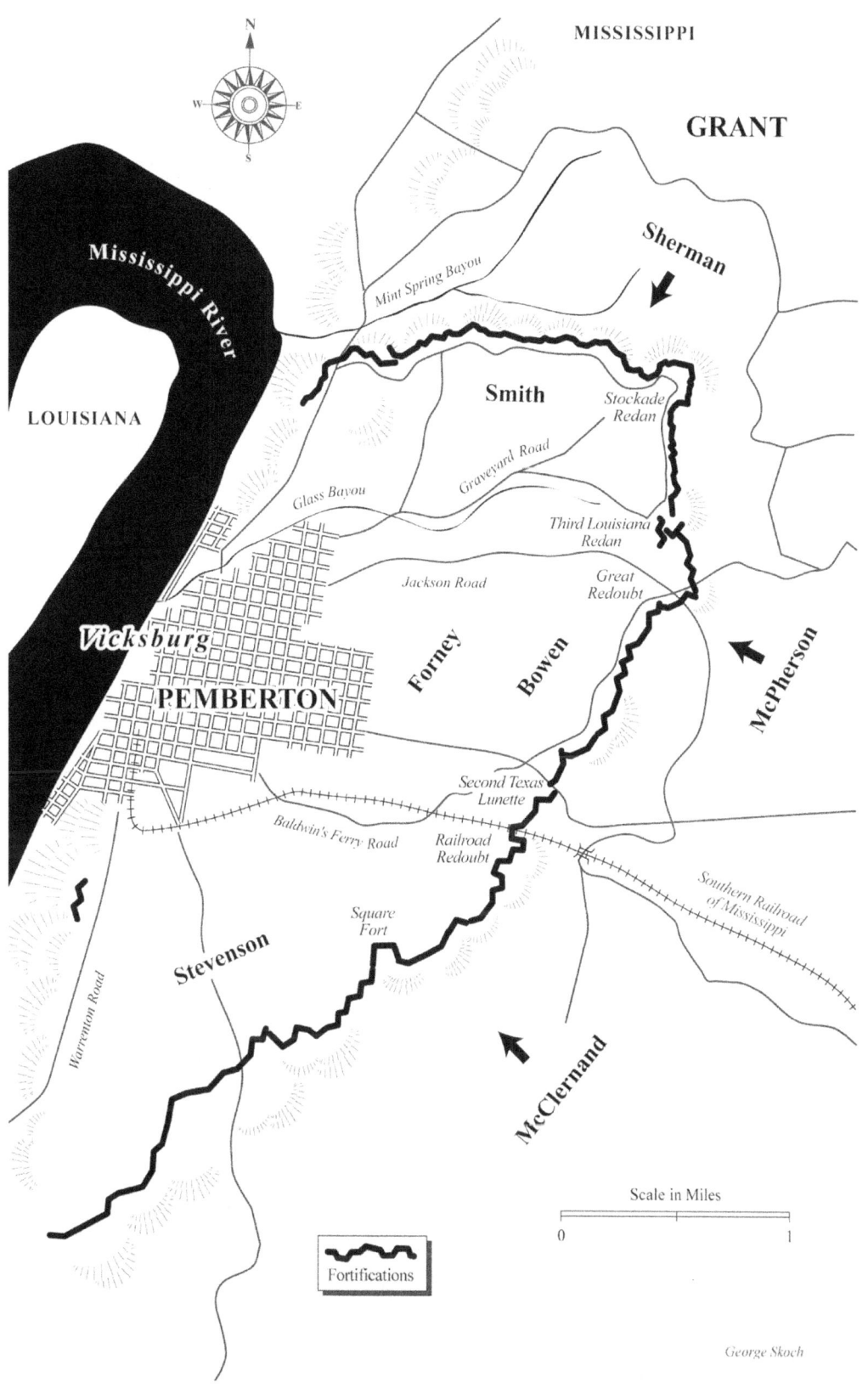

cost Sherman's corps 134 killed, 571 wounded, and 8 missing. Confederate casualties are not known but probably totaled less than 200 on all parts of the line. McPherson's and McClernand's corps, which launched only limited attacks that day, suffered a combined total of 23 killed and 206 wounded."[41]

The attack was repelled by three regiments and a battalion of Brigadier General Louis Hébert's troops. The attack was made in three battle lines, which reached the parapets near the artillery battery along Graveyard Road. Two Union flags were posted near the battery, but they were unable to be placed within the Confederate lines. After dark, the remaining Union soldiers withdrew to their lines. "Three attacks were made. In the first they were driven back; in the second the same result, and in the third they reached the parapet, as stated above. About 50 will cover the losses in front of this position, and perhaps one-fourth of these fatally," reported Confederate Major General John H. Forney of the attacks on May 19, 1863.[42] The attack on May 19 by Grant did not use the concentration of all his forces, but Grant had hoped the Confederate army was still disorganized after its recent defeats. However, the Southern defenders, now protected by the fortifications of Vicksburg, demonstrated their resolve, and repulsed the assault. Sherman's XV Corps did most of the fighting and suffered the majority of the casualties. The 11th Missouri Infantry fortunately missed the assault on the Confederate works at Vicksburg on May 19. The majority of the regiment was near the Black River Bridge, where it was placed in charge of guarding ammunition and artillery that had recently been captured at the battles which had occurred as the army advanced from Jackson to Vicksburg. They were also placed in charge of some prisoners who had been captured during the advance. As the regiment marched toward Vicksburg, they were supplied with 2 pounds of hardtack, ¾ pounds of salt pork, 1 ounce of coffee and 3 ounces of sugar and salt for each day they marched. The regiment reached its division on the northern part of the Union lines on May 21, and the officers and soldiers were informed they would be part of a second, more deliberate assault which was scheduled for the next day. The men of the 11th Missouri soon found the artillery bombardments were common, and those who exposed themselves were targets of the enemy's sharpshooters. It was reported soldiers were wounded as far as 800 yards from the Confederate defenses by sharpshooters and artillery fire.

May 22 Attack on Stockade Redan

The men looked over high hills and deep ravines as they observed the works they were ordered to assault. This had once been an area heavily timbered, but the trees had all been cut down. Anyone attacking the line of forts, parapets, and trenches had to advance across open ground and would be subjected to direct and enfilading fire. The defenses were also protected with artillery so positioned to cause the most damage to any attacking troops.

On May 22, Grant decided to launch a full-scale attack on the Confederate defenses with all three corps participating in the assault. General Grant felt the concentration of his entire force would overwhelm the Confederate defenders. Grant felt he needed to push again and break the defenses because he had a enemy to his front, but he also had General Joe Johnston's troops in his rear. On the northern part of the Union line, Sherman's XV Corps was scheduled to again attack Stockade Redan by way of the Graveyard Road, which was the only practical way to advance against the Confederate fortifications. The attack was ordered to begin at 10:00 A.M. with General Frank Blair' Second Division as the main attacking force. Facing the Union attack from Sherman were three Confederate brigades: Brigadier General Louis Hébert's brigade from Forney's division, Brigadier General Francis A. Shoup's brigade from M. L. Smith's division, and Colonel Francis Cockrell's brigade from Bowen's division.

The defenses around Vicksburg were formidable and included trenches, forts, redans, redoubts, and lunettes. Redans are fortifications with a projection or salient, and a lunette is a more circular, half-moon shaped fortification. The major defenses along the fortified Confederate line included Fort Hill, on a high bluff north of the city; the Stockade Redan, dominating the approach to the city on Graveyard Road from the northeast; the Third Louisiana Redan; the Great Redoubt; the Railroad Redoubt, Fort Garrott; and the South Fort. On the morning of the attack, Union sharpshooters had been placed within range of the Confederate defenses and twenty-seven artillery pieces were sighted onto their targets around Stockade Redan. Then the deadly work began and by the time of the attack, the Confederate artillery had been silenced and the parapet around the Stockade was partially destroyed.

The attack was an optimistic one. The plan called for 150 volunteers, the "Forlorn Hope," to dash forward with ladders to the parapet, and then they would assist those who followed. General Hugh Ewing's Third Brigade (30th Ohio, 37th Ohio, 47th Ohio, Fourth West Virginia) of Blair's division charged four abreast to the point of attack. But the optimistic attack soon became a nightmare of reality as the Confederate defenders "mowed it down. Only a handful of men reached the ditch" in front of the redan. The following regiments scattered around a "cut, which was soon choked with dead, wounded and demoralized men. Blair's attack had been stopped cold."[43] Blair had to improvise a way around his situation if he was to salvage his attack. So he sent another of his brigades into a ravine to attack another point on the Confederate line and he found himself in contact with McPherson's corps. This situation proved to be as impossible as his original one.

The assault on the Confederate works by the 55th Illinois Infantry of Colonel T. Kilby Smith's brigade was described by Lieutenant William Porter, "At 10 A.M. precisely we started, and proceeded rapidly, occupying but three minutes from the ravine to the bastion. Just as we entered the ditch, a captain and a lieutenant from the Sixth Missouri were shot by sharpshooters on our flank, severely wounding both. I immediately assumed command, and, with the colors firmly planted in the parapet by a private of the Eighth Missouri."[44] Porter recorded the most he could do was to prevent the Confederates from capturing their colors and wait for reinforcements. While some other men made it to the ditch in front of the redan, there was nothing that could be accomplished.

However, around 4:00 P.M., Sherman decided to send General James Tuttle's division to try to break the stalemate. Sherman could hear the firing from the assaults of McClernand's and McPherson's corps and it was reported to him that these forces had taken three of the enemy's forts and "that his flags floated on the stronghold of Vicksburg."[45] The anticipation of the second attack of May 22 was described by Sergeant Osborn Oldroyd, Twentieth Ohio Infantry. "The boys were expecting the order and busy divesting themselves of watches, rings, pictures, and other keepsakes, which were being placed in the custody of the cooks, who were not expected to go into action. I never saw such a scene before, nor do I ever want to see it again."[46]

When selecting the regiment to lead the assault on the Stockade Redan, Colonel William L. McMillen recorded, "I heard Gen. Grant direct Gen. Sherman to carry by assault, if it were possible, a strong earthwork commanding one of the approaches to the city, and to send a brigade with his best commander to do the work."[47] Sherman selected Joseph Mower's men to make the attack on Stockade Redan. Prior to the assault on Stockade Redan, General Mower met with General Sherman who pointed to the location of the assault and asked, "General Mower, can you carry those works?" Mower shook his head in a "peculiar way" and answered, "I can try." "Then do it," Sherman replied and the fate of the 11th Missouri Infantry was sealed.[48] Tuttle then met with General Mower and Brigadier General Charles Matthies, commanding

View along the Graveyard Road to the west toward Stockade Redan (Library of Congress).

the Third Brigade, to plan the strategy that would allow Mower's Second Brigade to make the assault and Matthies would support the attack. "The two brigades would advance by the flank down the road, and, as soon as a lodgment had been made, Mower would deploy to the right and Matthies to the left, and hold on till reinforced."[49]

The 11th Missouri Infantry was chosen to lead the brigade in the assault on the Rebel works. Specifically, the regiment was ordered to advance down the Graveyard Road in column formation and attack Stockade Redan. Stockade Redan was the key defensive fortification on the northern part of the Confederate line and was made up of 17-foot high earthen walls and a five-foot ditch at the base. The defenders at Stockade Redan were the 36th Mississippi Infantry of General Louis Hébert's Brigade and the Third Missouri Infantry (CSA) of Colonel Francis Cockrell's Brigade. The 11th Missouri had faced the 36th Mississippi Infantry in the Battle of Iuka in September 1862 and the Third

General Joseph Mower conferred with General Sherman before beginning the charge on Stockade Redan (courtesy Civil War Museum at Wilson's Creek National Battlefield).

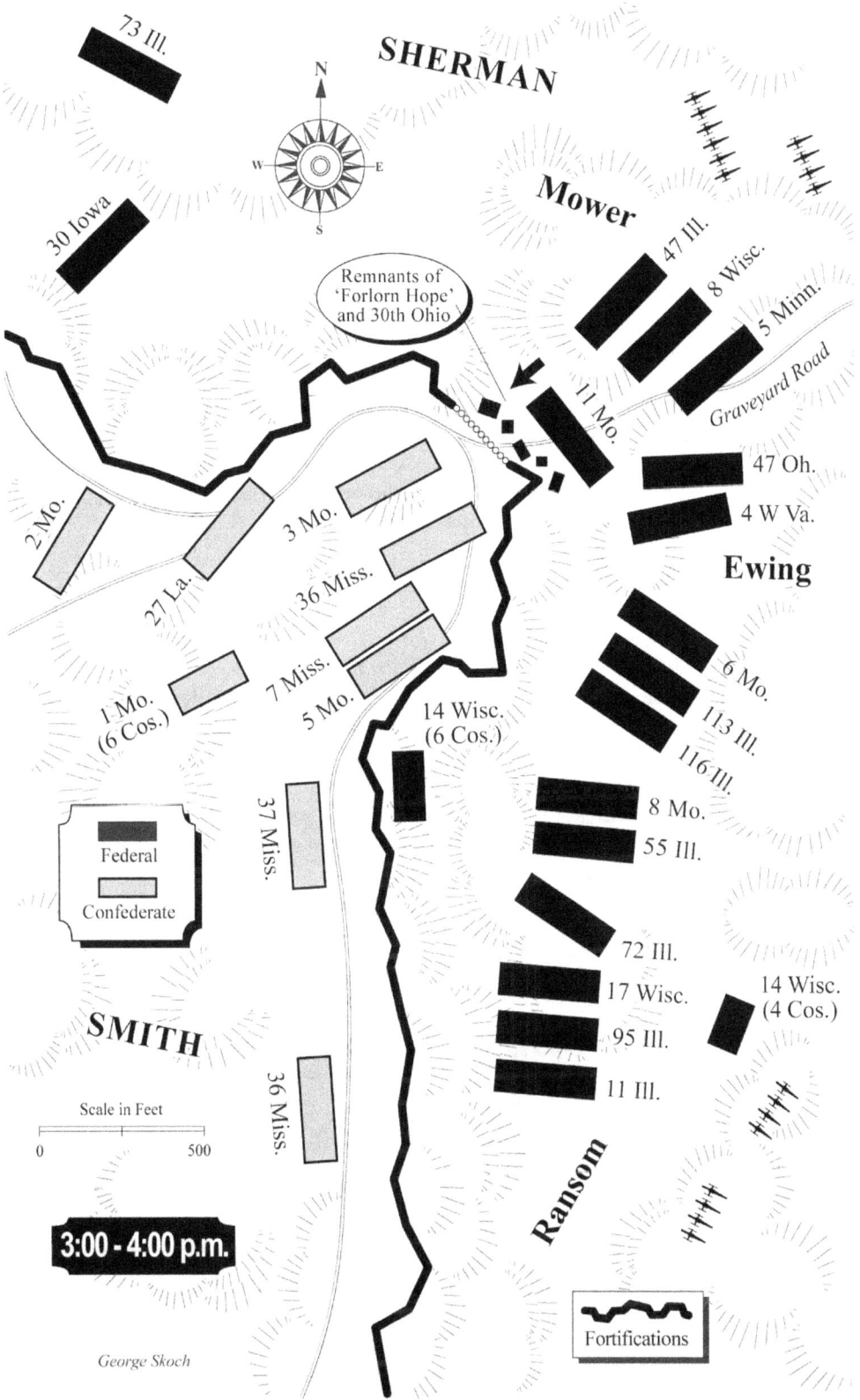

The 11th Missouri Infantry's attack at Stockade Redan, May 1863, 3:00 P.M.

Missouri on the afternoon on October 3 at Corinth. Mower's brigade marched four abreast with the 11th Missouri Infantry in the lead, followed by the 47th Illinois, the Eighth Wisconsin, and finally, the Fifth Minnesota.

At 4:00 P.M., the 11th Missouri Infantry made their assault, yelling as they attacked, but the same wall of musket and artillery fire awaited Mower's brigade that had met the morning's attackers. "The troops approached to within 150 yards of Stockade Redan before they were exposed to the Rebels' fire. The 'Eagle Brigade' soldiers emerged from the cut and met the same fate as the 'forlorn hope' and the two Ohio regiments. Ninety-two soldiers of the Eleventh Missouri and 38 men of the 47th Illinois were cut down. The narrow sunken road became increasingly encumbered with war's grisly harvest."[50] Duncan McCall of the 11th Missouri described the regiment's activities, "We went to double-quick to within three hundred yards, when the rebels opened on us with shot and shell, and their sharpshooters from behind their works were pouring volleys of rifle bullets into our ranks as we advanced. Whole ranks were shot down, either killed or wounded and only 30 reached the works. The colonel of the Eleventh [Andrew J. Weber] led the charge, and reached the outer ditch. While there the rebels threw a hand grenade, which tore off the front of his cap, doing him no other injury. The colors were planted on the outer works by a sergeant of company B."[51] Colonel William R. Gause of the Third Missouri Infantry, CSA, was the source of the grenades. The grenades were 12 pound artillery shells which killed or wounded twenty-two men. After a few had been thrown into the ditch, "the Yanks lobbed three of Gause's grenades back into the redan where they exploded."[52] By 5:00 P.M., Colonel James McCown's Fifth Missouri (CSA) moved into the primary defensive position within Stockade Redan.

Sergeant Joe Browning, Company H, 11th Missouri Infantry recorded the 11th Missouri's travels after leaving Jackson until the regiment advanced to Vicksburg. Browning recorded the attack on Stockade Redan, on "the memorable 22d day of May when the assault was made ... in the lead, started and went into the charge at right shoulder shift, double-quick, in column of regiment, with the enemy pouring an enfilading fire both right and left of the fort, and the larger siege guns pouring grape and canister into us at short range. We never faltered. On to the fort we went, and into the deadly ditch, where we found that there was nothing for us to do but try to keep the enemy from raking us with small artillery until darkness should make it so we could get out of that death trap."[53]

Sergeant Browning also related that Jack Warner was the member of the regiment that climbed the Southern parapet and planted the colors. Browning stated, "How the boys lived through that charge is a mystery to me to this day. We charged in plain view of the enemy, and went thru that cross fire from a strong line of infantry behind breastworks on both sides of that fort, and with grape and canister pouring into us."[54]

Lieutenant Porter of the 55th Illinois described their position where they had remained since mid-morning and now they were joined by the 11th Missouri Infantry. "We remained in this position, exposed to the fire from the flanks of the enemy, and a direct fire from the skirmishers of the First Brigade, till 4:30 P.M., when about 30 of the Eleventh Missouri, with their colonel, major, and 2 lieutenants, succeeded in reaching us with their colors, which they planted alongside of ours. The bearing of the two color-bearers was all that bravery and true courage could do, waving their colors in defiance of enemies and traitors, marching straight and unwavering to the fort through the most murderous fire I ever experienced. The rebels, in trying to dislodge us, commenced to use 12-pounder shells, burning the time and then rolling them into the ditch. We succeeded in throwing back three with our bayonets, which burst on the inside, causing the same effect they intended for us.... At about 7.30 P.M. I received a verbal order from Major-General Blair to fall back, which we did, but not till I had all my wounded safely removed."[55]

Vicksburg historian Edwin Bearss described the assault on Stockade Redan: "Feats of heroism as well as cowardice were common. Colonel Weber, accompanied by a number of stalwart men, reached the ditch, still occupied by survivors of the morning's storming party."[56] Another example of heroism was Lieutenant Menomen O'Donnell, serving as a part of the regimental staff for the 11th Missouri Infantry of May 22, 1863. Lieutenant O'Donnell was a native of Donegal County, Ireland, and was born in 1830. He immigrated to the United States in 1848 and traveled in various locations to make his fortune. By 1851 he had settled in Lawrence County, Illinois. Lieutenant Menomen O'Donnell received the Medal of Honor for his role in exhorting the 11th Missouri forward. He recorded, "The Eleventh Missouri led the advance. The enemy's guns had been booming for some time, but as soon as the Union advance was seen coming over the bluff; the fire seemed to double its former strength and fury. The ground was covered with the dead and wounded, and, not seeing my colors I felt like one lost in the wilderness. I called out: 'Where is the flag of the Eleventh Missouri?' A captain of an Ohio company answered: 'Lieutenant, your flag is over there!' then pointing still farther to the left he said: 'And the head of your regiment is at the fort.' I soon found the flag, and called all of the Eleventh Missouri, within sound of my voice, to come forward to the colors. Only forty-four appeared. I exhorted the boys to follow me to the fort. The color sergeant refused to carry the flag. Just as I was about to reach for it, brave Corporal Warner stepped forward, grabbed the flag, and to the fort it went with us. It was raised, but soon shot down, only to be again put up and floated on the rebel fort until dark. Twenty-four of the forty-four got to the fort. After arriving there we could do nothing but sit with our backs to the wall until darkness came, when under cover of the night, we finally got out and safely returned to camp."[57]

Another type of action may have doomed the attack to failure when Captain John T. Bowen, 47th Illinois, fled before the attack. Sergeant John Watts, Company A, of the 47th Illinois tried to rally his company. "Waving his hat and shouting encouragement, Watts succeeded in rallying the badly shaken company. But the damage had been done. Within less than a minute, the road cut became so jammed with soldiers that it was impossible for the regiments to the rear of the 47th Illinois to advance any farther."[58] Only the 11th Missouri and part of the 47th Illinois attacked Stockade Redan with over two-thirds of the brigade not participating. Mower sent a messenger to Sherman to explain the situation and both Mower and Sherman knew that the attack had failed. Sherman was quoted as saying, "This is murder; order those troops back."[59]

The records of Company I reported that Corporal Jack Warner carried the regimental flag through a "terrible storm of musketry, shell, & grape and canister" and mounted the parapet and waved the "Flag over the work. Also planting the flag in the embankment and leaving it floating until after dark."[60] Sergeant George Adams, Company I, recorded, "Eleventh in the lead and that brought Co. I in front for we moved by the right flank. We (Co. I and 3 other Cos) reached the fort, could not scale it, so we had to lay under the fort until dark."[61]

Captain Alonzo D. Hickok, of the Eighth Wisconsin Infantry, recalled that his regiment also planned to assault the Rebel works at Stockade Redan. The regiment began its charge by proceeding along a wagon road at the double-quick by flank, but they were "corralled" along some Confederate works where they also spent the rest of the day. Hickok reported, "We were on the side for glory. I attribute our failure to two causes: First, I think the entire brigade went by flank, not in line of battle; second, it was impossible to climb that steep, high bank of earth at the place we made our attack."[62]

The assault from the Confederate side of the line must have been magnificent and terrible as described by Colonel Francis Cockrell. "This assault was preceded by a most furious fire from the enemy's numerous batteries, of shell, grape and canister. The air was literally burdened with hissing missiles of death.... Nobly did the officers and soldiers of this brigade greet every

The attack at Vicksburg (Library of Congress).

assault of the enemy with defiant shouts and a deliberately aimed fire, and hurled them back in disorder. The enemy gained the ditch around the redan to the right of the stockade and occupied it for some time. Colonel Gause, of the Third Missouri Infantry, procured some fuse-shells, and, using them as hand-grenades, threw them into the ditch, where they exploded, killing and wounding some 22 of the enemy."[63] Cockrell reported that his brigade lost 28 men killed and 98 wounded with the Third Missouri Infantry suffering the greatest losses.

Sherman had felt his corps should be able to penetrate the Southern defenses. General Frank Blair said of the charge of the 11th Missouri Infantry, "Once again, the lead regiment was shot down upon exiting the road cut, and the follow-on troops again broke ranks and sought cover."[64] General Blair, whose division made the assaults against the Confederates on May 19 and May 22, recorded the futility and courage of the 11th Missouri Infantry in a report of the battle, "The active operations of the day were closed by an impetuous assault of the brigade of General Mower, of General Tuttle's

Colonel Francis Cockrell commanded the Confederate defenders at Stockade Redan on May 22 (Library of Congress).

The attack at Vicksburg (Library of Congress).

division, in your army corps, which rushed forward by the flank on the same road which had been attempted in the morning by the brigade of General H. Ewing. The attack was made with the greatest bravery and impetuosity, and was covered by a tremendous fire from our batteries, and by the sharpshooters of Ewing's and Giles A. Smith's brigades, and its failure only served to prove that it is impossible to carry this position by storm."[65]

Sherman recorded, "General Mower carried his brigade up bravely and well, but again arose a fire more severe, if possible, than that of the first assault, with exactly a similar result. The colors of the leading regiment, the Eleventh Missouri, were planted by the side of that of Blair's storming party, and remained there till withdrawn after nightfall by my orders."[66] Sherman's reason for the assault at 4:00 P.M. was an attempt to match the success of McClernand's and McPherson's corps, but the attack was for naught, as Sherman reported, "McClernand's report of success must have been premature, for I subsequently learned that both his and McPherson's assaults had failed to break through the enemy's line of intrenchments, and were equally unsuccessful as my own."[67]

The fighting reputation of Joseph Mower and his men resulted in their selection to make the assault on May 22. Cloyd Bryner, author of the history of the 47th Illinois, recalled a quote from General Sherman: "Our corps must be first in the breach; Mower will take the advance, a splendid tribute to the 'Eagle Brigade.' a fearful price for renown."[68] The 11th Missouri Infantry paid the price for their attack on Stockade Redan, which tore the heart out of the regiment with greater than 30 percent casualties in this forlorn assault. Duncan McCall wrote, "It was terrible day, for the regiment was exposed to a heavy fire, and fell back with a great loss without accomplishing anything."[69] The following is the list of soldiers killed and wounded in the assault:

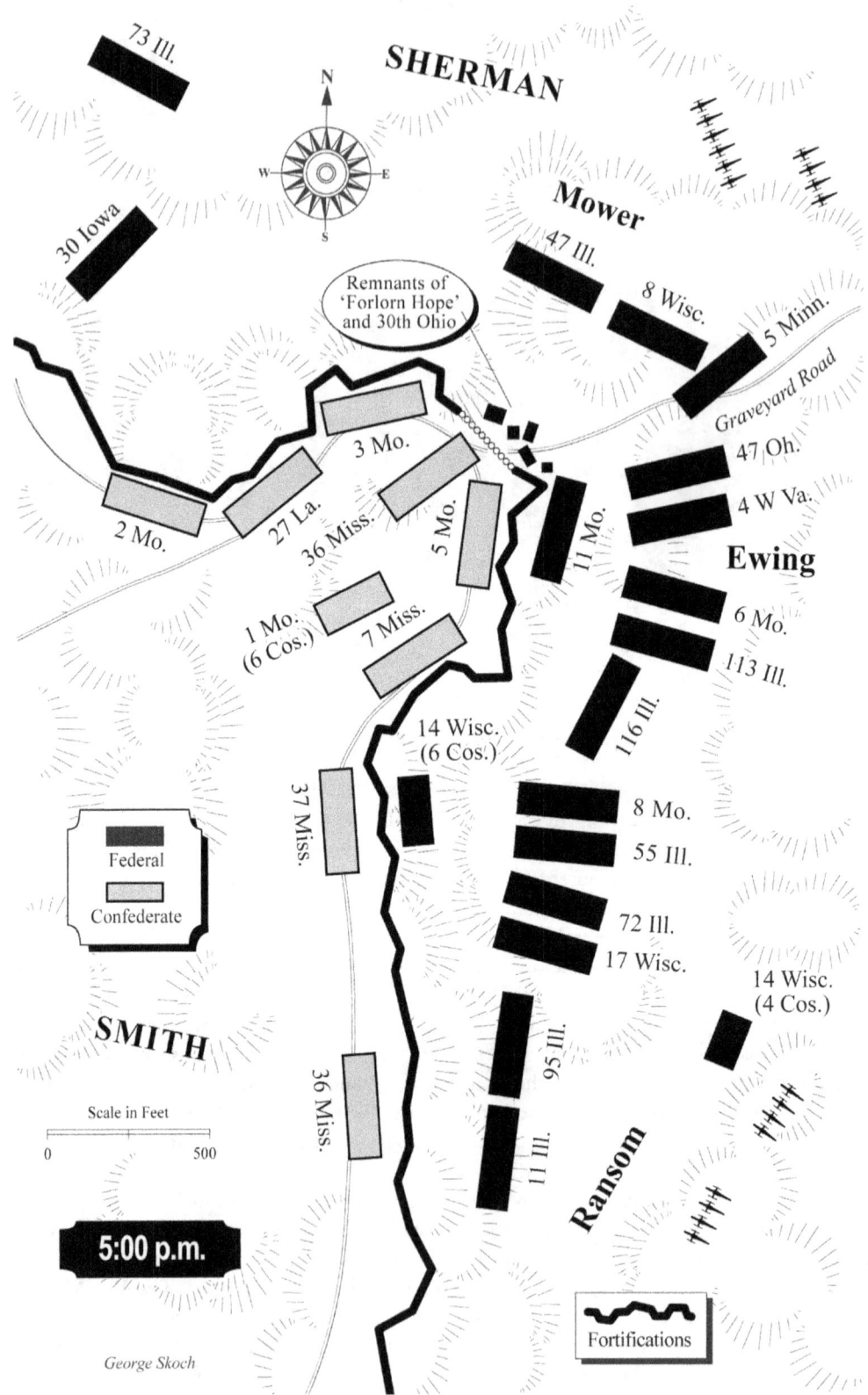

The 11th Missouri Infantry's attack at Stockade Redan, May 1863, 5:00 P.M.

Tabular Statement of Wounded in the Hospital 3rd Division 15th AC Dept. of the Tennessee on May 22, 1863[70]

Regimental Staff
Charles Brookings	Adjt.	Abdomen	Minié—Died

Company A
Whitney Clark	Corp.	Left thigh fracture	Minié—Died
John Corrie	Sgt.	Left arm near shoulder	Minié—Died
John Gould	Pvt.	Left Shoulder Severe	Minié
Samuel Heath	Pvt.	Back Severe	Minié—Died
William McGuire	Pvt.	Left Arm Slight	Minié
Constantine McMahan	Capt.	Right hand, thigh severely	Minié
Robert Myers	Pvt.	Both ankles, left knee Severe	Minié—Died
George Richards	Pvt.	KIA	
Daniel Sands	Pvt.	Thigh Severely	Minié—Died
Dennis Ward	Pvt.	KIA	
Clark, Whitney	Sgt.	Thigh Severely	Minié—Died
Aaron Williams	Pvt.	Left breast severe	Minié

Company B
William Davidson	Pvt.	Left Shoulder Flesh	Minié

Company C
Andrew Eagan	Pvt.	Head Slight	Minié
Smith Hinman	Pvt.	Finger Slight	Minié
Joseph Jones	Corp.	Left hand severe	Minié

Company D
William Erwin	Pvt.	Left leg	Minié
Dios Hagel	Pvt.	Head Slight	Shell
John Pridemore	Pvt.	Right Hip severe	Minié
Isaac Reeves	Pvt.	Right arm—amputation	Minié
Christopher Struckenschneider	Pvt.	Right Knee/Left foot Sev.	Minié—Died

Company E
John Baird	Sgt.	Hip, Shoulder Severe	Minié
Francis Behmeyer	Pvt.	Back (flesh) Severe	Minié
William Burgess	Pvt.	Right leg slight	Minié—Died
William Couch	Pvt.	Right Hand severe	Minié
Jacob Eppley	Pvt.	Arm and Breast Severe	Minié—Died
Geo W. Gaddy	Corp.	Neck Slight	Minié
Elijah Harmon	Pvt.	Lower Maxillary Severe	Minié—Died
Alonzo George W. Thomas	Corp.	Back and left leg severe	Minié—Died

Company F
Thomas D. Bayles	Pvt.	Left Thigh-flesh	Minié—Died
James Cunningham	Pvt.	KIA	
William McCleland	Capt.	Left thigh bone injured	Minié
Rueben Pettyjohn	Pvt.	KIA	
Cyrus Vickery	Pvt.	Right Cheek Severe	Minié
Lorenzo Winchester	Pvt.	Right Leg Flesh Wound	Minié

Company G
William Akin	Sgt.	Concussion	Shell
Miles Bishop	Pvt.	Hip, left arm severe	Minié—Died

Allen Dubois	Pvt.	Left leg	Minié
Augustus Grey	Sgt.	Face and shoulder Severe	Minié—Died
George Lehr (3rd wound)	Corp.	Right Ankle- amputated l leg	Minié
William Miles	Corp.	Left Foot Severe	Minié
Cyrus Miller	Sgt.	Finger Severely	Minié
General Pickrell	Pvt.	Finger Severe	Minié
William Thompson	Pvt.	Right thigh Severe	Minié

Company H

William Anderson	Drummer	Left Elbow(Flesh)	Minié
Samuel Daniels	Pvt.	Left Elbow (Fract.)	Minié
Lewis N Grey	1st Lt.	Right arm with bones Severe	Minié
John Irwin	Sgt.	Left eye Severe	Minié—Died
Jacob Johnson	Pvt.	Neck slight	Minié
John Mills	Pvt.		Minié—Died
Solomon Moler	Pvt.	Right Leg SevereShell—Died	
John Moran	Pvt.	Breast Severe	Minié—Died
William Ridgeley	Corp.	Right arm, Severely	Minié
D W Setchel	Sgt.	KIA	

Company I

Sam Beauchamp	Pvt.	Right thigh, flesh wounds	Minié
George Detrich	Pvt.	Shoulder Joint Severe	Minié
John Floyd	Pvt.	Right thigh, left hip, hand Sev	Minié—Died
James Hathorn	Pvt.	KIA	
William Jackson	Pvt.	KIA	
Stephen McPherson	Corp.	Left Shoulder (Flesh)	Minié
Cyrus Spicer	Sgt.	Left Groin Severe	Minié—Died
Josiah Sullins	Pvt.	Right Breast Left thigh Sev	Minié—Died
John Wyatt	Pvt.	Abdomen Severe	Minié—Died

Company K

James Johnson	Pvt.	Knee Flesh Wound	Minié
Harrison Twitty	Pvt.	Finger Left-hand Severe	Minié
Thaddeus Warner	Sgt.	Foot Slight	Minié

Compiled Service Record Additions of Casualties in the Vicksburg Campaign

James Brewer	Pvt.	G	Fingers	Severely
George Butler	Pvt.	E	Side	Slightly
James Cummins	Pvt.	G		KIA
W. W. Daniels	Pvt.	H		KIA
Walton W Finch	Sgt.	F	Leg	Slightly
Francis Hartman	Corp.	I	Head	Slightly
G. W. Lytle	Pvt.	E	Shoulder	Slightly
Horace M Malone	Pvt.	A	Toe	Slightly
William Daniels	Pvt.	H	Captured	
William Marion	Corp.	I	Leg	Severely
David O. Shoopman	Corp.	I	Thigh	Slightly
J. B. Severans	Sgt.	A	Leg	Slightly
John Seymour	Pvt.	E	Leg	Slightly

Based on the regimental morning reports, approximately 300 men of the 11th Missouri made the assault on Stockade Redan. The official losses for the 11th Missouri Infantry were seven killed and eighty-five wounded in this late assault on May 22. However, regimental records showed that many of the men who were wounded and removed to hospitals ultimately died. The final toll showed that 30 men died in the campaign against the Confederate forces at Vicksburg. Dr. Thomas Hawley described some of the carnage of the battlefields near Vicksburg. Hawley lamented he was so near the battle and stated the unpleasantness of having "to linger or live near the scent of bloody carnage where the ground is saturated with the life current of our fellow men, every hill is a cemetery and every gully becomes a receptacle of vigorous manhood but there limbs devoid of flesh refused a covering of mother earth protrude as if they were fair for monuments of fallen heroes who died victims to a false idea."[71]

Sherman's XV Corps lost 150 killed, 666 wounded and 42 missing on May 22. The wounded remained on the field of battle until May 25, when a cease-fire was declared to retrieve the wounded.

Corporal Joseph Jones, Company C, was severely wounded in the assault at Vicksburg and was discharged as a result (Abraham Presidential Library & Museum).

The advantage of the Confederate works was evident in the final tally. Grant's army lost approximately 3,200 men killed, wounded and missing to Pemberton's 500.

Return of Casualties in the Union Forces in the Assault on Vicksburg, May 22, 1863
Second Brigade Losses — Brigadier General Joseph Mower

	KILLED	WOUNDED	MISSING
47th Illinois	5	33	0
5th Minnesota	2	1	7
11th Missouri	7	85	0
8th Wisconsin	3	17	22
Total Second Brigade	17	136	29

After the attack on May 22, Pemberton still controlled the field to his front where the Union attack occurred. The gruesome fact was that the Union dead lay on the field of battle since the first assault on May 19, and it wasn't until May 25 that a truce allowed the dead to be removed from the field. The truce lasted for two and a half hours, during which time the combatants mingled with one another as if the life-and-death struggle hadn't occurred days before. After the burial details had accomplished their tasks, the blue and gray clad soldiers assumed their previous position within their respective lines.

Lieutenant Charles H. Brookings, regimental adjutant since the beginning of the war, was among the men killed in the 11th Missouri Infantry in its assault on May 22. Brookings, who began his military career as a captain in the 12th Illinois Infantry, was respected by the regiment, and the following statement was drafted to show the high esteem in which he was held: "Whereas in the sad events of war, we the officers of the Eleventh Mo Infty Vols. have been separated from our fellow officer Charles H. Brookings Adjutant of this Regiment by his untimely death occasioned from a wound inflicted by the enemy on the 22nd of May 1863 near the works of the rebels at Vicksburg and where as we are ever caused to remember the brave dead who have fallen.... Resolved That in the untimely death of our brave gallant officer Adjutant Charles H. Brookings we feel a deep grief while we find his place unfilled by his missing form in our columns and in whose death the Union has lost a true and gallant defender. Resolved That we deeply sympathize with his family and friends, that one of such faith & ability should so soon fall a martyr to the cause of his country to which he was most ardently devoted."[72]

On May 30, Regimental Surgeon, Dr. Thomas Hawley, was stationed at a hospital near Champion Hill. He described the situation of the siege, "As the sun grandly marches toward the zenith other sounds come booming to us ... proclaiming that the beleagured citadel still holds out with some resistance and that the outside forces are hailing iron and lead into their stronghold. It has been one continued roar since sun up and we are 20 miles from the army. Genl Grant has been mining and last night some say they heard a terrifick explosion which was supposed to the explosion of the mine. Then there would be a breach in their works and our forces could perhaps effect an entrance which was probably the cause of the heavy firing."[73] The siege of Vicksburg carried on.

Mechanicsburg, Mississippi, Expeditions

While Vicksburg remained under siege, the threat from Johnston's army was ever present. Johnston had a significant number of men, about 31,000, that threatened Grant's plans to capture Vicksburg. By late May, reconnaissance had estimated 6,000–10,000 Confederates

Assistant Surgeon Dr. Thomas Hawley's sketch of his living quarters during the Vicksburg Campaign (Missouri History Museum, St. Louis).

were poised at Mechanicsburg, Mississippi; and Grant needed to deal with this threat. He accomplished this by detailing a force of 12,000 men, commanded by Major General Francis Blair, to Mechanicsburg. The force was scheduled to include three brigades from each the XV and XVII Corps. Blair decided to split the force into two divisions, commanded by Brigadier General Joseph Mower and Brigadier General John McArthur. The troops were issued seven days rations and began their march. The divisions began marching independently and united their forces on May 28 in Sulfur Springs, Mississippi. Blair's cavalry discovered a disturbing rumor that "Lt. Gen. Ambrose P. Hill just reached Jackson with heavy reinforcements from the battle-hardened Army of Northern Virginia."[74] Even though the rumor was false, Blair thought he could now be facing 45,000 Confederates; however, Blair cautiously continued his march toward Mechanicsburg. The 11th Missouri, as part of Mower's Division, marched along, but it did not participate in any action with the enemy.

On May 28, the Union cavalry encountered Confederate Brigadier General John Adams' troops east of Mechanicsburg. General Adams threw his troops against the Union cavalry forcing the Federal cavalry back to Mechanicsburg; however, Adams was greatly outnumbered. As the Union infantry advanced, Adams disengaged his men and moved back east of the Big Black River. Grant, fearing that Blair would be destroyed by a superior Confederate force, urged him to disengage and return to Vicksburg. By May 30, the Union troops were marching back to Vicksburg, and as they marched back to the west, "a horde of blacks, at least, as numerous as Blair's force, deserted their masters and flocked along behind the column."[75] The march back to Haynes' Bluff on May 31 effectively ended the first expedition to Mechanicsburg, Mississippi.

A second Mechanicsburg expedition began for the 11th Missouri Infantry on June 3 as part of Brigadier General Nathan Kimball's force. General Mower moved his troops from their camp at Haynes' Bluff early on June 4. The expedition was designed to destroy the Way's Bluff railroad bridge which the Union forces had tried and failed to destroy on two previous attempts. The expedition utilized the Union navy to transport the infantry, including the 11th Missouri, and the cavalry to Satartia along the Yazoo River. Then these troops headed east to occupy Mechanicsburg. Mower's brigade disembarked at Satartia on June 4. The Eighth Wisconsin Infantry led the way for the brigade and skirmished throughout the afternoon with Confederate cavalry. The brigade was involved in combat with Confederate cavalry near Mechanicsburg, Mississippi, about 25 miles north and east of Vicksburg. Duncan McCall recalled, "Mechanicsburg was a small town with a few old houses in it, doing no business of importance. Everything appeared desolate and forsaken."[76] The only regiment involved in the skirmish was the Eighth Wisconsin. Upon reaching Mechanicsburg, the Confederate cavalry *en mass* moved to support a battery of artillery. This tactic delayed the Union advance, and on the next day the advance began again and Adams withdrew. However, again the threat of an attack from a superior Confederate force resulted in the Union troops withdrawing back to Vicksburg. The return march was very difficult due to the extremely hot conditions resulting in several cases of heatstroke. The soldiers of the regiment felt that the heat was so bad that marching was unendurable. The 11th Missouri, still reeling from the assault on Vicksburg, lost several men on the march near Mechanicsburg due to straggling and some were left behind. The Confederate cavalry quickly gobbled up anyone who was vulnerable. The 11th Missouri Infantry was the rear guard as the brigade marched from Mechanicsburg to Satartia and then to Haynes' Bluff. Duncan McCall recalled, "All cotton was burned during this march, also some corn and a few houses. One very fine house, occupied by a rebel, was destroyed. Everything of value was taken, because he aided in capturing some of our boys by making signals to a party of bushwhackers."[77]

The regimental records revealed that at least three men from the 11th Missouri were taken prisoner during the actions after the attack on Vicksburg.

George Gaddy	Company A	June 2, 1863
Samuel Leinhart	Company C	May 31, 1863
James Tooley	Company D	May 30, 1863

Action West of Vicksburg

In June, another Confederate threat developed in regard to Confederate forces from the Trans-Mississippi Department. This threat was being made against the Union troops in northeast Louisiana under the command of General Elias Dennis headquartered in Young's Point, Louisiana. The Confederate threat was from Major General John Walker's division, and when General Grant became aware of Walker's proximity to Vicksburg, he dispatched General Joseph Mower's brigade to assist in dealing with Walker's Confederates. Union reconnaissance discovered a concentration of Confederate troops at Richmond, Louisiana. Admiral David Porter and General Mower developed a joint army-navy plan to deal with Walker's Confederates there.

Union Brigadier General Alfred Ellet's Mississippi Marine Brigade joined Mower's Eagle Brigade on June 15, as they united their forces at Lum's Depot and advanced on Richmond, Louisiana. Discovering the Union advance and feeling he was outnumbered, Confederate General John Walker began withdrawing his forces, but he posted Lieutenant Colonel D. B. Culberson's 18th Texas Infantry to delay the Union advance. Ellet's Marine Brigade encountered the 18th Texas first and Mower rushed to his support. Mower detailed the Fifth Minnesota as skirmishers. As the Minnesotans advanced, they were surprised by a volley from the 18th Texas. The Confederates were reported to have been entrenched and were thought to be present in force. The 11th Missouri was moved into line with the other regiments of the brigade and advanced. Once the regiment pushed through a line of trees, the men observed the enemy retreating. The Union battle line soon advanced and the 18th Texas retreated. Walker withdrew his troops and the Union cavalry pursued the retreating Confederates for six miles. The Union troops burned Richmond before leaving.

Prisoners reported there were as many as 7,000 men threatening this position, although it was likely less than 2,000 men were in Walker's division. After the action against Walker at Richmond, the 11th Missouri with the other regiments of their brigade moved to Young's Point, Louisiana. Although the 11th Missouri had intended to return to Haynes' Bluff, rumors circulated that Pemberton intended to escape Vicksburg by using a flotilla of small boats. Grant felt he needed to keep Mower on the western side of the Mississippi River to prevent further threats from the Trans-Mississippi Confederates and to prevent any attempted escapes from Vicksburg. The 11th Missouri remained there until the surrender of the Vicksburg on July 4. Then the regiment moved to Big Black River Bridge east of Vicksburg by railroad on July 5.

Sergeant William Notestine wrote a letter to his family on June 12 about efforts and results of the Vicksburg campaign of the 11th Missouri. "The campaign is one extraordinary interest and also of unparalleled hardship.... The dust was suffocating and the heat was intolerable. We also had to do on half rations until the evacuation of Haines Bluff. Yet in compensation for all this we expect a great & glorius victory. We willingly endure the many privations of the campaign life when a great deal can be accomplished. Our Brigade which is the 2nd Brigade of Tuttle's Division & Sherman's Army Corps has been detached since the 23rd of May and we have had more than our share of marching. The Brid is wore out and run down and we were sent here for rest and to protect this side of the river which was threatened a few days ago. They had quite a fight up at Miliken Bend and a negro regiment saved the day driving off the rebles with great slaughter and saving our camp."[78]

Dr. Thomas Hawley, while looking over the morning reports, reflected on the situation of the regiment. "I was looking over one of the company reports books and find it numbered just over one year ago, 84 ... now 17." Hawley continued to reflect on his condition and the condition of the men in the regiment, "I am not sick, but emaciated from defective nutrition and want of proper diet."[79]

While assigned on the western side of the Mississippi River, the 11th Missouri Infantry observed magnificent artillery duels between the Union siege guns, including a 100-pound Parrot, and the defensives guns at Vicksburg. The regiment was involved in sharpshooting the Confederate artillerymen. A significant event occurred on June 29 for the 11th Missouri Infantry. The regiment was not destined to be commanded by a colonel for a long period of time throughout the Civil War. The regiment's first colonel was the David Bayles, followed by Joseph Plummer, Joseph Mower, and most recently by the much respected Andrew Weber. On June 29, the Confederates began shelling the regiment as it served as a guard for the brigade supplies and a shell fragment struck Colonel Andrew Weber in the head. It was thought that he had a concussion as a result of the wound, but Weber died on the morning of June 30. The medical report stated Colonel Weber died of compression of the brain. This was the final blow to a costly campaign for the regiment. Duncan McCall wrote of Andrew Weber, "He filled every place with honor to himself and with the esteem and friendship of his brother officers; a sober officer, taking pride in seeing his men appear well, the first to face danger; always kind and obliging, and never resorting to extreme measures, he won the good will of his men, who would follow him wherever he saw fit to lead them."[80] General Mower wrote of Colonel Weber, "Never demurring, for himself, he was ever on the alert for the welfare of those under his command. In battle, he was cool & watchful, prompt & brave whether in camp or in the field, he was an encouraging illustration of the fact that a good soldier may be an exemplary man. In years so young, he has left behind him for our imitation a distinguished example of patriotism, gallantry, unswerving integrity & unsullied honor."[81] Weber's remains were sent home, accompanied by his brother, George Weber, on July 2.

Siege of Vicksburg

Meanwhile, on the east side of the Mississippi River, the siege continued. After the repulse of the May 22 attack, Grant decided to classically lay siege to Vicksburg that lasted six weeks. Grant's forces dug trenches to face the Confederates trenches and siege batteries were established to shell Confederate strong points. Even the Union navy added its guns to the bombardment after May 22.

Although Pemberton held a very strong position in Vicksburg, once inside the defenses, he was in a position that only General Joe Johnston could relieve the siege; and Johnston did not have the forces to do that. As time passed, those besieged men began to realize that Johnston could not break the siege. Hunger and sickness became common. Diseases such as dysentery, diarrhea, malaria and other ailments were also common. As men died they were carried by wagons daily to the cemetery on the northeastern part of the city. Pemberton was forced to cut food and water rations as the siege continued, and by the end of June the defending Confederate soldiers lived on "only a handful of peas and rice per day."[82] Despite their closeness to the Mississippi River, water was also rationed.

Grant was not idle with his army as it was entrenched opposite Pemberton's works. Grant began digging his trenches to be in proximity to the Confederate lines, and in some cases, the trenches were only 100 yards away from the enemy. Grant made a desperate attempt to breach the Confederate line on June 25, when his men placed 2,200 pounds of black powder near the Confederate line and exploded this mine. Regiment after regiment assailed the Confederate defenders; but 26 hours later the battle was over and the Confederates had stopped this assault. Grant had another mine detonated on July 1, but it was not followed with an infantry assault. Within Vicksburg morale was low, and it was suspected that Grant would again attack the city on July 4. It was feared the defenders would not be able to stand another intense attack so Pemberton surrendered on July 4, 1863. Grant agreed to parole the entire garrison at Vicksburg. Soon after the fall of Vicksburg, the last remaining Confederate outpost on the Mississippi River, Port Hudson, surrendered to General Nathaniel Banks; and finally the Mississippi River was unencumbered from its source to New Orleans. Vicksburg was defeated and the Mississippi River was under complete control of the Union forces. It was during the final days of Siege of Vicksburg that another great battle was fought in Gettysburg, Pennsylvania, resulting in a Union victory.

Dr. Thomas Hawley reported the fall of Vicksburg in a letter from Young's Point, Louisiana, on July 5, "Glad tidings of great joy to you and all.... Yesterday, the 88th anniversary of our grand nation's birth has been doubly consecrated by the fall of the rebel forlorn hope, the last stronghold of the so called southern Confederacy, Vicksburg, the Great, the Mighty, has indeed fallen as I myself can bear testimony."[83]

The cost of the Siege of Vicksburg to the 11th Missouri Infantry was immeasurable. The regiment had suffered greatly, and still soldiers of the regiment struggled for their lives. Corporal Alonzo Thomas, company E, was wounded on May 22, 1863, during the failed assault on Stockade Redan and remained in the hospital during June. Private Thomas wrote to his father on June 21, 1863, about his recuperation, "My wounds are not doing quite so well as when I wrote before. The Dr in the ward I was in said that erysipelas was setting in and felt quite uneasy but it proved not to be erysipelas but matter forming just over the shin bone and it had to be lanced and it discharges a great deal that in connection with a slight fever weakens me very fast

Along the Big Black River, Mississippi, where the 11th Missouri was stationed after the Siege of Vicksburg (Library of Congress).

and then I have little appetite. I hope that I will take a turn for the better soon. I shall keep in as good spirits as possible and shall try to come home as I get able."[84] Corporal Thomas died on June 27, 1863.

Maybe the best summary for Vicksburg campaign stated: "For over forty days the brigade had been marching almost without rations, but living well by foraging; had bivouacked without tents; had been without change of clothing, many of the men shoeless; had tramped in the mud, forded streams, fought desperate battles and skirmished almost daily, and no man had been heard to utter a word of complaint. These were men of iron."[85]

11th Missouri Regimental Losses January 1, 1863 – June 30, 1863

	JANUARY–FEB–MARCH	APRIL	MAY	JUNE
Discharged	Bishop, Elisha (A)	Wade, Archibald Corp. (B)	Workman, Peter (C)	
	Newell, John A. (A)	Ross, Charles (B)	Reeves, Isaac (D)	
	Ell, Preston (B)	Hornsey, John (C)	Blackledge, Theodore (F)	
	Callaway, James (B)	Warden, Thomas (D)		
	Hall, Marion (B)	Eckey, William M. Corp (E)		
	Turner, Sylvester (B)	Fyffe, James A. Corp (G)		
	Crosman, Peter Sgt. (C)	Rivers, Joseph Corp (G)		
	Haas, William (C)	Henry, David Sgt. (H)		
	Martin, Robert (C)			
	Eaton, William S. (D)	Cunningham, James (F)		
	Friend, Samuel (D)			
	Hungate, John H. (D)			
	Beard, John (F)			
	Eckley, Alvin Corp (E)			
	Herrington, Zachariah (E)			
	Ogan, Joseph M. (E)			
	Wilkenson, Henry (E)			
	Lawson, John P. Sgt. (E)			
	Doyle, William (F)			
	Anderson, James (B)			
	Berkshire, Samuel (G)			
	Lewis, Franklin (G)			
	Mumpower, John (G)			
	Thompson, Alfred (G)			
	White, Silas (G)			
	McPherson, Anson Musician (I)			

	January–Feb–March	April	May	June
Died	McKinney, William (I)			
	Millstead, James M. (I)			
	Smith, Richard P. (I)			
	Campbell, Richard (K)			
	Pursley, Martin Corp (K)			
	Richie, William Corp (K)			
	Wade, James Corp. (K)			
	Buchanan, John (A)			
	Graham, John			
	Hanna, Joseph (B)			
	Seymour, Mortimer (E)		Clark, Whitney Corp (A)	Myers, Robert (A)
	Haines, James (B)		Corrie, John Sgt. (A)	Sands, Daniel Musician (A)
	Page, Eugene (B)		Cunningham, James (G)	Heath, Samuel (A)
	Plummer, Riel (A)		Harmon, Elijah (E)	Gray, Augustus Sgt. (G)
			Hathorn, James (I)	Spicer, Cyrus Sgt. (I)
	Collins, John (G)		Jackson, William (I)	Sullins, Josiah (I)
	Campbell, Anderson (K)		Pettyjohn, Reuben (F)	Mills, John (H)
	Price, Edward (K)		Richards, George (A)	Clark, Francis (A)
	Powell, Caleb (F)		Setchel, D. W. Sgt. (H)	Thomas, Alonzo Corp. (E)
	McGuire, John (C)		Ward, Dennis (A)	Floyd, John (I)
	Sutherland, William (F)		Wyatt, John Wagoner (I)	
			Irwin/Irvin, John Sgt. (H)	Underwood, John/James (A)
			Powell, John (F)	Johns, Alton (K)
			Eppley, Jacob (E)	
			Moran, John (H)	
			Bristo, Thomas (I)	
			Bishop, Miles (G)	
			Brookings, Charles Lt. (F&S)	
			Daniels, William (H)	
			Weber, A. J. Col. (F&S)	
Deserted	Bingham, John (C)	Dunning, Henry C. Sgt. (C)	Kellogg, Albert B. (C)	Andrews, William (C)
	Calmie, Taylor (C)	Dosing, John (C)	Caufield, Miner Corp. (F)	
	Capps, Thomas J. (C)			
	Cullin, John (C)			
	Davis, James (D)			

	January–Feb–March	April	May	June
	McCarty, Michael (D)			
	Owsley, Henry (D)			
	Smith, Thomas J. (F)			
	Gentle, William S. (F)			
Transferred Out	Hopper, Charles B. (E)			
	Holman, Gilbert (F)			
Resigned	Warner, Moses Capt. (C)			Kingsbury, Harley 2nd Lt. (H)
	Baldridge, Samuel Chaplain			

CHAPTER 6

End of the 11th Missouri and Reorganization

"We want a peace that will stand forever and ever."
— Sergeant Charles Treadway

After the Vicksburg Campaign was completed, the 11th Missouri Infantry was no longer the fighting regiment it had been before May 22. The unit had had key roles in Fredericktown, Point Pleasant, Iuka, Corinth, Jackson, and finally Vicksburg. In these engagements the regiment had always been the key regiment in the brigade and had always been chosen as the regiment that would lead the fight. It became apparent immediately after the Vicksburg attack on May 22 that, due to the loss of so many of their soldiers, other regiments should be placed in the primary position to engage the enemy. With the loss of Colonel Andrew J. Weber, regimental command passed to Lieutenant Colonel William Barnum. The 34-year-old William Barnum was elected as the captain of Company I as the regiment was formed in the fall of 1861. In May 1863, Barnum had been promoted to the rank of lieutenant colonel. William Barnum was a married attorney and merchant living in Springfield, Illinois, prior to the war. Barnum was born in New Jersey and had immigrated to Illinois. He was a businessman in Illinois prior to the war, including owning and managing the Barnum Hotel in Decatur, Illinois, and in Springfield he was a land agent before his enlistment. He was admitted to the bar in 1859. Now, only a few months after his promotion to the rank of lieutenant colonel, he commanded the 11th Missouri Infantry.

In August 1863, Captain Cyrenus Elliott, Company A, resigned his commission. Captain Elliott had served for 22 months without relief, and the Vicksburg campaign had finally sapped his strength. He was granted medical leave in June 1863 for no less than two months to enable him to recuperate, but he resigned on August 3 citing his poor physical condition. On August 4, 1st Lieutenant Menomen O'Donnell was promoted to rank of captain in Company A. O'Donnell had just proven his leadership skills and bravery in the assault on Stockade Redan and was rewarded with this promotion. Second Lieutenant William Pickrell was promoted to the rank of 1st lieutenant, and the company did not promote anyone to fill his old post. Also in August 1863, 2nd Lieutenant George Weber, Company B, was promoted to fill Charles Brookings' post as regimental adjutant after his death. No one was promoted to fill Weber's old post in the Company B.

Also in the summer of 1863, John Hathorn resigned his position as 2nd lieutenant in Com-

Lieutenant Colonel William Barnum assumed command of the 11th Missouri Infantry and led the regiment from July 1863 through August 1864 (author's collection).

pany I and Hathorn stated in his resignation letter that he was leaving the regiment "for the good of the service." His resignation was accepted in July 1863. He was not replaced until November 1863 when Charles Ethel was promoted to the rank of 1st lieutenant for Company I. The 20-year-old Ethel had been serving as a sergeant in Company I. Prior to his enlistment Ethel was a farmer from Bethel, Illinois.

After the fall of Vicksburg, Grant's army remained in place and awaited the next opportunity to engage their Southern foes. It wasn't until October when Grant had the opportunity to move when he was given command of the Union forces around Chattanooga, Tennessee. Along the Chickamauga Creek in northern Georgia, for three days in September 1863, the fury of General Braxton Bragg's Confederate Army was unleashed and soundly defeated the Union forces that had been stalking him since he left Perryville, Kentucky, in October 1862. At the Battle of Chickamauga during September 18–20, Southern forces capitalized on an errant order issued by Major General William Rosecrans to withdraw Brigadier General Thomas Wood's division out of the Union line, just as 10,000 Confederate soldiers were preparing to attack that very position. The result was the Union line rolled up around the breech and Rosecrans' army was forced to retreat to Chattanooga where they were besieged to the point of starvation. On September 23, Grant received a message ordering him to dispatch as many men as possible to the assistance of General William Rosecrans in Chattanooga. Grant immediately sent Major General William Sherman with part of two Corps toward the east. General Grant was then ordered to Louisville, Kentucky, where he met with Secretary of War Edwin Stanton and was made commander of the newly formed Military Division of Mississippi. This gave Grant control of most of the Union forces in the western theater. Rosecrans was removed as commander of the Union forces in Chattanooga when Grant arrived there. Grant made known his objective in Chattanooga: "hold Chattanooga at all hazards."[1] On October 23, 1863, Major General Ulysses Grant arrived at Chattanooga and began his personal command of the Union Military Division of the Mississippi. While the active theater of the war was moving eastward, the men of the 11th Missouri remained in Mississippi and Tennessee.

On July 20, 1863, Sergeant Charles Treadway, Company A, wrote of the conditions of the 11th Missouri Infantry, "We have seen a hard time since we commenced moving on to Vicksburg. We was fifty three days and nights marching through rain cold and heat and not a tent did we have in the whole time. Thare was several nights that it rained all night and we had to do as the cattle does in Illinois. Do the best that we could and that was not very good. Since our hard time is over the men is nearly all sick. Thare was a young man died in the Hospital last night by the name of Gibson he had a congestive chill and died in a short time. We are guarding a Rail Road Bridge on the Big Black River."[2] 20-year-old Private Calder Gibson died on July 3, 1863. Private Gibson was a member of Company D and was a Illinois native from Clay County, Illinois.

The 11th Missouri remained on guard duty on the Big Black River until October when Sherman's Corps moved in support of the Union forces near Chattanooga. The regiment was frightfully depleted and would never regain the large number of men that was present prior

Movement of Union supplies near the Big Black River (Library of Congress).

to the Battle of Vicksburg. The entire brigade was suffering the affects of the past two years. Even Ambrose Armitage of the Eighth Wisconsin noticed the condition of the regiments, "I never saw the Eighth Wisconsin and Eleventh Missouri so small as they are to night. They are simply squads. The Eleventh is smaller than we are."[3] On August 2, 1863, Dr. Hawley wrote a letter which described the continued poor condition of the men and resulted in some severe steps planned by the officers to "consolidate the ten companies in five.... Our regiment is far below the minimum. They have started on the march with 90 or 100 men, one tenth of what they should have."[4] Clearly the 11th Missouri was a shell of the regiment it had been. Dr. Hawley also expressed his thoughts about the horrors of the war that the regiment had been through: "Time still rolls on and we may feel assured it is the beginning of the end of this rebellion. God grant we may never have another and hasten the downfall of the present. The fine independent people of the northern states cannot have an idea of the terribleness of the horror of war."[5] The number of men that were present for duty had been reported regularly in the company morning reports since the regiment was formed in early August 1861, but as Dr. Hawley reported companies were consolidated to have an adequate number of men to function. The last month that all companies reported men ready for active duty was in August 1863, and at that point only 193 men and officers were present for duty. Only five companies had greater than 20 men present for duty, and the company with the fewest number of men present for duty was Company I with only 9 men.

During the time after the surrender of Vicksburg into the autumn, the 11th Missouri recuperated and rested, and the regiment's assignment was to guard the railroad and bridge on the Big Black River. Brigadier General Joseph Mower was sick and away from the brigade during this time. Captain Jesse Lloyd contracted smallpox during this period and recovered to again assume command of Company B. It wasn't until later in September that the regiment was again on the move. The regiment moved with Major General James McPherson's expedition to Canton, Mississippi, on October 14 through 20, 1863, and was involved in action at Bogue Chitto Creek on October 17. McPherson recorded, "The troops composing the expedition consisted of Logan's division (3,500 men), Tuttle's division (about 3,000), and the cavalry brigade (1,500 strong), under Colonel Winslow. On the morning of the 14th, Logan's division left Vicksburg and marched to the Big Black at Messinger's Ferry; Tuttle's division and the cavalry, under Colonel Winslow, concentrating the same day at the same point, ready to cross early in the morning."[6] General McPherson's forces advanced and encountered Confederate cavalry on October 15 near Brownsville, Mississippi. Early on October 16, McPherson's forces pushed aside Colonel John Griffith's 11th and Seventh Consolidated Arkansas Infantry. Later in the day, McPherson's force collided with the Confederate Brigadier General John Whitfield's infantry brigade positioned along the Canton Road, where the Bogue Chitto Creek crosses the Treadwell Plantation, with skirmishing and artillery exchanges occurring. On October 17, McPherson had concentrated his forces and prepared to engage the Confederate forces to his front, but the enemy withdrew.

Duncan McCall recalled the 11th Missouri formed their lines around the town of Brownsville, Mississippi, and then proceeded forward. "The roar of cannon broke upon our ears, but we could tell by the sounds that the firing was some distance ahead of us."[7] The regiment proceeded through a series of starts and stops as they advanced towards a retreating enemy. On October 17, the regiment advanced and the cavalry moved forward and came under artillery fire. The Confederates were in a defensive line at the top of a hill and, "it was a splendid sight to see the blue coats ascend the hill."[8] But the defenders retreated before the advancing infantry. The 11th Missouri was ordered back to the Black Water Bridge to assume the old task of protecting the railroad after marching for six days. The advance upon Canton,

Mississippi, was not without its action which was primarily assigned to the Union cavalry. However, McPherson, fearing Confederate reinforcements, decided to withdraw his forces. The entire expedition cost McPherson 5 killed, 15 wounded and an unrecorded number captured while straggling. The only reference relating to the 11th Missouri in this expedition was that the regiment was sent to guard the bridge over the Bogue Chitto Creek in a reserve capacity during the artillery and infantry exchanges on October 16.

The regiment moved to La Grange, Tennessee, in early November 1863. After returning to La Grange, Dr. Thomas Hawley wrote, "Truth is stranger than fiction after passing through the vicissitudes incident to an active camp life, I again find myself stationed in this once pretty village but now rendered desolate by the demon of War. It's colleges and seminary building destroyed, it churches desecrated, private dwellings ravaged until all of the former inhabitants have removed to more genial society."[9] Even Dr. Hawley used the La Grange Episcopal Church as his hospital. Joseph Mower's brigade was involved in scouting and pursuing Nathan Bedford Forrest's cavalry through December 24 and then remained at La Grange, Tennessee, until January 26, 1864. While in La Grange, Dr. Hawley criticized the medical care the soldiers were receiving in the larger hospitals in Memphis. He had 18 to 25 patients at his hospital at the Episcopal Church and he wrote, "We did not lose a man last month nor send any to Genl Hospital. All doing well as long as we remain at this station. I cannot trust the Hospital in Memphis. They kill nearly all the bad cases."[10]

In November, Elias Weir, 2nd Lieutenant, Company F, had two unfortunate events. First, he was informed that his wife had died in Illinois, which left his children without a parent; and secondly, he was diagnosed with chronic bronchitis that had been troubling him for several months. As a result, he tendered his resignation and left the regiment. In December 1863, 2nd Lieutenant Elmore Ridgely, Company E, resigned due to an infection of the lungs and he was not replaced.

On December 21, 1863, the regiment marched 20 miles to Purdy, Tennessee, with the 47th Illinois Infantry. The next night they found the two regiments near Jackson, Tennessee, having marched 30 miles that day. The third day they marched back to Corinth, where they were ordered back to La Grange, Tennessee. While seeking General Nathan Forrest's cavalry near Corinth, ironically it was reported that Forrest had crossed the railroad near La Grange which was the original location of the 11th Missouri Infantry.

The 11th Missouri Infantry was reorganized in December 1863, permanently removed from Sherman's XV Corps and became part of the Second Brigade, First Division, XVI Army Corps. This was the last time the regiment was reorganized, and it would remain part of the 16th Army Corps until mustered out in 1866.

Troops in the Department of the Tennessee, Maj. Gen. William T. Sherman, U.S.. Army, commanding, December 31, 1863[11]

FIRST DIVISION BRIG. GEN. JAMES M. TUTTLE
SECOND BRIGADE. BRIG. GEN. JOSEPH A. MOWER

47th Illinois, Col. John D. McClure
5th Minnesota, Col. Lucius F. Hubbard
11th Missouri, Lieut. Col. William L. Barnum
8th Wisconsin, Lieut. Col. John W. Jefferson

On January 26, 1864, the 11th Missouri and the brigade moved to Memphis and remained there long enough to be paid. They soon were loaded onto river transports and arrived at

Vicksburg, Mississippi, in early February. Next the regiment returned to the Big Black River Bridge where it had spent much of the last half of 1863. The odyssey for the regiment continued as the soldiers marched to Canton, Mississippi, on February 27–29 and then returned to Vicksburg in early March. The regiment's movement toward Canton was part of Sherman's Meridan, Mississippi, campaign. This was undertaken to put the Confederates in a defensive posture, destroy the Confederate infrastructure, remove Union soldiers from guarding the Mississippi River to participate in the active operations in Georgia, and destroy Major General Nathan Bedford Forrest's cavalry. Soon after the 11th Missouri returned to guard duty on the Big Black River in February 1864, the regiment left the Big Black River and was taken by rail car to Vicksburg and then moved by boat toward Memphis. Things never went smoothly, because, not only did the river boat hit a snag in the Mississippi River tearing a hole in the front of the boat, it was set on fire several times by a saboteur who was never identified. The fires were discovered and no serious damage resulted. Next, as the regiment moved by rail to La Grange, the cars were fired into by Confederates resulting in "a negro killed in the 11th Missouri, and two of the 5th Minnesota wounded, also a negro in the 3d Iowa battery was killed."[12] After reaching La Grange, the 11th Missouri Infantry went marching in an attempt to prevent Confederates from damaging the railroad. It was always difficult for infantry to deal with cavalry. Skirmishes erupted but as the engagement was prepared, the cavalry withdrew. Next, the 11th Missouri, along with the 47th Illinois Infantry, were loaded onto rail cars and moved to Corinth. At this point the 11th Missouri was still considered an active regiment, but practically the regiment no longer existed because it was split into two parts; the veterans and non-veterans. Those who enlisted in the 11th Missouri Infantry, enlisted for a term of three years. The end of the term of service for most of the regiment was August 6, 1864. At the end of the enlistment period, soldiers were offered an opportunity to continue their service in the army and become veterans, a term used to describe those soldiers who had served one three-year enlistment period and had reenlisted. Although the Union forces were clearly successful in their efforts in 1864 in the Civil War, the Confederate Army had a determined will to fight, and in many cases this will was intensified as these troops defended their home soil. So soldiers were still needed, and veterans' regiments were formed.

Despite orders that veterans' regiments were not be initiated prior to 90 days of the expiration of enlistments, there is evidence the regiment began making plans to become a veteran regiment as early as the summer of 1863. These plans went as far as having elections of officers to command the new regiment. The enlistment period for the 11th Missouri would not end until August 1864, thirteen months from the fall of Vicksburg. But the small number of men remaining in the regiment and lack of new recruits drastically reduced the viability of the regiment being moved into combat situations. However, the regiment continued to function within their brigade. Early in January 1864, communications between Lieutenant Colonel William Barnum and Colonel John Gray, Missouri Adjutant General, revealed as many as 325 men were committed to remaining in the veteran regiment and bounties were being planned to encourage the reenlistment. Many soldiers that were sick and exhausted in the campaign of the summer of 1863 had recuperated and returned to the regiment over the winter, increasing the number of soldiers present for duty.

As discussions by the regimental officers took place about reorganizing the regiment, issues began to surface, including the fact that after three years of marching, "most of the regiment preferred another arm of the service. Mostly cavalry."[13] William Barnum revealed in a letter to Colonel John Gray that he (Barnum) was also chosen unanimously to be the regimental commander of the newly forming veteran regiment. Barnum acknowledged he had found that progress to form the new veteran regiment to be "expedient," while acknowledging it was not according to proper military direction. Dissatisfaction was evident within the regiment by the actions that Barnum had taken, and he acknowledged the officers were not all pleased. In fact, Colonel Barnum had gone so far as to recommend the new officers of the companies in July 1863, and he withdrew recommendations because these were "in opposition to the wishes of the regiment as expressed. I have the honor to respectfully request permission to withdraw the same."[14] All was not well in the 11th Missouri Infantry, as revealed in Barnum's correspondence.

Several regiments actively planned to begin recruiting for the veteran regiments despite the restriction of a 90-day period prior to the end of the enlistment period. So prevalent was this problem of early recruitment activities, the XVI Corps Inspector General issued a circular on August 5, 1863, in which he stated, "Genl Grant desires me to say that the order does not contemplate, anything so destructive, as such a course would do to the old organization and that no recruiting officers will be permitted to open an office, or by any means, looking to the formation of a Veteran regt or regiments — until the term of the old regiments is within ninety days of expiration."[15]

The need to find recruits brought up nagging issues for the officers and men of the regiment. The 11th Missouri was remarkably unsuccessful in replacing the men lost during the war with new recruits, even though several recruiting groups had been dispatched back to Missouri and Illinois. Colonel Andrew Weber sent a request to the governor of Missouri pleading for more men after the Battle of Corinth, and Vicksburg campaign depleted the regiment even more. Earlier in the war the officers of the regiment sent a formal request that the designation of the 11th Missouri be changed to an Illinois regiment due to the overwhelming number of men from that state. The request was sent to the governor of Illinois on February 8, 1862, and signed by the Illinois officers, but the request was not approved. If the 11th Missouri intended to become a veteran regiment, they needed more men for that to be accomplished; and because so many of the regiment were from Illinois, it was found that Illinois was a potentially more fertile ground to find men to fill the regiment. A formal request was made to allow this recruitment within the state of Illinois. On March 28, 1864, Allen Fuller, Illinois Adjutant General, issued General Order No. 4, stating, "The Eleventh Missouri Infantry having been composed almost entirely of the Citizens of Illinois and said regiment having reenlisted as Veterans and placed to the credit of the State of Illinois, permission is hereby given to Colonel W. L. Barnum to recruit in the State of Illinois by said regiment. This permission is given with the expectation that said regiment will be transferred and hereafter know as an Illinois Regiment."[16] However, the name and designation of the 11th Missouri never changed. On April 30, 1864, the reenlisted portion of the 11th Missouri Infantry soon became known as the 11th Missouri Veteran Volunteer Infantry and was ordered to proceed to Cairo, Illinois, and report to the commanding officer of the 17th Army Corps.

In the meantime, life within the regiment continued. On March 1, 1864, Private Joseph Bay, Company K, was captured at Canton, Mississippi, and he was paroled at Savannah, Georgia, on November 30, 1864. The details of the capture are not recorded, but moving in any enemy territory was dangerous for the men of the 11th Missouri. On February 1, 1864, Private John Byrd, Company C, had also been taken prisoner at Canton, Mississippi. Byrd was returned to the regiment in May 1865 after being confined in prison in Goldsboro, North Carolina, for 15 months.

Those soldiers in the 11th Missouri who chose to reenlist to become veterans were offered furloughs before they started serving their new tour of duty. Special Field Order No. 14 issued on March 6, 1864, stated the 11th Missouri soldiers who reenlisted were "hereby ordered to proceed to Memphis Tenn where the arms, ordnance stores and other property excepting necessary cooking utensil, will be turned over when the Regiments will proceed with their officers to their respective states...the 11th Missouri to St. Louis Mo.... The men who have not reenlisted as Veterans will be assigned temporarily to other Regiments of the same states and will be provided with Descriptive Rolls."[17] For those who chose not to reenlist, or the non-veterans, their lot was to continue the war effort within other regiments. There were approximately 100 soldiers of the 11th Missouri Infantry who became non-veterans and were transferred to the 33rd Missouri Infantry. These men were soon marching as part of the 1,300 men of the 33rd Missouri Infantry in the Red River Campaign in Louisiana.

Red River Campaign

Special Order No. 43 issued on March 9, 1864, identified the men who had not reenlisted and were assigned to the 33rd Missouri Infantry[18]:

Sgt. Thomas Lackey	Co. A	Sgt. Jacob Severns	Co. A
Corp. Thomas Worstell	Co. A	Pvt. Peter Boulds	Co. A
Pvt. Charles Elliott	Co. A	Pvt. Thomas McGuire	Co. A
Pvt. Benjamin Matthews	Co. A	Pvt. John Gould	Co. A
Pvt. George Worstell	Co. A	Sgt. Clifton King	Co. B
Pvt. Stephen Cooper	Co. B	Corp. Joseph Coleman	Co. B
Corp. Thomas Stephens	Co. B	Corp. William Adams	Co. B
Pvt. Antonio Bush	Co. B	Pvt. Hiram Batchler	Co. B
Pvt. Julius Dunaway	Co. B	Pvt. George Graham	Co. B
Pvt. Jasper Gosses	Co. B	Pvt. Duncan McCall	Co. B
Pvt. Nathaniel Neer	Co. B	Pvt. Sanford Turley	Co. B
Sgt. John Lawrence	Co. C	Pvt. Daniel Cuppy	Co. C
Pvt. Samuel Leinhart	Co. C	Sgt. Phillip Heltman	Co. D
Sgt. John Fields	Co. D	Sgt. David McKnight	Co. D
Corp. Edward O'Neal	Co. D	Corp John Sexton	Co. D
Corp. Granville Williams	Co. D	Corp. Dios Hagle	Co. D
Pvt. Henry Brown	Co. D	Pvt. John Gross	Co. D
Pvt. J. McKinney	Co. D	Pvt. William McKnight	Co. D
Pvt. Francis Morgan	Co. D	Pvt. George Thatcher	Co. D
Pvt. James Tooley	Co. D	Sgt. John Bail	Co. E
Sgt. Adam Cottrell	Co. E	Corp. James Johnson	Co. E
Corp. James Seymour	Co. E	Corp. John Wilson	Co. E
Fifer John Crawford	Co. E	Wagoner William Lock	Co. E
Pvt. William Eckey	Co. E	Pvt. Henry Judy	Co. E
Pvt. Albert Knopf	Co. E	Pvt. Benjamin Rush	Co. E
Pvt. George Rush	Co. E	Pvt. John Seymour	Co. E
Pvt. Samuel Tade	Co. E	Corp. Morris Draper	Co. F
Pvt. Augustus Senkint	Co. F	Pvt. W M Black	Co. F
Pvt. John Hager	Co. G	Pvt. C W Owens	Co. G
Pvt. Charles W Owens	Co. G	Pvt. G E Rush	Co. G
Pvt. Joseph Rahm	Co. G	Pvt. John Williams	Co. G
Corp. Elias Browning	Co. H	Pvt. Allen McNeal	Co. H
Pvt. Alfred Logan	Co. H	Pvt. Samuel/Thos Adams	Co. H
Pvt. John McDonald	Co. H	Pvt. George York	Co. H
Corp. Columbus Wroe	Co. I	Pvt. Nemiah Bower	Co. I
Pvt. James Chapman	Co. I	Pvt. Jesse Henry	Co. I
Pvt. William Miller	Co. I	Pvt. William Maple	Co. I

Pvt. Charles Pike	Co. I	Pvt. Nicholas Russell	Co. I
Pvt. Matthew Bay	Co. K	Pvt. John W. Bay	Co. K
Pvt. Pleasant Bay	Co. K	Pvt. Daniel Gallagher	Co. K
Pvt. Henry Gines	Co. K	Pvt. James Gray	Co. K
Pvt. James Johnson	Co. K	Pvt. John Moor	Co. K
Pvt. Harrison Twitty	Co. K	Pvt. John Perry	Co. K

These 88 men, by General Mower's order, were transferred to the 33rd Missouri Infantry; and while the other men of the 11th Missouri were soon given furloughs, these men, along with General Mower, participated in one of the grandest defeats for the Union army in the Civil War. The Red River Campaign took place for over two months — March 10, 1864, through May 22, 1864. Gary Joiner, author of *Through the Howling Wind*, stated, "The Red River Campaign of 1864 in the Civil War was an overly ambitious attempt to send large Union army and navy forces deep into the interior of Louisiana, seize the Rebel capital of the state, and defeat the Confederate army guarding the region, enabling uninhibited access to Texas to the west."[19] Several reasons have been offered for the Red River Campaign, including controlling cotton trade, and even concerns and justification about this offensive as a way of preventing Maximilian of Mexico from annexing or invading the state of Texas. Nonetheless, the plans for this campaign began in January 1864, and the operation was launched in March under the command of Major General Nathaniel Banks. Banks, it was soon to be discovered, was not the man to lead his troops through Louisiana to capture Shreveport and then move westward to Texas. Banks, the former governor of Massachusetts, began the war by leading troops against Thomas "Stonewall" Jackson the battles of Winchester and Cedar Mountain. In December 1862, he was given command of the Department of the Gulf, and although he strove to come to Grant's aid at Vicksburg, he was unable to move his troops to participate in that siege. The Red River Campaign was designed to allow Banks to lead 17,000 soldiers up Bayou Teche; General Sherman, while actively campaigning in Georgia, agreed to send 10,000 troops up the Red River commanded by Major General Andrew J. Smith; and finally Major General Frederick Steele agreed to move southward from Little Rock with an additional 15,000 soldiers. The three forces planned to unite in Alexandria or Shreveport, Louisiana, and then turn west toward Texas. As the campaign unfolded, General Steele's force never participated in the operation due to their inability to coordinate their timing with the other two prongs of the attack. However, Steele's action in Arkansas occupied the minds of Confederate commanders. Steele's movements caused Lieutenant General Edmund Kirby Smith to reconsider redeploying the Confederate forces to Louisiana. As Steele pushed southward, his movements kept Major General Sterling Price's Confederate guessing his objective and many of his soldiers out of Louisiana.

The 11th Missouri Infantry soldiers, serving with the 33rd Missouri Infantry, were commanded by Colonel William Heath. The men of the 11th Missouri assigned to the 33rd Missouri were distributed throughout the regiment in various companies. The 33rd Missouri and the 35th Iowa Infantry, also containing non-veteran soldiers of the Eighth and 12th Iowa infantries, made up the regiments of the Third Brigade of the First Division commanded by Colonel Sylvester Hill. Hill reported to Major General Andrew J. Smith commanding the XVI Corps. Colonel Lucius Hubbard commanded the Second Brigade, which was made up of the 11th Missouri's old sister regiments of the Eighth Wisconsin, 47th Illinois and Fifth Minnesota infantries. The Third Division of Smith Corps was commanded by General Joseph Mower.

The Confederate forces opposing Banks in the Red River Campaign were part of Major General Kirby Smith's Army from the Trans-Mississippi Department, commanded in the field by Lieutenant General Theophilius Holmes in Camden Arkansas, Major General John Magruder occupying the Texas coastal area, and Major General Richard Taylor located in Louisiana. Kirby Smith had approximately 30,000 troops under his command.

The men of the 11th Missouri, while serving with the 33rd Missouri, still traveled closely with their old commander Joseph Mower, who commanded their brigade and the First Division, under the command of General A. J. Smith. Facing these troops were Richard Taylor's Confederates of J. G. Walker's division located near Markville and Brigadier General Alfred Moulton's Division located near Alexandria, as well as other various smaller detachments. General A. J. Smith's command left Vicksburg on March 10, 1864, and soon landed near Simmesport, Louisiana. With Admiral Porter's flotilla of gunboats and ironclads, Smith quickly encountered Fort De Russey, one of the first obstacles along the Red River. The soldiers of the 11th Missouri serving in the 33rd Missouri were transported on the gunboat *Hamilton*, landed at the mouth of Atchafalaya Bayou and were part of the Union force that moved forward against the Confederates at Fort De Russey near the Yellow Bayou. On March 14, A. J. Smith's XVI Corps troops captured Fort De Russey as they advanced into Louisiana toward Baton Rouge.

General Joseph Mower made mention of the 11th Missouri's Captain Menomen O'Donnell in his after-action report on the Battle of Fort De Russey. "I deem it my duty to mention the conduct of Captain O'Donnell, of my staff, who rendered me most efficient and valuable aid in putting troops into position. He was always ready when his services were required, and was one of the first in the enemy's works. We captured 260 men, as well as a large amount of ordnance and ordnance stores, among them ten guns, two of them 9-inch, one 32-pounder rifled and banded; the others of smaller caliber."[20] The 11th Missouri's Menomen O'Donnell had gallantly joined the attack on Stockade Redan in Vicksburg; but now in Louisiana, O'Donnell was "apparently the only man to charge the fort on horseback,"[21] again demonstrating legendary

The attack on Fort DeRussey (Florida Center for Instructional Technology).

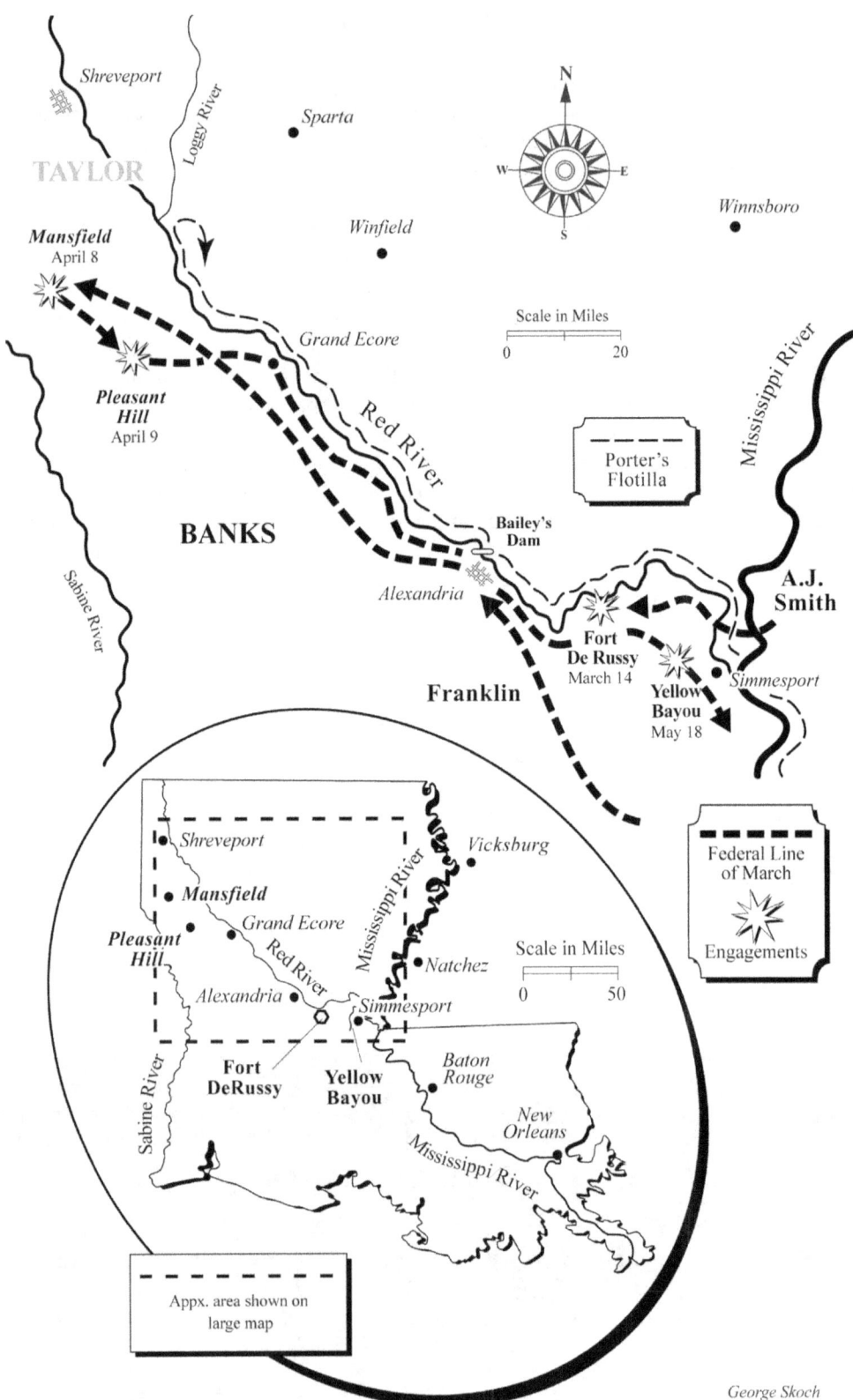

The Red River Campaign, March–May 1864.

bravery in the face of the enemy. O'Donnell recorded a conversation between General Joseph Mower and himself prior to the assault on Fort DeRussey,

> "Captain, I have received orders to go into that camp: what do you say?"
> "General, it is not for me to say what to do," O'Donnell answered.
> "I wish you would give me your opinion," he persisted.
> "General," I replied, "if I were in your place, I would capture Fort DeRussey before evening. If we don't the enemy will be gone before daylight."
> "Just my own opinion, General Mower said."[22]

Menomen O'Donnell was subsequently awarded the Medal of Honor for his actions at Vicksburg and Fort DeRussey.

The regiments were taken by gunboat up the Red River to Alexandria, but the trip was tediously slow. The boats could proceed no faster than five miles per hour. "The stream was very crooked and narrow, and might very easily be blockaded. The gunboats proceeded cautiously. Parker discovered there were torpedoes placed in the river, and four of these infernal machines were taken out before getting very close to them."[23] Civil War torpedoes were essentially floating mines and exploded when ships made contact with them. Then Smith moved to capture Alexandria on March 18, and General Banks joined this force at Alexandria. Banks' force included Ransom's XIII Corps, Major General William B. Franklin's XIX Corps, Brigadier General Albert Lee's cavalry division and four *Corps d'Afrique* regiments (73rd, 75th, 84th, and 92nd USCT). This force also possessed 13 batteries of artillery. All was going as planned, for now.

Andrew Smith, XVI Corps commander, was an excellent corps commander. Smith was born in 1815 in Bucks County, Pennsylvania, and he was a graduate of West Point, Class of 1838. Andrew Smith had participated in the Mexican War and also served in the army in the southwestern part of the United States. Smith was also referred to as "Whiskey Smith," but A. J. Smith was an outstanding commander, and led and trained rugged men who would stand and fight the enemy. His corps would be nicknamed Smith's Guerrillas for their fighting ability and efficiency in marching quickly to be in the action. Smith was described "of small stature, with rather brusque, abrupt manners, sometimes verging on irascibility, yet was popular with his troops, and shunned none of the hardships to which they were subjected."[24]

If General Nathaniel Banks had expected passive subordinates, he was disappointed with General A. J. Smith and General Joseph Mower. These were seasoned and excellent commanders. Friction began early in the Red

The wily Major General Andrew J. Smith commanded the Union XVI Corps (Library of Congress).

River Campaign, and while the XVI Corps waited for Banks to unite their forces, action was initiated against the Southern defenders. Sergeant Dios Hagle, 11th Missouri, Company D, reported, "Gen. Banks was not at all satisfied with the audacious course pursued by Gens. Smith and Mower."[25] Hagle recounted an event in which General Mower successfully captured a Confederate cavalry force which had been burning bridges to slow the Union advance. Mower kept his main force in the front of the Confederates, and during the night he successfully encircled the Confederate cavalry, which Hagle suspected to be the Second Louisiana Cavalry. At 2:00 A.M., a cavalry regiment and two pieces of artillery were found, and soldiers "with tired bodies, bleeding feet, and beating hearts, and without firing a gun," captured the camp.[26] Hagle reported the captured Confederates called their capture a "Yankee trick," and "it was believed that Gen. Banks looked upon it in somewhat the same way, as he gave no one credit for it, and from that time on during that memorable campaign he saw to it that Smith and Mower were kept in the rear."[27]

ARMY OF THE TENNESSEE (DETACHMENT)[28]
— BRIG. GEN. ANDREW J. SMITH
FIRST DIVISION, SIXTEENTH ARMY CORPS

Second Brigade — Col. Lucius F. Hubbard
47th Illinois, Col. John D. McClure
5th Minnesota, Maj. John C. Becht
8th Wisconsin, Lieut. John W. Jefferson

Third Brigade — Col. Sylvester G. Hill
35th Iowa, Lieut. Col. William B. Keeler
33d Missouri, Lieut. Col. William H. Heath
(Including the non-veteran 11th Missouri Infantry)

Next Banks advanced toward Shreveport, and the Confederates forces withdrew, but General Richard Taylor's forces were newly reinforced by those of Colonel Thomas Green's cavalry from Texas. The men of the 11th Missouri, as part of Smith's corps, were part of a skirmish which occurred at Grand Ecore and at least one casualty occurred — Captain Menomen O'Donnell was wounded in his arm. The skirmish resulted in a few Confederate prisoners being taken. By March 31, Banks' army advanced into Natchitoches, about 65 miles from Shreveport. Finally on April 8, the first significant clash between Banks and Taylor occurred near Pleasant Hill, Louisiana. The Confederate cavalry was driven back to Sabine Crossroads where Taylor organized a stiff defense utilizing the infantry divisions of Walker and Mouton. The Battle of Mansfield was fought on April 8, 1864. After Banks threw his troops at the Confederate defense, a counterattack won the day as Mouton's Division, the Texas Division and Major General John Major's cavalry charged into the Union line and the Federals were routed, resulting in a loss of 113 men killed, 581 wounded and 1,541 captured or missing compared to only a 1,000 for the Confederates. The Battle of Mansfield was a significant Confederate victory because a Confederate force of 8,800 defeated a superior Union force of 12,000 men. When the Battle of Mansfield was fought, the men of the 11th Missouri along with Smith's XVI Corps had been left to guard "Banks' everlasting train. It was train enough for 150,000 men, and it took all of Smith's army to guard while landing from the boats. We were soon in marching order, and on the 7th started, following Banks' grand army. Rain fell that day, laying the dust.... Reports began to be circulated through the regiment that the army under Banks was badly whipped, and things began to look gloomy, as the truth came to us that the 13th corps were all killed or captured, with all their cannon and wagons."[29] To stem the tide of the Confederate momentum, Federal reinforcements were sent forward. On the next day, General A. J. Smith's XVI Army Corps participated in the battle of Pleasant Hill, as Taylor tried to capitalize on his victory of the preceding day. Confidence was waning in Banks' ability to successfully lead the campaign, and as Duncan McCall, private in 11th Missouri, recorded, "As Banks could not command an army he gave the command to Smith [Commanding the XVI Corps] and Mower, who immediately formed their men in line of battle."[30] During the Battle of Pleasant Hill, the Confederates advanced toward the Union line, including the 33rd Missouri. Smith's western Union troops were thought by many to be the best Union troops in the war. The Confederates thought they were facing untested Union troops and mistakenly thought they were facing regiments from one corps, instead they faced Union regiments from three corps. "Taylor's cavalry had not observed Banks' column in its fullest extent prior to the battle. The scouts had not seen the banners of the 16th and 17th Corps, composed of Sherman's veterans."[31] The Confederate attack began around 3:00 P.M. on April 9, and at 5:00 P.M. the first Confederate charge into the Union positions began. The Confederate attack

Confederate General Richard Taylor faced Banks' Army during the Red River Campaign (Library of Congress).

gained initial momentum and pushed through the advanced Union regiments through the village of Pleasant Hill, but General A. J. Smith's Divisions were positioned to the rear of the village unnoticed by the Confederate attackers. When it appeared the Confederates would carry the day, "A. J. Smith then ordered his entire line to charge the Confederates."[32] As Smith's Corps moved forward, General Banks rode to him and said, "God bless you general, You have saved the army."[33] The Union counterattack drove the attackers backward and darkness ended the day.

The events of the Battle of Pleasant Hill for the 11th Missouri were recorded by Major George Van Beek of the 33rd Missouri. The 33rd Missouri Infantry was commanded by Lieutenant Colonel William Heath as the regiment entered the Battle of Pleasant Hill. At 3:00 P.M., the regiment was located about a mile to the rear of the town of Pleasant Hill and held the extreme right of the Third Brigade of the First Division of Smith's XVI Corps. The 33rd Missouri Infantry was in the rear of the 89th Indiana Infantry and maintained their position until 5:00 P.M., when they were ordered to the right of the Third Indiana battery. As the 33rd Missouri moved to support the battery, it came under a furious fire from the enemy, which had just broken through the first Union battle line and now focused their attention on the batteries. According to Major Van Beek, the Confederates "were pressing vigorously forward. The fire of the enemy becoming extremely severe, Lieutenant-Colonel Heath ordered the men to lie down to prevent an unnecessary loss of life. The enemy, now greatly encouraged by their success, continued advancing with renewed energy upon the retreating brigades, effectually preventing their reforming and at the same time breaking our second line. At this juncture my regiment was ordered to rise and charge the enemy."[34] While leading the charge, Lieutenant Colonel Heath received a severe head wound and command fell to Major Van Beek. The regiment advanced and the major directed the men to return fire from a prone position. Van Beek poured a deadly fire into the advancing Confederate line and firing from the prone position gave his soldiers the advantage of an accurate steady fire while presenting a small target for the advancing soldiers. "The enemy, being unable to withstand the effective and unerring fire now showered upon them by our troops, wavered."[35] Van Beek pressed forward and a four-gun Confederate battery began firing canister at his advancing regiment, but luckily firing over the charging 33rd Missouri Infantry. The Confederates the 33rd Missouri were facing were none other than the Ninth, 10th and 11th Missouri infantry regiments (CSA) according to prisoners. The 33rd Missouri pushed forward, taking the batteries and routing the infantry and gunners. At this point more inspiration appeared to the regiment when General Joseph Mower rode up to the 33rd Missouri Infantry and pointed his sword to the battery and encouraged the men forward. The men answered his call and steadily advanced forward in a solid line entering the woods intent on silencing the guns. The enemy gunners continued to fire at the advancing Union soldiers holding on as long as they could "obstinately contesting every inch of ground, until finding themselves irretrievably lost, fled, a panic-stricken mob, leaving horses, guns, equipments, and everything that impeded their progress upon the field."[36] Darkness made any further pursuit of the Confederates impractical, and the 33rd Missouri reformed on the edge of the woods and camped for the night on the field they had won during the struggle.

The participation of the soldiers of the 11th Missouri in the battle was also described in the report by Colonel Sylvester Hill, the brigade commander. When the brigade was ordered to rise and charge the enemy, the Confederate line had broken through the second Union line. The Union advance was made with a cheer and the line rushed forward. It was during this advance that Lieutenant Colonel William Heath was wounded in the head and was removed from the field, and command fell to Major George Van Beek who led the charge. Colonel Sylvester Hill recorded the brigade advanced and fired as they advanced with destructive volleys. The Confederate attackers were now defenders as the fresh Union line advanced, and so devastating were the Union volleys, the Confederate lines withered under the impact. "The brigade continued to advance, firing incessant and destructive volleys into the ranks of the enemy, who could no longer withstand the strong fire poured into them from our troops, began to waver, and were immediately charged very determinedly and compelled to fall back in great disorder, then followed closely by our troops."[37] The two regiments in Colonel Hill's Division recorded 78 casualties in the day's action. The Union loss at Pleasant Hill was "289 killed, 773 wounded, and 543 missing, for a total of 1605.... Confederate losses at Pleasant Hill as 1,200 killed and wounded and another 426 taken prisoner."[38]

The day after, the Battle of Pleasant Hill was described by Cloyd Bryner, author of the history of the 47th Illinois Infantry: "Sabbath morning saw a grewsome sight. Stark and pallid lay the dead faces upturned: gray-bearded men and beardless boys, the blue and the gray, side by side."[39]

After these battles, both sides were suffering from poor morale. By the end of April 9, both sides lost about 1,600 men, but the Confederate advance had been temporarily stopped. However, the strategic outcome of the battles on April 7–9 was that Banks decided to abandon his plan of moving any closer to Shreveport and immediately ordered a 25 mile retreat back to Natchitoches. General A. J. Smith's corps led the way. As Banks retreated, he finalized his decision to abandon his plan to capture Shreveport. By April 25, he had retreated and reached Alexandria clashing with the Confederate pursuers until May 13. The 33rd Missouri was involved in a skirmish at Marksville Prairie where some of the men of the 11th Missouri were wounded. At this point, Banks and his naval support of Admiral Porter began a general retreat and were harassed as they tried to escape. The Confederate forces continually harassed the retreating Union army out of Louisiana. Before the Union forces could totally withdraw, on May 18, General A. J. Smith decided to give battle to the forces attacking the rear of the column that he had been given responsibility of protecting. Under overall command of General Joseph Mower, the First and Third Divisions of Smith's XVI Corps stopped until their pursuers, Major General John Wharton's cavalry and Brigadier General Camille Polignac's infantry, reached the Federal line. Mower stopped and faced his pursuers. Polignac's soldiers made two attacks against Mower's force but were repulsed. The Union loss was estimated at 350 and the Confederates 608 at the battle at Yellow Bayou.

Again the actions of the soldiers of the 11th Missouri were recorded by Major George Van Beek of the 33rd Missouri Infantry. Van Beek reported that the 33rd Missouri's participation in the Battle of Yellow Bayou began at about 9:00 a. m., when the regiment was ordered to move from their position behind a levee on Avoyelles Bayou. The regiment moved to the center of the field just left of Battery M, 1st Missouri Light Artillery. The regiment remained in place only about a half an hour when butternut-clad soldiers were observed advancing forward with several pieces of artillery. Then, the 33rd Missouri was moved to the right of the Union line. Next, the advancing Confederates slammed into the Union skirmishers, sending them hurriedly back to the comfort of their line. Van Beek recorded that he was given orders to charge the enemy, which his regiment did with gusto, into an enemy firing with musket and artillery; but the 33rd Missouri successfully returned the fire and charged forward through a hail of shot and shell driving the enemy out of the timber and pushing them back to their reserves, "which were stationed midway of an open field and in rear of a sugar-mill and buildings of the plantation. Upon arriving at the field I received orders to fall back, under cover of the timber, and reform. This being accomplished, I was ordered to fall back to my first position in rear and on the edge of the above-mentioned timber. All this was accomplished under a heavy fire of the enemy's artillery. In the charge my regiment lost quite a number wounded."[40] As the Union line reformed, the Confederates reinforced, sent the skirmishers again scampering back to the line and a second Union charge was ordered. "I again charged with the brigade, again compelling the enemy to retire, which they did in a confused and disorganized mass, leaving behind them their dead and wounded and many prisoners in our possession. Owing to a misunderstanding of orders received I continued charging across the open field, and had advanced about 150 yards into the field, when I received orders to fall back and reform under cover of the woods. My loss in this charge was more severe than in the first, owing to our being in plain view and the enemy opening upon us with his artillery for the purpose of covering the retreat of his troops."[41] Major Van Beek reported he captured about 40 prisoners and was reinforced which allowed him to withdraw for ammunition. The regiment retired for the day and spent the night at Avoyelles Bayou.

By May 22 the disastrous Red River Campaign was over and General A. J. Smith's troops, including the men of the 11th Missouri, were heading for Vicksburg. The regimental records show that the detached men of the 11th Missouri were involved primarily in the Battle of Pleasant Hill and Yellow Bayou and the regiment was only lightly impacted. "Loss — one man wounded at Pleasant Hill."[42] Private William Maple, Company I, a farmer from Versailles, Illinois, was wounded in the Battle of Pleasant Hill, and John Evans, Company I, a shoemaker from Concord, Illinois, was recorded as being wounded in action at Bayou Glaize, Louisiana.

Meanwhile, for the reenlisting men of the 11th Missouri Infantry, the regimental records indicated the enlistees of the 11th Missouri Veteran Infantry were mustered on April 30 in St.

Louis and then traveled on the steamer *Des Moines* to Cairo, Illinois, on May 3. The regiment was transported to Memphis and arrived there on May 7, where they remained in camp, except to make an expedition into Arkansas to search for Rebels but no enemies were found. The only record of this event was from Dr. Thomas Hawley's letter written on May 7, "We are now returning from a fruitless search for Rebels in Ark, We left Memphis 4 days ago with a section of the 2nd Iowa Batt, 13 cav men and 250 of the 11th Mo I V V [Missouri Infantry Veteran Volunteers]. .. We went to Madison [with] no molestation, found the place all quiet."[43] The fate of the newly forming veteran regiment was unsure, and according to Dr. Hawley in letter on May 15, 1864, "We have yet been assigned to any brigade or division. The impression is prevalent that we will wait for our old command now up Red River and we cannot get much news from them as they are almost cut off from us."[44]

Regimental Changes April 1864

Unfortunately, 1st Lieutenant George Weber only served a few months when he was forced to resign his post as regimental adjutant due to the effects of an operation for fistula and generally debility. George Weber officially resigned his commission in April 1864. William Pickrell, 1st lieutenant, Company A, resigned in April 1864 after suffering from several bouts of typhoid-malarial fever. Also, 2nd Lieutenant Harrison Withrow, Company C, resigned in April 1864, citing personal matters that needed his attention at home. In Company G, Captain Charles Carter also resigned on April 28, 1864, and he was replaced with William Wallace who was promoted to the rank of Captain in Company G. The 34-year-old Wallace had previously held the rank of sergeant within the company. Wallace, a native of New York, was a blacksmith living in Lawrence County, Illinois, prior to the war. First Lieutenant David Bailey also resigned in April, stating that he had "contracted a disease" while in the service of the 11th Missouri which forced him to submit his resignation. Lieutenant Bailey suffered from malaria and camp diarrhea for more than eight months before his resignation. Company H fared no better at retaining officers. In March 1864, Captain William Boatright was transferred to the 71st USCT Infantry and commanded African American troops. In addition, 1st Lieutenant Lewis Gray submitted his resignation as a result of a gunshot wound that he had suffered during the Vicksburg campaign. These resignations allowed 2nd Lieutenant Edwin Applegate the opportunity for promotion to the rank of captain in Company H, which occurred in May 1864. Captain Applegate was quickly joined by 1st Lieutenant James McNeal. McNeal, an Ohio native, was 30 years old and was a saddler from Sumner, Illinois. In Company K, Captain William Stewart resigned his commission and was replaced with Cyrus Kendall, who had previously served as the company's 2nd lieutenant. 1st Lieutenant

Captain Edwin Applegate, 11th Missouri Infantry, a carpenter from Sumner, Illinois, led Company H (author's collection).

Charles Foster served the remainder of his term of enlistment and was mustered out of service.

In addition to Captain William Boatright, Sergeant Daniel DeWitt and Sergeant William Cusick transferred to the United States Color Troops. All three men were transferred with officer's rank. Both William Boatright and Daniel DeWitt later gained the rank of major in their new regiments. Daniel DeWitt was strongly supported, and each officer within the regiment signed a letter endorsing his promotion. Private Edwin Pendergast, Company B, and Private James Hussey, Company D, also enlisted in the USCT.

The Battle of Old River Lake, Arkansas

In May 1864, Confederate Major General John S. Maramduke began to plague the Federal river traffic near Greenville, Mississippi. Maramduke's force near Lake Village, Arkansas, was commanded by Colonel Colton Greene. In June 1864, the non-veterans of 11th Missouri Infantry were still part of the 33rd Missouri Infantry and the regiment was part of the First Division of the XVI Army Corps. The corps was commanded by General A. J. Smith, the Division was commanded by General Joseph Mower, and the Third Brigade was commanded by Major George Van Beek, who also commanded the 33rd Missouri Infantry. To deal with the troublesome Confederates, General Joseph Mower initiated an expedition to Lake Village, Arkansas. Mower's Second and Third Brigades landed at Sunnyside Landing, Arkansas, on the western side of the Mississippi River about 5 miles southwest of Greenville, Mississippi, at 6:00 A.M. on June 6. Mower began his march toward Lake Village, which was eight miles away; and about half way to his destination, he encountered resistance from Confederate skirmishers. Mower continued his advance until he was two miles from Lake Village when he found the Confederates on the opposite side of a bayou. The Confederate defenders held excellent position in an area of heavy timber and fired into the exposed Union lines as they approached. The Union battleline advanced to "within short musket-range of the enemy on the opposite side of the bayou, when they were met by a most galling fire from their artillery and musketry."[45] Major George Van Beek, 33rd Missouri Infantry, reported that his regiment, with detachments of the 11th Missouri Infantry, Eighth Iowa Infantry, and 12th Iowa Veteran Infantry, advanced on the Confederate position after 11 A.M. Van Beek recorded that "we soon found ourselves much exposed to a severe fire of shell and scrapnel."[46] Van Beek's brigade charged the Confederates from 150 yards away, but found that 75 yards from the enemy, a fence in their front shielded an impassable bayou 40 yards wide. Unable to advance further, both sides continued to fire away at one another from about 75 yards. Duncan McCall reported the viciousness of the fighting, and the brigade paid a significant price for their attack and inability to advance on the Confederates. Four men in the 33rd Missouri Infantry were wounded or killed with a single shell. The loss within the 33rd Missouri and the 35th Iowa was 80 casualties. McCall recalled, "One of their guns was marked. Our artillery did not render us any assistance. Eight guns were playing on us as we advanced, until we got close enough to them to use our guns, and they were forced to leave under a heavy fire. Their loss was not known. Five more of the 11th Mo., non-veterans, were wounded; two of them had to have a leg each amputated."[47] Both sides used their artillery to shell their opponent and after an hour the Confederate artillery "was silenced and that of the infantry ceased, with the exception of a few scattering shots."[48] Union reinforcements arrived and the defenders withdrew and then Mower proceeded to Lake Village without further incident.

Ambrose Armitage, Eighth Wisconsin Infantry, recorded in his diary, "We saw fifteen

Confederate Major General John S. Marmaduke, graduate of West Point and nephew of exiled Missouri governor Claiborne Fox Jackson (Library of Congress).

dead and thirty wounded rebels in a house we passed besides those who were carried away. Maraduke commanded the rebels. Col. Jefferson [8th Wisconsin Infantry commanding officer] had his horse killed and he was so drunk for awhile that he was placed under arrest, but is released again. This is the fourth time he has been in that condition in actions this spring."[49]

Two soldiers of the 11th Missouri died as a result of the action at Old River Lake. Columbus Wroe died on June 15 after his leg was amputated as result of his wounds. Wroe was a farmer from Bethel, Illinois. The other soldier who died of his wounds was Granville Williams, also a farmer, from Clay County, Illinois.[50]

Sergeant George Adams wrote of the account of Columbus Wroe's death in a letter of June 29, 1864: "One of the best boys of our company were wounded down the river. His leg were amputated between the hip joint and knee. Lived some 10 or 12 days. Died in hospital in Memphis. He were a friend of mine. He were a son of a widow name Wroe. He were my mess mate, a bed fellow and seemed next to a brother to me. He were a good example for a soulger."[51]

Battle of Tupelo

Away from the Red River Campaign of Louisiana and action in Arkansas, the focus now centered on Nathan Bedford Forrest's cavalry in Mississippi. The final conflict for the 11th Missouri Infantry involved the Battle of Tupelo in July 1864. As Sherman continued his march through Georgia toward Atlanta in the summer of 1864, it was important for the Union army that Major General Nathan Forrest be prevented from attacking their supply lines and from causing other damage for which he was particularly adept. Sherman wanted to keep Forrest busy in Mississippi to prevent his interference in the Union campaign in Georgia. Sherman sent a message to Major General George Thomas, commander of the Army of the Cumberland, on July 2 stating, "I see Forrest is at Tupelo; that the enemy has detected the fact that a heavy force, under A. J. Smith, is moving out of Memphis, as they suppose, to re-enforce us."[52] The expedition by General Andrew J. Smith was to draw "that devil" Forrest into a conflict. Sherman's hope was that Forrest would think that Smith was marching to join Sherman's armies in Georgia and attempt to prevent Smith's advance. In fact, Sherman had no other plan for Smith than to hold Forrest in place and perhaps to destroy his force. Smith's expedition would be the third attempt to control the Confederate cavalry that had been causing so much trouble. Brigadier General W. Sooy Smith was given this task during Sherman's Meridian Campaign early in 1864, and Smith was defeated at the Battle of Okolona, Mississippi, on February 22, 1864. The second attempt was made by Brigadier General Samuel Sturgis, who was defeated at the Battle of Brice's Crossroads on June 10, 1864. A. J. Smith was a wily, experienced general with excellent, well-trained troops under his command, and Smith was determined to show Forrest that he was indeed a different general than was Samuel Sturgis and Sooy Smith.

During this expedition, Sherman told Smith "to punish Forrest and the people now or risk compromising the effect of past victories."[53] Confederate General Joe Johnston needed Forrest out of Mississippi, and he wanted to "unleash him on the railroads in Sherman's rear," but Confederate President Jefferson Davis decided to keep him in Mississippi.[54] So, the stage was set as General Smith's divisions of the XVI Corp started their march toward Okolona, Mississippi, and Major General Nathan Forrest and Lieutenant General Stephen Dill Lee were there waiting for him.

On July 2, Sergeant Charles Treadway recorded that he anticipated no movement of the regiment until "the weather gets a little cooler. It is so hot here that it appears as though the earth will burn."[55] However, on July 5, General A. J. Smith's force consisted of the First Division commanded by General Joseph Mower, Colonel David Moore's Third Division, and Brigadier General Benjamin H. Grierson commanded the cavalry division. In addition, Colonel Edward Bouton commanded a brigade of United States Colored Troops. Smith's force consisted of about 14,000 men as they began their march.

As Smith moved toward Forrest, they reached Davis' Mill just inside the state of Mississippi on July 5, Ripley on July 7, New Albany on July 9 and was within five miles of Ponotoc on July 10 as the march continued in a general southward direction. As Smith's column moved southward, skirmishing intensified as Forrest tried to lure him toward Okolona where Forrest intended to fight him on his chosen terrain. Confederate generals Stephen Lee and Nathan Forrest decided that a battle with Smith could be successful, based on past victories over Sooy Smith and Samuel Sturgis, and so "decided to fight Smith where he showed an inclination to fight or attack at the first sign of retreat."[56] Dr. Thomas Hawley provided a gruesome description of the march through this part of Mississippi, "We passed over part of the same ground crossed as part of General Sturgess' forces. Could often see the wreck of a wagon, the skeleton of a mule or horse, a few muddy army blue rags. Looking closer in the bushes and gullies, we often saw bones of the human skeleton. A skull or other bones we distinguished. Some never buried at all, others in shallow pits that the pigs routed out and devoured the flesh. Then to hear the tales of many of the men who had run the gauntlet of death was truly distressing and exasperating. We could see houses burn without any compunction of conscience. Nearly all the household property was destroyed or captured. Gardens, orchards, fields near the road stripped."[57]

After remaining in Ponotoc for two days, on the evening of July 12, Smith decided to march eastward to Tupelo, sensing an ambush if he advanced further south. So it wasn't until the next morning on July 13 that Forrest and Lee discovered Smith marching toward Tupelo and away from Okolona. While Tupelo held no great strategic importance to Smith, Confederate stores and a railroad ran through the town the Confederates needed to defend. Lee and Forrest rapidly deployed their men to take advantage of Smith's column, which was stretched along the road toward Tupelo. Forrest's cavalry nipped at Smith's column and concentrated their efforts on the supply wagons. To meet Forrest's threat, Smith sent the 61st United States Colored Troops to ambush the Confederate cavalry that was harassing the Union column. After selecting a suitable ambush site, as Rebel horsemen advanced, the 61st USCT waited until Forrest's troopers got within "twelve paces before rising up, emptying many rebel saddles."[58] As the skirmishing intensified at the rear of the column, the 59th United States Colored Troops, the 11th Missouri Infantry and the 47th Illinois Infantry moved to the rear to protect the column from the cavalry actions.

CSA General Stephen Lee's men caught up to Smith's Column and decided that a concentrated attack into the column as it stretched along the road could cause some significant damage. At Burrow's Shop, also known as Camargo Crossroads, about 8 miles west of Tupelo, the Confederates attacked the Union center with men from Brigadier General James Chalmers division. Chalmers, while initially successful in killing some mules and disabling a couple of ambulances and wagons, was soon caught in a pinch between the Union soldiers behind the point of attack and the soldiers in front of the attack who stopped and moved to support the Union defenders. Chalmers was easily repulsed. Next, Confederate General Abraham Buford attacked Smith's column about six miles from Tupelo. Four brigades of Confederate cavalry attacked the supply train in an engagement that lasted about half an hour and again the Confederates were repulsed. General Mower reported that he sent the 11th Missouri Infantry to help with the repulse of the Confederate attack but the engagement was over by the time the regiment reached the supply train. Smith reported the losses: "The prisoners taken estimate their loss at this point at 500 killed, wounded, and missing. Our loss was 27 mules killed, 7 wagons broken by the carelessness of the team-

Brigade Commander Colonel Lucius Hubbard (Minnesota Historical Society).

General James Chalmers attacked the XVI Corps as they advanced on Tupelo (Library of Congress).

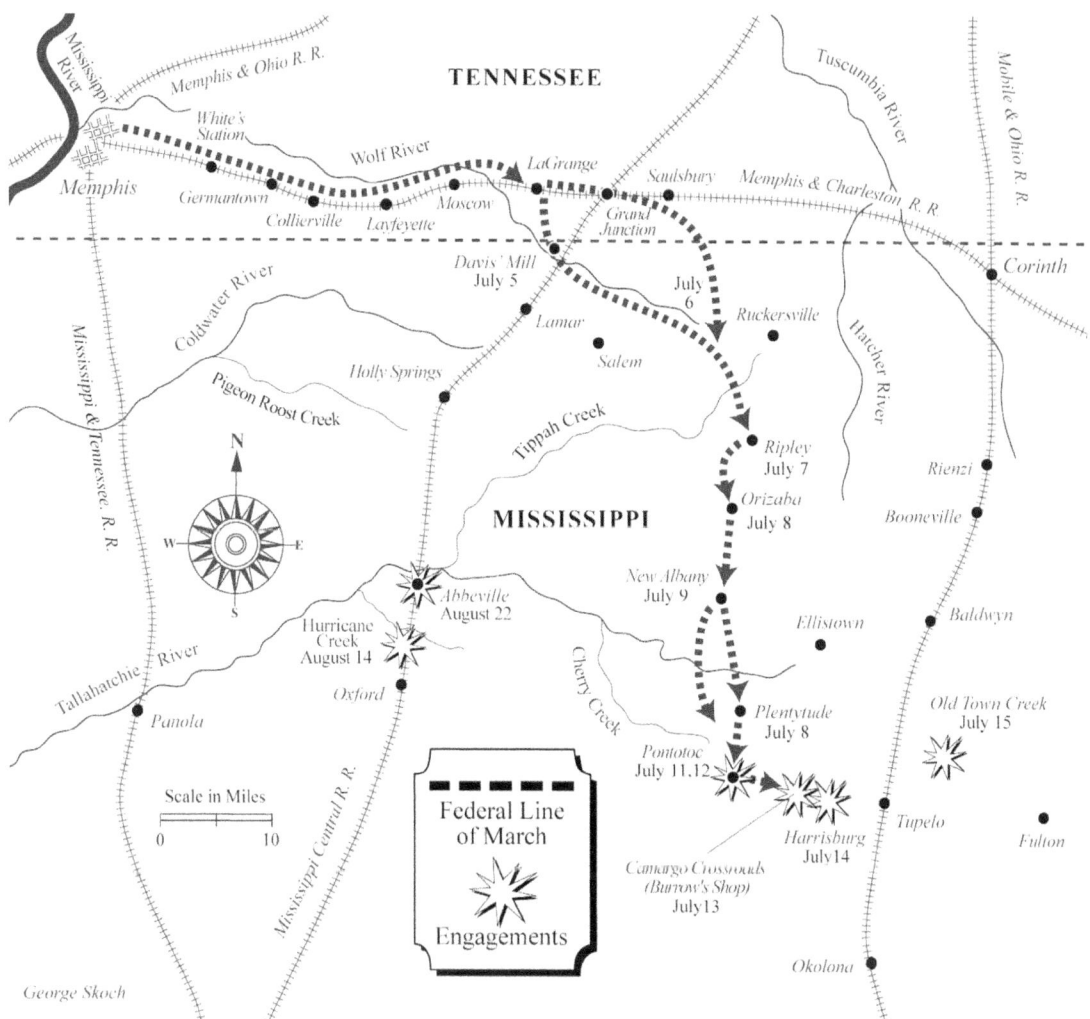

The XVI Corps' Tupelo and Oxford expeditions, July–August 1864.

sters and burned by order, after removing all stores from them and taking off the wheels and parts that could be of any service."[59] Buford reported, "After fighting him about an hour, suffering considerable loss, the enemy was heavily re-enforced and I was compelled to withdraw the brigade from action."[60] Duncan McCall reported that the Confederate attacks were repulsed, and "having tried the train to their satisfaction, and seeing that it would be impossible to get any of our hard-tack, took up a position in front of us, forming their lines across the road, with two batteries of artillery. In this way they divided the army."[61] These strategies did not delay the Union advance long, and Smith's troops advanced and took a defensive position at Harrisburg, west of Tupelo, and remained there for the night. The Union cavalry rode into Tupelo and destroyed the railroad.

The situation on the evening of July 13 was one of unpleasant decisions by Lee and Forrest. "If the Rebel commanders let him [Smith] be, Smith's men could wreck the railroad in Tupelo and destroy supplies desperately needed by the Confederacy. If they attacked head on, they would be going up against superior numbers who had terrain advantage."[62] Smith remained in place at Harrisburg and waited for Lee and Forrest to decide.

During the night of July 13, the Confederate forces moved into position to carry out a morning attack against Smith, who occupied a favorable defensive position being located on a ridge with an open field to their front. In addition, overnight Smith's troops threw up a light defensive works made of rails. On the right side of the Union line, which ran north to south, was General Mower's First Division, which included the 11th Missouri, and the left wing was defended by Colonel David Moore's Third Division. The Confederate attack was so designed that a general assault would occur all along the front of the Union right flank; but Forrest was to attack the extreme left flank and turn the Union line and possibly gain Smith's rear. The extreme left was held by the United States Colored Troops brigade commanded by Edward Bouton.

Facing Mower was Colonel Hinchie Mabry's Mississippi brigade and Colonel Tyree Bell's Tennessee brigade. Colonel David Moore was attacked by Colonel Edward Crossland's Kentucky brigade. Crossland initiated the attack as he stormed across the open field to Moore's front. The Confederate troops carried lighter carbines and shotguns during the assault as they faced the more powerful long-range muskets of the Union infantry. At this point in the war, a frontal assault into a heavily defended Union infantry line was futile, if not suicidal, and Crossland was easily repulsed. The impact of the repulse was so complete that a coordinated attack by Forrest became pointless, and Forrest abandoned his planned attack against Edward Bouton without informing Stephen D. Lee. As a result, the entire fire along the Union line was directed at Crossland who suffered greatly.

General A. J. Smith described the battle in his official report. At 7:30 A.M. the enemy was observed advancing on his troops stationed along the Pontotoc Road and drove the Union skirmishers back to their line. Smith allowed the advancing Confederate battle line to approach the Union defensive line to within 100 yards when the Union soldiers delivered a murderous volley. Then the Union soldiers began their work in deadly earnest as they rose and charged with bayonets, "driving the enemy with heavy loss from the field, killing more even as they were running than they did in the first volley. Here General Faulkner, of Kentucky, was killed."[63]

The second part of the Confederate attack was directed against General Joseph Mower's men including the 11th Missouri. The enemy advanced from the edge of a wooded area, which at least gave the Confederate soldiers

Lieutenant General Stephen D. Lee (Library of Congress).

a chance to approach the Union line. Smith recorded, "At first their lines could be distinguished separately, but as they advanced they lost all semblance of lines and the attack resembled a mob of huge magnitude. There was no skirmish line or main line or reserve, but seemed to be a foot race to see who should reach us first. They were allowed to approach, yelling and howling like Comanches, to within canister range, when the batteries of the First Division opened upon them. Their charge was evidently made with the intention to capture our batteries, and was gallantly made, but without order, organization, or skill. They would come forward and fall back, rally and forward again, with the like result."[64] The Confederate attack toward Mower and the 11th Missouri was a poorly executed attack by men who gave their full effort to accomplish their mission.

Colonel Hinchie Mabry who faced Mower wrote they "had constructed temporary fortifications on a strong position on the crest of a ridge."[65] Mabry also wrote, "A most terrific fire of small arms was opened on me when we were within 300 yards of the works. I immediately ordered a charge, but the heat was so intense and the distance so great that some men and officers fell exhausted and fainting along my line, while the fire from the enemy's line of works by both artillery and small-arms was so heavy and well directed that many were killed and wounded."[66] Mabry led the assault on Mower's line which was repulsed. Also, Bell assaulted the Union line but again he was easily repulsed.

Major General Nathan B. Forrest (Library of Congress).

Mower also counterattacked and drove the remaining Southern soldiers from the field. Smith reported that Mower found 270 dead Confederates soldiers in front of his position. The wounded from both sides were moved to several hospitals for proper care. Smith summed up the day, "My troops were so exhausted with the heat, fatigue, and short rations that it was not possible to press them farther. The loss of the enemy in this day's fighting could not fall short of 1,800 killed, wounded, and missing. 60 prisoners were captured unwounded, and have been turned over to the provost-marshal, District of Memphis, with complete lists. During the afternoon the enemy attempted to attack our rear from the east side of Tupelo, but were promptly driven back by General Grierson's cavalry."[67]

General Mower gave a report of the engagement on July 14: "The enemy commenced the attack at about 7:30 o'clock in the morning, coming down in line of battle along our front and opposite our left, moving in an irregular mass. I directed the fire to be retained until they approached quite near, and then opened on them with shell, canister, and musketry. The fight continued for about two hours and a half, when, finding that they would not approach any nearer our lines, I ordered the Third Brigade to charge on them. This was very gallantly done, and the enemy driven from the field with heavy loss."⁶⁸ The battle was fought in the hot Mississippi July sun, and Mower reported that both officers and soldiers suffered sunstroke while fighting.

The commander of the Second Brigade, Colonel Wilkin, was killed during the battle as he positioned the men of his brigade, and Colonel John McClure of the 47th Illinois Infantry assumed command of the brigade. McClure wrote the after-action report of the Battle of Tupelo for General Mower's Second Brigade. McClure reported the Second Brigade was held in reserve and formed in two lines behind the Fourth Brigade which was placed in the primary battle line. As the battle began, "we were, while there, under a heavy fire from the guns of the enemy, their shell, canister, etc., passing over the advanced forces and exploding around us."⁶⁹ The 11th Missouri Infantry and the 47th Illinois Infantry accompanied the supply train to Harrisburg to protect from another cavalry attack, and they remained with the train throughout the night. The 11th Missouri was held in a reserve role with the rest of the brigade throughout the battle and played no significant part in the fighting on July 14.

The 11th Missouri's Hospital Steward, Edward King, assisted Dr. Thomas Hawley in tending to the wounded after the Battle of Tupelo (author's collection).

Confederate General Stephen D. Lee reported of the Battle of Tupelo on July 14, 1864, from Okolona: "We attacked column of enemy under Smith, yesterday, on march from Pontotoc to Tupelo, causing him to burn many wagons. Attacked him in position at Tupelo this morning. Could not force his position. The battle was a drawn one, and lasted three hours. We are in a strong position, and can repulse an attack."⁷⁰

At sundown, the day appeared to be over and Smith withdrew his men for rest and hopefully a good night's sleep. However, at 11:00 P.M., Forrest's cavalry attempted a night attack, probably more for harassment sake than hope of doing any harm to Smith's troops. When the attack came, "it seemed as if the whole Federal army, had been waiting."⁷¹ The Confederate cavalry attacked the left flank of Smith's line that included Colonel Bouton's United States Colored Troops, and the Confederates quickly withdrew and the remainder of the night was peaceful.

After a successful day on July 14, the next morning General Andrew J. Smith found his food had spoiled, and much to his surprise, he had only one day's supply of rations for the troops. In addition to the problem with his provisions, he had only 100 rounds of artillery ammunition per gun which concerned him if the Confederates made another more serious assault on his forces. Faced with these problems, Smith decided to withdraw. On July 15, the oppressive heat continued from the previous day with numerous accounts of soldiers suffering from the affects of the heat. Despite the Union victory of the prior day, Confederate attacks began early in the day when they attacked the Union left flank. The 61st and 68th USCT met the attack and drove off the Confederates during the skirmish.

Building defenses to prevent a night attack (Library of Congress).

Smith remained in place until noon on July 15, when he started his movement away from Tupelo. Again Lee and Forrest harassed the Union movement as they had done on July 13. Mower's First Division skirmished with the dismounted Confederate cavalry as the Union began their march and as Mower's division crossed a creek bottom, the 11th Missouri came under artillery fire. The regiment recorded five casualties which occurred during the skirmish and artillery fire. Captain Menomen O'Donnell, Company A, had two horses shot from under him in the engagement resulting in a severe injury to his left shoulder when the horse fell.

Once the Confederates realized the Union forces were withdrawing, they hurried to find a way to inflict what harm they could. Smith's corps found it necessary to fight their way out of the ring of Confederates and accomplished this before the concentration of Stephen D. Lee's troops arrived. Most of this action occurred near Old Town Creek where the Confederates attacked the rear of Smith's column. Smith ordered reinforcements to meet this threat, and the Confederates withdrew from the action. It was at this time that General Forrest was wounded in this right foot. This action ended the second day's fighting near Tupelo.

The 11th Missouri's Captain William Cleland, who had been previously wounded at the Battle of Iuka and during the charge on Stockade Redan at Vicksburg, was wounded at the Battle of Tupelo. Duncan McCall recorded the incident where several men of the 11th Missouri were wounded while maintaining the rearguard as the regiment marched from Tupelo on July 15. "Here the 11th Missouri lost four men wounded, who were all struck by the same shell, a captain and three of his men, none of them dangerously wounded. Captain Clealand was struck twice, but will soon be able to take command of his company again."[72] Cleland was wounded more severely than McCall thought. Lieutenant Colonel William Barnum issued Special Order #27 on July 31, 1864, stating, "1st Captain William W Cleland has been seriously wounded at the Battle of Tupleo and rendered unfit for duty, he is hereby ordered to turn over all permanent property to 1st Lieut. George Quick who is hereby ordered to take command of said company."[73] However, Cleland recovered and remained with the regiment until the regiment was mustered out of service in 1866.

Losses of Mower's 2nd Brigade — Tupelo Expedition July 5–21, 1864[74]

	Killed	Wounded	Missing
47th Illinois	0	4	3
5th Minnesota	1	1	1
9th Minnesota	2	5	0
11th Missouri	0	5	0
8th Wisconsin	1	4	2
2nd Iowa Artillery	0	6	0
Total Second Brigade	4	25	6

General Smith recorded his thoughts regarding action at Tupelo: "The division commanders gallantly and faithfully discharged the duties assigned them with zeal and ability. I only ask that our country may always find such sons in her hour of need. General Mower was more fortunate than the others in being in the exact position where the hardest fighting occurred, and nobly bore the brunt and deserves the bays."[75]

The 11th Missouri Infantry recorded one officer and four soldiers were wounded in the Battle of Tupelo. The prolific letter writer, Dr. Thomas Hawley, recorded the action on July 13 and July 14 beginning with the attack on the Smith's column when the Confederates "got badly repulsed and severely punished. The attack on the flank of the moving column was directly on the rear of our regiment as it was turning an angle in the road. The Rebel cavalry rushed up and fired most of the balls whistling over our heads killing a man just behind the men and in front of the ambulance. No one of our regt hurt.... Next day they attacked us in force but Genl Smith & Mower had chosen a fine position and we thrashed them finally losing in all less than 300 and they nearly 1500. I had to work hard for a time."[76]

Sgt. Charles Treadway, Company A, wrote of the Battle of Tupelo, "Well it appears as things are going all right as far as I can learn. I haven't had any news for over a month as I have been on a long and hard march after Old Forrest. We found him at Tupelo Miss and gave him a complete whipping and have just got back to camp. We ware gone 87 days and all that time we ware cut off from news.... March was over two hundred miles and the weather was intensely hot and dry. We averaged 15 miles a day from the time we started until we returned. There was several sun struck. Our loss was about 300. The Rebs loss was twenty four hundred. I never saw such a victory gained we had the advantage in the ground and the Rebs charged us our company didn't lose any. Thare were 6 wounded in our Regt. one captain one corprell and 4 privates."[77]

Summary

The 11th Missouri Infantry ceased to exist on August 5, 1864, when the three-year term of enlistment expired for the soldiers. During the past three years, the regiment had experienced great victory, and the only real defeat for the regiment occurred while storming Stockade Redan on May 22, 1863. Even in that defeat the regiment demonstrated its pride and glory as they charged in a suicidal attack as Confederate fire ripped through the ranks of the regiment.

The regiment stood and never flinched at Fredericktown, Point Pleasant, Iuka, Corinth, Jackson, Vicksburg, and, finally, Tupelo. The regiment had excellent commanders and the men proved themselves worthy of their flag.

The 11th Missouri Infantry fielded 954 men, although they never went into battle with that number. The attrition of war, including, sickness, accident, capture, and battle losses eroded the men of this regiment. By the end of the three-year term, at least 150 men had died, giving their last full measure to preserve the Union. But from the ashes of the 11th Missouri Infantry would rise the 11th Regiment Missouri Veteran Infantry and this regiment had another 18 months of service remaining.

Maybe one of the best summaries of the first three years of service for the 11th Missouri comes from Sergeant Charles Treadway: "I see in yesterdays paper that the Confederate Government as the Rebs call it have sent in peace measures that they will come back to the Union if our government will let them keep their slaves that hasn't been freed by the war and all those has been freed by the war let them be free. Uncle Abe made them a reply that when thare was a peace made he wanted it made solid and firm so their wouldent be war in our country again. That is the kind of peace we soldiers want and no other. We want a peace that will stand forever and ever. Slavery is dead and well the South knows it and they are willing now to come back if we will let them have a portion of their slaves, if the slave is taken from the poor man let them be taken from the rich man. So says Abe, and in regard to our next President Lincoln is the man. He is the man that took hold of a broken lim and let him mend it. He will get a unanimous support in the Army he will get in the least 5 to one.... Instead of hallowing hurragh for Democract and hurragh for Republican let them all hurragh for the Union — stand firm to the constitution and laws and not be quarreiling over political issues."[78]

So for a lasting peace, the 11th Missouri had fought for three years and for the hope of mending a broken limb, the 11th Missouri Veteran Infantry would fight until 1866.

11th Missouri Infantry Regimental Losses July 1863–August 5, 1864

	JULY–SEPT 1863	OCTOBER–DEC	JAN–MAR 1864	APRIL–AUG 5
Discharged	Gould, Moses Wagoner (A)	Blackledge, Theodore (F)	Jones, Joseph Corp. (C)	
	Myers, Thomas (A)	Gillighan, James (F)	Anderson, Benjamin (E)	Wallace, William Sgt. (G)
	Back, John (C)	McCoy, Thomas Fifer (B)	Dougherty, Jefferson Sgt. (H)	Chapman, Daniel Corp. (I)
	Martin, Benjamin (C)	Rennick, Silas (F)	Cochran, Jacob Corp. (G)	Lehr, George (G)
	Rudicil, Jacob (C)	Donnell, Samuel (H)	Watson, Elijah (C)	Moore. John (K)
	Engledow, William C. (D)	Harman, Elijah (E)	Miles, William (G)	Perry, John (K)
	Robertson, James (F)	McGrady, William (K)	Pickerel, General (G)	Snoden, James (H)
	Jennings, James M. (G)	Winchester, Lorenzo (F)		
	Sherman, Charles (H)			
	Detrich, George (I)			
	Reed, Andrew (B)			
Died	Monyhon, Owen (A-K)	Severs/Seivert, William (A)	Creech, Voluntine (D)	Bridges, Jeremiah (B)

	JULY–SEPT 1863	OCTOBER–DEC	JAN–MAR 1864	APRIL–AUG 5
	Buchanan, Walter (A-K)	Baker, William (B)	Rinehart, John C. (D)	Williams, Granville (D)
	Kloffer, John (B)	Lucas, George Sgt. (C)	Delapp, Thomas (H)	Johns, Alton E. (K)
				Dewitt, Elijah (D)
	Snodgrass, James (B)	Butler, John (E)	Hunt, Thomas (K)	Fisher, Hiram (G)
	Morril, John/James (C)	Back, John (C)	Dudley, Joshua (H)	Wroe, Columbus (I)
	Gibson, Calder (D)	Bayles, Thomas (F)	Highsmith, Leander (G)	
	Gibson, Chester (D)	Hubbard, Benjamin (F)	Lawson, Victor (G)	
	McGuire, John (D)	Karn, John (C)	McGuire, William (A)	
	Stuckenschneider, Christopher (D)	Simmons, Charles (E)	Payne, Nathaniel (K)	
	Burgess, William (E)		Williams, William (D)	
	Pitman, Mills (F)			
	Moler, Solomon (H)			
	Beathard, Thomas (I)			
	Riley, Michael (K)			
	Scott, Samuel (K)			
	Miller, John (K)			
Deserted			Kelly, John (G)	Kelley/Kelly, Edward (F)
				Anderson, William A. Corp (H)
				Anderson, William Musician (H)
				Brewer, Joshua (G)
				Hicks, James (F)
				Martin, William (I)
Transferred Out		Mcguire, James (H)	Dixon, Henry (A)	
			Mcguire, George (A)	
			Hussey, James Musician (D)	
			Chasteen, Onias Corp. (F)	
			Selby, John T. (F)	
			Randall, John (F)	
			Geaghan, John (H-K)	
			Boatright, William Captain (H) to 71 USCT	
			Kerney, Timothy (H)	
			Laird, John H. (H)	
			Dewitt, Daniel Sgt. (I) to 71 USCT	
Resigned	Elliott, Cyrenus Capt. (A)		Bail, Abner Capt. (E)	Withrow, Harrison 2nd Lt. (C)
	Hathorn, John 2nd Lt. (I)		Weir, Elias W. 2nd Lt. (F)	Henry, George W. Capt. (D)
	Gannon, Edward 1st Lt. (G)		Gray, Lewis Lt. (H)	Cowperthwait, John 1st Lt. (D)

	JULY–SEPT 1863	OCTOBER–DEC	JAN–MAR 1864	APRIL–AUG 5
	Bailey, David (G)			Sappington, Mark L. 2nd Lt. (D)
				Wallace, William Capt. (G)
				Stewart, William S. Capt. (K)
Missing—				
POW			Byrd, John (C)	

CHAPTER 7

Abbeville, Pursuit of Price, and Battle of Nashville

"I was in the big battle at Nashville whare thousands sleep the sleep of the dead."
— Sergeant Charles Treadway

A New Beginning

The new 11th Regiment Missouri Veteran Volunteer Infantry was mustered into service, and this was a very different regiment than the one that served from 1861 until August 1864. Although in August 1864 the regiment contained about 300 of the soldiers from the old regiment, the Missouri Veteran Infantry became a regiment that received an influx of soldiers throughout the remaining term of service. Lieutenant Colonel William Barnum worked diligently to keep the identity of the regiment throughout 1864 and was successful. The reputation of the 11th Missouri Infantry as a fighting regiment was well-known and the Union army needed them. In August 1864, the new 11th Missouri Veteran Infantry consisted of reenlisting men from the 11th Missouri Infantry and one captain, 2 lieutenants and 180 soldiers from the Seventh Missouri Infantry. Colonel Barnum of the 11th Missouri and Lieutenant Colonel Robert Buchanan of the Seventh Missouri met and worked out an agreeable transfer of the men of the Seventh Missouri into the 11th Missouri Veteran Infantry. On June 12, 1864, Colonel Barnum explained in a letter to Colonel John Gray, Missouri Adjutant General, that the 11th Missouri had the lowest numbers needed to maintain its identity and the Seventh Missouri's numbers were too low to maintain the unit integrity. Barnum requested to have the Seventh Missouri integrated into his regiment, which was approved by August, but the Seventh Missouri Infantry did not physically join the regiment until December 10, 1864, per Special Order No. 153. At that time the regiment's combined strength was about 500 men. Colonel Barnum made similar requests to Colonel Gray to send the men of the Eighth Missouri Infantry and the Sixth Missouri Infantry to increase his numbers, but these requests were not approved. Soldiers from two other regiments (33rd Missouri Infantry and 124th Illinois Infantry) were added to the ranks of the 11th Missouri Veteran Infantry, but this did not occur until July 1865 for both regiments. Soldiers from both these units joined the 11th Missouri Infantry after the fighting was done. Also the regiment gained men over the next the eighteen months through recruits, draftees and substitutes. The draftees and substitutes came into the regiment at various times, and the cohesive, well-trained companies of the old regiment were a mixture of veterans and raw recruits in the new veteran regiment.

The flag of the 11th Missouri Veteran Volunteer Infantry (courtesy Missouri Department of Natural Resources).

Because the 11th Missouri Veteran Infantry had a relatively small number of men, it was not until December that the command structure of the regiment was fully formed. The initial commands structure of the regiment is shown below:

REGIMENTAL STAFF	AUGUST 1864–OCTOBER		
Colonel			
Lt. Colonel	Eli Bowyer		
Major	Modesta Green		
Adjutant	Walton Finch		
Quarter Master	Henry C. Applegate		
Surgeon	Melanchthon Fish		
Asst. Surgeon	Thomas Hawley		
Chaplain	Vacant		
Company A		*Company B*	
Captain	Constantine McMahan	Captain	Jesse Lloyd
1st Lieutenant	Barnabas Nigh	1st Lieutenant	
2nd Lieutenant		2nd Lieutenant	

Company C		***Company G***	
Captain	James Lott	Captain	William Wallace
1st Lieutenant	William Simmons	1st Lieutenant	George Quick
2nd Lieutenant		2nd Lieutenant	
Company D		***Company H***	
Captain	William Erwin	Captain	Edwin R Applegate
1st Lieutenant	Lyman Randall	1st Lieutenant	James McNeal
2nd Lieutenant		2nd Lieutenant	
Company E		***Company I***	
Captain	William Notestine	Captain	George Adams
1st Lieutenant	Levi Roney	1st Lieutenant	David O. Shoopman
2nd Lieutenant		2nd Lieutenant	
Company F		***Company K***	
Captain	William Cleland	Captain	Cyrus Kendall
1st Lieutenant	Charles Smith	1st Lieutenant	
2nd Lieutenant	Wilford McElyea	2nd Lieutenant	

For the regimental staff, gone was William Barnum who fought to make the 11th Missouri Veteran Regiment a reality. Colonel Barnum suffered from a series of physical aliments and chose to leave the regiment with the expiration of his term of service. Regimental command fell to one of the most unmilitary appearing lieutenant colonels in the Union army, Eli Bowyer; but Eli Bowyer was a thoughtful, dedicated and respected leader with three years' experience. The position of regimental colonel remained vacant until Bowyer was promoted in March 1865. Eli Bowyer had served as a surgeon in the regiment until he was promoted to major in 1863. Bowyer was born in Warren County, Ohio, on March 20, 1818. Bowyer taught school for two years prior to studying to become a physician. He graduated from the Ohio Medical College in Cincinnati in 1844 and moved to Mason, Ohio, to practice medicine. He moved to Indiana, and in 1860 settled in Olney, Illinois, as he tried to find a geographic location that helped improve his health.

Modesta Green, captain of Company C, was promoted to rank of regimental major. Walton Finch was promoted to position of regimental adjutant. Finch was previously a sergeant in Company F, and he was

Eli Bowyer was a physician, able leader, and well-respected commander of the 11th Missouri Veteran infantry in 1864 (author's collection).

a farmer from Xenia, Illinois, prior to his enlistment.

Dr. Thomas Hawley remained regimental surgeon despite what appears to be an indication he would have preferred to be mustered out. Dr. Hawley remained in Memphis from August 5 through August 12, awaiting the decision regarding whether he would be mustered out. Dr. Hawley discussed his request, "He would do all he could to have me mustered out as I wished it but he feared I could not get out as readily as medical officers are so scarce in the army."[1] Dr. Hawley was informed correctly because he did not leave the 11th Missouri infantry until January 1866.

The captain of Company A, future Medal of Honor winner, Menomen O'Donnell, was mustered out at the expiration of his term of service, and the only other officer in the company, William Pickrell, resigned in April 1864. Constantine McMahan assumed company command of Company A and was promoted to the rank of captain, and Barnabas Nigh was promoted to rank of 1st lieutenant. The company did not add a 2nd lieutenant until March 1865. Constantine McMahan was a native Illinoisan and was a farmer living in Bridgeport, Illinois, prior to the war. Fellow Bridgeport, Illinois, resident, Barnabas Nigh, a native of Ohio, was also a farmer prior to his enlistment. Both men had been part of the 11th Missouri Infantry since 1861.

Captain Constantine McMahan, Company A (courtesy Civil War Museum at Wilson's Creek National Battlefield).

The command of Company B remained unchanged as the regiment reformed in August. Captain Jesse Lloyd and 1st Lieutenant James Wilson remained as the officers of the company. In Company C, Modesta Green was promoted to major, and this allowed James Lott to assume company command. Captain Lott would remain as the sole officer until November. George Lucas was promoted from the ranks in Company C, but Lucas died of intermittent fever (typhoid pneumonia) in a general hospital at Jefferson Barracks in St. Louis before he could assume this role. George Lucas was a native of Massachusetts and listed Loami, Illinois, as his home. Lucas was teacher prior to the war.

Between April and August, all three of the officers of Company D resigned. In May, William Erwin was promoted to the rank of captain and commanded the company and remained the only officer of the company. Erwin, a native of Illinois, was a farmer residing in Clay County, Illinois, prior to the war. In October, 1st Lieutenant Lyman Randall was promoted to assist Captain Erwin. The 26-year-old Randall was a native of Maine who had been a farmer living in Clay County, Illinois, prior to the war. Company E was very similar to Company D, Captain Abner Bail, 1st Lieutenant Jacob Blew and 2nd Lieutenant Elmore Ridgely all resigned and Captain William Notestine was promoted to command the company. In October, Levi Roney was promoted to the rank of 1st lieutenant. Roney, a native of Ohio, had enlisted in the 11th Missouri Infantry at the age of 22 and was a farmer living in Stringtown, Illinois, prior to the war.

Company F retained Captain William Cleland and 2nd Lieutenant Wilford McElyea as company officers. First Lieutenant John Finlay was mustered out in August at the expiration of his term of service, and in October, Charles Smith was promoted to the rank of 1st lieutenant. Charles Smith was a 41-year-old stone cutter and resided in Xenia, Illinois, prior to his enlistment. Captain William Wallace retained command of Company G, but 1st Lieutenant David Bailey resigned in April. He was replaced by newly promoted

Lieutenant Wilford McElyea served with Company F for the remainder of the war (author's collection).

1st Lieutenant George Quick in May, and Lieutenant Quick remained with the regiment through the transition to the veteran regiment. The 25-year-old Quick was a farmer prior to his enlistment. The two officers of Company H, Captain Edwin Applegate and 1st Lieutenant James McNeal, retained their ranks during the reorganization of the regiment.

Both of Company I's officers, Captain Charles Osgood and Charles Ethel, resigned at the end of their term of service. Captain George Adams and 1st Lieutenant David O. Shoopman assumed the leadership positions of this company. Charles Adams was 35 years old when he enlisted in 1861 and he had been serving as a sergeant in Company I prior to his promotion. Adams was a native of Illinois and was a farmer living in Versailles, Illinois, prior to the war.

A new enlistee for the 11th Missouri, James A. Anderson, Company I, was a farmer from Illinois (courtesy Civil War Museum at Wilson's Creek National Battlefield).

David Shoopman had enlisted at the age of 23, and he had been a farmer living in Beardstown, Illinois, prior to his enlistment. Finally, Company K lost all three of the officers from April to August 1864. The single, new officer promoted was Captain Cyrus Kendall. Kendall remained the only officer in the company until 1865. Kendall, a Pennsylvania native, was 26 years old and had been an attorney living in Clay County, Illinois, prior to the war.

The Oxford, Mississippi, Expedition

During the months prior to December 1864, when the 11th Missouri Veteran Infantry was moved to Nashville, the soldiers were involved with various activities including an expedition to Oxford, Mississippi, for the entire month of August. The regiment was involved in skirmishes at Hurricane Creek, Mississippi, on August 14 and at Abbeville near College Hill on August 23. The regiment moved from Memphis to Duvall's Bluff, Arkansas, during the first week in September, and it marched to Brownsville September 10–11. Then the 11th Missouri marched through Arkansas and Missouri in pursuit of Price's army September 17 through November 13.

The new regiment remained as part of General Andrew J. Smith's XVI Army Corps; and more importantly, part of their beloved commander, General Joseph Mower's 1st Division. The 2nd Brigade continued to be commanded by the capable Colonel Lucius Hubbard.

Organization of Troops in the Department of the Tennessee [2]

16TH ARMY CORPS — MAJ. GEN. ANDREW J. SMITH
FIRST DIVISION — BRIG. GEN. JOSEPH A. MOWER

Second Brigade — Col. Lucius F. Hubbard
47th Illinois, Col. John D: McClure
5th Minnesota, Lieut. Col. William B. Gere
9th Minnesota, Maj. William Markham
11th Missouri, Maj. Eli Bowyer
8th Wisconsin, Lieut. Col. William B. Britton

In August 1864, the 11th Missouri left La Grange, Tennessee, and was involved in an expedition to Oxford, Mississippi, in an attempt to prevent the concentration and attack of the Rebel cavalry under command of Major General Nathan Bedford Forrest. General Smith's XVI Corps moved from Memphis to La Grange and marched toward Oxford, Mississippi. (See Map page 161.) It wasn't until August 14 that Hubbard's Second Brigade was involved in a skirmish at Hurricane Creek, Mississippi. Little is recorded about the skirmish at Hurricane Creek and the only 11th Missouri regimental records recorded "skirmishing with the enemy driving them across Hurricane Creek and then returned to camp."[3] Dr. Thomas Hawley recorded on August 14, 1864, the regiment "was marching towards Oxford after Mr. Rebels, found them in considerable force, drove them 7 miles after considerable artillery firing and heavy skirmishing.... No one hurt."[4] Cloyd Bryner, author of the history of the 47th Illinois Infantry, described the skirmish without much detail, "The fight lasted for two hours and the Confederates were driven for five miles toward Oxford. The rains were heavy and almost unintermittant."[5] The Union and Confederate batteries shelled each other through the afternoon, and the Union cavalry flanked the Confederates on "both sides, leaving the front open for a charge."[6]

While Smith's corps was seeking Confederate forces, they marched on Oxford, Mississippi, where the force of the Union army was felt when they burned "all the fine brick blocks fronting on the public square, and also the Courthouse, in one fine conflagration. The houses of some prominent official Rebels Confederates were also fired."[7]

Brigade commander Colonel Lucius Hubbard did not join the brigade until August 17 when the brigade was camped near Abbeville. As the brigade marched to Hurricane Creek, then to Oxford, and moved northward, the rear guard was attacked by Confederate cavalry on August 22. As the skirmishing at the rear of Hubbard's brigade increased, Hubbard sent reinforcements to deal with the situation. Interestingly, Hubbard does not refer to the 11th Missouri Veterans as part of his brigade; but the 11th Missouri regimental records show that "August 23 marched to Abbeville, skirmishing with and repulsing the enemy."[8] The skirmish on August 22 was described by Lyman Pierce of the Second Iowa cavalry. He explained that Smith was marching near Oxford, Mississippi, seeking the troublesome Confederate cavalry, when he received a message that General Nathan Forrest had just raided near Memphis. In the dispatch, Smith was ordered to return to Memphis. Pierce went on to explain the next events, "In compliance with this order, Smith returned to the Tallahatchie and started his train across the bridge near Waterford. Just as the third team got upon the bridge, it gave way, precipitating the teams into the water. This caused the army to bivouac until a new bridge could be constructed. Gen. Chalmers, who had followed our rear with a view of pouncing upon and capturing the rear guard, after the balance of the force should cross the river, was ignorant of this accident to the bridge, hence he waited until he supposed that the bulk of the army had had time to cross, when he furiously charged the rear. The pickets were not yet out, and the rebels came directly into the camp of the infantry, who quickly repulsed them with a loss of ten killed and nine wounded, left in our hands. The Federal loss was none killed and ten wounded. The cavalry pursued the retreating enemy back to Hurricane Creek. In this pursuit the Seventh Kansas lost one man killed."[9] On August 23, the 11th Missouri recorded one man wounded; Sergeant John M. Clements, Company B, was severely wounded in his left arm with a musket ball.

Colonel Hubbard explained, once he reinforced his rear guard, "an advance was ordered, which was made at double-quick. The enemy essayed to make a stand, but though in superior force succeeded only for a moment. A charge was made upon his line, which gave way in confusion and was driven for more than a mile in disorder, when the pursuit was abandoned, though the enemy continued to retreat, moving rapidly off to the music of the guns of the Second Iowa Battery. At sundown the command returned to camp."[10] Colonel Hubbard reported 15 wounded and that the enemy had "12 killed, that fell into our hands, many wounded, and some prisoners."[11] By August 29, the brigade was safely in La Grange, Tennessee. Dr. Thomas Hawley also recorded the action on Hurricane Creek: "The Brigade had quite a skirmish 7 miles south of here on Harry Carn Creek driving the Rebs off.... In Camp, had not been here half an hour when the enemy came upon us evidently thinking we were still crossing the River. Our boys were soon in line and heavy skirmishing commenced lasting all of another half or ¾ hour when Mr. Rebs beat a hasty retreat leaving about 12 killed and as many wounded in our hands. Also 8 or 10 prisoners.... Our loss was 12 or 13 in all. The Rebs carried off more than they left. I hear they got one of our wagons and ambulance. I had a chat with the prisoners. Rather intelligent, healthy men and say they are most agreeably disappointed in regard to our treatment of prisoners of war but are determined in their resistance to the old government and ... after their own terms they want their RIGHTS as usual ... poor deluded fellows."[12]

During both engagements on the expedition to Oxford, the Union forces were battling the Confederate cavalry forces of Brigadier General James Chalmers Division and the Second Cavalry Brigade commanded by Colonel Bill Wade, which included Seventh Tennessee Cavalry, 26th Tennessee Cavalry Battalion, Fifth Mississippi Cavalry, Seventh Mississippi Cavalry Regiment, and Willis' Cavalry Battalion. Chalmers, being outnumbered, could only seek opportunities to capitalize on any mistakes that Smith made.

The Pursuit of Price

In late August 1864, Major General Sterling Price, the 11th Missouri's old nemesis from the Battles of Iuka and Corinth, launched an aggressive attempt to disrupt the Union momentum in the west. Price's plan was to raid into Missouri, his home state, and attempt to win back Confederate supporters and also attempt to assist in the Atlanta campaign by diverting Union resources to Missouri and possibly allowing additional Confederate troops to move through Federal occupied territory in the mid-southern states. Price's plan included moving through a large arc that included attacking St. Louis, Jefferson City, sweeping across Missouri into Kansas and returning through the Indian Territory (Oklahoma) disrupting Union positions as he swept all before him in a massive cavalry raid.

Price's cavalry force of 12,000 horsemen entered Missouri on September 19, 1864, through southeastern Missouri. On September 27, Price unsuccessfully attacked a Union force at Fort Davidson, near Pilot Knob, Missouri, and guerrillas attacked Centralia, Missouri, in central Missouri. These actions caused the XVI Army Corps under command of Major General A. J. Smith to move in pursuit of Price; and thus began one of the 11th Missouri's longest, uneventful treks of the war. Price's force continued its east-west arc — striking Cuba, Missouri, on September 29, occupying Washington on October 2, skirmishing at Herman on October 3, and reaching the state capital on October 8. Then, Price continued his raid through October, striking Boonville, Glasgow, Sedalia, Lexington, and Independence. It wasn't until the Battle of Westport on October 23 that the momentum shifted, and instead of being on the offensive, Price began retreating back toward Arkansas, which he finally reached on December 2, 1864.

The 11th Missouri, again part of Colonel Lucius Hubbard's Second Brigade, A. J. Smith's XVI Corps, was sent in pursuit of Price. One of the most frustrating tasks in the Civil War was the pursuit of enemy cavalry by infantry; and this was no exception. The 11th Missouri and the brigade were first dispatched to St. Louis, and arrived in Cape Girardeau via riverboat on October 5. Dr. Hawley wrote on October 11, "Our stay in the city [St. Louis] has been so short I could hardly realize that we were so near home."[13] Next the regiment was sent to Jefferson City and arrived there on October 15, a week behind Price's cavalry. Then the brigade marched to Harrisonville, arriving there on October 26. The 11th Missouri marched to Independence and then into Kansas, only to return to Pleasant Hill, Missouri. Finally, the brigade marched eastward towards Warrensburg and embarked by rail back east and south. The 11th Missouri recorded that this marathon pursuit of Price resulted in an aggregate of 1,320 miles by rail, steamboat and foot. There are no indications the regiment participated in any direct combat during the odyssey.

Sergeant Charles Treadway described the regiment's pursuit of Price: "Marched to Brownsville Ark. We lay here for 4 days until all the wagons ware loaded then we took an Northeast direction and came out at Cape Girardeau Mo. got on some boats came up the River to St. Louis landed a few moments and then went ahead to Jefferson City took the cars and went to Salene Bridge which the Rebs had destroyed. Disembarked and marched to Sedalia thence to Lexington thence to Independence thence to Kansas City thence to Harrisonville thence to Warrensburg thence to Sedalia thence to Jefferson City thence to St. Louis."[14]

While Sterling Price wrote of his success of the raid through Missouri, it is generally considered to have been an unsuccessful foray northward. This was the last major offensive action by the Confederate Trans-Mississippi Department. Next, the 11th Missouri traveled to Nashville, departing on November 24, arriving on December 1, where their destiny lay on a hillside just south of the city. The men of the 11th Missouri were about to face their second bloodiest battle of the war; and maybe their finest hour.

Battle of Nashville

From May into September 1864, Major General William T. Sherman's Union armies steadily marched toward Atlanta; and Sherman fought a series of battles, finally besieging the city. Politically, 1864 had great significance because this was a presidential reelection year for Abraham Lincoln who was not optimistic about his chances to be reelected. Not only was Sherman stymied at Atlanta, Grant was stalemated at Richmond and Petersburg. Many Americans were pushing for an end to the war that had gone on for too long, and too many families had been touched by the casualties of the increasingly unpopular war. Sherman pushed onward toward Atlanta and General Joe Johnston was unable to hold back the sea of blue-coated Union soldiers. Finally, in July 1864, Johnston was relieved of his command and replaced with General John Bell Hood. John Hood was a native of Kentucky, born in 1831, and graduated from West Point in 1853. Hood had served in the army in the southwest part of the United States; but in 1861, Hood resigned his commission in the United States Army and joined the Confederate States of America. Hood served with Lee in the Army of Northern Virginia, and after the Battle of Gettysburg, he was assigned duty in Braxton Bragg's Army of Tennessee and participated in the Battle of Chickamauga. When Hood assumed command during the Atlanta campaign, his task was to keep Sherman from capturing Atlanta. The Battle of Jonesboro, Georgia, fought on September 1, resulted in the Union army cutting the last rail supply line into Atlanta. Realizing it was fruitless to defend the city any further, Hood abandoned Atlanta to the Union army. While Sherman was continuing his "march to the sea," Hood's Army of Tennessee moved to northwest Georgia and then to Florence, Alabama. On November 21, Hood began what was to be called the Tennessee Campaign, which would include battles at Spring Hill, Franklin, and finally, Nashville.

Hood's objective was to cut the supply line to Sherman and also to attempt to cut off and destroy either Major General George Thomas' force (19,000 men) in Nashville or Major General John Schofield's force (20,000 men) dispatched from eastern Tennessee to combine with Thomas' troops. Hood's army totaled greater than 30,000 men. Schofield moved toward Columbia, Tennessee, on the route to Nashville, but stopped and began to build defensive works when he became aware that Hood was near and a Confederate attack was imminent. Confederate Lieutenant General Stephen D. Lee began shelling Schofield's works in Columbia, while Hood, with 20,000 men, moved toward a Union force of 5,000 men commanded by Major General David Stanley at Spring Hill, Tennessee. Becoming aware of Hood's main force approaching Stanley's two divisions, Schofield moved to reinforce him. Stanley was attacked on November 29 and was able to repulse Major General Benjamin Cheatham's Confederates. Stanley then withdrew and joined Schofield's main force at Franklin, Tennessee. The Battle of Spring Hill was the prelude to the much more significant Battle of Franklin.

General Schofield had force-marched through the night and reached Franklin, Tennessee, at daybreak. At Franklin, only 20 miles from Nashville, Schofield was very close to his objective of uniting his forces with those of General Thomas. Despite the fact that General Stephen Lee's force and most of his artillery was not present, Hood was faced with a dilemma—allow Schofield to escape and join Thomas or to attack the smaller force that he faced at Franklin.

To make matters worse for Hood, he decided to make a frontal assault on a very strong defensive position, a tactic that was highly unlikely to be successful. In the entire Atlanta Campaign, only one frontal assault was successful in the three and half month campaign; but Hood decided to make the attack, beginning at 4:00 P.M. on November 30. The desperation and ferocity of the battle made this one of the bloodiest days of the war. The battle continued into the night, but by daybreak, the outcome was apparent. Hood had failed in his attempt to destroy Schofield, and in fact, had suffered 6,500 casualties, including 1,700 men killed, compared to Schofield's total losses of about 2,500 men. During the night, Schofield withdrew to his objective, successfully combining his forces with those of General George Thomas. In addition to the massive losses of Hood's army at Franklin were the great command losses that included fifteen Confederate generals (six killed or mortally wounded, eight wounded, and one captured) and 53 regimental commanders. The six generals killed or mortally wounded were Patrick Cleburne, John C. Carter, John Adams, Hiram B. Granbury, States Rights Gist, and Otho F. Strahl. The loss of these officers, particularly Major General Patrick Cleburne, to Hood was incalculable, because these officers had shown such an outstanding ability to lead men in battle this late in the war. Despite Hood's smaller army, he marched toward Nashville, stopped a few miles south of the city, and began to construct a series of defenses on which he hoped the Union army would throw themselves.

It was this series of events that led to the concentration of forces around Nashville, and the events that caused the 11th Missouri Veteran Infantry to be called from their pursuit of General Sterling Price to a major battle to its east. In October 1864, the 11th Missouri remained part of A. J. Smith's XVI Corps and were still assigned to the Second Brigade commanded by Lucius Hubbard, but one major change occurred. Brigadier General Joseph Mower, who had been part of the 11th's Missouri's life since May 1862, was gone. Recognition of his superior record, excellent leadership, and willingness to fight rewarded General Mower with a promotion to the rank of major general. Mower was transferred to the XVII Army Corps and he joined Sherman's army as it pushed eastward.

By December, additional officers were added to the rather thin ranks of the 11th Missouri in anticipation of receiving the replacements from the Seventh Missouri Infantry. The captain of Company B, Jesse Lloyd, was mustered out and William Followill, who previously served in the Seventh Missouri Infantry, was named captain of the company. Jesse Lloyd had several physical problems including a case of smallpox and infection of a wound. He had been removed from duty within the company as an attempt to restore his health, but this was not successful. In addition to the loss of Captain Lloyd in Company B, Benjamin F. Kelly was promoted to the rank of 1st lieutenant when 1st Lieutenant James Wilson resigned at the expiration of his term of enlistment. Benjamin Kelly was 23 years old and was a farmer from Sangamon County, Illinois, prior to his enlistment in the 11th Missouri in 1861. William Simmons was promoted to the rank of 1st Lieutenant in Company C. Simmons, 23 years old, was a carpenter from Springfield, Illinois. William Simmons had been serving as a sergeant in Company C before his promotion.

By December 1, 1864, the various components of the Union forces were converging on Nashville. General John Schofield's command, IV and XXIII Corps, marched into Nashville from their recent battle at Franklin. General George "Rock of Chickamauga" Thomas commanded the Union forces at Nashville. Thomas was a native Virginian who entered West Point in 1836, graduating in 1840, 12th in his class. He began his career in artillery and was involved in the Seminole War and the Mexican War. He taught at West Point and later participated in Indian warfare at Ft. Yuma in 1855. When the Civil War began, he chose to stay with the Union, not following the action of his native state of Virginia. He was promoted to brigadier general of volunteers in 1861 at 45 years of age, and became divisional commander of the Army of the Ohio. Thomas was promoted to command the Army of the Cumberland after successfully preventing the decimation of William Rosecrans' army by staging one of the most dramatic stands of the war around the Snodgrass Farm at Chickamauga. Thomas was formally given command of the Army of the Cumberland in October 1863, and this command successfully pushed Braxton Bragg's Confederate army off the seemingly impregnable Missionary Ridge in November 1863. Thomas continued to command the Army of the Cumberland throughout the Atlanta Campaign, and he was now called upon to deal with General John Bell Hood's army that was positioned south of Nashville. Although Thomas had excellent credentials as a general, Grant felt Thomas was too defensive minded and lacked confidence in him.

Right Wing, 16th Army Corps
November 14 to December 16 1864
Maj. Gen. Andrew J. Smith

FIRST DIVISION — BRIG. GEN. JOHN MCARTHUR
SECOND BRIGADE — COL. LUCIUS F. HUBBARD

5th Minnesota, Lieut. Col. William B. Gere
9th Minnesota, Col. Josiah F. Marsh
11th Missouri, Lieut. Col. Eli Bowyer, Major Modesta Green
8th Wisconsin, Lieut. Col. William B. Britton
Iowa Light Artillery, 2d Battery, Capt. Joseph R. Reed

As soon as the Union forces began arriving in Nashville, Thomas began to construct new defenses for the city of Nashville. He was unsure of the size of the Confederate army that was converging to his south and his situation was somewhat reminiscent of his experience at Chattanooga in September 1863, but this was vastly different. The city of Nashville was occupied by Union forces since 1862 and an extensive set of defenses had been constructed since that time, which included an "inner line" of defenses that boasted seven forts and redoubts. The "outer line" of defenses, about a mile from the inner defenses, was necessary because of the number of troops that were converging on Nashville. Nashville was the second most heavily fortified city in the United States at this time in the war, with only Washington D. C. being more heavily fortified. Thomas felt he needed to stay behind these defenses until he could concentrate his various forces and also determine the size of the enemy he was facing. Also, Thomas' army included the garrison of Nashville commanded by Brigadier General John Miller which contained 4,000 men. The 11th Missouri infantry arrived with the 9,000 men of General A J. Smith's XVI Army Corps by the end of November. General John Schofield's 24,000 men marched into Nashville on December 1. Major General James Steedman's Provisional Detachment from the District of Etowah arrived on December 1 with 8,500 soldiers. Finally, Major General James Wilson's 6,500 cavalrymen arrived in Nashville in December. Thomas clearly outnumbered Hood's 21,000 soldiers that arrived just south of Nashville on December 2.

Beginning in 1863, Missouri regiments were required to send a history of their activities during the year for the annual adjutant general's report, and the 11th Missouri's report was finalized on December 14 and reflected the uncertainty of the last two weeks of December near Nashville. Lieutenant Colonel Eli Bowyer's cover letter to the 1864 report for the 11th Missouri Infantry is found below:

Hd Quarts 11th Mo Vet Inf
Nashville Tenn Dec 14th / 64
Gen Jno B Gray
General

Please find enclosed the annual Regimental History of the Eleventh Mo V I. A simple narrative of marches and events as I understood you to request. Gen Hood's Army is still confronting us and may give us an additional part of interesting history to incorporate in the present year. The daily round of artillery and picket firing with an occasional reconnaissance. Of this however you are daily posted. The detachment of veterans of the 7th Mo is now being transferred to the Eleventh Mo Vet I. We got some good men I only regret the transfer on account of the disappointment of the officers of the 7th who had some expectations of filling up their regiment. The transfer was not brought about by the action of any of the officers present with the Eleventh Mo at this time. At least as far as my knowledge extends this accession will raise the number of the reg to over five hundred men that can be relied upon. We would be glad to have the Reg filled up with effective men. Can you do anything for us in that way? If so you will much oblige.[15]

The Seventh Missouri Infantry veterans, which were transferred to the 11th Missouri Infantry, had a distinguished career. They were part of the "Irish Seventh" and had been mustered into service in St. Louis in June 1861. They had served gallantly at Corinth and in multiple battles in the Vicksburg campaign, in addition to many other battles. These were veterans which fit well with the veterans of the 11th Missouri Infantry.

7th Missouri Infantry Soldiers Transferred into the 11th Missouri Infantry, December 1864

Soldier	Rank	Soldier	Rank
Company A		Arthur, John (1)	Cook
Allen, James	Pvt.	Blake, James	Pvt.
Berge/Birge, Alpheus W.	Pvt.	Curtis, John E.	Pvt.
		Daniels, John F.	Pvt.
Calder, William A.	Pvt.	Davis, Levi M.	Sgt.
Connors, John	Pvt.	Evans, Thomas	Pvt.
Cooper, Nathan	Sgt.	Followill, William P.	Captain
Dwyer, Edward	Musician	Geiles/Giles, James G.	Pvt.
German, Dennis	Pvt.	Goodrich, John	Pvt.
Graham, Edward L.	Pvt.	Heath, John B.	Sgt.
Hagan, Dennis	Pvt.	James, James W.	Corporal
Howell, George H.	Pvt.	Livingston, Napoleon B.	Musician
Long, James C.	Pvt.		
Minard, Nelson	Pvt.	Lockett, Thomas	Corporal
Morris, George	Pvt.	McGlassen, John	Pvt.
Murray, John	Pvt.	Morrow, Goldman J.	Corporal
Numach/Numerk, John	Pvt.	Nelson, Charles	Pvt.
		Quinn, John R.	Pvt.
O'Neil, Henry	Pvt.	Reynolds, Thomas	Pvt.
Raridan, Edward	Pvt.	Smith, Harmon/Herman	Pvt.
Raver, John	Pvt.	Talbott/Tolbott, Isaac A.	Pvt.
Riffle, George W.	Pvt.	Totzell, Valentine	Pvt.
Roach, Richard	Pvt.	Webb, Jehn/John	Pvt.
Roadbecker, Henry	Pvt.	Whitfield, Marshall (1)	Cook
Ryan, Thomas	Pvt.	Williams, James	Corporal
Smith, Jacob	Pvt.	Wroughton, George	Pvt.
Springer, Andrew U.	Pvt.	York, James J./Jefferson	Pvt.
Steward/Stewart, Jasper	Pvt.	**Company C**	
		Baker, Walter	Sgt.
Stewart/Stuart, John	Pvt.	Carless/Carlos, William	Pvt.
Welch, George W.	Corporal		
Westfall, Thomas F.	Pvt.	Dellon/Dillen/Dillen, Dennis	Pvt.
Company B			
Anderson, James C.	Pvt.	Doran, Patrick	Pvt.
Anderson, John J.	Pvt.	Flannagan, Patrick	Pvt.

Soldier	Rank	Soldier	Rank
Gannon, Thomas	Pvt.	Hurley/Harley, John	Pvt.
Jones, Robert	Pvt.	Keif, William	Pvt.
Kelly, Patrick	Pvt.	Kennedy, John	Pvt.
Lombard/Lumbard, John	Pvt.	Kinney, Henry	Pvt.
		Leahy, Patrick	Pvt.
Lynch, Martin	Pvt.	Mars, William H.	Pvt.
McCarty, Dennis	Pvt.	McGuire, James	Pvt.
McCormick, Lawrence	Pvt.	Padden/Paddin, Martin	Pvt.
Meyers, Augustus	Pvt.		
O'Reilly, John	Pvt.	Shultz, John	Pvt.
Riley/Rielley, John	Pvt.	Smith, John	Pvt.
Royester, John	Corporal	Taylor, John R.	Corporal
Ryan, Edward	Pvt.	White, Patrick	Pvt.
Shaw, Joseph	Pvt.	Wright, John	Pvt.
Sullivan, Patrick	Pvt.	**Company G**	
Welch, John	Pvt.	Bartch, Anton	Pvt.
Wright, Thomas	Pvt.	Cain, Robert P.	Pvt.
Company D		English, William E.	Pvt.
Atkinson, George	Pvt.	Haynes, George W.	Pvt.
Barnett, William	Sgt.	Highsmith, Richard M.	Pvt.
Connelly, Maurice	Pvt.		
Corcoran, Peter	Pvt.–Corporal	Hix, William	Pvt.
Cotterell, William	Pvt.	Kimberlin, Isaac N.	Pvt.
Dee, Maurice	Pvt.	Kueff, John W.	Pvt.
Dougherty, Felix	Pvt.	Meyers, James M.	Sgt.
Dugan, Peter	Pvt.	Powers, James	Pvt.
Granay, Cornelius	Pvt.	Sullivan, Thomas R.	Corporal
Herron, Thomas A.	Pvt.	Waggoner, Noah	Pvt.
Hyde, Patrick	Corporal	West, Andrew Jr.	Pvt.
Jacquess, Isaac	Pvt.	West, John M.	Corporal
Kelley/Kelly, James	Corporal	White, Edward N.	Corporal
Kelley/Kelly, Timothy	Corporal	**Company H**	
Keys, Michael	Pvt.	Baker, Joel D.	Pvt.
Kingston, William	Pvt.	Brinknell, Edward (1)	Pvt.
McBride, Joseph	Pvt.	Bunth, Christopher	Pvt.
McGinnis, John	Pvt.	McBride, Daniel	Pvt.
Murphey, Thomas	Pvt.	McCann, John	Pvt.
O' Donnell, Thomas	Sgt.	McDonald, Daniel	Pvt.
Company E		Ryan, James	Pvt.
Bolden, Thomas	Pvt.	Smith, Gilmour W.	Corporal
Brogan, John	Pvt.	Sumner, John B.	Corporal
Delevadwa/Delwadwo, Petro	Sgt.	**Company I**	
		Armstrong, John	1st Sgt.
Dowd, John	Pvt.	Breon, Patrick	Pvt.
Fairbanks, William H.	Pvt.	Davidhiser, Henry	Pvt.
Harper, William H.	Pvt.	Dulong, John	Pvt.
Harris, James	Corporal	Farrell, Christopher	Pvt.
Hays, Michael	Pvt.	Hurley, John	Pvt.
Hays, William	Pvt.–Cook	Logan, John	Pvt.

Soldier	Rank	Soldier	Rank
O'Neal, Patrick	Pvt.	Dolan, Francis	Sgt.
Rane/Raus, Bernard	Pvt.	Dougherty, Michael	Pvt.
Walsh, Garrett	Corporal	Hunt, Thomas	Pvt.
Company K		Jackson, Edmond M.	Sgt.
Alexander, Job. H.	Pvt.	Leddy, Bernard	Pvt.
Bagan, Frances	Pvt.	Maher, Lawrence	Pvt.
Blackmar, Richard	Corporal	McCauley, Alexander	Pvt.
Carterville, Adrian	Pvt.	McCready, Prosper	Pvt.
Cheney, William	Pvt.	Slyon, James	Pvt.
Connelly, Allen W.	Pvt.	Sharkey, Nicholas	Corporal
Clark, William F.	Musician	Upson, Nelson	Pvt.

It was quite a unique scenario that developed at Nashville in December 1864. A much smaller force was besieging a much larger force, but Hood felt he had no choice but to force an assault from General Thomas. "As long as the political focus was on Hood's northern invasion and siege of a major Federally occupied city, it was positive publicity and salve for Hood's injured ego. Yet, the military practicality of the matter was in serious doubt, as Hood knew all too well."[16] Hood hoped for reinforcements to bolster his army and to improve the chance of success of besieging Thomas. He knew the Union army would have to attack him. Selecting an excellent defensive line, Hood was in position to potentially defensively defeat the superior Union army. He planned to draw the Union army away from their strong defensive line and crush them as they attacked his defensive line. And in early December, Hood felt that he had the plan that would force Thomas' hand when he decided to attack the Union garrison at Murfreesboro, Tennessee. Thomas would have to allow the garrison of 8,000 to be defeated and captured by Hood's superior force, or he would have to attack Hood on the heights south of Nashville in a move to rescue the Union garrison at Murfreesboro.

Meanwhile, the external forces on the Union army at Nashville were also prompting action on the part of Thomas, and this prompting was coming by way of General Ulysses Grant. As previously mentioned, Grant did not have confidence in Thomas.

Eli Bowyer led the 11th Missouri in their first major engagement as a veteran regiment at Nashville in 1864 (USAMHI).

Although he felt he was an excellent defensive general, he did not think Thomas was a good offensive general. The exchange between Thomas and Grant over the two week period prior to the Battle of Nashville very nearly cost Thomas his command. On December 6, General Grant wired Thomas stating, "Attack Hood at once, and wait no longer for the remount of your cavalry."[17] Thomas felt facing Hood's Confederate cavalry, commanded by Major General Nathan Bedford Forrest, would require a rested and well-horsed Union cavalry, which he felt he lacked.

Action at Murfreesboro

Meanwhile the action around Murfreesboro was heating up. Major General Lovell Rousseau commanded the 8,000 men in the Union garrison at Murfreesboro. The action began around the town on December 1 when the Confederates cut the telegraph linking Murfreesboro to Nashville. Next the Confederates, who were systematically attacking railroad blockhouses, attacked a blockhouse just west of Murfreesboro. The Union cavalry moved to investigate the firing around the blockhouse and came under fire from Confederate infantry and artillery. The Union cavalry requested assistance from Rousseau, who responded by ordering three infantry regiments under commanded of Brigadier General Robert Milroy to advance on the blockhouse. Milroy encountered Confederate infantry, and after exchanging volleys, attacked and pushed the Confederates back. Milroy prudently moved back to Murfreesboro, because the infantry he has just encountered were three Florida infantry regiments, part of Major General William Bate's 1,600 man division. The ever aggressive Nathan Bedford Forrest, in conjunction with Bate, surrounded Murfreesboro. On December 7, Rousseau responded by again sending Milroy, this time with a force of 3,300 men, to relieve the siege on the town. After an exchange of volleys, Milroy's infantry charged and the broke the Confederate line, capturing 200 prisoners. Milroy again withdrew to Murfreesboro, and while this was less than a decisive victory, Rousseau successfully prevented Hood's plan of requiring Thomas to attack him to rescue Rousseau. Clearly, Rousseau did not need rescuing.

General John Bell Hood commanded the Confederate army at Nashville in December 1864 (Library of Congress).

Thomas Plans His Attack

While Hood planned to force Thomas in action, he made a serious mistake by sending Bate and Forrest away from his main force. This left only Confederate General James Chalmers' cavalry to protect the entire left flank of Hood's army at

Nashville, which was an impossible task covering an area of about three miles with only 900 cavalry. In addition, the anchors on the left of the Confederate line, Redoubt 4 and Redoubt 5, were virtually unprotected.

However, where Hood failed to force Thomas' hand, Grant succeeded. Grant threatened to relieve Thomas of his command if he did not attack Hood. During December 9–11, the weather worsened and became a factor that made Thomas reluctant to attack Hood; however, Thomas had decided to attack Hood. While awaiting the decision to initiate combat, the two warring armies faced very different situations. For Thomas' forces in Nashville, December was a time of waiting—first, anticipating Hood's attack on the city and when this did not occur, they waited for their attack on Hood. Nashville was well-supplied and offered good quarters for the troops. For Hood's men, the wait was more unpleasant. Unlike the Union soldiers who were well-housed in and around Nashville, the Confederates were camping on high, barren ground without adequate winter clothing, blankets and tents. The lack of shoes was "one of the Confederate army's most serious problems."[18] The temperatures fell into the teens as the defenders prepared for battle with Thomas' Federal troops

On December 11, General Thomas met with his commanders to prepare for offensive action against Hood commencing on December 13. Although some of Thomas' subordinates had also felt he was reluctant to attack Hood, at the end of this meeting there was no doubt about Thomas' commitment to take action. On December 13, General J. H. Wilson's cavalry took to the saddle and began to vex Hood who had, until this time, the initiative. As Hood began to anticipate an attack from Thomas, the question was where the attack would occur. The Union cavalry concerned Hood because it moved to the western part of the Confederate line. Hood had anticipated the Union strike would occur on his right (east). Hood began to shift his 25,000 men in an attempt to guess where Thomas would attack. The Confederate general still held the belief that Thomas wanted to relieve the pressure on Murfreesboro; but in fact, Thomas' objective was a few miles to his front—Hood's army. Hood had wanted Thomas to attack him, and he was about to get his wish.

The best advantage of the Confederate army was its defenses. Hood's defenses were formidable, which included "small enclosed redoubts capable of holding seventy-five to a hundred men, built of logs and earth, with embrasures for artillery."[19] However, Hood's shortage of men needed to adequately defend his position made the redoubts on the extreme left vulnerable targets for the attacking Union soldiers. In addition Redoubt 4 and Redoubt 5 were not completed. On the morning of December 14, the weather improved and the snow and ice melted leaving a muddy mess. Thomas sent a message to the War Department on December 14: "The ice having melted today, the enemy will be attacked tomorrow morning," and so, the fateful day for the Battle of Nashville was set for December 15, 1864.[20]

On the evening of December 14, General Thomas issued his plan for attack in Special Field Order No. 342, which outlined the actions for the components of his army. The orders called for the assault to begin as the weather permitted and ordered General Andrew J. Smith's XVI Corps to lead the assault on Hoods left flank. General Wilson's cavalry was to operate in conjunction with Smith in the assault, and he was also to deploy a portion of his command to protect the Union left flank in case Hood counterattacked. General Thomas Wood's IV Corps would attack along with Smith after uniting his right flank with Smith's left flank. General James Steedman's role was to protect Nashville from a counterattack, and his role was later modified to make a demonstration toward Hood. General Schofield was ordered to the trenches and later to provide support for Smith's attack. General John Miller's Nashville garrison was to protect the interior lines at Nashville. Finally, the orders designated that the attack would begin at 6:00 A.M. on December 15.[21]

The Union line at Nashville (Library of Congress).

Battle of Nashville, Day 1— December 15, 1864

Colonel Lucius Hubbard recorded his orders and the movement of the Third Brigade. He was directed to bring his brigade into readiness for the battle on December 15. His brigade began their march toward the enemy at 6:00 A.M., and they marched by columns to the front. By 8 A.M. the brigade was marching along Charlotte Pike. Colonel Lucius Hubbard recorded, "I moved out on the pike in column, by the flank, and about a mile from the point of starting was directed by General McArthur to move to the left across the country to the vicinity of the Hardin Pike, or until I should be able to connect with the line of the Third Brigade. In executing this movement I encountered a skirmish line of the enemy, which I was required to engage and push back. This, however, involved but little delay; the connection was readily formed and my line established upon the right of the Third Brigade."[22] The regiments were formed in the following order from right to left: Ninth Minnesota Infantry formed on the right, Fifth Minnesota Infantry, 11th Missouri Infantry, and Eighth Wisconsin Infantry on the left, with the Second Iowa Battery in reserve. Hubbard ordered a company from each of his regiments to be provided as skirmishers as the brigade marched toward the enemy.

Confusion resulted as units tried to get to their assigned positions for the attack on the Union right; but General James Steedman, while not bogged down with a wide sweeping move like A. J. Smith, began his attack on the left of the Union line at 8:00 A.M. Steedman's attack continued until noon when it ground to a halt, succeeding in slightly occupying the Confederate line on the eastern part of the battlefield, but making no other advance.

Meanwhile on the Union extreme right, the Union cavalry was unsuccessful in making progress against the outnumbered men of General Chalmers' cavalry on their front. The Fourth Infantry Corps, commanded by General Thomas Wood, located on the left of General

A.J. Smith's XVI Corps began their attack at 1:00 P.M. toward Montgomery Hill and was successful in capturing the hill by 2:00 P.M. without any losses. There they found the hill virtually unoccupied. Unknown to General Wood, Hood withdrew the Confederate line from Montgomery Hill a few days before the battle.

Next came General A. J. Smith's XVI Corps, a set of veteran soldiers who were "fond of boasting that they been to Vicksburg, Red River, Missouri, and about everywhere else in the South and West, and if A. J. ordered them to, they would to go to hell itself."[23] This would be the first battle the 11th Missouri would find General John McArthur leading their division, but McArthur was also an experienced soldier and had fought with the old 11th Missouri in the Battle of Corinth. The able Colonel Lucius Hubbard commanded their brigade and Lieutenant Colonel and Dr. Eli Bowyer led the regiment. The 11th Missouri, with their division, began their advance toward the Confederate extreme left defended by General A. P. Stewart's Corps. The 11th Missouri's Second Brigade was in the center of McArthur's Division as it approached the Confederate lines.

General John McArthur was "every bit as good a soldier as Mower, and many of his men proudly considered themselves the elite of the army" (Library of Congress).

Part of the attack made by the 11th Missouri was described by William H. Gilliard, Company F, who believed that he fired the first shot to begin the Battle of Nashville on this part of the Union line. "Early December 15, 1864, at Nashville, an army formed, with the cavalry, under the command of Hatch, covering the right flank. Cos. F and G of the 11th Mo. formed as skirmishers immediately in front of the regiment on the right flank of the infantry. The order to advance came, and we had gone about half a mile. At the foot of a hill stood a log cabin, with smoke curling out the chimney. In front of the cabin stood a Confederate sentienel at right-shoulder shift. I took aim and fired. Capt. Smith, who was a little to the rear, yelled; 'Gilliard what are you doing?' About this time 12 rebel guards ran out of the cabin, to be met by a volley from our skirmish line, the first volley in the opening of one of the greatest battles of the civil war, and I shall always believe that I fired the first shot."[24]

Around 2:15 P.M., the attack on the extreme left of the Confederate line began in earnest as the dismounted cavalrymen of Brigadier General Edward Hatch and the First Brigade of McArthur's Division, commanded by Colonel William McMillen (114th Illinois, 93rd Indiana,

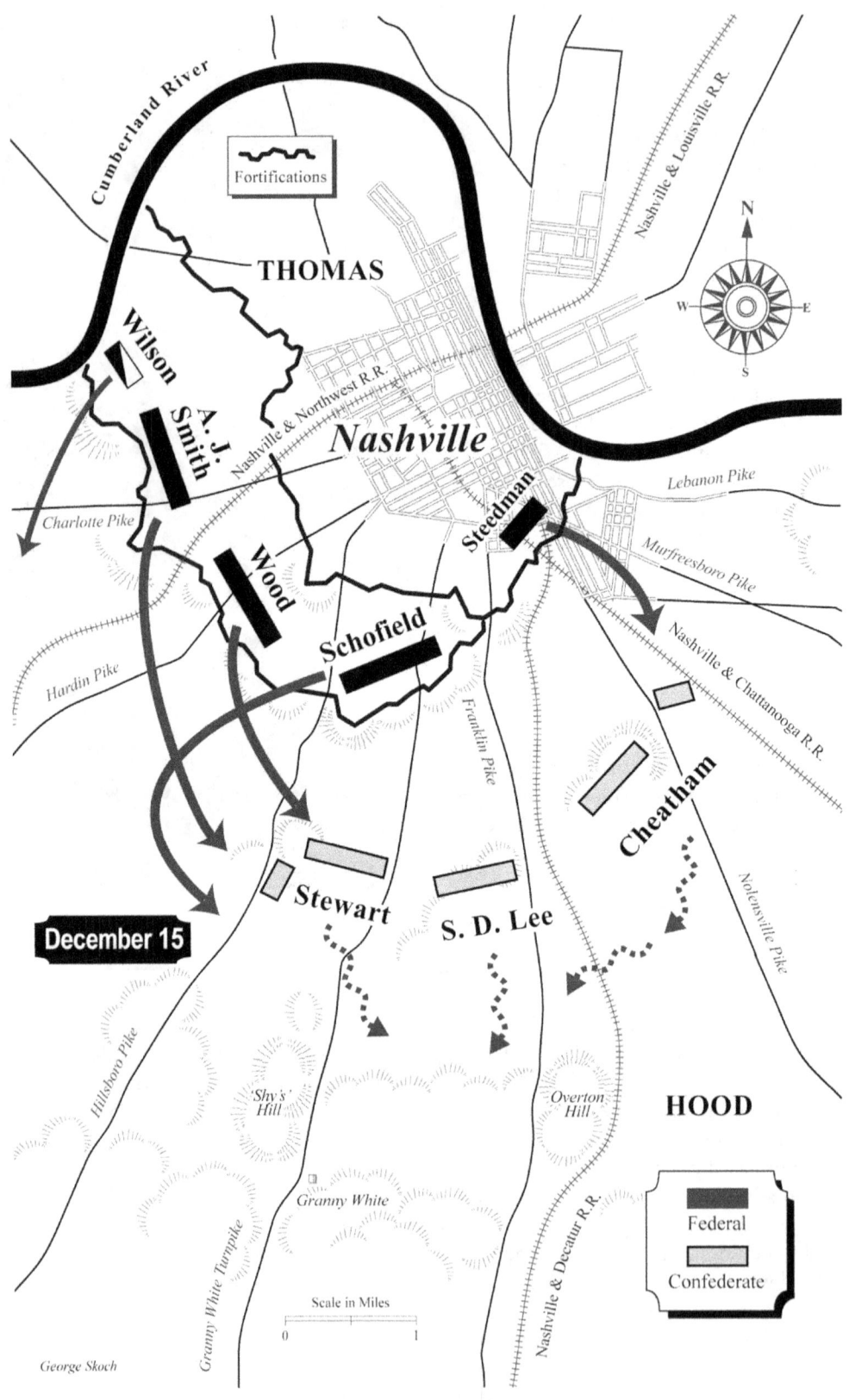

Battle of Nashville, December 15, 1864.

10th Minnesota, 72nd Ohio, 95th Ohio, and Cogswell's Light Artillery) attacked the Confederate line. Redoubt No. 5 had two 12-pound Napoleon cannons entrenched in the defenses. Located about 600 yards northeast was Redoubt No. 4, which faced the 11th Missouri and the regiments of the Second Brigade. Redoubt No. 4 contained four 12-pound cannons. These positions were defended by Major General Edward Walthall's Division. Specifically, Redoubt 4 was commanded by Captain John Lumsden and had about 150 defenders. The redoubt was bombarded for three hours by Union artillery, and it was quickly overwhelmed by Hatch and McMillan's brigades as they launched their attack. The first step in turning the Confederate left flank was accomplished. Redoubt No. 5 had been under construction the morning of the battle, and defended with about 100 men, was the second redoubt to fall.

The 11th Missouri faced the soldiers of General A. P. Stewart on the afternoon of December 15, 1864 (Library of Congress).

McArthur ordered the Second Brigade to support the attack on the Confederate left, and the brigade responded by charging toward Redoubt No. 4. Before Hubbard's men could reach Redoubt No. 4, Hatch's and McMillen's men charged by the flank on the redoubt. This freed Hubbard's men to charge past the redoubt and then move toward the east, but Hubbard realized that he needed to change his front to protect his unsupported left flank. Hubbard changed his front to face Brigadier General Daniel Reynolds' Confederate brigade (Fourth, Ninth and 25th Arkansas Infantry and the First and Second Arkansas Mounted Rifles). While Hubbard was moving to face Reynolds, McArthur ordered his Third Brigade an attack on Redoubt No. 3, located on the left of Hubbard, after seeing the success of the Union assault on Redoubts No. 4 and No. 5; and the Confederates quickly evacuated Redoubt No. 3. Next Colonel Sylvester Hill's Third Brigade turned their attention to Redoubt No. 2, which was also taken in short order, but Colonel Hill was shot and killed as the attack began. Redoubt 1, just north of Redoubt 2, was abandoned.

Around 4:00 P.M., Schofield's XXIII Corps was ordered to support the flank of XVI Corps' attack on the Confederate left flank. The XVI Corps moved toward the Confederate line, and a line of defenders was found behind a stone wall east and parallel to the Hillsboro Pike. Hubbard stated that the defenders "recoiled under our withering fire and fell back in disorder before the steady advance."[25] The first Confederate line was overwhelmed as the Union steadily moved forward. Hubbard claimed about 400 prisoners as they moved past the wall. As the brigade moved forward, they also captured two additional cannons that were unlimbered on a road, but Hubbard prudently decided not to advance further with his left flank unprotected. He changed his flank once he saw Confederate reinforcement moving forward. Hubbard formed his line on a crest to meet the approaching Confederate line and brought up the Second Iowa artillery, "whose effective practice checked the movements of the re-enforcing column of the enemy and served to increase the confusion of the retreat."[26]

As the Confederate reinforcements hastened to meet the Union attack, the focus of the

The Battle of Nashville (Florida Center for Instructional Technology).

battle shifted to an intense infantry regiment battle. Confederate General Daniel Reynolds' Arkansas Brigade directly faced the 11th Missouri's brigade, but other Union troops were converging on the angle held by Reynolds' brigade. As McArthur's division advanced, General Edward Walthall ordered Reynolds to retreat from his non-defendable position when he found himself being flanked on both ends of his line.

The action of the 11th Missouri was described by Major Modesta Green: "On the morning of December 15 the regiment, with the brigade, left camp near Nashville, and made a reconnaissance to the right and front, skirmishing with the enemy on the Charlotte pike, then passed to the left, taking position in line of battle in front of our former position. From here we advanced in support of Captain Reed's (Second Iowa) battery until the order was received to charge the rebel fort. The charge was made in handsome style. Company E, commanded by Captain Notestine, being in the advance, in line of skirmishers, were the first to enter the fort. (Captain Notestine was afterward badly wounded and had a leg amputated.) The regiment continued to advance until the second fort was taken by the cavalry and other troops on the right. Here we were allowed to rest a few moments, when we again moved forward. After advancing a short distance we came upon the enemy in line of battle on a hill; here another charge was made, in which the rebels were completely routed, and driven in perfect confusion a distance of three-quarters of a mile, officers and men behaving most gallantly, capturing many prisoners. Night coming on we were ordered to halt and remained in line of battle during the night, throwing up temporary earth-works."[27] The 11th Missouri began their attack at the Battle of Nashville with 325 officers and men reporting for duty.

William Notestine, who was wounded in the day's action, was the 23- year-old captain of Company E. Notestine was a railroader from Olney, Illinois, prior to the war. He was one of the original members of the 11th Missouri and had worked his way up through the ranks through the merit of his performance. Notestine was well liked in the regiment and was a personal friend of Dr. Thomas Hawley who bitterly lamented the serious wounding of his friend.

Colonel Hubbard recorded the action on December 15, when "Company E, Eleventh Missouri Infantry, Captain Notestine, engaged as skirmishers, advanced to within a dozen yards of the more advanced work of the enemy, from whence they drove the gunners from their pieces. By direction of the general commanding I gained a position as near the enemy's battery as practicable, formed the brigade in two lines, the Fifth and Ninth Minnesota constituting the first and the Eleventh Missouri and Eighth Wisconsin the second line, and prepared to assault the work. The brigade connected with the Union line on their right and together they advanced at the trot. The line crossed a deep gully and began to turn their right flank to the enemy. The enemy only held their position for a short time and began to retreat and brigade captured artillery that was abandoned. Captain Notestine's skirmishers, of the Eleventh Missouri, were the first to enter the work, and assisted in turning the captured guns upon the retreating enemy. I pursued as far as the Hillsborough pike, steadily driving everything in my front, and capturing many prisoners, my skirmishers the while pressing up the hill to the rear of the captured position, and entering the work of the enemy simultaneously with the troops upon my right."[28] The enemy along Hubbard's flank showed themselves to be full of fight and prepared to attack the brigade. Hubbard found himself in a perilous situation, with the enemy along his flank and extending to his rear. Hubbard had advanced so far that he was unsupported by friendly troops. Skirmishers from the Confederates were moving forward and encountered Hubbard's skirmishers. The Second Iowa Battery was valiantly shelling the advancing Confederates and protecting Hubbard's men. "The fire of the artillery, and the rapid advance of my skirmishers, two companies of which — Company D, Eighth Wisconsin, Captain Williams, and Company D, Eleventh Missouri, Captain Erwin — charged along the Hillsborough pike at a run, had a very demoralizing effect upon the enemy, who surrendered in large numbers, or retreated in utter disorder."[29] The two companies captured 450 prisoners, who were escorted to a holding area under General Thomas' control. The brigade established a new line across the Hillsborough Pike where it waited for the rest of the Union infantry to join it.

Around 4:30 P.M., General Thomas Wood's IV Corps moved against Redoubt No. 1 and captured it. The Confederate defenders were in full flight and only the early darkness of the December night stopped the fighting for the day. Before any additional movement could be made by the brigade, darkness had fallen and Hood had been forced to retreat during the evening. The Union troops moved east about a mile to the Granny White Pike. At the end of the day on December 15, a telegram was sent to Washington about the day's success. Questions remained about Hood's plans for the next day and whether he would withdraw or stay and fight. The decisions were made that evening — Hood felt he had no choice and decided to stay and fight reasoning that the South needed a victory in Nashville and there was nothing to be gained by retreating and being pursued by a superior force. For Thomas, the success of

December 15 convinced him even more that Hood could and would be defeated in the hills north of Brentwood, Tennessee.

Hood withdrew during the night and entrenched in front a group of hills. Hood concentrated and reinforced his flanks, and from west to east Cheatham's Corps, Stewart's Corps and Lee's Corps faced Schofield's XXIII, Smith's XVI, Wood's IV and Steedman's Provisional Corps. The new battle line was less than three miles long; and despite Thomas' optimism, the Confederate army had plenty of fight in it and had the added advantage of excellent defenses.

Ambrose Armitage, Eighth Wisconsin Infantry, recorded Hubbard's brigade settled in a muddy spot after the day's battle and was moved again into an equally muddy spot. "If any of us moved the rebels peppered us from their works. For six mortal hours we lay in this mud under close fire if any of us moved. My teeth chattered with cold."[30]

Battle of Nashville, Day 2 — December 16, 1864

On the morning of December 16, Smith's XVI Corps moved toward the Confederate breastworks and entrenchments only to come under artillery fire. Smith was reluctant to launch a frontal assault against these strong Confederate defenses. As he moved his infantry to within 600 yards of the Confederate defenses, he ordered his artillery to begin shelling the defensive positions. On Smith's right Schofield was also reluctant to initiate an attack fearing he did not have the troops to dislodge the entrenchments. Wood and Steedman's troops moved to the front by late morning. Finally, it was Wood and Steedman that initiated the attack on the right of the Confederate line because Wood thought that Overton Hill could be taken, which would allow him to turn the Confederate right flank. The attack began at 2:45 P.M., but Wood and Steedman were stopped in separate bloody attacks, which decimated many regiments of the United States Colored Troops (USCT).

Hubbard's brigade began the day about sunrise and advanced to find Hood's line in front of them. After advancing about a third of a mile, the Confederate line was encountered and Hubbard drew "from his line a very galling fire. I found him posted behind a line of works running parallel to my front and crossing the Granny White Pike at a right angle."[31] Next the brigade advanced until they were only 300 yards from the Confederate line near the Bradford House where the regiments could gain some cover. Hubbard then stacked his regiments by placing two regiments in the front with two regiments directly behind those. Next, the Second Iowa Battery, placed on a high point and to the rear of the brigade, began shelling the Confederate positions.

As mentioned, December 16 started early for the men of the 11th Missouri as described by Major Modesta Green: "The order to advance was given at an early hour on the morning of the 16th, and the regiment, together with the brigade to which it belongs, advanced in line of battle across an open field, but soon discovered that the enemy were strongly posted on the opposite side of the field behind formidable breast-works. After advancing about a half a mile under a heavy fire from the rebel skirmishers and sharpshooters, we came within range of the enemy's fire from their line of works and were ordered to halt and remain in line of battle. After remaining here a short time the regiment was ordered to change its position and form in rear of the Fifth Minnesota."[32] The regiment became exposed as the change in position was executed, and several of the men from the 11th Missouri were killed and wounded, the fire was so great from the Confederate line. A great loss occurred when Lieutenant Colonel Eli Bowyer was struck in the arm and leg with minié balls. Bowyer tried desperately to remain on the field but the wound was too great and he was removed to the hospital. Regimental control fell to Major Modesta Green who had previously served as captain of Company C until August. Green assumed command of the 11th Missouri in one of their greatest battles of the war.

On the Confederate left, the Union Second Cavalry Brigade, commanded by Colonel Datus Coon, attacked around noon. The dismounted cavalry made a long movement over high hills, but they were able to penetrate the flank and successfully unlimbered their cannons so that they could fire onto the Confederate troops entrenched on Shy's Hill. This action was to prove fateful for the battle on December 16.

One of the unsung heroes of the Union Army was General John McArthur. McArthur had an enviable record successfully leading his commands at Fort Donelson, Shiloh, Corinth, Vicksburg and now at Nashville, and he was a general who wanted to get in this fight. McArthur replaced the popular Joseph Mower; and while the division would miss Mower, McArthur was "every bit as good a soldier as Mower, and many of his men proudly considered themselves the elite of the army."[33] The 11th Missouri Infantry was very fortunate throughout the war of having such good commanders, and the regiment needed to regain the bravado they had before the Battle of Vicksburg. On the morning of December 16, McArthur felt he had detected a weakness in the Confederate line in his front. McArthur's sharp-eyed aggressiveness would make him the man of the hour. He had "observed that the enemy lines were not heavily defended here and that the enemy gunners could not sufficiently depress the muzzles of their cannons to use them effectively against the attacking infantry."[34] The weakness was the angle of the top of Compton Hill, also known as Shy's Hill. This was a steep rise that looked very formidable to the attacking troops. McArthur tried to convince Major General Darius Couch of Schofield's Corps to coordinate an attack with him, but he was unsuccessful. So, McArthur stayed in line and told his troops to dig rifle pits for protection from enemy fire. He remained in place, but McArthur was not to be denied; and at 2:30 P.M., he convinced Couch to occupy his place in line while McArthur charged the Confederate lines at Shy Hill.

At 2:30 P.M., McArthur ordered Colonel William McMillen's 1st Brigade and Colonel Lucius Hubbard's 2nd Brigade to charge the hill in their front. McMillan actually marched in front of Couch's position to start his attack. McArthur sent a message to General Andrew Smith of his intention to make this attack. Smith passed the message on to Thomas, who did not want the attack to occur; but before the order was returned to McArthur, the attack began.

One of the most ironic, and perhaps fateful, turns in the Battle of Nashville occurred just prior to McArthur's attack. Wilson's Union cavalry's success on Hood's left flank caused Hood to order the infantry to support the left flank. General A. P. Stewart complied with Hood's orders by sending General Daniel Reynolds infantry to accomplish this. "Not more than fifteen minutes after Reynolds' departure, the entire northern face of Shy's Hill seemed to vanish amid bursting shells."[35] Because Hood felt that Shy's Hill was one of his strongest positions, he had pulled four brigades to bolster other parts of the line, thus weakening the position that McArthur was planning to attack. General William Bate's division stretched themselves to fill in the most recently vacated position by Reynolds just as McArthur attacked. Receiving the order to charge, Hubbard's brigade obeyed amid shouts and yells, and the line of blue raced toward the Confederate line. The national and regimental standards flowed in the wind and the Union soldiers ran across 400 yards of open field. McArthur's Division suffered greatly for their frontal assault on Bate's Division. McMillan's brigade charge was on the western side of the attack, Hubbard was in the center, and Marshall, while not ordered to attack, attacked on the east. McMillan crashed into General Thomas Smith's Georgia and Tennessee Brigade overwhelming them in fierce hand-to-hand combat.

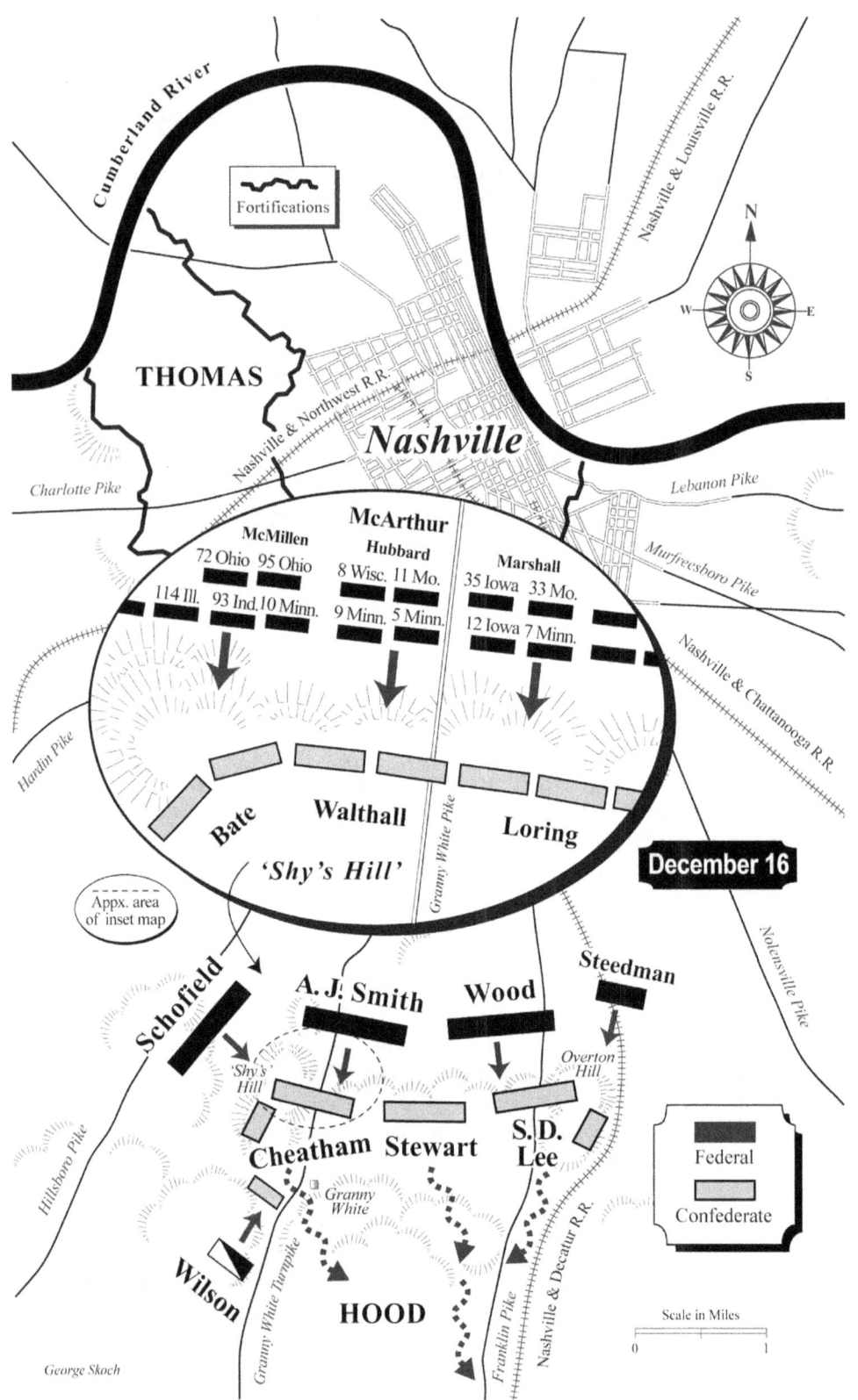

Battle of Nashville, December 16, 1864. McArthur's Division attacked and broke Hood's line near Shy's Hill.

The 11th Missouri, as part of Hubbard's brigade, clashed with Henry Jackson's Georgia brigade (25th, 29th, 30th Georgia, First Georgia Confederate, First Battalion Georgia Sharpshooters) and defenders from General Edward Walthall's division. Historian Wiley Sword stated the attack was a bloody task as the brigade "struggled to cross a muddy, 400-yards open field, only to be riddled from the east by repeated blasts of canister. A six-gun Confederate battery hidden in the underbrush along A. P. Stewart's line seemed to butcher these men at every step. The brown field was literally covered with blue-clad bodies in the wake of their advance."[36] Pointe Coupee Louisiana Battery, a four 12-pound Napoleon cannon battery, was located just east of the Granny White Pike and poured shot and canister into the attacking Union soldiers of Hubbard's Brigade.

Confederate General William Bate recorded the excruciating situation of being all but surrounded by Union soldiers. Bate was overextended and was preparing to face Union soldiers on all sides as he watched the Union lines approach his defenders. Bate realized that he was in a tight spot and sent a request for reinforcements but was told there were none to spare. He was on his own.

Bate recorded, "The general informed me that he had nothing that could possibly be spared, and desired me to extend still farther to the left, as he had to withdraw strength from his front to protect his left, which had been turned. About this time the brigade on the extreme left of our infantry line of battle was driven back, down the hill into the field in my rear, and the balls of the enemy were fired into the backs of (killing and wounding) my men. The lines on the left (as you go into Nashville) of the Granny White Pike at this juncture were the three sides of a square, the enemy shooting across the two parallel lines. My men were falling fast."[37] Bate joined his men in their defenses to inspire them to hold their lines, but Union soldiers were approaching his left and rear. He was encouraging his men to stand firm, when "about 4 P.M. the enemy with heavy force assaulted the line near the angle, and carried it at that point where Ector's brigade had built the light works, which were back from the brow of the hill and without obstructions; not, however, until the gallant and obstinate Colonel Shy and nearly half of his brave men had fallen, together with the largest part of the three right companies of the Thirty-seventh Georgia, which regiment constituted my extreme left. When the breach was made, this command — the consolidated fragments of the Second, Tenth, Fifteenth, Twentieth, Thirtieth, and Thirty-seventh Tennessee Regiments — still contested the ground, under Major Lucas, and, finally, when overwhelming numbers pressed them back, only sixty-five of the command escaped, and they not as a command, but individuals. The command was nearly annihilated."[38]

Once Bate's line was breached he knew he could not hold out against the surging Union attackers. His division began their retreat instantaneously, as if ordered to do so. Only two regiments, the 29th and 30th Georgia Infantry, refused to retreat and were surrounded. Bate valiantly tried to rally his men, but was unable to do so. General Benjamin Cheatham ordered Bate to reform his line along the Granny White Turnpike, but he found Union troops already firing into the new line. His men continued their retreat. Hood's army ceased to be, and the aftermath was described by Bate, "The whole army on this thoroughfare seemed to be one heterogeneous mass, and moving back without organization or government. Strenuous efforts were made by officers of all grades to rally and form line of battle, but in vain. The disorganized masses swept in confusion down the Franklin turnpike, amid the approaching darkness and drenching rain, until beyond Brentwood, when the fragments of commands were, in some measure, united, and bivouacked in groups for the night."[39]

Colonel Lucius Hubbard described the battle as it unfolded, "My line of advance lay across a corn-field, through every foot of which the men were exposed to a direct fire from the line of works in front and a cross-fire on either flank. My line was no sooner in motion than it was met by a most withering volley, and as the regiments struggled on through the muddy field, softened by the recent rain, their ranks were sadly decimated by the continuous fire they encountered. A battery on my left enfiladed my line, and with fearful accuracy poured its discharges of grape through the ranks. But seemingly unmindful of the storm of missiles they were breasting, the veterans of the Second Brigade did not falter, but, pressing steadily on, gained the works and carried them, in literal execution of the order they had received."[40] Hubbard reported the colors of the Fifth and Ninth Minnesota Infantry were placed in the Confederate defenses and next followed the flags of the 11th Missouri and Eighth Wisconsin. The 11th Missouri's Lieutenant William Simmons reported as the charge took place, the regiment in front of the 11th Missouri had taken so much fire that they wavered about 200 yards from the Confederate line. Then the 11th Missouri surged forward and past this regiment. As they advanced, Captain James Lott was shot from his horse, severely wounded in the groin and left arm. "Three times the colors of the 11th Missouri went down, each time picked up by another man. The last soldier who carried the flag had to hold the shivered flag staff together."[41] Hubbard's men suffered the worst of any of McArthur's brigades, losing nearly "300 officers and men from the 1,421 men who entered the fight."[42]

Major Modesta Green described the 11th Missouri's charge into Jackson and Walthall's awaiting muskets and cannons. The 11th Missouri Infantry's attack was made parallel to the Granny White Pike and just east of Shy's Hill. "We remained in this position until about 3 P.M., when the order was given to charge the rebel works. The order was no sooner given than the regiment started at a double-quick, charging through the open field for a distance of about 600 yards, under a most galling fire from the enemy. On reaching the works many prisoners were captured in the trenches, and many others either shot or captured while attempting to escape. A rebel battery of four guns was also captured here by the brigade, for which the Eleventh Missouri would respectfully claim, with the gallant brigade commander, its share of the honor. Two rebel flags were also captured by the regiment, one by Lieutenant Simmons and

Shy's Hill in a photograph from the 1880s (courtesy Nashville Battlefield Preservation Society).

the other by Corporal Parks, color guard. In making the charge the colors of the regiment were three times shot down, having one color-bearer killed and two wounded. The flag-staff was shot into three pieces by a rebel shell."[43] So great was the fire as the regiment charged, that Major Modesta Green had his horse shot from under him as he led the 11th Missouri into the battle. Major Green also received a serious wound to his temple and face. The Union line drove the Confederates from their works, and Green recorded that the regiment pursued the fleeing soldiers for about a mile after capturing many prisoners when they were ordered to stop and reform.

One of the 11th Missouri's men, Harrison N. Davis, First Sergeant, Company I, who carried their splintered colors across that fateful 400 yard field, recorded his dash, "I was Color-Sergeant for the 11th Mo.... I was in the charge the second day until I was wounded, when I gave the flag to a comrade, and he went only a few steps when he was wounded. The next man that took it went thru all right."[44] Jefferson Freakes was also a color bearer on December 16 and was killed in action as he carried the colors of the 11th Missouri toward Jackson and Walthall's waiting Confederate soldiers.

Jackson and Walthall, defending against the Hubbard attack, thought they had repulsed the attack, so devastating was the carnage, but at that point a "wild hurrah" went up on their left flank as McMillan broke through Smith's brigade. McMillan and Hubbard's successes made Marshall's attack relatively easy. The lines of Jackson and Walthall suddenly gave way. With the Confederates retreating from Shy's Hill, Hood's army melted toward the rear and the Battle of Nashville was over. General Edward Walthall recorded events of the afternoon of December 16: "The hill to my left just then was carried, and to save any part of my command an immediate withdrawal was necessary. To produce confusion in its accomplishment, the proximity of the enemy's flanking column, which had been observed by the troops, and the distance and rugged ground between them and the Franklin pike, known to them to be their only outlet, tended and conspired. Everywhere within my view the disorder was great and general, but it was inevitable, the surroundings considered."[45] Walthall stated that he tried to reorganize his troops as they ran toward Brentwood along the Franklin Turnpike and he was unsuccessful as he tried to piece together the various groups of his routed troops. While the 11th Missouri was charging across the field that had claimed so many lives, the Confederate defenders were by no means having an easy time themselves.

Colonel Lucius Hubbard recorded that the Eight Wisconsin and Ninth Minnesota captured three artillery pieces as they drove away their de-

Flag of the 29th Alabama captured by Lieutenant William Simmons, 11th Missouri Infantry (Alabama Department of Archives and History Montgomery, Alabama).

fenders. He ceased his pursuit as night fell on the hills south of Nashville. McArthur's attack was a total success, and by the end of December 16, he had captured 2 generals, 4,273 prisoners, and 24 cannons in two days.

The brigade loss during the two battles was:

Losses of Hubbard's 2nd Brigade — Battle of Nashville December 15–16, 1864[46]

	KILLED	WOUNDED	MISSING
2nd Iowa Artillery	0	1	0
5th Minnesota	14	92	1
9th Minnesota	8	50	0
11th Missouri	4	83	0
8th Wisconsin	7	55	0
Total Second Brigade	33	281	1

List of Casualties in 11th Missouri Inf Vet Vol in the Battle of Nashville, Tennessee. December 15–16, 1864 by W.H. Finch (Total 72 Killed & Wounded — 5 Killed) — Plus Compiled Service Records[47]

Regimental Staff
Eli Bowyer	Lt. Col.	Left Forearm	Partial recovery
Modesta Green	Maj.	Left Cheek	Slight

Company A
James Allen	Pvt.	Wounded in thigh	
Louis Breckle	Pvt.	Right thigh	
Edwin Cabe	Pvt.	Thigh	Slight
Benjamin Matthias	Pvt.	Face	Slight
William Mann	Pvt.	Hips	Severe
George Morris	Pvt.	Groin	Severe
Richard Roach	Pvt.	Leg	Slight
Thomas Webb	Pvt.	Head	Died

Company B
Squire Baker	Pvt.	Leg	Slight
Thomas Brown	Pvt.	Head	
John Constant	Pvt.	Hand and Arm	Slight
John Dunley	Pvt.	Abdomen	Died

Company C
Henry Bormlitz	Pvt.	Left leg	Slight
Horace Brown	Corp.	Left Elbow	Severe
Jefferson Freakes	Corp.	Killed	KIA
Thomas Hall	Corp.	Wrist	Severe
Joseph Heinman	Pvt.	Face	Serious
Smith Hinman	Pvt.	Left knee	Slight
John Lombard	Pvt.	Face/Shoulder	Died
James Lott	Capt.	Left Arm, groin	Severe
Owen Prentice	Pvt.	Left arm	Slight
Edward Ryan	Corp.	Arm	Severe

7. Abbeville, Pursuit of Price, and Battle of Nashville

Company D

William Barnett	Sgt.	Hand	
Peter Corcoran	Corp.		
Joseph Corder	Pvt.	Unknown	
William Cottrell	Pvt.	Knee	
William Englelow	Pvt.	Knee	Died
Patrick Hilde/Hyde	Corp.	Thigh, Arm	Severe
Ebenezer Hopkins	Sgt.		
Isaac Jacquess	Pvt.	Killed	KIA
Solomon Miller	Sgt.	Hand	
Thomas Murphey	Pvt.	Arm	
Henry Smith	Pvt.	Thigh	
David Wood	Pvt.	Thigh	

Company E

Amos Butler	Pvt.	Hand	
George Butler	Sgt.	Hand	
Petro Delevadwa	Sgt.	Wrist	
George Finnell	Pvt.	Arm	
Bentley Heisfind	Pvt.	Leg	Amputated — Died
Henry Judy	Pvt.	Unknown	
Holmes Knoph	Pvt.	Breast	Died
William Notestine	Capt.	Right Thigh	Amputated — Died
Martin Padden	Pvt.	Shoulder	
William Smith	Corp.	Breast	
Gottliebe Schieble	Pvt.	Arm Amputated	Died

Company F

Michael Caughan	Pvt.	Thigh	Slight
Charles Gilman	Pvt.	Thigh	Slight
John Holman	Pvt.	Leg Amputated	Died
Richard Sessions	Pvt.	Thigh	Died
Charles Smith	Capt.	Neck	Severe
Garrett Southerland	Pvt.	Right arm	

Company G

John Kirby	Pvt.	Leg	Severely
Joseph Kirkey	Pvt.	Leg	Severe
John Kueff/Kneff	Corp.	Hand	Severe
Solomon H. Norton	Pvt.	Face	Slight
Charles Robinson	Pvt.	Head	Amputated finger
James Smith	Corp.	Groin	Died
Amos Stewart	Corp.	Side and Leg	
William Wallace	Capt.	Foot	Slight

Company H

Samuel Conrad	Corp.	Concussion	
John Dulong	Pvt.	Arm	Amputated
Clark Goodman	Pvt.	Killed	KIA
Absalom Higgins	Pvt.	Foot	
Jacob Johnson	Pvt.	Thigh	Slight
Isaac Parker	Sgt.	Thigh	
John Parker	Pvt.	Mortally	

William Rainey	Pvt.	Hand	
William Ridgeley	Corp.	Groin	Slightly
Company I			
Henry Davidhiser	Corp.	Ankle	
Albert Adams	Pvt.	Thigh	Died
William Bascue	Pvt.	Side	Slight
Francis Baker	Pvt.	Left Breast	Absent
Daniel Chapman	Corp.	Hand	
Ed Cornwall	Pvt.	Back	
Harrison Davis	Sgt.	Leg	
Christopher Farrell	Pvt.	Abdomen	
Jacob Kline	Pvt.	Knee	
Marion Lung/Long	Pvt.	Side	Slight
Patrick OBrien	Pvt.	Ankle	
Martin OBrien	Pvt.	Knee	
Patrick ONeal	Pvt.	Leg	
Peter Plank	Pvt.	Hip	Serious
David Shoopman	1st Lt.	Thigh	
William Spicer	Corp.	Arm	
Company K			
Joseph Blond	Pvt.	Head	Died
John Blond	Pvt.	Chin	Slight
William Cheney	Sgt.	Knee	Slight
Dennis Coogan	Sgt.	Arm	Serious
John Crangle	Corp.	Chin	Slight
Cyrus Kendall	Capt.	Leg	Slight
Rueben Mills	Pvt.	Hip	Severely
George Scott	Pvt.	Chin	Slight
John R. Twitty	Pvt.	Mortally	
Nelson Upson	Pvt.	Unknown	

Sergeant Charles Treadway, Company A, recorded in a letter he wrote, "I was in the Big Battle at Nashville whare thousands sleep the sleep of the dead, though I was spared to pass through the terrific fires whare shot and shell and bullets flew in all directions and came through without being harmed. William Mann & Thomas Webb ware wounded, and some more that your not acquainted with. Thare ware 8 of Co. A wounded none killed.... Old Hood was so badly whipped at Nashville that he will lay quiet the rest of the winter."[48]

The 11th Missouri Infantry lost the second largest number of men in the brigade. Major Green, commanding the regiment in Colonel Bowyer's absence, concluded his record of the Battle of Nashville, "Here we remained until the morning of the 17th, when it was ascertained that the enemy were retreating, and we were ordered, with other troops, to follow in the pursuit. The losses in the regiment in the two days' fighting are 4 men killed and 83 wounded, including 10 commissioned officers.... During the fight every officer and man behaved with commendable coolness and bravery. No special mention can be made of individual acts of courage or bravery, as every officer and man behaved in the most praiseworthy manner."[49] Three members of the 11th Missouri Infantry were awarded the Medal of Honor for actions on December 16. Lieutenant William Simmons, Company C, captured the 34th Alabama Infantry flag. His citation stated that being the first to enter the works, he shot and wounded the enemy color bearer. The flag that Lieutenant Simmons captured was later correctly identified as the flag of the

29th Alabama Infantry. Corporal James W. Parks,' Company F, and Private George W. Welch's, Company A, citations stated they each captured a flag. The flags Parks and Welch captured were never conclusively identified.

There was correspondence supporting the recommendations for the commendation of the Medals of Honor.

Private James Parks, a resident of Xenia, Illinois, captured the flag in the entrenchments. "The rebel color-bearer having been shot from our lines, the colors were captured by the above-named soldier. It is not known to what regiment the flag belonged."[50]

George Welch, born in Ripley, Illinois, in 1845, is reported to have captured the flag of the 13th Alabama Infantry but it may never been known which flag was truly captured because this regiment was not present at the Battle of Nashville. Major Green reported, "The flag was being borne off the field as the enemy was retreating from their works, when the rebel color-bearer was struck by a shot from our lines, and the colors captured by the above-named man. It is not known to what regiment it belonged."[51]

Lieutenant William Simmons of Springfield, Illinois, stated during the Battle of Nashville that his captain, James Lott, was wounded. He commanded the assault and, "leaving my place as file closer, I sprang to the front and led the way, making straight for the flag. Being an exceptionally speedy runner at the time, I was first to reach the breastworks, and demanded the surrender of the colors. The Confederate sergeant attempted to run away with the prize and I was compelled to shoot, wounding him and thereby securing the flag."[52]

Private George Finnell, Company E, was wounded in the Battle of Nashville (courtesy Civil War Museum at Wilson's Creek National Battlefield).

The much underrated General Andrew Smith's personality was made clear in a conversation with General George Thomas during the Battle of Nashville. "It was in this fight, during a charge, that the troops of Smith in their ardor, pressing forward a little too rapidly, became slightly scattered, observing which General Thomas who was watching them remarked to Smith, 'General, I notice your men are not keeping good formation.' To which the grim and grizzled Smith replied, 'I only notice they are fighting like hell.'"[53] The bristly Smith was proud of the men he led.

Pursuit

Despite the great the success by Thomas at the Battle of Nashville, it was a bloody day for the 11th Missouri Infantry who paid a severe price for their charge. Regimental records recorded that four men were killed during the action and another 83 were wounded, including 10 officers. This was the second bloodiest day for the regiment with only the charge on Stockade Redan at Vicksburg being more costly. In addition to the four men who were killed in action, another twelve soldiers subsequently died of their wounds. The 11th Missouri, which now included men from the Seventh Missouri, suffered the second greatest losses of the brigade.

An example of the men who died subsequent of their wounds was Captain William Notestine who was wounded while leading the skirmishers on the afternoon on December 15. His leg was amputated above his knee and part of a letter written to his father has been preserved.[54]

> Dear Father
> ...My wounds is doing well. I sat up this morning 3½ hours and I am now sitting up at noon about the same I will be up at supper again. So you see that I improve....[55]

Lt. William Simmons picture taken when he was a sergeant. He was awarded the Medal of Honor for his actions at Nashville (courtesy Nancy Glaiberman).

Despite the optimism of his letter, William Notestine died on February 12, 1865, of "exhaustion from the amputation of thigh in consequent of gunshot fracture of femur." Colonel Eli Bowyer stated of William Notestine, "I think he was one of the best officers I knew."[56] It does appear that war claims the best. William Notestine's brother, James, grieved the death of his brother, but continued to serve with the 11th Missouri Infantry for the remainder of the war in Company E.

Captain William Notestine, Company E, was among the wounded (he then died) in the Battle of Nashville (courtesy Civil War Museum at Wilson's Creek National Battlefield).

11th Missouri Infantry Losses August 5, 1864, Through December 31, 1864

	AUG–SEPT 1864	OCTOBER	NOVEMBER	DECEMBER
Discharged	Worstell, Joseph (G)			Jenner, Edward (E)
	Ethel, Charles H. Lt. (I)			
	Finley, John T. Lt. (F)			
	Blew, Jacob Lt. (E)			
	O'Donnell, Menomen Capt. (A)			
Died	Lindsa, Leander J. (G)	Sutton, Thomas (1) (D)	Lucas, George Sgt. (C)	Webb, Thomas (A)
	Lightfoot, Benjamin Corp. (C)		Baker, Christopher (K)	Freakes, Jefferson Sgt. (C)
				Jacquess, Isaac (D)
	Cusick, William (A) to 61st USCT			Sessions, Richard (F)
	Lukekamper, Frederick (C)			Goodwin, Clark B. (H)
				Scheible, Gottleib (E)
				Knoph/Knopt, Holmes (E)
				Blonde, Joseph (K)
				Smith, James T. (G)
				West, John M. (G)
				Bridges, Jeremiah (B)
Deserted	Sanders, John (F)	Bigsby/Bixby, Nathaniel (D)	Winscott, James C. (1) (G)	Long, James C. (A)
		Shockley, Jasper (D)	Mcdaniel, George (H)	Murray, John (A)
		Trustey, William (D)		Bartch, Anton (G)
Resigned Transferred	Lloyd, Jesse D. Lt. (B)			
		Shepherd, Charles (G) to U.S. Naval Academy		

CHAPTER 8

Battle of Spanish Fort and the Occupation in Alabama

I have witnessed many a bloody battle field. I have stemmed the hardships and turmoils of the Bloody Strife, and the awful Strife is over.

Sergeant Charles Treadway

Pursuit of Hood and Conscripts

The 11th Missouri Infantry, as part of A. J. Smith's XVI Corps, pursued Hood's defeated army south from Nashville until December 28, and then went into winter quarters at Clifton, Tennessee, and Eastport, Mississippi, until February 7, 1865, when they began their last campaign — Mobile. However, efforts to strengthen the regiment had begun to pay rewards. The 11th Missouri received the much needed infusion of soldiers from the Seventh Missouri Infantry just prior to the Battle of Nashville, which paid dividends as the 11th Missouri stormed successfully into Hood's defenders. However, the regiment paid a butcher's bill, losing 87 men killed and wounded, in the two-day battle. The commanders of the 11th Missouri Infantry had been soliciting the governor of Missouri for two years to increase the recruits and transfers for the regiment. The 11th Missouri barely fielded 300 men prior to this infusion of transferees, and 325 soldiers participated in the battle in December, which resulted in the loss of almost 100 men. In addition to soldiers from the Seventh Missouri, beginning in November, the governor of Missouri made good his promise of sending new men to the regiment in the form of draftees and substitutes. The conscripts started arriving in November 1864, and they continued through March 1865 with slightly more than 500 men entering the regiment:

Date Of Enlistment	Number of Substitutes/Draftees Enlisted[1]
November 1864	23
December 1864	27
January 1865	173
February 1865	215
March 1865	55

Conscription was not a new concept to the Union army in 1864 and 1865. A pseudo draft was first used for Federal troops in August 1862 when the War Department issued a call for

300,000 militia to serve for nine months. The call for these volunteers required that by August 15, 1862, the soldiers were to be available to the army; and if the state had not met its quota, a "special draft" would be made up from the permanent militia of that state. While it would have been almost impossible to force this method of conscription, the pseudo draft was intended "rather as a whip to encourage volunteering."[2] While this pseudo draft was unsuccessful, what was learned from this exercise was utilized when the true draft was initiated in 1863. The lessons learned in 1862 were that "only Federal Officers should conduct the draft, and military service should be for a period of at least three years."[3]

By the time the United States government decided to initiate the draft, the Confederacy was already using this tool to keep their ranks filled. One of the criticisms of the policies of the Union army was the fact there was no system in place to keep existing regiments replenished when men were lost to desertion, death or discharge. Often times, new regiments were formed instead of refilling depleted ones. Finally, Senator Henry Wilson, chairman of the Committee on Military Affairs, "introduced a bill to enroll and call out the national forces; this bill was finally passed on March 3, 1863. By 'national forces' was meant all able-bodied male citizens of the United States and all aliens who had declared on oath their intention of becoming citizens between the ages of twenty and forty-five."[4] The proposed draft was planned to draw the draftee from a fair distribution without any particular group being overburdened. Also, drafted men were paid equally to volunteer soldiers, and the draftees were assigned where they were needed, including filling in ranks of depleted regiments, such as the 11th Missouri Infantry.

In addition to the use of the draft, two additional practices were utilized to encourage volunteers: (1) bounties and (2) the practice of purchasing substitutes for men who had been drafted. The U.S. government paid a bounty of $100 for recruits and often individual states added additional money to encourage men to enlist.

While efforts were made to make the draft fair and equitable, many criticized the draft for several reasons, and one of the major problems was substitution. A drafted man could agree to pay varying sums of money to an individual to enlist in his place, thus becoming his substitute. In these situations, the dedicated volunteers that enlisted in 1861–

A local advertisement regarding the practice of "Substitutes" for draftees (Library of Congress).

The draft created a new entrepreneur — the "substitute broker" (Library of Congress).

1862 were replaced with men motivated by financial gain. Two other issues resulted: (1) men entering the army made enlistees part of the "poor man's war," and (2) there was a new entrepreneur created, the "substitute broker," who found ways of furnishing substitutes on a commercial basis for those wishing to avoid the draft. One final part of the new draft allowed "men who were to be drafted the priviledge of purchasing exemption by paying a commutation fee of three hundred dollars."[5]

Drafts began in 1863 for the Union army, and the last draft was implemented on December 19, 1864, which required 300,000 men to be called into service. While all draftees' and substitutes' dates of enlistment cannot be identified for the 11th Missouri Infantry, the regimental records show the peak of new conscripts occurred during the first three months of 1865. While approximately a 1,000 men would be members of the 11th Missouri Veteran Infantry, about half of the soldiers were conscripts and another 210 were veteran transfers from other infantry regiments. It is also important to note during the first three years of service the 11th Missouri Infantry, there were only a very few deserters. This was very different with the new veteran infantry regiment. In the eighteen months the 11th Missouri Veteran Infantry was in service, there were 197 desertions and approximately 70 percent of those desertions were men who were substitutes or draftees.

The draftees and substitutes were, relatively, uniformly distributed across the individual companies.

Company	Draftees	Substitutes[6]
Company A	9	41
Company B	20	37
Company C	17	34
Company D	25	23
Company E	29	30
Company F	17	34
Company G	11	29
Company H	16	33
Company I	18	30
Company K	22	34
Total	184	325

As the war dragged on, the 11th Missouri's Sergeant Charles Treadway expressed the feelings of many people across the country and he reflected the national opinion in regard to conscripts entering the service of their country. "Thare are hundreds of young men at home that should be in the army and hundreds of old gray headed men in the Army that should be at home. ... I think the draft is the best plan, and then let every man stand his chance."[7]

Mobile Campaign

In January 1865, the war situation was gloomy for the Southern cause — General Robert E. Lee was besieged by Grant at Richmond, General Joe Johnston was trying to defend the Carolinas from the relentless William T. Sherman, and George Thomas had just defeated Hood's Army at Nashville. Hood's Confederate Army retreated from Nashville beginning on December 16, 1864, and the Union Army pursued the cold, wet, hungry and tired Rebel army until it crossed the Tennessee River on December 27. At that point General John Bell Hood relinquished command of his army. After Hood's resignation, one of the larger Confederate concentrations of troops was located at Mobile, Alabama, under the command of Dabney Maury. Mobile was one of the last Confederate ports still in Southern hands, and the forces at Mobile contained one of the last organized Confederate military forces which was not actively engaged. To concentrate their effective power, about 5,000 of Hood's troops were transferred to Maury's command. At this stage in the war, any concentration of Confederate forces quickly drew the attention of the Union commanders.

The 11th Missouri Infantry began the Mobile Campaign on February 7, 1865, when the soldiers boarded river transports and were carried to Vicksburg, Mississippi, arriving there on February 14. On February 19, the regiment was again transported by river transports to New Orleans and arrived there on February 21. After a two-day sea voyage, the regiment finally arrived at Dauphin Island located in Mobile Bay on March 7. The exit from New Orleans was a relief to many in the regiment and was expressed by Sergeant Charles Treadway: "I have seen enough of New Orleans to do me. One has to be very careful whare he puts his foot or he will mire or get snake bit. Snakes and alligators are thick as rabbits in the barns."[8] So, on March 7, the 11th Missouri was close enough to see Mobile and their final battle site, Spanish Fort. "By March 1865, Alabama's largest city of Mobile was the last seaport still held by the Confederacy. Although Union control of Mobile Bay, since August 1864, had rendered it useless for shipping, the city was still in Rebel hands."[9] The Union focus on Mobile had begun the previous summer, August 1864, when Admiral Farragut's warships moved into Mobile Bay and defeated the Confederate navy which had attempted to prevent their entry. Fort Morgan and Fort Gaines were captured by Union ground forces in August as well. The Union blockade caused shortages of daily staples for the citizens of Mobile and the city had already experienced a bread riot in 1863. The blockade made life even more difficult for the local population through the winter of 1864. "Long lines formed to buy goods, and fights frequently broke out as civilians, mostly women, pushed and shoved to get scarce items like cornmeal, wheat, flour, sugar and coffee."[10]

Mobile was fortified with three circles of earthen works that surrounded the land approaches to the city. Floating batteries and shore batteries protected the bay exposure. Two formidable defensive forts were located on the eastern side of Mobile Bay — Spanish Fort and Fort Blakeley. These forts were about seven miles east of the city. Mobile was strategically important because the port still proved to be a port for blockade runners which supplied the Southern troops, but it also was a concentration of Confederate soldiers. Finally, the next focus of the Union military offensive was Montgomery, Alabama, but a push in that direction would not be made as long as a concentrated Confederate military presence was active in Mobile, which could quickly be moved north to thwart any Union offensive. General Dabney Maury, the commander of the Confederate forces in Mobile, was an old foe of the 11th Missouri because Maury had commanded Confederate troops at both the battles Iuka and Corinth in 1862. Dabney Maury was born at Fredericksburg, Virginia, in 1822. He had served in the U.S. Army in the Mexican War where he was wounded but recuperated. Then he became an

General Dabney Maury commanded the Confederate forces at Mobile (Library of Congress).

instructor at West Point from 1847 through 1852. He served with the army in Oregon and Texas and he even authored a book, *Tactics for Mounted Rifles*. In addition to his actions at Iuka and Corinth, he had also participated in the Vicksburg campaign. So, Dabney Maury was not a stranger to the men of the 11th Missouri Infantry.

Major General Edward Canby commanded of the Union forces facing Dabney Maury. Edward Canby was born in Piatt's Landing, Kentucky, on November 9, 1817. He graduated from West Point in 1839 and served in the Second U.S. Infantry after he graduated. Canby saw action prior to the Civil War in the Seminole War in Florida and also in the Mexican War. Canby served in the adjutant general's office in California, and he had also served in Utah, New Mexico and Wyoming prior to the Civil War. Canby served in the American West at the beginning of the Civil War and commanded the Department of New Mexico. In May 1864 he was promoted to command the Military Division of Western Mississippi. In March 1865, General Canby had a force of about 45,000 men. The first column of 32,000 soldiers was the combined XIII Corps of Major General Gordon Granger and the XVI Corps of Major General A. J. Smith. A second column was commanded by Major General Frederick Steele with 13,000 men.

General Edward Canby commanded the Union forces at Mobile in 1865 (Library of Congress).

Characteristically for the Civil War, Canby was being prodded by General Ulysses Grant to take the offensive against Maury; but Canby complained of heavy rains and terrible road conditions, "The incessant rains we have had for the past month, and which show no signs of abatement, make it impractical to carry into effect the projected expedition."[11] However, in March Canby devised his strategy for the Mobile, Alabama, campaign. General Steele's column was ordered to march from western Florida and "feint toward Montgomery to divert Maury's cavalry away, then turn south to join Canby for operations against Spanish Fort and Blakeley."[12] Fish River on the eastern shore of Mobile Bay would serve as a rendezvous site for the XIII and XVI Army Corps. Mobile was not considered a strategic target for the Union army; however, Spanish Fort and Fort Blakeley were considered to be important targets. If Mobile could be quickly captured after the forts were taken, Canby was directed to do this. Otherwise, Mobile was to be ignored until a later time.

The Union offensive in the Mobile Campaign began on March 17, 1865. The 11th Missouri

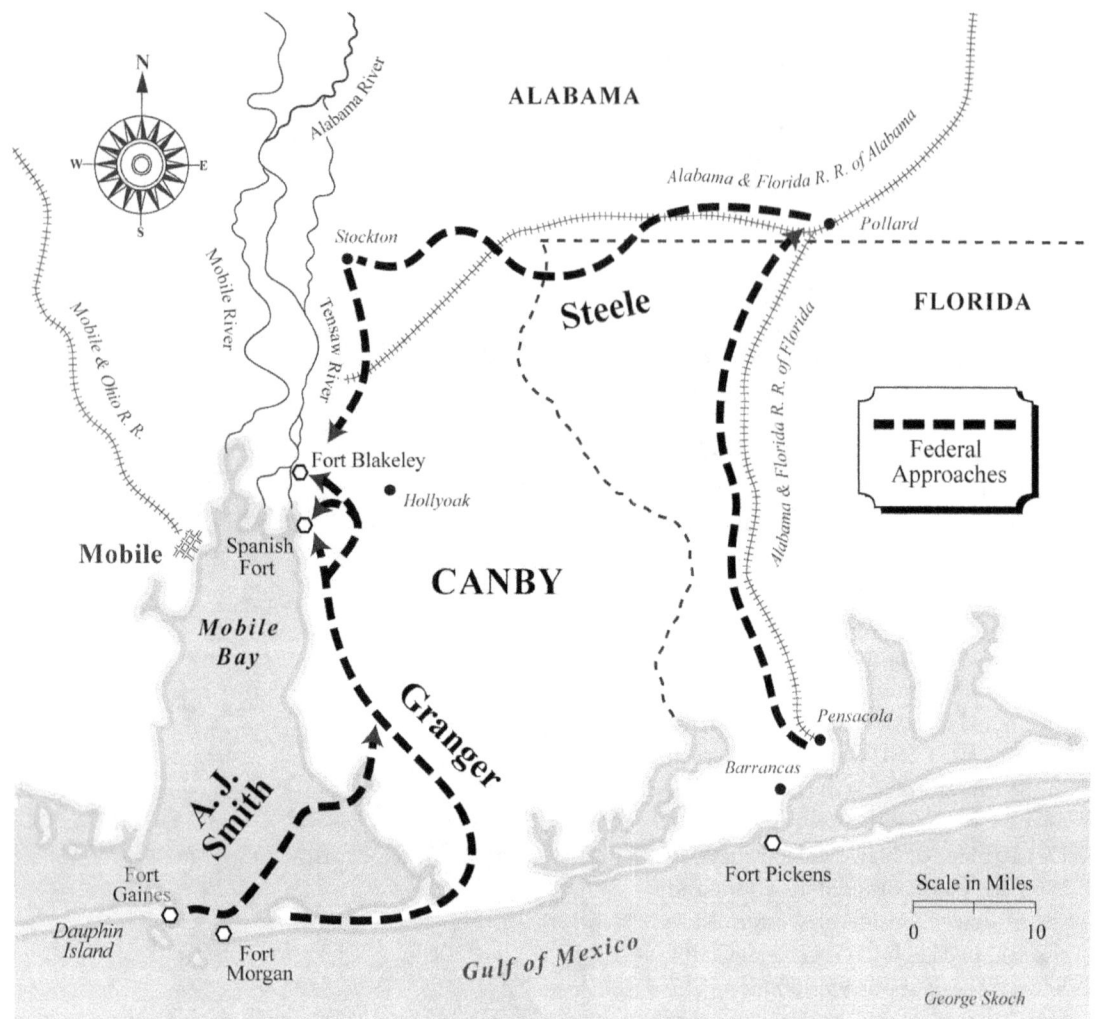

The Union advance on Spanish Fort and Fort Blakeley, March–April 1865.

Infantry, as part of Smith's XVI Corps, moved across Mobile Bay on March 19 and began disembarking on March 20. By March 22, the entire corps was on the eastern side of the bay and went into camp until Gordon Granger's corps reached their location. Granger's XIII Corps had a more arduous trek as they marched overland from Fort Morgan and along the eastern side of the shore until they approached Spanish Fort. Rainy weather and swampy conditions made the advance on Spanish Fort a difficult march. On March 27, the XVI Corps marched to initiate the siege of the two forts in conjunction with the XIII Corps. Once the two corps were in position, Canby pushed to encircle Spanish Fort, but the advancing Union troops were surprised when soldiers of the Louisiana Brigade charged out of Spanish Fort and temporarily pushed regiments of the XIII Corps backward. By March 28, Spanish Fort was fully encircled and the siege had begun.

To slow down the Union encirclement, Maury had planned to use his veteran infantry brigades to fight delaying actions outside the defenses of the forts. Brigadier General Frances Cockrell and Brigadier General Randall Gibson's divisions dug in and prepared to meet the Union columns, but the Union force was much larger than expected. Seeing the size of the advancing columns, the majority of the Confederate defenders scampered back to the defenses of the forts. Once the Confederate infantry entered the defenses of Spanish Fort, General Gibson assumed command of the 1,800 men defending the fort. The defenses at Spanish Fort were formidable. "Trees had been cleared and obstructions placed for the oncoming Federals. A tangled abates stretched about 15 feet deep along the whole front, and in front of the breastworks ran a ditch 8 feet wide and 5 feet deep. Rebel sharpshooters manned rifle pits scattered in the front of the six batteries or redoubts that crowned the crest of a red bluff running along the line."[13] The works were about a mile and half long.

16TH ARMY CORPS—MAJ. GEN. ANDREW J. SMITH
First Division— Brig. Gen. John McArthur

Second Brigade— Col. Lucius F. Hubbard
47th Illinois: Maj. Edward Bonham. Col. David W. Magee
5th Minnesota, Lieut. Col. William B. Gere
9th Minnesota, Col. Josiah F. Marsh
11th Missouri, Maj. Modesta J. Green
8th Wisconsin, Lieut. Col. William B. Britton

Commanding the First Division of Smith's XVI Corps was Brigadier General John McArthur, who had ably lead the division in Nashville and was considered an experienced and excellent commander. Again McArthur's Second Brigade was led by Colonel Lucius Hubbard, and the 11th Missouri was commanded by Major Modesta Green instead of Colonel Eli Bowyer, who was still recuperating from the wounds he had received in the Battle of Nashville. The Third Division of Smith's XVI Corps was commanded by Brigadier General Eugene Asa Carr. Carr and McArthur's divisions were selected to attack Spanish Fort on March 27 in hopes that a rapid attack might overwhelm the defenders. Although, the entire corps was not in place, McArthur agreed to the attack stating, "My division will go in there if ordered, but if the Rebels stay by their guns it will cost the lives of half my men."[14] As the 11th Missouri attacked with their division, Confederate General Gibson threw the full might of the artillery in his arsenal against the Union soldiers as the Federals charged the fort's defenses. Gibson's artillery included 6 heavy guns, 14 field cannons and 12 Coehorn mortars. Gibson reported 5 killed and 44 men wounded on March 27, and in this unsuccessful attack, the XVI Corps lost 91 men killed and many others wounded.

Historian C. C. Andrews wrote, "The troops advanced with alacrity, their banners unfurled. Their line was three miles in length, and presented a splendid appearance moving through the open woods."[15] McArthur's division immediately ran into resistance from the defenders but the attack pushed the defenders into their main works. During this attack the 11th Missouri Infantry suffered 12 casualties.[16]

There was no official report filed by Major Modesta Green of the 11th Missouri Infantry and the most detailed account to the actions of the 11th Missouri Infantry was the brigade report filed by Colonel Lucius Hubbard which stated, "On the 27th during the progress of the investment of Spanish Fort, the Second Brigade held a position in the center of, and advanced in line of battle with the First Division. A line of skirmishers deployed along my front met those of the enemy within perhaps a mile of the rebel defenses and engaged them actively, the latter slowly giving way, but contesting the ground quite stubbornly. The line of battle advanced by degrees until a position was secured within about 800 yards of the fort, the enemy the while delivering from his works a spirited fire of musketry and artillery. During the following night a line of investment was established and the command employed intrenching the position."[17]

The alignment of the Second Brigade presented a four-regiment front that included the Eighth Wisconsin Infantry, the 47th Illinois Infantry, Fifth Minnesota Infantry and the Ninth Minnesota Infantry. The 11th Missouri Infantry was positioned in a reserve role behind the four regiments.

Hubbard sent skirmishers forward during the evening and advanced to within 300 yards of the Confederate defenses. Then the brigade set about their daily tasks of entrenching their defenses and constructing artillery-proof structures where soldiers could withstand the barrages from the formidable Confederate artillery. By March 29, Hubbard's men were digging toward the Confederate defenses and also constructed a trench parallel to those Confederate defenses where he positioned a group of 250 sharpshooters, identified as the best marksman of the brigade. Under the command of Captain A. P. French of the Fifth Minnesota, these men set about their deadly task during the siege. These sharpshooters were particularly good at their duty and caused a great deal of injury to the Confederate artillerymen. So effective were these sharpshooters that the Confederate artillerymen abandoned their guns until the Union sniping subsided.

General Randall Gibson commanded Spanish Fort during the siege (Alabama Department of Archives and History Montgomery, Alabama).

After the failed assault on March 27, Canby decided to initiate a classical siege of Spanish Fort, and began digging trenches for protection of his men and for the purpose to getting closer to their enemy. The Confederate defenders also were actively involved with enhancing their entrenchments. Sharpshooters on both sides diligently picked off soldiers who inadvertently exposed themselves.

As the XIII and XVI Corps encircled Spanish Fort and Fort Blakeley, General Steele's column was making its march from the east. Steele began his march from Pensacola on March 20, but heavy rains caused any progress to be virtually impossible, and it wasn't until April that he reached Fort Blakeley. This fort was defended by 2,700 men and the defenses were somewhat similar to those of Spanish Fort, but there were nine redoubts and the earthen works ran about three miles around the defenses. The defenders boasted more than 40 pieces of artillery. It wasn't until April 3 that Fort Blakeley was fully encircled when Brigadier General Kenner Garrard's Division from the XVI Corps arrived from Spanish Fort.

The 11th Missouri trenched and waited patiently at Spanish Fort. "Old Spanish fort is a bastioned work, nearly enclosed, and built on a bluff whose shape projects abruptly to the water.

Opposite: The Siege of Spanish Fort.

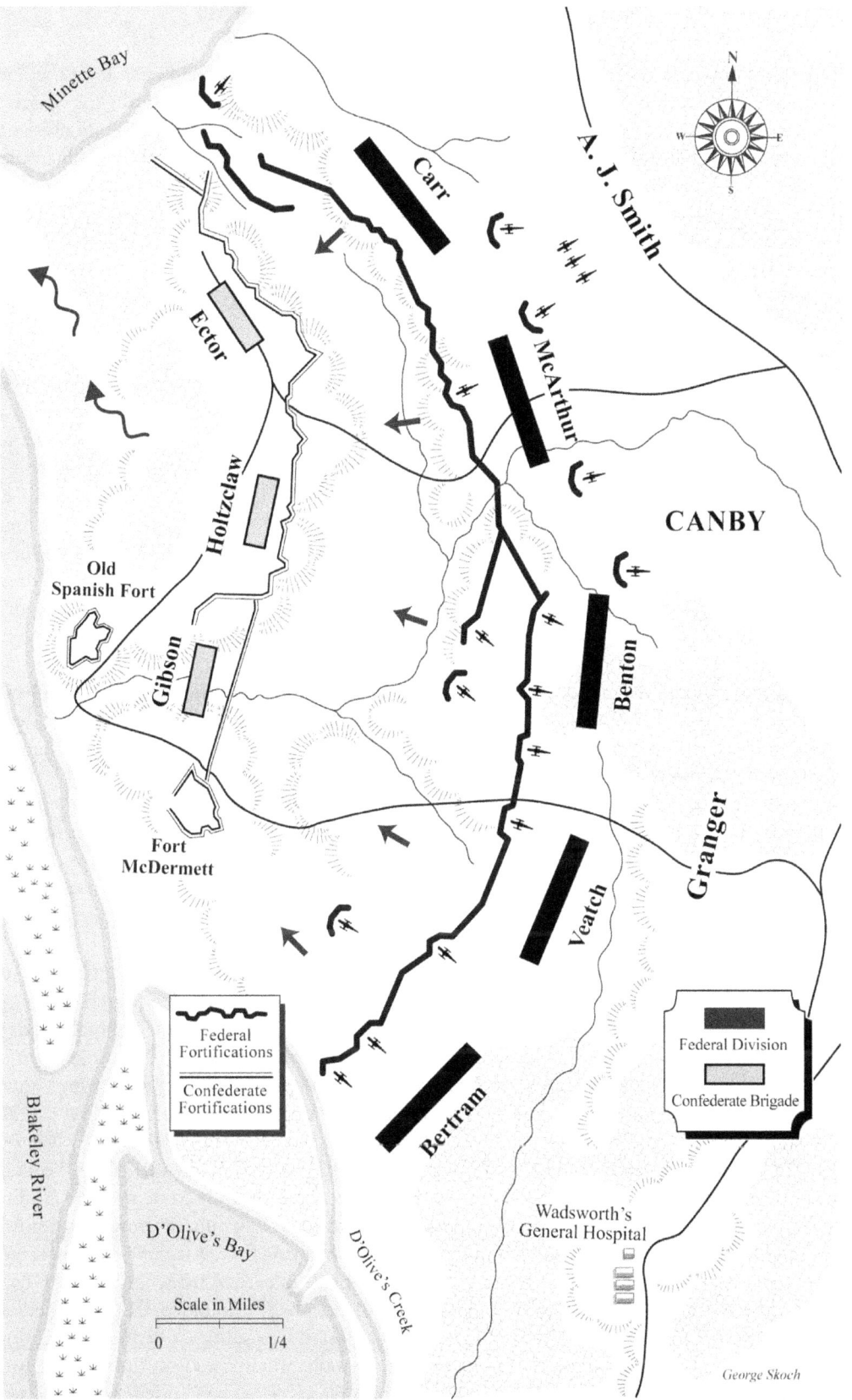

Its parapet, on the bay side, was partly natural, being made by excavating the earth from the side of the bluff, and was thirty feet in thickness."[18] Spanish Fort was originally built by the Spanish in 1780, and the fort itself was designated as Redoubt 1, and it was manned by the 22nd Louisiana Consolidated Infantry. The 22nd Louisiana also manned two batteries — Battery Huger and Battery Tracy. In addition, the 22nd Louisiana manned Fort McDermott (Redoubt 2) located about 400 yards on the southern part of the Confederate defenses. The center of the Spanish Fort defenses was anchored by Redoubt 3, manned by a company of the New Orleans Washington Artillery. Redoubts 4 and 5 were made up of the Phillips Battery and Garrity's Alabama Battery. Finally Redoubt 6 was manned by Lumsden's Alabama Battery. The 21st Alabama Infantry also occupied the defenses at Spanish Fort.

One of the few accounts of the Siege of Spanish Fort by a member of the 11th Missouri was found in a letter written by Captain George Adams on April 4, 1865: "Since then we marched 2 & ½ days built 2 breast works at night. On the 27 we came here. Had some fighting but the 4th had some to do. Only skirmishing. Very few men wounded — 28. We threw up works day & night. .... A skirmish had 2 men hurt. Terry lost two fingers but Cyrus [Baul] were hit with a spent ball. He is on duty now but not stout. He stays with the teams. So the Yanks has thrown up a great deal of dirt. It digs easy. Last eve from 5 to 7 P.M. the Yanks made a boom shell. Charge this for the first time reminded me much of Vicksburg. The rebs layed low when we are at work with all our artillery. Our Regt has had some 28 men killed & wounded. Most of them on 1,2, and 4 day. Casualty last 3 day very small."[19] Captain Adams referred to the mining efforts of the regiment in the letter and the siege was measured by days into the siege, e.g., Day 4 was the fourth day of the siege.

Captain Adams further described the action at Spanish Fort and the death of Captain William Erwin, Company D, "I hope I will be favored with the pleasure of greeting you in person my next birthday which will be my 30th one. If I don't get my call taken here. They have shot very close to me whilst at work. We lost one here. One fine Capt. at Nashville and one here. The one here is not ded but his arm is gone at his shoulder."[20] William Erwin was a 27-year-old farmer from Clay County, Illinois, and had served with the regiment since it was formed in August 1861. Captain Erwin died on April 7, 1865, as a result of his wounds. Erwin was one of four sons who fought for the Union due to the Confederate artillery. His brother John who also served with the 11th Missouri was discharged due to a physical disability in 1862, and another brother, Eli, was killed at Shiloh in April 1862 serving with 18th Missouri.

Daily exchanges of fire from musket and artillery occurred. Work parties dug trenches to approach the Confederate defenses and the artillery did the deadly work. On March 31, Confederate General Randall Gibson encouraged his defenders to maintain their morale under the intensifying siege, "Resolve to do your duty, every hour of each coming day, and with the blessing of Heaven we shall continue to achieve those successes which so far have crowned your efforts."[21] On the Union side of the line "the toil of the besiegers was incessant and severe" as the entrenchments continued.[22]

Initially, the Confederate artillery dominated the siege, but as the siege carried on, Federal heavy artillery arrived and began to bombard the Confederate forts. By March 31, the Union artillery began to be positioned to shell Spanish Fort, and soon 30-pound Parrotts, 20-pound Parrotts, and 8-inch mortars were hammering away at Spanish Fort. Artillery duels became commonplace, but a particularly vicious barrage took place in early April when "seventy-five cannons — thirty-eight siege guns and thirty-seven field pieces" pounded the Confederate defenses.[23] On April 6, the 11th Missouri Infantry reported one soldier killed in action. On April 8, the 13th day of the siege, the Union artillery again hammered away at the Confederate defenses and McArthur's division burrowed to within 60 yards of the Confederate defenses.

As the days passed, the end of the siege was in sight, and on April 8 Spanish Fort fell to Union control when 96 Union guns pounded the Confederate defenses from 5:30 to 7:30 P.M. Carr's Division probed forward in conjunction with the bombardment. As the Union troops pushed forward, the Confederate defenders tried to hold their line, but soon discovered that they were outnumbered and out-gunned. Nightfall saved the defenders of Spanish Fort who decided it was time to evacuate. By midnight the garrison escaped along the shore of Mobile Bay.

On April 9, General A. J. Smith sent McArthur's and Carr's divisions to join the siege of Fort Blakeley. The Union forces around Fort Blakeley attacked and successfully captured the fort in a bloody action on April 9, 1865. The 11th Missouri Veteran infantry did not play an active role in the siege at Fort Blakeley. The Union forces lost 116 killed and 659 wounded and missing in action at Fort Blakeley. The majority of the defenders at Fort Blakeley were captured. On the morning of April 12, General Dabney Maury removed the remainder of his forces from Mobile.

Colonel Lucius Hubbard reported, "During the siege of Spanish Fort the brigade excavated 7,000 cubic yards of earth, and expended 169,000 rounds of musket ammunition. The labors of the siege were very arduous. The men were worked by large details night and day upon fortifications and approaches, yet they bore their trials patiently, and cheerfully responded to every call of whatever character."[24] The casualty list for the 11th Missouri is not definitive. Fox's Regimental Losses reported 4 men were killed and another 17 were injured, but the Official Records report made by brigade commander Lucius Hubbard reported 1 officer and 5 enlisted men killed and 27 enlisted men wounded. Modesta Green recorded that Captain Erwin and five other soldiers died on April 9. Based on a search of the Compiled Service Records of the 11th Missouri, 27 were identified as killed and wounded in the siege at Spanish Fort.

Casuality List Spanish Fort[25]

Company A
Dace, Charles	Private	Head — Died of wounds

Company B
Abbott, Lyman,	Corporal	KIA
Totzell, Voluntine	Private	Leg
Armstrong, Washington	Private	Died of wounds

Company C
O'Reilly, John	Private	Died of wounds
Weech, John	Private	KIA
Wright, Thomas	Private	

Company D
Erwin, William	Captain	Died of wounds
Gross, John	Private	
House, James D	Private	Arm, hand
Pryfogle, Alexander	Private	
Woods, Robert	Private	Arm

Company F
Weinger/Weiman, John	Private	Arm — amputated

Company G
Edward Bullick	Private	Hand

Company H
Brown, George	Private–Chaplain	Slight
Crozier, John	Private	Arm

Fullen, Godfrey	Private	
Higgins, Absalom	Private	Head, legs
Kennedy, Moses	Private	Died Ft Gaines
McGuire, Michel	Private	Died of wounds
Spilkey, Edward	Corporal	Died of wounds

Company I

Davidhiser, Henry	Corporal	Ankle, leg
Lung, Marion	Private	Hand
O'Brien, Martin	Private	Knee
Williams, Allen	Private	Drowned — Died
Armstrong, John	Sergeant	
Davis, Harrison	Sergeant	

The wounds of the men ranged from slight to the severest, like those of Captain William Erwin who died after he lost his arm as a result of a cannon ball. Washington Armstrong died in June as a result of a gunshot wound to his right forefinger, which was amputated. In addition, the acting regimental Chaplain, George Brown, a minister and farmer from Missouri, was injured when a shell landed between him and another soldier. The other soldier was killed and Brown was wounded by the explosion, but the Rev. Brown was able to return to duty. General Andrew J. Smith reported his losses at Spanish Fort were 26 killed, 319 wounded and 3 missing.

The month of April 1865 recorded many significant events important to the history of the United States. April 1865 signaled the end of the Confederacy — Mobile fell into Union hands, Lee surrendered at Appomattox, General Joe Johnston surrendered to Sherman. Also in April 1865, President Abraham Lincoln was assassinated. Finally, on May 8, General Dabney Maury surrendered his forces. Based on all the actions going on across the country, the value of the lives lost at Spanish Fort and Fort Blakeley, from a historical standpoint, must be questioned. Historian Sean O'Brien stated, "The military operations against Mobile — with its costly siege at Spanish Fort and bloody storming of Fort Blakeley — was a needless one."[26] However, hindsight is perfect, but in the time of poor

The 11th Missouri Infantry's third chaplain, the Rev. George Brown (courtesy Civil War Museum at Wilson's Creek National Battlefield).

communications and an unknown future, those men who gave their lives and limbs at Mobile, did so performing to the best of their duty and honor based on the situation as they knew it.

Charles Treadway recorded on May 3, 1865, the regiment's movements before and after the Battle of Spanish Fort: "We left New Orleans on the 5th of March came across the Gulf to Dauphen Island at this post we ware detained 7 days. Thence we went across the bay and up Fish River about 40 miles. Disembarked and prepared for a long march and hard fighting. On the morning of the 26 of March the Army commenced moving our regiment being the advance Regiment of the Corps. We advanced about one mile when skirmishing ensued which was kept up all day. We drove the enemy about 8 miles this day. The day following we drove them 10 miles. On the 3 day we drove them in side of their fortifications. Now the tug of war commenced. We seiged them 12 days, when they came to the conclusion to surrender the Fort the name of this was Spanish Fort. Next move ware to take Fort Blakely which we succeeded in two days. Then we received orders to move to the place [Montgomery, Alabama]. We marched 240 miles through swamps and rain in one of the weariest marches of the war, we arrived here a week ago last Sunday."[27]

For the 11th Missouri, this proved be the last campaign of the war; but the regiment did not return home until January 1866. The regiment remained at Fort Blakeley until late April when it left to move northward to become part of the occupying Union force in the state of Alabama. The 11th Missouri Infantry soon became part of the Military District of Montgomery and was stationed at Demopolis, Alabama. The various regiments of the Second Brigade were placed in different Alabama cities to maintain the peace that had been so dearly won.

Occupation in Alabama

And so the Civil War ended for the 11th Missouri Infantry, but the regiment continued to serve as part of the United States Army until January 1866. As the 11th Missouri Infantry began its occupation of Alabama, the importance of discipline within the regiments was critical. Brigade Colonel Lucius Hubbard emphasized this by issuing General Order No. 19 on May 20, 1865, from his headquarters are Demopolis, Alabama: "Regimental commanders of this brigade are expected to exercise that degree of vigilance necessary to restrain the evil-disposed among their men from depredating and committing excesses upon citizens of the country. The most vigorous measures must be adopted to prevent lawlessness and outrage. If a proper degree of restraint cannot otherwise be secured, a strong guard will be posted around each regimental camp, and no soldier allowed to pass its limits except upon duty, or by special permission. The men must not be permitted to absent themselves at pleasure from camp and straggle at will about the country. The rules of discipline must be enforced, and the routine of duties rigidly observed. No soldier will be permitted to enter the house or yard of any citizen except by permission of an officer nor allowed more than a mile from camp except with the written permission of his regimental commander. The roll-calls prescribed in General Orders, No. 17, from these headquarters, will be observed, and every unauthorized absentee required to answer for the offense. Rigid rules are necessary to restrain the few bad men who embrace every opportunity to bring discredit upon themselves and their comrades. The good soldier will therefore readily submit to a severer discipline that the command may be saved from reproach."[28]

The Civil War in Alabama virtually destroyed the civil authority in the state and for a time anarchy reigned. The Union army was called to fill the void left by the absence of civil law. On June 7, 1865, the Military Division of the Tennessee was commanded by General George

Thomas, who had commanded this territory since 1863, and Thomas had administrative authority over Alabama. In 1865, the Department of Alabama was placed under the command of General C. R. Woods headquartered at Mobile. In early summer 1865, cities and the surrounding territory were formed into military districts ultimately reporting to General Woods. The military districts in Alabama were Mobile, Montgomery, Talladega and Huntsville. Under military control, the type of authority, either good or bad, was reflective of the character of the commander in charge of a specific geography. Fortunately President Andrew Johnson appointed Lewis Parsons as the provisional governor of Alabama on June 21, 1865, which was an important first step in establishing civilian rule in the state.

The Military District of Middle Alabama was commanded by General Henry Eugene Davies. Davies was a native New Yorker, being born in 1836, and a graduate of Columbia College in 1857. He began his military career as captain of the Fifth New York Infantry. Davies was faced with a less than desirable situation when he assumed command in May 1865. The discipline among the troops was very important in the relations between the local citizens and the occupying Union troops. As the war ended, these relations were not favorable. Charles Treadway expressed some of the actions and feelings in his May 3, 1865, letter, "But if thare is another Battle fought thare will be few prisoners taken. I have heard a great many Soldiers speak that they had taken the last prisoner that they ever would. Thare was two citizens shot in this town for saying bully for the man that shot the President. Thare was six killed in Mobile. Soldiers will not take such insults and I glorie in their spunk, it is a sad affair indeede though it is done and cant be helped."[29]

Life after the war in Alabama was unpleasant because the local citizens felt they were a part of a defeated country as the civil law was abolished and martial law became the law of the land. Again, on May 27, Charles Treadway wrote of the situation, "The South is almost destitute of any thing, their homes have been destroyed by fire. The Armies have taken all the stock and provision. Their Negrows have all run off and left them, and now they have been defeated in the war. And have to return home with their Confederate Scrip which they can not purchase a chew of tobacco with. Their Scrip is all that they have. Every since we have been here the Negrows have been coming in to our lines and both Officers and men have used their utmost endeavors to get them to return to their masters, and stay with them, we have persuaded a great many to return.... I hope I will be permited to live under Civil Law not Military, one that lives in a civil life has all the privaleges that he could wish and one that is subject to Military Discipline is like the Negrow, has no privaledges."[30]

In July 1865, the 11th Missouri received an influx of men into the regiment, and this time over 40 men were either transferred draftees/substitutes or veterans from the 33rd Missouri Infantry and the 124th Illinois Infantry. Because the Civil War was over, none of these men would ever face combat as part of the 11th Missouri Infantry.[31]

33RD MISSOURI TRANSFEREES		124TH ILLINOIS TRANSFEREES	
Company A		*Company C*	
Blackman, James R.	Pvt.	Fege/Fiege, Christian	Pvt.
Cabe, Edwin	Pvt.		
Nann/Nunn, William T.	Pvt.	Tormutz/Torunits, John	Pvt.
Smith, George	Pvt.	*Company D*	
Company C		Kufus, Christian	Pvt.
Curtis, Stephen A.	Pvt.	*Company E*	
Davis, Nelson	Pvt.	Helms, John	Pvt.–Corporal

33RD MISSOURI TRANSFEREES		124TH ILLINOIS TRANSFEREES	
Robin, Emile	Pvt.	Crider, Joseph C.	Pvt.
Graham, Francis M.	Pvt.	Kaple, Henry	Pvt.
Company D		King, John A.	Pvt.
Hopkins, Ebenezer	Corporal–Sgt.	Rhettmire, Christopher	Pvt.
		Seba, Frederick	Pvt.
Baker, Beverly R.	Pvt.	*Company F*	
Strother, Robert H.	Pvt.	Dappa, August	Pvt.
Company E		Eickenman/Eicherman, Herman	Pvt.
Deroin, Edward	Pvt.	Oggeschky, Lewis	Pvt.
Lee, John	Pvt.	*Company I*	
Willis, Fleming	Pvt.	Boesch, Jacob	Pvt.
May, Joseph C.	Pvt.	Ratkin, Fred	Pvt.
Company F		Schendler, Jacob	Pvt.
Green, John	Corporal	*Company K*	
Bullock, George W.	Pvt.	Emo, Peter	Pvt.
Barnes, John	Pvt.	Heffner, George	Pvt.
Failes, Alvin	Pvt.	Windland, Nicholas	Pvt.
Company G			
Hall, Hiram	Pvt.		
McGill, James	Pvt.		
Rettie/Retler, Joseph	Pvt.		
Norris, Abraham	Pvt.		
Company K			
Gogan, William	Pvt.		
Prior, George	Pvt.		
Winscott, William N.	Pvt.		

Throughout the long, hot Alabama summer, the attitudes among the soldiers of the regiment continued to deteriorate. Sergeant Charles Treadway recorded from Demopolis, Alabama, on June 19 1865, "We buried one of our company day before yesterday he was a German from Mo. by the name of John Unmach. He was a fine man, but now he has left the Armies of our Government and has gon to the Army above where war never is, and yesterday thare an other man went off and said he was going to drown him self, and we haven't seen him since. Thare is no doubt but what he lies in the Tombigbee River. He was a drafted man and he came to the conclusion that he never would be able to return home that he would die in the Army any how, he told me some 4 days ago that if he thought it was right that he would drown his self.... Oh how distressing it will be to his young wife in Mo."[32] Regimental records showed that John Unmach died July 17, 1865. Regimental records also record one suicide, but the soldier was not identified. Treadway went on record in a letter on July 10, 1865, "I do not like the climate nor the people."[33]

By August thoughts were directed toward home, Charles Treadway recorded in a letter on August 6 that the duty in Alabama was peaceful and work was light. "I know you are well aware that I am ancious to return home, not because I am tired of Soldiering, but mearly because my promise stands awaiting a future time. I did not come into the army for a Regular

Soldier I came to assist in putting down a rebellion which was brought upon our once happy homes. I came as a volunteer. I have witnessed many a bloody battle field. I have stemmed the hardships and turmoils of the Bloody Strife, and the awful Strife is over and I consider it right to discharge all volunteers."[34] As Treadway recorded, desertions were a major problem for the regiment. The records of the 11th Missouri Veteran Infantry's desertions for 1865 are listed in Appendix 2.

In August 1865 the Union army in Alabama was given the responsibility to administer the oath of allegiance to people who were either directly or indirectly involved in the rebellion against the United States. Those signing the oath were granted amnesty. There was a special section of the oath which bound those signing the oath to agree to support the provisions of the Emancipation Proclamation and to support the constitution of the United States. The state of Alabama was divided into 120 stations where the oath was administered.

By August, at least two members of the 11th Missouri Veteran Infantry lost their lives in the Military District of Montgomery. Details of these incidents are sketchy, but the first death was that of musician, Josiah Adams, Company H, who was killed on August 31, 1865. The 11th Missouri was camped near Tuscaloosa and Josiah Adams was involved in a fight with an ex–Confederate by the name of Cowan. During the altercation, Adams was shot in the head and died. The second incident was the murder of Private Julius Harrison, Company D. Originally Private Harrison was reported as missing from the regiment and listed as deserted but his body was found near a river and positively identified by two members of the regiment. His death was determined to be murder. Private Harrison is thought to have died on August 16, 1865. Clearly the relationship between the military and local citizens was precarious.

Final Regimental Officer Changes

As the war ended, there were a few regimental changes made during the final months of the 11th Missouri Infantry. In March 1865, Lieutenant Colonel Eli Bowyer was promoted colonel for the regiment and Major Modesta Green was also rewarded with a promotion to the rank of lieutenant colonel. Melanchton Fish resigned his commission as regimental surgeon on May 2, 1865, and Dr. Thomas Hawley was promoted to the rank of regimental surgeon on May 27, 1865. Finally, William Cleland was promoted to the rank of major in March, which allowed 1st Lieutenant Charles Smith to be promoted as captain of Company F. Second Lieutenant Wilford McElyea was promoted to the rank of 1st lieutenant and George A. Greenwood was promoted to the rank of 2nd lieutenant. Greenwood, a native of Tennessee, was 26 years old and had been a farmer from Xenia, Illinois, prior to the war.

On March 29, 1865, numerous promotions occurred within the 11th Missouri Infantry when a group of 2nd lieutenants were promoted on this date to completely fill the officer's ranks of the veteran regiment. In Company A, Henry Smith was promoted to the rank of 2nd lieutenant. Henry was 32 years old and had been with the regiment since the initial organization of the regiment. Smith was a Prussian by birth and was a farmer from Bridgeport, Illinois, prior to his enlistment. In Company B, Solomon Whitney was also promoted to the rank of 2nd lieutenant on the same date. Whitney, a native of New York, was a farmer from Sangamon County, Illinois, prior to the war. Daniel Walker was promoted to the rank of 2nd lieutenant in Company C. Walker was part of Company C throughout the war. In Company D, Charles W. Apperson was promoted to the rank of 2nd lieutenant. Apperson who originally enlisted as a corporal was a native of Illinois and was a farmer from Clay County, Illinois, prior to his enlistment. John F. Perry was promoted the rank of 2nd lieutenant in Company E. Perry, a native of Ohio, was a farmer from Olney, Illinois, and had advanced from his initial rank of private. Company G recorded the promotion of Thomas Mieure to the rank of 2nd lieutenant. Mieure was a 29-year-old farmer from Lawrenceville, Illinois, prior to the war and had been serving as a sergeant in the company prior to his promotion. In Company H, Robert Hamilton was promoted along with rest of the 2nd lieutenants. Hamilton, a native Scot, was a clerk from St. Louis at the time of his enlistment. Finally, McGuire Hathorn was promoted to the rank of 2nd lieutenant in Company I on the same date. Hathorn, a native of Ohio, was a farmer from Bethel, Illinois.

Company E needed to replace their captain William Notestine who died in February of wounds from the Battle of Nashville. In May, 1st Lieutenant Levi Roney was promoted to the rank of Captain, and John Myers was promoted to the rank of 1st lieutenant. The German-born Myers was a farmer from Calhoun, Illinois, prior to the war. Captain William Erwin of Company D died of his wounds in the Battle of Spanish Fort in April and Lyman Randall was promoted from his rank of 1st lieutenant to company command and the rank of captain in June 1865. James Tasker was promoted to the rank of 2nd lieutenant in June also. Tasker, a native of New York, was a stonecutter from Clay County, Illinois, prior to the war.

Second Lieutenant Solomon Whitney was promoted in March 1865 (Abraham Lincoln Presidential Library & Museum).

The final regimental changes occurred within Company K. Captain Cyrus Kendall resigned his commission on June 18, 1865, at the end of his term of service. He was officially replaced with Dennis E. Coogan who had previously declined a promotion in March 1865 due to his disability as a result of a wound he received in the Battle of Nashville. Captain Coogan was not able to physically perform his duties, but was promoted to that rank nonetheless. Coogan declined his promotion and was discharged due to his wounds. Dennis Coogan was a 30-year-old native of New York who resided in Franklin County, Missouri, prior to the war, where he was a farmer. George Robinson was promoted to the rank of 2nd lieutenant of Company K also in June, and then within two weeks he was promoted again to the rank of 1st lieutenant. George Robinson was also from Franklin County, Missouri, prior to the war. Robinson was born in Missouri and farming was his livelihood prior to the war. William Snow was promoted to the rank of 2nd lieutenant in June also. William Snow had been born in Kentucky and also was a farmer living in Franklin County, Missouri, prior to the war.

Mystery of William Cleland

One of the biggest mysteries in the history of the 11th Missouri Infantry was that of Major William Cleland's activities in Alabama after the end of the war. William Cleland had served with the regiment when it was formed from the First Missouri Rifles in 1861, where he served as a sergeant. A native of Massachusetts, Cleland worked as a clerk in St. Louis prior to the war. Cleland worked his way through the ranks during the Civil War, serving as a 2nd lieutenant, 1st lieutenant and captain of Company F. He was wounded in the Battle of Iuka when his horse was shot from under him and also during the Battle of Tupelo when he was wounded so severely he was removed from the regiment because he was deemed physically unfit for future duty. Cleland served as acting aide to Colonel Lucius Hubbard during the Battle of Nashville, and he was recognized as distinguishing himself by his actions. Finally, in the summer of 1865, he was appointed Acting Assistant Inspector General in the Military Department of Montgomery, being recommended for that role by Colonel Lucius Hubbard, the brigade commander.

Then things appear to have gone wrong. The first indication things were not going well for Major Cleland was a message from the Provost Marshall, Hunter Brooks, on October 29, 1865: "I have the within named officer and he acknowledges the arrest and leave on the first train on Oct 30 at 10 A.M. for Montgomery reporting to Maj Gen Davies."[35] The officer was Major William Cleland. The reason for the arrest was clarified when on November 8, General Henry Davies, commander of the Military District of Montgomery, wrote the following communication: "I have to report that Major Cleland A A J G at these Headquarters has never reported here pursuant to the request sent to you by telegram to have him arrested ten days ago. I find that he has most scandalously has abused his position as an officer and has availed himself to his official position to make unauthorized arrests of citizens and extort money as a condition of releasing them. I learn from some letters that have reached here since his disappearance that his wife lives at Flora, Clay Co., Illinois and I would request that the Commanding General of the Department asks for his arrest and return here under guard if he can be found at that place."[36]

Then the chase for Major Cleland began. The military authorities were also directed to look for the wayward major at his father's home in New York. General Davies indicated, "As the matter stands

Major William W. Cleland, left, and Lieutenant Colonel Modesta Green, right (author's collection).

I have to report him as having deserted and recommend his dismissal from the service."[37] On November 12, Major Cleland was reported to be in New Orleans, and the Provost Marshall there was alerted via telegraph from General Woods to arrest him if he could be found; but the officials in New Orleans reported Cleland had left New Orleans and was returning to Montgomery before he could be detained. Major Cleland's service record showed he was absent without leave in the months of November and December; however, he was mustered out with the regiment in January 1866.

The resolution of this affair is not known but there is no record Cleland faced a court-martial. William Cleland died very soon after the end of the war in 1867, and his official record showed no reference to this affair. Unfortunately, there are no surviving records of Cleland's side of this story; however, there were several instances of alleged wrong doing on the part of the Union army. The "local military authorities were directed to arrest persons who had been or might be charged with offences against officers, agents, citizens, and inhabitants of the United States.... Persons so arrested were to be confined by the military until a proper tribunal might be ready and willing to try them."[38] This certainly was a system that could be abused and could be open to allegations against those making the arrests. "Numerous complaints of arbitrary arrests and of the unwarranted seizure of private property" were reported as a result of the military situation in Alabama in 1865.[39]

No formal charges were ever brought against William Cleland, who had served throughout the war in every battle the 11th Missouri was involved, suffering severe wounds in numerous occasions as he steadily advanced in rank. The true events will never be known, but the explanation of this incident may be summarized in a letter from Thomas Hawley to his family in December 1865. "For these citizens deserve to be ordered around by darkies who they so much despise and indeed have despised us and treated us most shamefully but report most false & slanderous to the gov. and he to the cmdg general who was foolish enough to believe it."[40] This correspondence demonstrates the adversarial relationship with the local citizens of Alabama and the Union army. While it is impossible to conclusively show Dr. Hawley's letter related to William Cleland's situation, it appears to summarize the relationship the 11th Missouri Infantry shared with the citizens of Alabama.

Final Months of the 11th Missouri Infantry

Clearly by the fall of 1865, discipline and morale within the ranks was very poor; and this necessitated a firm admonishment of the officers to keep their troops in check. Major General Henry Davies issued General Order No. 35 on October 9, 1865, from the District of Montgomery: "The major general commanding has observed with great dissatisfaction the irregular discipline and general inattention to duty of which the officers and men of this command are guilty. The troops have been in permanent camp a sufficient period to fully remedy the irregularities that result from active campaign and to place the whole command in a condition of thorough discipline and complete equipment. He regrets to see little or nothing has been done by officers whose experience in the service would justify the expectations that they understood the duties of their position and their troops are still badly disciplined, poorly fed, and the appearance, and clothing many of them wear are unworthy of the name of soldiers."[41]

Dr. Thomas Hawley recorded in a letter to his family on August 25, 1865, "The soldiers are inclined to be insubordinate and discontented, want to go home, and leave these rebels to themselves."[42] Dr. Hawley reported that discord and fear was common and that cotton, livestock and other property changed hands rapidly and illegally in Alabama.

The discipline issue was echoed in letter written by Charles Treadway, from Marion,

Alabama, on October 29, 1865. "Thare is strong talk of the Regiment being mustered out in next month. Indeede if it does I will not cry you may be assured, for I am verry ancious to return home. It appears hard to me to serve in the Army when I know that I am not needed, and after serving through the whole war, I think it no more than just to liberate all the Vettern Troops as they have been from their homes and friends so long. Thare is more steeling go-ing on than I ever heard of. Thare is hardly a day but what we hear of something being stolen, or some one shot or stabed. We must take everything into consideration after war and such a continuous war as the later Revolution has been we may expect outrages being commited all over our land, not altogether in the Southern States.... The longer I am in the South the worse I hate the climate, if God spares me to get relieved from the Army I never will show my face in the South again, I do not like the people for one thing, and that is for aristocracy thare is hundred of young ladies in the Southern States that never put on their own gloves, not got a pan of water to wash them selves. They all have a Negrow to wait on them. Such pride as this does not suit me. You may rest assured that they do not like the Yankees as they call them.... The Rebel Soldiers and our boys gets along all right. Thare is some deserting nearly every day, thare has been 8 deserted from our company in the last month. Thare has been about 23 deserted since the first of last May. Our company consists of seventy six members at this time but it will not if we remain in service much longer for the boys think their time is out."[43]

Again on November 23, Sergeant Treadway explained the deteriorating morale within the regimental ranks, "I would be better satisfied if thare was no whiskey in the land although I do not use it myself, but thare is so much drunkness here. Thare is no time but one can see 5 or 6 drunk at a time and some times half of the Regiment and it is fight and quarrel all the time. Half of Co. C is drunk tonight and they have been fighting and quareling for the last hour. I am so digusted at drunk men I do not care whither I ever see any more intoxicating drink again or not."[44]

This concluded the letters of Charles Treadway. Charles Treadway sent a series of letters to his future wife, Elizabeth Moore, throughout the war. When the 11th Missouri Infantry was mustered out of service in January 1866, he lost no time in marrying Ms. Moore on February 8, 1866. Their time together was short because Sergeant Treadway died July 25, 1867, of consumption.

Although the war was over and the regiment's service was almost over, death still haunted the men. A letter written by the chaplain of the regiment, the Rev. George W. Brown to Mrs. Mary Norris, the widow of Abraham Norris of Palmyra, Missouri, recorded the sorrow for the men who died. "I am called upon to announce to you the death of your husband. Abraham Norris, who died this morning about 9 o'clock. He was sick a long time. In fact, ever since he was transferred from the 33RD MO. And all the time in the hospital. He was well taken care of. Nursed very tenderly, until death released him from suffering. He died fully in his senses and professed religion some 10 days ago. Requested me to inform you of the fact, and I am glad that you have this comfort in your sad affliction. That the Lord was pleased to have mercy upon him and lead him to Christ. Before his death he requested me to baptize him which I did. He expressed a willingness to die but said he would like to get well and return home."[45] The unfortunate Private Norris died of chronic diarrhea.

Another of the soldiers of the 11th Missouri Infantry, Captain George C. Adams, died on December 28, 1865, at the "residence of his father, E. H. Adams, near Versailles, Brown Co., Illinois."[46] Insight into the regiment was presented through a series of letters that were preserved from Captain Adams. Although men died throughout the war, it is always sad when soldiers died so near the end of their service. George Adams was 39 years old at the time of his death and had served faithfully throughout the war, first as sergeant and finally commanding Company I. He served through all the battles only to die a mere three weeks prior to the regiment mustering out of service.

The 11th Missouri continued their duty in Alabama serving by detachments at Tuscaloosa, Marion, Greensboro and Uniontown until October. The regiment was garrisoned at Demopolis until December 24 when it was moved to Memphis, and the regiment was mustered out January 15, 1866.

The final record of the 11th Missouri Infantry was a letter written by Colonel Eli Bowyer reporting the current address of the remaining officers of the regiment:

Olney Ill[47]
February 10th 1866
Col Simpson
A G of Mo
Sir
    Addresses of the officers of the 11th

Lt. Col. M J Green		Springfield, IL
Maj. Wm Cleland		Brooklyn, NY
Surg Thos Hawley		Olney, Ill
R S M I Swan		Bethel, Ill
Adjt W W French		Suttons Point Clay County, Ill
Chaplain G W Brown		Meramec Iron Works, Phelps Co. Mo
Capt. C McMahan	Co. A	Bridgeport Lawrence Co. Ill
1st Lt. B L Nigh	Co. A	Bridgeport Lawrence Co. Ill
Lt. W Smith	Co. A	St. Louis, MO
Capt. W B Followill	Co. B	
Lt. L A Whitney	Co. B	Chatham Sangamon Co. Ill
Lt. B F Kelley	Co. B	Springfield, Ill
Capt. Jas A Lott	Co. C	Springfield, Ill
Lt. W L Simmons	Co. C	Springfield, Ill
Lt. Dan Walker	Co. C	Springfield, Ill
Capt. L Randall	Co. D	Ingraham Clay Co. Ill
Lt. C W Apperson	Co. D	Louisville Clay Co. Ill
Lt. Tasker	Co. D	Louisville Clay Co. Ill
Capt. L D Roney	Co. E	Olney Ill
Lt. Myers	Co. E	Olney Ill
Lt. Perry	Co. E	Olney Ill
Capt. Charles Smith	Co. F	Xenia Clay Co. Ill
Lt. W McElyea	Co. F	Xenia Clay Co. Ill
Lt. Greenwood	Co. F	Xenia Clay Co. Ill
Capt. Wm Wallace	Co. G	Lawrenceville, Lawrence Co. Ill
Lt. George Quick	Co. G	Lawrenceville, Lawrence Co. Ill
Lt. T Meier	Co. G	Lawrenceville, Lawrence Co. Ill
Capt. E R Applegate	Co. H	Bridgeport, Lawrence Co. Ill
Lt. J McNeal	Co. H	Sumner Lawrence Co. Ill
Lt. Hamilton	Co. H	Sumner Lawrence Co. Il
Lt. Shoopman	Co. I	Bethel Morgan Co. Ill
Only surviving officer of this co.		
Lt. Geo E Robertson	Co. K	Bethel Morgan Co. Ill
Lt. W S Snow		Franklin, Mo

11th Missouri Infantry Regimental Losses 1865

	JAN–MARCH	APRIL–JUNE	JULY–SEPT.	OCT–DECEMBER
Discharged	Henson/Henston, Hiram (F)	Kelley/Kelly, Timothy Corp (D)	Jump, Riley (D)	Rogers, Barnett (H)
		King, George A. (F)	Judy, Henry (E)	Hyde, Patrick (D)
		Kline, Jacob L. (I)	Kelly, Patrick (C)	Roberts, Garrett (C)
		Keuff, John (G)	Kirkey, Joseph (G)	
		Lung, Marion S. (I)	Lee, Patrick (I)	
		Judy, Henry C. (E)	Mann, William (A)	
		Delevadwa/Delwadwo, Petro Sgt. (E)	Morehead, David (C)	
		Davidhiser, Henry Corp (I)	Young, Thomas (C)	
		McDaniel, Jackson (E)		
		Sullivan, Patrick (C)	Gravatt, John (D)	O'Keefe, Michael (K)
	Friend, William (E)	McKenna, Edward (A)	Schulte, Joseph (1) (K)	Hawkins, Robert (E)
	Rainey, William (H)	Gross, John (D)	Gillman, Charles (F)	Graham, Francis M. (1) (C)
		Wood, David (D)	Mathis, Leonard (H)	Rettie/Retler, Joseph (G)
		O'Brien, Martin (I)	Goldman, Francis M. (B)	Coon, George W. (K)
		Padden/Paddin, Martin (E)	Breckel, Louis (A)	Hicks, Joseph (K)
		McDanel, Jackson (E)	Williamson, Thomas (F)	Todd, Henry (K)
		Chapman, Daniel (E)	Richhart, Benjamin Alexander (E)	Adams, Thomas J. (E)
		Jones, Samuel (K)	Coogan, Dennis E. (Sgt) (K)	Blazer, Henry (E)
		Sutherland, Garrett (F)	Tate/Tait, Joseph L. (B)	Delong, John (A)
		Plank, Peter (I)	Gowan, John (F)	Riley, James (D)
		Weirman, John (F)	Wenze, Christopher (G)	Seaton, Robert (F)
			McClain, Dudley (H)	Ryan, James (H)
			McPherson, William (I)	Bay, Joseph (K)
			Alexander, Hiram (C)	Farrell, Christopher (I)
			Kelly, Patrick (C)	Todd, Henry (K)
			Mabery, Michael (C)	
			Stewart, Amos (H)	
			Blackford, Enoch (I)	
Died	Adams, Albert F. (I)	Phelps, James (K)	Snow, John (B)	Seigert, Fred A. (B) Date unknown
	Squires, Charles (I)	Sweet, Sylvester Corp. (C)	Clark, Teaddeus (I)	Fisher, Hiram (G) Date Unknown
	Morgan, William (K)	Allen, Samuel (A)	Keiker, John (C)	Owens, Charles W. Supposed died in prison- date unknown
		Freeny, Lawrence (K)	Adams, Josiah) Musician (H	Result, J. (I) date unknown
	Lombard/Lumbard, John (C)	Mcguire, Michael (H)	Rucker, John (H)	Miller, John (B) Date Unknown

8. Battle of Spanish Fort and the Occupation in Alabama

	Jan–March	April–June	July–Sept.	Oct–December
	Whitfield, Marshall (1) Cook (B)	O'Reilly, John (C)	Womack, William (A)	Adams, George C. Captain (I)
	Terrell/Terry, John (A)	Lutts, Joseph (G)	Laired, Alfred H. (E)	McCormick, John (D)
	Dunley/Dumley, John (B)	Weech/Weed, John (C)	Martin, John (K)	Monegan, Owen Corp. (K)
	Hathorn, Mcguire C. 2nd Lt. (I)	Erwin, William (1) (D)	Rollin, Buel S. (G)	Norris, Abraham (G)
	Will, James (unassigned)	Mosar, Peter (K)	Wilgus, William (H)	O'Keefe, Michael (K)
	Thompson, Stephen B. (A)	Jones, John T. (F)	Harrison, Julius (D)	Whitfield, Marshall (B)
	Engledow, Leland (1) (D) [Died of wounds after discharge]	Spilkey, Edward Corp. (H)	Keys, Michael (D)	
	Engledow, William C. (D)	Knobb, Adam (B)	Mccormick, John (D)	
	Crum, William (D)	Brown, James D. (I)		
	Heisfind, Bentley (E)	Armstrong, Washington (B)		
	Notestine, William Capt. (E)	Unmack, John (1) (A)		
	Pollard, John (I)	Wright, John W. (C)		
	Lanfrecht, Otto (K)	Burns, Rolin (D)		
	Michler/Miller, Ferdinand (A)	Thompson, Gailwood (B)		
	Holman, John (F)	Wethers, Isaac (D)		
	Brewer, James Corp (G)			
	Davis, William (K)			
	Payne, Nathaniel (K)			
	Kennedy, Moses (H)			
	Williams, Allen L. (I)			
	Abbott, Lyman Corp (B).			
	Dace/Dave, Charles (A)			
	Bender, Frederick (C)			
	Hix, William (G)			
	Brake, Benjamin (K)			
Deserted Killed In Action	Refer to Appendix 2			
Resigned		Foster, Charles Lt.	Finch, Walton H. (F&S) 1st Lt.	
		Fish, Melancthon, Surgeon	Kendall, Cyrus D. Capt. (K)	
			Applegate, Edwin Lt. (F&S)	
Transferred		O'Donal, Thomas Sgt. (D)		

Summary

The story of the Eleventh Missouri Infantry is one of an evolution of a group of men who came to the aid of their country and believed the Union had to be preserved at all costs. Most of the men who made up the regiment in 1861 were men from Illinois and Missouri, and these men wore the uniforms of the Union army proudly, with many paying the ultimate sacrifice for what they believed. The Eleventh Missouri never broke in any engagement, and the engagements were many, beginning with the Battle of Fredericktown, Missouri, and ending at the Battle of Spanish Fort.

The regiment was truly tested the first time at the Battle of Iuka when they stood against three charges from the Thirty-seventh Alabama and the Thirty-sixth Mississippi infantries and refused to give way. Next they were instrumental in halting Van Dorn's attempt to take Corinth and were involved in a bloody charge around Battery Robinett with seven members of their color guard shot down. Next was the legendary charge at Stockade Redan at Vicksburg when the regiment lost a third of its men in a murderous attack on an objective that could not be taken; but the regiment still ran through a hail of balls and shells refusing to be denied. The charge on Stockade Redan took the final toll on the Eleventh Missouri. It was a fighting regiment but it had finally lost too many men. Menomen O'Donnell was awarded the Medal of Honor for his actions at Vicksburg and during the Red River Campaign.

From the ruins of the Eleventh Missouri Infantry and Seventh Missouri Infantry came the Eleventh Missouri Veteran Infantry, which was again called upon at the Battle of Nashville to charge through 400 yards of shells and musket fire losing about 100 men, but refusing to be denied. Onward they ran and helped break the Confederate line at Shy's Hill that caused Hood to abandon any hope of victory. During this charge, three color bearers were shot down, only to have another man pick the flag of their country and race into the muzzles of guns of men who were intent on killing them. Three men of the regiment were awarded their nation's highest award, the Medal of Honor, for their efforts at the Battle of Nashville on December 16, 1864.

These were men who proved again and again that they would fight, even when they were outnumbered and even when victory was not possible.

The Eleventh Missouri Infantry was fortunate to have excellent leadership. Men like William Sherman and the unsung A. J. Smith as Corps commanders. They were even more fortunate to have Joseph Plummer, John McArthur and Joseph Mower as brigade and divisional commanders. Finally, the regiment was always blessed with excellent regimental colonels, including, Joseph Plummer, Joseph Mower, A. J. Weber, William Barnum and Eli Bowyer. The command structure under which the Eleventh Missouri Infantry fought guided this regiment and made it the fighting unit it was.

The American Civil War had such a devastating impact on the country when citizens of the United States were so separated by regional, political and social difference that they took up muskets and cannons against one another. This great country and principles on which it was founded were threatened, not from without, but within. The Eleventh Missouri Infantry was just one instrument that helped pull this country back together, even though many did not want that to happen. The Eleventh Missouri was just a group of farm boys that knew they had to stand up for their country. Many paid the ultimate sacrifice, their lives. Even though the records show 285 men killed from the regiment in the war, many men died shortly after returning home. For example, Lt. Colonel Modesta Green died at the age of 38 within 6 years of returning home of "old wounds." William Cleland was dead by 1867, at a young age, and also Jesse Lloyd died shortly after returning home. The list of casualties at battles like Iuka, Corinth, Vicksburg and Nashville contain scores of names of men killed in action, died of wounds, and amputations. The letters, the voices of the regiments are touching and tragic, from the hopeful, but dying Pvt. Alzono Thomas to Nathan Preston's letter about the death of William Chapman in which he wrote, "He died a true soldier. I deeply sympathize with you in your loss. You wanted to know if he was buried decently. He was buried as decently as he could under the circumstances." These were real men, simple men, with real feelings with real families.

When the 11th Missouri Infantry was mustered out in 1866, they left a proud history. They were a fighting regiment, and they were rough and they were rowdy. They were not a group that would have been pleasant to be around, but they were given a difficult and bloody job. There was none better than the 11th Missouri.

The story of the 11th Missouri Infantry needed to be told. One day a group of men proudly put on their blue uniforms of the 11th Missouri Infantry and for four and a half years willingly paid the ultimate sacrifice to protect their country. Let us never forget the men of the 11th Missouri Infantry and may their flag forever fly.

CHAPTER 9

Postwar Biographical Information

On January 17, 1866, the four and half year experience of the 11th Missouri Infantry was over. This history was the story of two regiments, and these two regiments contained the stories of more than 1,700 different men. So it is impossible to give postwar biographical information on all the men who made up the regiment, but the following biographical sketches include information that could be collected for the officers of the regiment with the rank of captain or higher.

Andrew Jackson Smith—As previously mentioned, the 11th Missouri Infantry, in their four and half years service, was blessed with excellent commanders. Although the 11th Missouri served in different corps, they were never more ably led than by General A. J. Smith. A. J. Smith is one of the most unsung Union generals of the Civil War. "Smith's Guerrillas" were veterans and hard-as-nails soldiers who would face anyone. It was quoted, "If A. J. ordered them to, they would to go to hell itself."[1] Smith, an outstanding commander, left the volunteer service in 1866 and was appointed colonel in the U.S. Seventh Cavalry serving in the western parts of the United States. He retired from the military in 1869 and became the postmaster in St. Louis, Missouri. Smith died on January 30, 1897, at the age of 81 and was buried in St. Louis.

Joseph Anthony Mower—Joseph "Wolf" Mower was aptly nicknamed. He was very effective in his role and was an excellent brigade and divisional commander in the Union army. General W. L. McMillen stated that Mower was "brave to a fault. Absolutely without any sense of danger, he seemed to relish above everything else that tumult of battle."[2] After leaving the 11th Missouri and the XVI corps, he commanded of the XX Army Corps. Mower was noted as having excellent service in the Battle of Bentonville, North Carolina. Mower left the volunteer infantry at the end of the war and entered the U.S. Infantry and served with the 39th U.S. Infantry and the 25th U.S. Infantry. He commanded the military district in eastern Texas and died of pneumonia in New Orleans in 1870.[3]

John McArthur—After Joseph Mower was promoted, the 11th Missouri Infantry was ably led by the Scottish-born John McArthur. John McArthur commanded the 11th Missouri's division, and his service was particularly notable in the Battle of Nashville as his division crashed into the Confederate line and won the day. After the war McArthur held several positions in the Chicago area. He was the Commissioner of Public Works of Chicago and the President of the Board of Education. He was also the postmaster of Chicago. General John McArthur died on May 15, 1906.[4]

Regimental Officers

Colonels

The officers and leaders of the 11th Missouri were from various walks of life, and after the war many returned to the same occupations. Within the 11th Missouri, the regiment had six colonels throughout the history of the regiment and only three of the colonels survived the war.

David Bayles — The unlucky David Bayles was instrumental in raising the 11th Missouri Infantry. Records show he was considered by some as a true patriot when the nation needed men like him to commit to the preservation of the Union. He was superseded as regimental colonel by Joseph Plummer in September 1861. Bayles fought to regain control of the regiment and was assigned to the regiment in 1862, but due to his ill health he could not assume command. He died early in 1863 never realizing his dream of leading the 11th Missouri Infantry into battle.

Joseph Plummer — Joseph Plummer was commissioned as the first colonel of the 11th Missouri Infantry on September 24, 1861, and assumed command of the regiment at its first station at Cape Girardeau, Missouri. When he arrived at Cape Girardeau, Colonel Plummer was carrying a remembrance from the Battle of Wilson's Creek, a wound that would ultimately be attributed as a cause for his death. Later he commanded the Fifth Division of Pope's Army at the siege of New Madrid and Island No. 10. Next he commanded a brigade within Stanley's Division at the siege at Corinth. One day before the anniversary of his wounding at the Battle of Wilson's Creek, Joseph Plummer died in Corinth, Mississippi, at the age of 45 years on August 9, 1862. He was the first of many excellent commanding officers that made the 11th Missouri Infantry the fighting regiment it was.[5]

Joseph Mower was the third regimental colonel.

Andrew Weber — Andrew Weber was initially part of the First Missouri Rifles which became the 11th Missouri. Weber gallantly led the regiment in the battles at Iuka, Corinth, Jackson, and, finally, Vicksburg where he died of his wounds. He gave his all and we "may well cherish, with pride, the memory of this young hero, who rose by talent, energy and industry to a position far above his years, and yielded his young and gifted life, a willing sacrifice on the altar of his country."[6]

William Barnum — 32-year-old William Barnum assumed the captaincy of Company I in September 1861. Barnum was an attorney and a married merchant living in Springfield, Illinois, prior to the war. He was born in New Jersey on August 24, 1829, and immigrated to Illinois, and moved back to Chicago after the war. He was married to Mary Davis Clark on October 18, 1854, in Springfield, Illinois. During the war, he was wounded in the right foot at the Battle of Corinth. Barnum was promoted to the rank of colonel on July 1, 1863. He was instrumental in commanding the regiment after the Siege of Vicksburg and was successful in forming the veteran regiment before his resignation in 1864. In 1867 he bought the insurance business of Lambert C. Hall and remained in the insurance business throughout his life. He later became the Secretary of Millers National Life Insurance Company. He lived in the U.S. Grant Hotel in San Diego for a short time in the early 1900s.[7] He lived at the Palmer Hotel in Chicago and then moved to the Lakota Hotel. He died on May 28, 1921.[8]

Eli Bowyer — The final colonel of the regiment was Dr. Eli Bowyer. Bowyer served as surgeon for the regiment and in 1863 was promoted to the rank of major. When the 11th Missouri

Veteran infantry was mustered into service, Bowyer assumed command of the regiment. He was wounded in the left arm and left leg in the Battle of Nashville and only partially recovered from his wound. He was brevetted brigadier general in March 1865. He was mustered out with his regiment in January 1866 at Memphis, Tennessee. "His patriotism, bravery, and ability as a commanding officer, are abundantly attested by his high testimonials from" the officers with which he served.[9] At the close of the war, Eli Bowyer returned to Olney, Illinois, and resumed his medical practice. In 1867 he was elected to the state legislature. He was active on the board of the Southern Normal University. He married Martha Cox in 1844, and he was member of the Presbyterian Church in Olney, Illinois.[10] In 1879, he was confirmed as postmaster for Olney, Illinois.[11] General Bowyer's health was reported to be shattered from the affects of the service during the war and he died March 6, 1886. It was said of him, "There was no public man whom the sword of criticism could penetrate more deeply or wound more thoroughly, nor was there any one who was more ready to defend unto the last his political or official acts with his own effective weapon."[12]

Lieutenant Colonels

William Panabaker—Colonel William Panabaker was one of the most interesting and versatile commanders in the war. Panabaker, a physician by occupation, was born in Virginia in 1822 and had served in the army during the Mexican War. He was also a Methodist minister who was instrumental in organizing, training and leading the regiment early in the war. This colorful individual led the 11th Missouri Infantry into their first full battle of the war, just two months after enlistment. He was thrown from a horse in the campaign near New Madrid injuring his back, and as a result he was discharged in 1862. He was a farmer and a doctor after the war. He was married to Mary Orr on October 3, 1855. After returning to Lawrence County, Dr. Panabaker helped to organize Grand Army of the Republic—Post 681 in Bridgeport, which was named the W. E. Panabaker Post. He died of tubercular disease on July 9, 1881, on his farm near Olive Branch Church in Illinois and was buried in the Olive Branch Cemetery.[13]

Modesta Green—Modesta Green was born in New Jersey and moved to Springfield, Illinois. He was a married carpenter before his enlistment. Green served throughout the war in the regiment and led the 11th Missouri Veteran Infantry through the hail of shot and shell at the Battle of Nashville. Lieutenant Colonel Modesta Green returned to Springfield after the war and made his living as a carpenter. He was a partner in the Green and Carver Carpentry business, which also sold paints, oil and glass. Green remained in Springfield until 1871 when he relocated to Omaha, Nebraska, as a postal clerk for the Union Pacific Railroad. Modesta James Green was born on June 24, 1836, and he died on January 19, 1875, at Omaha, Nebraska. Despite the fact that the original medical records of Modesta Green's injuries at the Battle of Nashville were noted as slight, he was shot in the temple and the fragment broke his nose and exited his face. Ultimately, his cause of death would be the "ulceration of the brain" due to the facial injury of this wound. He was just 38 years of age at his death.[14]

Majors

William Cleland—William Cleland began his military career as a sergeant in the First Missouri Rifles and worked his way through the ranks until he was promoted to the rank of major.

He was wounded at the Battle of Iuka, assault on Stockade Redan and finally severely injured in action after the Battle of Tupelo. Little is known of Cleland's activities after the war but the unfortunate major died in September 1867 in New Orleans shortly after he was mustered out of service. The cause of his death was not recorded but presumably the wounds he suffered in the war contributed to his death, as was the case with other officers of the regiment.[15]

Benjamin Livingston—The first captain of Company E was Benjamin Livingston. Benjamin Livingston was born in Tennessee in 1833. He was 28 years old and a lawyer living in Olney, Illinois, prior to the war, but he was soon elected as major for the 11th Missouri regiment. Livingston was forced to resign in April 1862 after contracting pulmonalis. After resigning from the 11th Missouri Infantry, he returned to Illinois. He lived in Kankakee from 1864 to 1869, then Cairo, Illinois, until 1879. Next he moved to Waldo, Florida, from 1879 to 1890. Then he moved to St. Petersburg where he resided until 1901 when he moved to California. Benjamin Livingston practiced law in these locations. While in Florida he was actively involved with real estate and orange growing. He died on February 16, 1909, of angina pectoris in Los Angeles, California.[16]

Surgeons

Thomas Smith—Dr. Thomas Smith resigned from the 11th Missouri Infantry in the spring of 1862 due to exhaustion from handling the medical needs of the regiment early in the war. Unfortunately in the summer of 1862, his second wife also died. By August of 1862, he recovered his strength and reenlisted in the 33rd Missouri Infantry and was chosen to be the regimental surgeon. By February 1863, his strength again failed and resigned again citing exhaustion.

He moved to Arkansas in 1864 as a family surgeon to a group of wealthy men who wanted to become cotton planters. In 1865, Thomas Smith remarried for the third time, and by 1868 he entered private practice. Also in 1868, he was a delegate to the constitutional convention in Arkansas and was assigned to the committee on education. In March 1868, he was chosen as the first state superintendent of instruction and held this position until 1873. Smith was recognized as directing the first "systematic enumeration of the school-age children and organized the school system" of Arkansas. He also organized the first professional association of teachers. Dr. Thomas Smith died at his home in Little Rock on August 17, 1885.[17]

Melancthon Fish—Dr. Fish, a native of New York, served with the 11th Missouri Infantry and also held various medical positions throughout the war. He studied medicine at Rush Medical College in Michigan and lived in Shanghai, China, where he served as U.S. Vice Consul prior to the war. Dr. Fish's connection to the United States Army continued after the war. He served on a contract basis from May 1866 through January 1871, and again from October 1872 into November 1872. His duties during these contracts were to "attend officers and their families residing in Oakland and Brooklyn [California]."[18] After leaving his military service he lived in Oakland, California, and held the position of professor of physiology in the Medical Department of the University of California. Dr. Fish died in California in March 22, 1891, of degeneration of the heart.

Thomas Hawley—Dr. Hawley was born February 20, 1837, in Dayton, Ohio, the son of the Rev. Nelson J. Hawley. Following his graduation from St. Louis Medical College in 1861, he served in the Civil War as a surgeon with the 111th Illinois Infantry and the 11th Missouri

Infantry. He married Caroline Joy of Delaware, Ohio, and established a medical practice in St. Louis after the war. Dr. Hawley was a much respected physician and was also a key member of the G. A. R. in St. Louis. He died July 24, 1918, in St. Louis.[19] The Thomas Hawley letters chronicled his Civil War experiences and provided invaluable insight into the character and the history of the regiment.

Chaplains

Joseph Brooks—The first chaplain for the 11th Missouri was Joseph Brooks, a Methodist minister who graduated from Asbury College in Indiana. He was known for his anti-slavery position prior to the war. Brooks began his Civil War service as the chaplain of the First Missouri Artillery and soon transferred to the 11th Missouri Infantry. He resigned from the regiment in 1862 and was appointed chaplain of the 33rd Missouri Infantry. Early in the Civil War, Brooks strongly supported the enlistment of African American troops. After leaving the 33rd Missouri Infantry, he served as chaplain of the Third Arkansas Colored Infantry.

Dr. Thomas Hawley practiced medicine in St. Louis after the Civil War (Missouri History Museum, St. Louis).

"After the war Mr. Brooks became a planter in Arkansas, and was a leader in the State constitutional convention of 1868. During the presidential canvass of that year an attempt was made to assassinate Mr. Brooks and Congressman C. C. Hines, which resulted in the death of the latter and the wounding of Mr. Brooks."[20] Brooks was elected to the state senate in 1870 and ran in a controversial election for governor in 1872 in which he forcibly took possession of the state house until he was removed by proclamation of President Grant. He was appointed postmaster of Little Rock and held that position until he died. The Rev. Brooks died in Little Rock on April 30, 1877, and was interred at Bellefontaine Cemetery in St. Louis.

Samuel Baldridge—The regiment's second chaplain was Samuel Coulter Baldridge, a native of Eugene, Indiana, who was born in 1829. He attended the New Albany Presbyterian Theological Seminary until 1852, and he completed his ministerial studies at Hanover College the same year. Baldridge became the pastor of a small rural congregation, the Wabash Church (Wabash County, Illinois), where he remained until 1857 at which time he went to the Friendsville (Illinois) Church. He was instrumental in recruiting his students at his Presbyterian Seminary in Friendsville into the service of the Union Army. The Rev. Baldridge had to close his Presbyterian Seminary when most of his students enlisted in the Union Army, many of them as part of Birge's Western Sharpshooters. Like Joseph Brooks, who preceded him as chaplain of the 11th Missouri, Samuel Baldridge was an ardent abolitionist. He served in the 11th Missouri in 1862.

After leaving the 11th Missouri Infantry, he returned to his ministerial duties at the Presbyterian churches of Wabash and Friendsville where he divided his time between them until

1866. In 1864 he became the principal of the Presbyterian Seminary but resigned at the end of the school term. He later accepted this position and held it from 1876 to 1880. In 1882 he moved to Cobden, Illinois, to serve as minister to the church there. He retired in 1891 and died in Hanover, Indiana, in 1898.[21]

George Brown—The third and final chaplain of the 11th Missouri Infantry, George Brown was born in Crawford County, Missouri, in 1833. He was 31 years old when he was drafted into the regiment. He was a minister and a farmer by occupation. Brown served as a private in Company H until July 1865 when he was promoted to assume the spiritual needs of the regiment. He was a "whole-souled Cumberland Presbyterian."[22] The Rev. Brown was nearly killed by a shell explosion at the siege of Spanish Fort and was moved from the battlefield to the hospital for treatment, where he soon recovered.

Brown returned to Missouri after the war and ultimately settled in Greenfield, Missouri, where he worked at the church and the Ozark College in Greenfield. He died on February 17, 1887. The president of the Ozark College, Thomas Toney, referred to the Rev. Brown as "a worthy man, no doubt a good soldier, an honored citizen, a noted minister, and a worthy subject."[23] At his death he left a wife and seven children.

Company Officers

Company A

Cyrenus Elliott—Captain Cyrenus Elliott assumed command of Company A after William Panabaker was promoted to the rank of lieutenant colonel for the regiment. Elliott served until August 3, 1863, when he resigned due to his increasingly poor physical condition. He had been granted a two-month medical leave in June in an attempt to regain his strength, but in August he resigned. Dr. Elliott was one of many physicians in the officer ranks of the 11th Missouri Infantry. After leaving the regiment he returned to Posey County, Indiana, to his practice. He and his wife raised three children and he was reputed to have the most extensive library in the county. Captain Elliott was the brother-in-law of Lieutenant Colonel William Panabaker. He married Rebecca Panabaker in 1841 and they had six children. His son, Cyrenus Elliott, Jr., also became a physician. The senior Elliott died on January 21, 1896, in Posey County, Indiana.[24]

Menomen O'Donnell—Menomen O'Donnell was born in Donegal County, Ireland, on April 30, 1830, and at the age of 18 he left Ireland and immigrated to the United States. He was involved in several different kinds of business. After his arrival in the United States, he worked in New England, the Midwest and Western states. In 1851 he purchased land in Lawrence County, Illinois, but during the 1850s he still traveled to several states. In 1858, he returned to Europe where he spent eight months in Italy and Spain. As the Civil War began, O'Donnell enlisted as a private in the 11th Missouri and was quickly elected to the rank of 1st lieutenant of Company A on July 20, 1861.[25]

Menomen O'Donnell served on General Mower's staff and was awarded the Medal of Honor for his actions at Vicksburg and during the assault on Fort DeRussey in the Red River Campaign. When the war was over, O'Donnell returned to his home and to peaceful occupations — farming and speculation. He was involved in the pork packing business while in Lawrence County, Illinois, after the war, but lost everything in the bad economy of 1873. He moved to Vincennes, Indiana, in 1879, where he was a feeder and shipper of livestock. He was a member of the Board of Supervisors in Vincennes and was the director and president of the Knox County Agricultural Society and the Knox Building Loan Association. He married Mary Bailey, and the couple raised five children. O'Donnell died on September 3, 1911, in Vincennes, Indiana.[26]

Constantine McMahan — Constantine McMahan was born in Richland County, Illinois, and was a farmer prior to the war. He began the war by enlisting as a corporal for three months in the Eighth Illinois Infantry. McMahan began his tenure in the 11th Missouri as a sergeant in Company A. He was promoted to the rank of captain in the veterans' regiment and was mustered out of service in January 1866.

He returned to Richland County, Illinois, after the war and remained there only a couple of years before relocating to Ohio from 1869 to 1871. In 1871 he moved to Canton, Missouri, and remained there until 1873 when he moved to Colorado. He remained in Colorado until 1897 when he moved to Kirkland, Arizona.[27] He remained in Kirkland until his death in 1915. McMahan worked with his two sons in mining in the Zonia area of Arizona and was highly regarded as a mining engineer. He died of a cerebral hemorrhage on May 24, 1915, after a successful career in the mining business in Colorado and Arizona.[28]

Company B

Jesse Lloyd — Jesse Lloyd was promoted to the rank of captain of Company B on April 21, 1862, when Andrew J. Weber was promoted to the rank of major. Lloyd served until November 26, 1864, when he was mustered out of service. Captain Lloyd had suffered for almost a year with physical maladies before he resigned. He was given medical leave due to erysipelas and smallpox and then he requested duty within the Provost Guard as an attempt to regain his health; but in November 1864 he finally was forced to resign his commission. The unfortunate Jesse Lloyd was never to regain his health and he died in April 1865, only six months after leaving the 11th Missouri Infantry. He left a wife and two children.[29]

William Thomas Followill (Fallowell) — Captain William T. Followill was 26 years old when he transferred from the Seventh Missouri Infantry in December 1864 just prior to the Battle of Nashville. He enlisted in the Seventh Missouri Infantry in June 1861 at the age of 22. He was born in Kentucky and lived in the town of Louisiana, Missouri, prior to the war. After the Civil War, he moved to Louisiana, Missouri, and married Mary McCarthy in 1868. They reared three children. He worked as a machinist in the town of Louisiana, Missouri. He died on July 18, 1899, in Louisiana, Missouri, of aortic insufficiency.[30, 31]

Company C

Moses Warner — Moses Warner was a native of Kentucky and he was the first captain of Company C. He served in that capacity until he resigned on February 4, 1863. Moses Warner had held several occupations prior to the war, including railroad conductor, city marshal of Springfield, Illinois, stone cutter, and policeman. He married Sarah Reynolds in 1857. Captain Warner received a gunshot wound to his thigh at the Battle of Iuka, and next lost the sight in one eye. This forced him to resign; but after recuperating, he enlisted in the 149th Illinois Infantry for one year at the rank of major. Soon after returning from the war, he died on December 27, 1867, from wounds and diseases contracted in his service during the Civil War.[32]

James Lott — James Lott was a native of Gettysburg, Pennsylvania, and was a carpenter and a stair maker by trade. He served in the Springfield Light Artillery in 1860 prior to enlisting in the 11th Missouri Infantry. James Lott was promoted to the rank of captain of Company C when the 11th Missouri Veteran Infantry was formed in August 1864, and he remained in that post throughout the remainder of the war. James Lott was from a strong Union-supporting family. His older brother, Henry Lott, who resided in Pennsylvania, received a captain's commission but after training his men he was unable to continue his military service because of poor health. One of his brothers, John Wesley Lott, was a part of the Iowa Infantry; another brother, George Washington Lott, served with the 55th Ohio Infantry and Ninth Ohio Cavalry; and finally, brother Peter Jacob Lott served in the 132nd Ohio Infantry. James Lott's father, Isaac Lott, enlisted at the age of 57. Although he falsely gave his age of 45, he served in the 61st Ohio Infantry, and passed through his hometown of Gettysburg during that campaign.

James Lott was severely wounded in the Battle of Nashville and required months of recuperation. After the war, James Lott returned to Springfield, Illinois. He died on December 6, 1910, age 80, at the Soldier's home in Danville, Illinois.[33]

Company D

Clark Hendee— After resigning his commission in 1862, Dr. Clark Hendee returned to Clay County, Illinois, but his Civil War service was not over. In February 1865, the 155th Illinois Infantry was organized from central Illinois and mustered into service for one year. The assistant surgeon of the regiment was Clark Hendee. The 155th Illinois Infantry spent their service protecting the railroads around Nashville, Tennessee. The regiment was mustered out of service in September 1865, and Dr. Hendee returned to his practice as a physician. He and his wife, Lucinda, raised five children. By 1870, they had moved to Fayette County, Illinois, and made their residence in LaClede. Dr. Hendee died at the age of 54 in 1880 in Fayette County.[34]

George Henry— George Henry was born on February 25, 1827, in Clarke County, Ohio, and was a resident of Clay County, Illinois, and an attorney prior to the war. Henry taught school in both Ohio and Illinois. He began preparing to become an attorney and was admitted to the bar in 1857. Then he moved to Clay County, Illinois, where he practiced law until he enlisted in the 11th Missouri Infantry in 1861.

After the war he was elected to the state senate for four years, and in 1877 he moved to Lake City, Colorado. He continued his occupation as an attorney and spent six years as a county judge. In 1887 he moved to Delta, Colorado, where he was employed as an attorney and a judge. "On April 2, 1857, Mr. Henry was married to Miss Rebecca A. Magner, a native of Indiana. They have had four children, two sons and two daughters. The sons, Lyman I. and William G., are living, and the daughters, Clara Frances and Mary Myrta, have died."[35] George Henry died on May 4, 1907.

Judge George Henry moved to Delta County, Colorado, after the war (courtesy Delta County Historical Society).

William Erwin—William Erwin enlisted in the 11th Missouri Infantry in 1861 as a sergeant and was promoted to the rank of captain of Company D in May 1863. Erwin remained in that post until he died of wounds he received in the Battle of Spanish Fort in Alabama on April 7, 1865. Erwin was an Illinois native and farmer residing in Clay County, Illinois, prior to his enlistment.[36]

Lyman Randall—Lyman Randall was born in Oxford County, Maine, in 1838. He moved to Illinois where he taught school and farmed prior to his enlistment in the 11th Missouri Infantry. He was promoted to the rank of captain of Company D on June 12, 1865, succeeding William Erwin. Randall remained captain of the company until he was mustered out of service in January 1866. In 1867, he married Mary Ingraham in Clay County, Illinois, and remained a farmer throughout his life; he died on July 2, 1918.[37]

Company E

Charles Hollister—Charles Hollister was promoted to the rank of captain of Company E on September 3, 1861, when Benjamin Livingston was promoted to regimental major. Charles Hollister lived in Olney, Illinois, prior to the war. He was killed in action at the Battle of Corinth on October 4, 1862, during the charge at Battery Robinett.[38]

Abner Bail—Abner Bail was promoted to the rank of captain after Charles Hollister's death at Corinth. Bail was promoted on October 15, 1862, and remained the company commander until his resignation on April 29, 1864. Bail returned home to Olney and lived with his wife, Catharine. He made his living as a harness maker. In 1900 he was a resident at the Soldiers and Sailors Home in Quincy, Illinois, and died on May 14, 1901, in Quincy from senile gangrene. Bail, a native of Ohio, was buried with military honors in Quincy.[39]

William Notestine—William Notestine enlisted in the 11th Missouri Infantry as a sergeant in Company E at the age of 19. Notestine was a native of Illinois and listed his occupation as a railroader. Notestine was promoted to the rank of captain of Company E in May 1864 and led the brigade's skirmishers against the enemy on the first day at the Battle of Nashville where he received a severe wound to his leg. William Notestine died of exhaustion in February 1865 as a result of this wound.[40]

Levi Roney—Levi Roney was promoted to the command of Company E after William Notestine's death. Born on September 17, 1840, in Coshocton County, Ohio, he moved to Richland County, Illinois, in 1856 with his family. Roney enlisted at the age of 22 and recorded that he was a single farmer living in Stringtown, Illinois. He was promoted to the rank of captain on May 27, 1865, and remained in that post until the end of the war.

After the Civil War ended, Levi Roney returned to Richland County, Illinois, and settled in German Township. In 1871 he married Elizina Hart, and he died in Olney on May 16 1910.[41] He was a farmer until he retired in 1898 and he moved to Olney, Illinois, where he lived until his death.[42]

Company F

Amos Singleton—Amos Singleton was the first captain of Company F. He was a 27-year-old carpenter, native of Ohio, living in Xenia, Illinois, at his enlistment. He served as company commander of Company F until he died on September 24, 1862, of wounds he received at the Battle of Iuka. His death left a wife, Mary, and four-year-old son, William R. The unfortunate story of the Singleton family continued later in the life of Mary Singleton who became a resident of the Illinois State Asylum for the Insane in Jacksonville, Illinois.[43]

Charles Smith—Charles Smith was a stonecutter living in Xenia, Illinois, when he enlisted in the 11th Missouri Infantry. He was born in Maryland in 1820 and was 38 years old when he enlisted. Smith was promoted to the rank of captain of Company F on May 27, 1865, when

William Cleland was promoted to the rank of major. After the war he remained in Xenia Township, Illinois, for the remainder of his life. Smith was a stone mason prior to the war and this remained his occupation after the war. He died on August 24, 1882.[44]

Company G

William Mieure — The 41-year-old William Mieure was the first captain of Company G and he listed his residence as Lawrenceville, Illinois. His occupation was merchant. Captain Mieure fell victim of typhoid fever early in the Civil War and died on November 4, 1861, while the regiment was located at Cape Girardeau, Missouri.

Charles Carter — Charles Carter was promoted to fill William Mieure's post on November 4, 1861, and remained captain of Company G until he resigned on April 28, 1864. A testament to the type of soldier he was, Captain Carter was placed under arrest for an administrative error on May 1863. This was prior to the assault on Jackson and Stockade Redan at Vicksburg. Carter appealed to General Gordon Granger to release him from arrest so that he could participate in the upcoming battles. He indicated in his appeal to Granger that he would carry a musket and join the ranks if needed.[45]

Dr. Carter was born in 1840 in Ohio. He had just graduated from the Kentucky School of Medicine in Louisville, prior to his enlistment in the 11th Missouri Infantry. He resigned from the regiment due to a disease of his eyes which continued to plague him after the war. Dr. Carter returned to Illinois after the war to practice medicine, and by all accounts he was an energetic and humorous person. After making a speech in Lawrence County about the bad affects of alcohol, there was some jealousy about his popularity after making the speech. He was criticized by another doctor, and his retort was that the other doctor's patients were "endowed with such robust and hardy constitutions that they recover in spite of his treatment."[46] He remained in practice in Lawrenceville through 1886 and then he moved to Kansas City, Missouri, for the remainder of his life. He died in Kansas City on March 26, 1910, of an abscess on his lung after a long career as a soldier and physician.[47]

William Wallace — The 32-year-old blacksmith from Lawrenceville, Illinois, enlisted in the 11th Missouri in August 1861 and was promoted to the rank of captain on May 3, 1864. Wallace was 5' 11" tall with dark hair and blue eyes. The New York–born Wallace held this post until the end of the war. Little is known of William Wallace after the Civil War. The last known record of him was in a message by Eli Bowyer that Wallace was living in Lawrence County, Illinois, in 1867.

Company H

Thomas Dollahan — Thomas Dollahan was the first captain of Company H. He resigned on June 17, 1862, suffering from several physical maladies including inflammation of the lungs, chronic diarrhea and hepatic disease. Born in 1828, he was a blacksmith prior to the war. The unfortunate Captain Dollahan never recovered from the physical problems that plagued him during the war. His son reported that his father was a stout individual before the war, but when he returned home he was a "living skelton."[48] He had gone to war weighing about 190 pounds and returned weighing about 120. Captain Dollahan died on January 1, 1873, in Jonesboro, Illinois, never having fully recovered his health.

William Boatright — William Boatright was promoted to the rank of captain on June 18, 1862, to replace Thomas Dollahan. He was instrumental in organizing a regiment that would become part of the 11th Missouri Infantry. Boatright held this post until he was transferred to the 71st USCT on March 20, 1864. After joining the 71st USCT, William Boatright was promoted to the rank of major. Just prior to the end of the war, Boatright married Miss Ellie Pierson. After the war, he lived in Sullivan, Indiana, and made farming his occupation. Major Boatright died on May 23, 1915.[49]

Edwin Applegate — The 20-year-old carpenter Edwin R. Applegate enlisted in the 11th Missouri Infantry in August 1861. He was a native of Ohio and was promoted to the rank of captain on May 24, 1864, after William Boatright was transferred. He remained at this post until the end of the war.

Edwin Applegate settled temporarily in St. Louis after the war, and then moved to Sumner, Illinois, where he clerked for a while. After clerking he earned his livelihood by buying and selling agricultural equipment. In 1871 he moved back to St. Louis where he kept the books of Payne Moody & Company. Next he moved to the Dakota Territory for two years. In 1889, he moved to Lawrence County, Missouri, where he began farming and later became a storekeeper and gauger for the Internal Revenue Service. He was married to Lucinda Brumfield from 1870 to 1873 and after his wife's death, he married her sister, Laura Brumfield. He also served as the president of the Bank of Verona.[50] On January 4, 1919, he died of apoplexy in Verona, Missouri.[51]

Company I

Charles Osgood — Charles Osgood was promoted to command Company I on May 16, 1863, after William Barnum was promoted to the rank of major. He was 23 years old and a resident of Bethel, Illinois, when he enlisted. He recorded that he was a married farmer and a native of Ohio. He resigned at the expiration of his term of service in August 1864, having been seriously wounded with a gunshot wound to the chest at Iuka. He later recuperated and completed his term of service.

Charles Osgood was a physician prior to the war, and after his resignation he returned home to Illinois to his residence in Jacksonville, Illinois.[52] In 1870 he had established his medical practice in Morgan County, Illinois. His pension record reveals that he later lived in Austin and Hempstead, Texas. In 1875, Dr. Osgood was living in Weatherford, Texas. He appears to have returned to Illinois in the late 1800s when he began drawing his pension through the Chicago Pension office, and in 1907 his address was Cincinnati, Ohio. Charles Osgood died on September 12, 1908, at Kennedy Heights, Ohio.[53] In his obituary, it was noted that he was always circumspect in regard to his family.

George C. Adams — George Adams was promoted to the rank of captain at the expiration of Charles Osgood's term of service. Adams had enlisted at the age of 38 years and was a farmer from Versailles, Illinois. He assumed command of Company I on October 11, 1864, and remained in that post until the end of the war. Captain Adams left a series of letters that relate the events of the regiment. He died on December 28, 1865, in the home of his father near Versailles, Illinois.

Company K

William Stewart — William Stewart was born in October 1831 in Franklin County, Indiana. Stewart attended Indiana Asbury College in Greencastle, Indiana. From 1856 to 1858 he studied law, probably at the Cincinnati Law School. He moved to St. Louis and established a law practice, which he continued until he enlisted in the First Missouri Rifles which later became the 11th Missouri Infantry. Stewart served on General Mower's staff and contracted "malarial poisoning from exposure" in the summer of 1863. He resigned his commission on April 30, 1864.

After his resignation Stewart was appointed lieutenant colonel of the Second Regiment of the City Guard of St. Louis. After the war Stewart practiced law in St. Louis until 1887. In 1887, he moved to Minneapolis, Colorado. He was appointed a judge while in Colorado and he was district attorney at the time of his death, as the result of a stroke, in 1897. Stewart lived on land he homesteaded and farmed, and was buried in the Minneapolis Cemetery near Walsh, Colorado.[54]

Cyrus Kendall — Cyrus Kendall was a native of Erie County, Pennsylvania. He was educated in Vermont until he was 17 and moved to Fayette County, Illinois, where he taught school in 1851, 1858, and 1859. He read law under W. W. Bishop and received notoriety when he defended John Lee in the Mountain Massacre case in which 120 men, women and children were murdered. In 1862 he married Rivilla Miller. Cyrus Kendall was a 23-year-old attorney living in Clay County, Illinois, when he enlisted in the 11th Missouri Infantry in 1861. Kendall was promoted to the rank of captain upon William Stewart's resignation and held this post until June 18, 1865.

Upon returning home after the war, he was involved with merchandising in Flora, Illinois, for a short period of time. In 1865 he was elected as County Court Clerk in Clay County, Illinois, and worked in the mercantile trade in Louisville. Then he moved to Newton in Jasper County, Illinois. From 1881 to 1900 he was a dry goods merchant in Jasper County. Kendall was instrumental in organizing the First National Bank and held the position of vice president.[55] He was the Assistant Secretary of the Illinois Senate in the 28th General Assembly and, "in his country's hour of need he was a gallant and faithful soldier, and honorably wore the blue of the Union. In times of peace he is both a successful businessman and an enterprising citizen."[56] Cyrus Kendall died in February 1919.

Dennis Coogan — The 26-year-old farmer from Franklin County, Missouri, enlisted in the 11th Missouri Infantry in 1861. Coogan was formally offered the command of Company K in 1865, but although the Adjutant General's report shows Coogan as captain of the company effective June 28, 1865, Coogan appears to have declined the promotion due to a severe wound he had received during the Battle of Nashville, which caused him to lose the use of his arm. Coogan was a native of New York. Dennis Coogan was married twice — first to Sarah Ritchey and next to Mary Ellen Richardson in 1879. He had a total of eleven children. After the war, he lived in Waynesville, Missouri, and Pulaski County and returned to his pre-war occupation of farmer. Dennis Coogan is thought to have died in 1901.[57]

Appendix A: 11th Missouri Volunteer Infantry Roster

Based on the Regimental Descriptive Book Located at the National Archives and Supplemented with the Regimental Descriptive Book located at the Missouri Archives and Regimental Cards Located at the Missouri Archives[1]

Regimental Staff

Soldier	Rank	Comment
Bayles, David	Colonel	Honorably discharged 1861.
Plummer, Joseph	Colonel	Promoted; died 8/1862.
Mower, Joseph	Colonel	Promoted to Brig. General.
Weber, Andrew	Colonel	Died of wounds 6/30/1963 Vicksburg.
Barnum, William	Colonel	
Panabaker, William	Lt. Colonel	Resigned 8/3/1862.
Livingston, Benjamin	Major	Resigned 4/11/1862.
Bowyer, Eli	Major	
Brookings, Charles	Adjutant	Died of wounds at Vicksburg.
Weber, George	Adjutant	Resigned 4/28/1864.
Henry, George	Quartermaster	Promoted to Captain Company D.
Pickrell, Abel	Quartermaster	
Smith, Thomas	Surgeon	Resigned 4/14/1862.
Fish, M. W.	Surgeon	
Bowyer, Eli	Asst. Surgeon	Promoted to Major.
Hawley, Thomas	Asst. Surgeon	
Brooks, Joseph	Chaplain	Resigned 4/11/1862.
Baldridge, Samuel	Chaplain	Resigned 1/7/1863.

Company A

Soldier	Rank	Age	Ht	Hair	Eyes	Occupation	Nativity	Place of Residence	Comment
Panabaker, William F.	Captain					Physician	Virginia	Bridgeport, IL	Resigned 12/3/1862; promoted to Lt. Col.
Elliott, Cyrenus	Captain					Physician	Ohio	Poseyville, IN	Resigned 8/3/1863.
O'Donnell, Menomen	Captain					Farmer	Ireland	Bridgeport, IL	Mustered out 8/9/1864; Medal of Honor Vicksburg.
Orr, Charles	1st Lt.					Farmer	Illinois	Bridgeport, IL	Resigned 10/31/1862.
Pickrell, William T.	2nd Lt.	25	5'8½"	Dark	Gray	Clerk	Illinois	Mechanicsburg, IL	Veteran.
Corrie, John S.	Sgt.	20	5'8"	Brown	Blue	Farmer	Illinois	Bridgeport, IL	Died of wounds received at Vicksburg 5/22/63.
Gould, George W.	Sgt.	19	5'8¼"	Light	Blue	Farmer	Ohio	Sumner, IL	Veteran.
Elliott, Charles D.	Sgt.	19	5'7½"	Light	Hazel	Miller	Ohio	Poseyville, IN	
French, Francis M.	1st Sgt.	22	5'5¾"	Brown	Blue	Farmer	Illinois	Sumner, IL	KIA 11/4/1862 Corinth, MS.

Soldier	*Rank*	*Age*	*Ht*	*Hair*	*Eyes*	*Occu-pation*	*Nativity*	*Place of Residence*	*Comment*
Johnson, Criddleton	Sgt.	24	5'10¼"	Light	Gray	Black-smith	Illinois	Sumner, IL	Mustered out 8/13/1864 to accept enlistment in 5th U.S. Hvy. Art.
Lackey, Thomas J.	Sgt.	21	5'6½"	Brown	Hazel	Farmer	Illinois	Bridgeport, IL	
McMahan, Constantine	Sgt.	22	5'11½"	Black	Hazel	Farmer	Illinois	Bridgeport, IL	Veteran; promoted to Sgt. 7/1/1863; wounded at Vicks-burg.
Nigh, Barnabas	Sgt.	20	5'9"	Brown	Gray	Farmer	Ohio	Bridgeport, IL	Veteran; promoted to Sgt. 10/1862.
Dutton, Daniel C.	Corporal	21	5'9"	Brown	Gray	Farmer	Ohio	Bridgeport, IL	Died of wounds from Battle of Iuka 10/6/1862.
Clark, Whitney	Corporal	21	5'5½"	Light	Gray	Farmer	Ohio	Sumner, IL	Died of wounds from Vicks-burg in Memphis 5/22/1863.
Cusick, William	Corporal	22	5'8"	Brown	Hazel	Farmer	Illinois	Bridgeport, IL	Veteran.
Lappin, John	Corporal	34	5'6"	Brown	Gray	Farmer	Pennsyl-vania	Bridgeport, IL	Veteran; wounded at Iuka.
Laughlin, William	Corporal	29	5'11"	Brown	Hazel	Farmer	Illinois	Bridgeport, IL	Died 12/19/1861 Cape Girardeau of paralysis.
Smith, Henry	Corporal	28	5'4¾"	Brown	Blue	Farmer	Prussia	Bridgeport, IL	Veteran.
Worstell, Thomas	Corporal	21	5'11"	Light	Hazel	Farmer	Ohio	Bridgeport, IL	
Treadway, Charles W.	Corporal	23	5'9¾"	Black	Blue	Farmer	Illinois	Bridgeport, IL	Veteran.
Gould, Moses R.	Wagoner	50	5'7"	Brown	Gray	Farmer	Ohio	Sumner, IL	Discharged 9/3/1863.
Bonner, Charles W.	Musician	23	5'5"	Brown	Gray	Farmer	Indiana	Bridgeport, IL	Discharged 11/28/1862 Davis Mills, MS.
French, Almond W.*	Musician	18	5'8"	Brown	Blue	Farmer	Illinois	Sumner, IL	Veteran.
French, Zeba*	Hospital Steward	23	5'9"	Dark	Hazel	Physician	Illinois	Sumner, IL	Mustered out 8/5/1864.
Addison, Aaron	Pvt.	22	5'10½"	Brown	Gray	Farmer	Illinois	Bridgeport, IL	Veteran.
Applegate, Henry C.	Pvt.	18	5'9¾"	Black	Hazel	Carpenter	Ohio	Sumner, IL	Veteran.
Appling, Winkfield L.	Pvt.	18	5'10¾"	Brown	Blue	Farmer	Kentucky	Sumner, IL	Veteran.
Askren, William	Pvt.	43	5'8¾"	Light	Gray	Farmer	Ohio	Bridgeport, IL	Discharged 6/21/1862, dis-ability Cape Girardeau.
Askren, Samuel	Pvt.	18	5'4"	Light	Gray	Farmer	Ohio	Bridgeport, IL	Discharged 12/3/1861, disabil-ity Cape Girardeau.
Besley, James	Pvt.	–	–	–	–	–	–	–	Transferred to Co. K 1/1862.
Bishop, Elisha S.	Pvt.	23	5'8"	Brown	Gray	Farmer	Indiana	Bridgeport, IL	Discharged 11/25/1862 (1/29/1863).
Brooks, Alexander	Pvt.	35	5'7"	Brown	Gray	Farmer	Ohio	Sumner, IL	Veteran; wounded at Battle of Iuka.
Boulds, Peter	Pvt.	20	5'6¼"	Dark	Hazel	Farmer	Ohio	Bridgeport, IL	
Bourn, Zacheus	Pvt.	19	5'8¼"	Light	Blue	Farmer	Indiana	Sumner, IL	Veteran.
Bourn, Samuel	Pvt.	20	5'8¾"	Light	Blue	Farmer	Indiana	Sumner, IL	Discharged 11/21/1862 St. Louis; wounded at Iuka.
Buchanan, John M.	Pvt.	20	5'11¾"	Light	Blue	Farmer	Illinois	Bridgeport, IL	Discharged 12/1862; wounded at Battle of Corinth.
Buchanan, Walter G.	Pvt.	20	5'10"	Dark	Gray	Farmer	Illinois	Bridgeport, IL	Died 8/8/1863 Camp Sher-man, MS.
Campbell, Richard	Pvt.	25	5'2"	Black	Gray	Farmer	Tennessee	Bridgeport, IL	Transferred to Co. K 1/1862.
Carroll, Jeremiah	Pvt.	33	5'8¾"	Brown	Gray	Farmer	Ireland	Hadley, IL	Transferred to Co. K 1/1862.
Chapman, Thomas L.	Pvt.	23	5'8"	Black	Gray	School-teacher	Illinois	Bridgeport, IL	Died of typhoid fever, St. Louis 6/15/1862.
Clark, Charles	Pvt.	23	5'9"	Black	Hazel	Farmer	Ohio	Sumner, IL	Wounded in the Battle of Fredericktown.
Clark, Francis	Pvt.	19	5'6¼"	Brown	Hazel	Farmer	Ohio	Sumner, IL	Died 6/25/1863 in Regt. Hospital, Young's Pt., LA.
Clifton, David	Pvt.	22	5'10"	Brown	Blue	Farmer	Indiana	Bridgeport, IL	Died 1/28/1862 of fever in Lawrence Co., IL.
Day, Elisha	Pvt.	20	6'1½"	Light	Hazel	Farmer	Ohio	Bridgeport, IL	Veteran; wounded at Battle of Corinth.
Dixon, Henry	Pvt.	18	6'	Black	Blue	Farmer	Ohio	Lawrenceville, IL	Transferred to Inv. Corps 3/15/1864.
Dover, Charles	Pvt.	25	5'3"	Black	Hazel	Farmer	Ireland	Bridgeport, IL	Transferred to Co. K 1/1862.

**Mentioned in Missouri Descriptive Roll but not in the National Archives.*

Soldier	*Rank*	*Age*	*Ht*	*Hair*	*Eyes*	*Occu-pation*	*Nativity*	*Place of Residence*	*Comment*
Davis, Edwin	Pvt.	–	–	–	–	–	–	–	Discharged.
Fish, Thomas J.	Pvt.	19	5'9¾"	Light	Hazel	Farmer	Illinois	Sumner, IL	Discharged 8/18/1862.
Galligher, Daniel	Pvt.	19	5'3¼"	Brown	Gray	Farmer	Ireland	Bridgeport, IL	Transferred to Co. K 1/1862.
Gould, John	Pvt.	18	5'7¼"	Brown	Gray	Farmer	Ohio	Sumner, IL	Wounded at Vicksburg.
Guines, Henry S.	Pvt.	18	5'8"	Light	Gray	Farmer	Illinois	Sumner, IL	Transferred to Co. K 1/1862.
Gutherie, John W.	Pvt.	20	5'5¼"	Brown	Blue	Farmer	Indiana	Bridgeport, IL	KIA 10/4/1862 Battle of Corinth.
Hanks, Samuel	Pvt.	21	5'9¼"	Brown	Gray	Farmer	Illinois	Bridgeport, IL	Mustered out 8/5/1864.
Heath, Edward	Pvt.	33	5'4"	Black	Hazel	Farmer	North Carolina	Sumner, IL	Veteran; wounded at Battle of Corinth.
Heath, Samuel H.	Pvt.	25	5'8"	Black	Gray	Farmer	Illinois	Sumner, IL	Died 6/12/1863 of wounds from Vicksburg.
Herthier/Werthier, Nathaniel	Pvt.	18	5'9"	Brown	Hazel	Farmer	Indiana	Bridgeport, IL	
Johnson, James	Pvt.	25	5'5¾"	Brown	Blue	Farmer	Ohio	Bridgeport, IL	Transferred to Co. K 1/1862.
Jones, Amos	Pvt.	–	–	–	–	–	–	–	
Kelley, George	Pvt.	18	5'7"	Black	Hazel	Farmer	Kentucky	Bridgeport, IL	Veteran.
Kelley, John	Pvt.	21	5'7½"	Brown	Blue	Farmer	Illinois	Bridgeport, IL	Veteran.
Lackey, William	Pvt.	31	5'6½"	Brown	Hazel	Farmer	Illinois	Bridgeport, IL	
Malone, Horace	Pvt.	18	5'9½"	Brown	Blue	Farmer	Illinois	Sumner, IL	Wounded at Vicksburg.
Malone, Thomas J.	Pvt.	20	5'10"	Brown	Blue	Farmer	Illinois	Sumner, IL	
Mann, William	Pvt.	21	5'11½"	Black	Gray	Farmer	Indiana	Bridgeport, IL	Veteran.
McAlpin, John	Pvt.	31	5'9¾"	Black	Gray	Farmer	Mississippi	Bridgeport, IL	Died 10/14/1862 of wounds from Battle of Corinth.
McCue, Patrick	Pvt.	20	5'5¾"	Light	Blue	Farmer	Ireland	Bridgeport, IL	Transferred to Co. K 1/1862; wounded at Battle of Corinth.
McGinley, John	Pvt.	–	–	–	–	–	–	–	Transferred to Co. K 1/1862.
McGready, William	Pvt.	21	5'8½"	Brown	Hazel	Peddler	Indiana	Bridgeport, IL	
McGuire, George W.	Pvt.	29	5'9¾"	Brown	Hazel	Cooper	Ohio	Bridgeport, IL	Transferred to Invalid Corps 3/15/1864.*
McGuire, Thomas	Pvt.	22	5'10¼"	Light	Gray	Farmer	Ohio	Bridgeport, IL	Mustered out 8/5/1864.
McGuire, William	Pvt.	23	5'11"	Light	Gray	Farmer	Ohio	Sumner, IL	Wounded at Vicksburg.
Mills, Reuben	Pvt.	36	6'	Brown	Gray	Farmer	Tennessee	Sumner, IL	Veteran; transferred to Co. K 1/1862.
Monyhon, Owen	Pvt.	–	–	–	–	–	–	–	Transferred to Co. K 1/1862.
Moore, George H.	Pvt.	20	5'9¼"	Brown	Gray	Farmer	Illinois	Sumner, IL	Died 9/1862 of wounds from Battle of Iuka.
Myers, Robert	Pvt.	21	5'11½"	Brown	Hazel	Farmer	Indiana	Bridgeport, IL	Died 6/11/1863 of wounds from Vicksburg; buried in Memphis Ntl. Cemetery.
Myers, Thomas	Pvt.	18	5'9½"	Black	Hazel	Farmer	–	Sumner, IL	Discharged 9/3/1863 Camp Sherman, MS.
Newell, John A.	Pvt.	45	5'7½"	Light	Gray	Farmer	Virginia	Bridgeport, IL	Discharged 1/7/1863 Evansville, IN.
Newell, Thomas	Pvt.	24	5'10¼"	Brown	Blue	Farmer	Illinois	Bridgeport, IL	Died 7/22/1862, Lawrence Co., IL, of consumption.
Nigh, Nathaniel	Pvt.	24	5'10¼"	Brown	Blue	Farmer	Ohio	Bridgeport, IL	Died 3/2/1862, inflammation of brain, Cape Girardeau.
Osborne, Marshall	Pvt.	35	5'8"	Black	Hazel	Farmer	Illinois	Bridgeport, IL	Transferred to Co. K 1/1862.
Perry, John G.	Pvt.	32	5'9½"	Light	Gray	Farmer	Virginia	Bridgeport, IL	Transferred to Co. K 1/1862.
Plummer, Riel B.	Pvt.	21	5'8¼"	Brown	Gray	Farmer	Maine	Venice, IL	Died 2/18/1863 of gunshot wounds from Battle of Corinth.
Raridan, Edward	Pvt.	21	5'7½"	Black	Hazel	Farmer	Illinois	Bridgeport, IL	Veteran.
Richards, George	Pvt.	20	5'11"	Brown	Gray	Farmer	Ohio	Bridgeport, IL	KIA 5/22/1863 Vicksburg, MS.
Sands, Daniel*	Pvt.	20	5'9"	Brown	Gray	Farmer	New York	Sumner, IL	Died 6/11/1863 of gunshot wounds from Vicksburg.
Severns, Jacob	Pvt.	21	5'7"	Black	Hazel	Farmer	Indiana	–	Wounded at Vicksburg.
Sivert, Wesley	Pvt.	19	5'9"	Brown	Blue	Farmer	Virginia	Bridgeport, IL	Wounded at Battle of Iuka.
Severs, William	Pvt.	22	5'11"	Brown	Gray	Farmer	Virginia	Bridgeport, IL	Died at Corinth, MS, of accidental gunshot wound.
Shaw, Oliver	Pvt.	30	5'7¾"	Brown	Blue	Farmer	Vermont	Bridgeport, IL	Discharged 7/1862 Evansville.
Sims, Jeremiah	Pvt.	38	5'9"	Brown	Blue	Farmer	Pennsylvania	Sumner, IL	

**Mentioned in Missouri Descriptive Roll but not in the National Archives.*

Soldier	*Rank*	*Age*	*Ht*	*Hair*	*Eyes*	*Occu-pation*	*Nativity*	*Place of Residence*	*Comment*
Smith, John	Pvt.	30	5'9¾"	Brown	Gray	Farmer	Germany	Sumner, IL	
Thompson, Stephen B.	Pvt.	18	5'9½"	Light	Gray	Farmer	Illinois	Bridgeport, IL	Veteran.
Turner, Marion/Marvin	Pvt.	18	5'10¼"	Light	Gray	Farmer	Illinois	Bridgeport, IL	Died 5/31/1862 Farmington, MS, of wounds.
Umfleet, Hiram	Pvt.	19	5'9½"	Light	Gray	Farmer	Illinois	Sumner, IL	
Umfleet, Hughey	Pvt.	18	5'7"	Light	Blue	Farmer	Indiana	Sumner, IL	
Underwood, James/John	Pvt.	18	5'9¾"	Sandy	Blue	Farmer	Illinois	Bridgeport, IL	Died 6/9/1863 Memphis.
Utter, Thomas	Pvt.	44	5'11¾"	Black	Blue	Miller	Illinois	Bridgeport, IL	Discharged 7/19/1862; disability; Camp Gaylord MS.
Ward, Dennis	Pvt.	28	5'5¼"	Light	Gray	Farmer	Ireland	Bridgeport, IL	KIA 5/22/1863 Vicksburg.
Webb, Thomas	Pvt.	18	5'11"	Light	Blue	Farmer	Kentucky	Bridgeport, IL	Veteran.
Wilkinson, Thomas	Pvt.	25	5'9½"	Brown	Blue	Farmer	Illinois	Bridgeport, IL	Died 9/2/1862 of wounds during Siege at Corinth.
Williams, Aaron	Pvt.	19	6'1"	Brown	Blue	Farmer	Illinois	Sumner, IL	Wounded at Vicksburg.
Williams, Benjamin	Pvt.	20	5'8"	Light	Blue	Farmer	Illinois	Venice, IL	Veteran.
Worley, Samuel	Pvt.	19	5'8½"	Brown	Gray	Farmer	Illinois	Bridgeport, IL	Veteran.
Worstell, George	Pvt.	25	5'7½"	Light	Gray	Farmer	Ohio	Bridgeport, IL	
Yates, Benjamin	Pvt.	20	5'4¾"	Brown	Hazel	Farmer	Illinois	Bridgeport, IL	Died 6/22/1862 Cape Girardeau.
Yates, Samuel	Pvt.	28	5'11¾"	Brown	Gray	Farmer	Indiana	Bridgeport, IL	Veteran.
Young, Benjamin	Pvt.	20	5'4¾"	Brown	Hazel	Farmer	Illinois	Bridgeport, IL	Died of fever at Cape Girardeau 1/22/1862.
Bridge, Alpheus*	Pvt.	–	–	–	–	–	–	–	Veteran.
Cabe, Edwin*	Pvt.	–	–	–	–	–	–	–	Veteran.
Duncan, Rice A.*	Pvt.	–	–	–	–	–	–	–	Veteran.
Holman, Gilbert*	Pvt.	–	–	–	–	–	–	–	Veteran.
Smith, George*	Pvt.	–	–	–	–	–	–	–	

Company B

Soldier	*Rank*	*Age*	*Ht*	*Hair*	*Eyes*	*Occu-pation*	*Nativity*	*Place of Residence*	*Comment*
Weber, Andrew J.	Captain-Colonel					Farmer	Illinois	Springfield, IL	Died 6/30/1863 of wounds at Vicksburg; promoted to Major.
Lloyd Jesse D.	Captain	24	5'7"	Black	Black	Merchant	Illinois	Springfield, IL	Promoted to Captain. 4/21/1862.
Wilson, James	1st Lt.	–	–	–	–	Farmer	Illinois	Springfield, IL	Promoted to 1st Lt. 4/21/1863.
Weber, George	2nd Lt.	–	–	–	–	Farmer	Illinois	Springfield, IL	Resigned 4/28/1864.
Cooper, Stephen	Sgt.	21	5'6"	Light	Blue	Farmer	Illinois	Sangamon County, IL	
Headly, John W.	Sgt.	24	6'1"	Light	Blue	Farmer	Indiana	Sangamon County, IL	Died 12/24/1861 of smallpox.
King, Clifton	Sgt.	21	6'	Dark	Dark	Farmer	Illinois	Sangamon County, IL	
Shutt, Thomas E.	Sgt.	21	5'10"	Light	Blue	Farmer	Virginia	Sangamon County, IL	
Wells, William B.	Sgt.	26	5'10"	Dark	Gray	Mechanic	New York	Chippewa, IL	POW Alabama; promoted to 1st Sgt. 4/21/1862.
Whitney, Solomon A.	Corporal	19	5'9"	Dark	Gray	Farmer	New York	Sangamon County, IL	Veteran.
Adams, William F.	Corporal	20	5'10½"	Dark	Blue	Farmer	Indiana	Sangamon County, IL	
Clark, David M.	Corporal	19	5'6¾"	Dark	Blue	Farmer	Indiana	Sangamon County, IL	Veteran.
Coleman, Joseph E.	Corporal	20	5'6½"	Dark	Dark	Farmer	Illinois	Sangamon County, IL	
Cooper, Henry	Corporal	19	5'5"	Light	Gray	Farmer	Illinois	Sangamon County, IL	Veteran.
Dennison, William	Corporal	21	5'8½"	Light	Blue	Farmer	Ireland	Sangamon County, IL	
Fletcher, William R.	Corporal	26	5'9⅞"	Black	Black	Farmer	Ohio	Sangamon County, IL	Veteran.
Helme, Thomas	Corporal	19	5'7"	Dark	Blue	Farmer	New York	Sangamon County, IL	Veteran.
Shepherd, Charles M.	Corporal	20	5'8"	Dark	Gray	Farmer	Illinois	Sangamon County, IL	
Steele, Thomas	Corporal	20	5'4½"	Light	Blue	Farmer	Indiana	Sangamon County, IL	Veteran.
Stephens/Stevens, Freeman C.	Corporal	21	5'5¾"	Light	Blue	Farmer	Illinois	Sangamon County, IL	
Wade, Archibald	Corporal	25	5'8"	Dark	Dark	Carpenter	Illinois	Sangamon County, IL	Discharged 4/25/1863, disability.
McCoy, Thomas	Fifer	22	4'8½"	Dark	Blue	Farmer	Ohio	Sangamon County, IL	Discharged 12/12/1863.*

**Mentioned in Missouri Descriptive Roll but not in the National Archives.*

Soldier	Rank	Age	Ht	Hair	Eyes	Occupation	Nativity	Place of Residence	Comment
Grandstaff, Isaac	Wagoner	28	5'10½"	Dark	Dark	Carpenter	Ohio	Sangamon County, IL	Died 12/20/1861 Cape Girardeau.
Abbott, Lyman	Pvt.	25	5'10"	Light	Blue	Farmer	New Hampshire	Sangamon County, IL	Veteran.
Armstrong, John B.	Pvt.	22	5'9¼"	Dark	Blue	Farmer	Ohio	Sangamon County, IL	Discharged 12/5/1861, disability.
Bachelor, Hiram	Pvt.	20	5'7"	Dark	Gray	Farmer	–	Sangamon County, IL	
Baily, Ervin F.	Pvt.	21	5'11¾"	Sandy	Gray	Farmer	Pennsylvania	Sangamon County, IL	Discharged 1/1863, disability.
Baker/Baher, Squire	Pvt.	19	5'10½"	Black	Blue	Farmer	Illinois	Sangamon County, IL	Veteran.
Baker, William M.	Pvt.	23	5'10½"	Black	Blue	Farmer	Illinois	Sangamon County, IL	Murdered 1/3/1863 by a citizen.
Bell, Preston	Pvt.	23	6'1"	Dark	Dark	Farmer	Illinois	Sangamon County, IL	Discharged 3/1863 for disability, Camp Butler.
Bridges, Jeremiah	Pvt.	21	5'8"	Dark	Blue	Farmer	Ireland	Sangamon County, IL	Died 6/1864 in hospital in Lexington, MO.*
Bridinger, William H.	Pvt.	18	5'5½"	Dark	Blue	Farmer	Ohio	Sangamon County, IL	Veteran.
Brown, Thomas	Pvt.	19	6'	Light	Blue	Farmer	Indiana	Sangamon County, IL	
Buck, John	Pvt.	38	5'10"	Light	Blue	Farmer	Germany	Sangamon County, IL	Veteran.
Buckley, William	Pvt.	25	5'6"	Dark	Blue	Farmer	Pennsylvania	Sangamon County, IL	Veteran.
Bush, Antonio	Pvt.	22	5'10"	Light	Blue	Farmer	Germany	Sangamon County, IL	Wounded at Battle of Iuka.
Callaway, James	Pvt.	27	5'11½"	Black	Blue	Farmer	New York	Sangamon County, IL	Discharged 1/14/1863 due to wounds in action at Battle of Corinth.
Cassady, David	Pvt.	39	5'5"	Dark	Black	–	Atlantic Ocean	Sangamon County, IL	Transferred to Co. K.
Clare, James F.	Pvt.	18	5'8"	Sandy	Blue	Farmer	Ireland	Sangamon County, IL	
Clements, John H.	Pvt.	20	5'6"	Dark	Gray	Printer	Illinois	Sangamon County, IL	
Constant, John E.	Pvt.	18	5'10¼"	Light	Gray	Farmer	Illinois	Sangamon County, IL	Veteran.
Cooly, Franklin	Pvt.	23	5'6"	Black	Black	Farmer	Virginia	Sangamon County, IL	
Coyke, John*	Pvt.	23	5'10½"	Dark	Gray	Hotel Runner	Ireland	Sangamon County, IL	
David, George H.	Pvt.	18	5'5"	Dark	Brown	Farmer	New York	Sangamon County, IL	Veteran.
Davidson, William H.	Pvt.	18	5'5"	Light	Blue	Farmer	Illinois	Sangamon County, IL	Veteran; wounded at Vicksburg.
Dawdrick, John	Pvt.	21	5'3½"	Light	Blue	Farmer	Pennsylvania	Cape Girardeau, MO	
Driscol, John	Pvt.	24	5'9½"	Dark	Blue	Farmer	Ireland	Sangamon County, IL	Wounded at Battle of Corinth.
Dunley/Dumley, John	Pvt.	21	5'7⅞"	Dark	Gray	Farmer	Kentucky	Sangamon County, IL	Veteran.
Dunnaway, Charles	Pvt.	22	5'5½"	Light	Gray	Farmer	Indiana	Sangamon County, IL	Discharged 6/1862.
Dunnaway, Julius	Pvt.	24	5'11¾"	Light	Gray	Farmer	Indiana	Sangamon County, IL	
English, Michael	Pvt.	20	5'7"	Dark	Dark	Farmer	Ireland	Sangamon County, IL	
Ford, William	Pvt.	18	5'10¼"	Light	Blue	Farmer	Illinois	Sangamon County, IL	Died 9/4/1861 of drowning.
Funderbark, David	Pvt.	21	5'8"	Black	Black	Farmer	Illinois	Sangamon County, IL	
Gallagher, John	Pvt.	20	5'4"	Light	Gray	Farmer	Vermont	Sangamon County, IL	
Geager, John	Pvt.	26	5'6¼"	Dark	Blue	Farmer	Ireland	Sangamon County, IL	Transferred by order of Gen. Halleck.
Gosses, Jasper	Pvt.	22	5'8"	Dark	Blue	Farmer	Pennsylvania	Sangamon County, IL	
Graham, George	Pvt.	22	6'	Dark	Blue	Farmer	Ohio	Sangamon County, IL	
Haas, Elias	Pvt.	23	5'7"	Light	Blue	Tailor	Bavaria	Sangamon County, IL	Discharged 5/20/1862.
Hailey, John	Pvt.	20	5'4"	Dark	Dark	Farmer	Illinois	Sangamon County, IL	Discharged 9/11/1862.
Haines, James B.	Pvt.	33	6'	Dark	Blue	Farmer	Kentucky	Sangamon County, IL	Died 2/14/1863 in Keokuk, IA, hospital.
Hall, Marion	Pvt.	18	5'4½"	Dark	Blue	Farmer	Ohio	Sangamon County, IL	Discharged 2/3/1863 due to wounds at Battle of Corinth.

*Mentioned in Missouri Descriptive Roll but not in the National Archives.

Soldier	Rank	Age	Ht	Hair	Eyes	Occupation	Nativity	Place of Residence	Comment
Hanna, Joseph	Pvt.	25	5'7½"	Dark	Gray	Farmer	Switzerland	Sangamon County, IL	Wounded at Battle of Corinth.
Hood, William F.	Pvt.	19	5'11"	Dark	Blue	Farmer	Kentucky	Sangamon County, IL	Discharged 9/14/1862.
Hunt, Thomas	Pvt.	26	5'4"	Brown	Blue	Farmer	Scotland	Sangamon County, IL	
Huttenheu/Huttenhow, William M.	Pvt.	21	5'6"	Light	Gray	Farmer	Illinois	Sangamon County, IL	Veteran.
John, Henry	Pvt.	22	5'6"	Light	Blue	Farmer	Bavaria	Sangamon County, IL	Veteran.
Jones, James	Pvt.	22	5'8"	Brown	Brown	–	–	–	
Kelley/Kelly, Benjamin	Pvt.	20	5'7½"	Dark	Dark	Farmer	Illinois	Sangamon County, IL	Veteran.
Kloffer, John	Pvt.	23	5'7"	Black	Black	Baker	Wurtemberg	Sangamon County, IL	Died 8/8/1863 Camp Sherman, MS.
Knobb, Adam	Pvt.	22	5'9"	Light	Blue	Soldier	Germany	–	
Madden, John W.	Pvt.	28	5'10"	Black	Blue	Farmer	Ohio	Sangamon County, IL	
May, John C.	Pvt.	18	5'7"	Light	Black	Painter	Illinois	Sangamon County, IL	Discharged by Writ of Habeas Corpus 1/27/1861.
McCall, Duncan	Pvt.	27	5'8"	Dark	Blue	Farmer	New York	Sangamon County, IL	
McMahan/McMann, Hugh	Pvt.	28	5'5½"	Gray	Blue	Farmer	Ireland	Sangamon County, IL	Discharged 11/1/1861.
Miller, John	Pvt.	24	5'8⅝"	Dark	Blue	Farmer	Pennsylvania	Sangamon County, IL	Discharged 11/1/1861, disability.
Neer/Neit, Nathaniel	Pvt.	18	5'5¼"	Dark	Gray	Farmer	Missouri	Sangamon County, IL	
Nichols, George W.	Pvt.	18	5'8¼"	Dark	Blue	Farmer	Ohio	Sangamon County, IL	Veteran.
O'Neil, Thomas	Pvt.	28	5'10"	Black	Blue	Farmer	Ireland	Sangamon County, IL	Company Wagoner.
Page, Eugene	Pvt.	23	6'1¼"	Black	Black	Farmer	Virginia	Sangamon County, IL	Died 2/16/1863 Memphis; buried in Ntl. Cemetery.
Pendergast, Edwin	Pvt.	23	5'10½"	Dark	Gray	Farmer	Louisiana	Sangamon County, IL	Transferred to Colored Infantry for promotion.
Pohlman, John	Pvt.	20	5'4½"	Dark	Blue	Farmer	Germany	Sangamon County, IL	Discharged 6/19/1862.
Pugh, Thomas*	Pvt.	20	5'6"	Light	Gray	Farmer	Tennessee	Sangamon County, IL	Veteran; wounded at Battle of Iuka.
Reed, Andrew	Pvt.	18	5'4½"	Dark	Gray	Farmer	Indiana	Sangamon County, IL	Died 8/5/1863 of wounds from Iuka.
Robinson, John B.	Pvt.	21	6'1"	Light	Blue	Farmer	Illinois	Sangamon County, IL	KIA 9/1862 Iuka.
Ross, Charles	Pvt.	19	5'11"	Black	Black	Farmer	Ohio	Sangamon County, IL	Discharged 4/8/1863 of wounds from Corinth; also wounded at Battle of Iuka.
Saunders, James	Pvt.	22	5'10"	Dark	Blue	Farmer	Kentucky	Sangamon County, IL	
Schaburg, Frederick	Pvt.	24	5'6"	Light	Blue	Farmer	Germany	Sangamon County, IL	KIA 9/18/1862 Iuka.
Smith, George	Pvt.	19	5'5"	Dark	Blue	Blacksmith	Illinois	Sangamon County, IL	Absent sick.
Smith, James C.	Pvt.	21	5'8½"	Dark	Blue	Farmer	Kentucky	Sangamon County, IL	KIA 10/8/1862 Corinth.
Smith, Joel F.	Pvt.	18	5'7"	Black	Dark	Farmer	Kentucky	Sangamon County, IL	KIA 10/4/1862 Corinth.
Smith, Samuel M.	Pvt.	22	5'7"	Dark	Dark	Farmer	Kentucky	Sangamon County, IL	Veteran.
Smithers, Henry	Pvt.	36	5'6"	Dark	Black	Farmer	England	Sangamon County, IL	Discharged 11/23/1862 for disability.
Smitson, Samuel M.	Pvt.	–	–	–	–	–	–	–	
Snodgrass, James	Pvt.	19	5'8½"	Dark	Blue	Farmer	Illinois	Sangamon County, IL	Died 7/16/1863 of chronic diarrhea; Vicksburg.
Talday/Tolday, Fleming	Pvt.	26	5'9½"	Dark	Gray	Farmer	Ohio	Sangamon County, IL	Veteran.
Turley, Sanford	Pvt.	18	5'6"	Sandy	Gray	Farmer	Illinois	Sangamon County, IL	
Turley, Theodore	Pvt.	21	5'9"	Dark	Gray	Farmer	Illinois	Sangamon County, IL	Died 11/16/1861 C. Girardeau of typhoid fever.
Turner, Sylvester	Pvt.	18	5'8"	Dark	Black	Farmer	Illinois	Sangamon County, IL	Discharged 2/26/1863, gunshot wound at Iuka.
Wagoner, George	Pvt.	21	5'5⅝"	Dark	Dark	Farmer	Illinois	Sangamon County, IL	
Wagoner, James*	Pvt.	28	5'10½"	Black	Black	Farmer	Illinois	Sangamon County, IL	Veteran.

*Mentioned in Missouri Descriptive Roll but not in the National Archives.

Soldier	*Rank*	*Age*	*Ht*	*Hair*	*Eyes*	*Occu-pation*	*Nativity*	*Place of Residence*	*Comment*
Anderson, James C.*	Pvt.	–	–	–	–	–	–	–	Veteran.
Arthur, John*	Pvt.	–	–	–	–	–	–	–	Veteran.
Busk, John*	Pvt.	–	–	–	–	–	–	–	
Clouts, William*	Pvt.	–	–	–	–	–	–	–	Veteran.
Eaton, W. N.*	Pvt.	–	–	–	–	–	–	–	
Goldman, Francis*	Pvt.	–	–	–	–	–	–	–	Veteran.

Company C

Soldier	*Rank*	*Age*	*Ht*	*Hair*	*Eyes*	*Occu-pation*	*Nativity*	*Place of Residence*	*Comment*
Warner, Moses	Captain	30	–	Black	Black	RR Conductor	Kentucky	Springfield, IL	Resigned 2/15/1863 disability; wounded at Battle of Iuka.
Green, Modesta J.	Captain	–	–	Black	–	Carpenter	New Jersey	Springfield, IL	Veteran.
Lott, James A.	1st Lt.	30	5'9"	Light	Blue	Carpenter	Pennsylvania	Springfield, IL	Veteran.
Perce, William	1st Lt.	–	–	–	–	Broom Maker	–	Springfield, IL	Resigned 4/11/1862, disability.
Walker, Daniel T.	2nd Lt.	–	–	–	–	–	–	–	Veteran.
Withrow, Harrison	2nd Lt.	21	6'	L. Brown	Gray	Farmer	Illinois	Loami, IL	Resigned 4/30/1864.
Brown, Horace E.	Sgt.	21	5'9½"	Dark	Black	Farmer	Illinois	Verdin, IL	Veteran.
Browning, Addison M.	Sgt.	44	6'⅜"	Black	Black	Physician	Kentucky	Loami, IL	Veteran.
Boyle, John	Sgt.	22	5'6"	Brown	Blue	Farmer	Ireland	Verdin, IL	
Crosman, Peter	Sgt.	40	5'4½"	Dark	Gray	Carpenter	New York	Loami, IL	Discharged 1/1/1863, disability.
Cutright, John B.	Sgt.	21	5'10"	Red	Hazel	Brickmaker	Ohio	Springfield, IL	Veteran; reduced in rank due to court-martial.
Dunning, Henry C.	Sgt.	25	5'7⅞"	Black	Dark	Carpenter	–	Loami, IL	Deserted 4/19/1863 Cairo, IL.
Lawrence, John A.	Sgt.	21	5'7¼"	Black	Dark	Manufacturer	Ohio	Springfield, IL	
Lucas, George M.	Sgt.	23	5'10"	Black	Dark	Teacher	Massachusetts	Loami, IL	Died of disease 11/14/1864.
Pickrell, Abel G.	Sgt.	28	5'8"	Light	Gray	Farmer	Illinois	Sangamon County, IL	
Pickrell, William T.	Sgt.–Major	25	5'8½"	Dark	Gray	Clerk	Illinois	Mechanicsburg, IL	
Roney, William T.	Sgt.	31	5'9¾"	Light	Blue	Millright	Pennsylvania	Springfield, IL	Veteran; wounded at Battle of Iuka.
Simmons, William T.	Sgt.	20	5'7"	Light	Dark	Carpenter	Illinois	Springfield, IL	Veteran; wounded at Battle of Corinth.
Walker, Daniel	Musician	41	5'6½"	Light	Blue	Carpenter	Indiana	Springfield, IL	Veteran.
Campbell, Robert D.	Corporal	23	5'8⅝"	Brown	Blue	Farmer	Illinois	Loami, IL	Veteran; reduced in rank for cause.
Eagan, Andrew	Corporal	21	5'10⅝"	Light	Blue	Laborer	Ireland	Verdin, IL	Veteran; wounded at Vicksburg.
Fairbanks, Charles S.	Corporal	21	5'7½"	L. Brown	Blue	Farmer	Ohio	Spring Creek, IL	Reduced in rank at his request.
Freakes, Jefferson	Corporal	23	5'5⅝"	Brown	Hazel	Farmer	Illinois	Lincoln, IL	Veteran.
Jones, Joseph	Corporal	25	5'9"	Brown	Blue	Carpenter	Illinois	Loami, IL	Mustered 3/4/1864 Davenport, IA; wounded at Vicksburg.
Lightfoot, Benjamin	Corporal	33	5'6¼"	Brown	Blue	Bricklayer	England	Springfield, IL	Died 8/13/1864 in hospital in Memphis; wounded at Battle of Corinth.
Morris, Gibson	Corporal	30	5'6½"	Black	Black	Carpenter	Kentucky	Loami, IL	Reduced in rank 3/3/1863 for cause.

**Mentioned in Missouri Descriptive Roll but not in the National Archives.*

Soldier	Rank	Age	Ht	Hair	Eyes	Occupation	Nativity	Place of Residence	Comment
Sweet, Sylvester H.	Corporal	21	6'½"	Black	Dark	Farmer	Illinois	Loami, IL	Veteran; reduced in rank at his request.
Graham, James A.	Musician	23	5'6⅝"	Light	Blue	Farmer	Illinois	Verdin, IL	Veteran.
Prentice, Owen D.	Pvt./	21	5'3"	Light	Blue	Printer	Illinois	Springfield, IL	Veteran; reduced in rank at his request.
Hime/Hine, John	Wagoner	39	5'8⅜"	Light	Blue	Laborer	Germany	Springfield, IL	Discharged 12/5/1862 due to wounds from Iuka.
Andrews, William	Pvt.	35	5'5⅝"	Light	Blue	Miller	Germany	Springfield, IL	Deserted second time Young's Point, LA, 6/21/1863.*
Back, John	Pvt.	20	5'9⅞"	Black	Dark	Farmer	Illinois	Loami, IL	Died 11/1863.
Barger, James N.	Pvt.	21	5'9½"	Dark	Hazel	Farmer	Illinois	Loami, IL	Discharged 11/19/1862, disability.
Beckman/Buckman, Charles H.	Pvt.	27	5'8½"	Brown	Hazel	Laborer	Germany	Springfield, IL	Died of disease 7/6/1862.
Bingham, John	Pvt.	20	5'6"	Brown	Dark	Teamster	Delaware	Springfield, IL	
Black, Andrew	Pvt.	33	5'6½"	Light	Blue	Laborer	Scotland	Springfield, IL	
Boemmlitz/Bomlitz, Henry	Pvt.	22	5'7⅞"	Brown	Blue	Farmer	Germany	Springfield, IL	
Bucklers, Herman	Pvt.	32	5'2½"	Light	Blue	Physician	Germany	Waverly, IL	Discharged 8/28/1861, disability.
Bullion, John	Pvt.	29	5'7¾"	Dark	Blue	Joiner	New York	Springfield, IL	
Calmie, Taylor	Pvt.	25	5'10½"	Brown	Dark	Farmer	France	Perryville, MO	Deserted 3/14/1863 Memphis.
Capps, Thomas J.	Pvt.	21	5'10¾"	Dark	Gray	Carpenter	Kentucky	Springfield, IL	
Clara/Clare, John	Pvt.	34	5'9¾"	Brown	Blue	Laborer	Ireland	Springfield, IL	
Craddock, William	Pvt.	28	5'3¼"	Brown	Blue	Gunsmith	Missouri	Springfield, IL	
Cullin, John	Pvt.	24	5'7¾"	Brown	Blue	Farmer	Ireland	Springfield, IL	Deserted 3/7/1863.
Cuppy, Daniel	Pvt.	30	5'11"	Black	Dark	Farmer	Illinois	Loami, IL	
Denezet, Morris	Pvt.	25	5'10"	Black	Black	Farmer	France	Perryville, MO	Killed 9/24/1861 in skirmish at Dallas, MO.
Dosing, John	Pvt.	20	5'6¾"	Light	Blue	Farmer	Prussia	Springfield, IL	Deserted 4/29/1863 Cairo, IL.*
Doty, William	Pvt.	31	5'4⅞"	Sandy	Gray	Farmer	New York	Williamsville, IL	Veteran.
Drenen/Drennan, Thomas	Pvt.	28	5'8¾"	Sandy	Gray	Carpenter	Illinois	Loami, IL	Veteran.
Egan, Andrew	Pvt.	21	5'10⅜"	Light	Blue	Laborer	Ireland	Verdin, IL	Veteran; wounded at Battle of Corinth.
Gable, Mat A.	Pvt.	28	5'6⅜"	Black	Black	Farmer	Indiana	Springfield, IL	Transferred to Co. K.
Gants/Gantz, Daniel	Pvt.	21	5'5¾"	Brown	Hazel	Farmer	Illinois	Mechanicsburg, IL	Veteran; wounded in Battle of Fredericktown.
Haas, William	Pvt.	40	6'1"	Dark	Dark	Farmer	Germany	Springfield	Discharged 2/22/1863 Germantown, TN.
Hainie, William	Pvt.	20	5'8¼"	Light	Blue	Laborer	Tennessee	Springfield	
Hall, Thomas M.	Pvt.	33	5'5½"	Dark	Blue	Laborer	Ireland	Mechanicsburg, IL	Veteran; wounded at Battle of Corinth.
Hami, William/John	Pvt.	39	5'8¾"	Light	Blue	Laborer	Germany	Springfield, IL	Discharged 11/15/1862 from wounds at Iuka.
Hanstey, James H.	Pvt.	25	5'8⅜"	Brown	Hazel	Bricklayer	Kentucky	Springfield, IL	
Hinman, Smith J.	Pvt.	25	6'1"	Dark	Dark	Farmer	Illinois	Loami, IL	Veteran; wounded at Vicksburg.
Hogue/Hoog, Martin	Pvt.	25	5'5½"	Dark	Blue	Laborer	Indiana	Springfield, IL	Veteran; wounded at Battle of Iuka.
Hornsey, John	Pvt.	43	5'6½"	Dark	Gray	Butcher	England	Springfield, IL	Discharged 4/10/1863 Young's Point.
Huffmaster, Daniel	Pvt.	20	5'7¼"	Black	Black	Farmer	Illinois	Loami, IL	Died of disease 3/18/1862 Cape Girardeau.
Jordan, John M.	Pvt.	26	5'10"	Light	Blue	Farmer	Illinois	Loami, IL	Died of disease 5/24/1862 Loami, IL.
Karn, John	Pvt.	23	5'5½"	Light	Blue	Laborer	Germany	Springfield	

*Mentioned in Missouri Descriptive Roll but not in the National Archives.

Soldier	*Rank*	*Age*	*Ht*	*Hair*	*Eyes*	*Occupation*	*Nativity*	*Place of Residence*	*Comment*
Kellogg, Albert B.	Pvt.	20	5'9½"	Light	Blue	Blacksmith	Ohio	Loami, IL	Deserted 5/25/1863 Richmond, LA.*
Kelly, Joseph	Pvt.	39	5'5½"	Brown	Blue	Laborer	Ireland	Springfield, IL	
Koch, Henry	Pvt.	37	5'4½"	Brown	Blue	Butcher	Germany	Springfield, IL	Discharged 12/30/1862 due to accidental wound.
Leinhart/Lienhart, Samuel*	Pvt.	29	5'6"	Black	Black	Laborer	Germany	Cape Girardeau, MO	Veteran; POW.
Little, William F.	Pvt.	17	5'3"	Light	Blue	Merchant	Illinois	Springfield, IL	Discharged at request by father.*
Lukeamper, Frederick	Pvt.	41	5'7½"	Brown	Blue	Miller	Germany	Springfield, IL	Veteran.
Lyons, John	Pvt.	37	5'8⅜"	Light	Blue	Farmer	Ireland	Springfield, IL	Died 6/9/1862 at Farmington, MS, of wounds from Siege of Corinth.
Manning, John W.	Pvt.	17	5'3"	Light	Blue	Clerk	Illinois	Springfield, IL	Discharged at request of father.*
Martin, Benjamin	Pvt.	43	5'4½"	Black	Blue	Farmer	Virginia	Springfield	Discharged 9/3/1863.
Martin, Robert	Pvt.	50	5'6½"	Dark	Dark	Farmer	Virginia	Dawson, IL	Discharged 1/1/1863.
McGuire, James	Pvt.	35	5'5⅝"	Brown	Hazel	Laborer	Ireland	Springfield, IL	Discharged 12/3/1861 Cape Girardeau.
McGuire, John	Pvt.	30	5'4"	Brown	Blue	Laborer	Ireland	Springfield, IL	
McHaley, Henry	Pvt.	25	5'9⅝"	Light	Blue	Farmer	S. Carolina	Springfield, IL	Wounded at Battle of Corinth.
Mehan, Patrick	Pvt.	28	5'6"	Black	Gray	Laborer	Ireland	Springfield, IL	Died 10/14/1862 of wounds from Corinth.
Meyers, Joseph	Pvt.	27	5'10"	Light	Blue	Farmer	Germany	Springfield, IL	Died of disease 11/27/1861 Cape Girardeau.
Michael, James	Pvt.	37	5'9¾"	Brown	Blue	Laborer	Ireland	Springfield, IL	
Morehead, David	Pvt.	32	5'10⅝"	Red	Blue	Blacksmith	Pennsylvania	Springfield, IL	Veteran.
Morril, John H./ James	Pvt.	23	5'5½"	Light	Blue	Farmer	Illinois	Springfield, IL	Died 9/11/863 at Camp Sherman, MS.*
Murry, John Metropolis, IL.*	Pvt.	27	5'3"	Light	Blue	Laborer	Pennsylvania	Springfield, IL	Deserted 4/20/1862
Neal, Samuel M.	Pvt.	25	5'9"	Light	Blue	Farmer	Illinois	Loami, IL	Veteran; wounded at Battle of Iuka and Battle of Corinth.
Redding, Thomas	Pvt.	24	5'5½"	Black	Brown	Stone Mason	New York	Springfield, IL	
Roberts, Garrett J.	Pvt.	24	5'11"	Dark	Blue	Farmer	Holland	Springfield, IL	Veteran.
Rose, John H.	Pvt.	22	5'3"	Brown	Blue	Tobacconist	Atlantic Ocean	Springfield, IL	Discharged 11/26/1862 of wounds from Iuka.*
Samson, William	Pvt.	44	5'5⅜"	Black	Dark	Laborer	England	Springfield, IL	Discharged 5/15/1862.
Scott, George C.	Pvt.	24	5'6¾"	Brown	Brown	Carpenter	Ohio	Springfield, IL	Veteran.
Seamon/Seemon, William P.	Pvt.	23	5'7⅝"	Light	Blue	Farmer	Illinois	Pleasant Plains, IL	Discharged 10/10/1862
Smith, John	Pvt.	25	5'7½"	Dark	Blue	Laborer	England	Springfield, IL	Died 11/28/1861 of disease.
Smith, Samuel/ Daniel	Pvt.	30	5'7"	Black	Black	Machinist	Ireland	Springfield, IL	Veteran.
Stratton, George H.	Pvt.	19	5'3"	Brown	Blue	Farmer	New York	Loami, IL	Veteran.
Sumpter, Samuel T.	Pvt.–Corp	21	5'5¼"	Dark	Blue	Farmer	Illinois	Mechanicsburg, IL	Veteran.
Sweet, Montgomery*	Pvt.	19	6'	Black	Black	Farmer	Illinois	Loami, IL	Discharged 11/15/1862 from wounds at Iuka.
Workman, Peter	Pvt.	22	5'9¾"	Light	Blue	Farmer	–	Loami, IL	Discharged 5/2/1863 gunshot wound, accident.
Yates, Will	Pvt.	26	5'8½"	Black	Black	Merchant	Illinois	Springfield, IL	Missing; desertion.*
Brulitz, Henry*	Pvt.	–	–	–	–	–	–	–	Veteran.
Byrd, John*	Pvt.	–	–	–	–	–	–	–	POW 3/1/1864; wounded at Battle of Iuka.
Graham/Gratian, Francis M.*	Pvt.	–	–	–	–	–	–	–	Veteran.
Letchner, Henry*	Pvt.	–	–	–	–	–	–	–	Veteran.

**Mentioned in Missouri Descriptive Roll but not in the National Archives.*

Soldier	Rank	Age	Ht	Hair	Eyes	Occupation	Nativity	Place of Residence	Comment
Mayberry, Michael*	Pvt.	–	–	–	–	–	–	–	Veteran.
Rudicil, Jacob*	Pvt.	–	–	–	–	–	–	–	Discharged 9/4/1863.
Ruker, John*	Pvt.	–	–	–	–	–	–	–	Veteran.
Seatron, Robert*	Pvt.	–	–	–	–	–	–	–	Veteran.

Company D

Soldier	Rank	Age	Ht	Hair	Eyes	Occupation	Nativity	Place of Residence	Comment
Hendee, Clark	Captain	36	5'7½"	Dark	Dark	Physician	Vermont	Clay Co., IL	Resigned 7/13/1862.
Henry, George W.	Captain	32	5'9"	Dark	Dark	Lawyer	Ohio	Clay Co., IL	Resigned 5/1/1864.
Kendall, Cyrus D.	Captain	23	5'8¾"	Dark	Gray	Lawyer	Pennsylvania	Clay Co., IL	Veteran.
Apperson, Charles W.	1st Lt.	20	5'5½"	Dark	Gray	Farmer	Illinois	Clay Co., IL	Veteran; wounded at Battle of Corinth.
Bentley, Clark G.	1st Lt.	33	5'10"	Dark	Blue	Painter	New York	Louisiana, MO	Resigned.
Cowperthwait, John	1st Lt.	26	5'9"	Black	Dark	Engineer	Missouri	St. Louis, MO	Resigned 5/26/1864; wounded at Battle of Iuka.
Sappington, Mark	2nd Lt.	31	5'6½"	Light	Blue	Minister	Missouri	Clay Co., IL	Resigned 6/23/1864.
Tasker, James	Sgt.	34	5'10½"	Dark	Gray	Stonecutter	New York	Clay Co., IL	Veteran.
Dewitt, John D.	Sgt.	29	5'8¼"	Black	Black	Blacksmith	Indiana	Clay Co., IL	
Erwin, William	Sgt.	23	6'3¾"	Light	Gray	Farmer	Illinois	Clay Co., IL	Veteran.
Fields, John	Sgt.	23	6'¼"	Dark	Blue	Teacher	Indiana	Clay Co., IL	
Heltman, Philip	1st Sgt.	26	5'8"	Light	Gray	Carpenter	Ohio	Clay Co., IL	
McKnight, David	Sgt.	21	5'10"	Dark	Dark	Farmer	Illinois	Clay Co., IL	Wounded at Battle of Corinth.
Randall, Lyman	Sgt.	23	5'7½"	Dark	Black	Farmer	Maine	Clay Co., IL	
Talifaro, Jones*	Sgt.	–	–	–	–	–	–	–	
Conley, James	Corporal	25	5'9"	Dark	Blue	Farmer	Indiana	Clay Co., IL	Died at Cape Girardeau 11/23/1861 of typhoid fever.
Dewitt, Elijah R.	Corporal	22	5'8½"	Light	Blue	Farmer	Indiana	Clay Co., IL	Died 6/27/1864; buried Memphis Ntl. Cemetery.*
Dyke, Calvin J.	Corporal	23	5'10"	Light	Gray	Farmer	Tennessee	Clay Co., IL	Veterans; reduced in rank.
Fields, Lancaster	Corporal	30	5'8¾"	Light	Blue	Farmer	Indiana	Clay Co., IL	Died 10/7/1862 of wounds from Battle of Corinth.
Fleece, James W.	Corporal	29	5'5"	Dark	Gray	Farmer	Kentucky	Louisiana, MO	Discharged 6/13/1862; disability.
Granville, William	Corporal	22	5'5½"	Light	Blue	Farmer	Ohio	Clay Co., IL	Veteran; dead.
McKnight, William T.	Corporal	22	5'9¾"	Dark	Gray	Farmer	Illinois	Clay Co., IL	Wounded at Battle of Corinth.
O'Neal, Edward	Corporal	19	5'6"	Dark	Blue	Farmer	Indiana	Clay Co., IL	
Sexton, John W.	Corporal	29	5'10"	Light	Gray	Farmer	Ohio	Franklin, MO	
Eaton, Newton J.*	Musician	18	5'4"	Light	Blue	Farmer	Illinois	Clay Co., IL	Veteran.
Hussey, James R.	Musician	23	5'7½"	Light	Gray	Carpenter	Maryland	Clay Co., IL	Transferred to 71st USCT 3/4/64.
Rinehart, John	Musician	25	5'5¾"	Dark	Gray	Farmer	Indiana	Clay Co., IL	Veteran.
Nimocks, Roland	Musician	30	5'8"	Dark	Blue	Carpenter	New York	Franklin, MO	Reduced to ranks.
Archer, Goran	Pvt.	19	5'4½"	Black	Black	Laborer	Missouri	Louisiana, MO	Transferred to Co. K.
Baker, Christopher	Pvt.	23	5'5½"	Light	Gray	Farmer	Missouri	St. Louis, MO	
Bigsby/Bixby, Nathaniel	Pvt.	24	5'8½"	Dark	Dark	Cooper	Indiana	Pike Co., IL	Veteran.
Bowen, Henry	Pvt.	31	5'9½"	Light	Gray	Farmer	New York	Franklin, MO	
Brown, Eloana	Pvt.	29	5'5½"	Red	Blue	Laborer	Illinois	Clay Co., IL	
Bryant, Cyrus	Pvt.	20	5'6¾"	Black	Dark	Farmer	Indiana	Clay Co., IL	Veteran.
Burton, Melkert H.	Pvt.	19	5'5¾"	Black	Gray	Farmer	Indiana	Clay Co., IL	Veteran; wounded at Battle of Iuka.
Carrick, Thomas	Pvt.	20	5'4"	Light	Blue	Carpenter	New York	Pike Co., IL	
Cooper, Adam P.	Pvt.	24	5'5¼"	Light	Blue	Farmer	Indiana	Pike Co., IL	Veteran.

*Mentioned in Missouri Descriptive Roll but not in the National Archives.

Soldier	Rank	Age	Ht	Hair	Eyes	Occupation	Nativity	Place of Residence	Comment
Corder, Joseph M.	Pvt.	28	5'5¾"	Light	Gray	Farmer	Tennessee	Clay Co., IL	Veteran.
Cross, Samuel F.	Pvt.	32	5'7½"	Light	Gray	Laborer	Tennessee	Madison, IL	
Coudery, John	Pvt.	25	5'5½"	Light	Gray	Farmer	Indiana	Clay Co., IL	Veteran.
Creech, Voluntine	Pvt.	21	5'10"	Light	Gray	Farmer	Virginia	Clay Co., IL	Died 1/17/1864 Lagrange, TN, buried in Memphis Ntl. Cemetery
Davis, James	Pvt.	19	5'6"	Light	Blue	Farmer	Tennessee	Pike Co., IL	Deserted 3/12/1863.
Dowell, Andrew W.	Pvt.	30	5'7"	Dark	Gray	Blacksmith	Virginia	Clay Co., IL	Veteran.
Eaton, William S.	Pvt.	40	5'8¼"	Light	Gray	Carpenter	Kentucky	Clay Co., IL	Discharged 3/17/1863.
Eddy, David S.	Pvt.	19	5'8"	Light	Blue	Farmer	Kentucky	Pike Co., IL	Veteran.
Engledow, Elander/Leland	Pvt.	18	5'8"	Light	Gray	Farmer	Tennessee	Clay Co., IL	Veteran; discharged 9/3/1863 (reenlisted).
Engledow, William C	Pvt.	22	5'6½"	Light	Gray	Farmer	Tennessee	Clay Co., IL	Veteran; discharged 9/3/1863.
Erwin, John	Pvt.	19	5'8¼"	Light	Blue	Farmer	Illinois	Clay Co., IL	Wounded at Vicksburg.
Fox, Henry	Pvt.	35	5'2"	Dark	Gray	Blacksmith	Germany	Pike Co., IL	
Friend, Samuel P.	Pvt.	20	5'9"	Dark	Dark	Farmer	Virginia	Clay Co., IL	Discharged; wounded at Battle of Corinth.
Froner/Frones,	Pvt.	20	6'½"	Light	Gray	Laborer	Indiana	Pike Co., IL	Veteran.
Gibson, Calder David	Pvt.	18	5'5"	Light	Gray	Farmer	Illinois	Clay Co., IL	Died 7/3/1863 of congestive cough; wounded at Battle of Corinth.
Gibson, Chester F.	Pvt.	19	5'9"	Light	Gray	Farmer	Illinois	Clay Co., IL	Died 7/18/1863 of congestive fever.
Gibson, Henry A.*	Pvt.	19	5'6"	Light	Blue	Farmer	Indiana	Clay Co., IL	Died 5/27/1862.
Gross, John	Pvt.	20	5'10"	Black	Black	Farmer	Indiana	Clay Co., IL	Veteran; wounded at Battle of Iuka.
Guenterman, Robert W.	Pvt.	–	–	–	–	–	–	–	Died 4/24/1862 of congestive chill.
Hagle, Dios C.	Pvt.	21	5'10"	Light	Blue	Farmer	Ohio	Wayne, IL	Wounded at Battle of Iuka and Vicksburg.
Harrison, Julius	Pvt.	22	5'8"	Dark	Gray	Farmer	Missouri	Crawford, MO	Veteran.
House, James	Pvt.	27	5'10"	Light	Blue	Carpenter	Indiana	Louisiana, MO	Veteran.
Hungate, George W.	Pvt.	20	5'6½"	Light	Gray	Farmer	Indiana	Clay Co., IL	Veteran.
Hungate, Jehn H.	Pvt.	18	5'6½"	Black	Black	Farmer	Indiana	Clay Co., IL	Discharged 3/10/1863.
Jarvis, Samuel	Pvt.	19	5'4½"	Dark	Dark	Farmer	Missouri	Gasconade, MO	Veteran.
Jump, George*	Pvt.	28	5'10"	Light	Gray	Farmer	Ohio	Pike Co., IL	Died 7/9/1862 of typhoid fever near Corinth.
Jump, Riley	Pvt.	19	5'5¾"	Light	Gray	Farmer	Ohio	Pike Co., IL	Veteran; wounded at Battle of Corinth.
Maxwell, Jesse	Pvt.	23	5'8¼"	Dark	Light	Farmer	Illinois	Clay Co., IL	
Maxwell, William	Pvt.	–	5'4½"	Dark	Black	Farmer	Illinois	Clay Co., IL	
McCarty, Michael*	Pvt.	32	5'4"	Light	Blue	Laborer	Ireland	Point Pleasant, MO	Deserted 3/12/1863.
McGaughey, Edward	Pvt.	22	5'8"	Black	Black	Farmer	Indiana	Clay Co., IL	Died 2/22/63 of typhoid fever.
McGuire, John	Pvt.	44	5'10"	Black	Gray	Laborer	Ireland	Franklin, MO	Died near Vicksburg 9/9/1863.*
McKinney, Jeremiah/James	Pvt.	19	5'8½"	Dark	Blue	Farmer	Illinois	Clay Co., IL	Discharged 11/9/1862 Cape Girardeau.
McKnelly, Crawford	Pvt.	20	5'8½"	Dark	Gray	Farmer	Illinois	Clay Co., IL	Died of wounds from Battle of Iuka.
Miller, Solomon	Pvt.	23	5'8½"	Light	Gray	Farmer	Indiana	Clay Co., IL	Veteran.
Morgan, Francis A.	Pvt.	24	5'6½"	Dark	Blue	Carpenter	Virginia	Clay Co., IL	Mustered out 8/4/1864.
Owsley, Henry	Pvt.	19	5'8½"	Dark	Blue	Farmer	Indiana	Pike Co., IL	Deserted 3/3/1863.*
Payne, Nathaniel	Pvt.	22	5'8¾"	Dark	Blue	Farmer	New York	Pike Co., IL	Veteran; transferred to Co. K.
Pettyjohn, Richard C.	Pvt.	19	5'11"	Dark	Dark	Farmer	Ohio	Wayne, IL	Died 10/25/1861.
Pointer, Washington	Pvt.	22	5'4¾"	Light	Gray	Farmer	Missouri	Gasconade, MO	Transferred to Co. K.
Pridemore, John H.	Pvt.	19	5'5"	Black	Gray	Farmer	Illinois	Clay Co., IL	Wounded at Battle of Corinth and Vicksburg.
Pryfogel, Alexander	Pvt.	20	5'9¾"	Light	Blue	Laborer	Illinois	Clay Co., IL	Veteran.

*Mentioned in Missouri Descriptive Roll but not in the National Archives.

Soldier	Rank	Age	Ht	Hair	Eyes	Occupation	Nativity	Place of Residence	Comment
Reeves, Isaac	Pvt.	19	5'7½"	Light	Blue	Farmer	Illinois	Clay Co., IL	Discharge 5/22/1863 for loss of arm Vicksburg.*
Rinehart, John C.	Pvt.	25	5'6"	Dark	Gray	Farmer	Indiana	Clay Co., IL	Died 1/19/1864, LaGrange, TN; buried Ntl Cemetery.*
Rinehart, Lewis	Pvt.	18	5'5¼"	Black	Black	Farmer	Indiana	Clay Co., IL	Veteran.
Rinehart, Lyman	Pvt.	23	5'7¼"	Dark	Black	Farmer	Maine	–	
Shelton, Charles V.	Pvt.	23	5'10"	Light	Blue	Farmer	Tennessee	Clay Co., IL	Veteran.
Shockley, Jasper	Pvt.	22	5'7"	Black	Gray	Farmer	California	Phelps Co., MO	Veteran; wounded at Battle of Iuka.
Smith, Henry	Pvt.	28	5'6½"	Light	Gray	Tailor	Ohio	St. Louis, MO	Veteran; wounded in Battle of Corinth.
Smith, Lewis	Pvt.	23	5'5½"	Light	Gray	Farmer	Virginia	Crawford, MO	Died 6/7/1862.
Smith, William	Pvt.	24	5'5½"	Dark	Gray	Farmer	N Carolina	Clay Co., IL	Died 6/9/1862.
Stuckenschneider, Christopher	Pvt.	27	5'10¾"	Dark	Dark	Carpenter	Germany	Franklin Co., MO	Died 7/6/1863 of wounds from Vicksburg.
Sutton, Thomas J.*	Pvt.	28	5'8"	Black	Black	Saddler	Kentucky	Boone Co., MO	Veteran.
Thatcher, George D.	Pvt.	17	5'7¼"	Dark	Gray	Cabinet Maker	Michigan	Clay Co., IL	
Tooley, James*	Pvt.	22	5'7¾"	Sandy	Gray	Farmer	Kentucky	Clay Co., IL	
Trustey, William*	Pvt.	32	5'¼"	Black	Dark	Farmer	Kentucky	Franklin Co., MO	Veteran.
Warden/Worden, George W.	Pvt.	19	5'7¾"	Light	Gray	Farmer	Tennessee	Gasconade, MO	Veteran.
Warden, Thomas*	Pvt.	26	5'9"	Light	Gray	Farmer	Tennessee	Gasconade, MO	Discharged 4/18/1863.
Warner, Thadeus C.*	Pvt.	24	5'9"	Light	Gray	Raft Pilot	Connecticut	Franklin Co., MO	Veteran.
Williams, Abraham*	Pvt.	19	5'5¼"	Light	Gray	Farmer	Ireland	Clay Co., IL	KIA 10/2/1862 Corinth.
Williams, Granville*	Pvt.	22	5'5½"	Light	Blue	Farmer	Ohio	Clay Co., IL	Died 6/26/1864 in Memphis of wounds from near Lake Village, AR.*
Williams, John*	Pvt.	24	5'9"	Dark	Blue	Blacksmith	Indiana	Louisiana, MO	Discharged 7/25/1862.*
Williams, William*	Pvt.	22	5'5"	Light	Gray	Farmer	Indiana	Clay Co., IL	
Wilson, Shelby*	Pvt.	21	5'8¾"	Black	Black	Farmer	Indiana	Clay Co., IL	
Wood, David*	Pvt.	21	5'10"	Light	Blue	Farmer	Missouri	Clay Co., IL	Veteran.
Wood, Robert*	Pvt.	23	5'10"	Dark	Blue	Farmer	Tennessee	Clay Co., IL	Veteran.
Bailey, Joshua*	Pvt.	–	–	–	–	–	–	–	
Cumandu, A L*	Pvt.	–	–	–	–	–	–	–	
Gillam, Daniel W.*	Pvt.	–	–	–	–	–	–	–	
Gravot, John*	Pvt.	–	–	–	–	–	–	–	
Martin, John*	Pvt.	–	–	–	–	–	–	–	
Masterson, Rusher*	Pvt.	–	–	–	–	–	–	–	
Morley, Henry*	Pvt.	–	–	–	–	–	–	–	
Sennor, John*	Pvt.	–	–	–	–	–	–	–	
White, George*	Pvt.	–	–	–	–	–	–	–	

Company E

Soldier	Rank	Age	Ht	Hair	Eyes	Occupation	Nativity	Place of Residence	Comment
Bail, Abner B.	Captain	–	–	–	–	Saddler	Ohio	Olney, IL	Resigned 3/30/1864.
Hollister, Charles	Captain	–	–	–	–	–	–	Olney, IL	KIA 10/4/1862 in Battle of Corinth.
Livingston, Benjamin F.	Captain/Major	–	–	–	–	Lawyer	–	Olney, IL	Resigned 4/11/1862.
Roney, Levi D.	Captain	22	5'7¾"	Brown	Hazel	Farmer	Ohio	Stringtown, IL	
Blew, Jacob	1st Lt.	–	–	–	–	Farmer	–	Claremont, IL	Mustered out 8/16/1864.
Perry, John F.	2nd Lt.	28	6'	Brown	Hazel	Farmer	Ohio	Olney, IL	Wounded at Battle of Iuka.
Bail, John D.	Sgt.	35	5'8"	Black	Hazel	Lawyer	Ohio	Olney, IL	Wounded at Battle of Iuka.
Cotterell, Abraham	Sgt.	27	6'1"	Dark	Gray	Farmer	Kentucky	Claremont, IL	
Meryhew, Charles W.	Sgt.	–	–	–	–	–	–	–	
Notestine, William F.	Sgt.	19	5'11"	Light	Gray	Railroader	Illinois	Olney, IL	Veteran.
Ridgley, Elmore	1st Sgt.	30	6'1"	Sandy	Gray	Carpenter	Ohio	Olney, IL	

*Mentioned in Missouri Descriptive Roll but not in the National Archives.

Soldier	Rank	Age	Ht	Hair	Eyes	Occupation	Nativity	Place of Residence	Comment
Tade, Samuel	Sgt.	18	5'4"	Black	Brown	Farmer	Illinois	Claremont, IL	Veteran.
Wright, James	Sgt.	44	6'	Gray	Gray	Physician		Fairview, IL	Discharged 7/25/1862 Farmington, MS.
Baird, John	Corporal	25	6'3"	Light	Gray	Laborer	Pennsylvania	Claremont, IL	Absent recruiting since 7/28/1861; wounded at Vicksburg.
Butler, George	Corporal	19	5'11½"	Brown	Brown	Farmer	Illinois	Stringtown, IL	Veteran; wounded at Vicksburg.
Crawford, John T.	Corporal	22	5'10"	Brown	Hazel	Hoop Maker	Pennsylvania	Fairview, IL	Reduced in rank at his request.
Eckey, William M.	Corporal	19	5'11"	Light	Blue	Farmer	Illinois	Fairview, IL	Discharged 4/6/1863 from wounds in Battle of Corinth.
Eckley, Alvin	Corporal	20	5'6"	Dark	Black	Farmer	Illinois	Fairview, IL	Discharged 1/3/1863 from wounds at Battle of Corinth.
Finnell, George T.	Corporal	20	5'7"	Sandy	Gray	Wagon maker	Virginia	Clay City, IL	Veteran.
Johnson, James	Corporal	23	5'10"	Brown	Gray	Farmer	Ohio	Stringtown, IL	
Seymour, James S.	Corporal	35	6'1¼"	Black	Gray	Saddler	Ohio	Stringtown, IL	
Smith, Ambrose F.	Corporal	39	5'7½"	Brown	Blue	Farmer	Ohio	Fairview, IL	
Thomas, Alonzo G. W.	Corporal	19	5'7½"	Black	Gray	Carpenter	New Jersey	Olney, IL	Died 6/27/1863 of gunshot wound from Vicksburg.
Wilson, John E.	Corporal	19	6'	Light	Blue	Farmer	Indiana	Fairview, IL	
Woods, George F.	Corporal	18	5'4"	Light	Gray	Farmer	Illinois	Olney, IL	
Burden, David	Musician	27	5'10½"	Light	Blue	Salesman	England	Fairview, IL	Veteran; reduced in rank at his request.
Bensley, Jesse	Musician	43	5'3"	Brown	Gray	Farmer	Pennsylvania	Olney, IL	Discharged 1/22/1863 Cape Girardeau; disability.
Treadway, John W.	Musician	29	5'7"	Black	Blue	Hoop maker	Indiana	Fairview, IL	Died 11/7/1861 Cape Girardeau from consumption.
Lock, William H.	Wagoner	18	5'10½"	Brown	Gray	Saddler	Ireland	Olney, IL	
Anderson, Andrew	Pvt.	19	5'8"	Black	Dark	Farmer	Indiana	Claremont, IL	Discharged 10/25/1862.
Anderson, Benjamin	Pvt.	24	5'5½"	Brown	Brown	Farmer	Indiana	Claremont, IL	
Bartley, Edward T.	Pvt.	21	6'6½"	Brown	Hazel	Carpenter	Ohio	Fairview, IL	Veteran.
Bartley, Thomas	Pvt.	18	5'2"	Brown	Gray	Farmer	Ohio	Fairview, IL	Discharged 6/11/1862.
Bay, John F.	Pvt.	24	5'5"	Light	Gray	Farmer	Missouri	St. Louis, MO	Veteran; wounded at Battle of Corinth.
Behymer, Francis M.	Pvt.	24	5'7"	Dark	Black	Farmer	Ohio	Noble, IL	Veteran; wounded at Vicksburg.
Bland, William	Pvt.	33	5'10"	Light	Hazel	Farmer	Tennessee	Carondolet, MO	Died 3/14/1862 at Point Pleasant of disease.
Blew, John	Pvt.	27	5'9"	Brown	Gray	Farmer	Indiana	Claremont, IL	Discharged 10/28/1862, disability.
Boughan, Henry C.	Pvt.	19	5'10½"	Light	Gray	Farmer	Ohio	Stringtown, IL	
Brown, Dennis	Pvt.	20	5'5"	Brown	Hazel	Clerk	Ireland	Hadley, IL	Discharged 12/3/1862; wounded at Battle of Corinth.
Burgess, William	Pvt.	23	5'9"	Light	Gray	Farmer	Indiana	Olney, IL	Died of disease 7/1863 Louisiana; wounded at Vicksburg.

*Mentioned in Missouri Descriptive Roll but not in the National Archives.

Appendix A

Soldier	Rank	Age	Ht	Hair	Eyes	Occupation	Nativity	Place of Residence	Comment
Butler, Amos	Pvt.	22	5'10"	Black	Hazel	Farmer	Ohio	Stringtown, IL	Veteran.
Butler, John	Pvt.	24	5'10"	Dark	Dark	Farmer	Ohio	Stringtown, IL	Died 11/4/1863, buried at Vicksburg Ntl. Cemetery.*
Clancy, Edward	Pvt.	18	5'5½"	Light	Blue	Railroader	Ireland	Olney, IL	Died of disease 3/23/1862 Olney, IL.
Colvin, Solomon	Pvt.	19	5'5"	Brown	Black	Farmer	Ohio	Fairview, IL	Veteran.
Couch, William H.	Pvt.	18	5'2"	Light	Brown	Farmer	Ohio	Clay City, IL	
Eckley, Ephraim M.	Pvt.	19	5'6"	Dark	Black	Wood Cutter	Indiana	Fairview, IL	Wounded at Battle of Corinth.
Eppley, Jacob R.	Pvt.	24	5'6½"	Red	Gray	Farmer	Pennsylvania	Olney, IL	Died of wounds 5/29/1863 during siege of Vicksburg.
Febrenbarger/Fehreubaker, Joseph F.	Pvt.	19	5'6"	Black	Gray	Farmer	Germany	Noble, IL	
Fitzgerald, James J.	Pvt.	18	5'6"	Dark	Hazel	Farmer	Illinois	Noble, IL	Deserted 2/1862 Jackson, TN.*
Freeze, Robert H.	Pvt.	28	5'9"	Dark	Blue	Painter	Pennsylvania	Olney, IL	
Gaddy, George W.	Pvt.	20	5'11"	Light	Gray	Farmer	Illinois	Olney, IL	Veteran; wounded at Vicksburg.
Gallaspie, Lewis M.	Pvt.	21	5'10"	Light	Blue	Farmer	Illinois	Claremont, IL	Veteran.
Gallaspie, Willis	Pvt.	23	5'6"	Light	Blue	Farmer	Illinois	Claremont, IL	Died of fever 11/7/1861.
Grate, George	Pvt.	25	5'8"	Light	Hazel	Plasterer	Pennsylvania	Olney, IL	KIA 5/29/1862 Siege of Corinth.
Hardy, William	Pvt.	19	5'8½"	Light	Gray	Farmer	Illinois	Paris, IL	
Harmon, Elijah	Pvt.	–	–	–	–	–	–	–	Died 5/22/1863 at Vicksburg of gunshot wound.*
Herrington, Zachariah	Pvt.	20	5'9"	Dark	Black	Farmer	Illinois	Claremont, IL	Discharged 2/6/1863 due to wounds on 10/4/1862 from Battle of Corinth.
Holt, John	Pvt.	44	5'10½"	Brown	Blue	Minister	Illinois	Fairview, IL	Deserted 4/20/1862 Paducah.*
Hood, George F.	Pvt.	18	5'4"	Light	Gray	Farmer	Illinois	Olney, IL	Veteran; wounded at Battle of Corinth.
Hopper, Charles B.	Pvt.	37	5'4½"	Brown	Blue	Shoemaker	Kentucky	Claremont, IL	Transferred 1/3/1863 to Mississippi Marine Brigade.
Howland, John E.	Pvt.	21	5'8"	Dark	Dark	Cooper	Ohio	Fairview, IL	Died 5/21/1862 of consumption in Fairview, IL.
Jones, Samuel S.	Pvt.	33	6'	Brown	Gray	Farmer	N Carolina	Claremont, IL	
Judy, Henry C.	Pvt.	18	5'8½"	Black	Black	Farmer	Ohio	Sumner, IL	
Judy, John	Pvt.	18	5'4½"	Sandy	Hazel	Farmer	Ohio	Stringtown, IL	Veteran.
Kirkham/Kirkland, William H.	Pvt.	37	5'7"	Dark	Black	Farmer	Kentucky	Noble, IL	Discharged 5/22/1862. Farmington, MS.
Kussing, J.*	Pvt.	–	–	–	–	–	–	–	Buried at Chattanooga National Cemetery.*
Lytle/Little, George W.	Pvt.	21	5'10"	Light	Gray	Farmer	Indiana	Jasper Co., IL	Wounded at Vicksburg.
Meyers, James K.	Pvt.	18	5'6"	Brown	Gray	Farmer	–	Paris, IL	Died of disease 10/13/1861 Cape Girardeau.
Meyers, John	Pvt.	30	5'6"	Brown	Gray	Farmer	Germany	Calhoun, IL	Veteran.
Ogan, Joseph M.	Pvt.	22	6'	Sandy	Gray	Farmer	Ohio	Stringtown, IL	Discharged for disability Germantown 2/23/1863.
Pear, John	Pvt.	27	5'6½"	Brown	Blue	Farmer	Ohio	Olney, IL	Discharged due to disability 11/8/1862.
Pease, John T.	Pvt.	44	5'8"	Brown	Gray	Shoemaker	Kentucky	Hadley, IL	Discharged due to disability 11/26/1862.

*Mentioned in Missouri Descriptive Roll but not in the National Archives.

Soldier	Rank	Age	Ht	Hair	Eyes	Occupation	Nativity	Place of Residence	Comment
Penton, James	Pvt.	38	6'	Gray	Blue	Laborer	Delaware	Olney, IL	
Perry, John	Pvt.	28	6'	Brown	Hazel	Farmer	Ohio	Olney, IL	
Price, Benjamin	Pvt.	26	5'8½"	Black	Hazel	Carpenter	Ohio	Olney, IL	Mustered out 8/5/64 Memphis.
Rollen, John D.	Pvt.	44	5'8"	Gray	Gray	Farmer	Kentucky	Olney, IL	Wounded at Battle of Corinth.
Rollin, William F.	Pvt.	19	5'9"	Light	Gray	Blacksmith	Tennessee	Olney, IL	
Rush, Benjamin F.	Pvt.	26	5'4"	Red	Hazel	Farmer	Pennsylvania	Fairview, IL	
Rush, George W.	Pvt.	22	5'7½"	Red	Gray	Farmer	Ohio	Fairview, IL	
Ryan, Alexander Z.	Pvt.	21	5'6"	Brown	Hazel	Farmer	Ohio	Stringtown, IL	Veteran.
Scheible, Gottlieb	Pvt.	22	5'8"	Light	Gray	Farmer	Germany	Cape Girardeau, MO	
Seymour, John W.	Pvt.	27	5'9½"	Dark	Black	Farmer	Ohio	Hadley, IL	Wounded at Vicksburg.
Seymour, Mortimer H.	Pvt.	19	5'9¾"	Brown	Blue	Farmer	Ohio	Hadley, IL	Died 1/17/1863 of disease in LaGrange.
Shepherd, John W.	Pvt.	20	5'1½"	Sandy	Gray	Machinist	Ohio	St. Louis, MO	Transferred to Co. K; discharged 5/64.*
Simmons, Charles	Pvt.	18	5'7"	Brown	Dark	Farmer	Illinois	Calhoun, IL	Died 10/1863.
Smith, William	Pvt.	18	5'7"	Dark	Blue	Farmer	Illinois	Hadley, IL	
Snuffin, William	Pvt.	19	6'½"	Brown	Gray	Farmer	Ohio	Olney, IL	
Staley, Ahart	Pvt.	32	5'10"	Black	Hazel	Blacksmith	Illinois	Fairview, IL	Mustered out 8/5/1864.
Studdewell, Bosworth/Boswwell	Pvt.	22	5'8"	Brown	Gray	Farmer	Illinois	Claremont, IL	
Tade, Alexander S.	Pvt.	18	5'2"	Light	Blue	Farmer	Illinois	Claremont, IL	Died 9/6/1861 Cape Girardeau of disease.
Taylor, Edward S.	Pvt.	19	5'10"	Brown	Dark	Farmer	Illinois	Stringtown, IL	Veteran.
Thompson, Nathan	Pvt.	19	5'2"	Light	Blue	Farmer	Ohio	Stringtown, IL	
Walker, Daniel	Pvt.	21	5'5"	Light	Blue	Farmer	Missouri	Olney, IL	Veteran.
Wilkenson, Henry	Pvt.	42	6'	Gray	Blue	Cooper	England	Stringtown, IL	Discharged 3/7/1863 disability Germantown.
Wilson, William O. B.	Pvt.	32	5'8"	Light	Blue	Farmer	Ohio	Stingtown, IL	Died 2/12/1862 of disease Cape Girardeau.
Barger, William H.*	Pvt.	–	–	–	–	–	–	–	
Fletcher, Jesse*	Pvt.	–	–	–	–	–	–	–	
Gardner, J. E.*	Pvt.	–	–	–	–	–	–	–	
Hause, James*	Pvt.	–	–	–	–	–	–	–	
Hickam, R. R.*	Pvt.	–	–	–	–	–	–	–	
Hunter, Squire*	Pvt.	–	–	–	–	–	–	–	
Meyer, Henry*	Pvt.	–	–	–	–	–	–	–	
Richpart, B. A.*	Pvt.	–	–	–	–	–	–	–	
Vaughn, Caswell*	Pvt.	–	–	–	–	–	–	–	

Company F

Soldier	Rank	Age	Ht	Hair	Eyes	Occupation	Nativity	Place of Residence	Comment
Singleton, Amos	Captain	–	–	–	–	–	–	–	Died of wounds received at Battle of Iuka.
Cleland, William	Captain	21	5'11½"	Dark	Blue	Bookkeeper	Massachusetts	St. Louis, MO	Wounded at Battle of Iuka, Vicksburg, and Battle of Tupelo.
Smith, Charles	Sgt.–Captain	38	5'7¾"	Black	Hazel	Stonecutter	Maryland	Xenia, IL	Resigned.
Colclasure, William	1st Lt.	–	–	–	–	–	–	–	Veteran.
Finley, John T.	1st Lt.	27	5'8¾"	–	–	Teacher	Indiana	Xenia, IL	Mustered out 8/15/1864.
Gannon, Edward	2nd Lt.	–	–	–	–	–	–	–	
McConnel, Benjamin	2nd Lt.	–	–	–	–	–	–	–	Resigned 8/31/1861.
Weir, Elias W.	2nd Lt.	44	5'7¾"	Brown	Blue	Physician	Pennsylvania	Xenia, IL	Resigned 4/34/1864.
Cunningham, John	Sgt.	24	5'9¼"	Light	Hazel	Farmer	Indiana	Xenia, IL	KIA 9/19/1863 Iuka.
Finch, Walton H.	Sgt.	21	5'7"	Auburn	Gray	Farmer	Illinois	Xenia, IL	Veteran; wounded at Vicksburg.

*Mentioned in Missouri Descriptive Roll but not in the National Archives.

Appendix A

Soldier	Rank	Age	Ht	Hair	Eyes	Occupation	Nativity	Place of Residence	Comment
Hand/Hant, Benjamin	Sgt.	18	5'9"	Auburn	Gray	Farmer	Indiana	Xenia, IL	Veteran.
Gavin, Ludovic	Sgt.	28	5'11¾"	Light	Hazel	Farmer	Scotland	Xenia, IL	Veteran.
Gray, George	Sgt.	26	5'5¾"	Auburn	Hazel	Ropemaker	Ireland	Xenia, IL	Veteran.
Holman, Robert H.	Sgt.	24	5'8¾"	Light	Blue	Blacksmith	Illinois	Xenia, IL	Reduced in rank at his request.
Lawson, John P.	Sgt.	21	5'10¼"	Sandy	Hazel	Farmer	Kentucky	Xenia, IL	Discharged 1/24/1863 Germantown, TN, of gunshot wounds from Iuka.
McElyea, Wilford	Sgt.	19	5'7¾"	Light	Gray	Farmer	Indiana	Xenia, IL	Veteran.
Renick, Silas	Sgt.	27	5'7¼"	Light	Gray	Farmer	Indiana	Xenia, IL	Discharged due to gunshot received while recruiting.
Smith, Richard	Sgt.	44	5'10¼"	Brown	Hazel	Shoemaker	England	Xenia, IL	KIA 10/21/1861 Fredericktown.
Bayles, Thomas	Corporal	26	5'5"	Auburn	Blue	Farmer	Kentucky	Xenia, IL	Died of wounds at Vicksburg.
Caufield, Miner	Corporal	19	5'8½"	Brown	Hazel	Farmer	Indiana	Xenia, IL	
Chasteen, Onias O.	Pvt./Corporal	19	5'5¾"	Black	Hazel	Farmer	Illinois	Xenia, IL	Transferred to invalid corps 3/15/1864.*
Cummins, William E.	Corporal	27	5'11"	Black	Hazel	Carpenter	N. Carolina	Xenia, IL	Died 8/2/1862 of chronic diarrhea Farmington, MS.
Draper, Benjamin	Pvt./Corporal	33	5'9"	Brown	Gray	Blacksmith	Indiana	Xenia, IL	Veteran; reduced in rank 8/12/1862.
Draper, Elias	Corporal	26	5'11"	Brown	Gray	Blacksmith	Indiana	Xenia, IL	Veteran; wounded at Battle of Iuka.
Draper, Morris	Corporal	31	5'8¼"	Brown	Blue	Farmer	Indiana	Xenia, IL	
Fair, James W.	Corporal	34	5'8¼"	Auburn	Hazel	Machinist	Illinois	Salem, IL	KIA 10/3/1862 during Battle of Corinth.
Glassman, Peter	Corporal	20	5'2"	Brown	Gray	Farmer	Kentucky	Xenia, IL	Veteran.
Greenwood, George	Corporal	22	5'7¼"	Light	Blue	Farmer	Tennessee	Xenia, IL	Veteran.
McDaniel, Columbus	Corporal	20	5'9"	Auburn	Hazel	Farmer	Illinois	Xenia, IL	Discharged 7/24/1862 disability.
McLean, Samuel S.	Pvt./Corporal	23	5'10"	Brown	Blue	Shoemaker	Ohio	Xenia, IL	Veteran; reduced in rank 9/21/1862.
Miller, Calvin R.	Corporal	18	5'9½"	Light	Gray	Cooper	Illinois	Xenia, IL	Veteran.
Sanders, John	Pvt./Corporal	27	5'4¾"	Black	Hazel	Blacksmith	Illinois	Salem, IL	Veteran.
Stevens, John H.	Pvt./Corporal	32	5'10"	Auburn	Gray	Cooper	Ohio	Xenia, IL	Reduced in rank 8/12/1862.
Sutherland, Garret	Pvt./Corporal	20	5'6¾"	Brown	Hazel	Farmer	Indiana	Xenia, IL	Died 9/3/1864 Memphis, TN; wounded at Battle of Iuka.
Ayres, William	Drummer	19	5'4"	Auburn	Brown	Farmer	New York	Xenia, IL	Died 5/9/1862 Xenia, IL.
Hubbard, Benjamin	Fifer	29	5'11"	Black	Hazel	Farmer	Indiana	Xenia, IL	
Jourdan, James M.	Drummer	18	5'3½"	Brown	Hazel	Shoemaker	Illinois	Xenia, IL	Veteran.
Robertson, William E.	Wagoner	21	5'8½"	Brown	Hazel	Farmer	Ohio	Xenia, IL	Veteran.
Vickery, Littleton	Pvt./Wagoner	28	5'7"	Light	Blue	Farmer	Illinois	Salem, IL	Veteran.
Ayres, Theodore	Pvt.	18	5'5¾"	Light	Blue	Farmer	Mississippi	Xenia, IL	
Babcock, James W.*	Pvt.	42	5'4½"	Auburn	Blue	Farmer	Ohio	Flora, IL	Discharged 8/5/1864.
Babcock, William	Pvt.	17	5'3¼"	Auburn	Gray	Farmer	Illinois	Flora, IL	
Bayles, Elijah J.	Pvt.	22	5'9¼"	Light	Blue	Farmer	Kentucky	Xenia, IL	Veteran.
Blackledge, Martin	Pvt.	22	5'11"	Auburn	Blue	Farmer	Indiana	Flora, IL	Died 7/8/1862 at Camp Gaylord, MS, of typhoid fever.
Blackledge, Gideon*	Pvt.	18	5'11½"	Light	Blue	Farmer	Illinois	Flora, IL	Discharged at St. Louis for disability.
Blackledge, Theodore	Pvt.	17	5'7½"	Light	Blue	Farmer	Illinois	Flora, IL	Discharged at Keokuk for disability 11/22/1863.
Burcher, Robert	Pvt.	24	5'8¾"	Black	Hazel	Blacksmith	Ohio	Flora, IL	
Croughan, Michael	Pvt./Corporal	18	5'2"	Brown	Gray	Farmer	Ireland	Xenia, IL	Veteran.

*Mentioned in Missouri Descriptive Roll but not in the National Archives.

Soldier	Rank	Age	Ht	Hair	Eyes	Occupation	Nativity	Place of Residence	Comment
Cunningham, James	Pvt.	22	5'8¾"	Auburn	Gray	Farmer	Indiana	Flora, IL	KIA Vicksburg.
Cunningham, William	Pvt.	29	5'11"	Black	Hazel	Carpenter	N. Carolina	Xenia, IL	Dead.
Decker, James	Pvt.	18	5'7½"	Brown	Gray	Farmer	Ohio	Flora, IL	
Doyle, William	Pvt.	44	5'4½"	Auburn	Hazel	Laborer	Ireland	Xenia, IL	Discharged St. Louis 1/28/1863 for disability; wounded in Battle of Iuka.
Draper, Elijah	Pvt.	27	5'9½"	Sandy	Blue	Blacksmith	Indiana	Xenia, IL	
Easley, Hiram	Pvt.	27	5'8¼"	Brown	Gray	Farmer	Illinois	Xenia, IL	Veteran.
Geuth, William S.	Pvt.	25	5'11½"	Brown	Hazel	Farmer	Indiana	Flora, IL	
Gillam, Jesse	Pvt.	22	5'5½"	Auburn	Hazel	Farmer	Tennessee	Xenia, IL	Veteran.
Gillard, William H.	Pvt.	18	5'2"	Brown	Gray	Farmer	Illinois	Xenia, IL	Veteran.
Gillighan, James	Pvt.	31	5'7½"	Brown	Hazel	Laborer	Ireland	Xenia, IL	Discharged 12/28/1863.
Gillman, Charles	Pvt.	17	5'2¾"	Light	Blue	Farmer	Illinois	Salem, IL	Veteran.
Grossman, William*	Pvt.	–	–	–	–	–	–	–	Promoted to Corporal 12/1862.
Hagel, George W.	Pvt.	24	5'8"	Light	Blue	Farmer	Ohio	Flora, IL	Veteran.
Halterman, Joseph	Pvt.	19	5'3¾"	Light	Blue	Farmer	Ohio	Flora, IL	Veteran.
Haltermont, Andrew R.	Pvt.	24	5'9"	Light	Blue	Farmer	Ohio	Flora, IL	Died 1/22/1862.
Harman, David	Pvt.	21	5'8¼"	Light	Gray	Farmer	Ohio	Xenia, IL	Discharged 12/28/1862 from wounds at Iuka.
Harmon, Peter	Pvt.	23	5'5¾"	Auburn	Hazel	Farmer	Ohio	Xenia, IL	Veteran.
Haws, Thomas	Pvt.	23	5'7¼"	Auburn	Hazel	Farmer	Illinois	Xenia, IL	Veteran; wounded during Siege of Corinth.
Henson, William	Pvt.	19	5'7½"	Light	Gray	Farmer	Tennessee	Xenia, IL	Convicted of AWOL; Veteran.
Holman, John	Pvt.	18	5'8½"	Light	Gray	Farmer	Illinois	Xenia, IL	Veteran.
Holman, Robert H.	Pvt.	24	5'8¾"	Light	Blue	Blacksmith	Illinois	Xenia, IL	
Jordan, Frederick W.	Pvt.	23	5'6½"	Brown	Hazel	Shoemaker	Illinois	Xenia, IL	Veteran.
Kelley/Kelly, Edward	Pvt.	28	5'3¼"	Brown	Hazel	Cooper	Ireland	Xenia, IL	Deserted 4/25/1864 St. Louis.*
Leach, Lewis	Pvt.	26	5'5"	Brown	Gray	Farmer	Ohio	Flora, IL	Veteran.
McLean, Jesse H.	Pvt.	18	5'7"	Brown	Hazel	Farmer	Ohio	Xenia, IL	Veteran; wounded in Battle of Iuka.
Meek, William H.	Pvt.	21	5'7¼"	Light	Blue	Farmer	Ohio	Xenia, IL	Veteran.
Montague, Lewis F.	Pvt.	20	5'7½"	Light	Gray	Farmer	Kentucky	Xenia, IL	Veteran.
Muller, Henry*	Pvt.	–	–	–	–	–	–	–	
Parks, James W.	Pvt.	22	5'6½"	Brown	Blue	Farmer	Ohio	Xenia, IL	
Pettyjohn, Rueben	Pvt.	39	5'10"	Auburn	Hazel	Farmer	Ohio	Xenia, IL	Instantly killed at Battle of Vicksburg 5/22/1863.
Pitman, Mills	Pvt.	27	6'½"	Brown	Hazel	Farmer	Tennessee	Flora, IL	Died at Blackwater Bridge 7/19/1863.
Powell, Caleb	Pvt.	19	5'7¾"	Brown	Hazel	Farmer	Ohio	Xenia, IL	Died 3/26/1863 Jackson, TN.
Powell, John	Pvt.	22	5'6½"	Auburn	Hazel	Farmer	Ohio	Xenia, IL	Died 5/25/1863 Grand Gulf, MS.
Powell, Thomas	Pvt.	27	5'6"	Brown	Hazel	Farmer	Ohio	Xenia, IL	Died 5/14/1862 St. Louis.
Power, Robert	Pvt.	18	5'9¾"	Auburn	Gray	Farmer	Kentucky	Xenia, IL	Died 8/9/1862 Farmington, MS.
Randall, John	Pvt.	20	5'7"	Dark	Hazel	Farmer	Ohio	Xenia, IL	Transferred to Signal Corps 1864.
Rusher, Benjamin	Pvt.	18	5'4¼"	Brown	Blue	Farmer	Indiana	Xenia, Il	Veteran.
Robertson, James	Pvt.	21	5'8½"	Light	Blue	Farmer	Tennessee	Xenia, IL	Discharged Memphis 8/12/1863; wounded in Battle of Iuka.
Robinson, Eugene	Pvt.	31	5'8"	Auburn	Blue	Carpenter	New York	Xenia, IL	Died 10/4/1862 at Corinth, MS, from wounds.
Selby, John T.	Pvt.	41	5'8"	Brown	Hazel	Farmer	Maryland	Flora, IL	Transferred to Inv. Corps 3/1864.
Senkint, Augustus	Pvt.	33	5'1½"	Brown	Hazel	Farmer	Germany	Xenia, IL	
Smith, Thomas J.	Pvt.	22	5'6¾"	Brown	Hazel	Carriage Maker	Indiana	Xenia, IL	Deserted 1/21/1863.*
Spurgeon, David S.	Pvt.	22	5'9¾"	Auburn	Hazel	Farmer	Indiana	Xenia, IL	
Stockwell, Peter	Pvt.	25	5'7"	Brown	Hazel	Laborer	England	Xenia, IL	
Sutherland, William P.	Pvt.	22	5'7¼"	Brown	Hazel	Farmer	Indiana	Xenia, IL	Died 3/24/1862 Jackson, TN.
Swango, John H.	Pvt.	23	5'10"	Black	Black	Farmer	Kentucky	Xenia, IL	
Tibbs, William D.	Pvt.	37	5'3½"	Black	Gray	Farmer	Kentucky	Xenia, IL	Discharged 3/21/1862.
Vickery, Cyrus J.	Pvt.	18	5'6½"	Auburn	Blue	Farmer	Illinois	Xenia, IL	Veteran; wounded at Vicksburg.
Walker, Richard*	Pvt.	–	–	–	–	–	–	–	

*Mentioned in Missouri Descriptive Roll but not in the National Archives.

Soldier	Rank	Age	Ht	Hair	Eyes	Occu-pation	Nativity	Place of Residence	Comment
Weirman, John H.	Pvt.	21	5'6"	Auburn	Blue	Farmer	Pennsylvania	Xenia, IL	
Williamson, Thomas*	Pvt.								
Winchester, Lorenzo D.	Pvt.	28	5'5"	Brown	Hazel	Farmer	Tennessee	Xenia, IL	Wounded at Vicksburg.
Gentle, William S.*	Pvt.	–	–	–	–	–	–	–	Deserted 3/4/1863 at Richmond, LA.
Haws, Gilbert*	Pvt.	–	–	–	–	–	–	–	
Holman, Gilbert*	Pvt.	–	–	–	–	–	–	–	Transferred to Veteran Reserve Corps 5/5/63.
Jordan, Thomas*	Pvt.	–	–	–	–	–	–	–	Died; buried Jefferson Barracks National Cemetery, St. Louis, MO.
Mattox, Joseph*	Pvt.	–	–	–	–	–	–	–	
Mattox, William*	Pvt.	–	–	–	–	–	–	–	

Company G

Soldier	Rank	Age	Ht	Hair	Eyes	Occu-pation	Nativity	Place of Residence	Comment
Mieure, William	Captain	41	5'10"	Black	Black	Merchant		Lawrenceville, IL	Died 11/5/1861 of typhoid fever Cape Girardeau.
Carter, Charles M.	Captain	21	5'10"	Auburn	Black	Physician	Ohio	Lawrenceville, IL	
Gannon, Edward	1st Lt.	25	5'8"	Auburn	Blue	Moulder	Pennsylvania	Cape Girardeau, MO	Resigned 7/22/1863.
Laird, Benjamin R.	2nd Lt.	40	5'8½"	Light	Blue	Lawyer	Pennsylvania	Lawrenceville, IL	Resigned.
Bailey, David	2nd Lt.	19	5'8"	Dark	Blue	Farmer	Missouri	St. Louis, MO	
Aikin, William J.	1st Sgt.	25	5'6"	Dark	Gray	Carpenter	Ohio	Lawrenceville, IL	Wounded at Vicksburg.
Gray, Augustus N.	Sgt.	31	5'8½"	Dark	Blue	Shoemaker	Pennsylvania	Lawrenceville, IL	Died 6/13/1863 of wounds received at Vicksburg.
Hopkins, Horatio N.	1st Sgt.	28	5'8"	Brown	Blue	Teacher	Connecticut	Lawrenceville, IL	Discharged 12/18/1861.
Mieure, Thomas	Sgt.	25	6'	Dark	Blue	Farmer	Illinois	Lawrenceville, IL	Veteran.
Miller, Cyrus	Sgt.	25	6'1"	Dark	Blue	Moulder	Pennsylvania	Lawrence Co., IL	Wounded at Vicksburg.
Priest, George E.	Sgt.	29	5'7"	Auburn	Blue	Engineer	Pennsylvania	Lawrenceville, IL	
Wallace, William	Sgt.	32	5'11"	Dark	Blue	Blacksmith	New York	Lawrenceville, IL	Mustered out 6/25/1864.
Beckshire, John	Corporal	34	5'7"	Auburn	Blue	Carpenter	Kentucky	Lawrence Co., IL	
Fyffe, James A.	Corporal	22	5'10"	Dark	Hazel	Farmer	Illinois	Lawrence Co., IL	Discharged 4/8/1863 from wounds at Corinth.
Lehr, George W.	Corporal	26	5'10"	Light	Blue	Farmer	Ohio	Lawrence Co., IL	Wounded in Battle of Iuka, Battle of Corinth, and Vicksburg.
Lidey, Emanuel	Corporal	25	5'9"	Black	Black	Farmer	Ohio	Lawrence Co., IL	Died 9/19/1862 at Battle of Iuka.
McKelvey, George	Corporal	35	5'7"	Black	Blue	Carpenter	Pennsylvania	Lawrenceville, IL	Died 11/5/1861 Cape Girardeau.
Norton, Patrick	Corporal	24	5'7"	Dark	Gray	Farmer	Ireland	Lawrence Co., IL	Wounded in Battle of Iuka.
Rivers, Joseph	Corporal	23	5'8"	Auburn	Gray	Painter	Canada	Lawrenceville, IL	Discharged 4/8/1863 from wounds at Corinth.
Shields, Samuel	Corporal	23	5'11"	Dark	Gray	Farmer	N. Carolina	Lawrenceville, IL	Died 7/12/1862 Paducah.
Urich, George	Corporal	22	5'7"	Black	Black	Farmer	Ohio	Lawrenceville, IL	
Barnett, Mark	Musician	20	5'4"	Dark	Black	Farmer	Indiana	Lawrenceville, IL	Veteran.
Mills, George J.	Musician	18	5'8"	Auburn	Gray	Farmer	Illinois	Lawrence Co. IL	Veteran.
Allender, James	Wagoner	42	5'11"	Dark	Gray	Merchant	Kentucky	Lawrenceville, IL	Discharged 3/7/1863.
Able, John D.	Pvt.	18	5'9½"	Light	Brown	Farmer	Indiana	Lawrence Co., IL	Veteran; wounded in Battle of Iuka.
Adams, General W.	Pvt.	18	5'6"	Dark	Hazel	Farmer	Illinois	Lawrence Co., IL	Veteran; wounded in Battle of Iuka.
Andrews, James	Pvt.	36	5'10½"	Auburn	Blue	Carpenter	Alabama	Lawrenceville, IL	
Bartch, Anton*	Pvt.	–	–	–	–	–	–	–	
Bates, Jones M.	Pvt.	22	5'7"	Dark	Gray	Farmer	Missouri	Lawrence Co., IL	Veteran.

*Mentioned in Missouri Descriptive Roll but not in the National Archives.

Soldier	Rank	Age	Ht	Hair	Eyes	Occupation	Nativity	Place of Residence	Comment
Bathe, John	Pvt.	28	5'6½"	Auburn	Hazel	Farmer	Indiana	Lawrence Co., IL	Died of disease St. Louis 5/10/1862.
Berkshire, Samuel*	Pvt.	–	–	–	–	–	–	–	Discharged 1/1/1863.
Bishop, Miles	Pvt.	20	5'3"	Light	Gray	Farmer	Illinois	Lawrence Co., IL	Died 5/27/1863 Vicksburg, MS.
Black, Joseph A.*	Pvt.	21	5'4"	Dark	Blue	Farmer	Kentucky	Lawrence Co., IL	Discharged 10/24/1862 Jackson, TN.
Black, Walter	Pvt.	26	5'9"	Light	Gray	Farmer	Kentucky	Lawrenceville, IL	
Branstuller, John B.	Pvt.	23	5'9"	Light	Gray	Farmer	Indiana	Lawrence Co., IL	Died St. Louis 5/3/1862.
Brewer, James	Pvt.	17	5'10"	Dark	Black	Farmer	Ohio	Sparta, IL	Veteran; wounded at Vicksburg.
Brown, Samuel	Pvt.	34	5'7"	Light	Blue	Farmer	England	Lawrenceville, IL	Drowned Cape Girardeau 8/21/1861.
Brunner, Granville	Pvt.	19	5'8"	Light	Black	Farmer	Kentucky	Lawrence Co., IL	Died of disease 8/20/1863 Camp Sherman, MS; wounded at Battle of Corinth.
Burrell, Albert	Pvt.	18	5'5"	Auburn	Black	Farmer	Illinois	Lawrence Co., IL	Veteran.
Clark, Bedford	Pvt.	21	5'4"	Dark	Black	Blacksmith	Illinois	Lawrenceville, IL	Died 10/20/1862 Jackson, TN, of wounds.
Cochran, Jacob	Pvt.	27	5'6"	Dark	Hazel	Carpenter	Pennsylvania	Lawrence Co., IL	Wounded in Battle of Iuka.
Cochran, John	Pvt.	24	5'8"	Dark	Gray	Farmer	Illinois	Lawrence Co., IL	Discharged 12/18/1861.
Collins, John	Pvt.	24	5'8"	Auburn	Brown	Farmer	Illinois	Lawrence Co., IL	Died 2/4/1863 Jackson, TN.
Cunningham/Cummings, James	Pvt.	23	5'8½"	Red	Gray	Farmer	Kentucky	Lawrence Co., IL	KIA 5/22/1863 Vicksburg, MS; wounded at Battle of Corinth.
Davis, William	Pvt.	32	5'9"	Light	Blue	Moulder	Ireland	Lawrenceville, IL	Died 7/24/1862 Farmington, MS.
Datis, George	Pvt.	23	5'7"	Light	Blue	Carpenter	Ohio	Lawrenceville, IL	
Deaver, Royal	Pvt.	23	6'	Dark	Gray	Farmer	Kentucky	Lawrence Co., IL	
Dubois, Allen	Pvt.	22	6'1"	Dark	Black	Farmer	Illinois	Lawrence Co., IL	Wounded at Vicksburg.
Eddleman, John H.	Pvt.	18	6'¼"	Auburn	Black	Farmer	Missouri	Scott County, MO	Veteran.
Flinn, Patrick	Pvt.	25	6'8"	Sandy	Blue	Moulder	Ireland	St. Louis, MO	Died 11/29/1862 Cape Girardeau.
Gillen, Charles A.	Pvt.	27	6'	Light	Gray	Farmer	Pennsylvania	Lawrence Co., IL	Discharged 11/10/1862.
Gipson, John	Pvt.	17	5'5"	Light	Gray	Farmer	Kentucky	Lawrence Co., IL	Veteran.
Hager, John H.	Pvt.	21	5'8"	Dark	Dark	Farmer	Illinois	Lawrence Co., IL	
Highsmith, Leander J.	Pvt.	18	5'6"	Light	Blue	Farmer	Illinois	Lawrence Co., IL	
Hoover, Jonathan	Pvt.	43	5'9"	Light	Blue	Farmer	Virginia	Lawrence Co., IL	Discharged 8/6/1862.
Haskins, William	Pvt.	18	5'8"	Light	Black	Farmer	Illinois	Lawrence Co., IL	Died 8/12/1862 Camp Gaylord, MS.
Jennings, James M.	Pvt.	28	5'11"	Light	Blue	Farmer	Ohio	Lawrence Co., IL	Discharged 9/4/1863.
Kirkey, Joseph*	Pvt.	21	5'8"	Black	Black	Farmer	Indiana	Lawrence Co., IL	Veteran.
Kueff, Edwin	Pvt.	23	5'6"	Dark	Hazel	Farmer	Ohio	Lawrence Co., IL	Veteran; wounded in Battle of Iuka.
Kyger, George W.	Pvt.	21	5'6"	Light	Gray	Farmer	Illinois	Lawrence Co., IL	Discharged 7/1862.
Kyger, William	Pvt.	25	5'9"	Dark	Gray	Farmer	Illinois	Lawrence Co., IL	Veteran.
Lambert, Hezekiah	Pvt.	19	5'5"	Dark	Hazel	Farmer	Kentucky	St. Louis, MO	Deserted 12/4/1862.*
Lawson, Elijah A.	Pvt.	43	5'6½"	Light	Blue	Farmer	Kentucky	Lawrence Co., IL	
Lawson, Victor	Pvt.	18	5'5"	Light	Blue	Farmer	Illinois	Lawrence Co., IL	
Lewis, Franklin	Pvt.	24	5'8"	Light	Blue	Farmer	Illinois	Lawrence Co., IL	Discharged 3/17/1863 of wounds from Iuka.
Lewis, James P.	Pvt.	19	5'10"	Light	Brown	Farmer	Illinois	Lawrence Co., IL	
Miles, William	Pvt.	25	6'	Auburn	Black	Farmer	Indiana	–	Wounded at Vicksburg.
Mullhall, James	Pvt.	22	5'9½"	Light	Blue	Mason	Ireland	Lawrence Co., IL	Died 3/18/1862 Cape Girardeau.
Mumpower, John T.	Pvt.	18	5'5"	Light	Blue	Farmer	Illinois	Lawrence Co., IL	Discharged 1/1/1863; wounded in Battle of Iuka.
Norton, Solomon H.	Pvt.	21	5'8"	Red	Blue	Farmer	Illinois	Lawrence Co., IL	Veteran.
Owens, Charles W.	Pvt.	18	5'7"	Dark	Blue	Farmer	Indiana	Lawrence Co., IL	Absent sick.
Pea, William	Pvt.	28	5'9"	Auburn	Dark	Farmer	Illinois	Lawrence Co., IL	

*Mentioned in Missouri Descriptive Roll but not in the National Archives.

Appendix A

Soldier	Rank	Age	Ht	Hair	Eyes	Occupation	Nativity	Place of Residence	Comment
Pickrell, General	Pvt.	21	5'8"	Dark	Gray	Farmer	Ohio	Lawrenceville, IL	Wounded at Vicksburg.
Powers, William	Pvt.	24	5'4"	Light	Hazel	Clerk	Illinois	Lawrenceville, IL	Discharged due to disability 10/10/1861.
Quick, George	Pvt.	22	5'7"	Black	Black	Farmer	Ohio	–	Wounded in Battle of Iuka.
Rahen, Joseph*	Pvt.	33	5'7"	Light	Blue	Plasterer	Pennsylvania	Lawrenceville, IL	Veteran.
Reams, Samuel	Pvt.	24	5'9"	Auburn	Hazel	Carpenter	Ohio	Lawrence Co., IL	Died 11/25/1862 Corinth, MS; wounded at Battle of Corinth.
Reaves, Samuel*	Pvt.	–	–	–	–	–	–	–	
Redick, James	Pvt.	38	5'5"	Black	Blue	Farmer	Missouri	Dallas, MO	Discharged 5/24/1862, disability.
Renix, George W.	Pvt.	26	5'9"	Dark	Black	Farmer	Illinois	Lawrence Co., IL	Died 5/4/1862 Lawrence Co., IL.
Rudicil, Jacob	Pvt.	21	5'11"	Light	Gray	Farmer	Missouri	Perryville, MO	Discharged 9/4/1863.
Sandiford, Samuel J.	Pvt.	26	5'9"	Light	Black	Farmer	Indiana	Lawrence Co., IL	Discharged 10/25/1862 Disability.
Smith, James T.	Pvt.	26	5'8½"	Light	Blue	Farmer	Ohio	Lawrence Co., IL	Veteran.
Stewart, Alexander Amos	Pvt.	19	5'5"	Light	Black	Farmer	Ohio	Lawrence Co., IL	Veteran.
Swagler, Lewis	Pvt.	26	5'4"	Dark	Dark	Farmer	Switzerland	Lawrence Co., IL	Discharged 11/22/1862 from wounds received at Iuka.
Tanquary, Thomas	Pvt.	18	5'6"	Light	Gray	Musician	Illinois	Lawrenceville, IL	Transferred 9/4/1861 to Band.
Thompson, Alfred	Pvt.	25	5'7"	Light	Blue	Farmer	Kentucky	Lawrence Co., IL	Discharged 1/15/1863 disability.
Thompson, John*	Pvt.	17	5'10"	Light	Blue	Farmer	Illinois	Lawrence Co., IL	Deserted 4/14/1862 New Madrid, MO.
Thompson, William	Pvt.	19	5'10"	Light	Gray	Farmer	Illinois	Lawrence Co., IL	Wounded at Vicksburg.
Thorn, William	Pvt.	19	5'6"	Auburn	Blue	Clerk	Illinois	Lawrenceville, IL	
Wallace, Thomas	Pvt.	18	5'5"	Auburn	Gray	Farmer	Ohio	Lawrence Co., IL	Veteran; wounded in Battle of Iuka.
Waller, Rollin T.	Pvt.	27	5'6"	Dark	Blue	Farmer	Illinois	Lawrence Co., IL	Veteran.
White, Silas	Pvt.	28	5'6"	Light	Blue	Wagon Maker	Ohio	Lawrenceville, IL	Discharged 2/28/1863, disability.
Williams, John M.	Pvt.	31	5'8"	Light	Gray	Farmer	Ohio	Lawrence Co., IL	
Worstell, Joseph	Pvt.	18	5'7"	Light	Blue	Farmer	Ohio	Lawrence Co., IL	Mustered 8/24/1864.
Young, Samuel	Pvt.	33	5'8"	Brown	hazel	Farmer	Kentucky	Lawrence Co., IL	Veteran.
Arney, John*	Pvt.	–	–	–	–	–	–	–	
Boyle, James*	Pvt.	–	–	–	–	–	–	–	
Hall, Hiram*	Pvt.	–	–	–	–	–	–	–	Veteran.
Hamilton, Jason*	Pvt.	–	–	–	–	–	–	–	
Kueff, Thomas*	Pvt.	–	–	–	–	–	–	–	
Lane, Charles*	Pvt.	–	–	–	–	–	–	–	
Miller, James*	Pvt.	–	–	–	–	–	–	–	
Perkins, Albert*	Pvt.	–	–	–	–	–	–	–	
Rettie/Retler, Joseph*	Pvt.	–	–	–	–	–	–	–	
Ross, Robert*	Pvt.	–	–	–	–	–	–	–	Veteran.
Ryan, John*	Pvt.	–	–	–	–	–	–	–	
Wright, Thomas*	Pvt.	–	–	–	–	–	–	–	
Yeatman, Cornelius*	Pvt.	–	–	–	–	–	–	–	
Young, Thomas*	Pvt.	–	–	–	–	–	–	–	

Company H

Soldier	Rank	Age	Ht	Hair	Eyes	Occupation	Nativity	Place of Residence	Comment
Applegate, Edwin R.	Captain	20	5'5"	Dark	Gray	Carpenter	Ohio	Sumner, IL	Veteran.
Boatright, William	Captain	25	–	–	–	–	–	–	Transferred 3/20/1864 to 71st USCT.
Dollahan, Thomas	Captain	–	–	–	–	–	–	–	Resigned 6/18/1862.
Gray, Lewis	1st Lt.	–	–	–	–	–	–	–	Discharged; wounded at Vicksburg.
Kingsbury, Harley	2nd Lt.	–	–	–	–	–	–	–	Resigned 6/26/1863.
Adams, Zachariah	Sgt.	22	5'9"	Light	Blue	Farmer	Illinois	Sumner, IL	
Bedford, Isaac	Sgt.	–	–	–	–	–	–	–	KIA Battle of Iuka.

*Mentioned in Missouri Descriptive Roll but not in the National Archives.

Soldier	Rank	Age	Ht	Hair	Eyes	Occupation	Nativity	Place of Residence	Comment
Browning, Joseph	Sgt.	19	5'7"	Dark	Gray	Farmer	Ohio	Sumner, IL	
Cleland, William	Sgt.	26	5'11½"	Dark	Blue	Bookkeeper	Massachusetts	St. Louis, MO	
Dougherty, Jefferson	Sgt.	21	5'10"	Dark	Blue	Farmer	Indiana	Sumner, IL	Discharged 1/26/1864.*
Goodman, Charles	Sgt.	19	5'7"	Light	Gray	Farmer	Ohio	Sumner, IL	
Hamilton, Robert	Sgt.	22	5'6"	Light	Blue	Clerk	Scotland	St. Louis, MO	
Henry, David P.	Sgt.	28	5'8"	Brown	Blue	Carpenter	Illinois	Sumner, IL	Discharged 4/7/1863; wounded at Battle of Corinth.
Irwin, John H.	Sgt.	28	5'11"	Dark	Gray	Harness Maker	Ohio	Sumner, IL	Died 5/23/1863 of wounds from Battle of Vicksburg.
McNeal/McNeil, James	Sgt.	28	5'8"	Dark	Hazel	Saddler	Ohio	Sumner, IL	Veteran.
Reed, Moses	Sgt.							Sumner, IL	
Setchel, D. W.	Sgt.	18	5'8"	Dark	Blue	Teacher	New York	Sumner, IL	KIA 5/22/1863 Vicksburg.
Anderson, William A.	Corporal	21	5'9"	Dark	Blue	Farmer	Illinois	Sumner, IL	
Browning, Elias	Corporal	21	5'9"	Dark	Gray	Farmer	Ohio	Sumner, IL	
Conrad, Samuel	Corporal	22	5'6"	Light	Blue	Farmer	Pennsylvania	Sumner, IL	Veteran.
Legg, George	Corporal	–	–	–	–	–	–	Sumner, IL	
Mathewson, William	Corporal	21	5'5"	Light	Blue	Farmer	Illinois	Sumner, IL	Veteran.
Ridgeley/Ridgley, William	Corporal	23	6'1"	Light	Gray	Farmer	Ohio	Sumner, IL	Veteran; wounded at Vicksburg.
Quinn, Michael	Corporal	22	5'5"	Dark	Blue	Farmer	Ireland	Sumner, IL	
Adams, Josiah	Musician	18	5'5"	Dark	Gray	Farmer	Illinois	Sumner, IL	Veteran; wounded in Battle of Iuka.
Anderson, William	Musician	19	5'4"	Dark	Gray	Farmer	New Mexico	St. Louis, MO	Wounded at Vicksburg.
Thomas, John J.	Wagoner	20	5'9"	Light	Blue	Blacksmith	Ohio	Sumner, IL	Veteran.
Anderson, Pvt. Franklin		24	5'5"	Light	Blue	Farmer	Ohio	Sumner, IL	Discharged 9/20/1862; wounded at Battle of Corinth.
Boler, Albert	Pvt.	20	5'6"	Light	Blue	Farmer	Germany	Sumner, IL	
Burvill, Francis M.	Pvt.	18	5'5½"	Dark	Blue	Farmer	Illinois	Sumner, IL	Veteran.
Conrad, John	Pvt.	20	5'6"	Light	Blue	Farmer	Illinois	Sumner, IL	Discharged 12/31/1862.
Daniels, George W.	Pvt.	18	5'7"	Dark	Hazel	Farmer	Ohio	Sumner, IL	Veteran.
Daniels, Samuel	Pvt.	19	5'8"	Light	Blue	Farmer	Illinois	Sumner, IL	Wounded in Battle of Iuka and Vicksburg.
Daniels, William H.	Pvt.	20	5'8"	Light	Blue	Farmer	Ohio	Sumner, IL	Veteran; captured at Vicksburg.
Delapp, Thomas	Pvt.	20	6'1"	Light	Blue	Farmer	Illinois	Sumner, IL	Died of disease in Richmond prison 3/27/1864.
Dudley, Joshua	Pvt.	18	5'6"	Dark	Hazel	Farmer	Illinois	Sumner, IL	
Ferguson, Anderson M.*	Pvt.	–	–	–	–	–	–	–	Died of disease 9/29/1861.
Fullen, Godfrey	Pvt.	23	6'	Light	Gray	Farmer	Indiana	Sumner, IL	Veteran.
Goodman, Henry	Pvt.	25	6'	Dark	Light	Farmer	Ohio	Sumner, IL	
Hicks, William	Pvt.	22	5'8"	Dark	Hazel	Farmer	Illinois	Sumner, IL	Died of disease 12/9/1861.
Higgins, George W.	Pvt.	21	6'	Light	Dark	Farmer	Illinois	Sumner, IL	Veteran.
Holmes, Marion	Pvt.	19	5'7"	Brown	Black	Farmer	Ohio	Sumner, IL	
Hume, Alexander	Pvt.	19	5'10"	Light	Blue	Shoemaker	Ohio	Sumner, IL	
Johns, Elias	Pvt.	32	6'	Red	Gray	Carpenter	Ohio	Sumner, IL	Deserted 9/15/1861.*
Johnson, Jacob	Pvt.	22	5'8"	Black	Blue	Farmer	Ohio	Sumner, IL	Veteran; wounded at Vicksburg.
Kaley, Henry P.	Pvt.	18	5'8"	Dark	Hazel	–	Ohio	Sumner, IL	Veteran; wounded in Battle of Iuka.
Kellogg, Elijah	Pvt.	22	5'7"	Red	Gray	Farmer	Illinois	Sumner, IL	Veteran.

*Mentioned in Missouri Descriptive Roll but not in the National Archives.

Soldier	Rank	Age	Ht	Hair	Eyes	Occupation	Nativity	Place of Residence	Comment
Kerney, Timothy	Pvt.	31	5'5"	Light	Blue	Miner	Scotland	St. Louis, MO	Transferred to Inv. Corps 3/5/1864*; wounded in Battle of Iuka.
Laird, John H.	Pvt.	30	5'8"	Auburn	Gray	Teacher	Maryland	St. Louis, MO	Transferred to Vet. Reserve Corps 4/10/64*; wounded at Battle of Corinth.
Lagow, Alfred G.	Pvt.	24	5'8"	Light	Gray	Printer	Indiana	Palestine, IL	Promoted to Corporal.
Longenecker, Addison	Pvt.	20	5'7"	Light	Blue	Farmer	Illinois	Sumner, IL	
Mann, Samuel P.	Pvt.	33	5'9"	Black	Hazel	Farmer	Ohio	Sumner, IL	
Martin, Henry C.	Pvt.	18	5'4"	Light	Blue	Farmer	Illinois	Sumner, IL	Veteran.
McColpin, George R.	Pvt.	27	5'8"	Dark	Hazel	Farmer	Illinois	Sumner, IL	Discharged 10/28/1862.
McDonel, John	Pvt.	23	5'7"	Dark	Gray	Farmer	Mississippi	Cape Girardeau., MO	Veteran.
McGuire, James	Pvt.	22	5'5¼"	Brown	Blue	Farmer	Ireland	St. Louis, MO	Transferred to Inv. Corps 2/63.*
McNeal, Allen	Pvt.	24	5'7"	Light	Blue	Blacksmith	Ohio	Sumner, IL	
McNeal, Fred E.	Pvt.	18	5'9"	Light	Blue	Farmer	Ohio	Sumner, IL	Veteran.
Meeker, Holsey	Pvt.	18	5'4"	Light	Hazel	Farmer	Indiana	Sumner, IL	Veteran.
Meeker, Thomas	Pvt.	18	5'6"	Dark	Dark	Farmer	Indiana	Sumner, IL	Veteran.
Mills, John H.	Pvt.	21	5'8"	Light	Blue	Farmer	Illinois	Sumner, IL	Died 6/20/1863 of wounds at Vicksburg, buried Mississippi River Ntl. Cemetery Memphis; wounded in Battle of Iuka.
Moler, Solomon	Pvt.	22	5'7"	Dark	Gray	Farmer	Ohio	Sumner, IL	Died of disease 7/22/1863; wounded at Vicksburg.
Moran, John	Pvt.	32	5'10"	Dark	Brown	Laborer	Indiana	St. Louis, MO	Died 5/31/1863 of wounds from Vicksburg, buried in Vicksburg Ntl. Cemetery; wounded in Battle of Iuka.
Morris, James	Pvt.	23	6'	Light	Blue	Farmer	Indiana	Sumner, IL	
Murphey, William	Pvt.	18	5'7"	Dark	Brown	Farmer	Illinois	Sumner, IL	
Parker, Isaac T. G.	Pvt.	23	5'7"	Black	Hazel	Farmer	Illinois	Sumner, IL	
Pearson, William B.	Pvt.	18	5'7"	Light	Blue	Farmer	Illinois	Sumner, IL	
Pollock, John	Pvt.	18	5'8"	Dark	Blue	Farmer	Ohio	Sumner, IL	
Pickering, Francis*	Pvt.	24	5'7"	Dark	Blue	Farmer	Ohio	Sumner, IL	Discharged 7/29/1862.
Pickering, James	Pvt.	22	5'8"	Light	Blue	Farmer	Ohio	Sumner, IL	Died 6/7/1862 of disease.
Richards, Jeremiah	Pvt.	21	5'8"	Dark	Gray	Farmer	Illinois	Sumner, IL	
Roaher/Rohar, David	Pvt.	24	5'10"	Light	Gray	Farmer	Illinois	Sumner, IL	Veteran.
Salisbury, David A.	Pvt.	22	5'7"	Light	Blue	Farmer	Illinois	Sumner, IL	Veteran.
Salisbury/Saulsbury, Orlando*	Pvt.	–	–	–	–	–	–	–	Discharged 9/26/1861, disability.
Scyoc, John V.	Pvt.	42	5'8½"	Light	Blue	Farmer	Pennsylvania	Sumner, IL	Discharged for disability 8/23/1862.
Sherman, Charles	Pvt.	22	5'6½"	Black	Blue	Schoolteacher	Ohio	Sumner, IL	Discharged 8/11/1863 for promotion.
Snoden, James	Pvt.	19	5'7"	Dark	Hazel	Farmer	Kentucky	Sumner, IL	
Spilkey, Edward	Pvt.	19	5'8"	Light	Blue	Farmer	Illinois	Sumner, IL	
Thompson, Alonzo H.	Pvt.	–	–	–	–	–	–	–	Discharged 10/20/1861, disability.
Treadway, Jacob	Pvt.	22	5'5"	Dark	Blue	Farmer	Indiana	Sumner, IL	Veteran.
Turner, Charles N.*	Pvt.	–	–	–	–	–	–	–	Deserted 8/27/1861.*
Waldrop, Ezekiel	Pvt.	22	5'10"	Dark	Gray	Farmer	Illinois	Sumner, IL	Discharged 8/20/1862, disability, wounded during Siege of Corinth.
Wisner, Benjamin*	Pvt.	–	–	–	–	–	–	–	–
Wolverton, Elza	Pvt.	21	5'4"	Dark	Blue	Farmer	Indiana	Sumner, IL	Transferred to Inv. Corps.
York, George	Pvt.	29	6'1½"	Dark	Blue	Farmer	Illinois	Sumner, IL	
York, Isaac N.*	Pvt.	–	–	–	–	–	–	–	Veteran.
Zimmerman, Luther	Pvt.	19	5'7"	Light	Blue	Farmer	Pennsylvania	Sumner, IL	Veteran.

*Mentioned in Missouri Descriptive Roll but not in the National Archives.

Soldier	Rank	Age	Ht	Hair	Eyes	Occupation	Nativity	Place of Residence	Comment
Adams, Samuel*	Pvt.	–	–	–	–	–	–	–	
Albright, William A.*	Pvt.	–	–	–	–	–	–	–	
Dephenbach, John*	Pvt.	–	–	–	–	–	–	–	
Diew, Franklin M.*	Pvt.	–	–	–	–	–	–	–	
Johnson, Mathew*	Pvt.	–	–	–	–	–	–	–	Veteran.
Kern/Keirn John*	Pvt.	–	–	–	–	–	–	–	Died 9/27/1861 Cape Girardeau.
McClain, Dudley*	Pvt.	–	–	–	–	–	–	–	
Rodhouse, Thomas W.*	Pvt.	–	–	–	–	–	–	–	
Young, William*	Pvt.	–	–	–	–	–	–	–	

Company I

Soldier	Rank	Age	Ht	Hair	Eyes	Occupation	Nativity	Place of Residence	Comment
Barnum, William L.	Capt–Colonel	32	–	–	–	Merchant	New Jersey	Springfield, IL	
Osgood, Charles H.	Captain	23	–	–	–	Physician	Ohio	Bethel, IL	Wounded in Battle of Iuka.
Hathorn, John	2nd Lt.	29	5'10"	Brown	Blue	Miller	Ohio	Bethel, IL	Resigned 7/5/1863.
Hathorn, McGuire	2nd Lt.	20	5'11½"	Sandy	Blue	Farmer	Ohio	Bethel, IL	Veteran.
Adams, George C.	Sgt.	35	5'8"	Light	Blue	Farmer	Illinois	Versailles, IL	
Boulden, William H.	Sgt.	25	5'10"	Light	Blue	Farmer	Illinois	Barry, IL	Veteran.
Courtney, Liberty	Sgt.	43	5'5"	Sandy	Blue	Carpenter	–	Bethel, IL	Discharged 11/15/1861.
Ethel, Charles H.	Sgt.	18	5'9"	Dark	Hazel	Farmer	Illinois	Bethel, IL	Mustered out 10/10/1864.
Hamilton, Noah P.	Sgt.	31	6'	Sandy	Blue	Farmer	Kentucky	Bethel, IL	Discharged 7/12/1862.
Davis, Harrison N.	1st Sgt.	22	5'8½"	Light	Black	Farmer	Maine	Bethel, IL	Veteran; wounded at Battle of Corinth.
Hummer, James	1st Sgt.	38	–	–	–	Minister	–	Bethel, IL	Resigned 5/17/1862.
Randall, Nelson	Sgt.	32	5'10½"	Brown	Black	Wagon Maker	Ohio	Bethel, IL	
Spicer, Cyrus J.	Sgt.	27	6'	Light	Blue	Farmer	Delaware	Barry, IL	Died 6/15/1863 of gunshot wound, Vicksburg; wounded in Battle of Iuka.
Swan, James M.	Sgt.	21	5'10"	Brown	Blue	Farmer	Ohio	Bethel, IL	
Warner, Wesley S.	Sgt.	22	6'	Dark	Hazel	Farmer	Illinois	Bethel, IL	Veteran.
Ethel, James H.	Corporal	26	5'6"	Sandy	Blue	–	Illinois	Bethel, IL	Died 5/13/1862 of chronic diarrhea.
Hummer, George W.	Corporal	30	6'1"	Black	Blue	Farmer	Virginia	Bethel, IL	Died 11/18/1861 Bethel, IL, of consumption.
Johnson, David B.	Corporal	25	6'2"	Black	Hazel	Farmer	Ohio	Barry, IL	Wounded at Battle of Corinth.
Pasley, David C.	Drummer	20	5'8"	Brown	Gray	Farmer	Illinois	Bethel, IL	
McPherson, Anson C.	Musician	25	5'8"	Sandy	Blue	Farmer	Illinois	Bethel, IL	Discharged 1/27/1863.
Wyatt, John	Wagoner	29	5'9"	Black	Black	Farmer	Illinois	Bethel, IL	KIA 5/22/1863 Vicksburg.
Bailey, John E.	Pvt.	30	5'8"	Auburn	Blue	Farmer	Kentucky	Bethel, IL	Veteran.
Bascue, William H.	Pvt.	19	5'5½"	Brown	Blue	Farmer	Virginia	Bethel, IL	Veteran.
Baul, Cyrus	Pvt.	18	5'8"	Brown	Blue	Farmer	Pennsylvania	Coopertown, IL	Veteran; wounded in Battle of Iuka.
Baymer, Albert	Pvt.	20	5'11¼"	Brown	Blue	Cooper	Maine	Bethel, IL	Died 11/1862 of wounds from Iuka.
Bennett, James	Pvt.	18	5'3½"	Black	Hazel	Farmer	Illinois	Meredosia, IL	Veteran.
Berry, Thomas	Pvt.	41	–	–	–	Farmer	–	Bethel, IL	Discharged 10/5/1861.
Beathard, Thomas	Pvt.	18	5'4½"	Light	Blue	Farmer	Ohio	Concord, IL	Died 7/17/1863 at Farmington of chronic diarrhea.
Beauchamp, Samuel	Pvt.	19	5'6½"	Dark	Blue	Farmer	Illinois	Meredosia, IL	Veteran; wounded at Vicksburg.
Boaryour, Thomas	Pvt.	28	5'6½"	Black	Gray	Farmer	Ireland	Morgan County, IL	
Bosley, Phillip	Pvt.	22	6'	Brown	Gray	Farmer	Illinois	Bethel, IL	Discharged 7/27/1862.
Bourn, Jeremiah*	Pvt.	28	5'9¼"	Brown	Blue	Farmer	Ohio	Morgan County, IL	
Bower, Edmond	Pvt.	21	5'11"	Black	Gray	Farmer	Illinois	Barry, IL	Died 6/17/1862 of wounds during the Siege of Corinth.

*Mentioned in Missouri Descriptive Roll but not in the National Archives.

Appendix A

Soldier	Rank	Age	Ht	Hair	Eyes	Occupation	Nativity	Place of Residence	Comment
Bower, Niemiah	Pvt.	18	5'7½"	Brown	Blue	Farmer	Ohio	–	
Byrnes, William	Pvt.	18	5'8"	Brown	Blue	Farmer	Ohio	Morgan County, IL	Died at Corinth 1/14/1862 of fever.
Capper/Copper, William H.	Pvt.	22	5'4½"	Light	Gray	Farmer	Ohio	Bethel, IL	Discharged 11/28/1862 for wounds of Battle of Iuka.
Chapman, James H.	Pvt.	30	5'6½"	Brown	Blue	Farmer	Illinois	Bethel, IL	Died 6/15/1862 of typhoid fever.
Chapman, Daniel S.	Pvt.	24	5'8½"	Brown	Blue	Farmer	Illinois	Bethel, IL	Veteran.
Chapman, William	Pvt.	18	5'8½"	Dark	Hazel	Farmer	Pennsylvania	Beardstown, IL	KIA 9/19/1862 Iuka.
Cine/Caine, Jacob	Pvt.	23	5'10"	Brown	Blue	Farmer	Virginia	Bethel, IL	Wounded at Battle of Corinth.
Clark, George	Pvt.	19	5'11"	Black	Hazel	Farmer	Ohio	Brown County, IL	
Clark, Thaddeus	Pvt.	22	5'9½"	Brown	Gray	Farmer	–	Bethel, IL	
Cornwall, Edward*	Pvt.	21	5'7½"	Brown	Gray	Farmer	Illinois	Barry, IL	Veteran.
Crim, George W.	Pvt.	22	6'	Black	Hazel	Farmer	Virginia	Concord, IL	Veteran.
Cutler, Thomas R.	Pvt.	18	5'6"	Black	Gray	Farmer	Illinois	Bethel, IL	Veteran.
Davis, William	Pvt.	–	–	–	–	–	–	–	Discharged 10/5/1861.
Detrich, George H.	Pvt.	31	5'4"	Black	Gray	Farmer	Germany	Beardstown, IL	Wounded at Vicksburg.
Easton, John G.	Pvt.	30	5'4"	Light	Blue	Farmer	Kentucky	Versailles, IL	Killed 9/19/1862 during Battle of Iuka.
Elliott, Edgar	Pvt.	36	5'6"	Black	Blue	–	Kentucky	Meredosia, IL	Died 11/10/1861 due to measles.
Evans, John	Pvt.	27	5'8½"	Auburn	Hazel	Shoemaker	England	Concord, IL	Wounded during the Red River Campaign.
Filey, William H.	Pvt.	21	5'9½"	Dark	Hazel	Farmer	Illinois	Concord, IL	Discharged 11/25/1862.
Floyd, John*	Pvt.	21	5'7½"	Sandy	Blue	Farmer	Ireland	Bethel, IL	Died 6/8/1863 of wounds from Siege of Vicksburg.*
Garmon, Robert	Pvt.	23	5'10"	Brown	Hazel	Farmer	Tennessee	Meredosia, IL	Died 10/23/1861 Cape Girardeau of measles.
Hackett, Thomas J.	Pvt.	26	5'4"	Brown	Blue	Minister	Ireland	Concord, IL	Veteran.
Hadsell, George M.	Pvt.	25	5'8½"	Brown	Blue	Farmer	New York	Barry, IL	Veteran.
Hartman, Frank H.	Pvt.	21	5'4"	Light	Blue	Farmer	Germany	Bethel, IL	Veteran; wounded at Vicksburg.
Hathhorn, James	Pvt.	23	5'10"	Brown	Blue	Farmer	Ohio	Bethel, IL	KIA 5/22/1863 Vicksburg.
Henderson, Francis M.	Pvt.	23	5'10"	Auburn	Blue	Farmer	Illinois	Bethel, IL	Discharged 5/20/1862.
Henry, Jesse W.	Pvt.	25	5'8"	Brown	Blue	Farmer	Illinois	Versailles, IL	
Jackson, William M.	Pvt.	18	5'7"	Brown	Blue	Farmer	England	Bethel, IL	KIA Vicksburg 5/22/1863.
Johnson, George H.	Pvt.	18	6'1½"	Black	Hazel	Farmer	Ohio	Barry, IL	Discharged 5/13/1862.*
Kimball, Joseph A.*	Pvt.	18	5'	–	–	–	–	Bethel, IL	Died 9/30/1861 of typhoid fever at St. Louis.
Kline, Jacob L.	Pvt.	18	5'9½"	Brown	Blue	Farmer	Pennsylvania	Concord, IL	Veteran.
Lake, Harrison	Pvt.	18	5'9"	Sandy	Blue	Farmer	Kentucky	Meredosia, IL	Veteran.
Lombard, Joseph	Pvt.	24	5'9½"	Brown	Blue	Teacher	Connecticut	Concord, IL	Discharged to enlist U.S. Medical Corps.*
Mackey, William A.	Pvt.	19	5'11"	Brown	Gray	Farmer	Missouri	Bethel, IL	Veteran.
Maple, William J.	Pvt.	20	5'7½"	Black	Gray	Farmer	Illinois	Versailles, IL	Veteran; wounded during Red River Campaign.
Marion, William H.	Pvt.	18	5'6"	Brown	Blue	Farmer	New Jersey	Barry, IL	Veteran; wounded at Vicksburg.
Mason, William T.	Pvt.	27	5'9½"	Brown	Black	Blacksmith	Illinois	Bethel, IL	Discharged 11/28/1862.
McKinney, William D.	Pvt.	24	5'11½"	Light	Blue	Farmer	Virginia	Aronsville, IL	Discharged 3/17/1863.
McPherson, Stephen	Pvt.	27	5'10½"	Sandy	Blue	Farmer	Virginia	Bethel, IL	Wounded at Vicksburg.
Messer, Levi	Pvt.	33	5'5½"	Black	Hazel	Farmer	Tennessee	Whitehall, IL	Wounded during the Siege of Corinth 5/1862.
Meyer, Andrew F.	Pvt.	27	6'	Brown	Blue	Farmer	Germany	Bethel, IL	
Miller, David C.*	Pvt.	18	5'5½"	Black	Hazel	Farmer	Tennessee	Concord, IL	Deserted 8/13/1861 Camp Scott, MO.*
Miller, William B.	Pvt.	29	5'4½"	Light	Blue	Farmer	Pennsylvania	Bethel, IL	Veteran.
Millstead, James M.	Pvt.	34	6'½"	Brown	Blue	Farmer	Illinois	Bethel, IL	Discharged 2/24/1863, disability.
Miras, John F.	Pvt.	22	5'10½"	Black	Black	Farmer	Illinois	Glasco, IL	Discharged 5/20/1862.

*Mentioned in Missouri Descriptive Roll but not in the National Archives.

Soldier	Rank	Age	Ht	Hair	Eyes	Occupation	Nativity	Place of Residence	Comment
Newman, Christopher	Pvt.	19	5'9"	Brown	Hazel	Farmer	Illinois	Bethel, IL	
O'Brien, Patrick	Pvt.	27	5'3½"	Black	Hazel	Farmer	Ireland	Concord, IL	Veteran.
Orr, Elijah B.*	Pvt.	20	5'10"	Dark	Hazel	Farmer	Illinois	Coopertown, IL	Died 9/29/1861 Cape Girardeau, measles.
Preston/Potter, Newton A.	Pvt.	24	5'10"	Light	Blue	Farmer	Ohio	Meredosia, IL	Veteran.
Plank, Peter	Pvt.	18	5'6½"	Brown	Blue	Farmer	Illinois	Concord, IL	
Reed, Cyrus M.	Pvt.	21	5'9"	Dark	Gray	Farmer	Illinois	Glasco, IL	
Result, J.*	Pvt.	–	–	–	–	–	–	–	Buried at National Cemetery Memphis.*
Rogers, George*	Pvt.	20	5'8½"	Light	Blue	Farmer	Illinois	Bethel, IL	
Rogers, Jeremiah*	Pvt.	18	5'9"	Light	Blue	Farmer	Illinois	Bethel, IL	
Rook, William	Pvt.	27	5'9½"	Light	Blue	Farmer	Illinois	Versailles, IL	Died 6/4/1862 in St. Louis of chronic disease.
Russell, Nicholas	Pvt.	24	5'5½"	Black	Hazel	Farmer	Germany	Bethel, IL	Died 10/23/1861 at Cape Girardeau.
Russell, James	Pvt.	23	–	Black	Black	Blacksmith		Bethel, IL	Died 10/23/1861.
Seager, John C.	Pvt.	20	5'6"	Light	Blue	Farmer	Germany	Bethel, IL	Discharged 11/29/1862, gunshot wound from Iuka.
Shoopman, David O.	Pvt.	23	6'	Dark	Blue	Farmer	Illinois	Beardstown, IL	Wounded at Vicksburg.
Shreves, Thomas J.	Pvt.	24	5'6"	Black	Brown	Cook	Pennsylvania	Meredosia, IL	Discharged 11/29/1862, disability.
Smith, Daniel	Pvt.	21	5'11"	Dark	Hazel	Farmer	Canada	Meredosia, IL	
Smith, Richard P.	Pvt.	34	5'10"	Black	Gray	Carpenter	Kentucky	Concord, IL	Discharged 2/23/1863, gun shot wound from Corinth.
Snowdon, Willis S.	Pvt.	33	5'8"	Light	Gray	Farmer	Kentucky	Exeter, IL	Discharged 8/2/1862, disability.
Spicer, William H.	Pvt.	23	5'9½"	Light	Blue	Farmer	Delaware	Barry, IL	
Springer, Job	Pvt.	25	5'11½"	Black	Hazel	Farmer	Virginia	Virginia, IL	
Sullins, Josiah M.	Pvt.	28	5'9"	Dark	Blue	Farmer	Tennessee	Bethel, IL	Died 6/2/1863 of wounds from Vicksburg.
Sweat, Nephi	Pvt.	24	5'10"	Dark	Blue	Farmer	Ohio	Exeter, IL	Discharged 7/27/1862, disability.
Thomas, Elijah	Pvt.	20	–	–	–	–	–	Meredosia, IL	
Thomas, Jeremiah L.	Pvt.	18	5'8½"	Light	Blue	Farmer	Illinois	Meredosia, IL	Discharged 7/7/1862, disability.
Thompson, Willis C.	Pvt.	20	5'8"	Dark	Black	Farmer	Missouri	Meredosia, IL	Died 3/3/1862 Commerce, MO.
Triebert, Christian	Pvt.	23	5'7"	Light	Gray	Farmer	Germany	Cass County, IL	Veteran.
Vance, Luther	Pvt.	18	5'8"	Sandy	Blue	Farmer	Ohio	Bethel, IL	Died 9/19/1862 of wounds at Iuka.
Wesser, Levi*	Pvt.	–	–	–	–	–	–	–	
Wroe/Rowe/Grove, Columbus	Pvt.	20	6'½"	Dark	Gray	Farmer	Illinois	Bethel, Il	Died 6/15/1864 of wounds near Lake Village, AR.
Wyatt, John	Pvt.	–	–	–	–	–	–	–	KIA 5/22/1863 Vicksburg.
Noble, William*									
Thompson, William*									
Thomas, James*									

Company K

Soldier	Rank	Age	Ht	Hair	Eyes	Occupation	Nativity	Place of Residence	Comment
Stewart, William S.	Captain	–	–	–	–	Lawyer	–	St. Louis, MO	Resigned 4/30/1864.
Kendall, Cyrus D.	Captain	23	5'8"	Brown	Gray	Lawyer	Pennsylvania	Clay Co., IL	Wounded at Battle of Corinth.
Foster, Charles	1st Lt.	–	–	–	–	Lawyer	–	St. Louis, MO	ADC General Lee 1863. Wounded in Battle of Iuka.
Duggans, Wilson A	1st Lt.	–	–	–	–	Merchant	–	Springfield, IL	
Snow, William S.	2nd Lt.	21	6'	Brown	Brown	Farmer	Kentucky	Franklin Co., MO	
Bay, Eli	Sgt.	36	5'9"	Brown	Blue	Farmer	Missouri	Franklin Co., MO	Veteran.
Coogan, Dennis E.	1st Sgt.	26	5'9¼"	Black	Blue	Farmer	New York	Franklin Co., MO	Veteran.
Manning, Thomas W.	Sgt.	22	6'½"	Brown	Brown	Miller	Tennessee	Franklin Co., MO	Accidentally killed 2/13/1862.
McClanahan, James	Sgt.	38	5'8"	Black	Black	Merchant	–	St. Louis, MO	Discharged 9/18/1862.

*Mentioned in Missouri Descriptive Roll but not in the National Archives.

Appendix A

Soldier	Rank	Age	Ht	Hair	Eyes	Occupation	Nativity	Place of Residence	Comment
Robertson, George C.	Sgt.	20	6'	Brown	Gray	Farmer	Missouri	St. Louis, MO	
Thorburn, Robert	Sgt.	27	5'8½"	Dark	Blue	Blacksmith	France	St. Louis, MO	Discharged 12/11/1862.
Wade, Albert M.	Sgt.	21	6'1½"	Brown	Blue	Farmer	Missouri	Franklin Co., MO	Died 5/10/1862 Farmington, MS.
Warner, Thadeus C.	Sgt.	24	5'9"	Light	Gray	Pilot	Connecticut	St. Louis, MO	Veteran; wounded at Vicksburg.
Cassady, David	Corporal	39	5'9"	Dark	Gray	Laborer	Atlantic Ocean	Sangamon County, IL	Veteran.
Crangle, John	Corporal	25	5'10½"	Dark	Hazel	Farmer	New York	Franklin Co., MO	Veteran.
Foster, John	Corporal	34	5'10"	Brown	Brown	Teamster	Vermont	St. Louis, MO	Wounded at Battle of Corinth.
Johns, Alton E.	Corporal	21	5'6"	Brown	Brown	Farmer	Missouri	Franklin Co., MO	Died 6/1864 Jefferson Barracks.*
McNash, William J.	Corporal	18	5'8"	Light	Blue	Nail Cutter	Virginia	St. Louis, MO	Veteran.
Pursley, Martin	Corporal	22	5'8"	Black	Hazel	Farmer	Missouri	Franklin Co., MO	Discharged 3/1863, casualty on file.
Richie, William J.	Corporal	22	5'7"	Brown	Blue	Farmer	Arkansas	Franklin Co., MO	Discharged 1/3/1863 Holly Springs.
Richie, Francis A.	Corporal	25	5'10½"	Dark	Blue	Farmer	Arkansas	Franklin Co., MO	Veteran.
Scranton, William	Corporal	21	5'4"	Brown	Blue	Farmer	Ohio	Rolla, MO	
Sullins, Nathan	Corporal	27	5'9"	Brown	Brown	Farmer	Missouri	Franklin Co., MO	Died of wounds at Vicksburg.
Tilton, William E.	Corporal	23	5'11"	Brown	Blue	Blacksmith	New York	Franklin Co., MO	Veteran.
Wade, James F.	Corporal	21	6'1"	Brown	Blue	Farmer	Missouri	Franklin Co., MO	Discharged 3/3/1863, disability Germantown, TN.
Montague, Lewis F.	Musician	20	5'7½"	Light	Gray	Farmer	Kentucky	Xenia, IL	Veteran.
Akers, Joseph*	Pvt.	22	5'5"	Dark	Blue	Miner	Illinois	Rolla, MO	Veteran.
Archer, Goran*	Pvt.	19	5'4½"	Black	Black	Laborer	Missouri	Pike Co., MO	
Babcock, William	Pvt.	17	5'3¾"	Auburn	Gray	Farmer	Illinois	Flora, IL	Discharged.
Bagan, Frances*	Pvt.	–	–	–	–	–	–	–	Veteran.
Baker, Christopher*	Pvt.	23	5'5½"	Light	Gray	Farmer	Missouri	St. Louis, MO	Died 10/1863 Vicksburg of consumption.
Bay, John S.*	Pvt.	21	5'5"	Light	Gray	Farmer	Missouri	Franklin Co., MO	Transferred to Co. E.
Bay, John W.	Pvt.	17	5'7"	Dark	Brown	Farmer	Missouri	Franklin Co., MO	Transferred to Co. E.
Bay, Joseph	Pvt.	19	5'8"	Light	Blue	Farmer	Missouri	Franklin Co., MO	Mustered out.
Bay, Martin	Pvt.	21	5'9"	Light	Blue	Farmer	Missouri	Franklin Co., MO	Died 5/10/1862 typhoid fever, buried at Jefferson Barracks St. Louis.
Bay, Mathew	Pvt.	21	5'5½"	Light	Blue	Farmer	Missouri	Franklin Co., MO	
Bay, Pleasant	Pvt.	21	5'6"	Brown	Blue	Farmer	Missouri	Franklin Co., MO	
Bay, William	Pvt.	32	5'6"	Brown	Blue	Farmer	Missouri	Franklin Co., MO	Discharged 12/5/1861.
Besley, James	Pvt.	18	5'9"	Black	Blue	Farmer	Illinois	Sumner, IL	Died 3/2/1862.
Blonde, Joseph	Pvt.	22	5'9"	Light	Blue	Farmer	France	Perryville, MO	Veteran.
Brown, William*	Pvt.	31	5'11"	Dark	Dark	Farmer	Tennessee	New Madrid, MO	
Bushner, Charles*	Pvt.	25	5'7"	Black	Black	Farmer	France	St. Louis, MO	
Bulling, John*	Pvt.	27	5'7¾"	Dark	Blue	Joiner	New York	Springfield, IL	
Campbell, Anderson	Pvt.	18	6'	Dark	Brown	Farmer	Tennessee	Sumner, IL	Died 3/12/1863 Germantown, TN.
Campbell, Richard*	Pvt.	35	6'2"	Black	Gray	Farmer	Tennessee	Sumner, IL	
Carroll, Jeremiah	Pvt.	33	5'8¾"	Brown	Gray	Farmer	Ireland	Sumner, IL	Died 4/20/1862 at Tennessee River.
Caughen, Bernard	Pvt.	18	5'5½"	Light	Hazel	Farmer	Missouri	Franklin Co., MO	Died 3/20/1862 Birds Point, MS.
Clear, James F.*	Pvt.	18	5'8"	Sandy	Blue	Farmer	Ireland	Sangamon Co., IL	Veteran.
Connelly, Allen W.*	Pvt.	–	–	–	–	–	–	–	
Deaton, Thomas*	Pvt.	23	5'10"	Light	Blue	Farmer	Kentucky	Point Pleasant, MO	

*Mentioned in Missouri Descriptive Roll but not in the National Archives.

11th Missouri Volunteer Infantry Roster

Soldier	Rank	Age	Ht	Hair	Eyes	Occupation	Nativity	Place of Residence	Comment
Donovan, Daniel*	Pvt.	–	–	–	–	–	–	–	Absent due to gunshot wound.
Dover, Charles*	Pvt.	25	5'3"	Black	Hazel	Farmer	Ireland	Bridgeport, IL	
Duncan, John M.	Pvt.	20	5'6"	Black	Black	Farmer	Missouri	Franklin Co., MO	Died 11/7/1861 Cape Girardeau.
Fisher, Jacob	Pvt.	16	5'5"	Black	Black	Farmer	Germany	Franklin Co., MO	
Gable, Alfred M.	Pvt.	36	5'6⅜"	Black	Black	Farmer	Indiana	Springfield, IL	Discharged 7/31/1863.
Galligher, Daniel	Pvt.	19	5'2¾"	Brown	Gray	Peddler	Ireland	Bridgeport, IL	
Geaghan, John*	Pvt.	26	5'6½"	Dark	Blue	Farmer	Ireland	Sangamon Co., IL	Transferred to Inv. Corp 3/15/1864.*
Gines, Henry S.*	Pvt.	18	5'8"	Light	Gray	Farmer	Illinois	Lawrence Co., IL	
Gordon, William H.*	Pvt.	–	–	–	–	–	–	–	
Gray, James M.	Pvt.	18	5'5"	Brown	Blue	Farmer	Missouri	Franklin Co., MO	
Green, George W.	Pvt.	18	5'5"	Light	Blue	Farmer	Missouri	Franklin Co., MO	Discharged 4/24/1862 Hamburg, TN.
Green, Hance	Pvt.	17	5'7"	Light	Hazel	Farmer	Missouri	Rolla, MO	Veteran.
Haltermont, Andrew R.	Pvt.	25	5'9"	Light	Blue	Farmer	Ohio	Flora, IL	Died 1/22/1862.
Hunt, Thomas*	Pvt.	26	5'4"	Brown	Blue	Farmer	Scotland	Sangamon Co., IL	
Johns, Sweptson	Pvt.	20	6'	Light	Gray	Farmer	Missouri	Franklin Co., MO	Died 9/30/1861 Cape Girardeau.
Johnson, James	Pvt.	25	5'5¾"	Brown	Blue	Farmer	Ohio	Bridgeport, IL	Wounded at Vicksburg.
Johnson, Eli	Pvt.	19	5'7½"	Dark	Blue	Farmer	Missouri	Franklin Co., MO	Died 5/31/1862 Farmington, MS.
Jones, Benjamin F.	Pvt.	–	–	–	–	–	–	–	
Maher, Lawrence	Pvt.	–	–	–	–	–	–	–	Veteran.
Manning, Talbot	Pvt.	22	6'1"	Light	Blue	Farmer	Missouri	Franklin Co., MO	Died.
McCue, Patrick*	Pvt.	20	5'5"	Light	Blue	Peddler	Ireland	Sumner, IL	Wounded at Battle of Corinth.
McCready, William*	Pvt.	21	5'8"	Black	Hazel	Peddler	Ireland	Sumner, IL	Mustered out as a veteran (also shown as died 12/17/1863).
McGinley, John	Pvt.	29	5'4½"	Black	Black	Farmer	Ireland	Sumner, IL	Discharged 11/22/1862.
Miller, John	Pvt.	24	5'8⅜"	Dark	Blue	Farmer	Tennessee	Sangamon Co., IL	Transferred to Co. K; died.
Mills, Reuben*	Pvt.	36	6'	Brown	Gray	Farmer	Tennessee	Sumner, IL	Veteran.
Monyhon, Owen	Pvt.	19	5'8½"	Brown	Hazel	Farmer	Illinois	Bridgeport, IL	Died 8/21/1863.*
More, John	Pvt.	31	5'7"	Black	Black	Farmer	Ireland	Rolla, MO	
Myers, Herman*	Pvt.	–	–	–	–	–	–	–	
Nicholson, George	Pvt.	17	5'5½"	Brown	Brown	Farmer	Scotland	Franklin Co., MO	
Osborne, Marshall	Pvt.	35	5'8"	Black	Hazel	Farmer	England	Sumner, IL	KIA Battle of Iuka 9/19/1862.
Payne, Nathaniel	Pvt.	22	5'8¾"	Dark	Blue	Farmer	New York	Pike Co., IL	Veteran.
Pointer, Washington*	Pvt.	22	5'4¾"	Light	Gray	Farmer	Missouri	Gasconade, MO	
Perry, John G.*	Pvt.	32	5'9½"	Light	Gray	Farmer	Virginia	Bridgeport, Il	
Price, Edward	Pvt.	37	5'7"	Brown	Blue	Farmer	Kentucky	Franklin Co., MO	Died 3/23/1863 Point Pleasant, MO.
Prior, George*	Pvt.	–	–	–	–	–	–	–	
Pursley, David W. M.	Pvt.	20	5'8"	Brown	Blue	Farmer	Missouri	Franklin Co., MO	Died 5/12/1862 Hamburg, TN.
Reed, Bluford*	Pvt.	–	–	–	–	–	–	–	
Riley, Michael	Pvt.	34	5'7½"	Brown	Blue	Farmer	Ireland	Rolla, MO	Died 8/5/1863 Camp Sherman of congestive fever.
Sampson, William	Pvt.	45	5'5¾"	Brown	Dark	Laborer	England	Sumner, IL	Discharged 5/15/1862.
Sauls, Ezekiel*	Pvt.	24	5'11"	Black	Black	Farmer	Illinois	New Madrid, MO	Deserted.*
Schriner, Herman	Pvt.	27	5'4½"	Brown	Blue	Gunsmith	Germany	Cape Girardeau, MO	Discharged 7/31/1862.
Scott, Samuel	Pvt.	25	5'5½"	Brown	Blue	Farmer	Ireland	Rolla, MO	Died 8/1/1863 Camp Sherman, MS.
Shepherd, John W.*	Pvt.	20	5'2"	Sandy	Gray	Machinist	Ohio	St. Louis, MO	Discharged 5/1864.
Smith, Emanuel*	Pvt.	28	6'	Sandy	Brown	Farmer	Indiana	New Madrid, MO	Deserted.*
Smith, John*	Pvt.	30	5'9¾"	Brown	Gray	Farmer	Germany	Sumner, IL	
Twitty, Harrison R.	Pvt.	21	5'5"	Brown	Blue	Farmer	Missouri	Franklin Co., MO	Wounded at Vicksburg.
Twitty, Thomas B.	Pvt.	18	5'7"	Brown	Gray	Farmer	Missouri	Franklin Co., MO	Veteran.
Umfleet, Hiram	Pvt.	19	5'9¼"	Light	Gray	Farmer	Illinois	Lawrence Co., IL	
Umfleet, Hughey*	Pvt.	18	5'7"	Light	Blue	Farmer	Indiana	Sumner, IL	
Wade, William H.	Pvt.	28	5'11"	Black	Black	Farmer	Missouri	Franklin Co., MO	Discharged 9/12/1862, disability Corinth.
Williams, John	Pvt.	24	5'9"	Dark	Blue	Blacksmith	Indiana	Louisiana, MO	Discharged 7/25/1862.

*Mentioned in Missouri Descriptive Roll but not in the National Archives.

Soldier	Rank	Age	Ht	Hair	Eyes	Occu-pation	Nativity	Place of Residence	Comment
Wilson, Douglas	Pvt.	26	5'5"	Brown	Hazel	Physician	Connecticut	Queuing, IL	Veteran.
Winscott, William N.*	Pvt.	–	–	–	–	–	–	–	Veteran.
Woodland, James	Pvt.	20	5'8"	Black	Blue	Farmer	Missouri	Franklin Co., MO	Discharged 8/2/1862 near Corinth.
Pruitt, Elijah*	Pvt.	–	–	–	–	–	–	–	–

*Mentioned in Missouri Descriptive Roll but not in the National Archives.

Appendix B: 11th Missouri Veteran Volunteer Infantry Roster

(Based on the Regimental Descriptive Book Located at the National Archives and Supplemented with the Regimental Descriptive Book Located at the Missouri Archives and Regimental Cards Located at the Missouri Archives)[1]

Regimental Staff

Bowyer, Eli	Colonel	Wounded in Battle of Nashville.
Green, Modesta	Lt. Colonel	Wounded in Battle of Nashville.
Cleland, William	Major	
Finch, Walton	Adjutant	Resigned 11/7/1865.
Applegate, H. C.	Quartermaster	Resigned 11/7/1865.
Swan, James	Quartermaster	
Fish, Melanchton	Surgeon	Mustered out 5/2/1865.
Hawley, Thomas	Surgeon	
Brown, George	Chaplain	Wounded in Siege of Spanish Fort.

Company A

Soldier	Rank	Age	Ht	Hair	Eyes	Occupation	Nativity	Comment
McMahan, Constantine	Captain	24	–	–	–	–	–	Mustered out 1/15/66 Memphis.
Nigh, Barney L./ Barnabas	1st Lt.	21	–	–	–	–	–	Mustered out 1/15/66 Memphis.
Smith, Henry	2nd Lt.	37	5'4¾"	Brown	Blue	Farmer	Prussia	Mustered out 1/15/66 Memphis.
Bouren / Bourn, Zacheus	Sgt.	21	5'9"	Light	Blue	Soldier	Indiana	Mustered out 1/15/66 Memphis, detached as 1st Sgt. with 61st U.S. Inf. since 6/9/1864.
Cooper, Nathan	Sgt.	22	5'7"	Brown	Hazel	Farmer	Kentucky	Mustered out 1/15/66 Memphis, 7th Missouri.
Gould, George W.	Sgt.	24	5'7"	Light	Blue	Soldier	Ohio	Mustered out 1/15/66 Memphis.
Lappin, John B.	Sgt.	36	5'6"	Brown	Gray	Soldier	Pennsylvania	Mustered out 1/15/66 Memphis.
Malone, Thomas	Sgt.	20	5'10"	Brown	Blue	Soldier	Illinois	Mustered out 1/15/66 Memphis.
Treadway, Charles W.	Sgt.	25	5'10"	Black	Blue	Soldier	Illinois	Mustered out 1/15/66 Memphis.
Appling, Winkfield	Corporal	20	5'8"	Brown	Blue	Soldier	–	Mustered out 1/15/66 Memphis.
Brooks, Alexander	Corporal	28	5'7"	Brown	Gray	Soldier	Ohio	Mustered out 1/15/66 Memphis, detached to Provost Guard 1865.
Day, Elisha	Corporal	22	6'1"	Light	Hazel	Soldier	Ohio	Mustered out 1/15/66 Memphis.
Cusick, William	Corporal	24	5'8"	Brown	Hazel	Soldier	Illinois	Mustered out 1/15/66 Memphis, detached to Provost Guard.
Dwyer, Edward	Musician	17	4'8"	Dark	Hazel	–	Missouri	Mustered out 1/15/66 Memphis, 7th Missouri.
French, Almond	Musician	18	5'8"	Brown	Blue	Soldier	Illinois	Mustered out 1/15/66 Memphis.
Williams, Benjamin	Wagoner	22	5'8"	Light	Blue	Soldier	Illinois	Mustered out 1/15/66 Memphis, substitute.

Appendix B

Soldier	Rank	Age	Ht	Hair	Eyes	Occupation	Nativity	Comment
Anderson, Jacob	Pvt.	18	5'7"	Brown	Brown	Farmer	Missouri	Mustered out 1/15/66 Memphis, substitute.
Baker, Charles	Pvt.	18	5'3½"	Brown	Gray	Farmer	Missouri	Mustered out 1/15/66 Memphis, substitute.
Blackman, James R.	Pvt.	33	–	–	–	–	–	Mustered out 1/15/66 Memphis, 33rd Missouri.
Breitenbach, Andrew	Pvt.	27	5'2"	Brown	Brown	–	Bavaria	Substitute.
Brinkley, William M.	Pvt.	18	5'9¼"	Light	Blue	Farmer	Kentucky	Mustered out 1/15/66 Memphis, substitute.
Calder, William A.	Pvt.	48	5'8"	Black	Black	Carpenter	Maryland	Mustered out 1/15/66 Memphis, 7th Missouri.
Cameron, John	Pvt.	28	5'6"	Dark	Black	Laborer	Canada	Mustered out 1/15/66 Memphis, substitute.
Dravel/Drewel, Henry	Pvt.	44	5'7"	Brown	Blue	Farmer	Prussia	Mustered out 1/15/66 Memphis, drafted.
Feil, Jacob	Pvt.	40	6'2"	Brown	Brown	Farmer	Germany	Mustered out 1/15/66 Memphis, drafted.
Graham, Edward L.	Pvt.	23	5'10"	Light	Blue	Carpenter	Illinois	Mustered out 1/15/66 Memphis, 7th Missouri.
Hagan, Dennis	Pvt.	23	5'5"	Brown	Gray	Laborer	Ireland	Mustered out 1/15/66 Memphis, 7th Missouri.
Hahn, John	Pvt.	18	5'5"	Brown	Gray	Laborer	Germany	Mustered out 1/15/66 Memphis, substitute.
Hamilton, John	Pvt.	22	5'9"	Brown	Brown	Soldier	Missouri	Mustered out 1/15/66 Memphis, drafted.
Howell, George H.	Pvt.	28	5'8"	Dark	Black	Carpenter	Alabama	Mustered out 1/15/66 Memphis, detached as nurse in post hospital, 7th Missouri.
Hunter, George W.	Pvt.	31	5'6"	Light	Blue	Carpenter	Scotland	Mustered out 1/15/66 Memphis, substitute.
Johns, Albert	Pvt.	26	5'7"	Black	Blue	Soldier	Missouri	Mustered out 1/15/66 Memphis, drafted.
Jones, George	Pvt.	20	5'8"	Red	Blue	–	Mississippi	Mustered out 1/15/66 Memphis.
Kammerman, John	Pvt.	33	5'5"	Brown	Brown	Laborer	Germany	Mustered out 1/15/66 Memphis, substitute.
Kelley/Kelly, George	Pvt.	23	5'7"	Brown	Blue	Soldier	Illinois	Mustered out 1/15/66 Memphis, substitute.
Kelley/Kelly, John	Pvt.	21	–	–	–	–	–	Mustered out 1/15/66 Memphis.
King, James A.	Pvt.	23	5'2½"	Dark	Gray	Farmer	Missouri	Mustered out 1/15/66 Memphis, substitute.
Klug/King, Adam	Pvt.	25	5'7"	Brown	Hazel	Farmer	Germany	Mustered out 1/15/66 Memphis, substitute.
Luman, Hiram T.	Pvt.	18	5'6"	Brown	Light	Farmer	Ohio	Substitute.
Malone, Horace	Pvt.	20	5'10"	Brown	Blue	Soldier	Illinois	Mustered out 1/15/66 Memphis.
Mathias, Benjamin F.	Pvt.	18	5'7"	Light	Gray	Farmer	Illinois	Mustered out 1/15/66 Memphis, wounded at Nashville.
McClanahan, William J.	Pvt.	18	5'6"	Black	Hazel	Farmer	Tennessee	Mustered out 1/15/66 Memphis, substitute.
McDonough, Hugh/John	Pvt.	31	5'4"	Dark	Gray	Laborer	Ireland	Mustered out 1/15/66 Memphis, substitute.
McMullen, John	Pvt.	19	5'2¼"	Brown	Blue	Laborer	Ireland	Substitute.
Minard, Nelson	Pvt.	44	5'10"	Brown	Blue	Mason	Kentucky	Mustered out 1/15/66 Memphis, 7th Missouri.
Moffat/Moffit, John M.	Pvt.	32	5'10"	Brown	Blue	Laborer	Ireland	Mustered out 1/15/66 Memphis, substitute.
Morris, George	Pvt.	21	5'10"	Brown	Gray	Cooper	Iowa	Mustered out 1/15/66 Memphis, wounded at Nashville, 7th Missouri.
Nortman, Julius	Pvt.	28	5'3"	Brown	Blue	Farmer	Germany	Mustered out 1/15/66 Memphis, drafted.
Numach/Numerk, John	Pvt.	27	5'9"	Brown	Blue	Farmer	Germany	
O'Neil, Henry	Pvt.	23	5'10"	Brown	Gray	Farmer	Pennsylvania	Under arrest awaiting trial, 7th Missouri.
Raridan, Edward	Pvt.	23	5'7"	Black	Hazel	Soldier	Illinois	Mustered out 1/15/66 Memphis, 7th Missouri.
Raver, John	Pvt.	31	5'6"	Brown	Black	Cooper	Canada	Mustered out 1/15/66 Memphis, 7th Missouri.
Reardon, Daniel	Pvt.	40	5'4"	Brown	Hazel	Laborer	Ireland	Mustered out 1/15/66 Memphis, substitute.
Redding, George W.	Pvt.	18	5'5"	Brown	Blue	Farmer	Missouri	Mustered out 1/15/66 Memphis, substitute.
Riffle, George W.	Pvt.	20	5'8"	Brown	Gray	Farmer	Virginia	Mustered out 1/15/66 Memphis, 7th Missouri.
Roadbecker, Henry	Pvt.	32	5'10"	Brown	Gray	Carpenter	Germany	Mustered out 1/15/66 Memphis, 7th Missouri.
Segrist, Jacob	Pvt.	22	5'3"	Dark	Gray	Saddler	Switzerland	Mustered out 1/15/66 Memphis, substitute.
Smith, Jacob	Pvt.	21	5'10"	Brown	Gray	Farmer	Illinois	Mustered out 1/15/66 Memphis, 7th Missouri.
Smutz, Andrew	Pvt.	20	5'11½"	Light	Blue	–	Germany	Mustered out 1/15/66 Memphis, substitute.
Stuckey, William	Pvt.	18	5'7"	Black	Brown	Farmer	Indiana	Mustered out 7/16/1865, substitute.
Weeks, Stephen L.	Pvt.	18	5'	Red	Gray	Farmer	Ohio	Mustered out 1/15/66 Memphis, substitute.
Westfall, Thomas F.	Pvt.	25	5'9"	Brown	Gray	Cooper	Ohio	Mustered out 1/15/66 Memphis, 7th Missouri.
Worley, Samuel	Pvt.	21	5'9"	Black	Blue	Soldier	Illinois	Mustered out 1/15/66 Memphis.
Yates, Samuel	Pvt.	30	6'	Brown	Gray	Soldier	Indiana	Mustered out 1/15/66 Memphis

Discharged

Soldier	Rank	Age	Ht	Hair	Eyes	Occupation	Nativity	Comment
O'Donnell, Menomen	Captain	31	–	–	–	–	–	Mustered out 8/9/1864, Medal of Honor.
Applegate, Henry C.	1st Lt.	20	5'10"	Brown	Hazel	Soldier	Ohio	Mustered out 1/15/66 Memphis.

Mentioned in Missouri Descriptive Roll but not in the National Archives.

Soldier	Rank	Age	Ht	Hair	Eyes	Occupation	Nativity	Comment
Berge/Birge, Alpheus W.	Pvt.	33	5'11"	Brown	Gray	–	Vermont	Mustered out 7/8/1865, 7th Missouri.
Breckel, Louis	Pvt.	23	5'3"	Brown	Blue	–	Germany	Discharged 8/15/1865 due to gunshot wound in Battle of Nashville, 7th Missouri.
Cabe, Edwin*	Pvt.	–	–	–	–	–	–	Wounded in the Battle of Nashville; end of term of service 10/2/1865, 33rd Missouri
Duncan, Rice A.	Pvt.	43	5'6½"	Brown	Gray	Farmer	Missouri	Mustered out 12/18/1865, drafted.
Mann, William	Pvt.	25	–	–	–	–	–	Mustered out 7/10/1865, wounded at Nashville.
McKenna, Edward A.	Pvt.	44	5'5"	Gray	Gray	Soldier	Ireland	Discharged 6/5/1865, substitute.
Nann/Nunn, William T.*	Pvt.	23	6'	Black	Gray	Soldier	Ireland	End of Service 10/3/1865, 33rd Missouri.
Sheal, Martin	Pvt.	40	5'2"	Brown	Brown	Soldier	Prussia	Mustered out 12/29/1865, substitute.
Smith, George*	Pvt.	–	–	–	–	–	–	Mustered out 10/11/1865, 33rd Missouri.

DIED

Soldier	Rank	Age	Ht	Hair	Eyes	Occupation	Nativity	Comment
Allen, Samuel	Pvt.	18	5'5½"	Black	Blue	Farmer	Ohio	Substitute, died 4/19/1865 Garrie, AL.
Dace/Dave, Charles	Pvt.	18	5'7½"	Light	Gray	Farmer	Tennessee	Killed 3/30/1865 in Siege of Spanish Fort, substitute.
Michler/Miller, Ferdinand	Pvt.	27	5'4"	Dark	Gray	Clerk	Hungary	Died of 2/3/1865 of heart disease Eastport, MS, substitute.
Terrell/Terry, John	Pvt.	28	5'6"	Light	Gray	Farmer		Died 1/20/1865, disease of lungs.
Thompson, Stephen B.	Pvt.	20	5'10"	Light	Gray	Soldier	Illinois	Died 1/24/1865 Lawrence Co., IL.
Unmack, John*	Pvt.	–	–	–	–	–	–	Died 6/17/1865 Demopolis, drafted.
Webb, Thomas	Pvt.	21	6'	Light	Blue	Soldier	Kentucky	Died 12/16/1864, wounded in Battle of Nashville.
Womack, William N.	Pvt.	28	5'8½"	Light	Gray	Farmer	Alabama	Died 7/8/1865, chronic diarrhea, Selma, drafted.

DESERTED

Soldier	Rank	Age	Ht	Hair	Eyes	Occupation	Nativity	Comment
Welch, George W.	Corporal	20	5'6"	Dark	Brown	Farmer	Iowa	Deserted 2/6/1865, 7th Missouri.
Allen, James	Pvt.	22	5'6"	Red	Hazel	Farmer	Missouri	Wounded in Battle of Nashville, deserted 9/28/65 Marion, AL, 7th Missouri.
Christian, William	Pvt.	25	5'8"	Dark	Blue	Farmer	Indiana	Deserted 11/7/1865 near Marion, AL.
Conaghan, Michael	Pvt.	33	5'7"	Brown	Gray	Tailor	Missouri	Deserted 2/9/1865 Cairo, IL, substitute.
Connors, John	Pvt.	35	5'7"	Brown	Hazel	Farmer	Ireland	Substitute not yet reported 2/65, 7th Missouri.
Dargan, John	Pvt.	22	5'11"	Brown	Blue	Boatman	Ireland	Deserted 2/9/1865 Cairo, IL.
Estis, Joseph R.	Pvt.	18	5'8½"	Light	Gray	Laborer	Missouri	Deserted, substitute.
Fuller, J. H.	Pvt.	18	5'2"	Light	Blue	Farmer	Missouri	Never reported, AWOL since 4/1865, substitute.
German, Dennis	Pvt.	40	5'4"	Brown	Blue	Farmer	Ireland	Deserted, absent sick, 7th Missouri.
Gilfoy, Michael	Pvt.	30	5'8"	Auburn	Gray	Laborer	Ireland	Deserted 6/25/1865 Demopolis, never reported, substitute.
Hagerty, John	Pvt.	23	5'2½"	Brown	Blue	Farmer	Ireland	Never reported, substitute.
Hurst, Joseph	Pvt.	–	–	–	–	–	–	Deserted 6/25/1865 Demopolis, drafted, substitute.
Kelly, Patrick	Pvt.	28	5'8"	Brown	Gray	Laborer	Ireland	Never reported, substitute.
Knack/Kuark, Theodore	Pvt.	21	5'4"	Dark	Blue	Clerk	Prussia	Never reported, substitute.
Long, James C.	Pvt.	31	5'10"	Brown	Brown	Boatman	Ireland	Deserter, never reported, 7th Missouri.
McDonald, Charles	Pvt.	24	5'9½"	Brown	Brown	Stonecutter	Canada	Deserted 12/2/1865, substitute.
Murray, John	Pvt.	25	5'5"	Black	Hazel	Laborer	Canada	Never reported, 7th Missouri.
Roach, Richard	Pvt.	21	5'8"	Brown	Gray	Laborer	Ireland	Deserted 9/28/1865 Demopolis, AL, wounded at Nashville, 7th Missouri.
Ryan, Thomas	Pvt.	30	5'8"	Brown	Dark	Laborer	Ireland	Deserted 5/29/1864, 7th Missouri.
Smith, Alfred	Pvt.	21	5'8"	Brown	Brown	Farmer	Missouri	Substitute.
Smith, Michael	Pvt.	21	5'9"	Black	Brown	Butcher	Ireland	Never reported for duty.
Springer, Andrew U.	Pvt.	37	5'10"	Brown	Gray	Farmer	Pennsylvania	Deserted 11/22/1865 Demopolis, TN, 7th Missouri.
Steward/Stewart, Jasper	Pvt.	26	5'5"	Brown	Brown	Farmer	Illinois	Deserted 9/15/1865 Demopolis, TN, 7th Missouri.

*Mentioned in Missouri Descriptive Roll but not in the National Archives.

Soldier	Rank	Age	Ht	Hair	Eyes	Occupation	Nativity	Comment
Stewart/Stuart, John	Pvt.	23	5'10"	Brown	Blue	Cooper	Illinois	Deserted 7/2/1865 Demopolis, AL, 7th Missouri.
Taylor, James	Pvt.	22	6'½"	Light	Gray	Farmer	Tennessee	Deserted 2/9/1865, substitute.
White, William	Pvt.	28	5'2"	Light	Blue	Farmer	Missouri	Deserted 2/9/1865 Cairo, IL.
Wilkinson, Thomas H.	Pvt.	27	5'6"	Sandy	Brown	–	Canada	Deserted 10/7/1865 Marion, AL, substitute.
Wilson, James	Pvt.	22	5'10"	Light	Blue	Clerk	Louisiana	Never reported, substitute.
Wullshlegen, John	Pvt.	40	5'6"	Black	Hazel	Farmer	Switzerland	Deserted 6/18/1865 Demopolis, drafted.

Transferred

Soldier	Rank	Age	Ht	Hair	Eyes	Occupation	Nativity	Comment
Johnson, Criddleton	Sgt.	24	5'10¼"	Light	Gray	Blacksmith	Illinois	Mustered out 8/13/1864 to accept enlistment in 5th U.S. Hvy Art.
Addison, Aaron	Pvt.	22	5'10½"	Brown	Gray	Farmer	Illinois	Bridgeport, IL.
Heineman, Martin	Pvt.	–	–	–	–	–	–	
Levi, Paul	Pvt.	18	–	–	–	–	–	
Luman, John B.	Pvt.	–	–	–	–	–	–	
Nance, James C.	Pvt.	18	–	–	–	–	–	Substitute.
Smith, John	Pvt.	30	5'9¾"	Brown	Gray	Farmer	Germany	
Worstell, George	Pvt.	24	5'7½"	Light	Gray	Farmer	Ohio	

Company B

Soldier	Rank	Age	Ht	Hair	Eyes	Occupation	Nativity	Comment
Fallowell, William	Captain	26	–	–	–	–	Kentucky	Mustered out 1/16/1866 Memphis, 7th MO Inf.
Kelley/Kelly, Benjamin F.	1st Lt.	22	–	–	–	–	–	Mustered out 1/16/1866 Memphis.
Whitney, Solomon	2nd Lt.	21	5'9"	Dark	Gray	Soldier	New York	Mustered out 1/16/1866 Memphis.
Brown, Thomas	Sgt.	21	6'¼"	Light	Blue	Soldier	Indiana	Mustered out 1/16/1866 Memphis, wounded in Battle of Nashville.
Clements, John H.	Sgt.	22	5'6"	Dark	Gray	Soldier	Illinois	Mustered out 1/16/1866 Memphis, wounded at Abbeville, MS, 8/1864.
Cooper, Henry	Sgt.	21	5'5"	Light	Gray	Soldier	Illinois	Mustered out 1/16/1866 Memphis.
Davis, Levi M.	Sgt.	21	–	–	–	–	–	Mustered out 1/16/1866 Memphis, 7th MO Inf.
Heath, John B.	Sgt.	22	5'10"	Brown	Brown	Farmer	Illinois	Mustered out 1/16/1866 Memphis, 7th MO Inf.
Baker/Baher, Squire W.	Corporal	21	5'10¼"	Black	Blue	Soldier	Illinois	Mustered out 1/16/1866 Memphis, wounded in the Battle of Nashville.
Clark, David M.	Corporal	21	5'6¾"	Dark	Blue	Soldier	–	Mustered out 1/16/1866 Memphis.
James, James W.	Corporal	22	5'9"	Brown	Brown	Farmer	Missouri	Mustered out 1/16/1866 Memphis, 7th MO Inf.
John, Henry	Corporal	24	5'6"	Light	Gray	Soldier	Bavaria	Mustered out 1/16/1866 Memphis.
Huttenheu/Huttenhow, William M.	Corporal	23	5'6"	Light	Gray	Soldier	Illinois	Mustered out 1/16/1866 Memphis.
Lockett, Thomas	Corporal	19	5'8"	Brown	Blue	Farmer	Tennessee	Mustered out 1/16/1866 Memphis, 7th MO Inf.
Morrow, Goldman J.	Corporal	20	5'8"	Brown	Gray	Farmer	Illinois	Mustered out 1/16/1866 Memphis, 7th MO Inf.
Williams, James	Corporal	21	5'10½"	Brown	Blue	Farmer	Illinois	Mustered out 1/16/1866 Memphis, 7th MO Inf.
Livingston, Napoleon B.	Musician	15	5'	Black	Black	–	Kentucky	Mustered out 1/16/1866 Memphis, 7th MO Inf.
Allison, Benjamin	Pvt.	18	5'5"	Dark	Dark	Farmer	Missouri	Mustered out 1/16/1866 Memphis, substitute, also recorded in Company K.
Anderson, John J.	Pvt.	21	5'10¼"	Dark	Blue	Farmer	Kentucky	Mustered out 1/16/1866 Memphis, 7th MO Inf.
Arthur, John*	Cook	28	–	–	–	–	–	Mustered out 1/16/1866 Memphis, 7th MO Inf.
Bandy, George W.	Pvt.	35	–	–	–	–	–	Mustered out 1/16/1866 Memphis, drafted.
Beck, Marion F.	Pvt.	32	5'5"	Brown	Hazel	Farmer	N. Carolina	Mustered out 1/16/1866 Memphis, drafted.
Blake, James	Pvt.	19	5'6½"	Auburn	Brown	Farmer	Illinois	Mustered out 1/16/1866 Memphis, 7th MO Inf.
Branson, Isaac	Pvt.	25	5'11"	Light	Blue	Farmer	Missouri	Mustered out 1/16/1866 Memphis, drafted.
Branson, William	Pvt.	29	5'11"	Light	Blue	Farmer	Missouri	Mustered out 1/16/1866 Memphis, drafted.
Bridinger, William H.	Pvt.	20	5'5½"	Light	Blue	Soldier	Ohio	Mustered out 1/16/1866 Memphis.
Buck, John	Pvt.	40	5'10"	Light	Blue	Soldier	Germany	Mustered out 1/16/1866 Memphis.
Buckley, William	Pvt.	27	5'6"	Dark	Blue	Soldier	Pennsylvania	Mustered out 1/16/1866 Memphis.

*Mentioned in Missouri Descriptive Roll but not in the National Archives.

Soldier	Rank	Age	Ht	Hair	Eyes	Occupation	Nativity	Comment
Bushling, Detrich	Pvt.	22	5'5"	Light	Blue	Soldier	Germany	Mustered out 1/16/1866 Memphis, substitute.
Carter, Robert	Pvt.	28	–	–	–	–	–	Mustered out 1/16/1866 Memphis, substitute.
Constant, John E.	Pvt.	20	5'6¼"	Light	Gray	Soldier	Illinois	Mustered out 1/16/1866 Memphis, wounded in Battle of Nashville.
Curtis, John E.	Pvt.	19	5'6½"	Dark	Brown	Farmer	Illinois	Absent confined in Selma, AL, 7th MO Inf.
Daniels, John F.	Pvt.	19	5'6"	Auburn	Black	Farmer	Illinois	Absent confined in Tuscaloosa, AL, 7th MO Inf.
David, George H.	Pvt.	20	5'5"	Dark	Brown	Soldier	New York	Mustered out 1/16/1866 Memphis.
Davis, Moses H.	Pvt.	24	–	–	–	–	–	Mustered out 1/16/1866 Memphis, drafted.
Davidson, William	Pvt.	21	5'5"	Light	Gray	Soldier	Illinois	Mustered out 1/16/1866 Memphis.
Ellis, John	Pvt.	33	5'9"	Brown	Hazel	Farmer	Tennessee	Mustered out 1/16/1866 Memphis, drafted.
Evans, Thomas	Pvt.	20	5'9½"	Brown	Black	Farmer	Ohio	Mustered out 1/16/1866 Memphis, 7th MO Inf.
Fitzgerald, Edward	Pvt.	42	5'6"	Brown	Hazel	Laborer	Ireland	Mustered out 1/16/1866 Memphis, substitute.
Geiles/Giles, James G.	Pvt.	50	5'6"	Gray	Gray	–	Virginia	Mustered out 1/16/1866 Memphis, 7th MO Inf.
Goodrich, John	Pvt.	19	5'8"	Dark	Dark	Farmer	Missouri	7th MO Inf.
Helme, Thomas	Pvt.	21	5'7"	Dark	Black	Soldier	New York	Mustered out 1/16/1866 Memphis.
Hogan, Thomas	Pvt.	35	5'5½"	Dark	Blue	Laborer	Ireland	Mustered out 1/16/1866 Memphis, substitute.
Holley, Charles W.	Pvt.	41	5'9½"	Dark	Blue	Laborer	Connecticut	Mustered out 1/16/1866 Memphis, substitute.
Ingram, Richard A.	Pvt.	39	5'9"	Brown	Blue	Farmer	S. Carolina	Mustered out 1/16/1866 Memphis, drafted.
Inker, Christian	Pvt.	33	5'7"	Brown	Hazel	Soldier	Switzerland	Mustered out 1/16/1866 Memphis.
Katthsmeyer, Julius	Pvt.	18	5'7"	Light	Blue	Baker	Germany	Mustered out 1/16/1866 Memphis, substitute.
Kenneck/Kimmick, Theodore	Pvt.	22	–	–	–	–	–	Mustered out 1/16/1866 Memphis, substitute.
Lankeman/Lankiman, Henry	Pvt.	34	–	Brown	Blue	Farmer	Hanover	Mustered out 1/16/1866 Memphis, drafted.
Massey, Charles	Pvt.	27	5'10"	Brown	Blue	Farmer	Missouri	Mustered out 1/16/1866 Memphis, drafted.
McGlassen, John	Pvt.	25	5'10"	Brown	Black	–	Illinois	Mustered out 1/16/1866 Memphis, 7th MO Inf.
Mulverhill, Jerry	Pvt.	23	5'9"	Brown	Gray	Farmer	Illinois	Mustered out 1/16/1866 Memphis, substitute.
Nelson, Charles	Pvt.	33	5'6"	Sandy	Brown	Farmer	Norway	Mustered out 1/16/1866 Memphis, 7th MO Inf.
Ousley, Pleasant	Pvt.	38	5'10"	Brown	Brown	Farmer	Pennsylvania	Mustered out 1/16/1866 Memphis, drafted.
Phillips, Thomas	Pvt.	27	–	–	–	–	–	Mustered out 1/16/1866 Memphis, substitute.
Piper/Peiper, Henry	Pvt.	28	–	–	–	–	–	Mustered out 1/16/1866 Memphis, drafted.
Quinn, John R.	Pvt.	18	5'	Brown	Hazel	Farmer	Ohio	Mustered out 1/16/1866 Memphis, 7th MO Inf.
Ross, John A.	Pvt.	30	–	–	–	–	–	Mustered out 1/16/1866 Memphis.
Reynolds, Allen L.	Pvt.	18	5'10"	Brown	Gray	Farmer	Missouri	Mustered out 1/16/1866 Memphis, substitute.
Reynolds, Thomas	Pvt.	32	–	–	–	–	–	Mustered out 1/16/1866 Memphis, 7th MO Inf.
Richardson, Alexander	Pvt.	26	–	–	–	–	–	AWOL 10/25/1865, drafted.
Schmidt, Adolph	Pvt.	27	5'5"	Brown	Hazel	Tanner	Germany	Mustered out 1/16/1866 Memphis, drafted.
Schmidt/Schmit, Christian	Pvt.	29	5'3¾"	Dark	Brown	Miller	Germany	Mustered out 1/16/1866 Memphis, substitute.
Smith, Harmon/Herman	Pvt.	30	5'8½"	Black	Brown	Farmer	Missouri	Mustered out 1/16/1866 Memphis, 7th MO Inf.
Smith, Samuel M.	Pvt.	24	5'7"	Dark	Dark	Soldier	Kentucky	Mustered out 1/16/1866 Memphis.
Steele, Thomas	Pvt.	20	5'4½"	Light	Blue	Soldier	Indiana	Mustered out 1/16/1866 Memphis.
Talbott/Tolbott, Isaac A.	Pvt.	23	5'9½"	Dark	Hazel	Farmer	Kentucky	Mustered out 1/16/1866 Memphis, 7th MO Inf.
Talday/Tolday, Fleming	Pvt.	26	5'9½"	Dark	Gray	Soldier	Ohio	Mustered out 1/16/1866 Memphis.
Totzell, Valentine	Pvt.	16	5'8"	Dark	Hazel	Farmer	Missouri	Mustered out 1/16/1866 Memphis, 7th MO Inf., wounded in Siege of Spanish Fort.
Veam/Vegom/Vigom, Charles	Pvt.	36	5'3½"	Dark	Hazel	Farmer	Canada	Mustered out 1/16/1866 Memphis, substitute.
Vogale/Vogeli, Fredolin	Pvt.	19	–	–	–	–	–	Mustered out 1/16/1866 Memphis.
Wallace, James	Pvt.	18	5'4"	Light	Blue	Farmer	Virginia	Mustered out 1/16/1866 Memphis, substitute.
Webb, Jehn/John	Pvt.	18	5'8"	Black	Black	Farmer	Illinois	Mustered out 1/16/1866 Memphis, 7th MO Inf.
Wehmeyer/Wemeyer, Ernest	Pvt.	19	–	–	–	–	–	Mustered out 1/16/1866 Memphis, substitute.
Wells, William B.	Pvt.	26	5'10"	Dark	Gray	Mechanic	New York	Mustered out 1/16/1866 Memphis.
Wroughton, George	Pvt.	22	5'8"	Sandy	Blue	Farmer	Illinois	Mustered out 1/16/1866 Memphis, 7th MO Inf.
York, James J./Jefferson	Pvt.	19	5'5½"	Light	Blue	Soldier	Kentucky	Mustered out 1/16/1866 Memphis, 7th MO Inf.

*Mentioned in Missouri Descriptive Roll but not in the National Archives.

Discharged

Soldier	Rank	Age	Ht	Hair	Eyes	Occupation	Nativity	Comment
Lloyd, Jesse D.	Captain	23	–	–	–	–	–	Mustered out 11/26/1864.
Anderson, James C.	Pvt.	18	5'3"	Dark	Brown	Farmer	Illinois	Discharged 6/11/1865 disability, 7th MO Inf.
Clouts, William	Pvt.	25	–	–	–	–	–	Mustered out 1/2/66, drafted.
Eaton, Washington N.	Pvt.	39	–	–	–	–	–	Mustered out 11/20/1865.
Goldman, Francis	Pvt.	18	5'9"	Light	Gray	Farmer	Missouri	Discharged 8/11/1865, substitute.
Porter, David	Pvt.	27	5'8"	Brown	Gray	Carpenter	Missouri	Mustered out 1/5/1866, substitute.
Pugh, Thomas	Pvt.	20	5'6"	Light	Gray	Farmer	Tennessee	Mustered out 3/2/1865.
Tate/Tait, Joseph	Pvt.	21	5'8½"	Brown	Blue	Farmer	Kentucky	Discharged 7/22/1865, substitute.
Thomas, James	Pvt.	19	6'½"	Black	Blue	Farmer	Missouri	Mustered out 11/20/1865, drafted.
Wagoner, James	Pvt.	24	5'10"	Black	Dark	Farmer	Illinois	Mustered out 3/3/1865.

Died

Soldier	Rank	Age	Ht	Hair	Eyes	Occupation	Nativity	Comment
Abbott, Lyman	Corporal	27	5'10½"	Dark	Blue	Soldier	New Hampshire	KIA 3/29/1865 Spanish Fort.
Armstrong, Washington	Pvt.	19	6'½"	Black	Brown	Farmer	Illinois	Died 6/14/1865 New Orleans Hospital, wounded in Siege of Spanish Fort, substitute.
Bridges, Jeremiah	Pvt.	21	5'8"	Dark	Blue	Farmer	Ireland	Died 1864 in hospital.
Dunley/Dumley, John	Pvt.	23	5'7⅞"	Dark	Gray	Soldier	Kentucky	KIA 12/16/1865 Nashville.
Knobb, Adam	Pvt.	22	5'9"	Light	Blue	Soldier	Germany	Died 5/25/1865 in hospital in Memphis.
Seigert, Fred A.	Pvt.	32	5'6"	Brown	Brown	–	Germany	Died on board steamer, substitute.
Snow, John	Pvt.	33	–	–	–	–	–	Died 9/4/1865 Tuscaloosa, drafted.
Thompson, Gailwood	Pvt.	18	–	–	–	–	–	Died 6/29/1865 Demopolis, substitute.
Whitfield, Marshall*	Cook	28	–	–	–	–	–	Died 11/8/1865 Selma, AL, 7th MO Inf.

Deserted

Soldier	Rank	Age	Ht	Hair	Eyes	Occupation	Nativity	Comment
Cole, Charles	Pvt.	22	5'11"	Red	Gray	Farmer	Ireland	Never reported to company, drafted.
Consadine, John	Pvt.	26	5'4¾"	Light	Blue	Laborer	Ireland	Deserted 1/28/1865, Eastport, MS, substitute.
Cooly, Franklin	Pvt.	20	5'6"	Black	Black	Soldier	Virginia	Deserted 7/8/1865 Demopolis, AL.
Dickerson, William	Pvt.	21	5'9"	Light	Brown	Laborer	Canada	Never reported, substitute.
Flinn, Thomas	Pvt.	26	5'9½"	Light	Brown	Laborer	Ireland	Never reported, substitute.
Jones, William J.	Pvt.	19	5'8"	Brown	Blue	Farmer	Mississippi	Deserted 1/28/1865 Eastport, MS, substitute.
Joyce, Thomas	Pvt.	28	5'4"	Brown	Gray	–	Ireland	Deserted 1/28/1865 Eastport, MS, substitute.
Kinney, Thomas	Pvt.	25	–	–	–	–	–	Never reported.
Mahoney, James	Pvt.	20	5'7"	Brown	Brown	Laborer	Ireland	Mustered out 1/4/1866, substitute.
McGinnis, Peter	Pvt.	25	5'3"	Brown	Blue	Laborer	Ireland	Never reported, substitute.
Mitchell, John	Pvt.	18	5'3½"	Brown	Blue	Laborer	Kentucky	Never reported, substitute.
Nichols, George W.	Pvt.	21	5'8¼"	Dark	Gray	Soldier	Missouri	Deserted 1/17/1865 Eastport, MS.
Roberts, Thomas	Pvt.	–	–	–	–	–	–	Deserted 2/20/1865 Cairo, IL, substitute.
Rook, Benjamin	Pvt.	18	–	–	–	–	–	Deserted 2/23/1865 Memphis, substitute.
Sheridan, David	Pvt.	28	–	–	–	–	–	Deserted 2/20/1865 Cairo, IL, substitute.
Sheridan, Thomas	Pvt.	25	–	–	–	–	–	Deserted 2/20/1865 Cairo, IL, substitute.
Smith, George	Pvt.	21	5'5"	Dark	Blue	Soldier	Illinois	Absent sick.
Snider, Augustus S.	Pvt.	26	5'5"	Brown	Gray	Soldier	–	Deserted 2/20/1865 Cairo, IL, substitute.
Wethers, Isaac*	Pvt.	38	–	–	–	–	–	Never reported, substitute.
Jones, James*	Pvt.	–	–	–	–	–	–	Drafted.
Lottman, Henry*	Pvt.	28	–	–	–	–	–	Drafted.
Rapp, John*	Pvt.	30	–	–	–	–	–	Drafted.

Company C

Soldier	Rank	Age	Ht	Hair	Eyes	Occupation	Nativity	Comment
Lott, James A.	Captain	30	5'9"	Light	Blue	Carpenter	Pennsylvania	Mustered out 1/15/66 Memphis, wounded in Battle of Nashville.
Simmons, William	1st Lt.	20	5'7"	Light	Dark	Carpenter	Illinois	Medal of Honor.

*Mentioned in Missouri Descriptive Roll but not in the National Archives.

Soldier	Rank	Age	Ht	Hair	Eyes	Occupation	Nativity	Comment
Walker, Daniel T.	2nd Lt.	38	–	–	–	–	–	Mustered out 1/15/66 Memphis.
Baker, Walter	Sgt.	20	5'8½"	Dark	Brown	Soldier	Ohio	7th Missouri.
Brown, Horace E.	Sgt.	21	5'9½"	Dark	Black	Soldier	Illinois	Wounded at Nashville, absent with leave since 12/4/1865.
Boyle, John	Sgt.	22	5'6"	Brown	Blue	Soldier	Ireland	
Egan, Andrew	Sgt.	21	5'10½"	Light	Blue	Soldier	Ireland	AWOL 12/1865, mustered out 1/15/66 Memphis.
Pickrell, William T.	Sgt.	25	5'8½"	Dark	Gray	Clerk	Illinois	
Roney, William T.	Sgt.	31	5'9¾"	Light	Blue	Soldier	Pennsylvania	Mustered out 1/15/66 Memphis.
Applegate, Lewis	Corporal	36	5'9"	Brown	Blue	Soldier	Ohio	Mustered out 1/15/66 Memphis.
Campbell, Robert	Corporal	23	5'8½"	Brown	Blue	Soldier	Illinois	Mustered out 1/15/66 Memphis.
Gants, Daniel	Corporal	21	5'6"	Light	Hazel	Soldier	Illinois	Mustered out 1/15/66 Memphis.
Hall, Thomas M.	Corporal	33	5'5½"	Dark	Blue	Soldier	Ireland	Wounded at Nashville, mustered out 1/15/66 Memphis.
Hinman, Smith J.	Corporal	26	6'1"	Dark	Dark	Soldier	Illinois	Mustered out 1/15/66 Memphis, wounded in Battle of Nashville.
Royester, John	Corporal	22	5'8½"	Dark	Brown	Laborer	Scotland	7th Missouri.
Scott, George C.	Corporal	24	5'6¾"	Brown	Brown	Soldier	Ohio	Mustered out 1/15/66 Memphis.
Stratton, George	Corporal	19	5'5"	Brown	Blue	Soldier	New York	Mustered out 1/15/66 Memphis.
Sumpter, Samuel	Corporal	21	5'5¼"	Dark	Blue	Soldier	Illinois	Mustered out 1/15/66 Memphis.
Graham, John T.	Musician	44	5'8"	Brown	Blue	Soldier	D C	Mustered out 1/15/66 Memphis.
Graham, James	Musician	23	5'6½"	Light	Blue	Soldier	Illinois	Mustered out 1/15/66 Memphis.
Walker, Daniel	Musician	18	5'6½"	Light	Blue	Carpenter	Indiana	
Bargeon, Levi	Pvt.	35	5'6"	Black	Brown	Mechanic	France	Mustered out 1/15/66 Memphis, substitute.
Beckham/Becham/Bickam, Andrew	Pvt.	27	5'6½"	Dark	Blue	Farmer	Missouri	Mustered out 1/15/66 Memphis, drafted.
Brown, John H.	Pvt.	24	5'9"	Brown	Hazel	Farmer	Kentucky	Mustered out 1/15/66 Memphis, drafted.
Bormiltz/Brulitz, Henry	Pvt.	22	5'7½"	Brown	Blue	Soldier	Germany	Mustered out 1/15/66 Memphis, wounded in Battle of Nashville.
Bruner, Martin C.	Pvt.	18	5'7½"	Dark	Blue	Farmer	Illinois	Mustered out 1/15/66 Memphis, substitute.
Copeland/Couplin, Jacob	Pvt.	18	5'6½"	Brown	Blue	Farmer	Mississippi	Mustered out 1/15/66 Memphis, substitute.
Curtis, Stephen A.	Pvt.	18	–	–	–	–	–	Mustered out 1/15/66 Memphis, 33rd Missouri.
Cutright, John B.	Pvt.	21	5'10"	Red	Blue	Soldier	Ohio	Mustered out 1/15/66 Memphis.
Davis, Nelson*	Pvt.	43	–	–	–	–	–	Mustered out 1/15/66 Memphis, 33rd Missouri.
Dierking/Durking, Durkin William	Pvt.	24	5'7½"	Brown	Blue	Farmer	At sea	Mustered out 1/15/66 Memphis, drafted.
Doran, Patrick	Pvt.	27	5'6½"	Brown	Blue	Laborer	Ireland	Mustered out 1/15/66 Memphis, 7th Missouri.
Doty, William	Pvt.	31	5'4½"	Red	Blue	Soldier	New York	Mustered out 1/15/66 Memphis.
Drenen/Drennan, Thomas	Pvt.	28	5'8¾"	Red	Gray	Soldier	Illinois	
Doyle, John	Pvt.	18	5'3"	Dark	Brown	Farmer	Illinois	Mustered out 1/15/66 Memphis. Substitute.
Eye, Laban	Pvt.	41	5'7½"	Brown	Hazel	Farmer	Virginia	Mustered out 1/15/66, drafted.
Fassler, David	Pvt.	23	5'10"	Brown	Blue	Farmer	Missouri	Mustered out 1/15/66 Memphis, drafted.
Fege/Fiege, Christian	Pvt.	26	5'5"	Brown	Gray	Farmer	Germany	Mustered out 1/15/66 Memphis, 124th Illinois, drafted.
Fleaths, Christian	Pvt.	30	5'5"	Brown	Brown	Farmer	Switzerland	Mustered out 1/15/66 Memphis, substitute.
Flinn/Flynn, John	Pvt.	33	5'3½"	Brown	Blue	Boatman	Ireland	Mustered out 1/15/66 Memphis, substitute.
Gannon, Thomas	Pvt.	14	4'3"	Fair	Blue	Drummer	Missouri	Mustered out 1/15/66 Memphis, 7th Missouri.
Graham, George	Pvt.	24	5'7½"	Brown	Blue	Soldier	Germany	Under arrest in Mobile since 12/20/65, mustered out 1/15/66 Memphis, substitute.
Hogue/Hoog, Martin	Pvt.	25	5'6"	Dark	Blue	Soldier	Indiana	Mustered out 1/15/66 Memphis.
Hudson, Constance	Pvt.	23	5'7"	Brown	Blue	Farmer	Arkansas	Mustered out 1/15/66 Memphis, drafted.
Hyman/Heinman, Joseph N.	Pvt.	18	5'3½"	Brown	Brown	Farmer	Missouri	Mustered out 1/15/66 Memphis, wounded in Battle of Nashville, substitute.
Jennin, August*	Pvt.	20	–	–	–	–	–	Mustered out 1/15/66 Memphis, substitute.
Johnson, James R.	Pvt.	18	5'	Light	Brown	Farmer	Missouri	Mustered out 1/15/66 Memphis, substitute.
Jones, Charles	Pvt.	39	–	–	–	–	–	Mustered out 1/15/66 Memphis, substitute.
Laflour, Adrian	Pvt.	21	5'6"	–	Light	Farmer	Alabama	Mustered out 1/15/66 Memphis, substitute.
Lechner, Henry	Pvt.	18	5'3¼"	Brown	Hazel	Butcher	Germany	Mustered out 1/4/66, substitute.

*Mentioned in Missouri Descriptive Roll but not in the National Archives.

Soldier	Rank	Age	Ht	Hair	Eyes	Occupation	Nativity	Comment
Leinhart/Lienhart, Samuel*	Pvt.	–	–	–	–	–	–	POW since 7/18/64, mustered out 1/15/66 Memphis.
Liecht, Jacob	Pvt.	27	5'2"	Black	Blue	Laborer	Prussia	Mustered out 1/15/66 Memphis, substitute.
Liecht, John	Pvt.	20	5'2"	Brown	Blue	Laborer	Prussia	Mustered out 1/15/66 Memphis, substitute.
Lynch, Martin	Pvt.	25	5'8"	Fair	Blue	Laborer	Ireland	Mustered out 1/15/66 Memphis, 7th Missouri.
Lyons, Nathan G.	Pvt.	24	5'9"	Sandy	Blue	Farmer	Tennessee	Mustered out 1/15/66 Memphis, drafted.
Mayberry, Michael*	Pvt.	18	5'	Dark	Gray	Farmer	Missouri	Mustered out 5/16/65 Memphis.
McCarty, Dennis	Pvt.	29	5'3½"	Fair	Gray	Laborer	Ireland	Mustered out 1/15/66 Memphis, 7th Missouri.
McCormick, Lawrence	Pvt.	30	6'	Light	Gray	Laborer	Ireland	Mustered out 1/15/66 Memphis, 7th Missouri.
Morehead, David	Pvt.	32	5'10½"	Red	Blue	Soldier	Tennessee	Mustered out 1/15/66 Memphis.
Neal, Samuel M.	Pvt.	27	5'9"	Light	Blue	Soldier	Illinois	Mustered out 1/15/66 Memphis.
O'Brien/O'Bryan, Dennis	Pvt.	33	5'4½"	Brown	Gray	Laborer	Ireland	Mustered out 1/15/66 Memphis, substitute.
Phillips, Thomas B.	Pvt.	39	5'3"	Dark	Gray	Laborer	England	Mustered out 1/15/66 Memphis, substitute.
Phillips, Wilson	Pvt.	26	5'7½"	Black	Blue	Farmer	Tennessee	Mustered out 1/15/66 Memphis, drafted.
Prentice, Owen D.	Pvt.	20	5'11"	Light	Blue	Soldier	Illinois	Mustered out 1/15/66 Memphis, wounded in Battle of Nashville.
Riley/Rielley, John	Pvt.	28	5'8"	Brown	Gray	Laborer	Ireland	Mustered out 1/15/66 Memphis, 7th Missouri.
Roberts, Garrett J.	Pvt.	22	5'11"	Dark	Blue	Soldier	Holland	Mustered out 1/15/66 Memphis.
Robin, Emile*	Pvt.	44	–	–	–	–	–	Mustered out 1/15/66 Memphis, 33rd Missouri.
Roland/Rowland, Joseph	Pvt.	36	5'10"	Brown	Hazel	Farmer	Missouri	Mustered out 1/15/66 Memphis, drafted.
Ryan, Edward	Pvt.	26	5'9"	Brown	Gray	Laborer	Ireland	Wounded at Nashville, mustered out 1/15/66 Memphis, 7th Missouri.
Sanders, Oliver	Pvt.	28	5'10"	Brown	Brown	Farmer	Missouri	Mustered out 1/15/66 Memphis, drafted.
Sellers, George	Pvt.	43	5'9"	Brown	Blue	Farmer	Indiana	Mustered out 1/15/66 Memphis, drafted.
Shaw, Joseph	Pvt.	15	5'	Light	Blue	Farmer	–	Mustered out 1/15/66 Memphis, 7th Missouri.
Smith, Samuel	Pvt.	30	5'7"	Black	Blue	Soldier	Ireland	Mustered out 1/15/66 Memphis.
Stoll, Charles	Pvt.	28	5'5"	Brown	Brown	Laborer	Switzerland	Mustered out 1/15/66 Memphis, substitute.
Tormutz/Torunits, John	Pvt.	40	5'7"	Brown	Hazel	Farmer	Germany	Mustered out 1/15/66 Memphis, 124th Illinois, drafted.
Walker, Charles E.	Pvt.	18	5'6"	Light	Blue	Farmer	Illinois	Mustered out 1/15/66 Memphis.
Watkins/Walkins, Ferrill	Pvt.	18	5'7½"	Dark	Blue	Farmer	Indiana	Mustered out 1/15/66 Memphis, substitute.
Webster, Josiah	Pvt.	21	5'10"	Brown	Blue	Farmer	Kentucky	Mustered out 1/15/66 Memphis, drafted.
West, Jesse	Pvt.	22	5'7"	Brown	Blue	Farmer	Tennessee	Mustered out 1/15/66 Memphis, drafted.
White, George	Pvt.	35	5'9"	Brown	Blue	Farmer	Tennessee	Substitute.
Wright, Thomas	Pvt.	31	5'8"	Sandy	Brown	Laborer	Ireland	Wounded at Spanish Fort, mustered out 1/15/66. Memphis, 7th Missouri

Discharged

Soldier	Rank	Age	Ht	Hair	Eyes	Occupation	Nativity	Comment
Alexander, Hiram	Pvt.	18	5'8"	Light	Blue	Farmer	Illinois	Discharged 7/10/1865 disability.
Berliner, Myers	Pvt.	20	5'11"	Dark	Fair	Clerk	Germany	Mustered out 1/2/66 Memphis, substitute.
Carless/Carlos, William	Pvt.	39	5'6"	Fair	Blue	Laborer	Ireland	Mustered out 11/25/65 Memphis, 7th Missouri.
Dellon/Dillen, Dennis	Pvt.	35	5'6"	Fair	Blue	Laborer	Ireland	Mustered out 11/16/65, 7th Missouri.
Flannagan, Patrick	Pvt.	35	5'5"	Black	Blue	Laborer	Ireland	Mustered out 5/14/1865, 7th Missouri.
Graham, Francis M.*	Pvt.	19	–	–	–	–	–	Discharged 12/31/1865. 33rd Missouri.
Jones, Robert	Pvt.	26	5'8"	Fair	Blue	Farmer	Georgia	Mustered out 10/30/1865, 7th Missouri.
Kelly, Patrick	Pvt.	32	5'10"	Fair	Gray	Laborer	Ireland	Discharged 7/10/1865, 7th Missouri.
Letchner, Henry*	Pvt.	–	–	–	–	–	–	Mustered out 1/15/66 Memphis.
Mabery, Michael	Pvt.	18	5'	Dark	Gray	Farmer	Missouri	Discharged Mound City 7/1865, substitute.
McEntire, John	Pvt.	28	5'4½"	Brown	Blue	Laborer	England	Mustered out 1/2/1866, substitute.
Meyers, Augustus	Pvt.	21	5'6½"	Fair	Blue	Laborer	Missouri	Mustered out 10/27/1865, 7th Missouri.
Reed, Thomas J.	Pvt.	29	5'6"	Brown	Gray	Farmer	Illinois	Mustered out 11/18/65, drafted.
Sites/Sight, Jonathan	Pvt.	22	5'9"	Brown	Brown	Farmer	Virginia	Mustered out 8/17/1865, drafted.
Sullivan, Patrick	Pvt.	24	5'6½"	Black	Blue	Laborer	Ireland	Discharged 6/30/1865 disability, 7th Missouri.

*Mentioned in Missouri Descriptive Roll but not in the National Archives.

DIED

Soldier	Rank	Age	Ht	Hair	Eyes	Occupation	Nativity	Comment
Freakes, Jefferson	Corporal	23	5'3½"	Brown	Blue	Soldier	Illinois	KIA Brentwood Hills 12/16/1864, Color Guard.
Lucas, George M.	Corporal	23	5'10"	Dark	Dark	Soldier	Massachusetts	Died at Jefferson Barracks 11/14/1864.
Sweet, Sylvester	Corporal	23	6'½"	Black	Dark	Soldier	Illinois	Died 4/17/1865 Memphis, TN.
Bender, Frederick	Pvt.	18	5'9"	Auburn	Gray	Farmer	Missouri	Died 3/4/1865, Vicksburg, buried at Vicksburg Natl. Cemetery, substitute.
Keiker, John	Pvt.	18	5'3½"	Dark	Blue	Farmer	Indiana	Died Marion AL 8/4/1865, substitute.
Lombard/Lumbard, John	Pvt.	28	6'1"	Dark	Blue	Laborer	Ireland	Died 1/18/1865 of wounds at Nashville, buried at Jeffersonville IN Ntl. Cemetery, 7th Missouri.
O'Reilly, John	Pvt.	26	5'6"	Brown	Gray	Soldier	Scotland	KIA Spanish Fort 4/4/1865, 7th Missouri.
Rucker, John*	Pvt.	–	–	–	–	–	–	Died 8/24/1865 Marion, AL.
Weech/Weed, John	Pvt.	26	5'7"	Dark	Blue	Farmer	Missouri	KIA Spanish Fort 4/5/1865, substitute.
Wright, John W.	Pvt.	44	–	–	–	–	–	Died 6/20/1865 Selma, AL, drafted.

DESERTED

Soldier	Rank	Age	Ht	Hair	Eyes	Occupation	Nativity	Comment
Bulger, James	Pvt.	30	6'½"	Brown	Blue	Soldier	Ireland	Deserted 2/9/1865 Paducah, substitute.
Byrd, John	Pvt.	20	5'9"	Brown	Gray	Soldier	Tennessee	POW 3/1/1864, Deserted 12/1/1865 Demopolis, AL.
Conley, James	Pvt.	26	5'4"	Brown	Gray	Laborer	Ireland	Deserted 2/9/1865 Paducah, KY, substitute.
Curbey/Kirby, Jerry	Pvt.	38	5'7"	Dark	Gray	Laborer	Ireland	Deserted 4/1/1865, substitute.
Feaurey/Feauscay, Francis	Pvt.	25	5'7"	Brown	Hazel	Soldier	France	Deserted 2/9/1865 Paducah, substitute.
Galony, Francis	Pvt.	42	5'7"	Brown	Hazel	Soldier	Hungary	Deserted 2/9/1865 Paducah, substitute.
Grarat/Gravat, John	Pvt.	30	6'1"	Brown	Gray	Farmer	Illinois	Deserted 4/1/1865, drafted.
Johnson, William	Pvt.	23	5'1"	Black	Blue	Soldier	Ireland	Deserted 2/9/1865 Paducah, substitute.
Rowe, John	Pvt.	–	–	–	–	–	–	Deserted 4/1/1865, substitute.
Welch, John	Pvt.	28	5'6"	Dark	Blue	Laborer	Ireland	Deserted 5/31/865, 7th Missouri.
Williams, John	Pvt.	24	5'9"	Brown	Blue	Farmer	Mississippi	Deserted 2/9/1865 Paducah, substitute.

Company D

Soldier	Rank	Age	Ht	Hair	Eyes	Occupation	Nativity	Comment
Randall, Lyman	Captain	–	5'7½"	Dark	Black	Farmer	Maine	
Apperson, Charles W.	1st Lt.	22	5'5½"	Dark	Gray	Farmer	Illinois	Mustered out 1/15/66 Memphis.
Tasker, James	2nd Lt.	36	5'10½"	Dark	Gray	Stonecutter	New York	Mustered out 1/15/66 Memphis.
Barnett, William	Sgt.	30	5'8"	Black	Gray	Laborer	Ireland	Mustered out 1/15/66 Memphis, 7th Missouri, wounded in Battle of Nashville.
Dyke, Calvin J.	Sgt.	25	5'10"	Light	Gray	Farmer	Tennessee	Mustered out 1/15/66 Memphis.
Hopkins, Ebenezer*	Sgt.	21	–	–	–	–	–	Wounded at Nashville, mustered out 1/15/66 Memphis, 33rd Missouri
Maxwell, William	Sgt.	23	5'11¼"	Light	Blue	Farmer	Illinois	Mustered out 1/15/66 Memphis.
Miller, Solomon	Sgt.	25	5'8½"	Light	Gray	–	Indiana	Mustered out 1/15/66 Memphis, wounded in Battle of Nashville.
O' Donnell, Thomas	Sgt.	21	–	–	–	–	–	7th Missouri.
Wood, Robert	Sgt.	25	5'10"	Dark	Blue	Farmer	Tennessee	Mustered out 1/15/66 Memphis, wounded in Siege of Spanish Fort.
Corcoran, Peter	Corporal	34	5'7½"	Black	Blue	Soldier	Ireland	Wounded in Nashville 12/1864, mustered out 1/15/66 Memphis, 7th Missouri.
Hyde, Patrick	Corporal	34	5'9"	Black	Gray	Stonecutter	Ireland	Mustered out 1/15/66 Memphis, wounded in Battle of Nashville, 7th Missouri.
Kelley/Kelly, James	Corporal	28	5'7"	Black	Black	Laborer	Ireland	Mustered out 1/15/66 Memphis, 7th Missouri.
Martin, John*	Corporal	20	–	–	–	–	–	Mustered out 1/15/66 Memphis.
Miller, Charles	Corporal	30	5'6"	Brown	Hazel	Laborer	Bavaria	Mustered out 1/15/66 Memphis, drafted.
Rinehart, Lewis	Pvt./Corporal	20	5'5¼"	Black	Black	Farmer	Indiana	Mustered out 1/15/66 Memphis.
Thomas, Francis M.	Pvt./Corporal	30	5'8"	Gray	Hazel	Farmer	Tennessee	Mustered out 1/15/66 Memphis, drafted.

*Mentioned in Missouri Descriptive Roll but not in the National Archives.

Soldier	Rank	Age	Ht	Hair	Eyes	Occupation	Nativity	Comment
Bryant, Cyrus	Musician	22	5'6¾"	Black	Dark	–	Indiana	Mustered out 1/15/66 Memphis.
Warden/Worden, George	Musician	21	5'7"	Light	Gray	–	Tennessee	Mustered out 1/15/66 Memphis.
Rhinehart, John*	Wagoner	27	5'6"	Dark	Gray	Farmer	Indiana	Mustered out 1/15/66 Memphis.
Baker, Beverly R.*	Pvt.	17	–	–	–	–	–	Mustered out 1/15/66 Memphis, 33rd Missouri.
Beck, Silas W.	Pvt.	30	5'3"	Brown	Blue	Farmer	N Carolina	Mustered out 1/15/66 Memphis, drafted.
Bracket, Charles	Pvt.	32	5'5½"	Brown	Hazel	Carpenter	Vermont	Mustered out 1/15/66 Memphis, substitute.
Brown, John T.	Pvt.	29	5'5"	Gray	Blue	Laborer	Ireland	Mustered out 1/15/66 Memphis, substitute.
Burton, Melkert H.	Pvt.	21	5'6¾"	Black	Gray	–	Indiana	Mustered out 1/15/66 Memphis.
Cline, Jacob	Pvt.	21	5'	Brown	Gray	Farmer	Germany	Mustered out 1/15/66 Memphis, substitute.
Connelly, Maurice	Pvt.	20	5'11"	Black	Gray	Soldier	Ireland	Mustered out 1/15/66 Memphis, 7th Missouri.
Cooper, George W.	Pvt.	43	5'5¾"	Brown	Blue	Stonecutter	England	Mustered out 1/15/66 Memphis, drafted.
Corder, Joseph	Pvt.	20	5'5¾"	Light	Gray	Soldier	Tennessee	Mustered out 1/15/66 Memphis, wounded in Battle of Nashville.
Cotterell, William	Pvt.	21	5'9"	Brown	Blue	Laborer	Georgia	Wounded in Nashville 12/1864, mustered out 1/15/66 Memphis, 7th Missouri
Coundery, John	Pvt.	25	5'5½"	Light	Gray	Soldier	Indiana	Mustered out 1/15/66 Memphis.
Cox, William D.	Pvt.	26	5'10"	Gray	Hazel	Farmer	Tennessee	Mustered out 1/15/66 Memphis, drafted.
Davis, Edward	Pvt.	33	5'9½"	Brown	Gray	–	Nova Scotia	Mustered out 1/15/66 Memphis.
Dee, Maurice	Pvt.	25	5'7"	Black	Gray	Soldier	Ireland	Mustered out 1/15/66 Memphis, 7th Missouri.
Dougherty, Felix	Pvt.	29	5'5"	Brown	Blue	Laborer	Ireland	Mustered out 1/15/66 Memphis, 7th Missouri.
Dowell, Andrew	Pvt.	32	5'7"	Dark	Gray	Soldier	Virginia	Mustered out 1/15/66 Memphis.
Eck, Herman	Pvt.	30	5'7"	Black	Gray	Miller	Germany	Mustered out 1/15/66 Memphis.
Eisanbuth, August	Pvt.	33	5'7"	Brown	Blue	Farmer	Germany	Mustered out 1/15/66 Memphis, drafted.
Frones/Froner, David	Pvt.	22	6'½"	Light	Gray	Chopper	Indiana	Mustered out 1/15/66 Memphis.
Granay, Cornelius	Pvt.	35	5'7½"	Sandy	Gray	Laborer	Ireland	Mustered out 1/15/66 Memphis, 7th Missouri.
Henderson, Frank	Pvt.	19	5'6"	Light	Blue	Laborer	England	Mustered out 1/15/66 Memphis, substitute.
Herron, Thomas A.	Pvt.	26	5'5"	Black	Blue	Laborer	Ireland	Mustered out 1/15/66 Memphis, 7th Missouri.
Hewitt, William G.	Pvt.	28	5'10"	Brown	Brown	Farmer	Missouri	Mustered out 1/15/66 Memphis, drafted.
House, James	Pvt.	29	5'10"	Light	Blue	Carpenter	Indiana	Mustered out 1/15/66 Memphis, wounded in Siege of Spanish Fort.
Hungate, George	Pvt.	22	5'6¼"	Light	Gray	Farmer	Indiana	Mustered out 1/15/66 Memphis.
Jarvis, Samuel	Pvt.	21	5'4½"	Dark	Dark	Farmer	Missouri	Mustered out 1/15/66 Memphis.
Johnson, Samuel	Pvt.	37	5'5"	Brown	Hazel	Farmer	–	Mustered out 1/15/66 Memphis, drafted.
Keith, Isham/Isam	Pvt.	43	6'2"	Dark	Blue	Farmer	Kentucky	Mustered out 1/15/66 Memphis, substitute.
Kingston, William	Pvt.	21	5'7"	Dark	Hazel	–	Missouri	Mustered out 1/15/66 Memphis, 7th Missouri.
Kufus, Christian	Pvt.	43	5'5"	Brown	Blue	Farmer	Prussia	Mustered out 1/15/66 Memphis, 124th Illinois.
McBride, Joseph	Pvt.	24	5'9½"	Brown	Blue	Bricklayer	Maryland	Mustered out 1/15/66 Memphis, 7th Missouri.
McGinnis, John	Pvt.	28	5'10½"	Brown	Hazel	Soldier	Ireland	Mustered out 1/15/66 Memphis, 7th Missouri.
Moore, Willis	Pvt.	30	5'5½"	Brown	Gray	Farmer	Prussia	Mustered out 1/15/66 Memphis, drafted.
Murphey, Thomas	Pvt.	26	6'1"	Dark	Blue	Laborer	Ireland	Mustered out 1/15/66 Memphis, 7th Missouri, wounded in Battle of Nashville.
Pryfogle, Alexander	Pvt.	22	5'9¾"	Light	Blue	Farmer	Illinois	Wounded at Spanish Fort, mustered out 1/15/66 Memphis.
Sennor, John*	Pvt.	27	5'¾"	Dark	Gray	Farmer	Indiana	Mustered out 12/30/65, substitute.
Sheedy, Michael	Pvt.	33	5'10"	Black	Brown	Laborer	Ireland	Mustered out 1/15/66 Memphis, substitute.
Shelton, Charles	Pvt.	25	5'10"	Light	Blue	Farmer	–	Mustered out 1/15/66 Memphis.
Smith, Andrew J.	Pvt.	20	5'9"	Brown	Hazel	Laborer	Indiana	Mustered out 1/15/66 Memphis, drafted.
Smith, Henry	Pvt.	28	5'6¼"	Light	Gray	Tailor	Ohio	Wounded at Nashville, mustered out 1/15/66 Memphis.
Strother, Robert H.*	Pvt.	18	–	–	–	–	–	Mustered out 1/15/66 Memphis, 33rd Missouri.
Tepperwean, William	Pvt.	35	5'6"	Black	Hazel	Carpenter	Germany	Mustered out 1/15/66 Memphis, substitute.
Thompson, John	Pvt.	18	5'1½"	Brown	Hazel	Laborer	New York	Mustered out 1/15/66 Memphis.
Wisdom, Sargent	Pvt.	34	5'6"	Brown	Blue	Farmer	Tennessee	Mustered out 1/15/66 Memphis, drafted.
Worth, George	Pvt.	19	5'8½"	Brown	Gray	Laborer	Canada	Mustered out 1/15/66 Memphis, substitute.

DISCHARGED

Soldier	Rank	Age	Ht	Hair	Eyes	Occupation	Nativity	Comment
Kelley/Kelly, Timothy	Corporal	19	5'7"	Black	Gray	Laborer	Connecticut	Discharged 6/25/1865, 7th Missouri.
Eaton, Newton J.	Musician	18	5'4"	Light	Blue	–	Illinois	Mustered out 1/6/1865.

*Mentioned in Missouri Descriptive Roll but not in the National Archives.

Soldier	Rank	Age	Ht	Hair	Eyes	Occupation	Nativity	Comment
Dugan, Peter	Pvt.	21	5'6½"	Black	Gray	Plasterer	Massachusetts	Mustered out 4/22/1865, 7th Missouri.
Gillam, Daniel W.	Pvt.	27	5'10"	Dark	Gray	Miner	Missouri	Mustered out 11/3/1865, drafted.
Gravatt, John	Pvt.	30	6'1"	Brown	Gray	Farmer	Illinois	Discharged 8/9/1865, drafted.
Gross, John	Pvt.	22	5'10"	Black	Black	Farmer	Indiana	Discharged for wounds at Spanish Fort 6/18/1865.
Jump, Riley	Pvt.	21	5'3¼"	Light	Gray	Farmer	Ohio	Discharged 9/7/1865 wounded near Albany, MS.
Lalnmandier, Augustus	Pvt.	28	5'7"	Dark	Hazel	Farmer	Missouri	Mustered out 11/3/1865, drafted.
Mertz, John	Pvt.	27	5'7"	Dark	Gray	Cooper	Germany	Mustered out 11/3/1865, drafted.
Morley, Henry	Pvt.	37	5'7"	Brown	Blue	Farmer	England	Mustered out 11/23/1865, drafted.
Murphey, Patrick	Pvt.	27	5'9½"	Brown	Blue	Laborer	Ireland	Mustered out 11/3/1865, drafted.
Paul, Peter	Pvt.	30	5'5½"	Brown	Hazel	Clerk	Germany	Service expired 11/3/1865, drafted.
Riley, James	Pvt.	29	5'	Black	Blue	Miner	Ireland	Dishonorable discharged, confined for 2 years Ft. Pickens, Al.
Rose, George W.	Pvt.	24	5'7½"	Light	Blue	Stonecutter	Ohio	Mustered out 11/3/1865, drafted.
Taake, Henry	Pvt.	21	5'6½"	Brown	Gray	Farmer	Prussia	Mustered out 12/23/1865, substitute.
Tenner, John	Pvt.	20	5'6"	Brown	Brown	Clerk	Saxony	Mustered out 12/30/1865, substitute.
Wood, David	Pvt.	23	5'10¼"	Light	Blue	Farmer	Missouri	Discharged 6/11/1865 of wounds from Nashville

Died

Soldier	Rank	Age	Ht	Hair	Eyes	Occupation	Nativity	Comment
Erwin, William*	Captain	25	5'8¼"	Light	Blue	Farmer	Illinois	Died 4/7/1865 of wounds during Battle of Spanish Fort.
Burns, Rolin	Pvt.	42	5'10"	Brown	Hazel	Farmer	S. Carolina	Died 6/23/1865 Demopolis, AL, drafted.
Crum, William	Pvt.	41	5'8"	Dark	Blue	Farmer	Indiana	Died 1/4/1865 Nashville, buried in Nashville Ntl. Cemetery.
Engledow, Leland*	Pvt.	18	5'8"	Light	Gray	Farmer	Tennessee	Died 1/29/1865 of wounds in action.
Engledow, William C.	Pvt.	24	5'6½"	Light	Gray	Farmer	Tennessee	Died of wounds in action 1/29/1865 at Nashville.
Harrison, Julius	Pvt.	24	5'8"	Dark	Gray	–	Missouri	Murdered 8/16/1865.
Jacquess, Isaac	Pvt.	24	5'9"	Brown	Blue	Farmer	Tennessee	KIA 12/16/1864 Nashville, 7th Missouri.
Keys, Michael	Pvt.	36	5'7"	Dark	Hazel	Farmer	Missouri	Died 11/1/1865 of consumption Demopolis, AL, 7th Missouri.
McCormick, John	Pvt.	20	5'8"	Blonde	Blue	Barkeeper	Ireland	Died 10/6/1865, substitute.
Rinehart, John C.	Pvt.	26	5'5¼"	Black	Black	Farmer	Indiana	Died 1/19/1864 LaGrange, buried Ntl. Cemetery
Sutton, Thomas*	Pvt.	28	5'8"	Black	Black	Saddler	Kentucky	Died 9/17/1864 Memphis, TN.

Deserted

Soldier	Rank	Age	Ht	Hair	Eyes	Occupation	Nativity	Comment
Atkinson, George	Pvt.	31	5'11½"	Light	Gray	–	Tennessee	Deserted 1/25/1865, 7th Missouri, drafted.
Bailey, Joshua	Pvt.	25	5'5"	Light	Gray	Laborer	Missouri	Deserted 7/6/1865, drafted.
Bigsby/Bixby, Nathaniel	Pvt.	26	5'8½"	Dark	Dark	Cooper	Indiana	Deserted 9/2/1864.
Burns, Patrick	Pvt.	22	5'4½"	Light	Gray	Boatman	Ireland	Deserted 3/15/1865, substitute.
Cadenbach, Joseph	Pvt.	22	5'8"	Blonde	Gray	Soldier	Germany	Deserted 2/10/1865.
Carey, James	Pvt.	22	5'6½"	Sandy	Gray	Boatman	Ireland	Deserted 3/15/1865, substitute.
Col/Coe, William	Pvt.	26	5'7"	Brown	Gray	Laborer	Ireland	Deserted 2/10/1865, substitute.
Cooper, Adam P.	Pvt.	26	5'5¼"	Light	Blue	Soldier	Indiana	Deserted 9/7/1865.
Cottrell, Joseph	Pvt.	26	5'9"	Gray	Blue	Farmer	Kentucky	Deserted 8/1/1865, drafted.
Esher, George	Pvt.	23	5'8"	Brown	Blue	Farmer	Mississippi	Deserted 1/27/1865, substitute.
Harlen, James	Pvt.	19	5'9"	Brown	Gray	Clerk	Florida	Deserted 3/15/1865, substitute.
Holst/Holts, John	Pvt.	21	5'4½"	Dark	Dark	Soldier	Missouri	Deserted 2/10/1865, substitute.
Jones, Joseph W.	Pvt.	21	5'10"	Brown	Hazel	Farmer	Tennessee	Deserted 4/26/1865, drafted.
Karey, James*	Pvt.	22	–	–	–	–	–	Deserted 3/15/1865.
Miller, Henry	Pvt.	23	5'5"	Brown	Brown	Waiter	Germany	Deserted 2/10/1865.
O'Hara, Martin	Pvt.	27	5'4"	Brown	Hazel	Laborer	Germany	Deserted 2/10/1865.
Seaman, Charles	Pvt.	22	5'9"	Brown	Blue	Laborer	England	Deserted 1/27/1865, substitute.
Shockley, Jasper	Pvt.	24	5'7"	Black	Gray	Teamster	California	Deserted 9/22/1864.
Singer, Joseph	Pvt.	22	5'7"	Brown	Brown	Boatman	Prussia	Deserted 1/27/1865, substitute.
Stuart, James H.	Pvt.	31	5'11"	Brown	Hazel	Farmer	Missouri	Deserted 9/15/1865, drafted.
Tate, John W.	Pvt.	18	5'5½"	Black	Blue	Farmer	Missouri	Deserted 8/1/1865, substitute.
Trustey, William	Pvt.	24	5'10¼"	Black	Dark	Farmer	Kentucky	Deserted 9/22/1864.

*Mentioned in Missouri Descriptive Roll but not in the National Archives.

Soldier	Rank	Age	Ht	Hair	Eyes	Occupation	Nativity	Comment
Turnbough, William	Pvt.	32	6'½"	Brown	Blue	Farmer	Missouri	Deserted 8/1/1865, drafted.
White, George W.	Pvt.	22	5'5"	Brown	Gray	Farmer	Ohio	Deserted 6/16/1865, substitute.

TRANSFERRED

Soldier	Rank	Age	Ht	Hair	Eyes	Occupation	Nativity	Comment
O'Donal/O'Donnel Thomas	Sgt.	21	5'7"	Light	Blue	Carriage Maker	Ireland	Transferred to Reserve Corps.

Company E

Soldier	Rank	Age	Ht	Hair	Eyes	Occupation	Nativity	Comment
Roney, Levi D.	Captain	24	5'8"	Brown	Hazel	Soldier	Ohio	
Meyers, John	1st Lt.	30	5'6"	Brown	Gray	Farmer	Germany	Mustered out 1/15/66 Memphis.
Perry, John F.	2nd Lt.	28	6'	Brown	Hazel	Soldier	Ohio	Commanded Co. B 1865.
Bartley, Edward T.	Sgt.	24	5'6½"	Brown	Hazel	Soldier	Ohio	Mustered out 1/15/66 Memphis.
Behymer, Francis	1st Sgt.	27	5'7"	Dark	Black	Soldier	Ohio	Mustered out 1/15/66 Memphis.
Butler, George	Sgt.	19	5'11½"	Brown	Brown	Soldier	Illinois	Mustered out 1/15/66 Memphis, wounded in Battle of Nashville.
Finnell, George T.	Sgt.	23	5'7"	Sandy	Gray	Soldier	Virginia	Wounded in Battle of Nashville 12/1864.
Judy, John	Sgt.	21	5'5"	Sandy	Hazel	Soldier	Ohio	
Smith, William	Sgt.	22	5'7"	Dark	Blue	–	Illinois	
Taylor, Edward S.	Sgt.	19	5'8"	Brown	Dark	Soldier	Illinois	Mustered out 1/15/66 Memphis.
Evans, William	Corporal	29	5'8"	Light	Gray	Farmer	Kentucky	Mustered out 1/15/66 Memphis.
Gallaspie/Gillespie, Lewis	Corporal	24	5'10"	Light	Blue	Soldier	Illinois	
Harris, James	Corporal	37	5'6"	Black	Gray	Laborer	Ireland	7th Missouri.
Helms, John	Corporal	32	5'7"	Brown	Brown	Farmer	Hanover	Mustered out 1/15/66 Memphis, 124th Illinois, drafted.
Hood, George F.	Corporal	21	5'4"	Light	Gray	Soldier	Illinois	Mustered out 1/15/66 Memphis.
Lane, Charles	Corporal	18	5'6"	Light	Brown	Farmer	Ohio	Mustered out 1/15/66 Memphis.
Ryan, Alexander	Corporal	24	5'6"	Brown	Hazel	Soldier	Ohio	Mustered out 1/15/66 Memphis.
Taylor, John R.	Corporal	20	5'4"	Light	Blue	Engineer	Missouri	Sentenced to 2 yrs. for desertion in 7/1864, 7th Missouri.
Colvin, Solomon	Musician	18	5'5"	Brown	Black	Soldier	Ohio	Mustered out 1/15/66 Memphis.
Baucum, Avery	Pvt.	25	5'11"	Brown	Gray	Farmer	Germany	Absent since 7/28/1865, drafted.
Bedle, Early	Pvt.	18	5'8"	Light	Gray	Farmer	Illinois	Convalescent camp 1864, mustered out 1/15/66 Memphis.
Berle, Prodas	Pvt.	26	5'3"	Brown	Gray	Photographer	Germany	Mustered out 1/15/66 Memphis, substitute.
Bolden, Thomas	Pvt.	22	5'8"	Brown	Gray	Laborer	England	Mustered out 1/15/66 Memphis, 7th Missouri.
Brogan, John	Pvt.	28	5'8½"	Brown	Gray	Soldier	Ireland	Mustered out 1/15/66 Memphis, 7th Missouri.
Burden, David*	Pvt.	27	5'10½"	Light	Blue	Salesman	England	Discharged 9/18/1865.
Butler, Amos	Pvt.	22	5'10"	Black	Hazel	Farmer	Ohio	Wounded in Battle of Nashville.
Conway, John	Pvt.	24	5'5"	Brown	Blue	Laborer	Ireland	Mustered out 1/15/66 Memphis, drafted.
Cordier, Celestin	Pvt.	40	5'8½"	Dark	Dark	Farmer	France	Absent since 7/28/1865, drafted.
Crider, Joseph C.	Pvt.	26	5'7"	Brown	Blue	Farmer	Missouri	Mustered out 1/15/66 Memphis, 124th Illinois, drafted.
Deroin, Edward	Pvt.	22	5'7½"	Dark	Dark	Ship carpenter	Missouri	Mustered out 1/15/66 Memphis, 33rd Missouri.
Duncan, William	Pvt.	38	5'9"	Brown	Brown	Laborer	N. Carolina	Mustered out 1/15/66 Memphis, drafted.
Fairbanks, Henry	Pvt.	55	5'9"	Light	Gray	Carpenter	Maine	AWOL 1/66, 7th Missouri.
Gaddy, George	Pvt.	23	5'11"	Light	Gray	Soldier	Illinois	Detached duty Alabama.
Garrison, Robert	Pvt.	28	5'8"	Brown	Hazel	Farmer	Missouri	Mustered out 1/15/66, drafted.
Hardy, William	Pvt.	21	5'8½"	Light	Gray	Soldier	Indiana	
Harper, William H.	Pvt.	22	5'6"	Light	Blue	Stonecutter	Massachusetts	Mustered out 1/15/66 Memphis, 7th Missouri.
Hays, Michael	Pvt.	30	5'8"	Brown	Hazel	Laborer	Ireland	Mustered out 1/15/66 Memphis, 7th Missouri.
Hays, William	Pvt./Cook	21	5'8"	Black	Black	Farmhand	Mississippi	7th Missouri.
Hurley/Harley, John	Pvt.	43	5'4½"	Brown	Gray	Laborer	Ireland	Mustered out 1/15/66 Memphis, 7th Missouri.
Johnson, Thomas B.	Pvt.	18	5'9½"	Brown	Gray	Farmer	Indiana	Mustered out 1/15/66 Memphis, substitute.
Jones, Doke	Pvt.	22	5'7"	Brown	Gray	Farmer	Pennsylvania	Mustered out 1/15/66 Memphis.

*Mentioned in Missouri Descriptive Roll but not in the National Archives.

Soldier	Rank	Age	Ht	Hair	Eyes	Occupation	Nativity	Comment
Kaple, Henry	Pvt.	22	5'3"	Brown	Blue	Shoemaker	Germany	Mustered out 1/15/66 Memphis, 124th Illinois.
Keif, William	Pvt.	19	5'8"	Light	Gray	–	Germany	Mustered out 1/15/66 Memphis, 7th Missouri.
Kemp/Komp, Albert	Pvt.	19	5'3"	Light	Blue	Clerk	Prussia	Mustered out 1/15/66 Memphis, substitute.
Kennedy, John	Pvt.	37	5'4½"	Gray	Brown	Tailor	Ireland	Mustered out 1/15/66 Memphis, 7th Missouri.
Kennedy, Mathew*	Pvt.	38	5'8"	Brown	Blue	Laborer	Ireland	Mustered out 1/15/66 Memphis, substitute.
Kennedy, William	Pvt.	21	5'4"	Brown	Blue	Soldier	Vermont	Mustered out 1/15/66 Memphis, substitute.
King, John A.	Pvt.	22	5'10"	Brown	Gray	Farmer	Hanover	Mustered out 1/15/66 Memphis, 124th Illinois.
Kinney, Henry	Pvt.	40	5'5"	Brown	Gray	Laborer	Ireland	Mustered out 1/15/66 Memphis, 7th Missouri.
Koeling, Gotlieb	Pvt.	24	5'4"	Brown	Blue	Sailor	Prussia	Mustered out 1/15/66 Memphis, substitute.
Lee, John	Pvt.	29	5'9½"	Dark	Gray	Laborer	Virginia	Mustered out 1/15/66 Memphis, 33rd Missouri.
Loher/Lohn, Benjamin	Pvt.	18	5'9"	Light	Blue	Farmer	Missouri	Substitute.
Long, John	Pvt.	33	6'1"	Brown	Gray	Farmer	Belgium	Mustered out 1/15/66 Memphis, substitute.
Major, Richard	Pvt.	25	5'4"	Brown	Hazel	Laborer	England	Mustered out 1/15/66 Memphis, drafted.
Mars, William H.	Pvt.	17	5'6"	Brown	Hazel	Laborer	Massachusetts	Mustered out 1/15/66 Memphis, 7th Missouri.
May, Joseph C.	Pvt.	18	5'11"	Brown	Gray	Farmer	Kentucky	Mustered out 1/15/66 Memphis, 33rd Missouri.
McGuire, James	Pvt.	40	5'6"	Light	Gray	Laborer	Ireland	Mustered out 1/15/66 Memphis, 7th Missouri.
Notestine, James	Pvt.	17	5'4"	Light	Blue	–	Illinois	Mustered out 1/15/66 Memphis.
Ogle, William	Pvt.	39	5'8"	Gray	Hazel	Farmer	Missouri	Mustered out 1/15/66 Memphis, drafted.
Price, William	Pvt.	24	5'9"	Brown	Gray	Soldier	Pennsylvania	Substitute.
Rhettmire, Christopher	Pvt.	24	5'6"	Brown	Gray	Farmer	Prussia	Mustered out 1/15/66 Memphis, 124th Illinois, drafted.
Schatte, Werner*	Pvt.	20	5'8"	Dark	Hazel	–	Switzerland	Substitute.
Seba, Frederick	Pvt.	22	5'8"	Brown	Hazel	Farmer	Hanover	Mustered out 1/15/66 Memphis, 124th Illinois, drafted.
Shultz, John	Pvt.	21	5'6½"	Brown	Brown	Laborer	Germany	Mustered out 1/15/66 Memphis, 7th Missouri.
Smith, John	Pvt.	37	5'7½"	Brown	Blue	Soldier	Denmark	Mustered out 1/15/66 Memphis, 7th Missouri.
Snoddy, Samuel	Pvt.	24	5'7"	Brown	Blue	Farmer	Tennessee	Mustered out 1/15/66 Memphis, drafted.
Stuteville, Bagwell	Pvt.	25	5'8"	Brown	Gray	Soldier	Illinois	Mustered out 1/15/66 Memphis.
Thompson, Nathan	Pvt.	18	5'2"	Light	Blue	Soldier	Ohio	Mustered out 1/15/66 Memphis.
Tibbs, George	Pvt.	25	5'9"	Brown	Gray	Farmer	Kentucky	Mustered out 1/15/66 Memphis, drafted.
Urbauck, John	Pvt.	25	5'3"	Dark	Blue	Farmer	Germany	Mustered out 1/15/66 Memphis, substitute.
Walker, Daniel	Pvt.	24	5'5"	Light	Blue	Soldier	Missouri	Mustered out 1/15/66 Memphis.
Werner, John T.	Pvt.	19	5'9"	Light	Brown	Clerk	Ohio	AWOL, substitute.
White, Patrick	Pvt.	35	5'9"	Brown	Brown	Laborer	Ireland	Mustered out 1/15/66 Memphis, 7th Missouri.
Willis, Fleming	Pvt.	35	5'11"	Brown	Brown	Farmer	Virginia	33rd Illinois.
Willoughby, John V.	Pvt.	29	5'7½"	Brown	Blue	Farmer	Tennessee	Mustered out 1/15/66 Memphis, drafted.
Witzig/Nitzig, James P.	Pvt.	38	5'5"	Light	Blue	Coppersmith	France	AWOL, drafted.
Wright, John	Pvt.	33	5'9"	Brown	Blue	Cooper	N. Carolina	Mustered out 1/15/66 Memphis, 7th Missouri, drafted.

DISCHARGED

Soldier	Rank	Age	Ht	Hair	Eyes	Occupation	Nativity	Comment
Blew, Jacob	1st Lt.	–	–	–	–	–	–	Mustered out 8/16/1864.
Perry, John F.	2nd Lt.	28	6'	Brown	Hazel	Farmer	Ohio	Commanded Co. B 1865.
Delevadwa/Delwadwo, Petro	Sgt.	36	5'5"	Light	Blue	Blacksmith	Italy	Discharged 4/11/1865 Memphis, wounded at Nashville, 7th Missouri.
Adams, Thomas J.	Pvt.	23	5'5"	Light	Gray	Farmer	Tennessee	Discharged 11/20/1865 disability, drafted.
Blazer, Henry	Pvt.	27	5'4"	Sandy	Blue	Farmer	Germany	Discharged 11/15/1865, drafted.
Dowd, John	Pvt.	27	5'7"	Brown	Gray	Soldier	Ireland	Mustered out 2/8/1865, 7th Missouri.
Fairbanks, William H.	Pvt.	22	5'8"	Light	Gray	Farmer	Maine	Shown as deserted 7/16/1865 Demopolis, later relieved of charge, 7th Missouri.
Fletcher, Jesse	Pvt.	37	5'8"	Brown	Hazel	Farmer	Missouri	Mustered out 12/2/1865 Montgomery, AL, drafted.
Friend, William H.	Pvt.	22	5'4½"	Light	Gray	Farmer	Ohio	Discharged 3/1865.
Hawkins, Robert H.	Pvt.	26	5'11"	Brown	Blue	Farmer	Missouri	Discharged 12/30/1865, shown as deserted 9/30/1865 in descriptive book, drafted.

*Mentioned in Missouri Descriptive Roll but not in the National Archives.

Soldier	Rank	Age	Ht	Hair	Eyes	Occupation	Nativity	Comment
Herse, James J.	Pvt.	18	5'10"	Light	Gray	Laborer	Illinois	Mustered out 1/15/66 Memphis, substitute.
Jenner, Edward	Pvt.	19	5'9"	Dark	Gray	Farmer	Illinois	Dishonorably discharge by general court-martial 12/29/1864 Jefferson City.
Judy, Henry C.	Pvt.	21	5'9"	Black	Black	Soldier	Ohio	Discharge 6/13/1865, wounded in Battle of Nashville.
Leahy, Patrick	Pvt.	23	5'4½"	Brown	Gray	Laborer	New York	Mustered out 2/1/1865, 7th Missouri.
McDanel, Jackson J.	Pvt.	26	5'7"	Dark	Dark	Farmer	S. Carolina	Discharged 5/25/1865 NY City, drafted.
Meyer, Henry	Pvt.	19	5'10"	Blonde	Gray	Clerk	Germany	Mustered out 1/5/66, substitute.
Padden/Paddin, Martin	Pvt.	24	5'8"	Brown	Gray	Laborer	Ireland	Wounded at Nashville, discharged 5/2/1865, 7th Missouri.
Richhart, Benjamin Alexander	Pvt.	26	5'6"	Brown	Blue	Farmer	Ohio	Discharged 7/21/1865 disability, drafted.

DIED

Soldier	Rank	Age	Ht	Hair	Eyes	Occupation	Nativity	Comment
Notestine, William F.	Captain	22	5'11"	Brown	Gray	Soldier	Ohio	Died 2/16/1865 of wounds from Nashville.
Heisfind, Bentley	Pvt.	17	5'8"	Dark	Gray	Farmer	Illinois	Died 1/8/1865 of wounds in Battle of Nashville.
Knoph/Knopt, Holmes	Pvt.	19	5'8"	Light	Blue	Farmer	Illinois	Died 12/22/1864 of wounds in Battle of Nashville.
Laired, Alfred H.	Pvt.	18	5'5¾"	Black	Black	Farmer	Pennsylvania	Died of disease 7/6/1865, buried at Marietta Ntl. Cemetery, substitute
Scheible, Gottlieb	Pvt.	25	5'8"	Light	Gray	Soldier	Germany	Died 12/20/1864 in Nashville.

DESERTED

Soldier	Rank	Age	Ht	Hair	Eyes	Occupation	Nativity	Comment
Canola, Charles	Pvt.	36	5'8"	Black	Gray	Miner	Italy	Deserted 2/23/1865 New Orleans.
Field, Thomas	Pvt.	25	5'7"	Brown	Blue	Laborer	England	Deserted 2/7/1865 Eastport, MS, substitute.
Flannagan, James	Pvt.	21	5'9"	Brown	Gray	Laborer	Ireland	Deserted 2/10/1865 Cairo, IL, substitute.
Gardaner/Gardner, James	Pvt.	24	5'7"	Brown	Blue	Farmer	Missouri	Deserted 7/19/1865 Demopolis, drafted.
Grady, Michael	Pvt.	23	5'8"	Black	Hazel	Boatman	Ireland	Deserted 2/27/1865 New Orleans, substitute.
Hager, Ignatz	Pvt.	35	5'8"	Brown	Hazel	–	Germany	Deserted 2/28/1865 New Orleans, substitute.
Haley/Hayley, Charles	Pvt.	27	5'6"	Brown	Gray	Painter	Canada	Deserted 2/10/1865 Cairo, IL, substitute.
Harris, John	Pvt.	20	5'6"	Brown	Blue	Laborer	Ireland	Deserted 1/25/1865 Paducah, drafted.
Hickam/Hickman, Robert	Pvt.	29	5'8"	Black	Blue	Farmer	Missouri	Deserted 7/19/1865 Demopolis, drafted.
Hunter, Squire	Pvt.	19	5'9½"	Brown	Blue	Laborer	Missouri	Deserted 7/11/1865, substitute.
Johnson, Edward	Pvt.	19	5'5"	Sandy	Blue	Laborer	Ireland	Deserted 9/18/1865 Marionville, AL, substitute.
Kepel, Frank	Pvt.	22	5'8"	Brown	Blue	Gardener	Hanover	Deserted 2/10/1865 Cairo, IL, substitute.
Latham, William	Pvt.	32	5'9"	Brown	Blue	Farmer	Indiana	Deserted 9/30/1865 Marion, AL, drafted.
Lewis, John	Pvt.	22	5'3½"	Brown	Hazel	Laborer	Ireland	Deserted 1/26/1865 Paducah, substitute.
Mack, William	Pvt.	36	5'1"	Brown	Blue	Soldier	Ireland	Deserted 3/4/1865 New Orleans, substitute.
McAuley, Daniel	Pvt.	21	5'6"	Black	Gray	Boatman	Scotland	Never reported, substitute.
Murphy, John	Pvt.	23	5'7"	Brown	Blue	Laborer	Ireland	Deserted 2/10/1865 Cairo, substitute.
Nallan/Nallen, William	Pvt.	25	5'5"	Dark	Blue	Laborer	Ireland	Substitute.
Owen, George	Pvt.	22	5'5½"	Brown	Blue	Sailor	Ireland	Deserted 1/26/1865 Paducah, KY, substitute.
Richerson, Charles	Pvt.	30	5'8"	Brown	Blue	Farmer	Tennessee	Deserted 11/27/1865 Demopolis, AL, drafted.
Shatty, Werner	Pvt.	20	5'8"	Dark	Hazel	Mason	Switzerland	Deserted 2/10/1865 Cairo, IL, substitute.
Vaughn, Caswell	Pvt.	36	5'7½"	Dark	Hazel	Farmer	Tennessee	Deserted 7/19/1865 Demopolis, drafted.
White, Charles	Pvt.	19	5'8"	Light	Blue	Farmer	Canada	Deserted 1/28/1865 East Port, MS.
White, William C.	Pvt.	24	5'8"	Brown	Brown	Farmer	Missouri	Deserted 11/27/1865 Demopolis, drafted.

Company F

Soldier	Rank	Age	Ht	Hair	Eyes	Occupation	Nativity	Comment
Smith, Charles	Captain	40	5'7"	Black	Hazel	Soldier	Maryland	Mustered out 1/15/66 Memphis, wounded in Battle of Nashville.

*Mentioned in Missouri Descriptive Roll but not in the National Archives.

Soldier	Rank	Age	Ht	Hair	Eyes	Occupation	Nativity	Comment
McElyea, Wilford	1st Lt.	22	5'7¾"	Light	Gray	Soldier	Indiana	Mustered out 1/15/66 Memphis.
Greenwood, George A.	2nd Lt.	24	5'7"	Light	Blue	Soldier	Tennessee	Mustered out 1/15/66 Memphis.
Caughan, Michael	Sgt.	20	5'2"	Brown	Gray	Soldier	Ireland	Mustered out 1/15/66 Memphis, wounded in Battle of Nashville.
Draper, Elias	Sgt.	28	5'11"	Brown	Gray	Soldier	Indiana	Mustered out 1/15/66 Memphis.
Hand/Hant, Benjamin L.	Sgt.	20	5'9"	Auburn	Gray	Soldier	Indiana	Mustered out 1/15/66 Memphis.
Holman, Gilbert	Sgt.	19	5'10"	Light	Blue	Farmer	Illinois	Transferred to Veteran Reserve Corps.
Gavin, Ludovic	Sgt.	30	5'11½"	Light	Hazel	Soldier	Scotland	Mustered out 1/15/66.
Gillard, William H.	Sgt.	26	5'9"	Light	Blue	Soldier	Illinois	Mustered out 1/15/66 Memphis.
Glassman, Peter	Sgt.	22	5'2"	Brown	Gray	Soldier	Kentucky	Mustered out 1/15/66 Memphis.
Colclasure, William	Corporal	36	5'8"	Light	Blue	Soldier	Tennessee	Reenlisted, mustered out 1/15/66 Memphis.
Gilman, Jesse	Corporal	24	5'5½"	Auburn	Hazel	Soldier	Pennsylvania	Mustered out 1/15/66 Memphis.
Green, John	Corporal	44	6'1"	Gray	Gray	Farmer	Pennsylvania	Mustered out 1/15/66 Memphis, 33rd Missouri.
Holman, Robert	Corporal	26	5'8¾"	Light	Blue	Soldier	Illinois	Mustered out 1/15/66 Memphis.
Lackey/Leackey, William H.	Corporal	22	5'7"	Brown	Blue	Farmer	Illinois	Mustered out 1/15/66 Memphis.
Leach, Lewis	Corporal	28	5'5"	Auburn	Hazel	Soldier	Ohio	Mustered out 1/15/66 Memphis.
Rasher, Benjamin/ Rusher	Corporal	20	5'5¼"	Brown	Blue	Soldier	Ohio	Mustered out 1/15/66 Memphis.
Stevens, John*	Corporal	–	5'10"	Auburn	Gray	Cooper	Ohio	
Ayres, William*	Drummer	19	–	–	–	–	–	
Robertson, William E.	Wagoner	23	5'8"	Brown	Hazel	Soldier	Ohio	
Vickery, Littleton	Wagoner	30	5'7"	Light	Blue	Soldier	Ohio	Mustered out 1/15/66 Memphis.
Bayles, Elijah J.	Pvt.	24	5'9¼"	Light	Blue	Soldier	Kentucky	Voluntary reduction in rank, mustered out 1/15/66 Memphis.
Bippis, John B.	Pvt.	40	5'6"	Brown	Blue	–	Germany	Mustered out 1/15/66 Memphis, substitute.
Bullock, George W.	Pvt.	45	5'11"	Black	Blue	Farmer	New York	Mustered out 1/15/66 Memphis, 33rd Missouri.
Conrad, Robert	Pvt.	28	5'7"	Brown	Blue	Blacksmith	Germany	Mustered out 1/15/66 Memphis, substitute.
Dappa, August	Pvt.	26	5'3"	Brown	Gray	Farmer	Switzerland	Mustered out 1/15/66 Memphis, transferred from 124th Illinois.
Draper, Benjamin	Pvt.	35	5'9"	Brown	Gray	Soldier	Indiana	Mustered out 1/15/66 Memphis.
Easley, Hiram	Pvt.	29	5'8¾"	Brown	Gray	Soldier	Illinois	Mustered out 1/15/66 Memphis.
Eickenman/ Eicherman, Herman	Pvt.	25	5'8"	Brown	Hazel	Farmer	Germany	Mustered out 1/15/66 Memphis, 124th Illinois, drafted.
Gibbs, Joseph C.	Pvt.	40	6'	Brown	Gray	Farmer	Virginia	Mustered out 1/15/66 Memphis.
Gray, George	Pvt.	28	5'5¼"	Auburn	Hazel	Soldier	Ireland	Mustered out 1/15/66 Memphis.
Hagel, George W.	Pvt.	26	5'8"	Light	Blue	Soldier	Ohio	Mustered out 1/15/66 Memphis.
Halterman, Joseph	Pvt.	20	5'2¾"	Light	Blue	Soldier	Ohio	Mustered out 1/15/66 Memphis.
Hamby, David S.	Pvt.	32	5'10"	Brown	Blue	Farmer	Missouri	Mustered out 1/15/66 Memphis, drafted.
Harmon, Peter	Pvt.	25	5'5¾"	Auburn	Hazel	Soldier	Ohio	Mustered out 1/15/66 Memphis.
Hawkins, William E.	Pvt.	41	5'11"	Brown	Blue	Farmer	Tennessee	Mustered out 1/15/66 Memphis, drafted.
Haws, Jefferson	Pvt.	18	5'5"	Brown	Gray	Farmer	Illinois	Mustered out 1/15/66 Memphis.
Haws, Thomas	Pvt.	25	5'7¼"	Auburn	Hazel	Soldier	Illinois	Mustered out 1/15/66 Memphis.
Henson, William	Pvt.	21	5'7½"	Light	Gray	Soldier	Tennessee	
Herman, John	Pvt.	30	5'6"	Brown	Blue	Laborer	Mississippi	Mustered out 1/15/66 Memphis, substitute.
Hoffman, Peter	Pvt.	30	5'8"	Brown	Hazel	Farmer	Prussia	Mustered out 1/15/66 Memphis, drafted.
Jordan, Frederick	Pvt.	25	5'6½"	Brown	Hazel	Soldier	Illinois	Mustered out 1/15/66 Memphis.
Keaton, William*	Pvt.	26	5'11"	Brown	Blue	Farmer	Tennessee	Mustered out 1/15/66 Memphis, drafted.
Manny, Jacob	Pvt.	43	5'5"	Brown	Blue	Farmer	Germany	Mustered out 1/15/66 Memphis, drafted.
Mattox, Joseph	Pvt.	39	5'7"	Gray	Blue	Soldier	Kentucky	Mustered out 1/15/66 Memphis.
McDonald, William	Pvt.	42	5'6"	Black	Gray	Farmer	Scotland	Mustered out 1/15/66 Memphis, substitute.
McGhee, James H.	Pvt.	26	5'8"	Brown	Gray	Farmer	Missouri	Mustered out 1/15/66 Memphis, drafted.
McLean, Samuel	Pvt.	25	5'10"	Brown	Blue	Soldier	Ohio	Mustered out 1/15/66 Memphis.
Meek, William H.	Pvt.	23	5'6¼"	Light	Blue	Soldier	Ohio	Mustered out 1/15/66 Memphis.
Meyer, Peter	Pvt.	31	5'7"	Brown	Gray	Farmer	Germany	Mustered out 1/15/66 Memphis, substitute.
Miller, Calvin R.	Pvt.	20	5'9½"	Light	Gray	Soldier	Illinois	Mustered out 1/15/66 Memphis.

*Mentioned in Missouri Descriptive Roll but not in the National Archives.

Soldier	Rank	Age	Ht	Hair	Eyes	Occupation	Nativity	Comment
Miller, John D.	Pvt.	30	5'10"	Brown	Hazel	Shoemaker	Germany	Mustered out 1/15/66 Memphis, drafted.
Myers, John	Pvt.	41	5'9"	Brown	Gray	Farmer	Kentucky	Mustered out 1/15/66 Memphis, drafted.
O'Brien/O'Brian, David	Pvt.	18	5'6"	Brown	Hazel	Blacksmith	Tennessee	On detached service Montgomery, AL, substitute.
Oggeschky, Lewis	Pvt.	37	5'5"	Brown	Blue	Farmer	Prussia	Mustered out 1/15/66 Memphis, 124th Illinois, drafted.
Parks, James W.	Pvt.	24	5'7½"	Brown	Blue	Soldier	Ohio	Medal of Honor, Nashville Capture of Flag.
Reilly, Edward*	Pvt.	25	5'3¼"	Brown	Hazel	Soldier	Ireland	
Rudy, John	Pvt.	38	5'6"	Brown	Blue	Farmer	Germany	Mustered out 1/15/66 Memphis, drafted.
Rusher, Masterson	Pvt.	26	5'8"	Black	Black	Farmer	Indiana	Sick in hospital 3/1865.
Senkint, Augustus	Pvt.	35	5'1½"	Brown	Hazel	Soldier	Germany	Mustered out 1/15/66 Memphis.
Sessions, Solomon	Pvt.	18	5'5"	Light	Blue	Farmer	Illinois	Mustered out 1/15/66 Memphis.
Smith, Andrew J.	Pvt.	40	5'11"	Brown	Blue	Farmer	Tennessee	Mustered out 1/15/66 Memphis, drafted.
Smith, William	Pvt.	34	5'7"	Brown	Blue	Farmer	Mississippi	Mustered out 1/15/66 Memphis, substitute.
Spurgeon, David	Pvt.	24	5'9¾"	Auburn	Hazel	Soldier	Indiana	Mustered out 1/15/66 Memphis.
Stockwell, Peter	Pvt.	27	5'7"	Brown	Hazel	Soldier	England	Mustered out 1/15/66 Memphis.
Swango, John H.	Pvt.	25	5'8"	Brown	Hazel	Soldier	Illinois	Mustered out 1/15/66 Memphis.
Taylor, George	Pvt.	18	5'1"	Black	Brown	Laborer	Ohio	Mustered out 1/15/66 Memphis, substitute.
Tilden, Joseph	Pvt.	18	5'7"	Brown	Blue	Farmer	Illinois	Mustered out 1/15/66 Memphis, substitute.
Wallace, James R.	Pvt.	30	5'8"	Brown	Blue	Farmer	Virginia	Mustered out 1/15/66 Memphis, substitute.
Walter, Michael	Pvt.	26	5'2"	Brown	Blue	Laborer	Germany	Mustered out 1/15/66 Memphis, substitute.
Weirman, John H.	Pvt.	23	5'5"	Auburn	Blue	Soldier	Pennsylvania	Wounded at Spanish Fort 3/27/1865.
Wiky, John	Pvt.	32	5'10"	Black	Brown	Boatman	Mississippi	Mustered out 1/15/66 Memphis, substitute.
Zeigler, Florentine	Pvt.	20	5'½"	Brown	Blue	Blacksmith	Germany	Mustered out 1/15/66 Memphis, substitute.

DISCHARGED

Soldier	Rank	Age	Ht	Hair	Eyes	Occupation	Nativity	Comment
Cleland, William	Captain	26	–	–	–	–	–	Promoted to Major.
Finley, John T.	1st Lt.	27	–	–	–	–	–	Mustered out 8/15/1864.
Finch, Walton H.	1st Lt.	23	5'7"	Auburn	Gray	Soldier	Illinois	Resigned 9/7/1865, promoted to Adjuvant
Allison, John H.	Pvt.	31	5'4½"	Black	Blue	Farmer	Virginia	Mustered out 11/6/1865, drafted.
Barnes, John	Pvt.	21	6'	Light	Blue	Farmer	Missouri	Mustered out 11/20/1865 Montgomery, AL, 33rd Missouri.
Bennes, John*	Pvt.	21	–	–	–	–	–	Mustered out 11/6/1865.
Besheer, Wade	Pvt.	18	5'5"	Brown	Hazel	Farmer	Tennessee	Mustered out 1/3/66 Memphis, substitute.
Cressman, William	Pvt.	39	5'7½"	Brown	Blue	Teamster	N. Carolina	Mustered out 11/6/1865, drafted.
Failes, Alvin	Pvt.	21	5'8"	Dark	Black	Blacksmith	Indiana	Mustered out 10/19/1865, 33rd Missouri.
Ford, Francis D.	Pvt.	38	5'6¼"	Brown	Blue	Farmer	Kentucky	Mustered out 11/6/1865, drafted.
Gillman, Charles	Pvt.	19	5'2¾"	Light	Blue	Soldier	Illinois	Discharged 8/24/1865. (Also shown as deserted same date as wounded in Battle of Nashville.)
Gowan, John	Pvt.	31	6'	Dark	Brown	Laborer	Canada	Discharged 7/18/1865, drafted.
Haws, Gilbert	Pvt.	21	5'7"	Black	Hazel	Farmer	Illinois	Mustered out 7/18/1865 from hospital.
Hellion, Edward	Pvt.	27	5'10"	Black	Blue	Farmer	Kentucky	Muster out 1/3/1866, substitute.
Henson/Henston, Hiram	Pvt.	36	5'8"	Auburn	Blue	Soldier	England	Discharged 3/13/1865.
Horton, Elias	Pvt.	19	5'7"	Brown	Gray	Farmer	Kentucky	Mustered out 1/3/1866, substitute.
King, George A.	Pvt.	18	5'9"	Brown	Blue	Farmer	–	Discharged 3/17/1865, substitute.
King, Robert J.	Pvt.	38	5'7"	Brown	Gray	Farmer	Tennessee	Mustered out 1/3/66, substitute.
Miller, Frank	Pvt.	30	5'¾"	Brown	Blue	Barber	Bavaria	Mustered out 11/6/1866 Montgomery, AL, drafted.
Seaton, Robert	Pvt.	18	5'10"	Black	Brown	Farmer	Missouri	Discharged by order of sec. of war, substitute.
Sutherland, Garrett	Pvt.	22	5'6¾"	Brown	Hazel	Soldier	Indiana	Discharged 4/18/1865, wounded in Battle of Nashville.
Williamson, Thomas	Pvt.	17	5'9"	Light	Gray	Farmer	Illinois	Discharged 7/7/1865.

*Mentioned in Missouri Descriptive Roll but not in the National Archives.

Died

Soldier	Rank	Age	Ht	Hair	Eyes	Occupation	Nativity	Comment
Holman, John	Pvt.	20	5'8½"	Light	Gray	Soldier	Illinois	Died 2/6/1865 at Nashville of wounds received in action.
Jones, John T.	Pvt.	20	5'8"	Brown	Hazel	Farmer	Illinois	Died 5/2/1865 chronic diarrhea.
Sessions, Richard	Pvt.	18	5'8"	Brown	Gray	Farmer	Illinois	KIA 12/16/1864 Nashville.

Deserted

Soldier	Rank	Age	Ht	Hair	Eyes	Occupation	Nativity	Comment
Borders, George	Pvt.	24	5'5"	Brown	Hazel	Laborer	Canada	Deserted 4/26/1865 Greenville, AL, substitute.
Harney, Brine	Pvt.	27	5'6"	Brown	Brown	Laborer	Ireland	Deserted 2/10/1865 Cairo, IL, substitute.
Horton, William	Pvt.	19	5'4½"	Black	Hazel	Farmer	Ireland	Deserted 3/5/1865 New Orleans, substitute.
Jeffers, James W.	Pvt.	22	5'11¼"	Light	Gray	Farmer	Virginia	Deserted 4/23/1865 Greenville, AL, substitute.
Johnson, Thomas	Pvt.	32	5'6"	Sandy	Blue	Laborer	Ireland	Deserted 2/22/1865 New Orleans, substitute.
Jones, Charles	Pvt.	28	5'10"	Dark	Hazel	Clerk	England	Deserted 4/25/1865 Alabama, substitute.
Jordan, William B.	Pvt.	18	5'4"	Light	Gray	Farmer	Illinois	Deserted 3/9/1865 Marion, AL.
Jourdan, James	Pvt.	20	5'3½"	Brown	Hazel	Soldier	Illinois	Deserted 9/6/1865 Marion, AL.
Learey, Edward	Pvt.	19	6'	Brown	Brown	Boatman	France	Deserted 3/5/1865 New Orleans, substitute.
Martin, Peter H.	Pvt.	21	5'5"	Black	Black	Soldier	New York	Deserted 3/16/1865 Ft. Gaines, AL, substitute.
McLean, Jesse H.	Pvt.	29	5'7"	Brown	Hazel	Soldier	Ohio	Deserted 10/1865, returned to duty and awaiting trial, mustered out 1/15/66 Memphis.
Miller, Henry	Pvt.	25	5'7"	Blonde	Blue	Laborer	Germany	Deserted 2/10/1865 Cairo, IL, substitute.
Moore, John	Pvt.	25	5'9"	Brown	Brown	Laborer	Mississippi	Deserted 2/10/1865 Cairo, IL, substitute.
Rainey, William	Pvt.	21	5'8"	Brown	Blue	Carpenter	Canada	Deserted 2/10/185 Cairo, IL, substitute.
Sanders, John	Pvt.	29	5'4¾"	Black	Hazel	Soldier	Illinois	Deserted 8/20/1864 from hospital.
Staettfield, Charles	Pvt.	21	5'8"	Light	Gray	Shoemaker	Prussia	Deserted 2/10/1865 at Cairo, IL, substitute.
Thomas, John	Pvt.	18	5'7"	Light	Hazel	Laborer	Kentucky	Deserted 2/10/1865 Cairo, IL, substitute.
Warrich, James	Pvt.	19	5'6½"	Brown	Blue	Laborer	Canada	Deserted 2/10/1865 Cairo, IL, substitute.
Williams, George	Pvt.	22	5'8"	Black	Hazel	Boatman	Ohio	Deserted 3/5/1865 New Orleans, substitute.

Company G

Soldier	Rank	Age	Ht	Hair	Eyes	Occupation	Nativity	Comment
Wallace, William	Captain	32	5'11"	Dark	Blue	Blacksmith	New York	Wounded in Battle of Nashville.
Quick, George	1st Lt.	34	5'7"	Black	Black	Soldier	Ohio	Mustered out 1/15/66 Memphis.
Mieure, Thomas	2nd Lt.	27	6'	Auburn	Blue	Soldier	Illinois	Mustered out 1/15/66 Memphis.
Barnett, Mark Q.	1st Sgt.	22	5'5"	Dark	Black	Soldier	Indiana	Mustered out 1/15/66 Memphis.
Bates, Jones M.	Sgt.	24	5'8"	Dark	Gray	Soldier	Missouri	Mustered out 1/15/66 Memphis.
Burrell, Albert	Sgt.	20	5'6"	Auburn	Black	Soldier	Illinois	Mustered out 1/15/66 Memphis.
Meyers, James M.	Sgt.	21	5'10"	Brown	Blue	Farmer	Indiana	Mustered out 1/15/66 Memphis, 7th Missouri.
Pickerell, William	Sgt.	21	5'8"	Black	Blue	Farmer	Ohio	Mustered out 1/15/66 Memphis.
Priest, George E.	Sgt.	25	5'7"	Light	Blue	Soldier	Pennsylvania	
Adams, General	Corporal	20	5'7"	Dark	Hazel	Soldier	Illinois	Mustered out 6/16/66 Memphis.
Eddleman, John	Corporal	20	6'	Auburn	Black	Soldier	Missouri	Mustered out 1/15/66 Memphis.
Gould, Thomas B.	Corporal	25	5'8"	Dark	Blue	Farmer	Illinois	Mustered out 1/15/66 Memphis.
Lewis, James P.	Corporal	21	5'11"	Light	Blue	Soldier	Illinois	
Norton, Solomon H.	Corporal	23	5'8"	Sandy	Blue	Soldier	Illinois	Mustered out 1/15/66 Memphis, wounded in Battle of Nashville.
Sullivan, Thomas R.	Corporal	21	5'3"	Dark	Gray	Soldier	Indiana	Mustered out 1/15/66 Memphis, 7th Missouri.
Waller, Rollin T.	Corporal	26	5'7"	Dark	Blue	Soldier	Illinois	Mustered out 1/15/66 Memphis.
Norton, Wellinton	Corporal	23	5'6"	Light	Black	Farmer	Illinois	
White, Edward N.	Corporal	37	5'10"	Light	Blue		Ohio	7th Missouri.
Mills, George J.	Musician	21	5'8"	Auburn	Gray	Soldier	Illinois	Mustered out 1/15/66 Memphis.
Andrews, James	Wagoner	35	5'10"	Auburn	Blue	Soldier	Kentucky	Mustered out 1/15/66 Memphis.
Bullick, Edward	Pvt.	18	6'½"	Brown	Gray	Farmer	Missouri	Mustered out 1/15/66 Memphis, substitute.
Cain, Robert P.	Pvt.	25	5'7"	Black	Black	Farmer	Ohio	Mustered out 1/15/66 Memphis, 7th Missouri.
Clark, John	Pvt.	19	5'10"	Brown	Brown	Farmer	Tennessee	Mustered out 1/15/66 Memphis, substitute.
Clark, William E.	Pvt.	18	5'6"	Light	Blue	Farmer	Illinois	Mustered out 1/15/66 Memphis.
Crammer, William P.*	Pvt.	33	–	–	–	–	–	Mustered out 1/15/66 Memphis, drafted.

*Mentioned in Missouri Descriptive Roll but not in the National Archives.

Soldier	Rank	Age	Ht	Hair	Eyes	Occupation	Nativity	Comment
English, William E.	Pvt.	21	5'9"	Sandy	Blue	Farmer	Pennsylvania	Mustered out 1/15/66 Memphis, 7th Missouri.
Fail, John	Pvt.	18	5'8"	Brown	Black	Soldier	Illinois	Mustered out 1/15/66 Memphis.
Fideman, Henry	Pvt.	19	5'10"	Brown	Gray	Soldier	New Jersey	Substitute.
Flanigan, Patrick	Pvt.	–	–	–	–	–	–	Substitute.
Florow, William	Pvt.	21	5'7"	–	–	Soldier	Indiana	Substitute.
Hamilton, Jason	Pvt.	18	5'7"	Brown	Hazel	Farmer	Ohio	Mustered out 1/15/66 Memphis.
Grissom, John D.	Pvt.	18	5'7"	Light	Hazel	Farmer	Missouri	Mustered out 1/15/66 Memphis, substitute.
Hastley, Asa	Pvt.	18	5'11"	Brown	Blue	Farmer	Tennessee	Mustered out 1/15/66 Memphis, substitute.
Haynes, George W.	Pvt.	22	5'11"	Brown	Blue	Farmer	Illinois	Mustered out 1/15/66 Memphis, 7th Missouri.
Highsmith, Richard M.	Pvt.	21	5'10"	Brown	Hazel	Farmer	Illinois	Mustered out 1/15/66 Memphis, 7th Missouri.
Kelly, Robert*	Pvt.	24	5'8½"	Brown	Blue	Laborer	Ireland	Mustered out 1/15/66 Memphis, drafted.
Kimberlin, Isaac N.	Pvt.	24	5'5"	Brown	Blue	Farmer	Indiana	Mustered out 1/15/66 Memphis, 7th Missouri.
Kirkey, Joseph	Pvt.	23	5'8"	Black	Black	Soldier	Indiana	Absent sick, wounded in Battle of Nashville.
Kueff, Edwin	Pvt.	27	5'7"	Dark	Hazel	Soldier	Ohio	Mustered out 1/15/66 Memphis.
Kyger, William	Pvt.	31	5'9"	Dark	Gray	Soldier	Illinois	Mustered out 1/15/66 Memphis.
Lane, Charles	Pvt.	30	5'9½"	Black	Black	Farmer	Missouri	
Lewis, John S.*	Pvt.	–	–	–	–	–	–	Mustered out 1/15/66 Memphis, substitute.
Meyer, John*	Pvt.	25	5'9"	Brown	Brown	Farmer	Germany	Mustered out 1/15/66 Memphis, substitute.
Meyers, Hiram H.	Pvt.	21	5'6"	Brown	Gray	Farmer	Pennsylvania	Mustered out 1/15/66 Memphis, drafted.
Ogden, Henry	Pvt.	18	5'3"	Dark	Dark	Farmer	Missouri	Mustered out 1/15/66 Memphis, substitute.
Oliver, John	Pvt.	–	–	–	–	–	–	Mustered out 1/15/66 Memphis, substitute.
Powers, James	Pvt.	32	5'6"	Brown	Blue	Laborer	Ireland	7th Missouri.
Ranagan, Theodore	Pvt.	21	5'7"	Black	Hazel	Glass blower	Massachusetts	Mustered out 1/15/66 Memphis, substitute.
Rader, Reuben	Cook	–	–	–	–	–	–	Mustered out 1/15/66 Memphis.
Reaves, Samuel*	Pvt.	–	–	–	–	–	–	
Rhodes, John T.*	Pvt.	34	–	–	–	–	–	Mustered out 1/15/66 Memphis, drafted.
Robinson, Charles J.	Pvt.	18	5'8"	Dark	Black	Farmer	Illinois	Mustered out 1/15/66 Memphis, wounded in Battle of Nashville.
Schneider, John	Pvt.	21	5'9"	Brown	Brown	–	Germany	Mustered out 1/15/66 Memphis, substitute.
Shepherd, Charles M.	Pvt.	18	5'6"	Dark	Dark	–	Illinois	Ordered to report to Naval School.
Simley, Nicholas*	Pvt.	–	–	–	–	–	–	Mustered out 1/15/66 Memphis, substitute.
Snelson, Andrew M.*	Pvt.	31	–	–	–	–	–	Mustered out 1/15/66 Memphis, drafted.
Spain, Theodore	Pvt.	–	–	–	–	–	–	Mustered out 1/15/66 Memphis, substitute.
Stewart, Robert E.	Pvt.	42	5'8"	Brown	Blue	–	Missouri	Mustered out 1/15/66 Memphis, drafted.
Sweeten, Stephen	Pvt.	24	5'9"	Brown	Hazel	–	Indiana	Mustered out 1/15/66 Memphis, drafted.
Trenley, Nicholas	Pvt.	18	5'4½"	Brown	Brown	Cigar Maker	Germany	Substitute.
Utt, James	Pvt.	18	5'3"	Brown	Blue	Farmer	Ohio	Mustered out 1/15/66 Memphis, substitute.
Wagoner, Christian	Pvt.	37	5'7"	Gray	Gray	–	Germany	
Waggoner, Noah	Pvt.	21	6'1"	Black	Dark	Farmer	Illinois	Mustered out 1/15/66 Memphis, 7th Missouri.
Wallace, Thomas	Pvt.	20	5'6"	Auburn	Blue	Soldier	Ohio	Mustered out 6/22/1865.
West, Andrew Jr.	Pvt.	19	5'5"	Light	Blue	Farmer	Canada	Mustered out 1/6/66 Memphis, 7th Missouri.
Yeatman, Cornelius	Pvt.	18	5'6"	Light	Gray	Farmer	Ohio	Mustered out 9/26/1865.
Yosh/Yost, William*	Pvt.	–	–	–	–	–	–	Mustered out 1/15/66 Memphis, substitute.
Young, Samuel	Pvt.	35	5'8"	Brown	Hazel	Soldier	Kentucky	Mustered out 1/15/66 Memphis.

Discharged

Soldier	Rank	Age	Ht	Hair	Eyes	Occupation	Nativity	Comment
Able, John D.	Pvt.	20	5'10"	Light	Brown	Soldier	Indiana	Mustered out 6/1/65. (Also shown as deserted.)
Arney, John	Pvt.	37	–	–	–	–	–	Mustered out 12/31/1865.
Finley, Thomas	Pvt.	–	–	–	–	–	–	Mustered out 11/15/1865 Montgomery, AL, drafted.
Gipson, John	Pvt.	19	5'8"	Light	Gray	Soldier	Kentucky	Mustered out 6/22/1865. (Also shown as deserted.)
Hall, Hiram	Pvt.	23	6'	Black	Blue	Farmer	Virginia	Mustered out 8/2/1865, 33rd Missouri.
Huffman, Thornton	Pvt.	18	6'1"	Brown	Blue	Farmer	Missouri	Mustered out 1/6/66 Memphis, substitute.
Hutchison, Clark	Pvt.	23	5'6½"	Brown	Gray	Farmer	Ohio	Muster out 11/20/1865, drafted.
Kueff, John W.	Pvt.	21	5'8"	Brown	Blue	Farmer	Indiana	Mustered out 7/17/1865, 7th Missouri, wounded in Battle of Nashville.

*Mentioned in Missouri Descriptive Roll but not in the National Archives.

Soldier	Rank	Age	Ht	Hair	Eyes	Occupation	Nativity	Comment
Kueff, Thomas	Pvt.	19	5'5"	Black	Gray	Farmer	Illinois	Mustered out 7/25/1865.
McGill, James	Pvt.	29	5'9¾"	Gray	Blue	Carpenter	Ireland	Mustered out 11/26/65, 33rd Missouri.
Miller, Samuel H.	Pvt.	22	5'4"	Sandy	Blue	Farmer	Indiana	Mustered out 11/26/1865, drafted.
Perkins, Albert	Pvt.	22	5'5½"	Black	Dark	Riverman	Indian Territory	Service expired 12/19/1865.
Rahen, Joseph	Pvt.	33	5'7"	Light	Blue	Plasterer	Pennsylvania	Mustered out 3/5/65, (Also shown as deserted.) Discharged 4/30/1865.
Rettie/Retler, Joseph	Pvt.	18	5'6"	Dark	Gray	Barber	Venezuela	Discharged 11/25/1865, 33rd Missouri.
Ross, Robert*	Pvt.	–	–	–	–	–	–	Mustered out 2/19/1865. (Also shown as deserted.)
Ryan, John	Pvt.	–	–	–	–	–	–	Mustered out 3/10/1865. (Also shown as deserted.)
Stewart, Amos	Pvt.	21	5'7"	Light	Blue	–	Ohio	Discharged 7/1/1865 disability, wounded in Battle of Nashville.
Travis, Israel	Pvt.	18	5'7½"	Black	Hazel	Laborer	Ohio	Mustered out 12/23/1865, drafted.
Wenze, Christopher	Pvt.	26	5'6¾"	Brown	Hazel	Stonecutter	Missouri	Discharged 7/15/1865.
Worstell, Joseph	Pvt.	20	5'7"	Light	Blue	Soldier	Ohio	Mustered 8/24/1864.
Young, Thomas	Pvt.	33	5'10"	Dark	Black	Farmer	Illinois	Mustered out 7/11/1865.

DIED

Soldier	Rank	Age	Ht	Hair	Eyes	Occupation	Nativity	Comment
Brewer, James	Corporal	19	5'10"	Dark	Black	Soldier	Ohio	Died 2/6/1865 in hospital in Louisville.
West, John M.	Corporal	22	5'10"	Black	Dark	Soldier	New York	Died 12/29/1864 Sumner, IL, 7th Missouri.
Fisher, Hiram	Pvt.	22	5'7"	Dark	Blue	Farmer	Illinois	Buried at Mississippi River Natl. Cemetery, TN.
Lindsa, Leander J	Pvt.	18	5'7"	Dark	Blue	Farmer	Illinois	Died 8/13/1864 Memphis, TN.
Lutts, Joseph	Pvt.	33	5'6½"	Brown	Hazel	Farmer	Germany	Died 4/4/1865 in hospital at Vicksburg.
Norris, Abraham	Pvt.	40	6'1"	Dark	Black	Farmer	Maryland	Died 12/21/1865 Demopolis, AL, 33rd Missouri.
Owens, Charles or Roland	Pvt.	18	5'5"	Dark	Gray	Farmer	Missouri	Supposed to have died in prison, substitute.
Rollin, Buel S.	Pvt.	18	5'11"	Brown	Brown	Farmer	Missouri	Died 7/2/1865 Marion, AL, buried National Cemetery
Smith, James T.	Pvt.	22	5'9"	Light	Blue	–	Ohio	Died 12/29/1864 Louisville, wounded in Battle of Nashville.

DESERTED

Soldier	Rank	Age	Ht	Hair	Eyes	Occupation	Nativity	Comment
Alexander, Richard	Pvt.	22	5'4"	Black	Brown	Soldier	Ohio	Deserted 3/3/1865 St. Louis, substitute.
Bartch, Anton	Pvt.	23	5'7"	Brown	Blue	–	Switzerland	Deserted 12/31/1864 Demopolis, AL, 7th Missouri.
Boyle, James*	Pvt.	34	–	–	–	–	–	Deserted 7/10/1865 Demopolis, AL.
Canley, Michael	Pvt.	27	5'6"	Brown	Brown	Ostler	Ireland	Deserted 3/1/1865 New Orleans.
Grasgin, Carl/Charles	Pvt.	19	5'9"	Brown	Gray	Clerk	Prussia	Deserted 2/12/1866 St. Louis, MO, substitute.
Hines, Edward	Pvt.	25	5'8"	Brown	Gray	Laborer	Ireland	Deserted 1/25/1865 Cairo, substitute.
Kelly, John	Pvt.	24	5'8½"	Brown	Blue	Laborer	Ireland	Deserted 12/7/1864 Cairo, IL, substitute.
Murry, John	Pvt.	18	5'9"	Brown	Gray	Laborer	Ireland	Deserted 3/16/1865.
Nash, William	Pvt.	28	5'6"	Dark	Dark	Laborer	Ireland	Deserted 3/1/1865, substitute.
Smith, Charles J.	Pvt.	19	5'9"	Red	Blue	–	Ireland	Deserted 1/25/1865 Cairo, IL, substitute.
Tosh, William	Pvt.	22	5'5¼"	Light	Gray	–	Canada	Deserted 1/17/1865 St. Louis, substitute.
Tully, William F.	Pvt.	29	5'10¼"	Brown	Blue	–	Canada	Deserted 1/9/1865.
Whallen, John	Pvt.	23	5'5½"	Light	Blue	Laborer	Ireland	Deserted 3/1/1865.
Winscott, James C.*	Pvt.	18	–	–	–	–	–	Deserted 11/16/1864, substitute.
Winston, Augustus F.*	Pvt.	–	–	–	–	–	–	Deserted 3/6/1865 St. Louis.

TRANSFERRED

Soldier	Rank	Age	Ht	Hair	Eyes	Occupation	Nativity	Comment
Aiken, William	Sgt.	25	5'6"	Dark	Gray	Soldier	Ohio	Transferred 1/1/1864.

Company H

Soldier	Rank	Age	Ht	Hair	Eyes	Occupation	Nativity	Comment
Applegate, Edwin	Capt.	22	5'5"	Dark	Gray	Carpenter	Ohio	Mustered out 1/15/66 Memphis.
McNeal, James	1st Lt.	30	5'8"	Black	Hazel	Soldier	Ohio	Mustered out 1/15/66 Memphis.

*Mentioned in Missouri Descriptive Roll but not in the National Archives.

Soldier	Rank	Age	Ht	Hair	Eyes	Occu-pation	Nativity	Comment
Hamilton, Robert	2nd Lt.	24	5'6"	Light	Blue	Soldier	Scotland	
Adams, Zachariah	Sgt.	24	5'9"	Light	Blue	Farmer	Illinois	AWOL since 12/3/65, no discharge furnished.
Browning, Joseph	Sgt.	23	5'7"	Dark	Gray	Soldier	Illinois	Mustered out 1/15/66 Memphis.
Conrad, Samuel	Sgt.	24	5'6"	Light	Blue	Soldier	Pennsylvania	Mustered out 1/15/66 Memphis, wounded in Battle of Nashville.
Parker, Isaac T. G.	Sgt.	25	5'7"	Black	Hazel	Soldier	Illinois	Mustered out 1/15/66 Memphis, wounded in Battle of Nashville.
Ridgeley/Ridgley, William	Sgt.	25	6'1"	Light	Gray	Soldier	Ohio	Mustered out 1/15/66 Memphis, wounded in Battle of Nashville.
Daniels, William H.	Corporal	22	5'8"	Light	Blue	Soldier	Ohio	Mustered out 1/15/66 Memphis.
Johnson, Jacob	Corporal	24	5'8"	Black	Blue	Soldier	Ohio	Mustered out 1/15/66 Memphis, wounded in Battle of Nashville.
Kaley, Henry P.	Corporal	20	5'5"	Dark	Hazel	Soldier	Ohio	Mustered out 1/15/66 Memphis.
Kellogg, Elijah	Corporal	24	5'7"	Red	Gray	Soldier	Illinois	Mustered out 1/15/66 Memphis.
McNeal, Frederick	Corporal	20	5'9"	Light	Blue	Soldier	Ohio	Mustered out 1/15/66 Memphis.
Smith, Gilmour W.	Corporal	24	6'1"	Black	Blue	Soldier	Illinois	Mustered out 1/15/66 Memphis, 7th Missouri.
Sumner, John B.	Corporal	27	5'7"	Sandy	Gray	Soldier	Illinois	Mustered out 1/15/66 Memphis, 7th Missouri.
Thomas, Johnson	Wagoner	22	5'6"	Sandy	Blue	Laborer	Ireland	Mustered out 1/15/66 Memphis.
Anderson, William	Pvt.	21	5'4"	Dark	Gray	Soldier	New Mexico	
Baker, Joel D.	Pvt.	28	5'6"	Brown	Hazel	Farmer	Ohio	Mustered out 1/15/66 Memphis, 7th Missouri.
Bennett, William M.	Pvt.	43	5'9"	Fair	Brown	Farmer	Missouri	Mustered out 1/15/66 Memphis, drafted.
Burvill, Francis M.	Pvt.	22	5'5½"	Dark	Blue	Soldier	Illinois	Mustered out 1/15/66 Memphis.
Beckett, Columbus	Pvt.	27	5'9"	Brown	Brown	Farmer	New Jersey	Mustered out 1/15/66 Memphis, drafted.
Brinknell, Edward*	Pvt.	24	5'8"	Brown	Blue	Soldier	Ireland	Mustered out 1/15/66 Memphis, 7th Missouri.
Bugh, John	Pvt.	33	5'9"	Black	Dark	–	Ohio	Mustered out 1/15/66 Memphis, substitute.
Bunth, Christopher	Pvt.	28	5'10"	Brown	Hazel	Boatman	Sweden	Mustered out 1/15/66 Memphis, 7th Missouri.
Cannady, Riley	Pvt.	18	5'9"	Light	Blue	Farmer	Illinois	Mustered out 1/15/66 Memphis.
Carroll, Lorenzo	Pvt.	21	5'9"	Dark	Hazel	Farmer	Ohio	Mustered out 1/15/66 Memphis.
Cooper, Isaac	Pvt.	35	5'10"	Brown	Gray	Farmer	Louisiana	Mustered out 1/15/66 Memphis, drafted.
Crozier, John	Pvt.	18	5'4"	Light	Black	Farmer	Illinois	Mustered out 1/15/66 Memphis, wounded in Siege of Spanish Fort.
Daniels, George	Pvt.	20	5'7"	Dark	Blue	Soldier	Ohio	Mustered out 1/15/66 Memphis.
Dechemeam/Decheneau, Louis	Pvt.	32	5'2"	Dark	Hazel	Farmer	Canada	Mustered out 1/15/66 Memphis, substitute.
Eaten, Robert B.	Pvt.	39	5'8"	Dark	Dark	Farmer	Missouri	Absent sick 4/1865, drafted.
Engle, John	Pvt.	42	5'8"	Gray	Black	Cigar maker	Germany	Mustered out 1/15/66 Memphis, substitute.
Fromme, George	Pvt.	44	5'6"	Brown	Gray	Farmer	Germany	Mustered out 1/15/66 Memphis, drafted.
Fullen, Godfrey	Pvt.	27	6'	Dark	Hazel	Soldier	Illinois	Wounded in the Siege of Spanish Fort, mustered out 1/15/66.
Harrison, John W.	Pvt.	29	5'6"	Brown	Black	Farmer	Missouri	Mustered out 1/15/66 Memphis, drafted.
Higgins, Absalom C.	Pvt.	20	5'7"	Black	Dark	Farmer	Illinois	Mustered out 1/15/66 Memphis, wounded in Battle of Nashville, wounded in Siege of Spanish Fort.
Higgins, George	Pvt.	23	6'	Light	Dark	Soldier	Illinois	Mustered out 1/15/66 Memphis.
Hoffman, John	Pvt.	42	5'5"	Light	Blue	–	Germany	Mustered out 1/15/66 Memphis, substitute.
Hutchings, James	Pvt.	21	5'6"	Black	Gray	Farmer	Illinois	Mustered out 1/15/66 Memphis.
Johnson, William A.	Pvt.	17	5'7"	Brown	Gray	Farmer	Missouri	Mustered out 1/15/66 Memphis, substitute.
Johnson, William H.	Pvt.	–	–	–	–	–	–	Mustered out 1/15/66 Memphis, substitute.
Keller, Columbus	Pvt.	18	5'6½"	Brown	Gray	Farmer	Illinois	AWOL, substitute.
Maples, James	Pvt.	40	5'4"	Brown	Gray	Farmer	Tennessee	Mustered out 1/15/66 Memphis, drafted.
Martin, Henry C.	Pvt.	20	5'4"	Light	Blue	Soldier	Illinois	Mustered out 1/15/66 Memphis.
Martin, Finley T.	Pvt.	18	5'7"	Dark	Dark	Farmer	Illinois	Mustered out 1/15/66 Memphis.
Mathewson, William O.	Pvt.	22	5'6"	Light	Blue	Soldier	Illinois	Mustered out 1/15/66 Memphis.
Meeker, Holsey	Pvt.	20	5'4"	Light	Hazel	Soldier	Indiana	Mustered out 1/15/66 Memphis.
Meeker, Thomas	Pvt.	20	5'6"	Dark	Dark	Soldier	Indiana	Mustered out 1/15/66 Memphis.
McAullfee, James	Pvt.	22	5'7"	Fair	Blue	Soldier	Ireland	Mustered out 1/15/66 Memphis, substitute.
McBride, Daniel	Pvt.	44	5'6"	Dark	Blue	Soldier	Ireland	Mustered out 1/15/66 Memphis, 7th Missouri.
McCann, John	Pvt.	28	5'5½"	Black	Blue	Laborer	Ireland	Mustered out 1/15/66 Memphis, 7th Missouri.

*Mentioned in Missouri Descriptive Roll but not in the National Archives.

Soldier	Rank	Age	Ht	Hair	Eyes	Occupation	Nativity	Comment
McDonald, Daniel	Pvt.	34	5'6"	Brown	Blue	Laborer	Ireland	Mustered out 1/15/66 Memphis, 7th Missouri.
McGrill, John	Pvt.	42	5'6"	Black	Light	Laborer	Ireland	Mustered out 1/15/66 Memphis, substitute.
Organ, James D.	Pvt.	21	5'9"	Dark	Hazel	Farmer	Illinois	Mustered out 1/15/66 Memphis.
Owens, Robert	Pvt.	18	5'3½"	Brown	Gray	Farmer	Missouri	Absent, sick, substitute.
Parker, John A.	Pvt.	19	5'6"	Auburn	Hazel	Farmer	Illinois	Wounded in Battle of Nashville.
Parker, George W.	Pvt.	22	5'7"	Sandy	Blue	Farmer	Illinois	
Pearson, William	Pvt.	20	5'7"	Light	Blue	Soldier	Illinois	
Poor, William	Pvt.	30	5'9"	Brown	Blue	Farmer	Kentucky	Mustered out 10/9/1865, drafted.
Quinn, Michael	Pvt.	24	5'5"	Dark	Blue	Soldier	Ireland	Mustered out 1/15/66 Memphis.
Riley, William	Pvt.	24	5'4"	Brown	Blue	Farmer	Indiana	Mustered out 1/15/66 Memphis, drafted.
Roaher/Rohar, David	Pvt.	26	5'10"	Light	Gray	Soldier	Illinois	Mustered out 1/15/66 Memphis.
Ryan, James	Pvt.	21	5'4½"	Brown	Hazel	Laborer	Ireland	Substitute.
Salisbury, David A.	Pvt.	21	5'7"	Light	Blue	Soldier	Illinois	Mustered out 1/15/66 Memphis.
Sweeney, John	Pvt.	18	5'6¾"	Brown	Hazel	Laborer	Ireland	Mustered out 1/15/66 Memphis, substitute.
Tigho, Peter	Pvt.	33	5'7"	Brown	Brown	Boatman	Canada	Mustered out 1/15/66 Memphis, substitute.
Treadway, Jacob	Pvt.	24	5'5"	Dark	Blue	Soldier	Indiana	Mustered out 1/15/66 Memphis.
Walters, Isaac N.	Pvt.	20	5'9"	Light	Blue	Farmer	Illinois	Mustered out 1/15/66 Memphis.
Wecker, Thomas*		20	–	–	–	–	–	Mustered out 1/15/66 Memphis.
White, Jefferson	Pvt.	26	5'7"	Brown	Gray	Farmer	Missouri	Mustered out 1/15/66 Memphis, drafted.
Wilson, Josiah M.	Pvt.	40	5'8½"	Brown	Blue	Farmer	Tennessee	Mustered out 1/15/66 Memphis, drafted.
Wisner, Benjamin*	Pvt.	–	–	–	–	–	–	Mustered out 1/15/66 Memphis.
Wyckoff, Fenton	Pvt.	38	5'6½"	Brown	Brown	Soldier	New Jersey	Mustered out 1/15/66 Memphis, substitute.
York, Isaac N.	Pvt.	27	6'	Dark	Blue	Soldier	Illinois	Mustered out 1/15/66 Memphis.

DISCHARGED

Soldier	Rank	Age	Ht	Hair	Eyes	Occupation	Nativity	Comment
Brown, George	Chaplain	31	5'8"	Brown	Blue	Farmer	Kentucky	Promoted Chaplain, mustered out 1/4/1865, wounded in Siege of Spanish Fort, drafted.
Albright, William A.	Pvt.	27	5'2½"	Brown	Blue	–	Ohio	Term of Service expired 12/5/1865, drafted.
Diew, Franklin M.	Pvt.	28	5'8½"	Brown	Blue	Carpenter	Louisiana	Mustered out 12/9/1865, substitute.
Mathis, Leonard	Pvt.	33	5'7"	Black	Blue	Farmer	Tennessee	Discharged 8/18/1865, drafted.
McClain, Dudley	Pvt.	–	–	–	–	–	–	Discharged 7/15/1865, substitute.
Pace, Benjamin	Pvt.	33	5'8"	Brown	Blue	Farmer	Kentucky	Service expired 11/15/1865, drafted.
Rainey, William H.	Pvt.	18	5'4½"	Dark	Dark	Farmer	Indiana	Discharged 1/1/65 disability, wounded in Battle of Nashville.
Rodhouse, Thomas W.	Pvt.	18	5'7"	Dark	Gray	Farmer	England	Mustered out 6/16/1865, substitute.
Rogers, Barnett	Pvt.	34	5'8½"	Black	Hazel	Farmer	Illinois	Discharged 12/9/1865, substitute.
Rush, John	Pvt.	24	5'6½"	Brown	Hazel	Farmer	Germany	Mustered out. 11/15/1865, drafted.
Ryan, James	Pvt.	28	5'8"	Black	Blue	Laborer	Illinois	Dishonorable discharged under arrest for Gen. Court-Martial, 7th Missouri.
Sims, Robert S.	Pvt.	18	5'11¾"	Brown	Black	Farmer	Missouri	Mustered out 11/18/1865, substitute.
Vanloren, Cornelius	Pvt.	32	5'5"	Black	Blue	Farmer	Holland	Mustered out 12/6/1865, substitute.
Zimmerman, Luther	Pvt.	21	5'7"	Light	Blue	Soldier	Pennsylvania	Mustered out 1/13/1865.

DIED

Soldier	Rank	Age	Ht	Hair	Eyes	Occupation	Nativity	Comment
Wilgus, William	Sgt.	24	5'11"	Black	Gray	Soldier	Pennsylvania	Died of disease 7/21/1865 Jackson, MS.
Spilkey, Edward	Corporal	21	5'7"	Light	Blue	Soldier	Illinois	Died 5/21/1865 due wounds in Siege of Spanish Fort.
Adams, Josiah	Musician	22	5'5"	Dark	Gray	Soldier	Illinois	Killed 8/31/1865.
Goodwin, Clark B.	Pvt.	24	5'7"	Dark	Hazel	Soldier	Indiana	KIA 12/16/1864 Battle of Nashville.
Kennedy, Moses	Pvt.	–	–	–	–	–	–	Died 3/19/1865 Fort Gaines, AL, substitute.
McGuire, Michael	Pvt.	34	5'3"	Sandy	Gray	Laborer	Ireland	Died of wounds 4/2/1865 from Siege of Spanish Fort, substitute.

DESERTED

Soldier	Rank	Age	Ht	Hair	Eyes	Occupation	Nativity	Comment
Anderson, William	Musician	23	5'9"	Dark	Blue	Soldier	Illinois	Deserted 7/18/1864.
Finch, James	Pvt.	23	5'7½"	Brown	Blue	Farmer	–	Deserted 6/24/1865, substitute.
Fitzpatrick, John	Pvt.	40	5'4½"	Light	Blue	Laborer	Ireland	Deserted 1/24/1865, substitute.
Hogan, Thomas	Pvt.	26	5'6"	Black	Brown	Farmer	Indiana	Deserted 1/27/1865, substitute.

*Mentioned in Missouri Descriptive Roll but not in the National Archives.

Soldier	Rank	Age	Ht	Hair	Eyes	Occupation	Nativity	Comment
Hunts, Charles	Pvt.	21	5'6"	Brown	Hazel	Laborer	Ireland	Deserted 2/10/1865, substitute.
James, G. W.	Pvt.	–	–	–	–	–	–	Deserted 3/16/1865, substitute.
Johnson, Mathew	Pvt.	–	–	–	–	–	–	Deserted 3/15/1865.
Johnson, Thomas*	Pvt.	22	–	–	–	–	–	Deserted 2/27/1865, substitute.
McArthur, Harrison	Pvt.	27	5'9"	Auburn	Blue	Farmer	Indiana	Deserted 3/16/1865, substitute.
McDaniel, George W.	Pvt.	18	5'5"	Auburn	Blue	Farmer	Illinois	Deserted 11/21/1864.
McDonald, Robert	Pvt.	41	5'10½"	Black	Gray	–	Scotland	Deserted 11/30/1865, substitute.
Taylor, William	Pvt.	19	5'3½"	Black	Hazel	–	Canada	Deserted 2/27/1865, substitute.
Walker, John	Pvt.	32	5'5"	Brown	Blue	Carpenter	Mississippi	Deserted 3/6/1865, substitute.
Williams, William	Pvt.	18	5'8¾"	Brown	Blue	Farmer	Germany	Deserted 1/24/1865, substitute.
Wright, Frank	Pvt.	28	5'7½"	Brown	Gray	–	Ireland	Deserted 2/7/1865, substitute.

Company I

Soldier	Rank	Age	Ht	Hair	Eyes	Occupation	Nativity	Comment
Adams, George C.	Captain	28	5'8"	Light	Blue	Soldier	Illinois	Died 12/1865.
Shoopman,	1st Lt.	26	6'	Dark	Blue	Soldier	Missouri	Mustered out 1/15/66 Memphis, wounded in Battle of Nashville.
Swan, James M.	Sgt./1st Lt.	23	5'10½"	Brown	Blue	Soldier	Ohio	Mustered out 1/15/66 Memphis.
Armstrong, John	1st Sgt.	21	5'7½"	Red	Blue	Laborer	Ireland	Mustered out 1/15/66 Memphis, wounded at Nashville and Spanish Fort, 7th Missouri.
Baul, Cyrus	Sgt.	19	6'	Brown	Blue	Soldier	Pennsylvania	Mustered out 1/15/66 Memphis, transferred to R Q M 5/1865.
Boulden, William	Corp./Sgt.	26	5'10½"	Sandy	Blue	Soldier	Delaware	Mustered out 1/15/66 Memphis.
Cornwell, Edward	Sgt.	23	5'7½"	Brown	Hazel	Soldier	Missouri	Wounded in Nashville 12/1864, mustered out 1/15/66. Memphis.
Davis, Harrison N.	Sgt.	25	5'8½"	Light	Blue	Soldier	Maine	Mustered out 1/15/66 Memphis, wounded at Nashville and Spanish Fort.
Warner, Wesley S.	Sgt.	24	6'½"	Dark	Hazel	Soldier	Illinois	Mustered out 1/15/66 Memphis.
Beauchamp, Samuel	Corporal	21	5'5"	Dark	Blue	Soldier	Illinois	Mustered out 1/15/66 Memphis.
Finson, Charles H.	Corporal	18	5'8½"	Light	Hazel	Farmer	Illinois	Mustered out 11/15/1865 Montgomery, AL.
Hackett, Thomas	Corporal	29	5'4"	Brown	Blue	Soldier	Ireland	Mustered out 1/15/66 Memphis. (Also shown as discharged for reason 3/20/1864.)
Hadsell, George	Corporal	28	5'8½"	Brown	Blue	Soldier	New York	Mustered out 1/15/66 Memphis.
Mackey, William	Corporal	22	5'11"	Brown	Gray	Soldier	Missouri	Mustered out 1/15/66 Memphis.
Marion, William H.	Corporal	20	5'7"	Brown	Blue	Soldier	New Jersey	Mustered out 1/15/66 Memphis.
Spicer, William H.	Corporal	26	5'7½"	Light	Blue	Soldier	Delaware	Mustered out 1/15/66 Memphis, wounded at Nashville.
Springer, Job	Corporal	27	5'10½"	Black	Hazel	Soldier	Virginia	Mustered out 1/15/66 Memphis.
Triebert, Christian	Corporal	26	5'7"	Light	Gray	Soldier	Germany	Mustered out 1/15/66 Memphis.
Pasley, David C.	Drummer	23	5'8"	Brown	Gray	Soldier	Illinois	Mustered out 1/15/66 Memphis.
Hartman, Franz	Fifer	23	5'3½"	Light	Blue	Soldier	Germany	Mustered out 1/15/66 Memphis.
Anderson, James	Pvt.	18	5'8"	Light	Gray	Farmer	Illinois	Mustered out 1/15/66 Memphis.
Arnold, Michael	Pvt.	24	5'8½"	Brown	Hazel	Farmer	Germany	Mustered out 1/15/66 Memphis, drafted.
Baker, Francis M.	Pvt.	18	5'7½"	Dark	Dark	Farmer	Illinois	Absent wounded in hospital Nashville 12/1864, wounded in Battle of Nashville.
Bennett, James	Pvt.	20	5'5½"	Black	Hazel	Soldier	Illinois	Mustered out 1/15/66 Memphis.
Bailey, John	Pvt.	33	5'8"	Auburn	Blue	Soldier	Kentucky	Mustered out 1/15/66 Memphis.
Basare/Bascue, William H.	Pvt.	22	5'6½"	Brown	Blue	Soldier	Virginia	Mustered out 1/15/66 Memphis. Wounded Dec 16, 1864 Nashville.
Boesch, Jacob	Pvt.	38	5'3"	Brown	Gray	Farmer	Switzerland	Mustered out 1/15/66 Memphis, drafted, 124th Illinois.
Brannon, John	Pvt.	33	5'6"	Brown	Brown	Stonecutter	Ireland	Mustered out 1/15/66 Memphis, substitute.
Breon, Patrick	Pvt.	30	5'7"	Dark	Blue	Laborer	Ireland	Mustered out 1/15/66 Memphis, 7th Missouri.
Brown, Michael	Pvt.	31	5'6"	Dark	Dark	Farmer	Ireland	Mustered out 1/15/66 Memphis.
Coffey, Campbell	Pvt.	34	5'10"	Brown	Blue	Farmer	Tennessee	Mustered out 1/15/66 Memphis, drafted.
Coffey, John	Pvt.	22	5'6"	Brown	Blue	Farmer	Missouri	Mustered out 1/15/66 Memphis, drafted.
Crim, George W.	Pvt.	25	6'	Black	Hazel	Soldier	Virginia	Mustered out 1/15/66 Memphis.
Cutler, Thomas R.	Pvt.	21	5'7"	Black	Gray	Soldier	Missouri	Mustered out 1/15/66 Memphis.
Dephenbach, John	Pvt.	21	5'10½"	Brown	Hazel	Farmer	Canada	Sick in hospital, substitute.

*Mentioned in Missouri Descriptive Roll but not in the National Archives.

Soldier	Rank	Age	Ht	Hair	Eyes	Occupation	Nativity	Comment
Duckett, Albert	Pvt.	18	5'9½"	Light	Light	Carpenter	Ohio	Mustered out 1/15/66 Memphis
Dulong, John	Pvt.	28	5'7"	Brown	Gray	Laborer	Canada	Wounded in Nashville 12/1864, 7th Missouri.
Grogan, James P.	Pvt.	43	5'9½"	Black	Hazel	Carpenter	–	Mustered out 1/15/66 Memphis, substitute.
Green, William T.	Pvt.	20	5'6"	Black	Gray	Farmer	England	Mustered out 1/15/66 Memphis, substitute.
Hosenfelt, Jacob	Pvt.	18	5'9"	Light	Gray	Farmer	Missouri	Mustered out 1/15/66 Memphis, substitute.
Hurley, John	Pvt.	29	5'7½"	Brown	Blue	Carpenter	Ireland	Mustered out 1/15/66 Memphis, 7th Missouri.
Hysner, Peter	Pvt.	18	5'6½"	Brown	Hazel	Farmer	Ohio	Mustered out 1/15/66 Memphis, substitute.
James, Thomas	Pvt.	26	6'1"	Brown	Dark	Farmer	Missouri	Deserted 7/7/1865 Demopolis, drafted.
Keller, August	Pvt.	19	5'8"	Brown	Dark	Farmer	Missouri	Mustered out 1/15/66 Memphis, substitute.
Kleinhaus, Leonard	Pvt.	43	5'5"	Brown	Hazel	Laborer	Germany	Mustered out 1/15/66 Memphis, drafted.
Lee, Patrick	Pvt.	24	5'8"	Fair	Blue	Painter	Ireland	Absent sick in hospital, 7th Missouri.
Logan, John	Pvt.	32	5'10"	Dark	Blue	Laborer	Ireland	Mustered out 1/15/66 Memphis, 7th Missouri.
Lake, Harrison	Pvt.	21	5'9"	Sandy	Blue	Soldier	Kentucky	Mustered out 1/15/66 Memphis.
Malotte, Ira	Pvt.	18	5'4½"	Dark	Dark	Farmer	Illinois	Mustered out 1/15/66 Memphis.
Marchade, Anton	Pvt.	27	5'4½"	Light	Gray	–	Prussia	Mustered out 1/15/66 Memphis, substitute.
Marion, Phillip	Pvt.	20	5'6"	Brown	Gray	Laborer	Germany	Mustered out 1/15/66 Memphis, substitute.
Michael, Martin	Pvt.	25	5'6"	Brown	Hazel	–	Germany	Mustered out 1/15/66 Memphis, drafted.
Milgers, Conrad	Pvt.	32	5'5¾"	Light	Blue	Cooper	Germany	Mustered out 1/15/66 Memphis, drafted.
Mitchell, John	Pvt.	40	6'	Light	Gray	Farmer	Missouri	Mustered out 1/15/66 Memphis, drafted.
Muligan, James A.	Pvt.	19	5'4"	Brown	Gray	Soldier	Pennsylvania	Mustered out 1/15/66 Memphis, substitute.
Nantz/Nanby, John T.	Pvt.	24	5'9½"	Brown	Blue	Laborer	Louisiana	AWOL, substitute.
O'Brien, Patrick	Pvt.	29	5'3½"	Black	Hazel	Soldier	Ireland	Mustered out 1/15/66 Memphis, wounded in Battle of Nashville.
O'Neal, Patrick	Pvt.	30	5'6"	Brown	Blue	Laborer	Ireland	Wounded at Nashville 12/16/1864, 7th Missouri.
Preston, Newton	Pvt.	27	5'10"	Light	Blue	Soldier	Ohio	Mustered out 1/15/66 Memphis.
Ratkin, Fred	Pvt.	42	5'1"	Black	Blue	–	Germany	Mustered out 1/15/66 Memphis, drafted, 124th Illinois.
Schendler, Jacob	Pvt.	39	–	–	–	–	–	Mustered out 1/15/66 Memphis, drafted, 124th Illinois.
Snyder, Jeremiah	Pvt.	18	5'5½"	Auburn	Gray	Farmer	Ohio	Mustered out 1/15/66 Memphis, substitute.
Squires, Charles	Pvt.	18	5'2½"	Brown	Blue	Laborer	Illinois	Substitute.
Striehenbine, Louis	Pvt.	22	5'9½"	Brown	Gray	Bookkeeper	Germany	Mustered out 1/15/66 Memphis, drafted.
Taylor, Rollins	Pvt.	18	5'8½"	Light	Hazel	Farmer	Illinois	Mustered out 1/15/66 Memphis.
Taylor, St Clair	Pvt.	19	5'5"	Light	Hazel	Farmer	Illinois	
Thomas, Elijah	Pvt.	21	5'8"	Dark	Blue	Soldier	Ohio	Mustered out 1/15/66 Memphis.
Vorlege, August	Pvt.	30	5'6"	Brown	Hazel	Carpenter	Germany	Mustered out 1/15/66 Memphis, substitute.
Walsh, Garrett	Pvt.	32	5'6"	Dark	Gray	Laborer	Germany	Mustered out 1/15/66 Memphis, 7th Missouri.
Wesser, Levi*	Pvt.	–	–	–	–	–	–	Substitute.
Williams, George	Pvt.	19	5'5"	Brown	Gray	Farmer	Tennessee	Mustered out 1/15/66 Memphis.
Wyatt, John*	Pvt.	–	–	–	–	–	–	

DISCHARGED

Soldier	Rank	Age	Ht	Hair	Eyes	Occupation	Nativity	Comment
Osgood, Charles	Captain	–	–	–	–	–	–	
Ethel, Charles H.	1st Lt.	18	–	–	–	–	–	Mustered out 10/10/1864.
Chapman, Daniel S.	Corporal	27	5'9½"	Brown	Blue	Soldier	Missouri	Gunshot wound at Nashville, discharged 5/25/1865.
Davidhiser, Henry	Corporal	36	5'6"	Dark	Gray	Teamster	Prussia	Discharge 5/25/1865, wounded in Battle of Nashville and Siege of Spanish Fort, 7th Missouri.
Blackford, Enoch M.	Pvt.	19	5'9½"	Light	Blue	Farmer	Missouri	Discharged 7/1865 St. Louis General Hospital, substitute.
Glover, Elijah	Pvt.	20	5'7"	Dark	Dark	Farmer	Missouri	Mustered out 9/20/1865, drafted.
Kline, Jacob L.	Pvt.	20	5'4"	Brown	Blue	Soldier	Tennessee	Discharged 5/25/1865, wounded in Battle of Nashville.
Lung, Marion S.	Pvt.	25	6'4½"	Black	Hazel	Laborer	Canada	Discharged 6/12/1865 due to wounds from Spanish Fort, wounded in Battle of Nashville, substitute.
McPherson, William E.	Pvt.	18	5'5½"	Light	Gray	Farmer	Illinois	Discharged 1865 Louisville.
Mole, William J.	Pvt.	18	5'5"	Light	Gray	Farmer	Missouri	Mustered out 8/5/1865, substitute.

*Mentioned in Missouri Descriptive Roll but not in the National Archives.

Soldier	Rank	Age	Ht	Hair	Eyes	Occupation	Nativity	Comment
O'Brien, Martin	Pvt.	30	5'11"	Black	Blue	Laborer	Ireland	Discharged Covington, KY, Hospital 6/2/1865, wounded in Battle of Nashville and Siege of Spanish Fort, 7th Missouri.
Plank, Peter	Pvt.	21	5'9"	Brown	Blue	Soldier	Missouri	Discharged due to wounds from Nashville.
Thompson, William L.	Pvt.	23	5'6"	Brown	Brown	Farmer	Arkansas	Mustered out 10/22/1865, drafted.

DIED

Soldier	Rank	Age	Ht	Hair	Eyes	Occupation	Nativity	Comment
Hathorn, Mcguire C.	2nd Lt.	23	6'	Sandy	Blue	Soldier	Indiana	Died 12/2/1865 in hospital Demopolis.
Adams, Albert F.	Pvt.	18	5'6½"	Brown	Gray	Farmer	Illinois	Died 1/10/65 of gunshot wound in Nashville, buried in Nashville National Cemetery.
Brown, James D.	Pvt.	31	5'5"	Brown	Gray	Farmer	Missouri	Died 5/6/1865 St. Francis, AL, pneumonia, drafted.
Clark, Teaddeus C. S.	Pvt.	24	5'9½"	Brown	Gray	Soldier	Illinois	Died 9/2/1865 in hospital in Marion, AL.
Pollard, John	Pvt.	37	5'5"	Brown	Blue	Farmer	Ireland	Died in hospital 2/22/1865 Vicksburg, drafted.
Result, J.	Pvt.	–	–	–	–	–	–	Buried at National Cemetery Memphis.
Williams, Allen L.	Pvt.	29	5'8½"	Brown	Hazel	Ranger	Canada	Died, drowned 3/22/1865 Mobile Bay, substitute.

DESERTED

Soldier	Rank	Age	Ht	Hair	Eyes	Occupation	Nativity	Comment
Bredenback, Sebastian	Pvt.	37	5'7"	Brown	Hazel	Laborer	Germany	Deserted 2/10/1865 Cairo, IL, drafted.
Clancy, John	Pvt.	34	5'6½"	Brown	Hazel	Laborer	Ireland	Deserted 4/4/1865 Blakeley, AL, substitute.
Colvin, George L.	Pvt.	18	5'9"	Sandy	Blue	Farmer	Illinois	Deserted 7/1/1865 Demopolis, AL, substitute.
Doyle, James	Pvt.	31	6'1"	Brown	Blue	Farmer	Missouri	Deserted 10/25/1865 Greenville, AL, drafted.
Farmer, Adolph M.	Pvt.	28	5'10"	Brown	Gray	Farmer	Alabama	Deserted 10/25/1865 Greensboro, AL, drafted.
Heman, William J.	Pvt.	35	5'4½"	Dark	Blue	Farmer	Germany	Deserted 3/1865 Vicksburg, substitute.
Herman, John	Pvt.	34	5'6"	Black	Blue	–	Missouri	Deserted 3/16/1865 Vicksburg, substitute.
Howard, George S.	Pvt.	26	5'11"	Light	Gray	Soldier	Kentucky	Deserted 3/16/1865 Vicksburg, substitute.
McDonald, John	Pvt.	30	5'9"	Brown	Hazel	–	Canada	Deserted 2/10/1865 Cairo, IL.
Moore, William P.	Pvt.	26	5'5"	Brown	Blue	Soldier	New York	Deserted 2/20/1865 Eastport, MS, substitute.
Moran, Patrick	Pvt.	23	5'11"	Brown	Hazel	Laborer	Ireland	Deserted 2/26/1865 New Orleans, substitute.
O'Brien, Christopher	Pvt.	35	5'7"	Brown	Gray	Laborer	Ireland	Deserted 1/25/1865 East Port, AL, substitute.
Pike, Charles J.	Pvt.	18	5'4"	Black	Gray	Cigar maker	Ohio	Deserted 11/5/1865 Greensboro, AL.
Rane/Raus, Bernard	Pvt.	29	5'9"	Light	Gray	Rope maker	Germany	Deserted 12/7/1865 Demopolis, AL, 7th Missouri.
Reed, Cyrus M.	Pvt.	23	5'9"	Dark	Gray	Soldier	Illinois	Deserted 7/29/1865 Tuscaloosa, AL.
Renfry, Mark	Pvt.	38	5'10"	Brown	Gray	Farmer	Kentucky	Deserted 10/25/1865 Greensboro, AL, drafted.
Squires, William K.	Pvt.	18	5'3"	Brown	Blue	Laborer	Ireland	Deserted 8/18/1865 Tuscaloosa, substitute.
Thomas, James*	Pvt.	–	–	–	–	–	–	Deserted 7/17/1865 Demopolis, AL.
Welch, John	Pvt.	28	5'3"	Light	Blue	Laborer	Ireland	Deserted 4/4/1865, substitute.
Wendler, Leo	Pvt.	21	5'9"	Light	Blue	Clerk		Deserted 12/9/1865 Demopolis, substitute.

TRANSFERRED

Soldier	Rank	Age	Ht	Hair	Eyes	Occupation	Nativity	Comment
Farrell, Christopher	Pvt.	29	5'4"	Dark	Blue	Laborer	Ireland	Mustered out 11/11/1865, wounded in Battle of Nashville, 7th Missouri.
King, Edward T.	Pvt.	26	5'9½"	Light	Light	Soldier	Connecticut	Mustered out 1/15/66 Memphis, transferred to hosp. Steward.

Company K

Soldier	Rank	Age	Ht	Hair	Eyes	Occupation	Nativity	Comment
Robertson, George C.	1st Lt.	20	6'	Brown	Gray	Soldier	Missouri	
Snow, William S.	2nd Lt.	21	6'	Brown	Brown	Soldier	New York	
Bay, Eli	Sgt.	36	5'9"	Brown	Blue	Soldier	Missouri	Mustered out 1/15/66 Memphis.
Crangle, John	Sgt.	25	5'10½"	Dark	Hazel	Soldier	New York	Mustered out 1/15/66 Memphis, wounded in Battle of Nashville.
Dolan, Francis	Sgt.	30	5'11"	Dark	Blue	Soldier	Ireland	Mustered out 1/15/66 Memphis, 7th Missouri.

*Mentioned in Missouri Descriptive Roll but not in the National Archives.

Soldier	Rank	Age	Ht	Hair	Eyes	Occupation	Nativity	Comment
Jackson, Edmond M.	Sgt.	28	5'6"	Light	Hazel	Soldier	New York	Mustered out 1/15/66 Memphis, 7th Missouri.
Richey, Francis A.	Sgt.	25	5'10½"	Dark	Blue	Soldier	Arkansas	Mustered out 1/15/66 Memphis.
Blackmar, Richard	Corporal	19	5'8"	Dark	Hazel	Soldier	Pennsylvania	Mustered out 1/15/66 Memphis, 7th Missouri.
Cassidy, David	Corporal	39	5'9"	Dark	Gray	Soldier	Atlantic Ocean	Mustered out 1/15/66 Memphis.
Connelly, Allen W.	Corporal	24	5'6"	Dark	Hazel	Soldier	Indiana	Mustered out 1/15/66 Memphis, 7th Missouri.
Sharkey, Nicholas	Corporal	28	5'7"	Light	Blue	Soldier	Ireland	Mustered out 1/15/66 Memphis, 7th Missouri.
Twitty, James R.	Corporal	19	6'	Brown	Hazel	Farmer	Missouri	Mustered out 1/15/66 Memphis, wounded in Battle of Nashville.
Wade, Lewis A.	Corporal	25	5'8"	Light	Blue	Farmer	Indiana	
Clark, William F.	Musician	24	5'6"	Dark	Hazel	Miller	Indiana	Mustered out 1/15/66 Memphis, 7th Missouri.
Ferguson, Joseph	Musician	18	4'5"	Light	Blue	Farmer	Illinois	Mustered out 1/15/66 Memphis.
Akers, Joseph	Pvt.	22	5'5"	Dark	Blue	Soldier	Illinois	Mustered out 6/16/66 Memphis.
Alexander, Job. H.	Pvt.	30	5'4"	Dark	Blue	Soldier	Pennsylvania	Mustered out 1/15/66 Memphis, 7th Missouri.
Anderson, Scott	Pvt.	21	5'10"	Brown	Hazel	Farmer	Missouri	Mustered out 1/15/66 Memphis, drafted.
Archer, Goran	Pvt.	19	5'8"	Black	Black	Soldier	Missouri	Mustered out 1/15/66 Memphis.
Bay, John S.	Pvt.	20	5'5"	Light	Gray	Soldier	Missouri	Mustered out 1/15/66 Memphis.
Blonde, John	Pvt.	–	–	–	–	–	–	Wounded in the Battle of Nashville.
Burgess, Henry I.	Pvt.	31	5'9"	Brown	Blue	Farmer	Missouri	Mustered out 1/15/66 Memphis, drafted.
Bushner, Charles	Pvt.	26	5'8"	Black	Black	Soldier	Canada	Mustered out 1/15/66 Memphis.
Carterville, Adrian	Pvt.	28	5'6"	Dark	Hazel	Soldier	Holland	Mustered out 1/15/66 Memphis, 7th Missouri.
Cheney, William	Pvt.	32	6'	Light	Blue	Soldier	Missouri	Mustered out 1/15/66 Memphis, wounded in Battle of Nashville, 7th Missouri.
Clear, James F.	Pvt.	18	5'8"	Red	Blue	Soldier	Ireland	Mustered out 1/15/66 Memphis.
Coyle, John	Pvt.	36	5'5"	Dark	Blue	Soldier	Ireland	Mustered out 1/15/66 Memphis, substitute.
Donovan, Daniel	Pvt.	35	5'7"	Black	Hazel	Laborer	Ireland	Absent due to confinement of General Court-Martial.
Dougherty, Michael	Pvt.	28	5'5"	Light	Blue	Soldier	Ireland	Mustered out 1/15/66 Memphis, 7th Missouri.
Edwards, James	Pvt.	18	5'5"	Light	Blue	Farmer	Illinois	Substitute.
Emo, Peter	Pvt.	–	–	–	–	–	–	Mustered out 1/15/66 Memphis, 124th Illinois, drafted.
Fisher, Jacob	Pvt.	18	5'5"	Black	Black	Soldier	Germany	Mustered out 1/15/66.
Gibson, George	Pvt.	18	5'10"	Black	Gray	Farmer	Missouri	Sick in hospital in Nashville, substitute.
Gillard, Charles H.	Pvt.	18	5'5"	Light	Gray	Farmer	Illinois	Mustered out 1/15/66 Memphis, substitute.
Gogan, William	Pvt.	22	5'5½"	Black	Blue	Boiler maker	Canada	Mustered out 1/15/66 Memphis, 33rd Missouri.
Green, Hance	Pvt.	19	5'7"	Light	Hazel	Soldier	Missouri	Mustered out 1/15/66 Memphis. (Also shown as discharged 7/26/1865.)
Heffner, George	Pvt.	–	–	–	–	–	–	Mustered out 1/15/66 Memphis, 124th Illinois, drafted.
Hendricks, Enos	Pvt.	37	5'6"	Brown	Blue	Farmer	Tennessee	Mustered out 1/15/66 Memphis, drafted.
Holding, James	Pvt.	35	5'8"	Red	Hazel	Laborer	Ireland	Mustered out 1/15/66 Memphis, substitute.
James, George W.	Pvt.	44	5'9"	Brown	Gray	Farmer	Tennessee	Mustered out 1/15/66 Memphis, drafted.
Leddy, Bernard	Pvt.	28	5'11"	Fair	Blue	Soldier	Ireland	Mustered out 1/15/66 Memphis, 7th Missouri.
Lesom, Solomon	Pvt.	20	5'6"	Red	Hazel	Laborer	Germany	Mustered out 1/15/66 Memphis, substitute.
McCauley, Alexander	Pvt.	25	5'7"	Dark	Blue	Soldier	Ireland	Mustered out 1/15/66 Memphis, 7th Missouri.
McCoy, Patrick	Pvt.	28	5'9"	Black	Gray	Clerk	Ireland	Mustered out 1/15/66 Memphis, substitute.
McCready, Prosper	Pvt.	28	6'	Dark	Hazel	Soldier	Ohio	Mustered out 1/15/66 Memphis, 7th Missouri.
McCready, William*	Pvt.	–	–	–	–	–	–	Mustered out 1/15/66 Memphis.
McGloughlan, Francis M.	Pvt.	28	5'10"	Brown	Blue	Farmer	Missouri	Mustered out 1/15/66 Memphis, drafted.
Mehan, John	Pvt.	18	5'4"	Brown	Gray	Farmer	Ireland	Mustered out 1/15/66 Memphis, substitute.
Mills, Reuben	Pvt.	36	6'	Sandy	Gray	Soldier	Tennessee	Mustered out 1/15/66 Memphis, wounded in Battle of Nashville.
Montague, Lewis F.	Pvt./Musician	22	5'7¾"	Light	Gray	Soldier	Kentucky	Mustered out 1/15/66 Memphis.
Mullhall, William	Pvt.	25	5'3¾"	Brown	Hazel	Miner	England	Mustered out 1/15/66 Memphis, substitute.
Myers, Frederick	Pvt.	18	5'6"	Brown	Hazel	Laborer	Germany	Mustered out 1/15/66 Memphis, substitute.
Myers, Herman*	Pvt.	–	–	–	–	–	–	
Myers, John	Pvt.	20	5'6"	Light	Gray	Boatman	Germany	

*Mentioned in Missouri Descriptive Roll but not in the National Archives.

Soldier	Rank	Age	Ht	Hair	Eyes	Occupation	Nativity	Comment
Pratt, Elijah*	Pvt.	–	–	–	–	–	–	AWOL since 6/14/1865. (No discharge furnished.)
Prior, George	Pvt.	44	5'8½"	Brown	Blue	Farmer	Kentucky	33rd Missouri.
Reaser, Phillip*	Pvt.	41	–	–	–	–	–	Mustered out 1/15/66 Memphis. Drafted.
Reed, Bluford	Pvt.	32	5'9"	Brown	Gray	Farmer	Tennessee	Absent sick, drafted.
Rychluski, Weiteg*	Pvt.	24	–	–	–	–	–	Mustered out 1/15/66 Memphis, substitute.
Scott, Anderson*	Pvt.	–	–	–	–	–	–	Mustered out 1/15/66 Memphis, drafted.
Scott, George C.	Pvt.	24	5'6¾"	Brown	Brown	Carpenter	Ohio	Wounded in Battle of Nashville.
Slyon, James	Pvt.	22	5'5"	Light	Blue	Soldier	Ireland	AWOL, 7th Missouri.
Tilton, William E.	Pvt.	25	5'11"	Brown	Blue	Soldier	New York	Mustered out 1/15/66 Memphis.
Twitty, Thomas B.	Pvt.	20	5'7"	Brown	Gray	Soldier	Missouri	Mustered out 1/15/66 Memphis.
Upson, Nelson	Pvt.	20	5'8"	Light	Blue	Soldier	New York	Mustered out 1/15/66 Memphis, wounded in Battle of Nashville, 7th Missouri.
Weinstein, August	Pvt.	30	5'5"	Black	Dark	Carpenter	Germany	Mustered out 1/15/66 Memphis, substitute.
Williams, Davis	Pvt.	18	5'5¾"	Brown	Blue	Farmer	Missouri	Substitute.
Wilson, Douglas	Pvt.	28	5'5"	Brown	Hazel	Soldier	Connecticut	Mustered 10/31/1865.
Windland, Nicholas	Pvt.	29	5'5"	Brown	Hazel	Farmer	France	Mustered out 1/15/66 Memphis, 124th Illinois, drafted.

Discharged

Soldier	Rank	Age	Ht	Hair	Eyes	Occupation	Nativity	Comment
Coogan, Dennis E.	Captain	26	5'9¾"	Black	Blue	Farmer	New York	Discharged 7/21/1865 due wounds from Battle of Nashville.
Kendall, Cyrus D.	Captain	23	–	–	–	–	–	Mustered out 7/1865, wounded in Battle of Nashville.
Foster, Charles	1st Lt.	20	–	–	–	–	–	ADC General Lee 1863 mustered out 6/15/1865.
Allison, Benjamin	Pvt.	18	–	–	–	–	–	
Anderson, Christopher C.	Pvt.	21	5'8¾"	Light	Blue	Farmer	Ohio	Term of service expired 11/23/1865, drafted.
Bagan, Frances	Pvt.	28	5'7"	Dark	Dark	Laborer	Ireland	Mustered out 5/25/1865, 7th Missouri.
Bay, Joseph	Pvt.	19	5'8"	Light	Blue	Soldier	Missouri	Absent with leave for purpose of mustered out.
Coon, George W.	Pvt.	21	6'2"	Dark	Black	Farmer	Ohio	Discharged 11/23/1865, drafted.
Gray, James	Pvt.	22	5'8"	Light	Blue	Laborer	Georgia	Mustered out 2/3/1865, (Also shown as deserted 2/3/1865 St. Louis.) Drafted.
Gyer, Hiram	Pvt.	18	5'4"	Brown	Brown	Farmer	Tennessee	Mustered out 1/4/66, substitute.
Hicks, Joseph	Pvt.	33	5'9¼"	Dark	Gray	Carpenter	N. Carolina	Discharged 11/24/1865, drafted.
Horton, William L.*	Pvt.	36	5'8¼"	Brown	Blue	Farmer	Kentucky	Mustered out 11/24/1865, drafted.
Jones, Benjamin F.	Pvt.	18	5'6"	Brown	Hazel	Farmer	Missouri	Mustered out 1/12/66, substitute.
Jones, Samuel	Pvt.	18	5'2"	Light	Gray	Farmer	Missouri	Discharged 5/1865.
Maher, Lawrence	Pvt.	40	6'¾"	Gray	Hazel	Laborer	Ireland	Mustered 4/7/1865, 7th Missouri.
Mahoney, James	Pvt.	20	5'7"	Brown	Brown	Boatman	Ireland	Mustered out 1/4/66, substitute.
Meyers, John*	Pvt.	20	5'2"	Brown	Brown	Carpenter	Germany	Mustered out 1/4/66, substitute.
Morgan, William G.	Pvt.	33	5'5¾"	Brown	Blue	Farmer	Missouri	Mustered out 11/24/1864, drafted.
O'Keefe, Michael	Pvt.	23	5'8¼"	Light	Blue	Laborer	Ireland	Discharged 12/8/1865 disability, substitute.
Palmer, Joseph	Pvt.	34	5'6"	Black	Brown	Cooper	Baden	Service expired 11/25/1865, drafted.
Schulte, Joseph*	Pvt.	–	–	–	–	–	–	Discharged 9/18/1865 disability, substitute.
Smith, John B.	Pvt.	24	5'6"	Brown	Blue	Laborer	Germany	Mustered out 12/20/1865, substitute.
Spencer, Cadwallader C.	Pvt.	40	5'9"	Black	Blue	Surgeon	Pennsylvania	Mustered out 7/16/1865, drafted.
Todd, Henry	Pvt.	18	5'6"	Brown	Gray	Farmer	Missouri	Discharged 11/20/1865 disability, substitute.
Waggoner, Christian	Pvt.	37	5'7"	Light	Gray	Laborer	Germany	Mustered out 1/4/66, substitute.

Died

Soldier	Rank	Age	Ht	Hair	Eyes	Occupation	Nativity	Comment
Monegan, Owen	Corporal	19	5'8½"	Brown	Hazel	Soldier	Ohio	Died of disease 11/2/1865 Demopolis, AL, buried at Marietta Ntl. Cemetery.
Blonde, Joseph	Pvt.	24	5'9"	Light	Blue	Soldier	France	Died of gunshot wounds in action 12/27/1864, Nashville Cemetery.

*Mentioned in Missouri Descriptive Roll but not in the National Archives.

Soldier	Rank	Age	Ht	Hair	Eyes	Occupation	Nativity	Comment
Brake, Benjamin F.	Pvt.	23	5'8"	Brown	Blue	Farmer	Tennessee	Died 2/2/1866, buried Jefferson Barracks, MO, substitute.
Davis, William	Pvt.	23	5'6"	Brown	Hazel	Farmer	Missouri	Died 3/10/1865 of disease, drafted.
Freeny, Lawrence	Pvt.	20	5'8¼"	Light	Blue	Laborer	Ireland	Died 4/19/1865, substitute.
Hunt, Thomas	Pvt.	28	5'4"	Brown	Blue	Soldier	Scotland	Died of wounds 1/28/1865, 7th Missouri.
Lanfrecht, Otto	Pvt.	37	5'6"	Brown	Blue	Soldier	Germany	Died of disease 2/24/1865, buried Memphis Ntl. Cemetery, substitute.
Martin, John	Pvt.	18	5'8"	Dark	Gray	Farmer	Missouri	Died of disease 7/18/1865 Jefferson Barracks, substitute.
Mosar, Peter	Pvt.	39	5'8"	Light	Gray	Teamster	France	Died of disease 5/15/1865 Selma, AL, buried in Marietta Ntl. Cemetery, drafted.
Payne, Nathaniel	Pvt.	24	5'8¾"	Dark	Blue	Soldier	New York	Died 3/17/1865 Memphis, buried in National Cemetery.
Phelps, James*	Pvt.	–	–	–	–	–	–	Died of disease 4/15/1865.

Deserted

Soldier	Rank	Age	Ht	Hair	Eyes	Occupation	Nativity	Comment
Adams, William	Pvt.	22	5'2"	Brown	Gray	Laborer	Ireland	Deserted 2/3/65 St. Louis, substitute.
Cinnerman, Frederick	Pvt.	22	5'4¼"	Light	Blue	Clerk	Germany	Deserted 12/4/1865 Demopolis, AL, substitute.
Cooper, William	Pvt.	23	5'4¼"	Brown	Gray	Driver	New Jersey	Deserted 1/16/1865, substitute.
Dever, Charles	Pvt.	27	5'5"	Black	Hazel	Soldier	Ireland	Deserted 11/24/1864.
Donahoe, John	Pvt.	30	5'4"	Brown	Hazel	Laborer	Ireland	Deserted 1/26/1865 St. Louis, substitute.
Johnson, William	Pvt.	25	6'	Brown	Blue	Farmer	Alabama	Deserted 2/9/1865 Cairo, IL, substitute.
McCue, Mathew	Pvt.	19	5'7"	Brown	Gray	Laborer	Missouri	Deserted 1/16/1865, substitute.
McNash, William	Pvt.	18	5'8"	Light	Blue	Soldier	Virginia	Deserted 2/11/1865.
Muse, John*	Pvt.	–	–	–	–	–	–	Deserted 2/5/1865.
Phillips, Thomas*	Pvt.	39	–	–	–	–	–	Deserted 2/15/1865 St. Louis, drafted.
Sheedy/Shidy, Michael	Pvt.	33	5'10"	Black	Blue	Laborer	Ireland	Deserted 2/15/1865 St. Louis, substitute.
Warner, Thadeus	Pvt.	26	5'9"	Light	Gray	Soldier	Connecticut	Deserted 4/27/1865, transferred from Co. D.
Winscott, William N.	Pvt.	21	5'9"	Dark	Blue	Carpenter	Missouri	Deserted 8/15/1865 Marion, AL, 33rd Missouri.

*Mentioned in Missouri Descriptive Roll but not in the National Archives.

Appendix C: Wartime Letters of Men of the 11th Missouri Infantry

Letter of Eugene Page

Eugene Page enlisted at 23 years of age. Eugene was a 6'1¼" unmarried farmer from Sangamon County, Illinois. Eugene was born in Virginia and was a private in Company B. Private Page died of smallpox on February 16, 1863. The following letter is located in the Civil War pension file of Private Page.

November the 27th 1862
Dear Mother
It is with greatest pleasure that I seat myself down to write you a few lines to let you know that I am well at this time and I do hope when these few lines come to hand that it may find you in the same state of health. Well I must tell you about my last soldiern I have been in. The biggest fight that has ever been in the west. But as it was God's will I came out sound while many of my friends fell around me. The fight commensed a little before sundown. Our regiment was marched up a little for dark, and [saw] too or three regiments running. There officers could not rally them. Our regiment stood and fought too brigades one [h]our and ten minutes. They charged on us too times. But we cent them back. Crossed bayonets several times. Our ammunition run out and we was ordered to fall back. Our killed and wounded was 80. The rebels was over three hundred. They said they had fought many a regiment but they never come cross one but what they could back before.

Well Mother, I reseved of the twenty third and the freight came off the twenty first. But I was very sorrow indeed to hear of my younger sisters death. Indeed I am sending my love to my other sisters and tell them to write to me.

The fight happened at Iuka, Mississippi and we are camped at Rianzy [Rienzi], Mississippi. Mother, please write soon without fail. I am going to start my girl's likeness to you, but I don't know if it will go or not. But if it does I want you to send me your likeness.

So I want to write a few lines to Samuel. I write the rest of this letter to him for he lives close to the office. Samuel, dear Sir, I now close my letter by writing a few lines. I reseved your letter with kindness. I was glad to hear that you was well. I can not write you much at this time, but I am going to send my girl's likeness to my mother and [she] will direct this letter to you and I will send the likeness and letter both at once and separate. So excuse my bad writing and spelling. Send me your and mothers likeness at this time.
Eugene Page

P. S.
No more at this time. Your beloved son until death.

William Notestine Letters

Captain William Notestine enlisted in the 11th Missouri Infantry at 19 years of age. Notestine enlisted as a sergeant, and in 1864 he was promoted to the rank of captain in Company E in the 11th Missouri Veteran Infantry. Notestine was a railroader in his civilian occupation and was a resident of Olney, Illinois. Captain Notestine died February 16, 1865, as result of his wound in the first day of the Battle of Nashville.

June 12 1863
Dear Father
I take the present opportunity to answer your kind and ever welcome letter. It has been a good while since I received it. Yet ever since we have been moving and have not had time to write to no one.
I wrote a letter to Uncle Jonas yesterday giving an account of our operations and told him to let you read it as I could not write to all at such length. The campaign is one of extraordinary interest and also of unparalleled hardship. The dust was suffocating and heat intolerable. We also had to do on half rations until the evacuation of Haines Bluff. Yet in compensation for all this we expect a great & glorious victory. We willingly endure the many privations of campaign life when a great deal can be accomplished. Our Brigade which is the 2nd Brigade of Tuttle's Division & Sherman's Army Corps has been detached since the 23rd of May and we have had more than our share of marching. The Brigade is wore out and run down and we were sent here for rest and to protect this side of the river which was threatened a few days ago. They had quite a fight up at Milliken's Bend and a Negro regiment saved the day driving off the rebles with great slaughter and saving our camp garrison equipage. The wounded in our company on the 22nd was 11. Sergeant John Baird wounded twice. Corporal [Alzono] George Thomas 3 times, once slightly. Jacob Eppley dangerously. Wm W. Couch finger shot off. George Gaddy once. Elijah Harmon seriously. F. Beyhamer seriously. G. W. Little seriously. Wm H. Barger slightly, John W. Seymour 3 times very slight. George Butler very slight. I hope to hear from you soon.
I remain as ever
Your son.
W. F. Notestine

1865 [Between January 1 and February 16, 1865]
Dear Father
I was overjoyed a few minutes ago by the receipt of a letter from you. The line I have received from you. It seemed as long as 21 days & I could not hear from you. But I expect to hear oftener. I have no consolation to expect in the letters, I guess. My wound is doing well. I sat up this morning 3 ½ hours and I am now sitting up at noon about the same. I will be up at supper again. So you see that I improve. (Letter ends here)

Letters of Alonzo G. W. Thomas

Corporal Alonzo George W. Thomas was born in New Jersey and made Olney, Illinois, his home prior to the war. Thomas enlisted in Company E at 19 years of age and was an unmarried carpenter prior to the war. Corporal Thomas was wounded in the assault on Vicksburg on May 22 and died as a result of his wounds on June 27, 1863. A description of Corporal Thomas' wounds was recorded in the previous letter by William Notestine.

Young's Point [Louisiana]
April 15, 1863
Mr. W. Thomas
Dear Father

We were paid for four months the 14th and receiving fifty two dollars, forty-five which I enclose. We are encamped nearly opposite the mouth of the Yazoo River. Have bin engaged with digging a canal for days past. Rather funny way to take Vicksburgh,
Yours
A G W Thomas

Memphis Tenn June 21, 1863
General Hospital Ward I
Dear Father

Your kind and welcome letter of June 16th has been received and gives me great pleasure to know that you are still well. My wounds are not doing quite so well as when I wrote you before. The Dr. in the ward I was in said the erysipelas was setting in and felt quite uneasy but it proved not be the erysipelas but matter forming just over the shin bone and it had to be lanced and it discharges a great deal that in connection with a slight fever weakens me very fast and then I have but very little appetite. I hope that I will take a turn for the better soon.

I shall keep in as good spirits as possible and shall try to come home as soon as I get able.

Sometime in April just before I left Duckport I expressed $45.00 to you. Did you receive it? I can think of nothing more this time. I will write as often as I can and hope you will do the same. Love to mother and the same to yourself from
Your son
A. G. W. Thomas

Letter of John Treadway

John Treadway, 29 years old, enlisted as a musician in Company E in the 11th Missouri Infantry in August 1861. Treadway was a married hoop maker living in Fairview, Illinois, prior to the war. John Treadway died of consumption November 7, 1861, at Cape Girardeau, Missouri.

August the 8 1861
Dear Wife

I am moved to Cape Gerdo [Girardeau], *40 miles above Caro. We was brought down here in a ferry. The news come to us that this place was about to be attaced. We started in one hour after we got the order. There is about three thousand troops here and there is four thousand secession troops in five miles of here. Do you see we are in a close place? We got to see a great many new things. The secessionists have all left there families and all half of the houses no one lives in. Some places they have run the union men off. There is a man and his wife in our company that they run off and took every thing they had. They ware poor folks and have one little boy two years old. There is not one of the company sick now.*

We are living in a large mill. There is three of them here that belonged to secessionists and they are all full of troops.

Aug the 10th

Since I commenced this I have bin in quite a battle. There was one reported killed and 2 wounded. I have seen the wonded men. One of them is shot through the shoulder close to the top of the lungs. It is thought he will get well. Some of our men was in a close place that is those that was on picet guard. John Crawford and Milt Akey was out. Then one of the guard fires. They have to all fire and then run to the main body of the army. Some of the guards saw some of the enemy and fired at them. All of the guard fired and the enemy then fired on them. Milt Akey fired his gun and started to run and there was a man shot at him not more than ten feet of Milt, rushed on him (illegible) and knocked him down and fought him untell they saw others running up then he run. It was a very bold act and shows that he will fight. But when he come to find he was one of our own men he is hurt very bad but not dangerous but the worst danger there was out [we] did not know that was a guard out there and as soon as they shot they thought that they was all enemys and they commenced firing at them. Capt. Hendy [Hendee] was struck with two balls. One only through his blanket and one tuched his arm and then he give orders to fire and then nearly all the regiment shot. John was running towards us and he found the balls flying so fast around him that they was cutting all the weeds down and then he got behind a wood pile but the main body of the enemy did not show themselves. They found that we was ready for them and they backed out. This was after night. We was taken out about eleven oclock up one hill and kept there untell morning. John Howland and me did not shoot. He said he did not here enemy orders to fire and I had laid down on the ground and went to sleep and the firing waked me up. I grabed my gun but I could not see any body to shoot at. There was one of the enemy shot. There was blood found where they stood and one horse found dead with bridle and saddle on. That was the only time there I have handled a gun since I have bin here, but I had no drum and I wanted something to do in the battle. There was two guns that there was no men for. So I took one of them.

I rote to you to send me your bad money for me to get good for it but I hope you have not sent it for if you have, it will not come to me now. Let me know whether you sent it or not. If you have sent it I will send Leudlow an order to get it and send you good money.

It is very likely that we will stay here all winter. If I was there we would get a room and send for you or come after you myself. Let me know how you would like to come and if I find out that we are going to stay all winter I will come after you. A good place to live.

Direct you letter to John Treadway
Cape Girardeau MO

Letters of John Collins

The 24-year-old John Collins enlisted in Company G of the 11th Missouri Infantry in August 1861. Collins was a single farmer from Lawrence County, Illinois. Private Collins died on February 4, 1863, in Jackson, Tennessee, of typhoid fever.

Camp Fremont
November 5th 1861
Dear Mr Watts Sir,

I take this opportunity of droping you a few lines for I have not heard any from you for so long I began to think you was all dead. I guess you will be very much surprised to hear of the death of George McKelvey who died last evening and also Captain Mieure today. I regret the loss of the loss of both of them. I suppose Capt. Mieure's remains will start home today or tomorrow. George will be buried in the graveyard. They was both sick about forty days with the fever. Our regiment was ordered away today but I do not know where they will go, but I think to Bloomfield.

I wrote to Lyle to hire a hand to gather his corn and get up mother's winter wood and if Lyle can't get a hand, I would like you would get one to help Lyle get the wood and gather her apples if they ain't gathered. If you get a hand then I would rather that you not pay over ten dollars a month. But write to me the amount you do have to pay and I will send you the money and I think we will get money in about ten days. I have nothing more . I would like to send you an account of our battle at Fredericktown. I am tired and I guess you have seen all about it before now. Please write as soon as this comes to hand and let me know how things are getting along, I have no more but give my love to Clementine. My paper give out and I must [illegible] so I can finish. I have wrote to you twice and have received no answer. One I sent by Patrick Norton and I would like to know how you are getting along. I want you to write as soon as you get this and let me know what Lyle and Tom as if they have hauled any winter wood. And if you have heard from James yet and what they are doing.

I sent that money home to you for safe-keeping, but if you need any of it for your own use you can use it and write to me that you have plenty of wood. I forgot to tell you that I seen Will Ryan and he was in the 21st Ill Rgt. And he said he would be glad to hear from you. He quartered at Pilot Knob Mo. I have no more to write any more as I want to write the rest to Lyle. So no more at present and I remain your affectionate son until death.
J. C. Collins
To Rachel Collins
P S
We heard out here that John Leason is married. Tell the folks to write for I would like to hear from them.

March 16, 1862
Point Pleasant
Army in the field eight miles below New Madrid on the River
Dear Mother
I take the pleasure of dropping you a few lines to let you know that I am on the land of the living. My health is tolerably good at the present considering the circumstances.

We left Commerce on the last day of February for New Madrid. After four days travel we reached Madrid. We surrounded the town and showed fight, but they did not come out to fight us. They only threw some shells at us which did not do us any hurt. We give them a few shots from our cannon and camped for the night in sight of the place. There was nothing happened for the army interest for several days until our heavy cannon arrived. The night before we commenced the attack, we planted our cannon and was ready and commenced to firing on them. There was continual roar from then on until about noon. When we dozed off we thought the fight had just begun. We intended to commence the next morning but behold to our surprise they had left in the night and we was left to take peaceable possession of the fort. We got all their cannon and some other stores. They heaved all they could in the river which we caught the next morning. The country here is very low and wet here. I guess we will go down the river before long. We are eight miles below Madrid on the river now. We captured a lot of sugar and molasses down here.

Mother I want you to write as soon as this comes to hand and let me know how you are getting along and how my things are getting along and whether James has sent any money home to pay his part of the taxes. I would like to know as soon as possible for it is tax paying time now. I cannot send money from here for it is hard to send letters from here. You must direct your letters to Cairo, Illinois to the Eleventh Mo. Regiment in Cairo Captain C. M. Carter and I will get them. Tell the folks to rite soon. Rite soon Mother as I will be anxious to hear from you. No more at present. But remain your affectionate son until death.
By, rite soon,
John C. Collins

[probably August-September 1862]
[Letter begins in the middle]
I was sorry that Woodworth had done so poorly. I was in hopes that he was the right kind of man. But he has proven to be worthless. If I could only see to my things myself, I would be a great deal better satisfied. But I will have to do the best I can. I want you to write to me as soon as this comes to hand and let me know that you are getting along. Whether you have plenty of wood and corn and other things. If you have not, I will get them for you. I do not want you to think that I won't. But anything that you stand in need of, let me know and I will try to furnish the money to get it. If it is not asking too much of you I would like for you to see to my wheat. That is if you can. I want to sell my wheat if I can get 6 bits a bushel for I want to make a payment to Watts this fall and I want to Reuis [re-issue] all the money that I can Reuis. That is the reason I want to sell my wheat and that I don't want for seed. Mother I want you to write and let me know things are getting along for I am very uneasy about things and my things and there is no one that I depend on but you and I would like for you to rite soon.

I have written to Tom Young and Malva. I got no answers yet so far. The rest of the folks you can *tell them it does not matter whether they write or not for it is clearly proven that they do not want to write. You have heard of the death of Colonel Plummer. He died at Camp Gaylord, Miss on the 9th of August. His death is very much lamented in his division. He was buried near camp. For a while it was a grand affair. Our regiment was one of the escorted the body. Uncle Jonathan Hoover got his discharge and started for home some time ago and I supposed he has reached home by this time. I wish you would tell Tom Tanqueray and Shepard that I am much obliged to them for writing so promptly. Mother, I want you to kiss the children for me and Sally in particular. I guess I will have to bring my letter to a close for this time hoping to hear from you soon.*

Believe me as your ever affectionate son,
John C. Collins

William Haskins Letters

Private William Haskins was 18 years old when he enlisted in Company G of the 11th Missouri Infantry. Haskins was a single farmer from Lawrence County, Illinois. He died on August 11, 1862, at Camp Gaylord, Mississippi, of "inflammation of stomach and bowels."

November 27, 1861
Camp Fremont, Missouri
Dear Father

It is with great pleasure that I sit down to write you a few lines to let you know that I am well at present and I hope these few lines find in you in the same state of health. I received your letter and was glad to hear from you and to hear from you that Aunt Mary is living with you. I was afraid she was turned out the door for they have been burning houses and turning women out of door in this state. They burned several houses in Fredericktown and burned one of the nicest houses you ever saw. All waste. It belonged to a widow woman and burned up all she had and turned her out in the street. You said that for me to send my money home and you would keep it and not spend it. I wonder if you do think that I would send my money home and let you keep it and not spend it. I will sent my money home and I want to pay Mr. Haney and then I want you to [do] what you please with the rest but I don't want you to keep it in your hands and not use it when you want it. If you don't pay your debts out of it and I hear that you don't I will come home and give hankers. You better reckon I haven't any money now but I will draw some before long and I have twenty fore dollars owing to me and I am owing twelve out of and then I will draw 26 dollars from the government and then I will send you about 20 of it and maybe I will send more and I don't want you to keep it and want money and have money in your hands. I can't think of much importance to write. I will have to quit writing. I want you to give my love to all and tell them to write as soon as they can. Tell Mandy Price to write to me if she pleases. I haven't heard from her since I have been here. You tell her that I send my love to her. So no more at present. Write as soon as you receive this.

W. A Haskins
Tell this you see
Remember although many miles apart

Cape Girardeau, MO
February 8, 1862
Dear Father,

It is again with pleasure that I take my pen in hand to inform you that I am still alive and enjoying a reasonable portion of health and I hope these few lines may find you all well. I received your letter last night and was glad to hear from you. Once more health is tolerably good at this present time. Charles A. Gillen has been at the hospital about a week but he is better. He is here in camp now and Walter Black is sick. He is at the hospital yet. There is some talk of us leaving here but I don't know whether we will or not. The 17th Ills Regt is going away from here today. They are going down to Cairo to be in the battle at Columbus. We keep taking in the Secessionist almost every day. The cavalry

fetched in twenty-one yesterday and killed several more. There has been a great battle at Fort Henry and Beauregard was taken prisoner. They first attacked by the gun boats from the river. They was driven out of there fort and the infantry pitched in and whipped them completely. Now I want you to tell all of the folks to write me and you do the same. I send my love to all inquiring friends. I will now bring my letter to a close. You wanted me to write how much money I sent. Well I sent $9 dollars. I think you will find it at the Depot at the express office. No more at present but remain your affectionate son forever.
W. A. Haskins

Camp 6 miles north of Corinth, MS
July 5, 1862
Dear Father,

It is with grate pleasure that I take this present opportunity of writing you a few lines to let you know that I am well and I hope these few lines may find the same. I received your kind letter and was glad to hear from you, but sorry to hear that Jackson had left you. I told him to stay with you and not to go to war for you was not able to do anything and he would help you along as much as he could.

Father I have sent you twenty five dollars by Aunt Harriet Allender. I expect you will hear about it before this comes to hand and I hope you will have it before this letter reaches you. I will try and send you some the next pay day. Write and let me know when you get it and tell me where Jack is and I will write to him and give him a piece of a fool's advice. Father, you write and tell me that if he knows where he is well off he will not go in for any longer than three months. Tell him that I said for him not to go in for three years service for he will make more to stay at home.

It is very sickly here at this time. It is so hot that the soldiers can't live hardly. So no more on that. Well something about the fourth of July, we did not have much of a time here. They were celebrating by firing cannons. There was a poor fellow that got his hand shot off and blowed about a rod and powder burned him until he was perfectly black. I can't think of anything of importance and I will have to bring my letter to a close. Give love to all the folks at Head Long. Tell Aunt Gany that I have wrote till I have got tired and some never write at all and I don't think I shall write to her anymore till she writes to me. I don't believe they think anything of me or they would write. Give my love to all the folks and tell them to write. So no more at present. Write as soon as you receive this letter and let me know if you receive that money.
WM A. Haskins

Camp Gaylord Missouri
July the 10th 1862
William A Haskins to A W Haskins
Dear Father

It is a great pleasure that I take my pen in hand to let you know that I am well at present and these few lines may find you in the same state of health. I received your kind letter and was glad to hear from you and that you was well as you were. Well, I will give the health of the boys. C. A .Gillen is sick and has been for some time. He was unlucky and got very bad yesterday by a limb falling from a tree. It struck him on the top of the head and knocked him down and senseless for some time. He is very bad today. His head is very sore and his neck is so stiff that he can't turn his head without giving him severe pain. George Mills is well and also Mark Barnett. There is several of the boys is sick. There was one of the men in the brass band that died yesterday and is to be buried today sometime. If you have not got the money when this comes to you, you go to Lawrenceville and inquire at the post office and if it is not there go to Harriet Allender and inquire of her what she done with it. There was 25 dollars all in 5 dollars bills. I expect we will be paid off this week or next and will send some more money. Tell Jack that I intend to send more money home than he does. The next six months to come I want you to let me know if you get that money so I won't be afraid to send more. You never let me know whether you got that I sent by Adams Express Company. If you did not, let me know and I won't send any more by express. I will send it to you in care of Thorn. Well I have to get and go and help Charlie Gillen to the hospital and now I will [close] my letter.

I saw Frances Pickering and he is pretty bad off. He can't hear scarcely at all. I believe that I have give you all the news. It is not worth my while of me trying to tell you anything about the war for you know what is a going on as well as we do ourselves.

We only get that once a day and they are two to 3 days old. The latest paper was the 1st and there was no news. Well I will have to bring my letter to a close. Write soon when you can and as often as you can. I would write oftener than I do if only I could get postage stamps but they are not to be got here no where. If you will send me some I will be much obliged. Don't send unless you get the money that I sent you. No more for present. Write soon and give my love to all the boys there and tell Harriet and William to write to me. Tell them that I wrote them and never received any answers from them and I will not write them until I get an answer. Give my love to all the Head Long folks. And tell them I would like to hear from them. Tell Uncle Howard and Cap to write if they please. Tell them I am not mad or anything like mad.

From William A. Haskins.

Camp Gaylord, MIS
Augt 11th [1862]

My old friend, with much regret I have to pen you a few lines to let you know that William Haskins is no more. He died about three o'clock today. The friends generally are well here. Some sickness among the soldiers. Roran Waller [Rollin Waller] was taken today the same way that William was and we have to carry him to the hospital now. He had inflammation of the stomach and bowels. My health is tolerable. Mark is well.

My respects to all the friends, yours truly,
Jas R. Allender

James Mulhall Letter

The Irish-born James Mulhall was a mason living in Lawrence County, Illinois, prior to the war. Mulhall was single and 22 years old at the time of his enlistment. He was a private and bugler in Company G when he died of congestion of the lungs at Cape Girardeau, Missouri, on March 15, 1862. The following letter was written by James Mulhall's sister, Jane.

December the 8, 1862
Dear Brother,
  I received your kind and welcome letter.
  Dear Brother, I thought you left Dubuque as you were so long before you wrote me. I am glad to hear of you being in good health. We are all at present. Thank God for it. Dear brother you will be surprised to hear that I am in Cape Girardeau. James was very sick so he wrote to me to come here. So I started for here last Friday week but he is well. No, only a bad coff but he is getting very well. He is chief bugler. He has no duty to do. I don't know how much he has a month, until he is paid. He has gotten but one month's pay and was only a private's pay. He is doing well if he only minds it. This is a very dangerous place at present. I can't tell you much about this place at present in my letter. I will be better able to let you know all particulars. Jamie sends his love to you and wants you to write to him. Write soon. No more at present. I remain your affectionate sister.
  Jane A. Mulhall

Abraham Norris Letter

The 40-year-old Abraham Norris joined the 11th Missouri Veteran Infantry after being transferred from the Thirty-third Missouri Infantry. Norris enlisted at Palmyra, Missouri, and was a member of Company G when he died of chronic diarrhea in Demopolis, Alabama. The following letter was written by the regimental chaplain, George Brown.

Demopolis, Ala
Dec 20th, 1865
Mrs. Mary Norris
Palmira, Mo

I am called upon to announce to you the death of your husband, Abraham Norris, who died this morning about 9 o'clock. He was sick a long time. In fact, ever since he was transferred from the 33rd MO. And all the time in the hospital. He was well taken care of. Nursed very tenderly, until death released him from suffering. He died fully in his senses and professed religion some 10 days ago. Requested me to inform you of the fact, and I am glad that you have this comfort in your sad affliction. That the Lord was pleased to have mercy upon him and lead him to Christ. Before his death he requested me to baptize him which I did. He expressed a willingness to die but said he would like to get well and return home.

Disease, chronic diarrhea.

His effects are in the hands of the Captain of his CO 'G' Capt. Wallace commanding, who will forward them all to you in due time. I know of nothing more in reference to the case at present worth communicating, and would say in conclusion that anything else you may want to know in regard to it I am ready to answer any and all questions, and give you all the information I can.

May the Son be with you in this bereavement.
Most respectfully yours,
G. W. Brown
Chaplain 11th MO. I. V. V.

Captain George C. Adams Letters

George Clinton Adams was 35 years old when he enlisted as a sergeant in the 11th Missouri Infantry. He was married and was a resident of Versailles, Illinois, prior to his enlistment. When the 11th Missouri Veteran Infantry was mustered, Adams was promoted to the rank of captain and commanded Company I. George Adams died on December 1865 at his home in Illinois. (The first three letters are located at the United States Military History Institute, and the last letter is housed at the Old Courthouse Museum in Vicksburg, Mississippi.)

La Grange
June 29, 1864
Sister Mary

I received your kind letter of the 17th of this month and were glad to hear that your health were good and the rest of the family are enjoying good health but you sayed that Mother's eyes were soer again. Do you think they are as same as they used to be some years hence? I were in hopes that she would not have another spell of the soer eyes again. You also sayed that Gran Ma's health were not as good as when I were home. This we have to make allowance for such is the path of old age for she has lived a long time but out lived her friends yet no never will she.

We moved from Memphis on the 17 of this month and have bin on or near the Memphis and Charlston R R and repairing the bridges burned by the rebs. We arrived here on the 27 inst doing some repairing here. We, the souldgers, don't work more than assist in the raising of a trestle now and then. There are a body of troops that is their business called pioneers or engineers corps. Some men have to do guard duty whilst they do the work.

The weather is very warm and dry here now but signs of rain. I got a letter from Perry yesterday the same time I got yours. I saw Wart Henry and the other boys the other day of the 119th and they were all well except Sam and Jim Brooks.

Jesse Henry is in moderate health now. He were quite unwell when he came to the company. One of the best boys of our company were wounded down the river. His leg were amputated between the hip joint and knee. Lived some 10 or 12 days. Died in hospital in Memphis. He were a friend of mine. He were a son of a widow name Wroe. He were my mess mate, a bed fellow and seemed next to a brother to me. He were a good example for a soulger. One of the recruits have died. He only lived some 2 days after taken some thing like the congestive on the brains. He were (I thought) the best one of the squad. A boy of 19 years and I had made a good deal of calculation on this future progress as a souldger as I had the drilling of the recruits. He were a son of a widow woman but his mother were married the 2nd time.

We expect to move from here soon & go down to Miss where Sturgus had a fight with the rebs. Frank is with us and is getting stout. I have had him out some a week for will do better here than in camp as he gets green applies and other things. I have tried to get him and 2 others sent back. When we start from here if we stop here few days and he improves like he has since he came from camp, he will go with us for he looks quite well. You sayed that kinman were in the 118 or 119 Ils. I can not tell which what camp is. Rite soon and give my love to all the folks that inquire after me. So no more. I am in the best of health and hoping when these few lines come to hand they may find you enjoying the same blessing.

From your well wished Brother
G C Adams

Benton Barracks, Mo.
Nov. 17th, 1864
Missy Mary Adams
Dear Sister

I recd your kind letter of the 28 ult. today. I were glad to hear from you and the rest of the connection. Also to hear that health were good. I did not understand whether you were at home or not. I have not had more than 3 letters (except official pay) for over 2 months, neither have & had chance to rite much. I not near the Miss River. [illegible] to Father and expressed a package from St. Louis to him but have not herd from either yet.

You spoke of Malinda as being on the mind yet. I am in hopes of her final recovery of heath. You sayed William York were at home to day. Do you mean [illegible] York or not? I have not heard from him for a long time. Neither have I heard one word from Levi Henry for 6 months. Is he not at home? Tell him I would like to hear from him. If he pleases. I heard from Jess a few days a go.

This is the seventeenth and Brother Perry's time is out with the 18th. I have a look out for him for he may come here to be discharged. It would be quite a treat to me for to see him, now here, as I have not seen him for over 3 years. It seems longer to me than the absents of many of my relatives. I begin to get anxious to see Frank but he has done much better than he would if he had been with me for we have marched hard. You spoke of helping shell corn. Were you only shelling for milking or for soil? I have no more to rite. Only I have had my rolls signed for six months pay and look for pay in 2 or 3 days. At least, Frank for 4 months pay at Memphis.

Then I will give you a few lines of our travel in Missouri only as I made mention of the marching in ARK in the letter to Father. We left St. Louis near the 11th of Oct. I were very sick as we went up the Missouri River. Same as I were at Memphis on my way home. So I were poorly while at Jefferson City and were sent to Sedalia Mo where I got one day behind, but went up overtaken them after a march of some 70 miles which I made in 2 days. We were through Independence in 4 miles of Kansas City. We were in Kansas one day only. I seen — near the lines of Kansas, the prettiest country I ever seen in my life. Not populated.

We had 1 big storm at Sedalia on our return here. It snowed all day and in the night until 10 o'clock, The snow were nearly knee deep. It were 15 inches on the level. It were warm the next day and water, snow & mud in the path were from 1 inch to 6 in deep. The officers on horse back broke the road and they only made the tracks and we went in two ranks. The snow were up to my overcoat tails on both sides of the little path. We marched at 7 P.M. Our trip in Mo by land were over 400 miles, ARK 350 besides the travel on water & R R of near 525 miles.

So no more at this time for I am not in a good fix to write as I am busy. You may think so when I tell you I worked until 5 A.M. on my rolls to git them ready. Rite soon. Believe me to be your affectionate,

Brother
G C Adams

Capt. I 11th Mo.
Tell Jess he may look for a letter.
Has he got his Blanket?

Near Spanish Fort Ala
April 4 1865
Sister Mary

I received your letter of the 17th ult. and were exceedingly glad to hear from some. Also to hear that the family were all well, as well as to learn that you did not forget to rite to me because I had not ritten to you in person when I rite to the family. I rite to all much to one as the other. I rite home quite oft times here when I have paper to do it with. My vouchers were left behind some time. I do not know when you would get them but all right.

I rote a letter to Erma on the 24th. Since then we marched 2 & ½ days builded 2 breast works at night. On the 27 we came here. Had some fighting but the 4th had some to do. Only skirmishing. Very few men wounded—28. We threw up works day & night. I only had [illegible] do out the time. A skirmish had 2 men hurt. Terry lost two fingers but Cyrus were hit with a spent ball. He is on duty now but not stout. He stays with the teams. So the Yanks has thrown up a great deal of dirt. It digs easy.

Last eve from 5 to 7 P.M. the Yanks made a boom shell. Charge this for the first time reminded me much of Vicksburg. The rebs layed low when [we] were at work with all our artillery. Our Regt has had some 28 men killed & wounded. Most of them on 1,2, and 4 day. Casualty last 3 day very small. I were glad to have you give me the account of the Cooperstown meeting. That is the first word I have heard of [illegible] for a long time. I suppose she were married ere long.

This leaves at the [illegible] you found me enjoying the blessing of good health and hoping these few lines may find you enjoying the same.
Believe me to be your
Loving Brother
G C Adams
Capt. 11 Mo VV

To his beloved sister
M A Adams
Versailles, Ills
Sister Emily

I were much delited at the idea of your making mention of our Mother's birthday. She is getting well advanced in years. I hope as she advances she may seem more dear to me. You spoke of sister Amanda's birthday. I hope I will be favored with the pleasure of greeting you in person my next birthday which will be my 30th one. If I don't get my call taken here. They have shot very close to me whilst at work. We lost one here. One fine Capt. at Nashville and one here. The one here is not ded but his arm is gone at his shoulder and his bone [illegible] The photos all you spoke of, it has no names, one of the company for Brother. Nothing more.
George

At Gen. Grant Hdqtr
in Rear of Vixburg, Miss
May 25th 1863
Miss E. S. Adams
Dear Sisteer

I recd your third letter of the 12 inst and very glad to here from home and to hear that you were all well and the rest of the folks to with Malinds Joel and Amands family.

I am in tolerable good health have ben quite unwell but marched all the time I were trobled with the flux for 10 days and since then my bowels are not in good fix but appetite good.

I would have riten sooner but we were a moving when we were not worttg to.

Jess is well and harty and rote a letter to his father one day and Recd one on the next day dated May the 12th.

I were glad to here that my money got home safe as it comes slow and much needed.

You sayed that Granmas health were good I were in hope that I would get to come home this summer for a few days but as it is looks doutfull now as we did not take Vixberg the first nor the second attempt but hope it is all for the better in the future so I will close hoping these few lines may all in good health you can rite oftine and I have to catch my opportunity from your affectionate Bro.

George

I will give you a little sketch of the try near young [Young's] Point we started on the 2nd of May and march down the Bajo on the west side of the Miss River we camped near Richmond the night I seen some of the 3rd Ills cav. fine weather marched early A.M. on the 6th and wrrored some 3 brigges the solgers ebanede. Some fine houses otone at home supposed to have 30 thousands dollars worth of furniture in it, it were burned. After our Brig passed somenice famrs here I seen corn some waist high one field some 4 to 5 hundred acres in looked fine we stopped in it some 3 hours and the teams destroyed a great deal of it. 7th we cross the river at Grand Gulf.

Marched at 11 A.M. warm and roads dustry and the brokensert county I ever seen the roads were cuts like railroad which made it good the hills farms out but corn looked well half boot top high corn on hills we would not think of sowing grass seede on for pasture if they ever plowed it I now not how all the arm.... ......are in corn we camped in the woods of miss once more. I marched at 3 P.M. and camped at Rocky Springs there we layed on the 10 with scarce rations. Leevi Heenry come an seen us also Joseph Heinnvan I marched at 6 A.M. and hard day march there. see Joseph Boot and several of the other boys we marched direct to Jackson. There and met or overtook the enemy near Miss Springs. on the eaven of the 13 we dress up the line of battle but the enemy clered the road here it rained on us some that night. 14th we marched early being th front. the Minn Regt in advance rain began to fall at near 7 A.M. and fell until 1 P.M. we found the enemy at a big home near 2 mills out of town drove them from there with skermishers and cannons and they stopped at their forts a short time and were drove from there with out a fight.

The 2nd Brig camped in the State yard and our company in the State house here we had plenty to eat and drink got all Secesh Knapsacks we waster (for we left ours) and they had clean cloes in them and ours were wet and muddy, 15 fine day dried up and cleaned. The officers took every thing in town were to eney use to the boys and tore up and burned the railroad. I no not how far and burned the penetentary they were one block owned by some Jews I guess blockade runners, were burned down there goods were took out first I think the citezons don the burning. common shoes were marked $15.00 common hat $30. flour $12.50 ti 14.75 per bbl cal. not less than $1.50 per yards. there were a woman the day before we come in there offered $20 for a pair of shoes and she dayed that day she had the pleasure of seeing them threw into the streets, guarding prekeretry are plaid as I hope. 16 there were a detail to role tabaco and sugar out in the street and knock them open all of this kind were disstroyed and all the Rail Road properly burned. we marched as 11 A.M. towards Big Black. Reached there on the 17 at 5 P.M. pioneers built a pontoon bridge. 18th the army finished crossline and we crossed over at Sun Set (as our brig were the last) 19 marched at 10 A.M. and reached our lines of battle at 8 P.M. our forces took Hanes Bluff.

22 there were and order to charge the enemys works at 10 A.M. efforts were made in the a m which we were not in but at 5 P.M. our Brig were ordered to Storm a fort of the enameys. the 11th in the lead and that brought Co. I in front for we moved by the right flank. We (Co. I and 3 other Cos) reached the fort, could not scale it, so we had to lay under the fort until dust when we stifed away our regt lossed good many killed and wounded (our co 12) None you new unless you new Same Beauchamp wounded I were not tutch we are beseageing the place now. Co. I were detail at Gen Grant head quarters to do guard and fatigue dewty, no not how long for our Brigade went last night to Haynes Bluff. I could say a great deal more but not this time as riteing privelges are few. I have paper, no envelope. I look for our knapsack and tents up soon then I can right. so no more

Your

G. C. Adams

William Chapman Letters

William Chapman, a Pennsylvania native, enlisted in the 11th Missouri Infantry at the age of 18. Private Chapman was an unmarried farmer who had lived in Beardstown, Illinois, prior to his enlistment. William Chapman died of wounds he received during the Battle of Iuka on September 19, 1862.

Thursday Aug the 8th 1861
Dear Parents
I take this opportunity of writing you a few lines to let you know where we are. We are at the Arsenal at St. Louis. We had a fine time of coming down here. We heard before we got here a mob would attack us a coming through St. Louis. But we marched through with flag a flying and never heard Jeff Davis cheers once. I was overjoyed when I saw Thomas in Naples. I hope he will stay with you. There is about 3000 soldiers here now. A great many have left here for the Barracks here. Our regiment is at Birds Point.
There is new companys coming in here all the time. This is a mighty fine place, where they can manufacture guns, canons and all sorts of arms. There was a man drowned this morning while in swimming. It ain't hotter here than it was up there last week. We don't have to drill in the heat of the day. We have plenty to eat and lots of fun and have a stone house to live in. They look for an attack on this place every day. They got a cecession Captain and 40 men as prisoners. They are a hard looking set. They are going to shoot the captain on Saturday. This is the nosiest place I ever saw. It is like climbing up hill to write. They are running against a fellar all the time. We have five men to cook for the whole company. We are going to be inspected this afternoon and get our uniforms and arms and be sworn in also. If any letters come for me, send them here. This is a mighty fine set of fellars in this company. Newton sends his love to all. They have taken several prisoners at St. Louis today and brought them here. Well I must close for they make so much noise that I can't half write. Give my love to all the children and Thomas. Tell him I will write before long. Give my love to Mrs. Davis, Martha and John and tell them I will write. Give my love to Wess and all inquiring friends. Write very soon. Direct your letters to me.
To: William H Chapman. In care of Capt. Barnum, Bayles Rifles Arsenal St. Louis
This is the way—. In care of Capt. Barnum, Bayles Rifles Arsenal St. Louis
Your affectionate son
William H Chapman
Give my love to Marga

Aug the 27 1861
Dear Brother
I thought I would write you a few lines to let you know that I am right side up with cane. I suppose that you got that letter and watch I sent you by Sam Mitchel. We are running around all the time. We get to see lots of country and have lots of fun. Well Thomas I have got no room here to write. Write. I told Pap all the perticulars. I want you to write and tell me all the news on the bottom. Tell them all I send my love to them. The boys sends all their love,
Your Brother
W H Chapman
Excuse this blotching

At St. Louis Arsenal
Aug the 27 1861
Dear Father
I take this present opportunity of writing to you. We arrived here last night about ten o'clock. We are going to leave here this afternoon for Cape Girardeau. Our regiment is there. We are ordered there immediately. We will go by water. The body of Gen Lyon came in last night the same time we did. We took lots of cecessionsts before we left Camp Moselle. There was preaching there last Sunday. There

were women, and children and nigars in large numbers. We had a good sermon. I had a tooth ache very bad last week. I got it pulled. I don't regret that I enlisted for a moment. It just suits me. We get fifteen dollars a month. As fast as I receive my pay I will send it right to you for it belongs to you not me. I hope Thomas will stay with you and help you shuck corn. We are going to whip them cowardly traitors in time to be there to break stalks next spring. Thousands of soldiers left here last night for Jefferson City. They are fighting there. I want to come home on a furlough next month if I can. Cape Girardeau is about 40 miles from this side of Cairo. We will be there by this time tomorrow. When you write to me, tell me how you are getting along and whether you have sold your corn and wheat yet or not. Whether that company has left Meredosia or not. I want to hear from home once a week any how. Edgar Elliott is in the hospital. You had better send me a little money to write with to or three times. We will get some next month. I could send without stamps but you aint sure of getting them that way. Well I must bring these few lines to a close for I have to cook to do our mess 48 hours. Give all my love to the children and Mother and Thomas and Mrs. Davis' folks. Newton sends his love to all and will write as soon as he gets at the Cape. Give my love to all inquiring friends. Please write as soon as you get this. Direct your letter to W. H. Chapman, First Rifles Missouri, Cape Girardeau in care of Capt. Barnum.

   from your son
Wm H Chapman

Camp Fremont
Cape Girardeau Mo
November the 8th 1861
Dear Mother

   I take this opportunity of writing you a few lines. I received your letter a few days ago. I would have answered your letter sooner but the very minute I received your letter they called for volunteers to go on scout. So I was right in. We returned yesterday evening. We took a good long tramp. The whole brigade volunteered. Started for Bloomfield. The report came that 18,000 rebels was there. We got to a small river call White River. We camped there for the night. The next morning the orders came for us to counter march or part of us. Our Colonel is the commander of the post. He said that he never ordered but one regiment out. There was a mistake but some where the 17th Ills and 11 Mo was ordered back and the balance went ahead to make a junction with troops from Birds Point. We haven't heard from them yet and we was going through what is called niger wood swamp. Some of our men lagged behind the whole brigade. The sneaking cecesionist is sniping all through them swamps. They shot two of them that was behind and shot at several more. A lot of us took out through the woods in search of them but you had just as well hunt for needles in a hay stack as one of them in the swamp. We took 15 prisoners. Some of them had furloughs from the rebel army. I am glad to hear your eyes are getting well. I hope I can get to come home for Christmas. Any how I am fatter now and feel better than I have ever been before. I like soldering the best kind but I like my country ten times better. Oh them infernal cecesionsts. Mother they are meanest looking people in God's creation. I can shoot them down like dogs for they are no better. I would like to be there to help you [with] molasses very well. I am glad pap got it made up. We have molasses here. Sometimes is hard. Schaffer preach the other night. He come up to see us last Sunday night and there was a meeting at Company A. We went up to Company A and they invited him to preach. He preached the best sermon I ever heard him preach. He give the gamblers fits. The balance of the brethren got in a good way. It made me think of home to see Schaffer stretch his big mouth. Nate says he is much obliged for sending him that ticket and piece of dress. He thinks Emily is coming out of the kinks. I don't think we will stay here long. I sent my likeness to you in a letter a few days ago and some money in one to Thomas. Tell me in your next letter whether you got them or not. I will get my likeness taken again in case and send it by Express before long. Tell Thomas that I think I could beat him shucking corn. This winter I will send him a cecesion breast pin to wear to remember me by . Well I must bring my letter to a close. Give my love to all the family and Mrs. Clavis folks and all inquiring friends. So please write as soon as you get this.

   Your affectionate son,
W H Chap
PS

Bad writing for this is a very bad pen.
Give my love to all. Tell pap I saw cypress and cypress knees and cane breaks he used to talk about

Camp Gaylord Miss
June 22 1862
Dear Mother
I take my pen in hand to write you a few lines to let you know how I am getting along. I am well & doing well as ever. I received your kind letter which came to hand some time ago but was unable to answer it till now on the account of one of our men was looking to go home every day. So I thought I would send by him & some money with it. I hate to risk it by mail but I don't see any other chance now. So I will risk six dollars. I have got more but I wont risk all at once. I wrote Thomas all the news the other day. So I won't have much to write. We are camped on the Tobigbe River on the Mobile railroad 10 miles west of Corinth. We have a nice place to camp. Every company has a good well. We are camped under large shady trees on high looking ground. It is thought that we will stay here all summer or till peace is declared. There is no mosquitoes of any account yet. But the whole earth & air is full of insects of every descriptions. Ann Laske wrote to Nate and said she heard that he was drunk & got put in the guard house. It is all a lie and it makes us know who told it. Nate hasn't been drunk or in the guard house since he has been in the service. I seen Thomas Miller the other day. He told me to send his best respects to all of the family. I must close for want of some thing to write about. Tell in your next one how much corn the old man has got in. Thank you for them flowers. Nate sends his love to all. Send your letters now to Murphy's brigade instead of Plummer's. I will tell you our position. If we move you will see it in the paper. Army of the Mississippi right wing commanded by Gen Rosecrans, Gen Stanley's Division, 2nd Brigade. Give my love to all the family & inquiring friends. Please excuse this poor writing from a poor pen
   from your son
   W H Chapman

Corinth Ms
Oct 15th 1862
Dear Friend
I received your letter yesterday & was truly glad to hear from you. Your letter found me in good health but not in the best of spirits since Henry was taken from us. I feel like I was lost. I thought as much of him as if he had been my brother but his battles is ended. He died a true soldier. I deeply sympathize with you in your loss. You wanted to know if he was buried decently. He was buried as decently as he could under the circumstances. He was buried with his blanket around him but his grave is sufficiently deep to keep him from being exposed. He has some money coming to him. Lt. Osgood has got what money notes he had. He has started home. He left this morning. You can see him by going to Morgan City. Henry got that letter you spoke of. We marched to Iuka. He had no time to answer it after he got it. I don't know all the things he left at the Cape but if you want me to I will write to the man he left them with to have the things expressed to you. He did not have much clothes with him. He was buried in his best. His things are here in his nap sack. There is one shirt & pr pants. He was like the rest of us in regard to clothes. We are short of clothes at present, but we will soon make a draw. It would be almost impossible to send his remains home as no remains are allowed to be carried on the R R at this time, and it is too far to send him any other way. I suppose that you have heard of the Battle of Corinth. Ere this thing our regt took a very active part in. It was another bloody time to witness. Our regt lost 80 killed and wounded. Our Co. had 3 men wounded but not seriously. Our Col [Mower] was wounded. I don't think we will have any more fights soon as the rebels are pretty well whipt out. I will send you an engraving of Iuka. I will make a dot where the Battle was. I have not yet received Thomas' letter. As soon as I do I will answer it. I expect we will stay here all winter. I heard today that our regiment is going to be transferred to heavy artillery as we have only got 180 effective men in the regt. I will close hoping to hear from you soon. My love to all the family and inquiring friends,
   From your friend
   N A Preston

In the Iuka House is where I helped take the wounded

Luther Vance Letters

Private Luther Vance was 18 years old and was farmer living in Clay County, Illinois, when he enlisted in Company I of the 11th Missouri Infantry. Private Vance died of wounds he received during the Battle of Iuka on September 19, 1862.

September the 20th 1861
Dear Sister
I thought I would write you a few lines to let you know I was well at present and hope these few lines find you the same. Father, I received your letter on the 18th. I was glad to hear from you and hear that you was well. We have been on a march. We have just got back to the Cape. We had a good time of it. I stood it first teate. We went to a little town called Perryville—We took 200 secesionest and made them take the oath. All but one. We kep him and fetched him to the Cape to have his trial. He belong in a secesionest company. We stade there about 5 days then went to Camp Jackson about 40 miles from Peryville. They told us that we would have a fight thare back. When we got thare [all] was quiet. Colonel Cook had just bin in thare and cleaned them out. So we didn't have no fight thare. We marched ahead on to the Cape without any fight.

Father, you wrote that you was going to buy that house of Bozier. I will help you all I can. I will send all money home that I draw. I cant tell how much it will be. We expect it every day but it may not come for a month. We will draw a suit of uniform today. It is a pretty nice suite. This is the second suit of cloth. We expect to put on our new suite this afternoon on dress parade. It is a nice home. I will come the first chance. I stood gard over a lot of seccionest the otherknight. I kept my gun cocked all night. I expect to have to shoot some of them.

I was sorry to hear that Uncle Patrick was dead.
Write soon I send my best respects to all you.
Good by
Luther Vance.
Tell the girls to write. You say give them hell but we cant ketch them.
Good by

Camp Fremont
Cape Girardeau
Oct the 9th 1861
My Dear Sister
I received your kind and welcome letter of the 3rd inst. on yesterday and was glad to hear that you were well which this leaves me in at present. My Dear Sister, I hope that you nor Father nor Mother will not think badly of me for going to fight in the defense. I know that I am in a good cause because so consequently I have no misgivings on this point. My term was for three years unless sooner discharged which I believe I will be for I have no idea this struggle will not last for three. I will send my likeness home just as soon as I can get it taken. I want that you will keep some of all you find. In hope that you will reserve some of them for me. I had quite a serious time of it since I last wrote to you. I had the measles but now I am well and out of danger. There were quite a number of the Boys had them the same time but are now well with the exception of a few. We have not got our money as yet but when I do, you may tell Father that I will send it to him as he directs.

I conclude for the present by sending my kind love to all my friends and relatives,
I remain as ever your loving and affectionate Brother
Luther Vance

Oct the 13th 1861
Dear Sister

I thought I would write to you. I have been sick this week with the measles but I am getting better pretty fast. I think I will be as well as ever in a few days. I was in the Hospital 6 days. I would like to see you all but I don't want to come home till payday. If I cant get off at payday I will send my money home.

You have know idea how Cape Girardeau looks. Big high breast works all around it and the cannon there is here and more coming every day. Thare was six big 24 pounders hauled up from the boat landing yesterday. It looks like the secessionst would get a part of it if they come here. Ben Todd and Ben Stoner and a lot more. I didn't hear they all has gone to California. Jim Dennis and Jo Haimes had a fight. Jim Dennis got his paw broke for being a secessionist. John Brewer is not here. I would like to be home next summer to work with you but I like it first rate here.

This general made a speech the other knight. He thought the war would be over in 3 months. Our Colonel has command of the post. His name is Colonel Plummer. We swaped off Old Bales [Bayles] for a man that knows what he is doing. The talk is that we will stay here this winter. If we do I will be at home this winter sometime. I would like if you could send me some postage stamps. They hant to be had here. Thare is so many soldiers here. I give a dime for this one. I would like to know whare Bill Eaby is. If he went with Boziers Co. or not. We had fresh beef for dinner which we have every three day. We haven't binn in the guard house yet.

Write soon. I remain your loving Brother. I send my best respect to all of you. Father and Mother and Sister and Brother .

Good By
Luther Vance to Jane Vance
I want all of you to see this letter
Good by

Oct 25th 1861
Dear Sister

I am well and harty and hope these few lines will find all of you the same.

The Boys hasent got back yet. They whipped Old Jeff Thompson and his band of thiefs. They killed Lowe, Jeff Thompson's partner. He was shot dead on the spot. Our Boys is after Jeff yet. If they get him they will use him pretty ruff. I think thare is 43 of our company gone. We cant tell when they will get back. We begin to want to see them pretty hard. We hope they will fetch him — Old Jeff. When they do return, I expect you will know more about the fight than we do. You can get the Mo Democrat and read all the news. We have got pay for the first month. I got 15 Dollars. I have sent one Dollar. I am going to send 10 dollars with Mr. Chapman when he goes. I don't know when he will go. He will leave it at Bethel. That is all at present. I remain your affectionate and loving brother,

Luther Vance

I want you to share some of that apple butter that you are talking about. I want one Barrel for my own use when I get home.

Dec 3rd 1861
Dear Sister

I once more take my pen in hand to address yours. These few lines to let you know that I am well at present and hope that this letter will find you enjoying the same blessing. I am still staying at Cape Girardeau and I expect to stay here this winter and gard the forts. Things are quite peaceable here. There is nothing new going on in this location of the country. The gunboats went down the river last Thursday and we are waiting here from it. I presume that they intend to take Columbus if they can. I should like to see you all and spend a weekend or two with you but General Halack says that he will give no furloughs anymore for six weeks and it is very uncertain whether he will give any then or not but I am very well satisfied as it is. Have nothing to do but stand twenty four hours in a week and help haul a little wood if I see fit. So good by for time. Write on sight of this and let me know how you are getting along.

Direct your letters to Cape Girardeau
Care of Capt. Barnum
Care 11th Mo Regt U.S. Vols

Cape Girardeau Mo
Jan 21st 1862
Dear Sister Jane

 I thought I would write you a few lines to let you know that I am well and in fine spirits and hope when these few lines reaches you it will find you enjoying good health. Well Jane, I have not much of any things of interest to tell you. Everything seems to be quiet here at present. Secesh are coming to the Cape every day from Jeff Thompson's camp. They are half starved, ragged looking set of traitors. They are getting tired of serving in an army where they don't get enough to eat and to wear. There was a force of about three hundred cavalry went out to scout out to Bloomfield fifty miles south west of here. They returned last Saturday night bringing in forty prisoners. The most of them were officers in the Rebel army. The Secesh is nearly played out in the part of the country and I hope it wont be long before it will be played out all over our Beloved Country. I should not wonder if they was fighting down at Columbus as we have heard heavy cannonading down the river for the last five or 6 days. If they are fighting, you will hear of it as soon as I can. We thought sometime ago that we would get to go south this winter but we are disappointed. We will have to stay here likely till spring and maybe longer. We have very good times here. Good comfortable quarters to stay in and plenty to eat and to wear and have plenty of fun such as it is. Since I commenced writing this letter I received a letter from home. They was all well when they wrote. Well Jane, I believe I have told you all the news that would interest you. So I will close hoping to hear from you soon. No more at present but remain your affectionate Brother,
 Luther Vance

Cape Girardeau Mo
Feb 13th 1862
Dear Sister

 I will devote a few moments in writing to you to let you know that I am well & in fine spirits and I would hope when these few lines reach you it will find you enjoying good health. I received your letter some two weeks ago and was glad to hear from you. I would of written to you sooner but I did not have any thing worth writing about. We are still in the fort & likely will stay here till we go away. The 17th Ills Regt left here last Saturday night. Report is that they have gone to Fort Henry on the Tennessee river. Our regt is all the infantry regt that is here now. A part of the 7th Ills Cavalry are here. They were out to Bloomfield fifty miles south west of here last week on a scout. While they was out there fifteen of them was detailed for picket guard. This went out to an Old Mill 6 miles from town. While there they was surrounded by one hundred rebels. They had to either fight or surrender and that would not be, so they fought them and whopt them bad. They killed 9 secesh and wounded a good many more. The Cavalry lost four men — two killed & one missing and one shot through the face and took part of his tongue off.

 Well Jane — it is the opinion of our leading men that the war will be over in three months. I am thinking the Secesh is nearly whipt out. They are losing now every battle that is fought. I think Columbus will go up the river in a few days. Well I believe I have told you all the news that would interest you. So I will close hoping to hear from you soon. I heard from home this week. They was all well. The weather is pleasant here now. The health of company is very good at present. I will close by requesting you to write soon. No more at present but remain your affectionate Brother,
 Luther Vance
 NB
 My worthy friend Newton A Preston sends his compliments and best wishes to you.

April 6th 1862
Point Pleasant Mo
Dear Sister Jane

 I will devote a few moments to you as I have written all the news to Father. I haven't much news to tell you. This is a very pleasant day and I am writing out in the cypress swamp on a log. The Spring is opened with its beauties. The Spring birds are singing their merry songs. The tall cypress trees are all leaving out finely. The peach trees are all in full bloom. The door yards in town and vicinity are full of green grass and flowers. It is quite reviving to see the Spring open after a long and [illegible] winter. The river has been very high but is falling just now.

Well Jane, I have written several letters to you and never got an answer yet. I don't know what is the reason. I wish you would write as soon as you get this and tell me all the news you can think of and tell me all about the girls. And if there is one wants to marry just tell them to send word down and let me know. I will close by sending my love to all. My friend Newton A Preston sends his compliments and best wishes to you.

So no more at present, but remain your Brother till Death,
Luther Vance

Poetry on the War

Hark I hear the canons roaring
Tis over on Kentucky shore
Many a Southern lady will be mourning
For her lover she'll see no more

Most anxiously they are awaiting
For their lover's return once more
But alas they see in a paper stating
That they were killed on Kentucky shore

Me thinks I hear them sighing
For their lover's, they are gone
Now their mangle forms are lying
Never more to look upon

I hope you will remember me
If you no more, my face shall see
And interest in your prayers I brave
That we may meet beyond the grave

Composed & written by
Newton Preston
Co. I 11th Regt Mo Vols

Presented to Miss Jane Vance
by her friend N A P

May 6th 1862
In Camp near Corinth
Dear Sister Jane

I will embrace a few moments in writing to you that I am well and hope these few lines will find you enjoying good health. I received yours of 17 and was truly glad to hear from you. We are now in camp 6 miles from Corinth. We have been advancing stoutly on the enemy at Corinth. This is the second day we have been here in camp at this place. I suppose we will be moving again tomorrow or next day on a little closer to the enemy. Some thinks there will not be much of a fight. And some thinks there will. We are bound to whip them out any way—be much or little. Our company was on picket guard night before last. We were within three miles of Corinth. We could hear the drum beating plain. The weather is quite warm down here. We cant stand it in the day time with our jackets on. The wheat is headed out and the corn has come up and the most of it plowed over once.

We are camped on a ridge close to a cotton field. We have plenty of good water, plenty of springs all around us but I would not like to live here. It is a hard looking country. Well Jane, as I am going to write some to Father, I will put in a few more words and bring my letter to a close. You wanted to know where Newton Preston come from. He came from Ohio but he was living in Meredosia when he enlisted. He sends you his best respects. He says he is going home with me when I go home and he sends you his thanks for your kind invitation you sent him and also for that nice jacket you sent. He thinks it was a very nice jacket. Well Jane, you think about the girls will back me out when I come up home.

Just wait till I get back and we see whether I back out or not. You said that you wanted to marry Jest Waite till the war is over and I think you will have no trouble in getting married. There is a certain nice young man in our company that has taken quite a fancy to your likeness. I will not tell you his name now but you know before long. Well Jane, I will close by sending my love to all the family and other enquiring friends.

 from your Brother,
 Luther Vance.

Corinth Miss Oct 8th 1862
Dear Friend Jane

 As your brother Luther was an intimate friend of mine I have took the painful duty of writing you concerning him. On 19th of Sept we attacked Gen Price's forces at Iuka. Our regt was ordered to the front a little before sundown. Luther was close to me in the ranks. The firing was so hot and the smoke was so thick that I could not tell who was shot. The Battle lasted till after dark. I did not see Luther after we commenced firing. Dan Smith & Sam Beauchamp took Luther off the field the morning after the fight he was wounded. A ball had struck him on the top of the head. He had no other wounds about him. He was perfectly sensible and talked to the Boys. He appeared to be getting along well when the Boys left him. The regt went on after Price so the Boys was compelled to leave him but he was left in good hands.

 I suppose you have heard before this that he is dead. If he is I haven't heard of it yet. I was detailed the next day to wait on the wounded. Our regimental Doctor told me that Luther was fine and doing well in one of the hospitals. I looked for him but could not find him but there had been a great many of the wounded has been taken up north. He might have been among them. I am in hopes that he is still living and doing well for he was one of my best friends. I will write to you again as soon as I can hear about him.

 He had no valuables in his nap sack but your likeness that I took care of for fear the nap sack might fall into the hands of the rebels. His nap sack is put away for safe keeping with the rest of the wounded boys things. If you request it I will send the likeness to you. If not I will keep it as remembrance of the owner and will deem it a sacred gift unless Luther should get well. If he does, which I sincerely hope he will, I will return it to him. I will close by requesting you to write soon. The [next] time I write I will give you the full details of the late Battle. Good by for the present from your friend.

 The Lord blessed our army with another great victory,
 N A Preston

Corinth Ms Oct 26th 1862
 Dear Friend Jane

 I will take the opportunity of writing you. I received your kind letter yesterday and was truly glad to hear from the sister of my unfortunate friend, Luther. Although it gives me pain to write you the sad news. But I consider it my duty to rite to you. Luther died a few days after he was shot. He was buried at Iuka. That is what I heard yesterday that was the report that the doctors sent in yesterday. I suppose it is true. I have not heard till yesterday what had become of him. I tell you I felt bad when I heard it for I thought as much of him as if he had been my Brother. Many is the dark and stormy night we have stood together on guard watching our treacherous foe but he has done now never more to join our social [illegible]. I deeply sympathize with you in his loss but let us cherish his memory. Let us bear in mind that he was a true soldier and never knew what it was to turn his back to the enemy. My Dear friend I cannot express my feelings on this subject— Lieut Osgood is at home now— Your Father can see him in regard to his money and cloths. He was wounded in the Battle. He will stay at home a good while I suppose. I have not seen your Father yet. I am in hopes that I will get to see him before he goes back home.

 I think as you do about a soldier have a hard time but that cant be helpt. Our glorious country will have to be saved and the sooner the better. I am willing to do my part towards saving it. I am in hopes that this bloody war will soon come to a close and we can live in peace hereafter. What a good time we could all have this winter if the war [was] to close now but it seems very likely that we will be in service for some time yet. It is quite cold here now. We had quite a snow storm here last night. The health *is very good here now. I suppose you have already heard of our victory here at Corinth. It was another Bloody fight. I heard that they was coming again soon to take the place but they will meet with a warm reception if they come to see us. Jane wanted to know about the 27 Ills. I heard about three weeks ago they was in Nashville Tennessee. There is where they started for when they left Tuscumbia. I think it is very likely that they are there. Communication from there has been cut off by the rebels for some time. I suppose that is the reason you have not heard from then for so long. I am much obliged to you for that likeness and will remember the giver. I believe I have written all the news that would interest you. So I will close. I would very much like to hear from you soon. That is if you have no objections to write. By for the present from your sincere friend and well wisher*

Newton A Preston

Washington and Anderson Campbell Letters

Private Anderson Campbell was born in Tennessee and had moved to Sumner, Illinois, prior to the Civil. Anderson Campbell was 18 years old when he enlisted in Company K, and he was a farmer. Anderson Campbell died of smallpox on March 8, 1863. Anderson Campbell's pension records showed he served in the war with his father, Washington Campbell, although the regimental rolls of the 11th Missouri Infantry do not show his name. The pension records also showed Washington Campbell survived the war.

June the 9th 1862
Dear Father

It is with great pleasure that I take my pen in hand to let you know that I am well at this time hoping that when these few lines come to hand they will find you all well. I am well and harty now and well satisfied. I want you to write soon and send me Thomas' likeness and George's too and I will send you mine as soon as I can get it taken. We are in Missippi under marching orders now. I gess you have heard that Corinth is evacuated and the rebels is gone and we are going to start after them in the morning. We have been on gard for 48 hours. I seen Mark Cooper and George Greenlee and all of the boys and they are all well now. I think the secesh is about plaid out and it is getting dark and I must quite writing soon.

Anderson Campbell

Washington Campbell [Washington is not listed in the 11th Missouri roster or shown as a member of the regiment. It is likely he was either illiterate or prompted Anderson to write the letters.]

October 13th 1862

Dear Father I received your kind letter on the 29 of Sept. I am well and hearty. Hoping that when these few lines comes to hand will find you all well and hearty. I want you to write me soon and let [me] no how you are getting along. I was not killed nor wounded. John McAlpin was wounded. Hyramm Umfleet is wounded. I supposed that you heard [Marshall] Osborne was killed at Iuka Springs. He never shot of his gun. We just marched up in line to the edge of woods and he was shot before we fired a shot. We are at Corinth Miss now. We have a battle at Corinth. We fight two day in the morning of the second day just before day light the boys bilt a fire up there. The rebels commenced and continued until day light and then they retreated back into the woods and left one piece of cannon — 20 pounds brass gun.... They was skirmishing about half the day and then made charge on one of our forts and tuck it and we tuck it back in about 20 minutes. The rebels charged again but missed it and then we fight about one hour. Then the rebels ran. I have nothing of importance to write. I am going to send you a peace of a rebel flag in this letter. I want you to write me soon and send me some postage stamps for I am out of them and can't write any more until I get some. I must bring this letter to a close so no more at present.

Anderson Campbell
Washington Campbell

Notes

Chapter 1

1. William Parrish, *History of Missouri Vol. III, 1860–1875* (Columbia: University of Missouri Press, 1997), 4.
2. *Ibid.*, 12.
3. *Ibid.*, 4.
4. *Ibid.*, 22.
5. Floyd A. Showmaker, *A History of Missouri and Missourians* (Columbia, MO: Walter Ridgeway, 1922), 155–156.
6. Harvey Carter and Norma Peterson, "William Stewart Letters, January 13, 1861 to December 4, 1862," *Missouri Historical Review* 61 (January 1967): 226.
7. John Frémont, "Proclamation," *Missouri Democrat*, September 3, 1861.
8. Merrill E. Gates, *Men of Mark in America*, Vol. II (Washington, DC: Men of Mark, 1906), 278–279.
9. Duncan McCall, *Three Years in the Service: Record of the Doings of the 11th Reg. Missouri* (Springfield, MO: Johnson & Bradford, 1864), 4.
10. William S. Stewart, Letter Collection, Papers, 1861–1864 (C2991). August 8, 1861, Western Historical Manuscript Collection, University of Missouri, Columbia, State Historical Society of Missouri.
11. Stewart, Letter, August 10, 1861.
12. John Treadway, Letter, August 8 and 10, 1861, Civil War Pension File, National Archives.
13. Thomas Hawley, Letter, August 25, 1861, Thomas Hawley Papers, 1856–1867 (A0666), Missouri Historical Society, St. Louis.
14. *Annual Report of the Adjutant General of the State of Missouri, December 31, 1863* (Jefferson City, MO: W. A. Curry, 1864) 263.
15. McCall, *Three Years in the Service*, 6.
16. Luther Vance, Letter, September 20, 1861, Civil War Pension File, National Archives.
17. Jeremiah Miller, Compiled Service Records, Missouri Volunteer Union Soldiers, 1962, National Archives.
18. "Skirmish at Dallas," *Camp Fremont Register* 1, no. 1 (September 25, 1861), Civil War Papers Folio, Wisconsin Historical Society, Madison.
19. *Ibid.*
20. Stewart, Letter, September 26, 1861.
21. Hawley, Letter, September 8, 1861, Thomas Hawley Papers, 1856–1867.
22. David Bayles, Special Order 277, July 17, 1871, Civil War Pension Record, National Archives.
23. George Cullum, *Biographical Register of the Officers and Graduates of U.S. Military Academy*, Vol. II. (Cambridge, MA: Houghton Mifflin, 1891), 85–86.
24. McCall, *Three Years in the Service*, 4.
25. David Bayles, Special Order 37, January 23, 1863, Civil War Pension Record, National Archives.
26. Hawley, Letter, September 29, 1861, Thomas Hawley Papers, 1856–1867.
27. *Ibid.*, October 2, 1861.
28. Joseph Plummer, General Order No. 20, October 2, 1861, Eleventh Missouri Order Book, National Archives.
29. Nancy Williams, ed., *Arkansas Biography: A Collection of Notable Lives* (Fayetteville: University of Arkansas Press, 2000), 41–42.
30. Clara Kennan, "Dr. Thomas Smith. Forgotten Man of Arkansas Education," *Arkansas Historical Quarterly* 20, no. 4 (1961): 309–310.
31. General Order No. 21, October 3, 1861, Eleventh Missouri Order Book, National Archives.
32. James McGhee, "'A Damned Tight Place': General Jeff Thompson Confronts the Federals at Fredericktown, Missouri," *Missouri Historical Review* (April 2009): 150.
33. Doris Land Mueller, *Missouri's Swamp Fox of the Confederacy* (Columbia: University of Missouri Press, 2007), 9–20.
34. M. Jeff Thompson, *Official Records*, vol. 3, 223.
35. *Ibid.*, 224.
36. William Carlin, *The War of the Rebellion: A Compilation of the Official Records of the Union and Confederate Armies*," vol. 3 (U.S. Government Printing Office, 1880–1891), 202.
37. U.S. Grant, *Official Records*, vol. 3, 204.
38. E. M. Joel, *Official Records*, vol. 3, 205.
39. Carlin, *Official Records*, vol. 3, 220.
40. Thompson, *Official Records*, vol. 3, 225.
41. *Ibid.*, 227.
42. McGhee, "A Damned Tight Place," 154.
43. *Ibid.*, 153–154.
44. McCall, *Three Years in the Service*, 6.
45. Frank Moore and Edward Everett, *The Rebellion Record: a Diary of American Events: Battle of Fredericktown, Missouri*, vol. 1 (New York: G. P. Putnam and Henry Holt, 1864), 493.
46. McCall, *Three Years in the Service*, 6.
47. McGhee, "A Damned Tight Place," 154.
48. Tom Kirkwood, *A History of Lawrence County Physicians and a Review of Medicine as Practiced 100 Years Ago*

(Lawrence County Historical Society; Repr., Evansville, IN: Unigraphic, 1975), 19–20.

49. Carlin *Official Records*, vol. 3, 218.
50. William Cleland, "Victory at Fredericktown, Mo," *Chelsea Telegraph and Pioneer*, November 9, 1861, p. 2, col. 4.
51. McCall, *Three Years in the Service*, 6.
52. McGhee, "A Damned Tight Place," 155.
53. William Panabaker, *Official Records*, vol. 3, 214.
54. R. C. Arnett, "The Battle of Fredericktown," October 21, 1917, *Democrat-News*, 1–4.
55. C. C. Marsh, *Official Records*, vol. 3, 212.
56. Stewart, Letter, October 26, 1861.
57. Cleland, "Victory at Fredericktown."
58. Thompson, *Official Records*, vol. 3, 227.
59. Joseph Plummer, *Official Records*, vol. 3, 208.
60. *Ibid.*, 209.
61. Thompson, *Official Records*, vol. 3, 226.
62. R. C. Arnett, "The Battle of Fredericktown."
63. Panabaker, *Official Records*, vol. 3, 215.
64. Charles Clark, Compiled Service Records, Missouri Volunteer Union Soldiers, 1962, National Archives.
65. *Ibid.*
66. Cleland, "Victory at Fredericktown."
67. "Battle in Missouri," *New York Times*, October 28, 1861.
68. Stewart, Letter, October 26, 1861.
69. U.S. Grant, *Official Records*, vol. 3, 209.
70. *Ibid.*, 210.

Chapter 2

1. Treadway, Charles, "The Letters of Charles Wesley Treadway," January 2, 1862, in *Foot Prints: Past and Present*, vol. 9 (Olney, IL: Richland County Genealogical and Historical Society, 1986).
2. Hawley, Letter, November 24, 1861, Thomas Hawley Papers, 1856–1867.
3. *Ibid.*, November 30, 1861.
4. *Ibid.*, January 4, 1862.
5. William Mieure, Compiled Service Records, Missouri Volunteer Union Soldiers, 1962, National Archives.
6. John Collins, Letter, November 5, 1861, Civil War Pension File, National Archives.
7. Charles Carter, Compiled Service Records, Missouri Volunteer Union Soldiers, 1962, National Archives.
8. Benjamin Laird, Court Martial Record (KK-127), National Archives.
9. Stewart, Letter, January 12, 1862.
10. Eleventh Missouri Infantry Morning Reports, National Archives.
11. McCall, *Three Years in the Service*, 6.
12. Stewart, Letter, February 25, 1862.
13. Schulyer Hamilton, *Official Records*, vol. 8, 102.
14. Stewart, Letter, March 13, 1862.
15. McCall, *Three Years in the Service*, 7.
16. Stewart, Letter, March 13, 1862.
17. Larry J. Daniel and Lynn Bock, *Island No. 10* (Tuscaloosa: University of Alabama Press, 1996), 51.
18. *Ibid.*, 52.
19. Cloyd Bryner, *Bugle Echoes: The History of the Illinois 47th* (Springfield, IL: Phillips Bros., 1905), 37.
20. McCall, *Three Years in the Service*, 7.
21. Stewart, Letter, March 29, 1862.
22. William Snow, "Adventure at New Madrid," *National Tribune*, March 21, 1912.
23. Daniel, *Island No. 10*, 110.
24. Alden Carter, *Brother to the Eagle: The Civil War Journal of Sgt. Ambrose Armitage, 8th Wisconsin Infantry* (Bangor, ME: Booklocker, 2006), 85.
25. Eleventh Missouri Infantry Descriptive Record Book, National Archives.
26. Stewart, Letter, April 11, 1862.
27. McCall, *Three Years in the Service*, 8.
28. Stewart, Letter, April 22, 1862.
29. Jeremiah Carroll, Civil War Pension Record, National Archives.
30. Thomas Smith, April 4, 1862, Compiled Service Records, Missouri Volunteer Union Soldiers, 1962, National Archives.
31. Joseph Brooks, Letter, April 1, 1862, Compiled Service Records, Missouri Volunteer Union Soldiers, 1962, National Archives.
32. William Perce, Letter, April 3, 1862, Compiled Service Records, Missouri Volunteer Union Soldiers, 1962, National Archives.
33. James Lott, *Illinois State Journal*, April 17, 1860, p. 3, col. 2.
34. Charles Brookings, Letter, April 14, 1862, Eleventh Missouri Infantry Folder, Missouri Archives. Jefferson City.
35. *Official Records*, vol. 11, 147.
36. David Stanley, *Official Records*, vol. 10, 720.
37. Patton Anderson, *Official Records*, vol. 10, 801.
38. McCall, *Three Years in the Service*, 8.
39. *Ibid.*
40. Joseph Mower, May 5, 1862, Eleventh Missouri Order Book, National Archives.
41. John Loomis, *Official Records*, vol. 10, 806.
42. *Ibid.*
43. McCall, *Three Years in the Service*, 8.
44. Daniel Ruggles, *Official Records*, vol. 10, 809.
45. John Pope, *Official Records*, vol. 11, 173.
46. John Loomis, *Official Records*, vol. 10, 806.
47. *Ibid.*
48. *Ibid.*
49. *Ibid.*
50. *Ibid.*
51. Pope, *Official Records*, vol. 11, 176.
52. Stewart, Letter, May, 20, 1862.
53. McCall, *Three Years in the Service*, 8.
54. Loomis, *Official Records*, vol. 10, 805–807.
55. *Ibid.*
56. Ruggles, *Official Records*, vol. 10, 811.
57. Pope, *Official Records*, vol. 11, 176.
58. Stanley, *Official Records*, vol. 10, 721.
59. General Order No. 46, May 14, 1862, Eleventh Missouri Order Book, National Archives.
60. Mower, May 6, 1862, Company D Orders, Eleventh Missouri Order Book, National Archives.
61. Stacy Allen, "Corinth: Crossroads of the Western Confederacy," *Blue and Gray* 6, XIX, no. 6 (2007): 24.
62. Abraham Lincoln, *Official Records*, vol. 10, 667.
63. Stanley, *Official Records*, vol. 10, 722–723.
64. *Ibid.*
65. McCall, *Three Years in the Service*, 9.
66. Henry Halleck, *Official Records*, vol. 10, 668.
67. William Fox, *Regimental Losses in the American Civil War 1861–1865* (NY: Albany Publishing, 1889), 413.
68. Anderson Campbell, Letter, June 9, 1862, Civil War Pension File, National Archives.
69. James Scott, Letter, June 18, 1862, Civil War Pension File, National Archives.
70. *Ibid.*
71. Harley Kingsbury, June 12, 1862, Compiled Service Records, Missouri Volunteer Union Soldiers, 1962, National Archives.

72. Wilson Duggans, June 13, 1862, Compiled Service Records, Missouri Volunteer Union Soldiers, 1962, National Archives.
73. Stewart, Letter, June 13, 1862.
74. *Ibid.*
75. William Haskins, Letter, July 5, 1862, Civil War Pension File, National Archives.
76. Jack Welsh, *Medical Histories of Union Generals* (Ohio: Kent State University Press, 1996), 261.
77. McCall, *Three Years in the Service*, 9.
78. Stewart, Letter, August 23, 1862.
79. Clark Hendee, Letter, July 10, 1862, Compiled Service Records, Missouri Volunteer Union Soldiers, 1962, National Archives.
80. David McKnight, 1862, Civil War Diary of Sgt. David McKnight, February 1, 1862–March 21, 1864, Missouri Historical Museum, St. Louis.

Chapter 3

1. Peter Cozzens, *The Darkest Days of the War: The Battles of Iuka and Corinth* (Chapel Hill: University of North Carolina Press, 1997), 37.
2. *Ibid.*, 43
3. Sterling Price, *Official Records*, vol. 24, 120.
4. Braxton Bragg, *Official Records*, vol. 25, 676.
5. Cozzens, *The Darkest Days of the War*, 51.
6. Charles Hamilton, *Opposing Forces at Iuka, Miss.: Battles and Leaders of the Civil War*, Vol. II (New York: Century, 1887), 736.
7. Wayne Calhoun Temple, *A Chaplain in the 11th Missouri Infantry* (Harrowgate, TN: Lincoln Memorial University Press, 1962), 81–88. Taken from article in *Lincoln Herald*, vol. 64 (Summer 1962).
8. Stewart, Letter, September 9, 1862.
9. Cozzens, *The Darkest Days of the War*, 62.
10. *Ibid.*
11. W. H. Gilliard, "The Battle of Iuka," *National Tribune*, June 26, 1902, p. 3.
12. Sterling Price, *Official Records*, vol. 27, 229–30.
13. Steven Dossman, *Campaign for Corinth: Blood in Mississippi* (Abilene, TX: McWhitney Foundation Press, 2006), 63.
14. Cozzens, *The Darkest Days of the War*, 87.
15. *Ibid.*, 90.
16. *Ibid.*, 91.
17. *Ibid.*, 92.
18. Eleventh Missouri Infantry Morning Reports, National Archives.
19. Cozzens, *The Darkest Days of the War*, 111.
20. Andrew J. Weber, *Official Records*, vol. 24, 88.
21. *Ibid.*
22. *Ibid.*
23. *Ibid.*
24. Temple, *A Chaplain in the 11th Missouri Infantry*, 83.
25. Stewart, Letter, September 23, 1862.
26. William Rosecrans, *Official Records*, vol. 24, 74.
27. *Ibid.*, 75.
28. David Stanley, *Official Records*, vol. 24, 82.
29. Mower, *Official Records*, vol. 24, 85.
30. Amos Singleton, Civil War Pension Record, National Archives.
31. Eugene Page, Letter, November 27, 1862, Civil War Pension Record, National Archives.
32. Stewart, Letter, September 23, 1862.
33. Eleventh Missouri Descriptive Roll, National Archives.
34. Compiled Service Records, Missouri Volunteer Union Soldiers, 1962, National Archives.
35. Weber, *Official Records*, vol. 24, 88.
36. Thomas Hawley Papers, 1856–1867.
37. Anderson Campbell, Letter, October 13, 1862, Civil War Pension Record, National Archives.
38. Newton Preston, Letter, October 15, 1862, in William Chapman Pension File, National Archives.
39. Treadway, "The Letters of Charles Wesley Treadway," 130.
40. Dossman, *Campaign for Corinth*, 79.
41. "That Precious Blanket," *National Tribune*, October 4, 1906.
42. Cozzens, *The Darkest Days of the War*, 122.
43. Edward Ord, *Official Records*, vol. 24, 119.
44. Stewart, Letter, September 23, 1862.

Chapter 4

1. Treadway, "The Letters of Charles Wesley Treadway," 130.
2. Cozzens, *The Darkest Days of the War*, 137.
3. William Rosecrans, *Battles and Leaders of the Civil War*, Vol. II (New York: Century, 1887), 741.
4. *Ibid.* p. 743.
5. Cozzens, *The Darkest Days of the War*, 327–328.
6. *Ibid.*, 326–327.
7. Bryner, *Bugle Echoes*, 57.
8. Cozzens, *The Darkest Days of the War*, 158.
9. *Ibid.*, 166.
10. *Ibid.*, 200.
11. Stanley, *Official Records*, vol. 24, 179.
12. McCall, *Three Years in the Service*, 12.
13. Cozzens, *The Darkest Days of the War*, 210.
14. Weber, *Official Records*, vol. 24, 201–202.
15. McCall, *Three Years in the Service*, 12.
16. Dossman, *Campaign for Corinth*, 105.
17. Bryner, *Bugle Echoes*, 60.
18. Rosecrans, *Battles and Leaders of the Civil War*, 748
19. Rosecrans, *Official Records*, vol. 24, 169.
20. Allen, "Corinth: Crossroads of the Western Confederacy," 54.
21. Weber, *Official Records*, vol. 24, 202.
22. McCall, *Three Years in the Service*, 12.
23. *Ibid.*, 13.
24. George Henry, Company D Eleventh Missouri Report, October 1862, Compiled Service Records, Missouri Volunteer Union Soldiers, 1962, National Archives.
25. Rosecrans, *Official Records*, vol. 24, 169.
26. Cozzens, *The Darkest Days of the War*, 256.
27. Weber, *Official Records*, vol. 24, 202.
28. Dossman, *Campaign for Corinth*, 117.
29. Dabney Maury, *Official Records*, vol. 24, 395.
30. John Sprague, *Official Records*, vol. 24, 191.
31. McCall, *Three Years in the Service*, 13.
32. Cozzens, *The Darkest Days of the War*, 261.
33. *Ibid.*, 264.
34. Weber, *Official Records*, vol. 24, 202.
35. John Fuller, *Official Records*, vol. 24, 185.
36. Weber, *Official Records*, vol. 24, 202.
37. McCall, *Three Years in the Service*, 13.
38. James McNeal, "Charge of the Texans: An 11th Mo. Officer Tells of Incidents Around Battery Robinette," *National Tribune*, January 5, 1899.
39. William Snow, "Battle of Corinth," *National Tribune*, July 26, 1906.
40. E. M. Eckley, "Battle of Corinth: A View from the

11th Mo.'s and 56th Ill.'s Standpoints," *National Tribune*, August 7, 1884.
41. George Henry, "The 11th Mo. at Corinth," *National Tribune*, June 28, 1894.
42. *Ibid.*
43. McNeal, "Charge of the Texans."
44. *Ibid.*
45. McCall, *Three Years in the Service*, 13
46. Company D Records, October 1862, Compiled Service Records, Missouri Volunteer Union Soldiers, 1962, National Archives.
47. Company K Records, October 1862, Compiled Service Records, Missouri Volunteer Union Soldiers, 1962, National Archives.
48. John Fuller, *Official Records*, vol. 24, 186–187.
49. McCall, *Three Years in the Service*, 14.
50. "Corinth: What One Comrade Knows about Battery Robinett," *National Tribune*, March 15, 1894.
51. Stewart, Letter, October 12, 1862.
52. *Ibid.*
53. Mower, *Official Records*, vol. 24, 198.
54. *Ibid.*
55. Rosecrans, *Battles and Leaders of the Civil War*, 752.
56. Cozzens, *The Darkest Days of the War*, 236.
57. Price, *Official Records*, vol. 24, 388.
58. Anderson, Letter, October 13, 1862, Civil War Pension Record, National Archives.
59. Dossman, *Campaign for Corinth*, 133.
60. Andrew J. Weber, Letter, October 30, 1862, Missouri State Archives, Eleventh Missouri Infantry Folder, Jefferson City.
61. Preston, Letter, October 15, 1862, in William Chapman Civil War Pension Record.
62. *Ibid.*, October 26, 1862, in William Chapman Civil War Pension Record.

Chapter 5

1. McCall, *Three Years in the Service*, 14.
2. *Ibid.*
3. *Ibid.*
4. Hawley, Letter, February 27, 1863, Thomas Hawley Papers, 1856–1867.
5. Stewart, Letter, November 27, 1862.
6. Temple, *A Chaplain in the 11th Missouri Infantry*, 85.
7. Robert Murphy, *Official Records*, vol. 24, 509.
8. Peter Workman, February 7, 1865, Pension Record, National Archives.
9. Hawley, Letter, January 31, 1863, Thomas Hawley Papers, 1856–1867.
10. McCall, *Three Years in the Service*, 16.
11. Alden Carter, *Brother to the Eagle*, 239.
12. Hawley, Letter, January 3, 1863, Thomas Hawley Papers, 1856–1867.
13. Samuel Baldridge, Resignation Letter, November 12, 1862, Compiled Service Records, Missouri Volunteer Union Soldiers, 1962, National Archives.
14. Benjamin Laird, Resignation Letter, November 12, 1862, Compiled Service Records, Missouri Volunteer Union Soldiers, 1962, National Archives.
15. Temple, *A Chaplain in the 11th Missouri Infantry*, 85.
16. Joseph Jones, "Some Ruffianly Soldiers," *National Tribune*, June 2, 1904.
17. *Ibid.*
18. McCall, *Three Years in the Service*, 18.
19. Joseph Jones, "Almost a Scrap," *National Tribune*, April 11, 1901.
20. Bryner, *Bugle Echoes*, 76.
21. Treadway, "The Letters of Charles Wesley Treadway," 128.
22. Alonzo Thomas, Letter, April 15, 1863, Civil War Pension Record, National Archives.
23. Henry O'Neil, "Running the Batteries: Thrilling Moments Under Continuous Fire of Hundreds of Guns," *National Tribune*, January 26, 1899.
24. *Official Records*, vol. 37, 152.
25. A. A. Stuart, *Iowa Colonels and Regiments: Being a History of Iowa Regiments in the War of the Rebellion* (Des Moines, IA: Mills, 1865), 58.
26. George C. Adams, Letter, May 25, 1863, Old Courthouse Museum, Vicksburg, MS.
27. Kenneth Williams *Grant Rises in the West: From Iuka to Vicksburg, 1862–1863* (Lincoln, NE: Bison, 1997), 371.
28. John Tuttle, *Official Records*, vol. 36, 759.
29. *Ibid.*
30. Company C Records, May 1863, Compiled Service Records, Missouri Volunteer Union Soldiers, 1962, National Archives.
31. Lucius Hubbard, *Official Records*, vol. 36, 767–768.
32. McCall, *Three Years in the Service*, 21.
33. Joseph Johnston, *Official Records*, vol. 36, 215.
34. William Sherman, *Official Records*, vol. 36, 754–755.
35. Joe Browning, "A Charge at Fort Hill," *National Tribune*, September 29, 1910.
36. Sherman, *Official Records*, vol. 36, 754.
37. McCall, *Three Years in the Service*, 21.
38. Alden Carter, *Brother to the Eagle*, 282
39. *Ibid.*, 284.
40. Michael Ballard, *Vicksburg: The Campaign that Opened the Mississippi* (Chapel Hill: University of North Carolina Press, 2004), 281.
41. *Ibid.*
42. John Forney, *Official Records*, vol. 37, 359.
43. Christopher Gabel, *Staff Ride Handbook for The Vicksburg Campaign: December 1862–July 1863* (CSI/CGSC Press, 2001), 165.
44. William Porter, *Official Records*, vol. 37, 273.
45. Sherman, *Official Records*, vol. 36, 757.
46. A. A. Hoehling, *Vicksburg — 47 Days of Siege* (Englewood Cliffs, NJ: Prentice Hall, 1969), 36.
47. "Gen. Joseph Mower; His dauntless bravery — An incident of the Vicksburg Assault," *New York Times*, June 4, 1883.
48. Bryner, *Bugle Echoes*, 85.
49. Edwin Bearss, *The Campaign for Vicksburg: Unvexed to the Sea*, Vol. III (Dayton, OH: Morningside House, 1991), 841.
50. *Ibid.*
51. McCall, *Three Years in the Service*, 23.
52. Bearss, *The Campaign for Vicksburg*, 842.
53. Browning, "A Charge at Fort Hill."
54. *Ibid.*
55. Porter, *Official Records*, vol. 37, 273.
56. Bearss, *The Campaign for Vicksburg*, 842.
57. Walter Beyer and Oscar Keydel, *Deeds of Valor: How America's Heroes Won the Medal of Honor*, Vol. I (Detroit: Perrien-Keydel, 1901), 200–201.
58. Bearss, *The Campaign for Vicksburg*, 842.
59. Ballard, *Vicksburg: The Campaign that Opened the Mississippi*, 345.
60. Company I Report, Compiled Service Records, Missouri Volunteer Union Soldiers, 1962, National Archives.

61. George C. Adams, Letter, May 25, 1863.
62. A. D. Hickok, "On Wrong side of the Works," *National Tribune*, September 29, 1910.
63. Francis Cockrell, *Official Records*, vol. 37, 415.
64. Frank Blair, *Official Records*, vol. 37, 258.
65. *Ibid*.
66. Sherman, *Official Records* Vol. 36, 757.
67. *Ibid*.
68. Bryner, *Bugle Echoes*, 86.
69. McCall, *Three Years in the Service*, 23.
70. Thomas Hawley, Hospital Casualty List — Vicksburg, Thomas Hawley Papers, 1856–1867.
71. Hawley, Letter, June 7, 1863, Thomas Hawley Papers, 1856–1867.
72. Eleventh Missouri Infantry Correspondence Book, July 2, 1863, National Archives.
73. Hawley, Letter, May 30, 1863, Thomas Hawley Papers, 1856–1867.
74. Bearss, *The Campaign for Vicksburg*, 1001.
75. *Ibid*.
76. McCall, *Three Years in the Service*, 23.
77. *Ibid*., 25.
78. William Notestine, Letter, June 12, 1863, Civil War Pension File, National Archives.
79. Hawley, Letter, June 21, 1863, Thomas Hawley Papers, 1856–1867.
80. McCall, *Three Years in the Service*, 26.
81. Mower, July 1, 1863, Eleventh Missouri Infantry Correspondence File, National Archives.
82. William Shea and Terrence Wenschel, *Vicksburg is the Key: The Struggle for the Mississippi River* (Lincoln: University of Nebraska Press, 2003), 171.
83. Hawley, Letter, July 5, 1863, Thomas Hawley Papers, 1856–1867.
84. Alonzo Thomas, Letter, June 27, 1863, Pension Record, National Archives.
85. Bryner, *Bugle Echoes*, 89.

Chapter 6

1. T. E. Vineyard, *Battles of the Civil War* (Chicago: Hammond Press, 1914), 110.
2. Treadway, "The Letters of Charles Wesley Treadway," 129.
3. Alden Carter, *Brother to the Eagle*, 322.
4. Hawley, Letter, August 2, 1863, Thomas Hawley Papers, 1856–1867.
5. *Ibid*., July 26, 1863.
6. James McPherson, *Official Records*, vol. 51, 802–803.
7. McCall, *Three Years in the Service*, 27.
8. *Ibid*.
9. Hawley, Letter, November 14, 1863, Thomas Hawley Papers, 1856–1867.
10. *Ibid*., December 5, 1863.
11. *Official Records*, vol. 57, 168.
12. McCall, *Three Years in the Service*, 28
13. William Barnum, Letter to Colonel John Gray, February 4, 1864, Missouri Archives, Eleventh Missouri Infantry Folder, Jefferson City.
14. *Ibid*.
15. Circular, August 5, 1864, Order Book, Eleventh Missouri Infantry, National Archives.
16. Arthur Fuller, General Order No. 4, March 28, 1864, Order Book, Eleventh Missouri Infantry, National Archives.
17. Special Field Order No. 14, March 6, 1864, Eleventh Missouri Correspondence Book, National Archives.
18. Joseph Mower, Special Order No. 43, March 9, 1864, Order Book, Eleventh Missouri Infantry, National Archives.
19. Gary Joiner, *Through the Howling Wildness* (Knoxville: University of Tennessee, 2006), XVII.
20. Mower, *Official Records*, vol. 61, 317.
21. Steven Mayeux, *Earthen Walls, Iron Men* (Knoxville: University of Tennessee Press, 2007), 183.
22. Beyer, *Deeds of Valor*, 201.
23. McCall, *Three Years in the Service*, 31.
24. Leslie Perry, "Major General Andrew Jackson Smith," excerpted from *Twenty-eighth Annual Reunion of the Association Graduates of the United States Military Academy at West Point New York* (Saginaw, MI: Seeman & Peters, 1896), 53.
25. Dios Hagle, "The Red River Campaign," *National Tribune*, April 1, 1886.
26. *Ibid*.
27. *Ibid*.
28. *Official Records*, vol. 61, 172.
29. McCall, *Three Years in the Service*, 32.
30. *Ibid*., 33.
31. Joiner, *Through the Howling Wildness*, 97.
32. *Ibid*., 104.
33. *Ibid*., 108.
34. George Van Beek, *Official Records*, vol. 61, 335–336.
35. *Ibid*.
36. *Ibid*.
37. Sylvester Hill, *Official Records*, vol. 61, 328.
38. Joiner, *Through the Howling Wildness*, 107.
39. Bryner, *Bugle Echoes*, 106.
40. Van Beek, *Official Records*, vol. 61, 337–8.
41. *Ibid*.
42. Field and Staff Record, Compiled Service Records, Missouri Volunteer Union Soldiers, 1962, National Archives.
43. Hawley, Letter, May 7, 1864, Thomas Hawley Papers, 1856–1867.
44. *Ibid*., May 15, 1864.
45. Mower, *Official Records*, vol. 61, 971.
46. Van Beek, *Official Records*, vol. 61, 976.
47. McCall, *Three Years in the Service*, 40.
48. Mower, *Official Records*, vol. 61, 971.
49. Bryner, *Bugle Echoes*, 446.
50. Field and Staff Record, Compiled Service Records, Missouri Volunteer Union Soldiers, 1962, National Archives.
51. George Adams, Letter, June 29, 1864, Mary Adams — CWTI Collection, 2nd series, United States Army Military History Institute, Carlisle, PA.
52. Sherman, *Official Records*, vol. 76, 16–17.
53. Michael Ballard, *The Battle of Tupelo, Mississippi — July 14–15, 1864* (Tupelo: Northeast Mississippi Historical and Genealogical Society, 2009), 5.
54. *Ibid*., 6.
55. Treadway, "The Letters of Charles Wesley Treadway," 140–141.
56. Ballard, *The Battle of Tupelo*, 10.
57. Hawley, Letter, July 21, 1864, Thomas Hawley Papers, 1856–1867.
58. Ballard, *The Battle of Tupelo*, 15.
59. A. J. Smith, *Official Records*, vol. 77, 251.
60. Ballard, *The Battle of Tupelo*, 17.
61. McCall, *Three Years in the Service*, 37.
62. Ballard, *The Battle of Tupelo*, 18.
63. A. J. Smith, *Official Records*, vol. 77, 251–252.
64. *Ibid*.
65. Ballard, *The Battle of Tupelo*, 25.
66. *Ibid*., 26.

67. A. J. Smith, *Official Records*, vol. 77, 251–252.
68. Mower, *Official Records*, vol. 77, 257.
69. John McClure, *Official Records*, vol. 77, 265–266.
70. Stephen Lee, *Official Records*, vol. 77, 320.
71. Ballard, *The Battle of Tupelo*, 28.
72. McCall, *Three Years in the Service*, 39.
73. Barnum, Special Order #27, July 31, 1864, Missouri Order Book, National Archives.
74. Mower, *Official Records*, vol. 77, 257.
75. A. J. Smith, *Official Records*, vol. 77, 251–252.
76. Hawley, Letter, July 21, 1864, Thomas Hawley Papers, 1856–1867.
77. Treadway, Letter, July 24, 1864, "The Letters of Charles Wesley Treadway," 142–144.
78. *Ibid.*

Chapter 7

1. Hawley, Letter, August 15, 1864, Thomas Hawley Papers, 1856–1867.
2. *Official Records*, vol. 78, 332.
3. Field and Staff Record, Compiled Service Records, Missouri Volunteer Union Soldiers, 1962, National Archives.
4. Hawley, Letter, August 16, 1864, Thomas Hawley Papers, 1856–1867.
5. Bryner, *Bugle Echoes*, 137.
6. Alden Carter, *Brother to the Eagle*, 472.
7. "Gen. A. J. Smith Expedition: The Movement into Mississippi," *New York Times*, September 10, 1864.
8. Compiled Service Records, Missouri Volunteer Union Soldiers, 1962, National Archives.
9. Lyman Pierce, *History of the 2nd Iowa Cavalry* (Burlington, IA: Hawk-Eye Steam, 1865), 113–114.
10. Hubbard, *Official Records*, vol. 77, 373–374.
11. *Ibid.*
12. Hawley, Letter, August 25, 1864, Thomas Hawley Papers, 1856–1867.
13. *Ibid.*, August 10, 1864.
14. Treadway, "The Letters of Charles Wesley Treadway," 145–146.
15. Eli Bowyer, Letter, December 14, 1864, *Missouri Report to the Adjutant General*, Eleventh Missouri Infantry Folder, Missouri State Archives, Jefferson City.
16. Wiley Sword, *Embrace an Angry Wind: The Confederacy's Last Hurrah: Spring Hill, Franklin, and Nashville* (New York: HarperCollins, 1992), 280.
17. Ulysses Grant, *Official Records*, vol. 94, 70.
18. Sword, *Embrace an Angry Wind*, 305.
19. *Ibid.*, 316.
20. George Thomas, *Official Records*, vol. 94, 180.
21. George Thomas, General Order No. 342, *Official Records*, vol. 93, 37–38.
22. Hubbard, *Official Records*, vol. 93, 454–455.
23. Sword, *Embrace an Angry Wind*, 331.
24. W. H. Gilliard, "The First Shot at Nashville," *National Tribune*, September 28, 1911.
25. Hubbard, *Official Records*, vol. 93, 454–455.
26. *Ibid.*
27. Modesta Green, *Official Records*, vol. 93, 445.
28. Hubbard, *Official Records*, vol. 93, 454–455.
29. *Ibid.*
30. Armitage, *Official Records*, vol. 93, 519.
31. Hubbard, *Official Records*, vol. 93, 454–455.
32. Green, *Official Records*, vol. 93, 445.
33. Sword, *Embrace an Angry Wind*, 365.
34. *Ibid.*
35. *Ibid.*, 369.
36. *Ibid.*, 374.
37. William Bate, *Official Records*, vol. 93, 749–750.
38. *Ibid.*
39. *Ibid.*
40. Hubbard, *Official Records*, vol. 93, 454–455.
41. Sword, *Embrace an Angry Wind*, 375.
42. *Ibid.*
43. Green, *Official Records*, vol. 93, 445.
44. H. N. Davis, "Hubbard's Brigade," *National Tribune*, November 23, 1916.
45. Edward Walthall, *Official Records*, vol. 93, 723–724.
46. Hubbard, *Official Records*, vol. 93, 449.
47. Thomas Hawley, Battle of Nashville Casualty List, Thomas Hawley Papers, 1856–1867.
48. Treadway, "The Letters of Charles Wesley Treadway," 147.
49. Green, *Official Records*, vol. 93, 445.
50. *Ibid.*, 456.
51. *Ibid.*
52. Beyer, *Deeds of Valor*, 468.
53. Bryner, *Bugle Echoes*, 150.
54. Notestine, Civil War Pension Record, National Archives.
55. *Ibid.*
56. *Ibid.*

Chapter 8

1. Eleventh Missouri Infantry Descriptive Rolls, National Archives.
2. Francis Lord, *They Fought for the Union* (Harrisburg, PA: Stackpole, 1960), 4.
3. *Ibid.*
4. *Ibid.*, 5.
5. *Ibid.*, 6.
6. Eleventh Missouri Infantry Descriptive Rolls.
7. Treadway, "The Letters of Charles Wesley Treadway," 148.
8. *Ibid.*
9. Sean Michael O'Brien, *Mobile, 1865: Last Stand of the Confederacy* (Westport, CT: Praeger, 2001), 12.
10. *Ibid.*, 24.
11. Edward Canby, *Official Records*, vol. 103, 812.
12. O'Brien, *Last Stand of the Confederacy*, 34.
13. *Ibid.*, 45.
14. *Ibid.*, 134.
15. C. C. Andrews, *History of the Campaign of Mobile* (New York: D. Van Nostrand, 1889), 52.
16. *Ibid.*, 54.
17. Hubbard, *Official Records*, vol. 103, 239.
18. Andrews, *History of the Campaign of Mobile*, 48.
19. George Adams, Letter, April 4, 1865, Mary Adams — CWTI Collection.
20. *Ibid.*
21. Andrews, *History of the Campaign of Mobile*, 87.
22. *Ibid.*, 135.
23. *Ibid.*, 144.
24. Hubbard, *Official Records*, vol. 103, 240.
25. Field and Staff Record, Compiled Service Records, Missouri Volunteer Union Soldiers, 1962, National Archives.
26. O'Brien, *Last Stand of the Confederacy*, 223.
27. Treadway, Letter, May 3, 1865, "The Letters of Charles Wesley Treadway," 153–155.
28. Hubbard, General Order No. 19, May 20, 1865, *Official Records*, vol. 104, 855–856.

29. Treadway, Letter, May 3, 1865, "The Letters of Charles Wesley Treadway," 153–155.
30. Ibid., May 27, 1865, 156–157.
31. Descriptive Rolls, Eleventh Missouri Infantry.
32. Treadway, Letter, June 19, 1865, "The Letters of Charles Wesley Treadway," 158–159.
33. Ibid., July 10, 1865, 162–163.
34. Ibid., August 6, 1865, 167–168.
35. Hunter Brooks, Letter, October 29, 1865, Compiled Service Records, Missouri Volunteer Union Soldiers, 1962, National Archives.
36. Henry Davies, Letter, November 8, 1865, Compiled Service Records, Missouri Volunteer Union Soldiers, 1962, National Archives.
37. Ibid.
38. Walter L. Fleming, *Civil War and Reconstruction in Alabama* (New York: Columbia University Press, 1905), 416.
39. Ibid., 415
40. Thomas Hawley, Letter, December 22, 1865, Hawley Papers, 1794–1953 (bulk 1857–1953), Duke University, Durham, NC.
41. Davies, General Order No. 35, October 9, 1865, Eleventh Missouri Infantry Order Book, National Archives.
42. Hawley, Letter, August 25, 1865, Thomas Hawley Papers, 1856–1867.
43. Treadway, Letter, October 29, 1865, "The Letters of Charles Wesley Treadway," 171–177.
44. Ibid., November 30, 1865, 179–181.
45. G. W. Brown, Letter, December 20, 1865, in Abraham Norris Civil War Pension Record, National Archives.
46. George Adams, Field and Staff Record, Compiled Service Records, Missouri Volunteer Union Soldiers, 1962, National Archives.
47. Eli Bowyer, Letter, February 10, 1866, Eleventh Missouri Infantry, Missouri State Archives.

Chapter 9

1. Sword, *Embrace an Angry Wind*, 331.
2. "Joseph A. Mower: His Dauntless Bravery," *New York Times*, June 4, 1883
3. William Ellis, ed., *Norwich University, 1819–1911*, Vol. 2 (Montpelier, VT: Capital City Press, 1911), 401.
4. "Gen. John McArthur Dead: Was a Gallant Officer in Civil War and Ex-Postmaster of Chicago," New York Times, May 17, 1906.
5. George Cullum, *Biographical Register of the Officers and Graduates of U.S. Military Academy*, Vol. II (Cambridge, MA: Houghton Mifflin, 1891), 85–86.
6. John Power, *History of Early Settlers of Sangamon County* (Springfield, IL: Edwin A. Wilson, 1876), 760.
7. Barnum, Civil War Pension Record, National Archives.
8. "W. L. Barnum, Insurance Man, Succumbs at 91," *Chicago Tribune*, May 29, 1921, p. 15, col. 2.
9. *Counties of Cumberland, Jasper and Richland, Illinois — Historical and Biographical* (Chicago: F. A. Battey, 1884), 731–733.
10. Ibid.
11. "Forty-Sixth Congress," *The New York Times*, December 16, 1879.
12. "Eli Bowyer," *Olney Times*, March 10, 1886.
13. Kirkwood, *A History of Lawrence County Physicians*, 19–20.
14. Green, Modesta. Civil War Pension Record, National Archives.
15. William W. Cleland, Death Certificate, 1867, Number 194, Louisiana State Archives. Baton Rouge.
16. , Benjamin Livingston, Civil War Pension Record, National Archives.
17. Kennan, "Forgotten Man of Arkansas Education," 303–317.
18. Melancthon Fish, Civil War Pension Record, National Archives.
19. Thomas Hawley Papers, 1856–1867
20. Nancy Williams, ed., *Arkansas Biography*.
21. Temple, *A Chaplain in the 11th Missouri Infantry*, 81–88.
22. George Brown, Civil War Pension Record, National Archives.
23. Ibid.
24. "Another Pioneer Completes Life's Labors and Passes to His Happy Reward," *Poseyville News* (IN), January 24, 1896.
25. "Biographical Sketches of Citizens of Lawrence County, Illinois," In *Atlas of Lawrence Co. Illinois* (Edwardsville, IL: W. R. Brink, 1875), 25.
26. *History of the Catholic Church in Indiana*, Vol. II (Logansport, IN: A. W. Bowen, 1898), 1136–1139.
27. Constantine McMahan, Civil War Pension Record, National Archives.
28. "Fatal Illness Overtakes Good Man. Captain M'Mahon Ends Life at Zonia from a Stroke of Paralysis: Age 81 Years," *Prescott Journal Miner*, June 1, 1915, p. 3, col. 4.
29. Joseph Wallace, *Index to Past and Present of the City of Springfield and Sangamon County, Illinois* (Chicago: S. J. Clarke, 1904), 779.
30. William T. Followill, Civil War Pension Record, National Archives.
31. "William T. Followill," *Louisiana Press Journal*, July 20, 1889.
32. Moses Warner, Civil War Pension Record, National Archives.
33. James A. Lott, "Obituary," *Illinois State Journal*, December 8, 1910, p. 9.
34. United States Census Records, 1870, 1880.
35. *Progressive Men of Western Colorado* (Chicago, IL: A. W. Bowen, 1905), 366–367.
36. *History of Wayne and Clay Counties, Illinois* (Chicago: Globe, 1884), 186.
37. *Portrait and Biographical Record of Effingham, Jasper and Richland Counties Illinois, Containing Biographical Sketches of Prominent and Representative Citizens, Governors of the State and Presidents of the United States* (Chicago: Chapman Brothers, 1887), 574.
38. Descriptive Rolls, Eleventh Missouri Infantry, National Archives.
39. United States Census Records, 1900, 1910.
40. Notestine, Civil War Pension Record, National Archives.
41. *Portrait and Biographical Record of Effingham, Jasper and Richland Counties*, 584.
42. "Capt. L. D. Roney Died Monday. Veteran of the Civil War Took Part in Many Active Engagements," *Olney Advocate*, May 18, 1910.
43. Amos Singleton, Civil War Pension Record, National Archives.
44. Charles Smith, Civil War Pension Record, National Archives.
45. Charles Carter, Compiled Service Records, Missouri Volunteer Union Soldiers, 1962, National Archives.
46. Kirkwood, *A History of Lawrence County Physicians*, 31.

47. Charles Carter, Civil War Pension Record, National Archives.
48. Thomas Dollahan, Civil War Pension Record, National Archives.
49. "William Boatright," *Sullivan Union* (IN), May 16, 1915.
50. A. W. Haswell, *The Ozark Region: Its History and Its People*, Vol. III (Springfield, MO: Interstate Historical Society, 1971), 41–43.
51. Edwin Applegate, Death Certificate, January 4, 1919, State of Missouri, Jefferson City.
52. Charles Osgood, Civil War Pension Record, National Archives.
53. "Dr. Osgood. Hero of the Civil War and Former Practicing Physician, Died after Long Life," *Cincinnati Enquirer*, September 14, 1908, p. 10. col. 4.
54. Harvey and Peterson, "William S. Stewart Letters," 192–197.
55. "Captain C. D. Kendall Death Takes Out a Lending Citizen," *Newton Press*, February 25, 1919.
56. *Portrait and Biographical Record of Effingham, Jasper and Richland Counties*, 260.
57. Dennis Coogan, Civil War Pension Record, National Archives.

Appendix A

1. Based on the Regimental Descriptive Book located at the National Archives and Supplemented with the Regimental Descriptive Book located at the Missouri Archives and Regimental Cards located at the Missouri Archives.

Appendix B

1. Based on the Regimental Descriptive Book located at the National Archives and Supplemented with the Regimental Descriptive Book located at the Missouri Archives and Regimental Cards located at the Missouri Archives.

Bibliography

Adams, George. Compiled Service Records, Missouri Volunteer Union Soldiers. National Archives.
———. Letter, June 29, 1864. Mary Adams — CWTI Collection 2nd series, United States Army Military History Institute, Carlisle, PA.
Adams, George C. Letter, May 25, 1863. Old Courthouse Museum, Vicksburg, MS.
Allen, Stacy. "Corinth: Crossroads of the Western Confederacy." *Blue and Gray* 6, XIX, no. 6 (2007).
Anderson, Campbell. Letter, October 13, 1862. Civil War Pension Record. National Archives.
Anderson, Patton. *Official Records*. Vol. 10.
Andrews, C. C. *History of the Campaign of Mobile*. New York: D. Van Nostrand, 1889.
Annual Report of the Adjutant General of the State of Missouri, December 31, 1863. Jefferson City, MO: W. A. Curry, 1864.
"Another Pioneer Completes Life's Labors and Passes to His Happy Reward." *Poseyville News* (IN), January 24, 1896.
Applegate, Edwin. Death Certificate, January 4, 1919. Jefferson City, MO.
Arnett, R. C. "The Battle of Fredericktown," October 21, 1917, *Democrat-News*. State Historical Society of Missouri.
Baldridge, Samuel. Resignation letter, November 12, 1862. Compiled Service Records, Missouri Volunteer Union Soldiers. National Archives.
Ballard, Michael. *The Battle of Tupelo, Mississippi — July 14–15, 1864*. Tupelo: Northeast Mississippi Historical and Genealogical Society, 2009.
———. *Vicksburg: The Campaign that Opened the Mississippi*. Chapel Hill: University of North Carolina Press, 2004.
Barnum, William. Civil War Pension Record. National Archives.
———. Letter to Colonel John Gray, February 4, 1864. Eleventh Missouri Infantry Folder. Missouri Archives, Jefferson City.
———. Special Order 27, July 31, 1864. Missouri Order Book. National Archives.
Bate, William. *Official Records*. Vol. 93, pp. 749–750.
"Battle in Missouri." *New York Times*, October 28, 1861.
Bayles, David. Special Order 37, January 23, 1863. Civil War Pension Record. National Archives.
———. Special Order 277, July 17, 1871. Civil War Pension Record. National Archives.

Bearss, Edwin. *The Campaign for Vicksburg: Unvexed to the Sea*. Vol. III. Dayton, OH: Morningside House, 1991.
Beyer, Walter, and Oscar Keydel. *Deeds of Valor: How America's Heroes Won the Medal of Honor*. Vol. I. Detroit: Perrien-Keydel, 1901.
"Biographical Sketches of Citizens of Lawrence County, Illinois." In *Atlas of Lawrence Co. Illinois*. Edwardsville, IL: W. R. Brink, 1875.
Blair, Frank. *Official Records*. Vol. 37, p. 258.
Bowyer, Eli. Letter, February 10, 1866. Eleventh Missouri Infantry Folder. Missouri State Archives, Jefferson City.
———. Letter. *Missouri Report to the Adjutant General, December 14, 1864*. Eleventh Missouri Infantry Folder. Missouri State Archives, Jefferson City.
Bragg, Braxton. *Official Records*. Vol. 25, p. 676.
Brookings, Charles. Letter, April 14, 1862. Eleventh Missouri Infantry Folder. Missouri Archives, Jefferson City.
Brooks, Joseph. Letter, April 1, 1862. Compiled Service Records, Missouri Volunteer Union Soldiers. National Archives.
Brooks, Hunter. Letter, October 29, 1865. Compiled Service Records, Missouri Volunteer Union Soldiers. National Archives.
Brown, G. W. Civil War Pension Record. National Archives.
Brown, George. Abraham Norris Civil War Pension Record, December 20, 1865. National Archives.
Browning, Joe. "A Charge at Fort Hill." *National Tribune*, September 29, 1910.
Bryner, Cloyd. *Bugle Echoes: the History of the Illinois 47th*. Springfield, IL: Phillips Bros., 1905.
Campbell, Anderson. Letter, June 9, 1862. Civil War Pension File. National Archives.
———. Letter, October 13, 1862. Civil War Pension Record. National Archives.
Canby, Edward. *Official Records*. Vol. 103, p. 812.
"Captain C. D. Kendall Death Takes Out a Lending Citizen." *Newton Press*, February 25, 1919.
"Capt. L. D. Roney Died Monday. Veteran of the Civil War Took Part in Many Active Engagements." *Olney Advocate*, May 18, 1910.
Carlin, William. *Official Records*. Vol. 3.
Carroll, Jeremiah. Civil War Pension Record. National Archives.
Carter, Alden. *Brother to the Eagle: The Civil War Journal of Sgt. Ambrose Armitage, 8th Wisconsin Infantry*. Bangor, ME: Booklocker, 2006.

Carter, Charles. Civil War Pension Record. National Archives.
_____. Compiled Service Records, Missouri Volunteer Union Soldiers. National Archives.
Carter, Harvey, and Norma Peterson. William S. Stewart letters, January 13, 1861 to December 4, 1862. *Missouri Historical Review.* Vol. 61, pp. 192–226.
Clark, Charles. Compiled Service Records, Missouri Volunteer Union Soldiers. National Archives.
Cleland, William. "Victory at Fredericktown, Mo." *Chelsea Telegraph and Pioneer*, November 9, 1861, p. 2, col. 4.
Cleland, William W. Death Certificate, 1867, No. 194. Louisiana State Archives, Baton Rouge.
Cockrell, Francis. *Official Records.* Vol. 37, p. 415.
Collins, John. Letter, November 5, 1861. Civil War Pension File. National Archives.
Company C Records. May 1863. Compiled Service Records, Missouri Volunteer Union Soldiers. National Archives.
Company D Records. October 1862. Compiled Service Records, Missouri Volunteer Union Soldiers. National Archives.
Company I Report. Compiled Service Records, Missouri Volunteer Union Soldiers. National Archives.
Company K Records. October 1862. Compiled Service Records, Missouri Volunteer Union Soldiers. National Archives.
Compiled Service Records, Missouri Volunteer Union Soldiers. National Archives.
Coogan, Dennis. Civil War Pension Record. National Archives.
"Corinth: What One Comrade Knows about Battery Robinett." *National Tribune*, March 15, 1894.
Counties of Cumberland, Jasper and Richland, Illinois — Historical and Biographical. Chicago: F. A. Battey, 1884.
Cozzens, Peter. *The Darkest Days of the War: The Battles of Iuka and Corinth.* Chapel Hill: University of North Carolina Press, 1997.
Cullum, George. *Biographical Register of the Officers and Graduates of U.S. Military Academy.* Vol. II. Cambridge, MA: Houghton Mifflin, 1891.
Daniel, Larry J., and Lynn Bock. *Island No. 10.* Tuscaloosa: University of Alabama Press, 1996.
Davies, Henry. General Order 35, October 9, 1865. Eleventh Missouri Infantry Order Book. National Archives.
_____. Letter, November 8, 1865. Compiled Service Records, Missouri Volunteer Union Soldiers. National Archives.
Davis, H. N. "Hubbard's Brigade." *National Tribune*, November 23, 1916.
"Dr. Osgood, Hero of the Civil War and Former Practicing Physician, Died after Long Life." *Cincinnati Enquirer*, September 14, 1908, p. 10, col. 4.
Dollahan, Thomas. Civil War Pension Record. National Archives.
Dossman, Steven. *Campaign for Corinth: Blood in Mississippi.* Abilene, TX: McWhitney Foundation Press, 2006.
Duggans, Wilson. June 13, 1862. Compiled Service Records, Missouri Volunteer Union Soldiers. National Archives.
Eckley, E. M. "Battle of Corinth: A View from the 11th Mo.'s and 56th Ill.'s Standpoints." *National Tribune*, August 7, 1884.
Eleventh Missouri Infantry Correspondence Book. July 2, 1863–March 6, 1864. National Archives.
Eleventh Missouri Infantry Correspondence Book. Special Field Order 14, March 6, 1864. National Archives.
Eleventh Missouri Infantry Descriptive Roll Book. National Archives.
Eleventh Missouri Infantry Morning Reports. National Archives.
Eleventh Missouri Infantry Order Book, August 5, 1864. Circular. National Archives.
Eleventh Missouri Order Book. General Order 21, October 3, 1861. National Archives.
Eleventh Missouri Order Book. General Order 46. May 14, 1862. National Archives.
"Eli Bowyer." *Olney Times*, March 10, 1886.
Ellis, William, ed. *Norwich University, 1819–1911.* Vol. 2. Montpelier, VT: Capital City Press, 1911.
"Fatal Illness Overtakes Good Man. Captain M'Mahon Ends Life at Zonia from a Stroke of Paralysis: Age 81 Years." *Prescott Journal Miner*, June 1, 1915, p. 3, col. 4.
Fish, Melancthon. Civil War Pension Record. National Archives.
Fleming, Walter L. *Civil War and Reconstruction in Alabama.* New York: Columbia University Press, 1905.
Followill, William. Civil War Pension Record. National Archives.
Forney, John. *Official Records.* Vol. 37, p. 359.
"Forty-Sixth Congress," *The New York Times*, December 16, 1879.
Fox, William. *Regimental Losses in the American Civil War, 1861–1865.* NY: Albany Publishing, 1889.
Fremont, John. "Proclamation." *Missouri Democrat*, September 3, 1861.
Fuller, Arthur. General Order 4, March 28, 1864. Eleventh Missouri Infantry Order Book. National Archives.
Fuller, John. *Official Records.* Vol. 24, pp. 185–187.
Gabel, Christopher. *Staff Ride Handbook for the Vicksburg Campaign: December 1862–July 1863.* CSI/CGSC Press, 2001.
Gates, Merrill E. *Men of Mark in America.* Vol. II. Washington, D.C.: Men of Mark Publishing, 1906.
"Gen. A. J. Smith Expedition: The Movement into Mississippi." *New York Times*, September 10, 1864.
"Gen. John McArthur Dead: Was a Gallant Officer in Civil War and Ex-Postmaster of Chicago." *New York Times*, May 17, 1906.
"Gen. Joseph Mower: His Dauntless Bravery — An incident of the Vicksburg Assault." *New York Times*, June 4, 1883.
Gilliard, W. H. "The Battle of Iuka." *National Tribune*, June 26, 1902.
_____. "The First Shot at Nashville." *National Tribune*, September 28, 1911.
Grant, Ulysses. *Official Records.* Vol. 94, p. 70.
_____. *Official Records.* Vol. 3, pp. 204, 209–210.
Green, Modesta. Civil War Pension Record. National Archives.
_____. *Official Records.* Vol. 93, pp. 445–446.
Hagle, Dios. "The Red River Campaign." *National Tribune*, April 1, 1886.
Halleck, Henry. *Official Records.* Vol. 10, p. 668.
Hamilton, Charles. *Opposing Forces at Iuka, Miss.: Battles and Leaders of the Civil War.* Vol. II. New York: Century, 1887.
Hamilton, Schuyler. *Official Records.* Vol. 8, p. 102.
Haskins, William. Letter, July 5, 1862. Civil War Pension File. National Archives.
Haswell, A. W. *The Ozark Region: Its History and Its People.* Vol. III. Springfield, MO: Interstate Historical Society, 1971.
Hawley, Thomas. Battle of Nashville Casualty List. Thomas Hawley Papers, 1856–1867. A0666. Missouri Historical Society Archives, St. Louis.
_____. Hospital Casualty List — Vicksburg. Thomas Hawley Papers, 1856–1867. A0666. Missouri Historical Society Archives, St. Louis.

_____. Letter, December 22, 1865. Hawley Papers, 1794–1953 (bulk 1857–1953). Duke University, Durham, NC.

_____. Thomas Hawley Papers, 1856–1867. A0666. Missouri Historical Society Archives, St. Louis.

Hendee, Clark. Letter, July 10, 1862. Compiled Service Records, Missouri Volunteer Union Soldiers. National Archives.

Henry, George. Company D Eleventh Missouri Report, October 1862. Compiled Service Records, Missouri Volunteer Union Soldiers. National Archives.

_____. "The 11th MO. at Corinth." *National Tribune*, June 28, 1894.

Hickok, A. D. "On Wrong Side of the Works." *National Tribune*, September 29, 1910.

Hill, Sylvester. *Official Records.* Vol. 61, p. 328.

History of the Catholic Church in Indiana. Vol. II. Logansport, IN: A. W. Bowen, 1898.

History of Wayne and Clay Counties, Illinois. Chicago: Globe, 1884.

Hoehling, A. A. *Vicksburg—47 Days of Siege.* Englewood Cliffs, NJ: Prentice Hall, 1969.

Hubbard, Lucius. General Order 19, May 20, 1865. *Official Records.* Vol. 104, pp. 855–856.

_____. *Official Records.* Vol. 36, pp. 767–768.

_____. *Official Records.* Vol. 77, pp. 373–374.

_____. *Official Records.* Vol. 93, pp. 449, 454–455.

_____. *Official Records.* Vol. 103, pp. 239–240.

"James A. Lott Obituary." *Illinois State Journal*, December 8, 1910, p. 9.

Joel. E. M. *Official Records.* Vol. 3, p. 205.

Johnston, Joseph. *Official Records.* Vol. 36, p. 215.

Joiner, Gary. *Through the Howling Wildness.* Knoxville: University of Tennessee, 2006.

Jones, Joseph. "Almost a Scrap." *National Tribune*, April 11, 1901.

_____. "Some Ruffianly Soldiers." *National Tribune*, June 2, 1904.

"Joseph A. Mower: His Dauntless Bravery." *New York Times*, June 4, 1883.

Kennan, Clara. "Dr. Thomas Smith: Forgotten Man of Arkansas Education." *Arkansas Historical Quarterly* 20, no. 4 (1961).

Kingsbury, Harley. June 12, 1862. Compiled Service Records, Missouri Volunteer Union Soldiers. National Archives.

Kirkwood, Tom. *A History of Lawrence County Physicians and a Review of Medicine as Practiced 100 Years Ago.* Lawrence County Historical Society. Reprint, Evansville, IN: Unigraphic, 1975.

Laird, Benjamin. Court Martial Record, (KK-127). National Archives.

_____. Resignation letter, November 12, 1862. Compiled Service Records, Missouri Volunteer Union Soldiers. National Archives.

Lee, Stephen. *Official Records.* Vol. 77, p. 320.

Lincoln, Abraham. *Official Records.* Vol. 10, p. 667.

Livingston, Benjamin. Civil War Pension Record. National Archives.

Loomis, John. *Official Records.* Vol. 10, pp. 805–807.

Lord, Francis. *They Fought for the Union.* Harrisburg, PA: Stackpole, 1960.

Lott, James A. "Obituary." *Illinois State Journal*, April 17, 1860, p. 3, col. 2.

Marsh, C. C. *Official Records.* Vol. 3, p. 212.

Maury, Dabney. *Official Records.* Vol. 24, p. 395.

Mayeux, Steven. *Earthen Walls, Iron Men.* Knoxville: University of Tennessee Press, 2007.

McCall, Duncan. *Three Years in the Service: Record of the Doings of the 11th Reg. Missouri.* Springfield, MO: Johnson & Bradford, 1864.

McClure, John. *Official Records.* Vol. 77, pp. 265–266.

McGhee, James E. "'A Damned Tight Place': General Jeff Thompson Confronts the Federals at Fredericktown, Missouri." *Missouri Historical Review* (April 2009).

McKnight, David. Civil War Diary of Sgt. David McKnight, February 1, 1862–March 21, 1864. Missouri Historical Museum, St. Louis.

McMahan, Constantine. Civil War Pension Record. National Archives.

McNeal, James. "Charge of the Texans: An 11th Mo. Officer Tells of Incidents Around Battery Robinette." *National Tribune*, January 5, 1899.

_____. "The 11th Mo.'s Part: Comrade McNeal Endeavors to Show Where the Credit Should Be Given as to the Fighting at Robinett." *National Tribune*, June 29, 1899.

McPherson, James. *Official Records.* Vol. 51, pp. 802–803.

Mieure, William. Compiled Service Records, Missouri Volunteer Union Soldiers. National Archives.

Miller, Jeremiah. Compiled Service Records, Missouri Volunteer Union Soldiers. National Archives.

Moore, Frank, and Edward Everett. *The Rebellion Record: a Diary of American Events: Battle of Fredericktown, Missouri.* Vol. 1. New York: G. P. Putnam and Henry Holt, 1864.

Mower, Joseph. Company D Orders, May 6, 1862. Eleventh Missouri Order Book. National Archives.

_____. Eleventh Missouri Infantry Correspondence File, July 1, 1863. National Archives.

_____. May 5, 1862. Eleventh Missouri Order Book. National Archives.

_____. *Official Records.* Vol. 24, p. 85, 198.

_____. *Official Records.* Vol. 61, pp. 317, 971.

_____. *Official Records.* Vol. 77, p. 257.

_____. Special Order No. 43, March 9, 1864. Eleventh Missouri Order Book. National Archives.

Mueller, Doris Land. *Missouri's Swamp Fox of the Confederacy.* Columbia: University of Missouri Press, 2007.

Murphy, Robert. *Official Records.* Vol. 24, p. 509.

Notestine, William. Letter, June 12, 1863; 1865. Civil War Pension File. National Archives.

O'Brien, Sean Michael. *Mobile, 1865: Last Stand of the Confederacy.* Westport, CT: Praeger, 2001.

Official Records. Vol. 37, p. 152.

Official Records. Vol. 57, p. 168.

Official Records. Vol. 61, p. 172.

Official Records. Vol. 78, p. 322.

O'Neil, Henry. "Running the Batteries: Thrilling Moments Under Continuous Fire of Hundreds of Guns." *National Tribune*, January 26, 1899.

Ord, Edward. *Official Records.* Vol. 24, p. 119.

Osgood, Charles. Civil War Pension Record. National Archives.

Page, Eugene. Letter, November 27, 1862. Civil War Pension Record. National Archives.

Panabaker, William. *Official Records.* Vol. 3, pp. 214–215.

Parrish, William. *History of Missouri, 1860–1875.* Vol. III. Columbia: University of Missouri Press, 1997.

Perce, William. Letter, April 3, 1862. Compiled Service Records, Missouri Volunteer Union Soldiers. National Archives.

Perry, Leslie. "Major General Andrew Jackson Smith." Excerpted from *Twenty-eighth Annual Reunion of the Association Graduates of the United States Military Academy at West Point New York.* Saginaw, MI: Seeman & Peters, 1896.

Pierce, Lyman. *History of the 2nd Iowa Cavalry*. Burlington, IA: Hawk-Eye Steam, 1865.
Plummer, Joseph. General Order 20, October 2, 1861. Eleventh Missouri Order Book. National Archives.
_____. *Official Records*. Vol. 3, p. 208.
Pope, John. *Official Records*. Vol. 11, pp. 173, 176.
Porter, William. *Official Records*. Vol. 37, p. 273.
Portrait and Biographical Record of Effingham, Jasper and Richland Counties Illinois, Containing Biographical Sketches of Prominent and Representative Citizens, Governors of the State and Presidents of the United States. Chicago: Chapman Brothers, 1887.
Power, John. *History of Early Settlers of Sangamon County*. Springfield, IL: Edwin A. Wilson, 1876.
Preston, Newton. Letter, October 8, 1862, October 26, 1862. Luther Vance Civil War Pension Record. National Archives.
_____. Letter, October 15, 1862, October 26, 1862. William Chapman Civil War Pension Record. National Archives.
Price, Sterling. *Official Records*. Vol. 24, pp. 120, 388.
_____. *Official Records*. Vol. 27, pp. 229–230.
Progressive Men of Western Colorado. Chicago, IL: A. W. Bowen, 1905.
Rosecrans, William. *Battles and Leaders of the Civil War*. Vol. II. New York: Century, 1887.
_____. *Official Records*. Vol. 24, pp. 74–75, 169.
Ruggles, Daniel. *Official Records*. Vol. 10, pp. 809, 811.
Scott, James. Letter, June 18, 1862. Civil War Pension File. National Archives.
Shea, William, and Terrence Wenschel. *Vicksburg is the Key: The Struggle for the Mississippi River*. Lincoln: University of Nebraska Press, 2003.
Sherman, William *Official Records*. Vol. 36, pp. 754–745, 757.
_____. *Official Records*. Vol. 76, pp. 16–17.
Showmaker, Floyd A. *A History of Missouri and Missourians*. Columbia, MO: Walter Ridgeway, 1922.
Singleton, Amos. Civil War Pension Record. National Archives.
"Skirmish at Dallas." *Camp Fremont Register* 1, no. 1 (September 25, 1861). Civil War Papers Folio. Wisconsin Historical Society.
Smith, A. J. *Official Records*. Vol. 77, pp. 251–252.
Smith, Charles. Civil War Pension Record. National Archives.
Smith, Thomas. Letter, April 4, 1862. Compiled Service Records, Missouri Volunteer Union Soldiers. National Archives.
Snow, William. "Adventure at New Madrid." *National Tribune*, March 21, 1912.
_____. "Battle of Corinth." *National Tribune*, July 26, 1906.
Sprague, John. *Official Records*. Vol. 24, p. 191.
Stanley, David. *Official Records*. Vol. 10, pp. 720–723.
_____. *Official Records*. Vol. 24, pp. 82, 179.
Stewart, William S. Papers, 1861–1864, Letter Collection (C2991). Western Historical Manuscript Collection.
University of Missouri, Columbia, State Historical Society of Missouri.
Stuart, A. A. *Iowa Colonels and Regiments: Being a History of Iowa Regiments in the War of the Rebellion*. Des Moines, IA: Mills, 1865.
Sword, Wiley. *Embrace an Angry Wind: The Confederacy's Last Hurrah: Spring Hill, Franklin, and Nashville*. New York: HarperCollins, 1992.
Temple, Wayne Calhoun. *A Chaplain in the 11th Missouri Infantry*. Harrowgate, TN: Lincoln Memorial University Press, 1962. From an article in *Lincoln Herald*, vol. 64, Summer 1962.
"That Precious Blanket." *National Tribune*, October 4, 1906.
Thomas, Alonzo. Letter, April 15, 1863. Civil War Pension Record. National Archives.
_____. Letter, June 27, 1863. Civil War Pension Record. National Archives.
Thomas, George. General Order 342. *Official Records*. Vol. 93, pp. 37–38.
_____. *Official Records*. Vol. 94, p. 180.
Thompson, M. Jeff. *Official Records*. Vol. 3, pp. 223–227.
Treadway, Charles. "The Letters of Charles Wesley Treadway." In *Foot Prints: Past and Present*. Vol. 9. Olney, IL: Richland County Genealogical and Historical Society, 1986.
Treadway, John. Letters, August 8 and 10, 1861. Civil War Pension File. National Archives.
Tuttle, John. *Official Records*. Vol. 36, p. 759.
United States Census Records, 1870, 1880, 1900, 1910.
Van Beek, George. *Official Records*. Vol. 61, pp. 335–338, 976.
Vance, Luther. Civil War Letters. Civil War Pension File. National Archives.
Vineyard, T. E. *Battles of the Civil War*. Chicago: Hammond Press, 1914.
Wallace, Joseph. *Index to Past and Present of the City of Springfield and Sangamon County, Illinois*. Chicago: S. J. Clarke, 1904.
Walthall, Edward. *Official Records*. Vol. 93, pp. 723–724.
Warner, Moses. Civil War Pension File. National Archives.
Weber, Andrew. Letter, October 30, 1862. 11th Missouri Infantry Folder. Missouri State Archives. Jefferson City.
_____. *Official Records*. Vol. 24, pp. 88, 201–202.
Welsh, Jack. *Medical Histories of Union Generals*. OH: Kent State University Press, 1996.
"William Boatright." *Sullivan Union* (IN), May 16, 1915.
"William T. Followill." *Louisiana Press Journal*, July 20, 1899.
Williams, Kenneth. *Grant Rises in the West: From Iuka to Vicksburg, 1862–1863*. Lincoln, NE: Bison, 1997.
Williams, Nancy, ed. *Arkansas Biography: A Collection of Notable Lives*. Fayetteville: University of Arkansas Press, 2000.
"W. L. Barnum, Insurance Man, Succumbs at 91." *Chicago Tribune*, May 29, 1921, p. 15, col. 2.
Workman, Peter. February 7, 1865. Pension Record. National Archives.

Index

Numbers in ***bold italics*** indicate pages with photographs.

Abbeville Skirmish 176
Adams, George 113, 125, 158, 174, 214, 224, 240; letters 307–310
Adams, John 133
Akey, Milt 13
Alabama: 38th Infantry 71–72. 74; 42nd Infantry 88, 93; occupation of 217–224
Alexander, John 26
Anderson, Patton 48
Apperson, Charles 220
Applegate, Edwin 56, ***156***, 174, 240
Arkansas: 3rd Infantry 89; 4th Infantry 189; 9th Infantry 189; 11/7 Infantry 143; 14/17 Infantry 70; 15th Infantry 88, 93; 23rd Infantry 88, 93; 25th Infantry 189; 1st Mounted Rifles 189; 2nd Mounted Rifles 189
Armitage, Ambrose 116, 143, 157–158, 192
Armstrong, Frank 64, 67, 69, 83
Arnett, R.C. 30, 33

Bail, Abner 11, 17, 20, 108, 173, 238
Bailey, David 108, 156, 174
Baker, William Moses 107
Baldridge, Samuel 58, 65, 74, 234
Banks, Nathaniel 148–156, 158–64
Barnum, William 12, 17, 21, 111, 140–***141***, 165, 170, 172, 228, 231
Bascue, William 106
Bate, William 195
Battery Robinette 93–97, 99–100
Bay, Joseph 146
Bayles, David 10–12, 15–17, 231
Beauregard, Pierre 45, 47, 53, 57, 62
Belmont, battle of 38
Bentley, Clark 11, 17, 19, 36
Blair, Frank 5, 8, 12, 118, 120, 133

Blew, Jacob 11, 17, 20, 108, 173
Boatright, William 11, 17, 21, 56, 156–157, 239
Bogue Chitto Creek 144
Bouton, Edward 159, 162, 165
Bowen, John 112
Bowyer, Eli 11, 17, 24, 47–48, 108, 111, ***172***, 180, 200, 220, 228, 231
Bragg, Braxton 62–64, 141
Brookings, Charles 11, 17, 109, 131
Brooks, Joseph 11, 13, 17, 22, ***23***, 46–47, 234
Brown, George 216, 224, 235
Brown, Horace 102
Brown, Samuel 14
Browning, Joe 116, 124
Bryner, Cloyd 40–41, 87, 127, 175
Burcher, Robert 24
Byrd, John 146

Camp Fremont Register 14
Camp Jackson 6
Campbell, Anderson 56, 78, 100; letters 319
Canby Edward 209–213
Canton Expedition 143–145
Carlin, William 25–***26***, 28
Carroll, Jeremiah 45
Carter, Charles 11, 17, 21, 29, 36–37, 156, 239
Chalmers, James 176, 186
Champion Hill, battle of 117
Chapman, William 229; letters 311–314
Chickamauga, battle of 141
Clark, Charles 33
Cleland, Williams 29, 32–33, 47, 57, 67, 75, 108, 165, 174, 220–223, 228, 232–233
Cloclasure, William 11, 17, 20, 57
Cockrell, Francis 120, 122, 125
Cogswell's Light Artillery 189
Collins, John 36; letters 302–304

Coogan, Dennis 221, 241
Copper, William 76
Corinth 45–46; battle of 81–103; casualties 97–98; maps 85, 91, 94; siege 48–55
Cowperthwait, John W. 17, 20, 36–37, 75
Crawford, John 13
Crocker, Marcellus 88

Davies, Thomas 84, 87–88, 92
Davis, Harrison 197
Davis Bridge, battle of 101
Denizet, Morris 14
Dennis, Elias 134
DeWitt, Daniel 157
Dollahan, Thomas 11, 17, 21, 29, 56, 239
Dowdell, James 75
Draftees 201–207
Ducatel's Orleans Guards 50
Duggans, Wilson 12, 17, 22, 40, 57

Eagle Brigade 42–43, 124, 127
Eckley, Ephraim 96
Ellet, Alfred 134
Elliott, Cyrenus 17, 18, 140, 235
Erwin, William 173, 191, 214–216, 237
Ethel, Charles 141, 174

Fair, James 97
Filley, Oliver 5
Finch, Walton 172
Finlay, John 57, 174
Fish, Melancthon 46–48, 220, 233
Followill, William 179, 236
Ford, William 14
Forrest, Nathan B. 144–145, 158–164, 167, 175–176, 184
Fort Blakeley *see* Mobile Campaign
Fort DeRussey: capture 149
Foster, Charles 12, 17, 21, 75

333

Franklin, battle of 178–179
Freakes, Jefferson 197
Fredericktown: battle of 24–34; Big River Bridge skirmish 25; casualties 32; command determination 27; 11th Missouri companies positions 29; forces 28; map 31
Frémont, John C. 7, 8, 16
Frémont's Proclamation 8–9
French, Francis 97
Frost, Daniel 6
Fyffe, James 96

Gamble, Hamilton 7, 8
Gannon, Edward 17, 37, 47
Gantz, Daniel 33
Gause, William 124, 126
Georgia: 1st Battalion Georgia Sharpshooters 195; 1st Georgia Confederate 195; 25th Infantry 195; 29th Infantry 195; 30th Georgia 195
Gibson, Calder 142
Gibson, Randall 210–213
Gillard, William 67, 187
Gillen, Charles 57
Gould, George *34*
Grant, Ulysses 26, 34, 38, 62–63, 67–69, 79–80, 82, 92, 105–106, 111–112, 117, 135–136, 141–142, 183–184
Gray, Lewis 56, 156
Green, Modesta 11, 17, 19, 47, 109, 111, 172–173, 190, 192, 196–197, 200, 211, 215, 228, 232
Greene, Alexander 74
Greenwood, George 220
Grierson, Benjamin 159, 163
Guthrie, John 97

Hall, Willard 7
Hamilton, Charles 64, 67–69, 79, 84, 87, 90
Hamilton, Robert 221
Harney-Price Agreement 7
Haskins, William 57; letters 304–306
Hathorn, John 47, 140
Hawkins' Missouri Cavalry 28
Hawley, Thomas 13–14, 16–17, *23*, 24, 35, 75, 105, 107, 110, 131–132, 135–136, 143–144, 159, 166, 173, 175, 191, 220, 223, 233–234
Hébert, Louis 70–72, 79, 83, 120, 122
Hendee, Clark 11–13, 17, 29, 57, 237; resignation letter 58
Henry, George 11, 17, 19, 57, 93, 96, 237
Hodgson's Artillery 50
Hollister, Charles 17, 97, 108, 238
Holly Springs: raid 106
Hood, John Bell 178–180, 184–201

Hubbard, Lucius 115, 176–177, 186, 189, 191–193, 195–197, 211–217
Hulbert, Stephen 101
Hummer, James 12, 17, 21, 29, 47
Hurricane Creek: skirmish at 176
Hussey, James 157

Illinois: 2nd Artillery 43; 7th Cavalry 42; 17th Infantry 28–32; 20th Infantry 28–32; 21st Infantry 26, 28–29; 26th Infantry 49, 51–52, 65, 72, 90; 27th Infantry 43; 33rd Infantry 28–29, 31–32; 38th Infantry 26, 28–29; 47th Infantry 40, 49, 51–52, 65, 72, 89–90, 108, 124–125, 148, 160, 164, 175, 212; 52nd Infantry 89; 55th Infantry 121, 124; 114th Infantry 187; 124th Infantry 170
Indiana: 1st Indiana Cavalry 26, 28–29, 31–32; 48th Infantry 70–73; 93rd Infantry 187
Iowa: 2nd Artillery *see* Spoor's Battery 65, 115, 191; 2nd Cavalry 51; 5th Infantry 70–72; 7th Infantry 89; 10th Infantry 71; 11th Infantry 88; 13th Infantry 88; 15th Infantry 88; 16th Infantry 70–72, 88; 17th Infantry 72; 35th Infantry 157–158
Island Number 10: map 41; siege 38–46
Iuka: battle of 61–80; casualties 76–77; map 73

Jackson, Claiborne Fox 5–7
Jackson, Oscar 93
Jackson, battle of (May 1863) 112–117
Johnston, Albert Sidney 24, 45, 159, 216
Johnston, Joseph 115, 135, 178
Jones, Joseph 109, *131*

Kelly, Benjamin 179
Kendall, Cyrus 57, 156, 175, 221, 241
Kimball, Nathan 133
Kingsbury, Harley 11, 17, 21, 56
Koch, Henry 42

Laird, Benjamin 11, 17, 21, 108; court martial 37
Langen's Cavalry 28
Laughlin, William 35
Lee, Stephen Dill 159–164, 178
Lightfoot, Benjamin 101
Lincoln, Abraham 53; call for volunteers 6; 1861 election 5
Little, Henry 65, 71–72
Livingston, Benjamin 11, 15, 17, 18, 20, 37, 47, 233
Lloyd, Jesse 11, 17, 47, 143, 173, 179, 228, 236

Loomis, John 42, 48–53, 104, 106
Lott, James *47*, 174, 236
Louisiana: 2nd Cavalry 152; 3rd Infantry 70–71; 22nd Infantry 214
Lovell, Mansfield 83, 87, 92
Lowe, Aden 28–32
Lucas, George 173
Lyon, Nathaniel 6–7, 9, 11

Mackall, William 44
Manning, Thomas 44
Mansfield: battle of 152
Matthies, Charles 121–122
Maury, Dabney 65, 79, 89, 92–93, 208–213
McArthur, John 88, 133, 187, 189–190, 193, 195, 228, 230
McCall, Duncan 12–13, 16, 28, 30, 39–40, 42, 48, 50, 52, 55, 69, 89–90, 93, 95–96, 104, 107, 116, 127, 133, 135, 143, 157, 161, 165
McClernand, John 62, 113, 117, 120, 127
McConnell, Benjamin 11, 20
McCown, James 124
McCready, William 17
McDonel, John 63
McElyea, Wilford 174, 220
McGinley, John 17
McGown, John 38, 42–43
McKean, Thomas 84, 87, 92
McKelvey, George 36
McKnight, David 58
McMahan, Constantine *173*, 236
McMillen, William 121, 187, 193
McNeal, James 96, 156, 174
McPherson, James 112–113, 117, 120, 127, 143–144
Mechanicsburg expeditions 132–134
Michigan: 1st Cavalry 40; 2nd Cavalry 40; 3rd Artillery (Dee's) 54, 65; 3rd Cavalry 69
Mieure, Thomas 221, 239
Mieure, William 11, 17, 21, 36–37
Minnesota: 4th Infantry 70, 73; 5th Infantry 88, 115, 124, 148, 186, 196, 212; 5th Light Artillery 88; 9th Infantry 186, 196, 212; 10th Infantry 189, 197
Mississippi: 1st Partisan Rangers 69; 7th Battalion 90; 35th Infantry 88, 93; 36th Mississippi 71–72, 74, 122; 37th Infantry 71–72, 74; 38th Infantry 71; 40th Infantry 70–71; 43rd Infantry 90
Missouri (Confederate/State Guard): 2nd Dragoons 28; 2nd Infantry 28; 3rd Cavalry 28, 90; 3rd Infantry 28, 30, 89–90, 122, 124; 4th Infantry 28, 90; 5th Infantry 124; 6th

Infantry 90; Jennings Battalion 28; Rapley's Battalion 28
Missouri (Union): 1st Missouri Rifles 10, 22; 7th Infantry 112, 170, 180–182; 10th Infantry 71; 21st Infantry 88; 26th Infantry 70–71, 89; 29th Infantry 26; 33rd Infantry 148–158, 170; Missouri Light Artillery 28, 40
Missouri, 11th Regiment: battle of Corinth 81–103; battle of Iuka 65–80; battle of Nashville 178–201; battle of Old Lake 157–158; battle of Tupelo 158–166; Canton Expedition 143–145; charge on Stockade Redan 124–132; flag 172; general Order Number 46 53; march to Point Pleasant 40; Mechanicsburg Expeditions 132–134; Mobile Campaigns 207–217; occupation of Alabama 217 224; plans for Reorganization 145–146; Richmond Expedition 134–135; roster of officers 11–12; roster of soldiers 243–270; roster of veteran regiment 271–297; skirmish at Cape Girardeau 12–13; skirmish at Dallas 14; skirmish at Farmington 49–55; soldiers in Red River Campaign 147; substitutes and Draftees 204–207; transfer of 7th Missouri 180–182; Vicksburg Campaign 104–132
Moore, David 159, 162
Mosquito Point 45
Mower, Joseph 42, 46, 61, 81, 104–105, 107–108, 112, 228, 230; assault on Stockade Redan 121–122, 127; battle of Corinth 88–90; battle of Iuka 66–67, 69, 72, 74–76; battle of Jackson 115–117; battle of Old Lake 157–158; battle of Tupelo 163–164, 166; capture 99; convalescence 143; death of A.J. Weber 135; Mechanicsburg Expedition 133; Oxford Expedition 175; promotion and Transfer 179; Red River Expedition 149–156; siege of Corinth 49–50, 52, 54; skirmish West of Vicksburg 134
Mulhall, James 306
Murfreesoro: Confederate attacks 184
Murphy, Robert 48, 58, 65, 106
Myers, John 221

Nashville: battle 178–201; casualties 198; map 188
New Madrid, siege of *see* Island No. 10
Nicholson, George 44

Nigh, Barnabas 173
Norris, Abraham 224; letter 306–307
Notestine, William 134, 174, 190–191, 202, 221, 238; letters 300

O'Donnell, Menomen 11, 17–18, 29, 42, 125, 140, 149, 165, 173, 235
Ohio: 11th Artillery 70–72; 13th Infantry 121; 17th Infantry 71; 20th Infantry 121; 27th Infantry 92–93, 95; 37th Infantry 121; 39th Infantry 54, 92–93; 43rd Infantry 92–93; 47th Infantry 121; 63rd Infantry 92–93, 95; 72nd Infantry 189; 80th 71–72
Old Abe 42–43, 90
Old Lake, Arkansas: battle of 157–158
Oliver, John 87–88
O'Neil, Henry 112
Ord, Edward 63, 65–69, 79–80
Orr, Charles 11, 17, 18, 108
Osgood 12, 17, 21, 47, 75, 111, 174, 240
Oxford Expedition 175

Page, Eugene 75–76; letter 299–300
Paine, Eleazer 49
Palmer, David 40, 52, 53
Panabaker, William 11, 15, 17–18, 28–30, 33, 38, 46, 48, 58, 232
Parks, James 201
Pemberton, John 105, 117, 135
Pendergast, Edwin 157
Perce, William 11, 17, 19, 47
Perry, John 220
Perryville Expedition 13–14
Phifer, C.W. 89–90, 93
Pickrell, Able 57, 106
Pickrell, William 108, 140, 156, 173
Pillow, Gideon 38
Pleasant Hill, battle of 153
Plummer, Joseph 12, 15–**16**, 17, 46, 228, 231; death 57; Fredericktown Campaign 27–32, 34, 37, 48–49; Island No. 10 38–44
Point Coulee Artillery Battery 40
Point Pleasant *see* Island No. 10
Polk, Leonidas 24
Pope, John 38–40, 42–43, 48–51, 53–54, 57, 62
Powell, Caleb 33
Powell, John 33
Powell's Battery 40
Prentice, Owen 108
Preston, Newton 78, 102, 228
Price, Sterling 7, 49, 61, 63–69, 79–83, 92, 100; Missouri Raid 177
Pursell's Howitzers 28

Quick, George 166, 174

Randall, Lyman 173, 238
Raymond, battle of 113
Red River Campaign 147–156; map 150
Renick, Silas 58
Reynolds, Daniel 189–190, 193
Reynolds, Thomas 5
Ridgely, Elmore 108, 144, 173
Robinson George 221
Rogers, William 95–96
Roney, Levi 174, 221, 238
Rosecrans, William 62–65, 67–68, 74, 79–80, 87–88, 92, 97, 99, 105
Ross, Leonard 27–33, 105–106
Rousseau, Lovell 184
Ruggles, Daniel 49–50, 53

Sanborn, John 69–72
Sappington, Mark 36
Saxton, Rufus 10, 12
Schofield, John 33, 178–180, 185
Scott, James 56
Sherman, William 53, 105, 112–113, 115–117, 120, 126–127, 158, 178, 228
Shiloh, battle of 45
Shoopman, David 174
Sievert, William 101
Simmons, William 179, 196, 200, **201**
Singleton, Amos 11, 17, 20, 29, 75, 108, 238
Slaton, William 74
Smith, A.J. 148–156, 159–164, 166, 175, 177, 179, 187, 192–193, 201, 204, 209–213, 215, 228, 230
Smith, Charles 174, 220, 238
Smith, Henry 220
Smith, James 97
Smith, Joel 97
Smith, Richard 33
Smith, Thomas 11, 13, 15, 17, 23–24, 36, 46, 233
Snow, William 42, 96, 221
Spanish Fort *see* Mobile Campaign
Spoor's Battery 51
Sprague, John 93–94
Stanley, David 40, 42, 49–50, 52, 54, 64–65, 67–**68**, 72, 75, 79–80, 84, 87–88, 92–93, 99, 104–105, 178
Steedman, James 180, 186, 192
Stewart, William 8, 12, 14, 17, 22, 29–30, 33–34, 39–40, 42, 45, 52, 57–58, 65, 75–76, 80, 97, 156, 192, 240
Stewart's Cavalry 28, 30
Stirman's Sharpshooters 89
Stockade Redan: assaults 118–132

Substitutes 201–207
Sullivan, Jeremiah 71

Tasker, James 221
Taylor's Battery 28
Texas: 3rd Cavalry (dismounted) 70–71; 6th Cavalry 89; 9th Cavalry 89; 2nd Infantry 88, 93, 95–96; 18th Infantry 134; 1st Texas Legion 70–71
Thomas, Alzono 110, 136–137, 229; letters 300–301
Thomas, George 178–180, 183–186, 192, 201–202
Thompson, M. Jeff: battle of Fredericktown 24–**25**, 33, 39
Treadway, Charles 35, 78, 110, 142, 159, 166, 177, 200, 217–219, 223–224
Treadway, John 13; letter 301–302
Trudeau, James 38
Tupelo, battle of 158–166
Tuttle, James 112–113, 115, 143–144

United States: 1st Infantry 42, 90; 13th Infantry 118
USCT: 59th Infantry 160; 61st Infantry 160, 164; 68th Infantry 164

Van Beek, George 153–158
Vance, Luther 14; letters 314–319
VanDorn, Earl 63–64, 66, 68, 79, 81–84, 87, 90, 92, 97, 101; Holly Springs raid 106; siege of Corinth 49–50, 53
Vicksburg Campaign 105–137; casualties 129–131; defenses 121; *see also* Stockade Redan
Vicksburg Canal 110

Walker, Daniel 220
Walker, John 134
Wallace, William 156, 239
Walthall, Edward 189, 195, 197
Warner, Jack 124–125
Warner, Moses 11, 14, 17, 19, 29, 75, 111, 236

Weber, Andrew J. (A.J.) 11, 17, **18**, 29, 47, 58, 66, 72, 74, 81, 90, 92, 95, 101–102, 108, 111, 125, 135, 140, 228, 231
Weber, George 47, 140, 156
Weir, Elias 108, 144
Welch, George 200
West Virginia: 4th Infantry 121
Whitney, Solomon 220
Williams, Abraham 97
Wilson, James 11, 17–18, 173
Wilson, Gen. James H. 180, 185
Wilson's Creek, battle of 9
Wisconsin: 12th Artillery 71; 8th Infantry 28–29, 42–43, 49–52, 65–66, 72, 89–90, 116, 124–125, 133, 143, 148, 157–158, 186, 192, 196–197; 16th Infantry 88
Withrow, Harrison 111, 156
Workman, Peter 106–107
Wroe, Columbus 158

Yellow Bayou, battle of 155

www.ingramcontent.com/pod-product-compliance
Lightning Source LLC
Chambersburg PA
CBHW081537300426
44116CB00015B/2662